THE COLLEC

F. A. Hayek

VOLUME XV

THE MARKET AND OTHER ORDERS

PLAN OF THE COLLECTED WORKS
Edited by Bruce Caldwell

The plan is provisional. Minor alterations may occur in titles of individual books,
and additional volumes may be added.

THE COLLECTED WORKS OF

F. A. Hayek

VOLUME XV

THE MARKET AND
OTHER ORDERS

EDITED BY

BRUCE CALDWELL

The University of Chicago Press

The University of Chicago Press, Chicago 60637
The University of Chicago Press, Ltd., London

© 2014 by The Estate of F. A. Hayek
All rights reserved. Published 2014.
Paperback edition 2017
Printed in the United States of America

23 22 21 20 19 18 17   2 3 4 5 6

ISBN-13: 978-0-226-08955-3 (cloth)
ISBN-13: 978-0-226-52731-4 (paper)
ISBN-13: 978-0-226-08969-0 (e-book)
DOI: 10.7208/chicago/9780226089690.001.0001

Library of Congress Cataloging-in-Publication Data

Hayek, Friedrich A. von (Friedrich August), 1899–1992, author.
  [Works. Selections]
  The market and other orders / F. A. Hayek ; edited by Bruce Caldwell.
      pages cm — (Collected works of F. A. Hayek ; volume XV)
  Includes bibliographical references and index.
  ISBN 978-0-226-08955-3 (cloth : alkaline paper) — ISBN 978-0-226-08969-0 (e-book)
1. Economics. 2. Order. 3. Order (Philosophy) 4. Free enterprise. 5. Rule of law. I. Caldwell,
Bruce, 1952– editor. II. Title. III. Series: Hayek, Friedrich A. von (Friedrich August), 1899–
1992. Works. 1988 ; v. 15.
HB171.H4265 2014
330.092—dc23

2013023564

♾ This paper meets the requirements of ANSI/NISO Z39.48-1992 (Permanence of Paper).

THE COLLECTED WORKS OF F. A. HAYEK

Founding Editor: W. W. Bartley III
General Editor: Bruce Caldwell

Published with the support of

The Hoover Institution on War, Revolution, and Peace
Stanford University

The Cato Institute

The Earhart Foundation

The Pierre F. and Enid Goodrich Foundation

The Heritage Foundation

The Morris Foundation, Little Rock

CONTENTS

EDITORIAL FOREWORD

This volume collects papers that span much of the career of Friedrich Hayek. Most of them are taken from three previous collections: *Individualism and Economic Order* (1948), *Studies in Philosophy, Politics and Economics* (1967), and *New Studies in Philosophy, Politics, Economics and the History of Ideas* (1978). I hope that the editor's introduction will make clear the rationale behind the selection.

Because Hayek's papers have appeared in both British and American publications, the question as to which conventions to follow regarding spelling and punctuation naturally arises. We have chosen to follow a "mixed system" that uses as a model the conventions followed in the 1967 *Studies* volume. Typographical errors have been silently corrected, as have minor inaccuracies in Hayek's quoting of others. More significant errors are noted. Because each of the chapters stands alone, the usual practice of providing a full reference at the first quotation and abbreviated ones thereafter holds only within each chapter.

I gratefully acknowledge the assistance of Jack Bladel, Eric Howard, Hansjoerg Klausinger, Jeremy Shearmur, and Michael Wohlgemuth in tracking down obscure references. Michaël Assous, Claire Caldwell, Hansjoerg Klausinger, John Lewis, and James Murphy translated passages from French, German, Latin, and Greek. Angela Zemonek, Sam Caldwell, and Matt Panhans aided me in preparing the final manuscript. Participants at the HOPE Workshop at Duke University in January 2012 provided comments on my editor's introduction. Faculty at the Advanced Austrian Economics seminar at the Foundation for Economic Education in August 2009, participants at the Fund for the Study of Spontaneous Orders meeting in February 2009 on "Manifestations of Spontaneous Order in Politics and Society", and Paul Lewis all provided comments on an earlier version. My thanks to them all.

I have been working on this manuscript for a number of years, and as a result, quite a few people at the University of Chicago Press have contributed to bringing it to press. My thanks to David Pervin, John Tryneski, Joe Jackson, Shenyun Wu, Rhonda Smith, Kelly Finefrock-Creed, and Carissa Vardanian for their good work and support.

All of the previously published pieces appeared in University of Chicago Press volumes with the exception of "The Primacy of the Abstract" and the related "Discussion." My thanks to the estate of Arthur Koestler for granting permission to quote this material.

This book is dedicated to John Lewis, who died of cancer in December 2011.

Bruce Caldwell

INTRODUCTION

This fifteenth volume in *The Collected Works of F. A. Hayek* assembles papers published over a goodly portion of Friedrich A. Hayek's lengthy career, the first appearing in 1937, the last in 1975. The papers were written for a variety of purposes and reasons. Some commemorated special occasions: a presidential address before the London Economics Club, inaugural speeches at the Universities of Salzburg and Freiburg, contributions to volumes honouring his friends Karl Popper and Jacques Rueff, and his Nobel Prize address. Others were simply independent contributions to knowledge.

The number of topics covered is large. There are his justly famous articles on the so-called 'knowledge problem.' But there are also papers on other aspects of economics, on the philosophy of science and of social science, on the physiology of the brain, on the methods of economists, on the origins of various social institutions, on theories of law, on intellectual history, on the responsibilities of teachers, and more. It is striking how easily Hayek glides from one area into another within the same article: he evidently saw linkages among all of these fields. I hope in this introduction to show, in what may at first appear to be a mishmash, the gradual emergence of and, indeed, the underlying *order* to be discovered in Hayek's ideas.

The papers are presented roughly in chronological order of publication, with one clear exception. The paper chosen as the prologue, "Kinds of Rationalism", was a lecture that Hayek delivered at Rikkyo University, Japan, on April 27, 1964. It is a wholly representative contribution. Though Hayek's focus is a critique of what he dubs "rationalist constructivism", he explores all manner of other ideas: the misuse of words like 'planning' and 'social' (especially when the latter is conjoined with the word 'justice'), John Maynard Keynes's rejection in his writings on 'his early beliefs' of moral rules, the relation of rules to orders, a call for collaboration among specialists in law, economics, and social philosophy, and so on. And befitting a prologue, it contains what is perhaps Hayek's first statement that many of these seemingly unrelated topics are in fact very much of a piece. He also suggests that his first glimmer of the underlying unity dates back to the paper that is chapter 1 of this volume, his 1936 presidential address before the London Economics Club, "Economics and Knowledge":

> This brings me to what in my personal development was the starting point of all these reflections, and which may explain why, though at one time a very pure and narrow economic theorist, I was led from technical economics into all kinds of questions usually regarded as philosophical. When I look back, it seems to have all begun, nearly thirty years ago, with an essay on "Economics and Knowledge" in which I examined what seemed to me some of the central difficulties of pure economic theory. Its main conclusion was that the task of economic theory was to explain how an overall order of economic activity was achieved which utilized a large amount of knowledge which was not concentrated in any one mind but existed only as the separate knowledge of thousands or millions of different individuals. But it was still a long way from this to an adequate insight into the relations between the abstract rules which the individual follows in his actions, and the abstract overall order which is formed as a result of his responding, within the limits imposed upon him by those abstract rules, to the concrete particular circumstances which he encounters. It was only through a re-examination of the age-old concept of freedom under the law, the basic conception of traditional liberalism, and of the problems of the philosophy of law which this raises, that I have reached what now seems to me a tolerably clear picture of the nature of the spontaneous order of which liberal economists have so long been talking.[1]

The title of this volume is *The Market and Other Orders*. Though there will be many sub-themes in the papers, as one would expect given that they were written at different times, and for different audiences and purposes, a principal theme, as Hayek states above, is his discovery of orders in many sorts of unrelated phenomena in both the natural world and in the social relations and institutions that compose a part of that world, orders that emerge due to rule-following on the part of the relevant constituent elements. That insight is what lends coherence to a volume that covers so many apparently disparate topics. The social theory that is the ultimate result is impressive both in its breadth and its originality. It will also be evident, however, that its construction was a laborious task, and one in which the repetition of themes is not absent.

I begin by tracing the development of these ideas in Hayek's work in economics in the 1930's and 1940's. Next comes his integration of certain key insights into his contributions to political theory and other areas. It is often said that Hayek abandoned economics when he turned to political theory, but I will show that this is not true: he continued to try to apply these insights

---

[1] F. A. Hayek, "Kinds of Rationalism", this volume, pp. 49–50.

in his economic contributions in *A Grammar of the Economic Calculus*, a work that was, however, never published.[2] Finally, I will show the full blossoming of Hayek's treatment of complex adaptive systems, or spontaneous orders, and his recommendations for how to study them, in the pieces that comprise the concluding section.

Part I. The Early Ideas

Hayek arrived as a visiting professor at the London School of Economics (LSE) in the fall of 1931 and was appointed the next year as the Tooke Chair of Economic Science and Statistics. In his first few years at LSE he engaged in a number of debates: with John Maynard Keynes over their respective theories of money and of the business cycle, with the American economist Frank Knight and others over their respective theories of capital, and with socialists of various stripes over the prospects for a socialized economy.[3] During this period there was also an active discussion over the importance of expectations, which saw the participation of Hayek, Oskar Morgenstern, and assorted Swedish and other economists over the meaning to be attributed to the term 'perfect foresight.' In 1936 Hayek became president of the London Economic Club and was invited to prepare an address to be delivered on November 10 of that year. Hayek titled the address "Economics and Knowledge" and in it wove together themes that had been occupying him in recent years. The paper was published three months later in the journal *Economica*.[4]

In later reminiscences Hayek told of "a certain excitement" that accompanied his writing of the paper:

> It was really the beginning of my looking at things in a new light. If you asked me, I would say that up until that moment I was developing conventional ideas. With the '37 lecture to the Economics Club in London, my Presidential Address, which is "Economics and Knowledge", I started my own way of thinking. . . .

[2] The closest Hayek came to writing up the ideas that would have been incorporated in the book were his four lectures at the University of Virginia in 1961, collectively titled A New Look at Economic Theory. The lectures are published for the first time in the appendix.

[3] For the details, see volumes 6 through 12 of F. A. Hayek, *The Collected Works of F. A. Hayek* (Chicago: University of Chicago Press; London: Routledge), and the associated editor's introductions.

[4] F. A. Hayek, "Economics and Knowledge", *Economica*, n.s., vol. 4, February 1937, pp. 33–54, reprinted in F. A. Hayek, *Individualism and Economic Order* (Chicago: University of Chicago Press, 1948), pp. 33–56. The *Economica* version contained footnotes that were deleted in the 1948 reprinting. The 1948 version also contained some slight wording changes. The 1948 wording was used for the present text, but the removed footnotes have been restored in the text below, in brackets.

And it was with a feeling of sudden illumination, sudden enlightenment that I—I wrote that lecture in a certain excitement. I was aware that I was putting down things which were fairly well known in a new form, and perhaps it was the most exciting moment in my career when I saw it in print.[5]

"Economics and Knowledge" concerns, as its title suggests, the rôle of assumptions about knowledge in economic analysis. In the standard analysis of his day, which Hayek termed 'static equilibrium theory', it was typically assumed that all agents have access to the same, objectively correct knowledge. During the early 1930's a number of economists began to question this assumption, particularly because it seemed inadequate to handle the question of expectations: Did access to full information extend also into the future? As Oskar Morgenstern pointed out, the assumption produces some bizarre results.[6] For example, if one assumes perfect foresight, one assumes not only that an agent knows what all other agents will do, but also that all of them know what the original agent will do, now and in the future. The question arises: How can such a world ever get *out* of equilibrium?

To address the problem, Hayek begins by distinguishing equilibrium for an individual and equilibrium for a society, and between the subjective perceptions of an agent versus an outside observer's 'objective' knowledge of a situation. Equilibrium for an individual agent is not a problem: at any given moment, an agent is in equilibrium with respect to the agent's own subjective perceptions, even if these do not match up with objective reality. (Note that an agent's perceptions may change from moment to moment, as learning takes place, but *at any given moment*, the agent is in equilibrium with respect to the knowledge available at the moment of decision.) For a *society* to be in equilibrium, however, much more is required: namely, the plans of many individual agents must be co-ordinated. For that to occur, subjective perceptions must be made consonant with objective reality. If societal equilibrium is our concern, then, "the question why the data in the subjective sense of the term should ever come to correspond to the objective data is one of the main problems we have to answer."[7]

Hayek defines societal equilibrium in terms of a compatibility of plans,

---

[5] F. A. Hayek, "Nobel Prize-Winning Economist", ed. Armen Alchian (transcript of an interview conducted in 1978 under the auspices of the Oral History Program, University Library, University of California–Los Angeles, 1983 [transcript no. 300/224, Department of Special Collections, Charles E. Young Research Library, UCLA]), pp. 425–26.

[6] Oskar Morgenstern, "Vollkommene Voraussicht und wirtschaftliches Gleichwicht", *Zeitschrift für Nationalökonomie*, vol. 4, 1934, pp. 337ff. A translation of this paper is now available as "Perfect Foresight and Economic Equilibrium", in *Selected Economic Writings of Oskar Morgenstern*, ed. Andrew Schotter (New York: New York University Press, 1976), pp. 169–83.

[7] F. A. Hayek, "Economics and Knowledge", this volume, p. 63.

a situation in which foresight is "in a special sense" correct. This occurs automatically in a world in which all agents have access to complete, correct information. Hayek posits instead a world in which knowledge is divided or dispersed (i.e., different agents have access to different bits of knowledge) and in which knowledge claims are subjectively-held (i.e., they can be wrong). It is a world in which adjustment to new information is constantly occurring.

One could still tell an equilibrium story if one assumes that agents have subjectively-held knowledge. There, a movement to equilibrium would entail subjective data becoming objective data. Through a process of error elimination, one would reach a final equilibrium state in which there exists a mutual compatibility of expectations.

If one adds in the dispersion of knowledge in a world of constant change, however, the whole notion of a movement towards a static final equilibrium becomes a forced metaphor. In such a world, the dispersion of knowledge is not some temporary condition that gets eliminated once and for all by movement to a final resting point. It is a permanent condition. If all agents act on different bits of knowledge, and inhabit a world in which data is constantly changing, the real question is how the fragments of data that exist in many different minds can ever get co-ordinated. In this situation the "central question" becomes, "How can the combination of fragments of knowledge existing in different minds bring about results which, if they were to be brought about deliberately, would require a knowledge on the part of the directing mind which no single person can possess?"[8]

Hayek does not answer the question in his seminal paper. How social coordination is possible in a world of dispersed knowledge, of error, and of constant change, would indeed become the central question in Hayek's work to follow.[9]

* * *

As the war approached, Hayek began another project, grand in scale, a two-volume tome that was to carry the title *The Abuse and Decline of Reason*. In it he would show how the twin doctrines of socialism and scientism—the latter being the application of the methods of the natural sciences in domains in which they were not appropriate, namely, the social sciences—had grown up together and become ever more intertwined as they spread from France to Germany, England, and the United States. In the fall of 1940 he began work on a theoretical analysis of scientism that was to have been the first chapter

[8] Ibid., p. 76.

[9] There is a burgeoning secondary literature on the paper and its importance for the development of Hayek's thought; for those who want to investigate further, see Bruce Caldwell, *Hayek's Challenge: An Intellectual History of F. A. Hayek* (Chicago: University of Chicago Press, 2004), chapter 10, and the citations therein.

of the book. The chapter ultimately grew into the much more extended essay "Scientism and the Study of Society", a paper that was published in three instalments in *Economica* from 1942 to 1944.[10] Somewhere between the first and second instalment Hayek wrote "The Facts of the Social Sciences", the second chapter in the present collection. The first two sections of "Facts" are a précis of the positions taken in the larger piece.

Hayek reports that he presented "Facts" on November 19, 1942, before the Cambridge University Moral Sciences Club, a philosophical discussion group that was dominated by two eminent philosophers, Hayek's cousin Ludwig Wittgenstein and G. E. Moore.[11] Given his audience, it is of no little interest that Hayek begins by noting that he had started out his career as a social scientist "thoroughly imbued with a belief in the universal validity of the methods of the natural sciences."[12] He apparently wanted to make sure that the philosophers understood that he appreciated the power of natural scientific methods in their proper domain. It was only when such methods were applied within the social sciences that, in Hayek's opinion, one was led into error.

Hayek's key argument is that the facts of the social sciences differ from those of the natural sciences and therefore require a different method for understanding them. The objects of human activity—his examples include things like "tools, food, medicine, weapons, words, sentences, communications, and acts of production"[13]—depend not on objective properties but on people's interpretations. In a like manner, when we interpret the actions of another human, either in everyday life or in our capacity as social scientists, we do so in terms of the opinions or intentions that we ascribe to the acting person, something that we do employing the analogy of our own mind. This is especially evident when we try to make sense of a culture that is very different from our own. Significantly, in such exercises we use abstract rather than concrete concepts to understand the actions that we observe:

[10] F. A. Hayek, "Scientism and the Study of Society", *Economica*, n.s., vol. 9, August 1942, pp. 267–91; ibid., vol. 10, February 1943, pp. 34–63; ibid., vol. 11, February 1944, pp. 27–39; reprinted in *The Counter-Revolution of Science: Studies on the Abuse of Reason* (Glencoe, IL: Free Press, 1952; reprinted, Indianapolis, IN: Liberty Fund, 1979); now see F. A. Hayek, *Studies on the Abuse and Decline of Reason*, ed. Bruce Caldwell, vol. 13 (2010) of *The Collected Works of F. A. Hayek*, chapters 1–10. The *Abuse of Reason* project was never completed; for more on its history, see the editor's introduction to *Studies on the Abuse and Decline of Reason*.

[11] When the Battle of Britain began in fall 1940, LSE was evacuated to Peterhouse, Cambridge, where it remained for the duration. Hayek in reminiscences talked about the various times he encountered his cousin, but he never mentioned Wittgenstein as having attended his talk before the club.

[12] F. A. Hayek, "The Facts of the Social Sciences", this volume, p. 78.

[13] Ibid., p. 80.

When we say that a person possesses food or money, or that he utters a word, we imply that he knows that the first can be eaten, that the second can be used to buy something with, and that the third can be understood. . . .

My knowledge of the everyday things around me, of the particular ways in which we express ideas or emotions, will be of little use in interpreting the behaviour of the inhabitants of Tierra del Fuego. But my understanding of what I mean by a means to an end, by food or a weapon, a word or a sign, and probably even an exchange or a gift, will still be useful and even essential in my attempt to understand what they do.[14]

In short, classifications using abstract categories, and interpretations using those categories or models, play key rôles in our understanding of human action. These ideas would recur in Hayek's 1952 book on psychology, *The Sensory Order*, as well as in later essays found in this volume.[15]

Hayek anticipates the objection that we should instead derive all of our knowledge from observation and experience. In the last section of "Facts" he tries to refute the claim, laying out his own criticisms of what he would refer to in the February 1943 instalment of the "Scientism" essay as the collectivism, historicism, and objectivism of the scientistic approach.

In "The Facts of the Social Sciences" Hayek comes as close as he would ever come to endorsing the position of Ludwig von Mises on methodology. One sees this in his description of the relationship between theory and history, in his claim that there can be no testing of the theories of the social sciences, and perhaps especially in the fact that he approvingly uses the term '*a priori*'— though it should be added immediately that when he uses the phrase, it is in reference to the mental classification system of the mind, so he is using it in a way quite different from that of Mises.[16]

Throughout the essay Hayek always puts the contrast he is drawing in terms of the differences between the methods of the natural and the social sciences.

---

[14] Ibid., pp. 82, 85.

[15] F. A. Hayek, *The Sensory Order: An Inquiry into the Foundations of Theoretical Psychology* (Chicago: University of Chicago Press, 1952); a *Collected Works* edition is anticipated. Hayek's 'interpretive turn' here and in other work has itself led to various interpretations of his ideas in the secondary literature; some see it as evidence of his support for hermeneutics and others as a flirtation with post-modernism. See, e.g., G. B. Madison, "Hayek and the Interpretive Turn", *Critical Review*, vol. 3, Spring 1989, pp. 169–85; Theodore Burczak, "The Postmodern Moments of F. A. Hayek's Economics", *Economics and Philosophy*, vol. 10, April 1994, pp. 31–58. For criticism of these views, see Caldwell, *Hayek's Challenge*, appendix D.

[16] For more on the Mises-Hayek relationship regarding methodology, see Caldwell, *Hayek's Challenge*, pp. 220–23; and Caldwell, "A Skirmish in the Popper Wars: Hutchison versus Caldwell on Hayek, Popper, Mises, and Methodology", *Journal of Economic Methodology*, vol. 16, September 2009, pp. 315–24.

He will later talk about these differences in terms of methods that are appropriate for the study of simple versus complex phenomena.

* * *

As the war drew to a close, Hayek returned to the problem that he had introduced in "Economics and Knowledge", one he now described as the "problem of the utilization of knowledge which is not given to anyone in its totality."[17] In "The Use of Knowledge in Society", Hayek shows how freely-adjusting market-formed prices can help to solve the problem of co-ordinating human activity in a world of dispersed, subjectively-held knowledge.

Hayek sets up the problem as follows: If one wants to design an efficiently-operating economic system in a world of dispersed knowledge, is it better to take a centralized or a decentralized approach? The answer depends on which one is better at utilizing knowledge, and that in its turn depends on which sort of knowledge is most important in an economic system. Many people when they hear the word 'knowledge' immediately think of scientific knowledge or some other form of specialized expertise. But in an economic system, a much more significant kind of knowledge is the kind that everyday participants in the market system possess, what Hayek calls "the knowledge of the particular circumstances of time and place."[18] This knowledge is hugely important in a world of constant change, because knowledge of changes in local conditions is essential if one is to make the right decisions in a market environment.

But there is a catch. The person who has localized knowledge has a very restricted view. That person has little idea of what is going on in the system as a whole. This brings the real problem to the forefront: How can a single person use not only personal knowledge but also the localized knowledge that exists in all the brains of all the other agents in the system? It would be (to say the least) difficult for a central authority to collect all of this kind of knowledge, especially if it is constantly changing. Can we figure out a way to employ it?

It is here that the price system comes in. The 'man in the street' might possess only local, as opposed to global, knowledge. But in a free market system, what is going on in the system as a whole is reflected in the prices that the individual confronts every day in the market. Hayek illustrates his claim with his 'tin example', in which he shows that millions of market participants react 'in the right direction' when there is a change in the price of a good or resource, even though they may not know anything about what caused the change.[19]

---

[17] F. A. Hayek, "The Use of Knowledge in Society", this volume, p. 94.

[18] Ibid., p. 95.

[19] The tin example was first used by Hayek in "The Economics of Planning", a paper published in an Oxford student publication in 1941. See F. A. Hayek, "The Economics of Planning", in *Socialism and War: Essays, Documents, Reviews*, ed. Bruce Caldwell, vol. 10 (1997) of *The Collected Works of F. A. Hayek*, pp. 141–47.

Though he does not use the phrase, what Hayek is describing in the tin example is, quite evidently, a spontaneous order.

"The Use of Knowledge in Society" is Hayek's most famous paper, one frequently referenced as a seminal early contribution by economic theorists working in the economics of information.[20] The clarity of Hayek's presentation makes it equally accessible to students. In the annals of the history of economic thought, Hayek's tin example of how markets use dispersed information should rightly be placed alongside Adam Smith's 'pin factory' illustration of how the division of labour allows for huge increases in output.

Hayek draws some methodological conclusions. At the beginning of the paper, and much in keeping with ideas he expressed in "The Facts of the Social Sciences", he says that the very character of the fundamental problem had "been obscured rather than illuminated by many of the recent refinements in economic theory", refinements that he links to "an erroneous transfer to social phenomena of the habits of thought we have developed in dealing with the phenomena of nature."[21] Later in the paper he also notes how the use of static equilibrium analysis, which abstracts from change, "has made us somewhat blind to the true function of the price mechanism and led us to apply rather misleading standards in judging its efficiency."[22] Hayek would continue this theme in "The Meaning of Competition."

* * *

In July 1941 Hayek wrote to his old university friend Fritz Machlup, who was then living in Washington, D.C., and working at the Department of Commerce. Hayek had read an article by Machlup concerning competition and responded to it as follows: "I was particularly pleased to see that your developments fit in so well with my methodological views and that in many ways they border on views on competition which I hoped myself some time to develop. You more or less imply what I always stress, that competition is a process and

[20] See, e.g., Sanford Grossman, *The Informational Role of Prices* (Boston: MIT Press, 1989), pp. 1, 32, 108, 134; Leonid Hurwicz, "Economic Planning and the Knowledge Problem: A Comment", *Cato Journal*, vol. 4, Fall 1984, p. 419; Joseph Stiglitz, "The Contribution of the Economics of Information to Twentieth Century Economics", *The Quarterly Journal of Economics*, vol. 115, November 2000, pp. 1446–48, 1468–69. These authors, however, interpret Hayek as focusing on the informational properties of *equilibrium* prices, whereas—as we will see in "The Meaning of Competition"—his actual concern is with the signaling function of *disequilibrium* prices. Hayek's ideas on knowledge have also generated a vast secondary literature among those sympathetic to the Austrian view. Two representative examples are Esteban Thomsen, *Prices and Knowledge: A Market-Process Perspective* (London: Routledge, 1992), and Israel Kirzner, "Entrepreneurial Discovery and the Competitive Market Process: An Austrian Approach", *Journal of Economic Literature*, vol. 35, March 1997, pp. 60–85.

[21] Hayek, "Use of Knowledge in Society", this volume, p. 94.

[22] Ibid., p. 100.

not a state, and that if it were ever 'perfect' in the strict sense it would at the same time disappear."[23] It is no accident, then, that in his paper "The Meaning of Competition" Hayek in his first footnote cites a paper by Machlup, praising him for bringing the discussion of the meaning of competition "back to earth."[24]

In the aftermath of the war, the question of the regulation of industry was a key policy issue. Economists typically assert that competition leads to efficient market outcomes, for it forces firms to produce the goods that consumers desire at minimal costs. Firms that either produce the wrong goods relative to consumers' wants, or do so at costs higher than those of their competitors, do not survive in the market. The theoretical model that economists use to capture this common-sensical notion is the theory of perfect competition. That model (or, more precisely, its misuse in discussions about appropriate policy towards business) is Hayek's target in the article:

> It appears to be generally held that the so-called theory of 'perfect competition' provides the appropriate model for judging the effectiveness of competition in real life and that, to the extent that real competition differs from that model, it is undesirable and even harmful.
>
> For this attitude there seems to me to exist very little justification.[25]

For Hayek, "competition is by its nature a dynamic process whose essential characteristics are assumed away by the assumptions underlying static analysis."[26] Proposals to 'remedy' the imperfect competition that one finds in the real world—for example, by imposing 'orderly competition', by the compulsory standardization of products, or, in the most extreme case, by nationalizing industries deemed insufficiently competitive—reveal the dangers of taking the theoretical models too seriously.

Hayek notes that, paradoxically, our everyday notion of what competition entails is wholly absent from the economic theory of perfect competition. There is no rivalry or striving, no attempts to undercut a competitor or differentiate a product; in short, "'perfect' competition means indeed the absence of all competitive activities."[27] The larger methodological point is evident:

---

[23] F. A. Hayek to Fritz Machlup, July 31, 1941, Machlup Collection, box 43, folder 15, Hoover Institution Archives, Stanford University, Calif. (hereafter cited as Hoover Institution Archives). A similar position was taken by Schumpeter: see Joseph Schumpeter, *Capitalism, Socialism, and Democracy* (New York: Harper and Brothers, 1942; 3rd ed., New York: Harper and Row, 1950), chapter 7.

[24] F. A. Hayek, "The Meaning of Competition", this volume, p. 105.

[25] Ibid.

[26] Ibid., p. 107.

[27] Ibid., p. 109.

static equilibrium theory, with its focus on long-run outcomes when all adjustments have been made, obscures the fact that the forces of competition actually operate during periods of *disequilibrium*. Competition is the more important, the less perfect is the market. Attempts to replicate the artificial world of perfect competition are a recipe for policy disaster, for they can lead, in the pursuit of perfection, to the suppression of competition as it actually exists in the real world.

* * *

Hayek reprinted the four chapters just reviewed here in his 1948 collection *Individualism and Economic Order*. As noted above, "The Facts of the Social Sciences" connects up with his *Abuse of Reason* project. But the three other papers belong together. In "Economics and Knowledge" Hayek asserts that, to answer the question of how a movement towards societal equilibrium might ever come about in a world of dispersed knowledge and constant change, we will need to learn more about the *kinds* of knowledge that individuals must possess, and the *process* by which individuals will acquire them. In "The Use of Knowledge in Society", Hayek answers the first question: it is not scientific knowledge but specific knowledge of time and place that is most important. In "The Meaning of Competition", he answers the second: it is the market process—that is, the process of market competition—through which such specific knowledge is discovered and transmitted to others.

There were other essays in *Individualism and Economic Order*, including the three that constituted his contribution to the socialist calculation debate.[28] Even at this early stage, Hayek was integrating arguments about the correct methods of the social sciences with specific claims about the limits of certain theoretical concepts in economics and their potential for misleading us in terms of policy. The breadth of his vision would only increase in coming years.

Part II. From Chicago to Freiburg: Further Development

Having achieved his 'fifteen minutes of fame' with the publication of *The Road to Serfdom* in 1944,[29] from the summer of 1945 through much of the rest of the decade Hayek worked on a book on theoretical psychology that finally was

---

[28] Hayek, *Individualism and Economic Order*. Hayek's essays on socialism are collected in F. A. Hayek, *Socialism and War*, vol. 10 (1997) of *The Collected Works of F. A. Hayek*.

[29] F. A. Hayek, *The Road to Serfdom: Texts and Documents*, ed. Bruce Caldwell, vol. 2 (2007) of *The Collected Works of F. A. Hayek*. It is probably more accurate to say that the *Reader's Digest* condensation of the book in 1945 is what led to his international fame; for more on this, see the editor's introduction to *The Road to Serfdom*. His other activities in this period included organizing the first

published in 1952 as *The Sensory Order*. In 1950 Hayek left LSE for a position on the Committee on Social Thought at the University of Chicago, where he would remain for twelve years. This would be a critical decade for the development of his thought.

Beginning in October 1950, Hayek would organize each fall a two-quarter-long seminar on a topic of his choosing. The first two, titled "Equality and Justice" and "The Liberal Tradition", covered themes in political theory, philosophy, and history. These and subsequent seminars provided Hayek with the requisite background for his next great book. In November 1953 he told Fritz Machlup that the book would be titled *Greater Than Man: The Creative Powers of a Free Civilization*.[30] The next year, while on a seven-month trip with his wife to Italy and Greece, replicating to the day a journey that had been taken one hundred years before by John Stuart Mill,[31] Hayek took a side trip to Egypt to deliver four lectures at the National Bank of Cairo. He published them in 1955 as *The Political Ideal of the Rule of Law*. In later reminiscences Hayek recounted how the Cairo lectures helped him to organize his ideas for what would finally become *The Constitution of Liberty*: "Shortly after the conclusion of our journey, I had before me a clear plan for a book on liberty arranged round the Cairo lectures. In the three succeeding years, I wrote drafts of each of the three parts of *The Constitution of Liberty*, revising the whole during the winter of 1958–59, so that I was able to take the finished manuscript to my American publishers on my sixtieth birthday, May 8, 1959."[32]

In the Cairo lectures Hayek begins with classical treatments of the notion of "equality before the law", then traces the history of British liberalism and the further development of the concept of the rule of law from early statements in the seventeenth century through its establishment in the eighteenth. Next he discusses the American contribution of a Bill of Rights incorporated into a written constitution, then explores the German notion of a *Rechtsstaat*, the

---

meeting of the Mont Pèlerin Society and completing a book on the John Stuart Mill–Harriet Taylor correspondence.

[30] F. A. Hayek to Fritz Machlup, November 19, 1953, Machlup Collection, box 44, folder 1, Hoover Institution Archives. The name of the book would change to *The Constitution of Liberty*, but Hayek managed to incorporate the subtitle, using it as the title of chapter 2 of the book.

[31] Hayek's diary of the trip may be found in the Hayek Collection, box 125, folder 2, Hoover Institution Archives.

[32] F. A. Hayek, *Hayek on Hayek: An Autobiographical Dialogue*, ed. Stephen Kresge and Leif Wenar (Chicago: University of Chicago Press, and London: Routledge, 1994), p. 130. F. A. Hayek, *The Constitution of Liberty* (Chicago: University of Chicago Press, 1960); now see *The Constitution of Liberty*, ed. Ronald Hamowy, vol. 16 (2011) of *The Collected Works of F. A. Hayek*. In a "Memorandum on Plans for Work" dated November 1955, Hayek originally thought that there would be two books, the other titled *Greater Than Man: The Creative Powers of a Free Civilization*. But he ultimately integrated the themes he would have treated there into *The Constitution of Liberty*. For the "Memorandum", see the Hayek Collection, box 93, folder 11, Hoover Institution Archives.

attempt to place the administrative apparatus of the national state under the rule of law. Hayek goes on to identify the key attributes of the rule of law (e.g., the rule of law as a meta-principle; the importance of its generality, certainty, and equality of enforcement[33]) and concludes with a description of its decline in the late nineteenth and early twentieth centuries. The core middle chapters of *The Constitution of Liberty* (chapters 11 through 16) would draw directly on the ideas first expressed in *The Political Ideal of the Rule of Law*.

Our main concern, though, is with the statements Hayek makes in his lectures about the relationship between rules (which in this case are laws) and the orders that rule-following behaviour creates. At the beginning of the third lecture, Hayek notes the human tendency to see an intentional design behind every orderly pattern, a tendency that can mislead:

> It is a deeply ingrained tendency of the human mind that whenever it discovers an orderly pattern, it believes that this must have been designed by a mind like itself and assumes that there can be no order without such conscious design. But if a multitude of individual elements obey certain general laws, this may of course produce a definite order of the whole mass without the interference of an outside force. This applies to the laws obeyed by men no less than to the laws of nature; and however much the two meanings of the term law may have moved apart, if we look for a moment at the most general aspects of that relationship, the general nature of our problem would be placed in a clearer light.[34]

In nature, orders may form even when we cannot make precise predictions about the behaviour or movements of the individual elements that compose the order. Because of the dispersion of knowledge, "this is precisely the problem" that we face "in creating an order in society."[35]

---

[33] Hayek's reliance on the rule of law for restraining coercion by government has been criticized. See, e.g., Ronald Hamowy, "The Hayekian Model of Government in an Open Society", in *The Political Sociology of Freedom: Adam Ferguson and F. A. Hayek* (Cheltenham, UK: Edward Elgar, 2005), p. 235: "It has been shown that no purely formal criteria of the sort Hayek has offered, that is, that all laws be general, predictable, and certain, can effectively curtail the extent of governmental intrusion. . . . Only by placing unequivocal, substantive limitations on what laws may be enacted would it be possible to control the areas in which the legislature may intervene, and, even then, one would still require a vigilant and suspicious judiciary to ride herd on the legislature. The decisions concerning which areas must be off limits to the legislature can be made only on the basis of a theory of rights, which logically precedes a theory of government. This is a conception that Hayek, for some reason, fails to come to grips with." For an earlier version of his critique, see Ronald Hamowy, "Hayek's Concept of Freedom", *New Individualist Review*, vol. 1, April 1961, pp. 28–31.

[34] F. A. Hayek, *The Political Ideal of the Rule of Law*, this volume, p. 160.

[35] Ibid., p. 161.

The Political Ideal of the Rule of Law is, then, one of the first places in which Hayek moves beyond market phenomena to apply the idea that individual elements, by following rules, may give rise to orders. It is also the first place that the phrase (though not the concept of!) 'spontaneous order' appears in Hayek's work.[36] The ideas noted above are incorporated into *The Constitution of Liberty* in chapter 10, which is titled, appropriately enough, "Laws, Commands, and Order."

* * *

In the same year as the Cairo lectures Hayek published "Degrees of Explanation" in the *British Journal for the Philosophy of Science*. His subject, as in the "Scientism" essay, is scientific method. But instead of enumerating the differences between the natural and the social sciences as he had done in the earlier work, Hayek notes characteristics that *all* sciences share in common. For example, all theoretical sciences construct hypothetico-deductive systems. Such systems cannot be verified, but because they forbid certain events, they can be falsified. Explanation and prediction are two aspects of the same scientific procedure. And so on.

Only after discussing what all sciences share does he get to where the sciences differ, which is in the *degree* of explanation that each is able to achieve (hence the title of the paper) by using these methods. In particular, sciences that study complex phenomena are able to provide only a range, or pattern, of predicted values rather than specific predictions of particular events. Put another way, they are able to offer only an explanation of the principle by which a process works, and thereby to predict only certain types of outcomes. Because they forbid certain types of outcomes, such theories are still weakly testable, so they are still scientific. But precise prediction, often seen as the hallmark of science, is in such cases impossible.

In the "Scientism" essay Hayek had drawn a dividing line between the natural and the social sciences. In "Degrees of Explanation" the dividing line is between those sciences that study relatively simple phenomena and those that study relatively complex phenomena. What is the significance, if any, of the switch?

The principal reason for the change, and it is an important one, is that the distinction as Hayek had originally drawn it was inconsistent with the prevailing philosophy of science of his day, which insisted that there was a unity of scientific method. Hayek's friend Karl Popper had advocated the unity of science thesis in "The Poverty of Historicism", thereby implicitly criticizing Hayek's bifurcation of the methods of the natural and social sciences.[37] When

---

[36] Ibid.

[37] Karl Popper, "The Poverty of Historicism, III", *Economica*, n.s., vol. 12, May 1945, pp. 78–82; reprinted, *The Poverty of Historicism*, 2nd ed. (London: Routledge, 1960), pp. 130–31.

The Counter-Revolution of Science was published in 1952, in a review the philosopher Ernest Nagel explicitly attacked this part of Hayek's argument.[38] Hayek doubtless also received criticism during his 1952 seminar at Chicago, which was on the methods of the sciences.[39] Hayek wanted to retain the idea that in sciences like economics it was often the case that only pattern predictions or explanations of the principle were possible, but the distinction between natural and social science was not the right way to draw the line.

The mathematician Warren Weaver showed Hayek the way out. Weaver was a referee for Hayek's paper at the *British Journal* and sent Hayek a lengthy report criticizing his presentation. He included with the report a copy of his 1948 paper "Science and Complexity."[40] In that paper Weaver had argued that, up until about 1900, the physical sciences had dealt principally with simple phenomena, isolating and representing mathematically only a few variables. The physical sciences then moved to the study of phenomena of 'disorganized complexity' in which millions of variables interact randomly and to which probability theory and statistical methods could fruitfully be applied. The next stage, one just entered at the time of Weaver's paper, would take up phenomena of 'organized complexity.' In such phenomena, millions of variables are again encountered, but the variables are inter-related rather than independent, so that the usual statistical methods do not apply. According to Weaver, such phenomena exist in a variety of fields, and new methods will be needed for their investigation. Weaver's distinction provided Hayek with a way to emphasize the limits faced by the social sciences without making them seem any less scientific. From this time forward, Hayek virtually always referenced Weaver's paper when he discussed the study of complex phenomena. And he would almost always use the simple-versus-complex distinction when describing methodological differences among the sciences.

Karl Popper is mentioned frequently in the article, and it would therefore be easy to take Hayek at his word when he says in an early footnote that "in many respects what follows is little more than an elaboration of some of Popper's ideas."[41] And indeed Popper had helped him by suggesting that what Hayek had (in Popper's view) rightfully criticized in "Scientism" were not truly the methods of the natural sciences but rather the inaccurate reconstructions of philosophical observers.[42]

---

[38] Ernest Nagel, "Review of F. A. Hayek, *The Counter-Revolution of Science*", *Journal of Philosophy*, vol. 49, August 1952, pp. 560–65.

[39] For more on the seminar, see Caldwell, *Hayek's Challenge*, pp. 298–99.

[40] Warren Weaver, "Science and Complexity", *American Scientist*, vol. 36, October 1948, pp. 536–44. Note that the first citation in Hayek's article is to Weaver's paper. Weaver's referee report may be found in the Hayek Collection, box 137, folder 10, Hoover Institution Archives.

[41] F. A. Hayek, "Degrees of Explanation", this volume, p. 196, note 3.

[42] In *The Poverty of Historicism* (1960), Popper redefined Hayek's "scientism" as "the imitation of *what certain people mistake* for the method and language of science" (p. 105, emphasis in the

But it is also evident that as soon as one accepts that there are "degrees of explanation", strict falsifiability as a criterion for assessing theories becomes much harder to apply. The implications are consequential: "Because such theories are difficult to disprove, the elimination of inferior rival theories will be a slow affair, bound up closely with the argumentative skill and persuasiveness of those who employ them. There can be no crucial experiments which decide between them. There will be opportunities for grave abuses: possibilities for pretentious, over-elaborate theories which no simple test but only the good sense of those equally competent in the field can refute."[43] Furthermore, this state of affairs will not change with the progress of science; to think otherwise "would be a complete misunderstanding of the argument of this essay."[44]

A final point: evolutionary theory appears prominently in this paper as an exemplar of a science that studies complex phenomena. Evolutionary theory would come to play an increasingly important rôle in Hayek's explanations of how spontaneous orders form.

* * *

It is a commonplace that Hayek stopped working on economics and turned instead to political philosophy in the 1950's and 1960's. Like many commonplaces, it is untrue. Reproduced in figure I.1 is a hand-drawn book cover for *A Grammar of the Economic Calculus*. The date on the cover suggests that as early as 1952 he envisaged writing a book on economics. Notes for "Topics and Problems" to be covered in the book also exist, and include such things as economics and engineering, measurement, choice, equivalence, opportunity cost, as well as their "Corresponding Fallacies", among these the notions of objective value, an optimum, energetics, and the just price.[45] In his 1955 "Memorandum on Plans for Work" Hayek included the book as a possible project: "I do hope not completely to abandon my work on technical economics. I had long thought that the next book in that field would be *A Grammar of the Economic Calculus*—a sort of rigorous introduction into the basic logic of economics intended mainly for scientists and people with a scientifically trained mind. But although I have collected a good deal of material for this, it still proves very refractory to shaping in a book."[46]

---

original). That Hayek accepted this move is evident in, e.g., his "Preface to the Italian Edition of *The Counter-Revolution of Science*", (ms., Hayek Collection, box 129, folder 12, Hoover Institution Archives), where he states, "Sir Karl Popper has by his critique of 'inductivism' convinced me that the natural sciences did in fact not follow the method which most of its practitioners believed that they did employ." For a similar acknowledgement, cf. his preface to *Studies in Philosophy, Politics and Economics* (Chicago: University of Chicago Press, 1967), p. viii.
[43] F. A. Hayek, "Degrees of Explanation", this volume, p. 210.
[44] Ibid.
[45] Hayek Collection, box 129, folders 5 and 6, Hoover Institution Archives.
[46] "Memorandum on Plans for Work, November 1955", Hayek Collection, box 93, folder 11, Hoover Institution Archives.

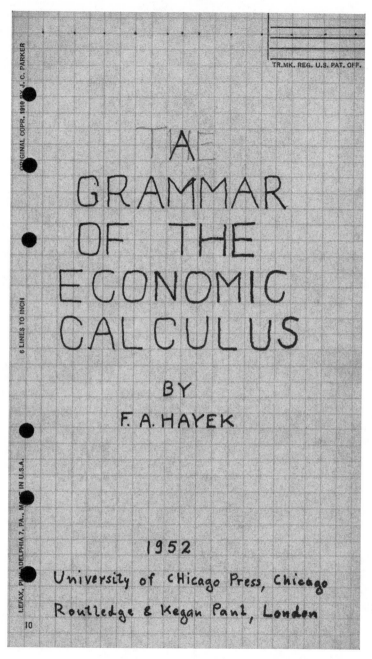

Figure I.1   Book cover hand-drawn by F. A. Hayek. Friedrich A. von Hayek Papers, box 129, folder 5, Hoover Institution Archives.

Four years later he had changed the title to *A New Look at Economic Theory* and stated that it would be a much simpler book, "merely an outline of the economic calculus followed by an examination of the working of the money economy."[47] A year later, however, he had another change in direction, telling Karl Popper that he hoped to restate his views on the nature of economic theory using "the conception of higher level regularities", an idea that he felt would be "fruitful far beyond the field of economics." He went on to say, "I suspect it is really what Bertalanffy with his General Systems Theory was after and the conception itself was of course already implied in my 'Degrees of Explanation.' It continues to become clearer, though I have not yet got an altogether satisfactory formulation of what I am after."[48]

The next year, in spring 1961, Hayek delivered four lectures at the University of Virginia on the subject.[49] This was Hayek's attempt to further integrate his new ideas about complex orders into his work in economics, where in fact his first insights had come.

Hayek's starting point is the claim that many economic phenomena are in fact organized but undesigned complex orders. In the second half of the first lecture, and in the second lecture, Hayek examines what he calls "the economic calculus"—that is, the tools that economists use to describe "the patterns (or the regularity or the order) which we find in the economic phenomena."[50] He provides some diagrams to capture these, some of them familiar because they are used in undergraduate textbooks, others of his own invention—the latter are mostly used to clarify the logic of choice. The economic calculus, then, consists of those parts of economic theory that attempt to portray analytically a certain structure—namely, "the interrelation of the decisions about resource allocation in conditions where all the relevant facts are known to a single mind."[51] Its usefulness is displayed in the third lecture, in which Hayek

[47] "Memorandum on Plans for Work, November 1959", Hayek Collection, box 93, folder 11, Hoover Institution Archives.

[48] Hayek to Popper, February 27, 1960, Hayek Collection, box 44, folder 2, Hoover Institution Archives. A founder of general systems theory, the Austrian-born biologist Ludwig Bertalanffy (1901–1972) was a friend of Hayek's and had offered him comments on *The Sensory Order* when it was in manuscript form.

[49] Hayek's lectures were sponsored by the Thomas Jefferson Center for Studies in Political Economy. The month before giving the first of his lectures, Hayek attended a conference, "Scientific Alternatives to Communism", at the University of Notre Dame. He presented a paper titled "Economic Order and Freedom" in which he explored his developing ideas about complex phenomena in a comparison between a centrally planned and market economy. The ideas about complex phenomena show up again in his Virginia lectures, as well as in "The Theory of Complex Phenomena." The Notre Dame paper was also never published; it may be found in the Hayek Collection, box 108, folder 1, Hoover Institution Archives.

[50] F. A. Hayek, A New Look at Economic Theory, "Lecture II. The Economic Calculus", this volume, p. 387.

[51] Ibid., "Lecture IV. The Communication Function of the Market", p. 415.

discusses choices among technologies that face developing countries. In the last lecture he contrasts the assumptions made when employing the economic calculus with those applicable in "the world of action" in which "not only different people have different knowledge but where their actions lead constantly to the acquisition of new knowledge",[52] and where the communication rôle of the market comes into play.

The lectures help clarify exactly what Hayek meant by claiming that many economic phenomena are unplanned, complex adaptive orders and emphasizing that the economic calculus, though useful for some purposes, is less helpful for analyzing the formation of such orders. But he never published them. Why not?

It is clear from the text of the lectures that Hayek felt that, though he had been able to restate some earlier insights, he had not really advanced the discussion in the way that he had hoped when he had written to Popper. This was confirmed by James Buchanan, Hayek's host at the University of Virginia, who later reflected on the talks: "These lectures were failures, at least by Professor Hayek's own standards. Those who listened to them were, of course, rewarded by a careful review of the earlier analysis of knowledge in relation to economic interaction. But Hayek was unable to go beyond that which he had developed two decades before; no new insights emerged as he reviewed the earlier thought processes. His announced ambitions were thwarted."[53]

Instead of publishing the lectures, Hayek incorporated parts of them in later writings. Because they are of considerable historical interest, and indeed advance our understanding of the development of Hayek's ideas, the four talks are reproduced in the appendix to this volume.

* * *

In 1962 Hayek accepted a professorship at the University of Freiburg, an appointment that would also provide a modest lifetime pension. This was important as a practical matter for him, as he was not to receive a pension from the University of Chicago, only a lump-sum payment for his years on the faculty. He delivered his inaugural lecture, "The Economy, Science and Politics", on June 18, 1962. The address is at once a pedagogic statement about proper teaching practices and a meditation on the place of the economist in public life. But Hayek also deals with methodological issues, asking what can be known by economists, a theme that he links to his developing views on complex phenomena.

Within economics Hayek had always been a theorist. The move to Freiburg

---

[52] Ibid.

[53] James Buchanan, "I Did Not Call Him 'Fritz': Personal Recollections of Professor F. A. v. Hayek", *Constitutional Political Economy*, vol. 3, 1992, p. 131.

marked yet another departure from his earlier paths, for his charge there was to lecture on economic policy. Things become complicated when one moves from the realm of pure theory to the evaluation of policy. To evaluate policy, value judgments must be made.

Hayek accordingly begins with a statement about the proper rôle of value judgments in science. He endorses the standard Austrian view, one derived from the writings of the German sociologist and economist Max Weber, that positive claims must be kept separate from normative ones.[54] When evaluating policy, one starts with positive questions, where the key goal is to clarify the expected consequences of one's policy decisions. Hayek here is underlining that fundamental insight of economics, that policies must be evaluated by their actual, rather than their intended, results.[55]

Of course, figuring out what those results are going to be is difficult when one deals with something as complex as an economy. Though we may have abstract theoretical models that represent mathematically the structure of economic phenomena, rarely are we in a position to fill in the variables with data. As he had maintained in "Degrees of Explanation", often the best we can do is to determine the general character of the order, or to offer a prediction about its general arrangement. Hayek takes swipes at Paretian general equilibrium theory, or "the mathematical theory of prices", as well as at Keynesian macroeconomics.[56] Instead of longing for the will-o'-the-wisp of precise prediction, which would require that we have more knowledge than we could ever attain, we should content ourselves with our general knowledge, which is, after all, often quite useful. Hayek provides a pedagogic twist to make the point:

> Not because he knows so much, but because he knows how much he would have to know in order to interfere successfully, and because he knows that he will never know all the relevant circumstances, it would seem that the economist should refrain from recommending isolated acts of interference even in conditions in which the theory tells him that they may sometimes be beneficial. . . .
>
> It is no accident that in our subject the term 'principles' is so often used

[54] Weber had developed his views on value-freedom while chastising his German historical school colleagues for injecting value judgments into their lectures. For more on this, see Caldwell, *Hayek's Challenge*, chapter 4.

[55] Perhaps this was best said by Henry Simons, who noted in the syllabus for his principles of economics course, "Economics is primarily useful, both to the student and to the political leader, as a prophylactic against popular fallacies." See Henry Calvert Simons, *The Simons' Syllabus*, ed. Gordon Tullock (Fairfax, VA: Center for the Study of Public Choice, George Mason University, 1983), p. 3.

[56] F. A. Hayek, "The Economy, Science and Politics", this volume, pp. 223–24.

in the titles of general treatises. Especially so far as economic policy is concerned, principles are practically all that we have to contribute.[57]

*   *   *

In 1963 Hayek returned to the University of Chicago to give a series of lectures under the sponsorship of the Charles R. Walgreen Foundation.[58] Two of the lectures are reminiscences of economics in 1920's Vienna and 1930's London and have been published previously in the *Collected Works* series.[59] Another, titled "Types of Theoretical Thinking", appears to be an early version of what was eventually reworked, retitled, and published as "Two Types of Mind."[60] Another lecture, "Economists and Philosophers", documents how most of the economists in the British tradition from the Scottish Enlightenment through the early twentieth century had also made contributions that one might broadly describe as philosophical. Given this history, Hayek laments the scientistic turn away from philosophy that took place in the twentieth century. In doing so, he provides in the second half of the lecture a discussion of the study of complex orders that repeats arguments found in other papers in this volume. "Economists and Philosophers" is reproduced for the first time in the appendix.[61]

*   *   *

The final selection in the second part of this volume is "Rules, Perception and Intelligibility", a paper first published in 1962 in the *Proceedings of the British Academy*. It is a remarkable piece in which Hayek integrates insights from a wide diversity of fields, among them linguistics, ethology, Gestalt psychology,

[57] Ibid., p. 227.

[58] George Stigler, who occupied the Walgreen Chair and was in charge of the funds provided by the foundation, was his host. For more on Stigler's rôle at Chicago, see Edward Nik-Khah, "George Stigler, the Graduate School of Business, and the Pillars of the Chicago School", in *Building Chicago Economics: New Perspectives on the History of America's Most Powerful Economics Program*, ed. Robert Van Horn, Philip Mirowski, and Thomas A. Stapleford (Cambridge: Cambridge University Press, 2011), pp. 116–47.

[59] F. A. Hayek, "The Economics of the 1920's as Seen from Vienna", *The Fortunes of Liberalism: Essays on Austrian Economics and the Ideal of Freedom*, ed. Peter Klein, vol. 4 (1992) of *The Collected Works of F. A. Hayek*, pp. 19–38; and Hayek, "The Economics of the 1930's as Seen from London", *Contra Keynes and Cambridge: Essays, Correspondence*, ed. Bruce Caldwell, vol. 9 (1995) of *The Collected Works of F. A. Hayek*, pp. 49–63.

[60] F. A. Hayek, "Two Types of Mind" [1975], reprinted in *The Trend of Economic Thinking: Essays on Political Economists and Economic History*, ed. W. W. Bartley III and Stephen Kresge, vol. 3 (1991) of *The Collected Works of F. A. Hayek*, pp. 49–55.

[61] F. A. Hayek, "Economists and Philosophers", Hayek Collection, box 138, folder 12, Hoover Institution Archives; and Hayek, "Types of Theoretical Thinking", Hayek Collection, box 138, folder 15, Hoover Institution Archives.

THE MARKET AND OTHER ORDERS

physiology, biology, aesthetics, the methodology of the social sciences, and the philosophy of mind.

Hayek's starting point is that all animals, including humans, follow rules of which they are not aware. Two examples he provides are the ability of small children to learn to speak using rules of grammar that they know nothing of but which are themselves exceedingly complex, and our ability to identify emotional states by the facial expressions of people who are widely different in appearance.[62] Both skills depend on our ability to recognize abstract patterns and follow abstract rules. Drawing on the psychological theory he had developed in *The Sensory Order*, Hayek proposes a physiological basis for these abilities in the workings of the hierarchical structure of the brain. Hayek postulates that there are multiple chains of rules, on both the perceptual side and the motor side, and their totality is what ultimately leads to a disposition to act: "It is the total of such activated rules (or conditions imposed upon further action) which constitutes what is called the 'set' (disposition) of the organism at any particular moment, and the significance of newly received signals consists in the manner in which they modify this complex of rules."[63]

Hayek ends his piece by asking whether we will ever be in a position to specify all the rules that guide our perception and action. He thinks that the answer is no, postulating that conscious thought is itself governed by rules of which we are necessarily unconscious. Hayek notes that this supports a claim that he made in both the "Scientism" essay and in *The Sensory Order* (some twenty and ten years earlier, respectively) that any system of classification would have to be of a greater degree of complexity than the object that it attempts to classify, which he feels implies that it is impossible for the brain to provide anything more than an explanation of the principle by which the brain operates.[64] The mind is yet another instance of a complex order, one that follows rules that we cannot specify but which allow us to navigate in that complex order known as society, which itself contains a host of rule-constrained orders: language, the economic system, the legal system, our system of morals, and so on. Complex orders are everywhere. The next year Hayek would write "Kinds of Rationalism", which placed the further articulation of these insights prominently and permanently on his agenda.

[62] This example about recognizing faces appears in both "Scientism", p. 110, and in "Facts of the Social Sciences", this volume, p. 84.

[63] F. A. Hayek, "Rules, Perception and Intelligibility", this volume, p. 247.

[64] Ibid., pp. 250–51. Hayek's discussion earlier in the paper of "dispositions" to act also helped to bridge the gap between neuronal connections in the brain and the end result of intentional action, a problem that he had grappled with, unsuccessfully, in his incomplete paper "Within Systems and about Systems." That paper will be reprinted for the first time in the *Collected Works* edition of *The Sensory Order*.

Part III. A General Theory of Orders, with Applications

Though completed in December 1961 (that is, in the same year as the Virginia lectures), "The Theory of Complex Phenomena" was not published until 1964, when it appeared in a festschrift volume for Karl Popper. In the paper Hayek accomplishes at least part of the goal that he had identified in his 1960 letter to Popper, that of providing a more complete statement of the themes first covered in "Degrees of Explanation."

Hayek's goal is to distinguish clearly the difference between sciences that study simple phenomena versus those that study complex phenomena. Complexity arises both because "the minimum number of distinct variables a formula or model must possess in order to reproduce the characteristic patterns of structures" increases, and due to the fact of "the 'emergence' of 'new' patterns as a result of the increase in the number of elements between which simple relations exist."[65] In such instances one cannot get sufficient data to make anything more than a pattern prediction. Because the elements are interconnected, statistical techniques which disregard that "the relative position of the different elements in a structure may matter" are "impotent to deal with pattern complexity."[66]

At the end of the paper Hayek makes two important claims. He notes that, because a society's system of values and morals is also the product of an evolutionary process, "we have no more ground to ascribe to them eternal existence than to the human race itself."[67] He is quick to add, however, that—just as the mind cannot explain consciousness—there is no way to get outside of our own cultural heritage, no way to know how the values that govern us emerged through time. He concludes that this should produce in us a certain humility towards the values that have survived the millennia. The applicability of an evolutionary theory of complex phenomena to the explanation of the origins of human moral codes—a theme that would be highlighted in later work— was by this point quite clearly on Hayek's agenda.[68]

The second insight was in regard to how we should react to our ignorance when it comes to the study of complex phenomena. Hayek asserts that knowledge of the limits of our knowledge is itself an important type of knowledge: "Once we explicitly recognize that the understanding of the general mecha-

---

[65] F. A. Hayek, "The Theory of Complex Phenomena", this volume, pp. 261–62. This is the first instance where Hayek specifically identifies emergent phenomena as giving rise to complexity.
[66] Ibid., pp. 264–65.
[67] Ibid., p. 273.
[68] See, e.g., F. A. Hayek, *Law, Legislation and Liberty*, vol. 3, *The Political Order of a Free People* (Chicago: University of Chicago Press, 1979), epilogue; and Hayek, *The Fatal Conceit*, ed. W. W. Bartley III, vol. 1 (1988) of *The Collected Works of F. A. Hayek*.

nism which produces patterns of a certain kind is not merely a tool for specific predictions but important in its own right, and that it may provide important guides to action (or sometimes indications of the desirability of no action), we may indeed find that this limited knowledge is most valuable."[69]

* * *

Perhaps Hayek's most ambitious attempt to investigate the varieties of fields in which spontaneous orders might be found is the "Analogy Symposium", a meeting he organized that took place at the Villa Serbelloni in Bellagio, Italy, on April 17–24, 1966. In his initial proposal, Hayek describes the purpose of the academic gathering as

> a symposium on unconscious rules governing conscious action. The discussion would have to start by considering the rôle which rules not known to the actor play in physical skills, language, law and morals, the visual arts with the aim of throwing light on
> - the cultural transmission of unformulated rules (i.e., their acquisition without explicit teaching)
> - the requirement of the common possession of unformulated rules for the intelligibility of communications
> - the general problem of pre-conscious learning from experience (the formation and alteration of an unconscious framework within which conscious thought moves).[70]

Unfortunately, many of those invited to the symposium could not come. The next year, though, Hayek published "Notes on the Evolution of Systems of Rules of Conduct", which carries the subtitle "The Interplay between Rules of Individual Conduct and the Social Order of Actions." The article is Hayek's clearest attempt to provide a statement at the highest level of generality of the relationship between rules and orders, and of their evolution.

Hayek begins by noting that he would use "the pairs of concepts 'order and its elements' and 'groups and individuals' inter-changeably", thereby underlining the fact that orders occur everywhere, not just in human societies.[71] He then lays out the links between complex spontaneously-forming orders, evolution, and rule-following behaviour.[72]

---

[69] Hayek, "Theory of Complex Phenomena", this volume, p. 275.

[70] Hayek Collection, box 65, folder 7, Hoover Institution Archives.

[71] F. A. Hayek, "Notes on the Evolution of Systems of Rules of Conduct: The Interplay between Rules of Individual Conduct and the Social Order of Actions", this volume, p. 278, note 2.

[72] The summary draws directly on a similar one found in Caldwell, *Hayek's Challenge*, pp. 309–10.

1. Orders of various sorts exist in nature. An order occurs when the actions of various elements or members of a group are co-ordinated or brought into mutual adjustment.

2. Sometimes orders occur without anyone consciously designing them. Such spontaneous orders come into being as the result of the individual elements following rules, rules that do not aim at creating the resulting order as a goal.

3. We can say a number of things about the rules that can generate spontaneous orders:

   a. Rules are often simple and often take the form of prohibitions.

   b. Individuals, even when they are capable of speech, need not know that they *are* following rules, or even if they do, need not be able to *articulate* the rules.

   c. Individuals often cannot say *why* they are following the rules that they do nor can they see what the actual *results* of the rules are.

   d. Not all rules lead to order, and those that lead to an order in a given environment may become dysfunctional if the environment changes. In fleshing this out, Hayek again introduces the notion of emergent phenomena.[73]

4. Given what has been said about rules, it should be evident that typically they are not consciously selected by individuals aiming at an order. Rather, rules persist when the groups in which they are practiced persist.[74]

5. The past history of a group, which includes the environments it faced in the past and its past rules, determines what rules will be followed in the present and the corresponding nature of the order.

6. Orders vary in complexity. Social orders are among the most complex: "Societies differ from simpler complex structures by the fact that their elements are themselves complex structures whose chance to persist depends on (or at least is improved by) their being part of the more comprehensive structure."[75]

7. When dealing with complex orders, often the best we can do is to provide an "explanation of the principle" by which they operate. Precise predictions will not be possible; only "pattern predictions" about the range of phenomena to expect will be available.

---

[73] See Hayek, "Notes on the Evolution of Systems of Rules of Conduct", pp. 282–83: "A change of environment may require, if the whole is to persist, a change in the order of the group and therefore in the rules of conduct of the individuals; and a spontaneous change of the rules of individual conduct and of the resulting order may enable the group to persist in circumstances which, without such change, would have led to its destruction." I thank Will Christie for bringing the importance of this passage to my attention.

[74] As he put it, in both "animal and human societies . . . the genetic (and in a great measure also the cultural) *transmission* of rules of conduct takes place *from individual to individual*, while what may be called the natural *selection* of rules will operate on the basis of the greater or lesser efficiency of the resulting *order of the group*." Ibid., p. 279, emphasis in the original. Though Hayek does not use the term 'group selection' in the article, the idea is clearly present, and he approvingly cites the work of a prominent advocate of the theory, V. C. Wynn-Edwards, on p. 282, note 8.

[75] Ibid., p. 288.

8. As such, the theories we develop to explain complex orders will forbid fewer events, and thus will be less falsifiable, than those that deal with simple phenomena. As Hayek puts it in "The Theory of Complex Phenomena", this creates a dichotomy among the sciences: "The advance of science will thus have to proceed in two different directions: while it is certainly desirable to make our theories as falsifiable as possible, we must also push forward into fields where, as we advance, the degree of falsifiability necessarily decreases. This is the price we have to pay for an advance into the field of complex phenomena."[76]

* * *

Intellectual history was always an important component of Hayek's work. Indeed, his great unfinished *Abuse of Reason* project was intended to show that ideas matter, that the course of Western history was forever changed by the contemporaneous dual emergence of scientism and socialism. In "The Results of Human Action but Not of Human Design" Hayek asks a related question in intellectual history: Why have people so often lost sight of spontaneous orders? Though René Descartes (always identified by Hayek as the father of rationalist constructivism) was the one who got us off track in the modern era, Hayek here traces the misstep all the way back to the distinction made by Greek philosophers between the natural and the artificial, where the latter meant 'constructed by man.' This apparently common-sensical distinction misses, of course, all those phenomena which arise, in the phrase used in his essay's title, as a result of human action but not of human design.

Much of the paper is devoted to showing how Descartes's subversion was followed by a revival of the concept of order by the Spanish Schoolmen and by British moral philosophers like Adam Smith and David Hume, as well as by some whose names are less well recognized like Josiah Tucker and Adam Ferguson.[77] These men gradually "built up a social theory which made the undesigned results of individual action its central object, and in particular provided a comprehensive theory of the spontaneous order of the market."[78] This idea, ever after associated with Adam Smith's metaphor of "the invisible hand", was derided by social theorists in the nineteenth century, who claimed (falsely, according to Hayek) that it implied a natural harmony of interests. Only later was it revived by the Austrian economist Carl Menger, though he

---

[76] Hayek, "Theory of Complex Phenomena", this volume, p. 264.

[77] Hayek first began referencing the Scottish Enlightenment philosophers for their insights into spontaneously forming social orders in his 1945 essay, "Individualism: True and False", which he had intended to be the opening chapter of the *Abuse of Reason* volume. The essay is reprinted as a prelude in Hayek, *Studies on the Abuse and Decline of Reason*. Ferguson was the originator of the phrase "the result of human action, but not the execution of any human design."

[78] F. A. Hayek, "The Results of Human Action but Not of Human Design", this volume, p. 296.

too began from the insights of a jurist, in this instance the founder of the German historical school of law, Friedrich Karl von Savigny. Hayek tells an evolutionary story about why certain social institutions formed and survived—they developed "in a particular way because the co-ordination of the actions of the parts which they secured proved more effective than the alternative institutions with which they had competed and which they had displaced. The theory of evolution of traditions and habits which made the formation of spontaneous orders possible stands therefore in a close relation to the theory of evolution of the particular kinds of spontaneous orders which we call organisms, and has in fact provided the essential concepts on which the latter was built."[79]

In the last part of the article Hayek laments the fact that these insights, by now well-established in the theoretical social sciences, seem to have had very little impact in the field of jurisprudence—an ironic fact, given their origins. In that field the dominant philosophy, legal positivism, views all rules of justice as having been produced by deliberate invention or design. Hayek would further develop his critique of legal positivism, something already begun in *The Constitution of Liberty*, in the second volume of his *Law, Legislation and Liberty* trilogy.[80]

* * *

"Competition as a Discovery Procedure" ties together two of Hayek's great themes, the knowledge problem and the idea of competition, and thereby complements his earlier essays "The Use of Knowledge in Society" and "The Meaning of Competition."[81] Hayek states the relationship early on, in a decidedly paradoxical way: "If anyone really knew all about what economic theory calls the *data*, competition would indeed be a very wasteful method of securing adjustment to these facts."[82] It is precisely because we are ignorant of virtually all of the data—which is simply to say, there is a dispersion of knowledge—that competition as a discovery procedure comes into its own.

Hayek illustrates the point with an example. As every Economics 101 student is (or should be) taught, the beginning of economic reasoning is the fundamental fact of scarcity.[83] But how do we come to discover which goods are

---

[79] Ibid., p. 298.

[80] See Hayek, *Constitution of Liberty*, vol. 16 (2011) of *The Collected Works of F. A. Hayek*, pp. 347–350; and Hayek, *The Mirage of Social Justice*, vol. 2 of *Law, Legislation and Liberty* (Chicago: University of Chicago Press, 1976), chapter 8.

[81] It might also be interpreted as Hayek's attempt to state in a more concise form some of the arguments from his Virginia lectures.

[82] F. A. Hayek, "Competition as a Discovery Procedure", this volume, p. 304.

[83] Scarcity makes choice among alternatives necessary; the cost of every choice is the highest-valued alternative that must be foregone, so that all choices have opportunity costs; economics is the study of choice in a world of scarcity.

scarce? We owe this knowledge to the forces of competition: "Which goods are scarce goods, or which things are goods, and how scarce or valuable they are—these are precisely the things which competition has to discover."[84] He notes further that some dislike the market order because of its impersonal nature, and others because it has no purpose of its own. But these attributes are in fact virtues, for the adjustments made every day as the result of impersonal market forces allow millions of individuals to make use of the knowledge possessed by millions of other individuals—as expressed through relative prices—in the pursuit of their *own* purposes and goals.

Hayek notes the analogy between the forces of competition in the market and the process of scientific discovery. Both are efficient engines of discovery, but because we can never know in advance what will be discovered, there is no way to test empirically the claim that they are better than other procedures for discovering knowledge. He also expresses a preference for the term 'order' over 'equilibrium' in describing the competitive market process. 'Equilibrium' is, according to Hayek, "a somewhat unfortunate term, because such an equilibrium presupposes that the facts have already all been discovered and competition therefore has ceased."[85] The term 'order' emphasizes the mutual adjustment of plans that takes place in complex, self-organizing systems. All such systems use negative feedback—in the case of economics, a disappointment of expectations—to generate adjustments in 'the proper direction.' The market is not perfect in doing this, but it is often good enough, and "we do injustice to the achievement of the market if we judge it, as it were, from above, by comparing it with an ideal standard which we have no known way of achieving."[86]

* * *

"The Primacy of the Abstract" was prepared for a symposium organized by Arthur Koestler in Alpbach in the Tyrolean mountains in 1968.[87] In his preface Koestler, a self-described "trespasser from the humanist camp",[88] provides a

---

[84] Hayek, "Competition as a Discovery Procedure", p. 306.

[85] Ibid., p. 308. In an address at LSE in 1981, Hayek would go even further, abandoning the term 'equilibrium' and embracing instead the metaphor of a stream. The address, titled "The Flow of Goods and Services", now appears in *Business Cycles, Part II*, ed. Hansjoerg Klausinger, vol. 8 (2012) of *The Collected Works of F. A. Hayek*.

[86] Hayek, "Competition as a Discovery Procedure", p. 309.

[87] Hungarian-born author Arthur Koestler (1905–1983), author of the anti-totalitarian novel *Darkness at Noon* (1940), owned a home in Alpbach. He had been among those invited by Hayek to the Analogy Seminar, but he did not attend. The Tyrolean mountain village of Alpbach had been the host to a summer school since 1945, at which Hayek was a frequent participant.

[88] Arthur Koestler, "Opening Remarks", in *The Alpach Symposium 1968, Beyond Reductionism: New Perspectives in the Life Sciences*, ed. Arthur Koestler and J. R. Smythies (New York: Macmillan, 1970), p. 1. Koestler had just published *The Ghost in the Machine* (New York: Macmillan, 1967) in which he criticized behaviourism and, in introducing the concept of the 'holon', argued that hierarchy

rationale for the volume: in a variety of symposia that he had attended over the past decade he had detected among at least some scientists "a certain discontent with the prevailing philosophical bias which—whether explicitly formulated or tacitly implied—seems to linger on as a heritage from the nineteenth century, although the new insights gained by contemporary research have reduced it to an anachronism."[89] What they had been critical of was "what von Bertalanffy called the robotomorphic view of man, or more soberly, the insufficient emancipation of the life sciences from the mechanistic concepts of nineteenth-century physics, and the resulting crudely reductionist philosophy."[90] Evidently, Hayek was among like-minded scholars at the meeting. "The Primacy of the Abstract" is based on the notes he used for his talk and continues themes he had introduced in "Rules, Perception and Intelligibility."

Hayek starts with an apparently paradoxical claim: all of the things that we usually think of as concrete are actually the product of an abstraction— namely, the super-imposition of a structure of classification. The reason that we do not recognize the primacy of the abstract is because in our subjective conscious experience, "concrete particulars occupy the central place and the abstractions appear to be derived from them."[91] Hayek's main contention is "that the mind must be capable of performing abstract operations in order to be able to perceive particulars, and that this capacity appears long before we can speak of a conscious awareness of particulars. Subjectively, we live in a concrete world. . . . But when we want to explain what makes us tick, we must start with the abstract relations governing the order which, as a whole, gives particulars their distinct place."[92] Hayek argues that well-known results from a variety of contemporary fields—ethology, psychology, the phenomenon known as 'knowing how', and linguistics are among those he cites—support the claim, as do observations made by social theorists at least as far back as Adam Ferguson. This, of course, is ground Hayek had covered in "Rules, Perception and Intelligibility."

But there is also much that is new, or at least clarified, in the paper. First among these is Hayek's extended discussion in section 4 of the key concept of 'disposition.' For Hayek, the notion of an abstraction is the inclination to respond to certain classes of stimuli not with a specific response but with responses of a certain kind. "A disposition will thus, strictly speaking, not be directed towards a particular action, but towards an action possessing certain

---

plays an essential rôle in the organization of biological organisms, from the simplest of them all the way up to societies.

[89] Koestler, "Preface", *The Alpbach Symposium*, p. vii.

[90] Koestler, "Opening Remarks", *The Alpbach Symposium*, p. 2. Bertalanffy was among those who attended the symposium.

[91] F. A. Hayek, "The Primacy of the Abstract", this volume, p. 315.

[92] Ibid., p. 316.

properties, and it will be the concurrent effect of many such dispositions which will determine the various attributes of a particular action."[93]

A second implication is that our rich sensory experience is not the starting point for, but the result of, abstraction. This would imply that, for example, a human infant does not experience reality as—in the expression made famous by William James—a "blooming, buzzing confusion", which may be interpreted as meaning that the baby could fully perceive particulars but not order them. If Hayek's theory is correct, it is more likely that the infant would experience a structured world in which the particulars are indistinct. "The baby and the animal certainly do not live in the same sensory world in which we live. But this is so, not because, though their 'sense data' are the same, they have not yet been able to derive from them as many abstractions as we have done, but because of the much thinner net of ordering relations which they possess—because the much smaller number of abstract classes under which they can subsume their impressions makes the qualities which their supposedly elementary sensations possess much less rich."[94]

A third implication is that our conscious experience is not the pinnacle of mental events, because much of what takes place in our minds—the ordering and classifying of stimuli, which Hayek dubs "super-conscious" processes— "governs our conscious processes without appearing in them."[95] This is the principal reason why we will never be able fully to explain the operation of the brain but only the principle by which it operates.

A final conclusion that Hayek draws is that the formation of what feels like a new abstraction is necessarily simply the discovery of something that already guides our mental operations. He notes that this approach to understanding creativity may have some commonalities with the concept of "bisociation" in Koestler's *The Act of Creation*.[96] Unfortunately, in the equally rich discussion of Hayek's paper, Koestler does not take up Hayek's point.

* * *

In 1969 Hayek moved to Salzburg, Austria. "The Errors of Constructivism" was his inaugural lecture at the University of Salzburg, delivered on January 27, 1970. In it Hayek contrasts constructivism, the idea that, because man has created his institutions, he must be able deliberately to alter them, with the competing idea that though all of our social institutions are the results of

---

[93] Ibid., p. 319.

[94] Ibid., pp. 322–23. This claim generated a considerable amount of comment in the ensuing discussion.

[95] Ibid., p. 323.

[96] In *The Act of Creation* (London: Hutchison, 1964), Koestler argued that humour, scientific discovery, and artistic creation all follow a basic pattern—bisociative thinking—in which, through a creative leap, a connection is made among previously unconnected frames of reference.

human action, not all are a result of human design. The latter view implies that man did not create civilization with his reason, but that reason and civilization arose together. Given his theme, the paper may be viewed as a companion piece to his 1967 paper "The Results of Human Action but Not of Human Design."

But it is more than this, for it is a highly integrative piece. Hayek sought to spell out for his new colleagues the variety of areas in which he had been working over the past decade and to show how they cohered. He cites no less than nine of his own previously published works, which is perhaps a record (for him) of self-citation in a single article. Hayek so liked "The Errors of Constructivism" that he chose it as the lead piece for his 1978 collection *New Studies in Philosophy, Politics, Economics, and the History of Ideas.*[97]

Note too that Hayek foreshadows in the paper a number of themes that he would include in his trilogy *Law, Legislation, and Liberty,* especially concerning the relationship between legal institutions and the workings of markets, and the damage that had been done by utilitarian and legal positivist theorists whose work had as a modern consequence Hayek's bête noire, the concept of "social justice." Indeed, when it was published in the 1978 collection, Hayek included a footnote citation to the first volume of the trilogy.[98] He also briefly touches on an idea that he would develop much more fully in *The Fatal Conceit,* one concerning the origins of our economic institutions: "None of our ancestors could have known that the protection of property and contracts would lead to an extensive division of labour, specialization and the establishment of markets, or that the extension to outsiders of rules initially applicable only to members of the same tribe would tend towards the formation of a world economy."[99] There are few better summaries of Hayek's late work than "The Errors of Constructivism."

* * *

Hayek also included "Nature vs. Nurture Once Again" in his 1978 collection, and given that it is simply a short comment on a book by the British biologist and geneticist C. D. Darlington, one might wonder why.[100] The reason, I think,

---

[97] F. A. Hayek, *New Studies in Philosophy, Politics, Economics, and the History of Ideas* (Chicago: University of Chicago Press, 1978).

[98] F. A. Hayek, "The Errors of Constructivism", this volume, p. 343, note 13.

[99] Ibid., p. 346. Cf. Hayek, *The Fatal Conceit.*

[100] Darlington is a figure not without interest. He was a close friend of J. B. S. Haldane, one of Hayek's "men of science", but later split with Haldane over the Lysenko affair, in which scientific authorities in the Soviet Union outlawed the teaching of genetics. In later work Darlington endorsed the idea that different races had different character and cultural attributes. This may help to explain the reaction of the reviewer in the *New Statesman* that Hayek mentions at the end of his short piece.

is that the review provided him with the opportunity to illustrate some of the implications of his views—in this case, for the time-worn debate over the relative importance of nature versus nurture.

Darlington analyses human history from the vantage point of a geneticist and argues that distinct innate capacities are the key determinant of that history. Though Hayek applauds the book as a nice remedy to behaviourism, he thinks that Darlington has erred in overemphasizing the rôle of the genetic factor. The key to Darlington's error is his belief that "all actions that are not guided by conscious reason must be genetically determined. He operates with the simple dichotomy between, on the one hand, the genetically determined, innate, instinctive, or unconscious capacities (terms which are treated as equivalent), and, on the other hand, rational or learned activities."[101]

As one might guess, Hayek thinks that there is more to it than a simple choice between our genetic heritage and consciously-learned behaviour. He cites the imitative behaviour of infants as an example of pre-rational learning, and notes that once such learning takes place, "the transmission of abilities takes a new form—vastly superior to genetic transmission precisely because it includes the transmission of acquired characteristics which genetic transmission does not."[102] Hayek observes that much that is learned is not consciously acquired, and that group selection plays a key rôle in cultural evolution.

Towards the end of the review Hayek notes that there is no test that would reveal how much of our culture depends on the innate properties of individuals and how much has been culturally transmitted. And, writing in 1971, a time of campus unrest when many traditional values were being challenged, he remarks rather dolefully, "If we had, it would probably show how precarious the stability of our present civilization is, precisely because it rests largely on cultural traditions which can be more rapidly destroyed than the genetic endowment of populations."[103]

* * *

In 1974 Hayek was awarded, jointly with the Swedish economist Gunnar Myrdal, the Bank of Sweden Nobel Memorial Prize in Economics. The joint award, doubtless intended to achieve a certain ideological balance, was less than fully satisfying for the two recipients.[104] "The Pretence of Knowledge" is Hayek's Nobel address, so predictably it focuses on economics. But befitting its

[101] F. A. Hayek, "Nature vs. Nurture Once Again", this volume, p. 358.

[102] Ibid.

[103] Ibid., p. 360.

[104] After Milton Friedman got the prize in 1976, Myrdal stated publicly that it should be abolished: How could economics be a science, when people like Friedman and Hayek—whom Myrdal viewed as reactionaries—could receive the award? For a translation of his article, see Gunnar Myrdal, "The Nobel Prize in Economic Science", *Challenge*, March–April 1977, pp. 50–52.

position as the final paper of this volume, it contains all of the usual Hayekian themes.

The address was delivered in December 1974, when "the chief practical problem" economists faced was accelerating inflation.[105] In Hayek's view, the problem was brought on by undertaking policies that most economists supported and promoted: "As a profession we have made a mess of things."[106]

Scientism was the source of economists' errors by causing them to think that a theory must make reference to quantitative data to be truly scientific. A second problem was their assumption that simple relationships between aggregate statistical concepts exist—in this case, between total employment and aggregate demand. But with markets economists are dealing with essentially complex phenomena. The assumption that they must, to be 'scientific', only use theories for which they have data may well cause them to choose a false theory: "The correlation between aggregate demand and total employment, for instance, may only be approximate, but as it is the *only* one on which we have quantitative data, it is accepted as the only causal connection that counts. On this standard there may thus well exist better 'scientific' evidence for a false theory, which will be accepted because it is more 'scientific', than for a valid explanation, which is rejected because there is no sufficient quantitative evidence for it."[107] The "now fashionable theory" that follows from this view is that unemployment can be "lastingly cured" by inflationary policies (i.e., by stimulative monetary policy).[108]

In Hayek's view "extensive unemployment" occurs when the structure of prices and wages has become distorted, usually due to some form of price fixing, either by monopolies or the government.[109] When this happens, changes in relative prices are necessary to restore equilibrium. But admittedly, one does not and cannot know the particular structure of wages and prices that will restore equilibrium. Another way of putting this is that although one may have mathematical models that reveal the structure of the economy, one can never fill in the necessary numerical values of the variables. This is the price one pays when dealing with essentially complex phenomena, a phrase that Hayek uses over and over again in the lecture. As in earlier pieces, he defines "essentially complex phenomena" as those for which the number of relevant

---

For his part, in his banquet speech in 1974 Hayek said that had he been consulted on whether to establish the prize, "I should have decidedly advised against it."

[105] F. A. Hayek, "The Pretence of Knowledge", this volume, p. 362. Hayek emphasizes inflation, but unemployment was also a problem. By December 1974, at least in the United States, the great stagflation of the 1970's was well underway.

[106] Ibid.

[107] Ibid., pp. 363–64.

[108] Ibid., p. 364.

[109] Under 'monopolies' Hayek would include both industrial monopolies and labour unions.

variables is large, but for which statistical techniques are inappropriate because they are phenomena of "organized complexity."[110]

In short, in his Nobel lecture Hayek presents an abbreviated version of the policy implications of the Austrian theory of the business cycle within the framework of his own theories about the dangers of scientism when confronting essentially complex phenomena. Evidently, this theory offers very little solace for those who wish to intervene in the economy to tame the business cycle.[111] Hayek recognizes that this is not going to be a popular message:

> What I mainly wanted to bring out by the topical illustration is that certainly in my field, but I believe also generally in the sciences of man, what looks superficially like the most scientific procedure is often the most unscientific, and, beyond this, that in these fields there are definite limits to what we can expect science to achieve. . . . In contrast to the exhilaration which the discoveries of the physical sciences tend to produce, the insights which we gain from the study of society more often have a dampening effect on our aspirations.[112]

Hayek concludes his Nobel lecture with a sentence that captures well the variety of themes that he addresses, both here and in earlier work: "The recognition of the insuperable limits to his knowledge ought indeed to teach the student of society a lesson in humility which should guard him against becoming an accomplice in men's fatal striving to control society—a striving which makes him not only a tyrant over his fellows, but which may well make him the destroyer of a civilization which no brain has designed but which has grown from the free efforts of millions of individuals."[113] This will strike many readers as overly dramatic—but he was writing in a dramatic time. Stagflation had underlined the difficulties of successfully applying the most 'scientific' macroeconomic doctrine of the day, Keynesian demand management policy. For some it was a signal that capitalism had failed, and for others it showed that a more sophisticated theory of how the economy operated was necessary. Hayek had such a theory, but its implications were decidedly modest. It is perhaps a

[110]Ibid., p. 365. Note that Warren Weaver is referenced when Hayek speaks of "phenomena of organized complexity."
[111]It is worth noting that Hayek's warnings about the likely effect of "the continuous injection of additional amounts of money" into the system were born out by the experience of the U.S. economy under the 'stop-go' policies that reigned throughout the 1970's.
[112]Ibid., p. 368.
[113]Ibid., p. 372. In using the phrase "tyrant over his fellows", Hayek may have been invoking Keynes's defence of income inequality in the concluding chapter of *The General Theory* where Keynes says, "It is better that a man should tyrannise over his bank balance than over his fellow-citizens." See J. M. Keynes, *The General Theory of Employment, Interest, and Money* (London: Macmillan, 1936), p. 374.

testimony to the veracity of his insights that he recognized that few would ever accept it—the human attachment to scientism does not fade so easily.

* * *

The papers gathered together in this volume offer a compelling documentary account of the slow but steady development of F. A. Hayek's views on how to study complex spontaneous orders. He first encountered the idea while thinking about how a market system might work to co-ordinate human action in a world in which knowledge was both dispersed and subjectively held. But as he came to realize, such orders are ubiquitous: they can be found in nature, and they are integral for understanding the development of many of our most important social, cultural, and economic institutions. Their very ubiquity has profound implications. What are the characteristics of spontaneous orders? What is the best way to study them? What limitations do we face when we try to predict their course or to control them? And what are the implications of the answers to these questions for how we should think about the organization of society? In answering these questions, Hayek provided scientific grounding for his arguments about the limitations of planning and the importance of nurturing that set of institutions that would allow societies, and the individuals that comprise them, better to flourish.

The title of this volume is *The Market and Other Orders*. The title is meant to highlight Hayek's own path: he began with the market order, then became aware of the existence of orders in many other areas. It is also meant to allude to the title of Hayek's 1948 collection *Individualism and Economic Order*, where some of the early papers were first gathered together. It should be evident that the chapters in this volume are some of Hayek's most important papers, and, to close on a personal note, they are very much my favourites.

Bruce Caldwell
Durham, North Carolina
November 2012

THE MARKET AND OTHER ORDERS

KINDS OF RATIONALISM[1]

I

In the course of my critical examination of certain dominant beliefs of our time I have sometimes had to make a difficult choice. It often happens that quite specific demands are labelled by a perfectly good word which in its more general sense describes a thoroughly desirable and generally approved activity. Indeed the specific demands which I find necessary to oppose are often the result of the belief that, if a certain attitude is usually beneficial, it must be beneficial in all applications. The difficulty which this creates for the critic of current beliefs I have first encountered in connection with the word 'planning.'[2] That we should think out beforehand what we are going to do, that a sensible ordering of our lives demands that we should have a clear conception of our aims before we start acting, seems so obvious that it appears difficult to believe that the demand for planning should ever be wrong. All economic activity, in particular, is planning decisions about the use of resources for all the competing ends. It would, therefore, seem particularly absurd for an economist to oppose 'planning' in this most general sense of the word.

But in the 1920's and 1930's this good word had come to be widely used in a narrower and more specific sense. It had become the accepted slogan for the demand, not that each of us should intelligently plan his economic activities, but that the economic activities of all should be centrally directed according to a single plan laid down by a central authority. 'Planning' thus meant central collectivist planning, and the discussion whether to plan or not to plan referred

---

[1] A lecture delivered on April 27, 1964, at Rikkyo University, Tokyo, and published in *The Economic Studies Quarterly*, Tokyo, vol. 15, March 1965, pp. 1–12. [Reprinted in F. A. Hayek, *Studies in Philosophy, Politics and Economics* (Chicago: University of Chicago Press, 1967), pp. 82–95.—Ed.]

[2] [Cf., e.g., Hayek's discussion of "the mist of confusion and ambiguity which enshrouds the term 'planning'" in "Freedom and the Economic System" [1939], reprinted in F. A. Hayek, *Socialism and War: Essays Documents, Reviews*, ed. Bruce Caldwell, vol. 10 (1997) of *The Collected Works of F. A. Hayek* (Chicago: University of Chicago Press; London: Routledge), pp. 193–200, as well as his discussion of planning in section 2 of "The Use of Knowledge in Society", reprinted in this volume as chapter 3.—Ed.]

exclusively to this issue. This circumstance, that the good word 'planning' had been appropriated by the central planners for their particular schemes, created for the opponents of these proposals a delicate problem. Were they to try to rescue the good word for its legitimate uses, insisting that a free economy rested on the separate plans of many individuals, and indeed gave the individual more scope for planning his life than a centrally planned system? Or ought they to accept the narrow sense in which the term had come to be used and to direct their criticism simply against 'planning'?

Rightly or wrongly, I decided, somewhat to the discomfort of my friends, that things had already gone too far and that it was too late to vindicate the word for its legitimate uses. Just as my opponents argued simply for planning, meaning thereby central planning of all economic activity, I directed my criticism simply against 'planning'—leaving to my adversaries the advantage of the good word and laying myself open to the charge of opposing the use of our intelligence in the ordering of our affairs. Yet I still believe that as things then were, such a head-on attack on 'planning' was necessary to dethrone what had become a shibboleth.

More recently, I have encountered similar difficulties with the blessed word 'social.' Like 'planning' it is one of the fashionable good words of our time, and in its original meaning of belonging to society it could be a very useful word. But in its modern usage in such connections as 'social justice' (one would have thought that all justice is a social phenomenon!), or when our social duties are contrasted with mere moral duties, it has become one of the most confusing and harmful words of our time, not only itself empty of content and capable of being given any arbitrary content one likes, but depriving all terms with which it is combined (as in the German *soziale Marktwirtschaft* or *sozialer Rechtsstaat*) of any definite content.[3] In consequence I felt obliged to take a position against the word 'social', and to demonstrate that in particular the concept of social justice had no meaning whatever, calling up a misleading mirage which clear-thinking people ought to avoid. But this attack on one of the sacred idols of our time again made many people regard me as an irresponsible extremist, entirely out of sympathy with the spirit of our time.

One more example of such a good word which, if it had not been given a special meaning, I should readily have used to describe my own position, but which I felt forced to turn against, is 'positive' or 'positivist.' Again the special sense which has been given to it has created a situation where I felt forced to leave this perfectly good word to my opponents and find myself an 'anti-

---

[3] [The phrases translate as "social market economy" and "social rule of law." For more on this, see Hayek's chapter entitled "Our Poisoned Language" in F. A. Hayek, *The Fatal Conceit: The Errors of Socialism*, ed. W. W. Bartley III, vol. 1 (1988) of *The Collected Works of F. A. Hayek*, especially pp. 114–19.—Ed.]

positivist', although what I defend is quite as much positive science as the doctrines of the self-appointed positivists.

II

I am now, however, involved in another conflict of opinion where I do not dare to do the same without a good deal of explanation. The general social philosophy which I hold has sometimes been described as anti-rationalist, and at least with regard to my main intellectual forebears in this respect, Bernard Mandeville, David Hume and Carl Menger, I have, like others, occasionally myself used that term.[4] Yet this has given rise to so many misunderstandings that it seems to me now a dangerous and misleading expression which ought to be avoided.

We have to deal here once again with a situation in which one group of thinkers have effectively claimed for themselves the only proper use of the good word and have in consequence come to be called rationalists. It was almost inevitable that those who did not agree with their views on the proper use of reason should have been labelled 'anti-rationalists.' This gave the impression as if the latter rated reason less highly, while in fact they were anxious to make reason more effective and pleaded that an effective use of reason required a proper insight into the limits of the effective use of individual reason in regulating relations between many reasonable beings.

There seems to me to exist a sort of rationalism which, by not recognizing these limits of the powers of individual reason, in fact tends to make human reason a less effective instrument than it could be. This sort of rationalism is a comparatively new phenomenon, though its roots go back to ancient Greek philosophy. Its modern influence, however, begins only in the sixteenth and seventeenth century and particularly with the formulation of its main tenets by the French philosopher René Descartes.[5] It was mainly through him that the

---

[4][Hayek refers to the Dutch physician Bernard Mandeville (1670–1733), the Scottish philosopher David Hume (1711–1776), and the founder of the Austrian school of economics, Carl Menger (1840–1921). Hayek discusses the tradition here identified in his 1945 Finlay lecture, "Individualism: True and False", reprinted in *Studies on the Abuse and Decline of Reason: Texts and Documents*, ed. Bruce Caldwell, vol. 13 (2010) of *The Collected Works of F. A. Hayek*, pp. 46–74. See also his essays "Dr. Bernard Mandeville (1670–1733)" and "The Legal and Political Philosophy of David Hume (1711–1776)", chapters 6 and 7, respectively, of *The Trend of Economic Thinking: Essays on Political Economists and Economic History*, ed. W. W. Bartley III and Stephen Kresge, vol. 3 (1991) of *The Collected Works of F. A. Hayek*, as well as "Carl Menger (1840–1921)" and "The Place of Menger's *Grundsätze* in the History of Economic Thought", reprinted as chapter 2 of *The Fortunes of Liberalism: Essays on Austrian Economics and the Ideal of Freedom*, ed. Peter Klein, vol. 4 (1992) of *The Collected Works of F. A. Hayek.*—Ed.]

[5][Hayek identifies the French philosopher René Descartes (1596–1650) as a key figure in the development of the modern rationalist position in "Individualism: True and False."—Ed.]

very term 'reason' changed its meaning. To the medieval thinkers reason had meant mainly a capacity to recognize truth, especially moral truth,[6] when they met it, rather than a capacity of deductive reasoning from explicit premises. And they were very much aware that many of the institutions of civilization were not the inventions of the reason but what, in explicit contrast to all that was invented, they called 'natural', i.e., spontaneously grown.

It was against this older natural law theory which did recognize that much of the institution of civilization was not the product of deliberate human design that the new rationalism of Francis Bacon, Thomas Hobbes and particularly René Descartes contended that all the useful human institutions were and ought to be deliberate creation of conscious reason.[7] This reason was conceived as to the Cartesian *esprit géométrique*, a capacity of the mind to arrive at the truth by a deductive process from a few obvious and undoubtable premises.

It seems to me that the best name for this kind of naïve rationalism is rationalist constructivism. It is a view which in the social sphere has since wrought unmeasurable harm, whatever its great achievements in the sphere of technology may have been. (If it be thought that by labelling this view 'constructivism' I am once again presenting my opponents with a good word, I should plead that this term was used in precisely this sense already by one of the greatest of the nineteenth-century liberals, W. E. Gladstone.[8] He used it as a

[6]Cf. John Locke, *Essays on the Laws of Nature* [1676], ed. W. von Leyden (Oxford: Clarendon Press, 1954), p. 111: "By reason, however, I do not think is meant here that faculty of the understanding which forms trains of thought and deduces proofs, but certain definite principles of action from which spring all virtues and whatever is necessary for the proper moulding of morals."

[7][For a time the Lord Chancellor of England, Francis Bacon (1561–1626) is remembered today for his writings on scientific method. Hayek makes his own views on Bacon clear in "Francis Bacon: Progenitor of Scientism", chapter 5 of *The Trend of Economic Thinking*. The English philosopher Thomas Hobbes (1588–1679) provided a social contract theory of the state, in which individuals cede their natural rights to the sovereign in order to avoid the "war of all against all" that would exist in the state of nature.—Ed.]

[8][The British statesman William Ewart Gladstone (1809–1898) served as the Liberal prime minister on four different occasions. As Hayek admits in "The Errors of Constructivism", this volume, p. 338, note 3, he never succeeded in finding Gladstone's reference to constructivism in the latter's published works. He may have been thinking about Gladstone's letter of February 11, 1885, to Lord Acton, where Gladstone says of the liberalism of his day, "Its pet idea is what they call construction, that is to say, taking into the hands of the state the business of the individual man." See *Selections from the Correspondence of the First Lord Acton*, ed. John Neville Figgis and Reginald Vere Laurence (London: Longmans, Green, 1917), vol. 1, p. 239. I thank Jack Bladel for tracking this down, and also for his plausible conjecture that Hayek may have run across the quote while reading John Morley's biography of Gladstone; see John Morley, *The Life of William Ewart Gladstone* (New York: Macmillan, 1904), vol. 3, p. 173.—Ed.]

name for the attitude for which in the past I had no better term than the 'engineering type of mind.' 'Constructivism' now seems to me the best label for the practical attitude which regularly accompanies what in the field of theory I have described as 'scientism.'[9])

The ascendancy of this view in the seventeenth century implied in fact a relapse into an earlier naïve way of thinking, into a view which habitually assumed a personal inventor for all human institutions, be it language or writing, laws or morals. It is no accident that Cartesian rationalism was completely blind to the forces of historical evolution. And what it applied to the past it proclaimed as programme for the future: that man in the full knowledge of what he was doing should deliberately create such a civilization and social order as the process of his reason enabled him to design. Rationalism in this sense is the doctrine which assumes that all institutions which benefit humanity have in the past and ought in the future to be invented in clear awareness of the desirable effects that they produce; that they are to be approved and respected only to the extent that we can show that the particular effects they will produce in any given situation are preferable to the effects another arrangement would produce; that we have it in our power so to shape our institutions that of all possible sets of results that which we prefer to all others will be realized; and that our reason should never resort to automatic or mechanical devices when conscious consideration of all factors would make preferable an outcome different from that of the spontaneous process. It is from this kind of social rationalism or constructivism that all modern socialism, planning and totalitarianism derives.

III

Our issue may now be pointed by asking whether, as Cartesian rationalism and all its descendents assume, human civilization is the product of human reason, or whether it is not the other way round and we should regard human reason as the product of a civilization which was not deliberately made by man but which had rather grown by a process of evolution. This is, of course, in a way a 'hen or egg' kind of question—nobody will deny that the two phenomena constantly interact. But the typical view of Cartesian rationalism is to insist throughout on the first interpretation, on a pre-existing human reason designing institutions. From the 'social contract' to the view that law is the

---

[9] Cf. my *The Counter-Revolution of Science* (Glencoe, Ill., Free Press, 1952). [Hayek refers to his essay, "Scientism and the Study of Society", now reprinted in *Studies on the Abuse and Decline of Reason*, pp. 75–166.—Ed.]

creation of the State, and that because we have made our institutions we can also change them at will, the whole thinking of our modern age is permeated by the offspring of this tradition. It is characteristic of this view also that it has no place for social theory proper: because the problems of social theory arise out of the fact that the individual efforts of man do often produce an order which, although unintended and unforeseen, turns out to be indispensable for the realization of what men strive for.

It deserves mention that in this respect the two hundred and more years of effort of social and particularly economic theorists are now receiving unexpected support from the new science of social anthropology: its investigations show in more and more fields how what has long been regarded as the invention of reason was in fact the outcome of a process of evolution and selection very similar to that which we find in the biological field. I called it a new science—but in fact the social anthropologists merely continue work which Mandeville, Hume, and his successors among the Scottish philosophers had commenced, but which was largely forgotten when their later followers more and more confined themselves to the narrow field of economics.[10]

In its more general form the main result of this development is thus the insight that even man's capacity to think is not a natural endowment of the individual but a cultural heritage, something transmitted not biologically but through example and teaching—mainly through, and implicit in, the teaching of language. The extent to which the language which we learn in early childhood determines our whole manner of thinking and our view and interpretation of the world is probably much greater than we are yet aware of. It is not merely that the knowledge of earlier generations is communicated to us through the medium of language; the structure of the language itself implies certain views about the nature of the world; and by learning a particular language we acquire a certain picture of the world, a framework of our thinking within which we henceforth move without being aware of it. As we learn as children to use our language according to rules which we do not explicitly know, so we learn with language not only to act according to the rules of language, but according to many other rules of interpreting the world and of acting appropriately, rules which will guide us though we have never explicitly formulated them. This phenomenon of implicit learning is clearly one of the most important parts of cultural transmission, but one which we as yet only imperfectly understand.

---

[10] [For more on the antecedents of social and cultural anthropology, see F. A. Hayek, *Rules and Order*, vol. 1 (1973) of *Law, Legislation and Liberty* (Chicago: University of Chicago Press, and Routledge: London, 1973–1979), pp. 22–24, 74–76, and notes therein.—Ed.]

IV

The fact to which I have just referred probably means that in all our thinking we are guided (or even operated) by rules of which we are not aware, and that our conscious reason can therefore always take account only of some of the circumstances which determine our actions. That rational thought was only one element among those which guide us has of course long been recognized. It was expressed in the scholastic maxim that *ratio non est judex, sed instrumentum*—that reason is not the judge but an instrument. But clear awareness came only with David Hume's demonstration (directed against the constructivist rationalism of his time) that "the rules of morality . . . are not conclusions of our reason."[11] This applies, of course, to all our values, which are the ends which reason serves but which reason cannot determine. This does not mean that reason has no function in deciding in conflicts of values—and all moral problems are problems created by conflicts of values. But nothing shows better the limited rôle of reason in this connection than a closer analysis of how we decide such conflicts. Reason can only help us to see what are the alternatives before us, which are the values which are in conflict, or which of them are true ultimate values and which are, as is often the case, only mediate values which derive their importance from serving other values. Once this task is accomplished, however, reason cannot help us further. It must accept as given the values which it is made to serve.

That values nevertheless serve a function or 'purpose' which scientific analysis may be able to discover is a different matter. It will help to distinguish further between the different types of rationalism if we examine somewhat more closely the character of these attempts to explain why we hold the values which we do. The best known of these theories concerning moral rules is utilitarianism. It occurs in two forms which provide the best illustration of the difference between the legitimate use of reason in the discussion of values and that false 'constructivist' rationalism which ignores the limitations that are set to the powers of reason.

Utilitarianism appears in its first and legitimate form in the work of the same David Hume who was so emphatic that "reason of itself is utterly impotent" to create moral rules, but who at the same time insisted that the obedience to moral and legal rules which nobody had invented or designed for that purpose was essential for the successful pursuit of men's aims in society.[12] He showed that certain abstract rules of conduct came to prevail because those

---

[11] [David Hume, *A Treatise of Human Nature*, in *The Philosophical Works*, ed. T. H. Green and T. H. Grose, new rev. ed. (London: Longmans, Green, 1890), vol. 2, p. 235.—Ed.]

[12] [Ibid. This and the previous passage quoted by Hayek appear in the first section of Book III, "Of Morals", of Hume's *Treatise*. In the second section of the book, titled "Of Justice and Injustice", Hume discusses the origins and effects of those moral and legal rules (in particular, the

groups who adopted them became as a result more effective in maintaining themselves. What he stressed in this respect was above all the superiority of an order which will result when each member obeys the same abstract rules, even without understanding their significance, compared with a condition in which each individual action was decided on the grounds of expediency, i.e., by explicitly considering all the concrete consequences of a particular action. Hume is not concerned with any recognizable utility of the particular action, but only with the utility of a universal application of certain abstract rules including those particular instances in which the immediate known results of obeying the rules are not desirable. His reason for this is that human intelligence is quite insufficient to comprehend all the details of the complex human society, and it is this inadequacy of our reason to arrange such an order in detail which forces us to be content with abstract rules; and further that no single human intelligence is capable of inventing the most appropriate abstract rules because those rules which have evolved in the process of growth of society embody the experience of many more trials and errors than any individual mind could acquire.

Authors in the Cartesian tradition like Helvétius and Beccaria, or their English followers Bentham and Austin down to G. E. Moore, turned this *generic utilitarianism*, which searched for the utility embodied in the abstract rules evolved by successive generations, into a *particularist utilitarianism* which in its ultimate consequences amounts to a demand that every action should be judged in full awareness of all its foreseeable results—a view which in the last resort tends to dispense with all abstract rules and leads to the claim that man can achieve a desirable order of society by concretely arranging all its parts in full knowledge of all the relevant facts.[13] While the generic utilitarianism of Hume thus rests on a recognition of the limitations of our reason and expects its fullest use from a strict obedience to abstract rules, the constructivist particularist

---

stability of possession, the transference of property by consent, and the performance of promises) that are essential for the successful pursuit of men's aims in society.—Ed.]

[13] [The French philosopher Claude Adrien Helvétius (1715–1771) argued in his 1758 book *On Mind* that the two main principles of human activity are the pursuit of pleasure and the avoidance of pain. Cesare, Marquis of Beccaria-Bonesana (1738–1794) was an Italian legal reformer. His book *Crimes and Punishments* (1764), in which he argued against the death penalty and torture on utilitarian grounds, greatly influenced the English philosopher, jurist, and social reformer Jeremy Bentham (1748–1832), who is often described as the founder of utilitarianism. The English jurist John Austin (1790–1859) developed an analytical approach to jurisprudence and is one of the founders of legal positivism. The Cambridge philosopher G. E. Moore's (1873–1958) book *Principia Ethica* was lauded by John Maynard Keynes as providing the moral foundations for those "early beliefs" to which Hayek alludes later in this chapter. Hayek provides an extended critique of particularistic, or act, utilitarianism as developed by Bentham and his followers in *The Mirage of Social Justice*, vol. 2 (1976) of *Law, Legislation and Liberty*, pp. 17–23, and an equally critical assessment of legal positivism on pp. 44–59.—Ed.]

utilitarianism rests on the belief that reason is capable of directly manipulating all the details of a complex society.

V

The attitudes of the different kinds of rationalism to abstraction require somewhat fuller discussion because they are the source of frequent confusion. Perhaps the difference is best explained by saying that those who recognize the limits of the powers of reason want to use abstraction to extend it by achieving at least some degree of order in the complex of human affairs, where they know it is impossible to master the full detail, while the constructivist rationalist values abstraction only as an instrument in determining particulars. To the first, as Tocqueville expressed it, "general ideas are no proof of the strength, but rather of the insufficiency of the human intellect", to the second they are a tool which is to give us unlimited power over the particular.[14] In the philosophy of science this difference manifests itself in the belief of the adherents of the second view that the value of a theory must be judged by its capacity to predict particular events, i.e., on our ability to fill in the general pattern described by the theory with sufficient concrete facts to specify its particular manifestation, while of course the prediction that a kind of pattern will appear is also a falsifiable statement. In moral philosophy the constructivist rationalist tends to disdain any reliance on abstract mechanical rules and to regard as truly rational only behaviour such as is based on decisions which judge each particular situation 'on its merits', and chooses between alternatives in concrete evaluation of the known consequences of the various possibilities.

It is fairly obvious that this kind of rationalism must lead to the destruction of all moral values and to the belief that the individual should be guided only by his personal evaluation of the particular ends he pursues, and that it tends to justify all means by the ends pursued. The state of mind which it produces has been well described in an autobiographical essay by the late Lord Keynes. Describing the views he and his friends had held in the early years of the century—and he himself admittedly still held thirty years later—he wrote:

[14] [Alexis de Tocqueville, *Democracy in America*, translated by Henry Reeve, revised by Francis Bowen, ed. Philipps Bradley (New York: A. A. Knopf, 1945), vol. 2, book 1, chapter 3, p. 13. The chapter is titled, "Why the Americans Show More Aptitude for General Ideas Than Their Forefathers, the English." French historian and political thinker Alexis Charles Henri Clérel de Tocqueville (1805–1859) argued in *Democracy in America* (1835, 1840) and *The Old Regime and the French Revolution* (1856) that the quest for social equality under democracy brings with it a growth in the centralization of government, and that administrative centralization and bureaucratization lead inevitably to a reduction of individual liberties. In keeping with standard usage, Hayek's reference to 'De Tocqueville' has been changed to 'Tocqueville.'—Ed.]

We entirely repudiated a personal liability on us to obey general rules. We claimed the right to judge every individual case on its merits, and the wisdom, experience and self-control to do so successfully. This was a very important part of our faith, violently and aggressively held, and for the outer world it was our most obvious and dangerous characteristic. We repudiated entirely customary morals, conventions and traditional wisdom. We were, that is to say, in the strict sense of the term, immoralists. The consequences of being found out had, of course, to be considered for what they were worth. But we recognized no moral obligation on us, no inner sanction, to conform or to obey. Before heaven we claimed to be our own judge in our own case.[15]

It is to be noticed that this statement implies not only a rejection of traditional moral rules but of all commitment to any kind of binding abstract rules of conduct, moral or other. It implies the claim that man's intelligence is adequate to order his life successfully without availing himself of the aid which general rules or principles can give him, in other words, the claim that man is capable of co-ordinating his activities successfully through a full explicit evaluation of the consequences of all possible alternatives of action, and in full knowledge of all the circumstances. This, of course, involves not only a colossal presumption concerning our intellectual powers, but also a complete misconception of the kind of world in which we live. It treats our practical problems as if we knew all the facts and the task of coping with them were a purely intellectual one. I am afraid much of modern social theory also has been deprived of value by this same assumption. The crucial fact of our lives is that we are *not* omniscient, that we have from moment to moment to adjust ourselves to new facts which we have not known before, and that we can therefore not order our lives according to a preconceived detailed plan in which every particular action is beforehand rationally adjusted to every other.

Since our whole life consists in facing ever new and unforeseeable circumstances, we cannot make it orderly by deciding in advance all the particular actions we shall take. The only manner in which we can in fact give our lives some order is to adopt certain abstract rules or principles for guidance, and then strictly adhere to the rules we have adopted in our dealing with the new situations as they arise. Our actions form a coherent and rational pattern, not because they have been decided upon as part of a single plan thought-out beforehand, but because in each successive decision we limit our range of choice by the same abstract rules.

---

[15] J. M. Keynes, *Two Memoirs: Dr. Melchior: A Defeated Enemy, and My Early Beliefs*, Introduction by D. Garnett (London: Rupert Hart-Davis, 1949), pp. 97–98. [Though Keynes ends the paragraph quoted above with the sentence "I remain, and will always remain, an immoralist", he also states that his early views about what human nature was like were "disastrously mistaken."—Ed.]

Considering how important is this adherence to rules in making our lives orderly, it is curious how little the connection between such abstract rules and the achievement of an overall order has been studied. We all know of course that in fact we have learned to act according to rules in order to give our successive action some coherence, that we adopt general rules for our lives not only to save us the trouble of reconsidering certain questions every time they arise, but mainly because only thus can we produce something like a rational whole. I cannot attempt here a more systematic discussion of the relation between the abstract rules followed in all the separate decisions and the abstract overall pattern which will thereby result. But there is one signifi-cant point I must mention briefly. If we want in this manner to achieve an overall order of our affairs, it is requisite that we follow the general rule in all instances and not only when there is no special reason to do otherwise. This may imply that we must deliberately disregard some knowledge of particular consequences which obedience to the rule in the given instance may produce. Here I think a true insight into the significance of behaviour according to rules demands a much more rigid adherence to them than would be conceded by the constructivist rationalists who would accept abstract rules at best as a substitute for a decision in full evaluation of all the particular circumstances and would regard it as desirable to depart from the rules whenever there is special reason for doing so.

Lest I be misunderstood I ought here briefly to say that when I speak of rig-idly adhering to rules I do of course not mean isolated single rules but always a whole system of rules where often one rule will modify the consequences which we have to draw from another. More precisely, I ought to speak of a hierarchy of rules of different degrees of importance. But I cannot here go further into this important question than is necessary to prevent the misunder-standing that any one rule in isolation will normally be sufficient to solve our problems.

VI

What I have said about the need of abstract rules for the co-ordination of the successive actions of any man's life in ever new and unforeseen circumstances applies even more to the co-ordination of the actions of many different indi-viduals in concrete circumstances which are known only partially to each indi-vidual and become known to him only as they arise. This brings me to what in my personal development was the starting point of all these reflections, and which may explain why, though at one time a very pure and narrow economic theorist, I was led from technical economics into all kinds of questions usually regarded as philosophical. When I look back, it seems to have all begun, nearly thirty years ago, with an essay on "Economics and Knowledge"[16] in which I examined what seemed to me some of the central difficulties of pure economic theory. Its main conclusion was that the task of economic theory was to explain how an overall order of economic activity was achieved which utilized a large amount of knowledge which was not concentrated in any one mind but existed only as the separate knowledge of thousands or millions of different individuals. But it was still a long way from this to an adequate insight into the relations between the abstract rules which the individual follows in his actions, and the abstract overall order which is formed as a result of his responding, within the limits imposed upon him by those abstract rules, to the concrete particular circumstances which he encounters. It was only through a re-examination of the age-old concept of freedom under the law, the basic conception of traditional liberalism, and of the problems of the philosophy of law which this raises, that I have reached what now seems to me a tolerably clear picture of the nature of the spontaneous order of which liberal economists have so long been talking.

It turns out to be an instance of a general method of indirectly creating an order in situations where the phenomena are far too complex to allow us the creation of an order by separately putting each element in its appropriate place. It is a sort of order over the particular manifestation of which we have little control, because the rules which determine it determine only its abstract character, while the detail depends on the particular circumstances known only to its individual members. It is therefore an order which we cannot improve upon but only disturb by attempting to change by deliberate arrangement any one part of it. The only way in which we can effectively improve it is by improving the abstract rules which guide the individuals. This, however, is of necessity a slow and difficult task, because most of the rules which do govern existing society are not the result of our deliberate making, and in consequence we often understand only very imperfectly what depends on them. As I have mentioned before, they are the product of a slow process of evolution in the course of which much more experience and knowledge has been precipitated in them than any one person can fully know. This means that, before we can hope successfully to improve them, we must learn to comprehend much better than we do now in what manner the man-made rules and the spontaneous forces of society interact. This will require not only a much closer collaboration between the specialists in economics, law and social philosophy than we have had in recent times; even after we have achieved this, all we can hope for will be a slow experimental process of gradual improvement rather than any opportunity for drastic change.

---

[16] F. A. Hayek, "Economics and Knowledge", *Economica*, n.s., vol. 4, February 1937, pp. 33–54, reprinted in *Individualism and Economic Order* (Chicago: University of Chicago Press, 1948), pp. 33–56. [Now see this volume, chapter 1.—Ed.]

It is perhaps understandable that constructivist rationalists, in their pride in the great powers of human reason, should have revolted against the demand for a submission to rules whose significance they do not fully understand, and which produce an order which we cannot predict in detail. That we should not be able fully to shape human affairs according to our wishes went much against the grain of generations which believed that by the full use of his reason man could make himself fully master of his fate. It seems, however, that this desire to make everything subject to rational control, far from achieving the maximal use of reason, is rather an abuse of reason based on a misconception of its powers, and in the end leads to a destruction of that free interplay of many minds on which the growth of reason nourishes itself. True rational insight into the rôle of conscious reason seems indeed to indicate that one of the most important uses is the recognition of the proper limits of rational control. As the great Montesquieu clearly pointed out at the height of the 'age of reason': *la raison même a besoin de limites.*[17]

VII

In conclusion I would like to say a few words in explanation of why I have chosen this particular topic for what I regard as my chief public address in Japan—the address to the University which has so graciously received me as one of its members. I do not think I am wrong in thinking that the cult of the explicit use of reason, which has been so important an element in the development of European civilization during the last three hundred years, has not played the same rôle in the indigenous Japanese evolution. Nor can it probably be denied that the deliberate use of reason as a critical instrument in the seventeenth, eighteenth and nineteenth centuries is perhaps the main cause of the more rapid development of the European civilization. It was therefore only natural that, when Japanese thinkers began to study the different strands in the development of European thought, they should have been most attracted by those schools which seemed to represent this rationalist tradition in its most extreme and explicit form. To those who were seeking the secret of Western rationalism, the study of the most extreme form of it, what I have called constructivist rationalism and what I regard as an illegitimate and er-

---

[17] [The actual phrase is "le vertu même a besoin de limites" (i.e., "virtue itself has need of limits"). The line may be found in the French social and political theorist Charles de Secondat, Baron de la Brède et de Montesquieu's (1689–1755) *L'Esprit des lois* [1748], or see *The Spirit of the Laws*, translated by Thomas Nugent (New York: Hafner, 1949), vol. 1, book 11, chapter 4, p. 150. The phrase comes in a discussion of the abuse of power and is followed by the sentence "To prevent this abuse, it is necessary from the very nature of things that power should be a check to power."—Ed.]

roneous exaggeration of a characteristic element of the European tradition, was bound to appear as the most promising path to the discovery of this secret.

Thus it came about that of the various traditions of European philosophy that which goes back to Plato in ancient Greece and then was revived by Descartes and Hobbes in the seventeenth century and which, with Rousseau, Hegel, and Marx and later the philosophical and legal positivists, had carried this cult of reason furthest, was most widely studied by the Japanese.[18] The chief purpose of what I have said was to warn you that the very schools which have carried furthest what may seem most characteristic of the European tradition may have gone as far wrong in one direction as those who have not fully appreciated the value of conscious reason have gone in another. Reason is like a dangerous explosive which, handled cautiously, will be most beneficial, but if handled incautiously may blow up a civilization.

Fortunately, this constructivist rationalism is not the only philosophy which the European tradition has to offer—even if it must be admitted that it has tinged the views of some of its greatest philosophers, including even Immanuel Kant. But at least outside the communist world (where constructivist rationalism has indeed blown up a civilization) you will also find another, more modest and less ambitious tradition, a tradition which is less given to building magnificent philosophical systems but which has probably done more to create the foundation of modern European civilization and particularly the political order of liberalism (while constructivist rationalism has always and everywhere been profoundly anti-liberal). It is a tradition which also goes back to classical antiquity, to Aristotle and Cicero, which was transmitted to our modern age mainly through the work of St. Thomas Aquinas, and during the last few centuries was developed mainly by political philosophers. In the eighteenth century it was mainly opponents of Cartesian rationalism like Montesquieu, David Hume and the Scottish philosophers of his school, in particular Adam Smith, who built up a true theory of society and of the rôle of reason in the growth of civilization. We owe much also to the great classical German liberals, Kant and Humboldt, who, however, as is true also of Bentham and the English utilitarians, did not wholly escape the fatal attraction of Rousseau and French rationalism. In its purer form we then find the political philosophy of

---

[18] [Here and in the next paragraph Hayek seeks to distinguish for his Japanese audience those members of the rationalist constructivist tradition, who are his chief target in the essay, from members of his own preferred tradition, which he calls at various points "individualism true" (in the Finlay lecture), the "British tradition", and "the evolutionary conception"—both of the latter are found in *The Constitution of Liberty*, ed. Ronald Hamowy, vol. 16 (2011) of *The Collected Works of F. A. Hayek*, chapter 4. Hayek's neat division of so many past thinkers into two camps has not met with universal approval; for just one example, the linking of Descartes with Hegel and Marx seems particularly ill-conceived. Cf. the editor's introduction to Hayek, *Studies on the Abuse and Decline of Reason*, p. 13, note 33, and pp. 39–40, note 115.—Ed.]

this school once more in Alexis de Tocqueville and Lord Acton; and the foundation of its social theory was clearly restated, for the first time after David Hume, in the work of the founder of the Austrian School of Economics, Carl Menger. Among contemporary philosophers it is particularly Professor Karl R. Popper who has provided important new philosophical foundations for this strand of thought. He has coined for it the name 'critical rationalism', which I think very happily expresses the contrast to the naïve rationalism or constructivism. It seems to me the best term for describing the general position which I regard as the most reasonable one.

It was one of the chief aims of my talk to draw your attention to this tradition. I believe that if you will examine it you will find less that is new and startling in it than earlier generations of Japanese found in the extreme rationalism of the Descartes-Hegel-Marx school. You may find it at first less fascinating and exciting—it does not carry with it the peculiar fascination or even intoxication which the cult of pure reason engenders. But I hope you will find it not only more congenial. It seems to me that, because it is not a one-sided exaggeration which has its roots in a peculiar phase of European intellectual development, but provides a true theory of human nature, it should offer a foundation to the development of which your own experience should enable you to make important contributions. It is a view of mind and society which provides an appropriate place for the rôle which tradition and custom play in their development. It makes us see much to which those brought up on the crude forms of rationalism are often blind. It shows us that sometimes grown institutions which nobody has invented may provide a better framework for cultural growth than more sophisticated designs.

President Matsushita,[19] on another occasion, asked me a question which goes right to the heart of the matter but which I was not then at once able to answer. He asked, if I understood him rightly, whether a people who relied on convention rather than invention for its institutions may not sometimes provide more freedom for the individual and therefore more scope for evolution than those who attempted deliberately to construct all institutions, or tried to remake them according to the principles of reason. I believe the answer is Yes. Until we have learnt to recognize the proper limits of reason in the arrangement of social affairs, there is great danger that in trying to force on society what we think is a rational pattern we may smother that freedom which is the main condition for gradual improvement.

---

[19]Dr. Masatoshi Matsushita, president of Rikkyo University, who took the chair when this lecture was delivered.

PART I

THE EARLY IDEAS

ONE

ECONOMICS AND KNOWLEDGE[1]

I

The ambiguity of the title of this paper is not accidental. Its main subject is, of course, the rôle which assumptions and propositions about the knowledge possessed by the different members of society play in economic analysis. But this is by no means unconnected with the other question which might be discussed under the same title—the question to what extent formal economic analysis conveys any knowledge about what happens in the real world. Indeed, my main contention will be that the tautologies, of which formal equilibrium analysis in economics essentially consists, can be turned into propositions which tell us anything about causation in the real world only in so far as we are able to fill those formal propositions with definite statements about how knowledge is acquired and communicated. In short, I shall contend that the empirical element in economic theory—the only part which is concerned not merely with implications but with causes and effects and which leads therefore to conclusions which, at any rate in principle, are capable of verification[2]— consists of propositions about the acquisition of knowledge.

Perhaps I should begin by reminding you of the interesting fact that in quite

[1] Presidential address delivered before the London Economic Club, November 10th, 1936. Reprinted from *Economica*, n.s., vol. 4, February 1937, pp. 33–54. [This essay was reprinted in F. A. Hayek, *Individualism and Economic Order* (Chicago: University of Chicago Press, 1948), pp. 33–56.—Ed.]

[2] Or rather falsification. Cf. Karl Popper, *Logik der Forschung* (Vienna: Springer, 1935) *passim*. [The Austrian philosopher of science Karl Popper (1902–1994) introduced falsifiability as a criterion of demarcation between scientific and non-scientific statements in section 6 of *Logik*, pp. 12–14; cf. Popper, *The Logic of Scientific Discovery* (New York: Basic Books, 1959), pp. 40–42. Soon after its publication Gottfried Haberler gave Hayek a copy of Popper's book, and this led to an invitation to Popper to present an early draft of *The Poverty of Historicism* in Hayek's seminar at the London School of Economics (LSE) in June 1936. Hayek later reported that he added this footnote reference to falsification while his own paper was in galley proofs. F. A. Hayek to T. W. Hutchison, May 15, 1983, in the Friedrich A. von Hayek papers, box 26, folder 8, Hoover Institution Archives, Stanford University, Calif.—Ed.]

a number of the more recent attempts made in different fields to push theoretical investigation beyond the limits of traditional equilibrium analysis, the answer has soon proved to turn on the assumptions which we make with regard to a point which, if not identical with mine, is at least part of it, namely, with regard to foresight. I think that the field in which, as one would expect, the discussion of the assumptions concerning foresight first attracted wider attention was the theory of risk.[3] The stimulus which was exercised in this connection by the work of Frank H. Knight may yet prove to have a profound influence far beyond its special field.[4] Not much later the assumptions to be made concerning foresight proved to be of fundamental importance for the solution of the puzzles of the theory of imperfect competition, the questions of duopoly and oligopoly. Since then, it has become more and more obvious that, in the treatment of the more 'dynamic' questions of money and industrial fluctuations, the assumptions to be made about foresight and 'anticipations' play an equally central rôle and that in particular the concepts which were taken over into these fields from pure equilibrium analysis, like those of an equilibrium rate of interest, could be properly defined only in terms of assumptions concerning foresight. The situation seems here to be that, before we can explain why people commit mistakes, we must first explain why they should ever be right.

In general, it seems that we have come to a point where we all realize that the concept of equilibrium itself can be made definite and clear only in terms of assumptions concerning foresight, although we may not yet all agree what exactly these essential assumptions are. This question will occupy me later in this essay. At the moment I am concerned only to show that at the present juncture, whether we want to define the boundaries of economic statics or whether we want to go beyond it, we cannot escape the vexed problem of the exact position which assumptions about foresight are to have in our reasoning. Can this be merely an accident?

As I have already suggested, the reason for this seems to me to be that we have to deal here only with a special aspect of a much wider question which we ought to have faced at a much earlier stage. Questions essentially similar to those mentioned arise in fact as soon as we try to apply the system of tautologies—those series of propositions which are necessarily true because they are merely transformations of the assumptions from which we start and

[3] A more complete survey of the process by which the significance of anticipations was gradually introduced into economic analysis would probably have to begin with Irving Fisher's *Appreciation and Interest* (New York: Macmillan, 1896).

[4] [Hayek refers to Frank Knight, *Risk, Uncertainty, and Profit* (New York: Houghton Mifflin, 1921). The American economist Frank Knight (1885–1972) was a dominant figure in the 'Old'—that is, pre–Second World War—Chicago School of Economics. His book was a standard text at LSE in the inter-war years.—Ed.]

which constitute the main content of equilibrium analysis[5]—to the situation of a society consisting of several independent persons. I have long felt that the concept of equilibrium itself and the methods which we employ in pure analysis have a clear meaning only when confined to the analysis of the action of a single person and that we are really passing into a different sphere and silently introducing a new element of altogether different character when we apply it to the explanation of the interactions of a number of different individuals.

I am certain there are many who regard with impatience and distrust the whole tendency, which is inherent in all modern equilibrium analysis, to turn economics into a branch of pure logic, a set of self-evident propositions which, like mathematics or geometry, are subject to no other test but internal consistency. But it seems that, if only this process is carried far enough, it carries its own remedy with it. In distilling from our reasoning about the facts of economic life those parts which are truly *a priori*, we not only isolate one element of our reasoning as a sort of Pure Logic of Choice in all its purity but we also isolate, and emphasize the importance of, another element which has been too much neglected. My criticism of the recent tendencies to make economic theory more and more formal is not that they have gone too far but that they have not yet been carried far enough to complete the isolation of this branch of logic and to restore to its rightful place the investigation of causal processes, using formal economic theory as a tool in the same way as mathematics.

[5] [The following footnote from the original *Economica* article was deleted in the 1948 version: I should like to make it clear from the outset that I use the term 'equilibrium analysis' throughout this paper in the narrower sense in which it is equivalent to what Professor Hans Mayer has christened the 'functional' (as distinguished from the 'causal-genetic') approach, and to what used to be loosely described as the 'mathematical school.' It is round this approach that most of the theoretical discussions of the past ten or fifteen years have taken place. It is true that Professor Mayer has held out before us the prospect of another, 'causal-genetic' approach, but it can hardly be denied that this is still largely a promise. It should, however, be mentioned here that some of the most stimulating suggestions on problems closely related to those treated here have come from his circle. Cf. Hans Mayer, "Der Erkenntniswert der funktionellen Preistheorien: Kritische und positive Untersuchungen zum Preisproblem", in Hans Mayer, ed. *Die Wirtschaftstheorie der Gegenwart* (Vienna: Springer, 1932), vol. 2, pp. 147–239; P. N. Rosenstein-Rodan, "Das Zeitmoment in der mathematischen Theorie des wirtschaftlichen Gleichgewichtes", *Zeitschrift für Nationalökonomie*, vol. 1, May 1929, pp. 129–42; and "The Role of Time in Economic Theory", *Economica*, n.s., vol. 1, February 1934, pp. 77–97.
For a translation of Hans Mayer's article, see "The Cognitive Value of Functional Price Theories: Critical and Positive Investigations Concerning the Price Problem", translated by Patrick Camiller, in *Classics in Austrian Economics*, vol. 2, *The Interwar Period*, ed. Israel Kirzner (London: William Pickering, 1994), pp. 55–168.—Ed.]

II

But before I can prove my contention that the tautological propositions of pure equilibrium analysis as such are not directly applicable to the explanation of social relations, I must first show that the concept of equilibrium *has* a clear meaning if applied to the actions of a single individual and what this meaning is. Against my contention it might be argued that it is precisely here that the concept of equilibrium is of no significance, because, if one wanted to apply it, all one could say would be that an isolated person was always in equilibrium. But this last statement, although a truism, shows nothing but the way in which the concept of equilibrium is typically misused. What is relevant is not whether a person as such is or is not in equilibrium but which of his actions stand in equilibrium relationships to each other. All propositions of equilibrium analysis, such as the proposition that relative values will correspond to relative costs, or that a person will equalize the marginal returns of any one factor in its different uses, are propositions about the relations between actions. Actions of a person can be said to be in equilibrium in so far as they can be understood as part of one plan. Only if this is the case, only if all these actions have been decided upon at one and the same moment, and in consideration of the same set of circumstances, have our statements about their interconnections, which we deduce from our assumptions about the knowledge and the preferences of the person, any application. It is important to remember that the so-called 'data', from which we set out in this sort of analysis, are (apart from his tastes) all facts given to the person in question, the things as they are known to (or believed by) him to exist, and not, strictly speaking, objective facts. It is only because of this that the propositions we deduce are necessarily *a priori* valid and that we preserve the consistency of the argument.[6]

The two main conclusions from these considerations are, first, that, since equilibrium relations exist between the successive actions of a person only in so far as they are part of the execution of the same plan, any change in the relevant knowledge of the person, that is, any change which leads him to alter his plan, disrupts the equilibrium relation between his actions taken before and those taken after the change in his knowledge. In other words, the equilibrium relationship comprises only his actions during the period in which his anticipations prove correct. Second, that, since equilibrium is a relationship between actions, and since the actions of one person must necessarily take place successively in time, it is obvious that the passage of time is essential to give the concept of equilibrium any meaning. This deserves mention, since

---

[6]Cf., on this point particularly, Ludwig von Mises, *Grundprobleme der Nationalökonomie* (Jena: Gustav Fischer, 1933), pp. 22ff, 158ff. [Cf. Ludwig von Mises, *Epistemological Problems of Economics*, translated by George Reisman (Princeton, NJ: D. Van Nostrand, 1960), pp. 23ff, 170ff.—Ed.]

many economists appear to have been unable to find a place for time in equilibrium analysis and consequently have suggested that equilibrium must be conceived as timeless. This seems to me to be a meaningless statement.

III

Now, in spite of what I have said before about the doubtful meaning of equilibrium analysis in this sense if applied to the conditions of a competitive society, I do not, of course, want to deny that the concept was originally introduced precisely to describe the idea of some sort of balance between the actions of different individuals. All I have argued so far is that the sense in which we use the concept of equilibrium to describe the interdependence of the different actions of one person does not immediately admit of application to the relations between actions of different people. The question really is what use we make of it when we speak of equilibrium with reference to a competitive system.

The first answer which would seem to follow from our approach is that equilibrium in this connection exists if the actions of all members of the society over a period are all executions of their respective individual plans on which each decided at the beginning of the period. But, when we inquire further what exactly this implies, it appears that this answer raises more difficulties than it solves. There is no special difficulty about the concept of an isolated person (or a group of persons directed by one of them) acting over a period according to a preconceived plan. In this case, the plan need not satisfy any special criteria in order that its execution be conceivable. It may, of course, be based on wrong assumptions concerning the external facts and on this account may have to be changed. But there will always be a conceivable set of external events which would make it possible to execute the plan as originally conceived.

The situation is, however, different with plans determined upon simultaneously but independently by a number of persons. In the first instance, in order that all these plans can be carried out, it is necessary for them to be based on the expectation of the same set of external events, since, if different people were to base their plans on conflicting expectations, no set of external events could make the execution of all these plans possible. And, second, in a society based on exchange their plans will to a considerable extent provide for actions which require corresponding actions on the part of other individuals. This means that the plans of different individuals must in a special sense be compatible if it is to be even conceivable that they should be able to carry all of them out.[7] Or, to put the same thing in different words, since some of the data

---

[7] It has long been a subject of wonder to me why there should, to my knowledge, have been no systematic attempts in sociology to analyse social relations in terms of correspondence and non-

THE MARKET AND OTHER ORDERS

on which any one person will base his plans will be the expectation that other people will act in a particular way, it is essential for the compatibility of the different plans that the plans of the one contain exactly those actions which form the data for the plans of the other.

In the traditional treatment of equilibrium analysis part of this difficulty is apparently avoided by the assumption that the data, in the form of demand schedules representing individual tastes and technical facts, are equally given to all individuals and that their acting on the same premises will somehow lead to their plans becoming adapted to each other. That this does not really overcome the difficulty created by the fact that one person's actions are the other person's data, and that it involves to some degree circular reasoning, has often been pointed out. What, however, seems so far to have escaped notice is that this whole procedure involves a confusion of a much more general character, of which the point just mentioned is merely a special instance, and which is due to an equivocation of the term 'datum.' The data which here are supposed to be objective facts and the same for all people are evidently no longer the same thing as the data which formed the starting point for the tautological transformations of the Pure Logic of Choice. There 'data' meant those facts, and only those facts, which were present in the mind of the acting person, and only this subjective interpretation of the term 'datum' made those propositions necessary truths. 'Datum' meant given, known, to the person under consideration. But in the transition from the analysis of the action of an individual to the analysis of the situation in a society the concept has undergone an insidious change of meaning.

---

correspondence, or compatibility and non-compatibility, of individual aims and desires. [In the original *Economica* article, the footnote continued as follows:

It seems that the mathematical technique of *analysis situs* (topology) and particularly such concepts developed by it as that of *homeomorphism* might prove very useful in this connection, although it may appear doubtful whether even this technique, at any rate in the present state of its development, is adequate to the complexity of the structures with which we have to deal. A first attempt made recently in this direction by an eminent mathematician (Karl Menger, *Moral, Wille und Weltgestaltung: Grundlegung zur Logik der Sitten* [Vienna: Springer, 1934]) has so far not yet led to very illuminating results. But we may look forward with interest to the treatise on exact sociological theory which Professor Menger has promised for the near future. (Cf., "Einige neuere Fortschritte in der exakten Behandlung sozialwissenschaftlicher Probleme", in *Neuere Fortschritte in den exakten Wissenschaften* [Leipzig: F. Deuticke, 1936], p. 132.)

For a translation of Menger's 1934 book, see *Morality, Decision, and Social Organization: Toward a Logic of Ethics*, based on a translation by Eric van der Schalie (Dordrecht: D. Reidel, 1974).—Ed.]

IV

The confusion about the concept of a datum is at the bottom of so many of our difficulties in this field that it is necessary to consider it in somewhat more detail. Datum means, of course, something given, but the question which is left open, and which in the social sciences is capable of two different answers, is to *whom* the facts are supposed to be given.[8] Economists appear subconsciously always to have been somewhat uneasy about this point and to have reassured themselves against the feeling that they did not quite know to whom the facts were given by underlining the fact that they *were* given—even by using such pleonastic expressions as 'given data.' But this does not answer the question whether the facts referred to are supposed to be given to the observing economist or to the persons whose actions he wants to explain, and, if to the latter, whether it is assumed that the same facts are known to all the different persons in the system or whether the 'data' for the different persons may be different.

There seems to be no possible doubt that these two concepts of 'data', on the one hand, in the sense of the objective real facts, as the observing economist is supposed to know them, and, on the other, in the subjective sense, as things known to the persons whose behaviour we try to explain, are really fundamentally different and ought to be carefully distinguished. And, as we shall see, the question why the data in the subjective sense of the term should ever come to correspond to the objective data is one of the main problems we have to answer.

The usefulness of the distinction becomes immediately apparent when we apply it to the question of what we can mean by the concept of a society being at any one moment in a state of equilibrium. There are evidently two senses in which it can be said that the subjective data, given to the different persons, and the individual plans, which necessarily follow from them, are in agreement. We may mean merely that these plans are mutually compatible and that there is consequently a conceivable set of external events which will allow all people to carry out their plans and not cause any disappointments. If this mutual compatibility of intentions were not given, and if in consequence no set of external events could satisfy all expectations, we could clearly say that this is not a state of equilibrium. We have a situation where a revision of the plans on the part of at least some people is inevitable, or, to use a phrase which in the

---

[8] [As Hayek later recounted, "My whole thinking on this started with my old friend Freddy Benham joking about economists speaking about given data just to reassure themselves that what was given was really given. That led me, in part, to ask to whom were the data really given." See F. A. Hayek, *Hayek on Hayek: An Autobiographical Dialogue*, ed. Stephen Kresge and Leif Wenar (Chicago: University of Chicago Press, 1994), p. 147. Frederic Benham (1900–1962) was a colleague of Hayek at LSE.—Ed.]

past has had a rather vague meaning, but which seems to fit this case perfectly, where 'endogenous' disturbances are inevitable.

There still remains, however, the other question of whether the individual sets of subjective data correspond to the objective data and whether, in consequence, the expectations on which plans were based are borne out by the facts. If correspondence between data in this sense were required for equilibrium, it would never be possible to decide otherwise than retrospectively, at the end of the period for which people have planned, whether at the beginning the society has been in equilibrium. It seems to be more in conformity with established usage to say in such a case that the equilibrium, as defined in the first sense, may be disturbed by an unforeseen development of the (objective) data and to describe this as an exogenous disturbance. In fact, it seems hardly possible to attach any definite meaning to the much used concept of a change in the (objective) data unless we distinguish between external developments in conformity with, and those different from, what has been expected, and define as a 'change' any divergence of the actual from the expected development, irrespective of whether it means a 'change' in some absolute sense. If, for example, the alternations of the seasons suddenly ceased and the weather remained constant from a certain day onward, this would certainly represent a change of data in our sense, that is, a change relative to expectations, although in an absolute sense it would not represent a change but rather an absence of change. But all this means that we can speak of a change in data only if equilibrium in the first sense exists, that is, if expectations coincide. If they conflicted, any development of the external facts might bear out somebody's expectations and disappoint those of others, and there would be no possibility of deciding what was a change in the objective data.[9]

V

For a society, then, we *can* speak of a *state* of equilibrium at a point of time— but it means only that the different plans which the individuals composing it have made for action in time are mutually compatible. And equilibrium will continue, once it exists, so long as the external data correspond to the common expectations of all the members of the society. The continuance of a state of equilibrium in this sense is then not dependent on the objective data being constant in an absolute sense and is not necessarily confined to a stationary

---

[9] Cf. the present author's article, "The Maintenance of Capital", *Economica*, n.s., vol. 2, May 1935, p. 265. [Cf. F. A. Hayek, "The Maintenance of Capital", in *Essays on Capital and Interest*, ed. Lawrence H. White, vol. 11 (forthcoming) of *The Collected Works of F. A. Hayek* (Chicago: University of Chicago Press; London: Routledge).—Ed.]

process. Equilibrium analysis becomes in principle applicable to a progressive society and to those inter-temporal price relationships which have given us so much trouble in recent times.[10]

These considerations seem to throw considerable light on the relationship between equilibrium and foresight, which has been somewhat hotly debated in recent times.[11] It appears that the concept of equilibrium merely means that the foresight of the different members of the society is in a special sense correct. It must be correct in the sense that every person's plan is based on the expectation of just those actions of other people which those other people intend to perform and that all these plans are based on the expectation of the same set of external facts, so that under certain conditions nobody will have any reason to change his plans. Correct foresight is then not, as it has sometimes been understood, a precondition which must exist in order that equilibrium may be arrived at. It is rather the defining characteristic of a state of equilibrium. Nor

---

[10]This separation of the concept of equilibrium from that of a stationary state seems to me to be no more than the necessary outcome of a process which has been going on for a fairly long time. That this association of the two concepts is not essential but only due to historical reasons is today probably generally felt. If complete separation has not yet been effected, it is apparently only because no alternative definition of a state of equilibrium has yet been suggested which has made it possible to state in a general form those propositions of equilibrium analysis which are essentially independent of the concept of a stationary state. Yet it is evident that most of the propositions of equilibrium analysis are not supposed to be applicable only in that stationary state which will probably never be reached. The process of separation seems to have begun with Marshall and his distinction between long- and short- run equilibriums. Cf. statements like this: "For the nature of the equilibrium itself, and that of the causes by which it is determined, depend on the length of the period over which the market is taken to extend." Alfred Marshall, *Principles of Economics: An Introductory Volume*, 7th ed. (London: Macmillan, 1916), Book V, chapter 1, section 6, p. 330. The idea of a state of equilibrium which was not a stationary state was already inherent in my "Das intertemporale Gleichgewichtssystem der Preise und die Bewegungen des 'Geldwertes'", *Weltwirtschaftliches Archiv*, vol. 28, July 1928, pp. 3–76, and is, of course, essential if we want to use the equilibrium apparatus for the explanation of any of the phenomena connected with 'investment.' [For the English version of Hayek's paper, see F. A. Hayek, "Intertemporal Price Equilibrium and Movements in the Value of Money", in *Good Money, Part I: The New World*, ed. Stephen Kresge, vol. 5 (1999) of *The Collected Works of F. A. Hayek*, pp. 186–227.—Ed.] On the whole matter much historical information will be found in Ewald Schams, "Komparative Statik", *Zeitschrift für Nationalökonomie*, vol. 2, August 1930, pp. 27–61. [Hayek added the following citations to the 1948 version: "See also Frank H. Knight, *The Ethics of Competition, and Other Essays* (London: Allen and Unwin, 1935), p. 175; and for some further developments since this essay was first published, the present author's *The Pure Theory of Capital*, chapter 2." For the last, see F. A. Hayek, *The Pure Theory of Capital*, ed. Lawrence H. White, vol. 12 (2007) of *The Collected Works of F. A. Hayek.*—Ed.]

[11]Cf. particularly Oskar Morgenstern, "Vollkommene Voraussicht und wirtschaftliches Gleichgewicht", *Zeitschrift für Nationalökonomie*, vol. 6, August 1935, pp. 337ff. [Cf. Oskar Morgenstern, "Perfect Foresight and Economic Equilibrium", translated by Frank Knight, in *Selected Writings of Oskar Morgenstern*, ed. Andrew Schotter (New York: New York University Press, 1976), pp. 169–83.—Ed.]

need foresight for this purpose be perfect in the sense that it need extend into the indefinite future or that everybody must foresee everything correctly. We should rather say that equilibrium will last so long as the anticipations prove correct and that they need to be correct only on those points which are relevant for the decisions of the individuals. But on this question of what is relevant foresight or knowledge, more later.

Before I proceed further I should probably stop for a moment to illustrate by a concrete example what I have just said about the meaning of a state of equilibrium and how it can be disturbed. Consider the preparations which will be going on at any moment for the production of houses. Brickmakers, plumbers, and others will all be producing materials which in each case will correspond to a certain quantity of houses for which just this quantity of the particular material will be required. Similarly we may conceive of prospective buyers as accumulating savings which will enable them at certain dates to buy a certain number of houses. If all these activities represent preparations for the production (and acquisition) of the same amount of houses, we can say that there is equilibrium between them in the sense that all the people engaged in them may find that they can carry out their plans.[12] This need not be so, because other circumstances which are not part of their plan of action may turn out to be different from what they expected. Part of the materials may be destroyed by an accident, weather conditions may make building impossible, or an invention may alter the proportions in which the different factors are wanted. This is what we call a change in the (external) data, which disturbs the equilibrium which has existed. But if the different plans were from the beginning incompatible, it is inevitable, whatever happens, that somebody's

---

[12]Another example of more general importance would, of course, be the correspondence between 'investment' and 'saving' in the sense of the proportion (in terms of relative cost) in which entrepreneurs provide producers' goods and consumers' goods for a particular date, and the proportion in which consumers in general will at this date distribute their resources between producers' goods and consumers' goods. (Cf. my essays, "Price Expectations, Monetary Disturbances, and Malinvestment" [1933], reprinted in *Profits, Interest, and Investment* (London: Routledge, 1939 [reprinted, Clifton, NJ: Kelley, 1975—Ed.]), pp. 135–56, and "The Maintenance of Capital" [1935], in the same volume, pp. 83–134. [In the *Economica* version the citations given here were "Preiserwartungen, monetäre Störungen and Fehlinvestitionen", *Ekonomisk Tidskrift*, vol. 34, 1935 (French translation: "Prévisions de Prix, Perturbations monétaires et faux Investissements", *Revue des Sciences Economiques*, October, 1935, pp. 165–81), and "The Maintenance of Capital", *Economica*, n.s., vol. 2, August 1935, pp. 241–76. I was unable to find the listed article in *Ekonomisk Tidskrift.*—Ed.] It may be of interest in this connection to mention that in the course of investigations of the same field, which led the present author to these speculations, that of the theory of crises, the great French sociologist Gabriel de Tarde stressed the "contradiction de croyances" or "contradiction de jugements" or "contradictions des esperances" as the main cause of these phenomena (*Psychologie Economique* [Paris: F. Alcan, 1902], vol. 2, pp. 128–91. Cf. also Norbert Pinkus, *Das Problem des Normalen in der Nationalökonomie* [Leipzig: Duncker und Humblot, 1906], pp. 252 and 275).

plans will be upset and have to be altered and that in consequence the whole complex of actions over the period will not show those characteristics which apply if all the actions of each individual can be understood as part of a single individual plan, which he has made at the beginning.[13]

VI

When in all this I emphasize the distinction between mere inter-compatibility of the individual plans[14] and the correspondence between them and the actual external facts or objective data, I do not, of course, mean to suggest that the subjective inter-agreement is not in some way brought about by the external facts. There would, of course, be no reason why the subjective data of different people should ever correspond unless they were due to the experience of the same objective facts. But the point is that pure equilibrium analysis is not concerned with the way in which this correspondence is brought about. In the description of an existing state of equilibrium which it provides, it is simply assumed that the subjective data coincide with the objective facts. The equilibrium relationships cannot be deduced merely from the objective facts, since the analysis of what people will do can start only from what is known to them. Nor can equilibrium analysis start merely from a given set of subjective data, since the subjective data of different people would be either compatible or incompatible, that is, they would already determine whether equilibrium did or did not exist.

We shall not get much further here unless we ask for the reasons for our concern with the admittedly fictitious state of equilibrium. Whatever may occasionally have been said by over-pure economists, there seems to be no possible doubt that the only justification for this is the supposed existence of a tendency towards equilibrium. It is only by this assertion that such a tendency exists that

[13]It is an interesting question, but one which I cannot discuss here, whether, in order that we can speak of equilibrium, every single individual must be right, or whether it would not be sufficient if, in consequence of a compensation of errors in different directions, quantities of the different commodities coming on the market were the same as if every individual had been right. It seems to me as if equilibrium in the strict sense would require the first condition to be satisfied, but I can conceive that a wider concept, requiring only the second condition, might occasionally be useful. A fuller discussion of this problem would have to consider the whole question of the significance which some economists (including Pareto) attach to the law of great numbers in this connection. On the general point see P. N. Rosenstein-Rodan, "The Co-ordination of the General Theories of Money and Price", *Economica*, n.s., vol. 3, August, 1936, pp. 257–80.

[14]Or, since in view of the tautological character of the Pure Logic of Choice, 'individual plans' and 'subjective data' can be used interchangeably, the agreement between the subjective data of the different individuals.

economics ceases to be an exercise in pure logic and becomes an empirical science; and it is to economics as an empirical science that we must now turn.

In the light of our analysis of the meaning of a state of equilibrium it should be easy to say what is the real content of the assertion that a tendency towards equilibrium exists. It can hardly mean anything but that, under certain conditions, the knowledge and intentions of the different members of society are supposed to come more and more into agreement or, to put the same thing in less general and less exact but more concrete terms, that the expectations of the people and particularly of the entrepreneurs will become more and more correct. In this form the assertion of the existence of a tendency towards equilibrium is clearly an empirical proposition, that is, an assertion about what happens in the real world which ought, at least in principle, to be capable of verification. And it gives our somewhat abstract statement a rather plausible common-sense meaning. The only trouble is that we are still pretty much in the dark about (*a*) the *conditions* under which this tendency is supposed to exist and (*b*) the nature of the *process* by which individual knowledge is changed.

VII

In the usual presentations of equilibrium analysis it is generally made to appear as if these questions of how the equilibrium comes about were solved. But, if we look closer, it soon becomes evident that these apparent demonstrations amount to no more than the apparent proof of what is already assumed.[15] The device generally adopted for this purpose is the assumption of a perfect market where every event becomes known instantaneously to every member. It is necessary to remember here that the perfect market which is required to satisfy the assumptions of equilibrium analysis must not be confined to the particular markets of all the individual commodities; the whole economic system must be assumed to be one perfect market in which everybody knows everything. The assumption of a perfect market, then, means nothing less than that all the members of the community, even if they are not supposed to be strictly omniscient, are at least supposed to know automatically all that is relevant for their decisions. It seems that that skeleton in our cupboard, the 'economic man', whom we have exorcised with prayer and fasting, has returned through the back door in the form of a quasi-omniscient individual.

The statement that, if people know everything, they are in equilibrium is

---

[15] This seems to be implicitly admitted, although hardly consciously recognized, when in recent times it is frequently stressed that equilibrium analysis only describes the conditions of equilibrium without attempting to derive the position of equilibrium from the data. Equilibrium analysis in this sense would, of course, be pure logic and contain no assertions about the real world.

true simply because that is how we define equilibrium. The assumption of a perfect market in this sense is just another way of saying that equilibrium exists but does not get us any nearer an explanation of when and how such a state will come about. It is clear that, if we want to make the assertion that, under certain conditions, people will approach that state, we must explain by what process they will acquire the necessary knowledge. Of course, any assumption about the actual acquisition of knowledge in the course of this process will also be of a hypothetical character. But this does not mean that all such assumptions are equally justified. We have to deal here with assumptions about causation, so that what we assume must not only be regarded as possible (which is certainly not the case if we just regard people as omniscient) but must also be regarded as likely to be true; and it must be possible, at least in principle, to demonstrate that it is true in particular cases.

The significant point here is that it is these apparently subsidiary hypotheses or assumptions that people do learn from experience, and about how they acquire knowledge, which constitute the empirical content of our propositions about what happens in the real world. They usually appear disguised and incomplete as a description of the type of market to which our proposition refers; but this is only one, though perhaps the most important, aspect of the more general problem of how knowledge is acquired and communicated. The important point of which economists frequently do not seem to be aware is that the nature of these hypotheses is in many respects rather different from the more general assumptions from which the Pure Logic of Choice starts. The main differences seem to me to be two:

First, the assumptions from which the Pure Logic of Choice starts are facts which we know to be common to all human thought. They may be regarded as axioms which define or delimit the field within which we are able to understand or mentally to reconstruct the processes of thought of other people. They are therefore universally applicable to the field in which we are interested—although, of course, where *in concreto* the limits of this field are is an empirical question. They refer to a type of human action (what we commonly call 'rational', or even merely 'conscious', as distinguished from 'instinctive' action) rather than to the particular conditions under which this action is undertaken. But the assumptions or hypotheses, which we have to introduce when we want to explain the social processes, concern the relation of the thought of an individual to the outside world, the question to what extent and how his knowledge corresponds to the external facts. And the hypotheses must necessarily run in terms of assertions about causal connections, about how experience creates knowledge.

Second, while in the field of the Pure Logic of Choice our analysis can be made exhaustive, that is, while we can here develop a formal apparatus which covers all conceivable situations, the supplementary hypotheses must of necessity be selective, that is, we must select from the infinite variety of possible situations such ideal types as for some reason we regard as specially relevant to conditions in the real world.[16] Of course, we could also develop a separate science, the subject matter of which was *per definitionem* confined to a 'perfect market' or some similarly defined object, just as the Logic of Choice applies only to persons who have to allot limited means among a variety of ends. For the field so defined our propositions would again become *a priori* true, but for such a procedure we should lack the justification which consists in the assumption that the situation in the real world is similar to what we assume it to be.

VIII

I must now turn to the question of what are the concrete hypotheses concerning the conditions under which people are supposed to acquire the relevant knowledge and the process by which they are supposed to acquire it. If it were at all clear what the hypotheses usually employed in this respect were, we should have to scrutinize them in two respects: we should have to investigate whether they were necessary and sufficient to explain a movement towards equilibrium, and we should have to show to what extent they were borne out by reality. But I am afraid that I am now getting to a stage where it becomes exceedingly difficult to say what exactly are the assumptions on the basis of which we assert that there will be a tendency towards equilibrium and to claim that our analysis has an application to the real world.[17] I cannot pretend that

[16]The distinction drawn here may help to solve the old difference between economists and sociologists about the rôle which 'ideal types' play in the reasoning of economic theory. The sociologists used to emphasize that the usual procedure of economic theory involved the assumption of particular ideal types, while the economic theorist pointed out that his reasoning was of such generality that he need not make use of any 'ideal types.' The truth seems to be that within the field of the Pure Logic of Choice, in which the economist was largely interested, he was right in his assertion but that, as soon as he wanted to use it for the explanation of a social process, he had to use 'ideal types' of one sort or another. [Hayek has in mind here the differing views of the sociologist Max Weber and the economist Ludwig von Mises on the proper usage of the ideal type construct. For more on this, see Ludwig von Mises, *Human Action: A Treatise on Economics*, 3rd ed. (Chicago: Henry Regnery, 1966), part 1, chapter 2, section 9, "On Ideal Types."—Ed.]

[17]The older economists were often more explicit on this point than their successors. See, e.g., Adam Smith, *An Inquiry into the Nature and Causes of the Wealth of Nations* [1776], ed. Edwin Cannan (London: Methuen, 1904), vol. 1, p. 116 [See now Adam Smith, *An Inquiry into the Nature and Causes of the Wealth of Nations*, ed. W. B. Todd, vol. 2 of *The Glasgow Edition of the Works and Correspondence of Adam Smith* (Glasgow: University of Glasgow, 1976; reprinted, Indianapolis, IN: Liberty Fund, 1981), book 1, chapter 10, p. 131.—Ed.], "In order, however, that this equality [of wages] may take place in the whole of their advantages or disadvantages, three things are requisite even where there is the most perfect freedom. First, the employments must be well known and long established in the neighbourhood . . ."; or David Ricardo, in *Letters of David Ricardo to Thomas Rob-*

I have as yet got much further on this point. Consequently, all I can do is to ask a number of questions to which we shall have to find an answer if we want to be clear about the significance of our argument.

The only condition about the necessity of which for the establishment of an equilibrium economists seem to be fairly agreed is the 'constancy of the data.' But after what we have seen about the vagueness of the concept of 'datum' we shall suspect, and rightly, that this does not get us much further. Even if we assume—as we probably must—that here the term is used in its objective sense (which includes, it will be remembered, the preferences of the different individuals) it is by no means clear that this is either required or sufficient in order that people shall actually acquire the necessary knowledge or that it was meant as a statement of the conditions under which they will do so. It is rather significant that, at any rate, some authors feel it necessary to add 'perfect knowledge' as an additional and separate condition.[18] Indeed, we shall see that constancy of the objective data is neither a necessary nor a sufficient condition. That it cannot be a necessary condition follows from the facts, first, that nobody would want to interpret it in the absolute sense that nothing must ever happen in the world, and, second, that, as we have seen, as soon as we want to include changes which occur periodically or perhaps even changes which proceed at a constant rate, the only way in which we can define constancy is with reference to expectations. All that this condition amounts to, then, is that there must be some discernible regularity in the world which makes it possible to predict events correctly. But, while this is clearly not sufficient to prove that people will learn to foresee events correctly, the same is true to a hardly less degree even about constancy of data in an absolute sense. For any one individual, constancy of the data does in no way mean constancy of all the facts independent of himself, since, of course, only the tastes and not the actions of the other people can in this sense be assumed to be constant. As all those other people will change their decisions as they gain experience about the external facts and about other people's actions, there is no reason why these processes of successive changes should ever come to an end. These difficulties are well

---

ert *Malthus, 1810–1823* (Oxford: Clarendon Press, 1887), Letter of October 22, 1811, p. 18 [See now David Ricardo, *Letters 1810–1815*, ed. Piero Sraffa with the collaboration of M. H. Dobb, vol. 6 (1952) of *The Works and Correspondence of David Ricardo* (Cambridge: Cambridge University Press for the Royal Economic Society, 1951–1973; reprinted, Indianapolis, IN: Liberty Fund, 2004), p. 64. Hayek added the bracketed material.—Ed.], "It would be no answer to me to say that men were ignorant of the best and cheapest mode of conducting their business and paying their debts, because that is a question of fact not of science, and might be urged against almost every proposition in Political Economy." [This footnote was not present in the original 1937 *Economica* version.—Ed.]

[18] See Nicholas Kaldor, "A Classificatory Note on the Determinateness of Equilibrium", *Review of Economic Studies*, vol. 1, February 1934, p. 123.

known,[19] and I mention them here only to remind you how little we actually know about the conditions under which an equilibrium will ever be reached. But I do not propose to follow this line of approach further, though not because this question of the empirical probability that people will learn (that is, that their subjective data will come to correspond with each other and with the objective facts) is lacking in unsolved and highly interesting problems. The reason is rather that there seems to me to be another and more fruitful way of approach to the central problem.

IX

The questions I have just discussed concerning the conditions under which people are likely to acquire the necessary knowledge, and the process by which they will acquire it, have at least received some attention in past discussions. But there is a further question which seems to me to be at least equally important but which appears to have received no attention at all, and that is how much knowledge and what sort of knowledge the different individuals must possess in order that we may be able to speak of equilibrium. It is clear that, if the concept is to have any empirical significance, it cannot presuppose that everybody knows everything. I have already had to use the undefined term 'relevant knowledge', that is, the knowledge which is relevant to a particular person. But what is this relevant knowledge? It can hardly mean simply the knowledge which actually influenced his actions, because his decisions might have been different not only if, for instance, the knowledge he possessed had been correct instead of incorrect but also if he had possessed knowledge about altogether different fields.

Clearly there is here a problem of the *division of knowledge*[20] which is quite analogous to, and at least as important as, the problem of the division of labour. But, while the latter has been one of the main subjects of investigation ever since the beginning of our science, the former has been as completely neglected, although it seems to me to be the really central problem of eco-

---

[19] Ibid., *passim.*

[20] Cf. Ludwig von Mises, *Die Gemeinwirtschaft: Untersuchungen über den Sozialismus*, 2nd ed. (Jena: Gustav Fischer, 1932), p. 96: "Die Verteilung der Verfügungsgewalt über die wirtschaftlichen Güter der arbeitsteilig wirtschaftenden Sozialwirtschaft auf viele Individuen bewirkt eine Arte geistiger Arbeitsteilung, ohne die Produktionsrechnung und Wirtschaft nich möglich wären." [This footnote did not appear in the original 1937 *Economica* version. In Ludwig von Mises, *Socialism: An Economic and Sociological Analysis*, translated by J. Kahane (London: Jonathan Cape, 1969; reprinted, Indianapolis, IN: LibertyClassics, 1981), p. 101, the quoted passage is rendered: "In societies based on the division of labour, the distribution of property rights effects a kind of mental division of labour, without which neither economy nor systematic production would be possible."—Ed.]

nomics as a social science.[21] The problem which we pretend to solve is how the spontaneous interaction of a number of people, each possessing only bits of knowledge, brings about a state of affairs in which prices correspond to costs, etc., and which could be brought about by deliberate direction only by somebody who possessed the combined knowledge of all those individuals. Experience shows us that something of this sort does happen, since the empirical observation that prices do tend to correspond to costs was the beginning of our science. But in our analysis, instead of showing what bits of information the different persons must possess in order to bring about that result, we fall in effect back on the assumption that everybody knows everything and so evade any real solution of the problem.

Before, however, I can proceed further to consider this division of knowledge among different persons, it is necessary to become more specific about the sort of knowledge which is relevant in this connection. It has become customary among economists to stress only the need of knowledge of prices, apparently because—as a consequence of the confusions between objective and subjective data—the complete knowledge of the objective facts was taken for granted. In recent times even the knowledge of current prices has been taken so much for granted that the only connection in which the question of knowledge has been regarded as problematic has been the anticipation of future prices. But, as I have already indicated at the beginning of this essay, price expectations and even the knowledge of current prices are only a very small section of the problem of knowledge as I see it. The wider aspect of the problem of knowledge with which I am concerned is the knowledge of the basic fact of how the different commodities can be obtained and used,[22] and under what

---

[21] [The following footnote from the original *Economica* article was deleted in the 1948 version: "I am not certain, but I hope, that the distinction between the Pure Logic of Choice and economics as a social science is essentially the same distinction as that which Professor A. Amonn has in mind when he stresses again and again that a *'Theorie des Wirtschaftens'* is not yet a *'Theorie der Volkswirtschaft.'*" Hayek may be referring here to Alfred Amonn's *Objekt und Grundbegriffe der theoretischen Nationalökonomie*, 2nd ed. (Vienna: Deuticke, 1927; reprinted with an introduction by T. W. Hutchison, Vienna: Böhlau, 1996). There in section 2, chapter 4, pp. 78–96, Amonn distinguishes between 'Wirtschaft' and 'Volkswirtschaft' as the objects of economic science. Specifically, he associates 'Wirtschaft' with the economy of the individual in contrast to'Volkswirtschaft', which refers to the economy within a framework of social relations. 'Wirtschaft' might then be translated as 'isolated economy', and 'Volkswirtschaft' as 'social' or 'national economy.' I thank Hansjoerg Klausinger for tracking down and making sense of this citation.—Ed.]

[22] Knowledge in this sense is more than what is usually described as skill, and the division of knowledge of which we here speak more than is meant by the division of labour. To put it shortly, 'skill' refers only to the knowledge of which a person makes use in his trade, while the further knowledge about which we must know something in order to be able to say anything about the processes in society is the knowledge of alternative possibilities of action of which he makes no direct use. It may be added that knowledge, in the sense in which the term is here used, is identical with foresight only in the sense in which all knowledge is capacity to predict.

conditions they are actually obtained and used, that is, the general question of why the subjective data to the different persons correspond to the objective facts. Our problem of knowledge here is just the existence of this correspondence which in much of current equilibrium analysis is simply assumed to exist, but which we have to explain if we want to show why the propositions, which are necessarily true about the attitude of a person towards things which he believes to have certain properties, should come to be true of the actions of society with regard to things which either do possess these properties, or which, for some reason we shall have to explain, are commonly believed by the members of society to possess these properties.[23]

But, to revert to the special problem I have been discussing, the amount of knowledge different individuals must possess in order that equilibrium may prevail (or the 'relevant' knowledge they must possess): we shall get nearer to an answer if we remember how it can become apparent either that equilibrium did not exist or that it is being disturbed. We have seen that the equilibrium connections will be severed if any person changes his plans, either because his tastes change (which does not concern us here) or because new facts become known to him. But there are evidently two different ways in which he may learn of new facts that make him change his plans, which for our purposes are of altogether different significance. He may learn of the new facts as it were by accident, that is, in a way which is not a necessary consequence of his attempt to execute his original plan, or it may be inevitable that in the course of his attempt he will find that the facts are different from what he expected. It is obvious that, in order that he may proceed according to plan, his knowledge needs to be correct only on the points on which it will necessarily be confirmed or corrected in the course of the execution of the plan. But he may have no knowledge of things which, if he possessed it, would certainly affect his plan.

The conclusion, then, which we must draw is that the relevant knowledge

---

[23]That all propositions of economic theory refer to things which are defined in terms of human attitudes towards them, that is, that the 'sugar' about which economic theory may occasionally speak is not defined by its 'objective' qualities but by the fact that people believe that it will serve certain needs of theirs in a certain way, is the source of all sorts of difficulties and confusions, particularly in connection with the problem of 'verification.' It is, of course, also in this connection that the contrast between the *verstehende* social science and the behaviourist approach becomes so glaring. I am not certain that the behaviourists in the social sciences are quite aware of *how* much of the traditional approach they would have to abandon if they wanted to be consistent or that they would want to adhere to it consistently if they were aware of this. It would, for instance, imply that propositions of the theory of money would have to refer exclusively to, say, 'round discs of metal, bearing a certain stamp', or some similarly defined physical object or group of objects. [Hayek takes up some of these same issues in "The Facts of the Social Sciences", chapter 2 of this volume, and in his war-time essay "Scientism and the Study of Society" that is cited there.—Ed.]

which he must possess in order that equilibrium may prevail is the knowledge which he is bound to acquire in view of the position in which he originally is, and the plans which he then makes. It is certainly not all the knowledge which, if he acquired it by accident, would be useful to him and lead to a change in his plan. We may therefore very well have a position of equilibrium only because some people have no chance of learning about facts which, if they knew them, would induce them to alter their plans. Or, in other words, it is only relative to the knowledge which a person is bound to acquire in the course of the attempt to carry out his original plan that an equilibrium is likely to be reached.

While such a position represents in one sense a position of equilibrium, it is clear that it is not an equilibrium in the special sense in which equilibrium is regarded as a sort of optimum position. In order that the results of the combination of individual bits of knowledge should be comparable to the results of direction by an omniscient dictator, further conditions must apparently be introduced.[24] While it should be possible to define the amount of knowledge which individuals must possess in order that this result should be obtained, I know of no real attempt in this direction. One condition would probably be that each of the alternative uses of any sort of resources is known to the owner of some such resources actually used for another purpose and that in this way all the different uses of these resources are connected, either directly or indirectly.[25] But I mention this condition only as an instance of how it will in most cases be sufficient that in each field there is a certain margin of people who possess among them all the relevant knowledge. To elaborate this further

---

[24] These conditions are usually described as absence of 'frictions.' In a recently published article, "The Quantity of Capital and the Rate of Interest: II", *Journal of Political Economy*, vol. 44, October 1936, p. 638, Frank H. Knight rightly points out that "'error' is the usual meaning of friction in economic discussion."

[25] This would be one, but probably not yet a sufficient, condition to ensure that, with a given state of demand, the marginal productivity of the different factors of production in their different uses should be equalized and that in this sense an equilibrium of production should be brought about. That it is not necessary, as one might think, that every possible alternative use of any kind of resources should be known to at least one among the owners of each group of such resources which are used for one particular purpose is due to the fact that the alternatives known to the owners of the resources in a particular use are reflected in the prices of these resources. In this way it may be a sufficient distribution of knowledge of the alternative uses, $m, n, o, \ldots y, z$, of a commodity, if A, who uses the quantity of these resources in his possession for m, knows of n, and B, who uses his for n, knows of m, while C, who uses his for o, knows of n, etc., until we get to L, who uses his for z, but knows only of y. I am not clear to what extent in addition to this a particular distribution of the knowledge of the different proportions is required in which different factors can be combined in the production of any one commodity. For complete equilibrium additional assumptions will be required about the knowledge which consumers possess about the serviceability of the commodities for the satisfaction of their wants.

would be an interesting and a very important task but a task that would far exceed the limits of this paper.

Although what I have said on this point has been largely in the form of a criticism, I do not want to appear unduly despondent about what we have already achieved. Even if we have jumped over an essential link in our argument, I still believe that, by what is implicit in its reasoning, economics has come nearer than any other social science to an answer to that central question of all social sciences: How can the combination of fragments of knowledge existing in different minds bring about results which, if they were to be brought about deliberately, would require a knowledge on the part of the directing mind which no single person can possess? To show that in this sense the spontaneous actions of individuals will, under conditions which we can define, bring about a distribution of resources which can be understood as if it were made according to a single plan, although nobody has planned it, seems to me indeed an answer to the problem which has sometimes been metaphorically described as that of the 'social mind.' But we must not be surprised that such claims have usually been rejected,[26] since we have not based them on the right grounds.

There is only one more point in this connection which I should like to mention. This is that, if the tendency towards equilibrium, which on empirical grounds we have reason to believe to exist, is only towards an equilibrium relative to that knowledge which people will acquire in the course of their economic activity, and if any other change of knowledge must be regarded as a 'change in the data' in the usual sense of the term, which falls outside the sphere of equilibrium analysis, this would mean that equilibrium analysis can really tell us nothing about the significance of such changes in knowledge, and it would also go far to account for the fact that pure analysis seems to have so extraordinarily little to say about institutions, such as the press, the purpose of which is to communicate knowledge. It might even explain why the preoccupation with pure analysis should so frequently create a peculiar blindness to the rôle played in real life by such institutions as advertising.

X

With these rather desultory remarks on topics which would deserve much more careful examination I must conclude my survey of these problems. There are only one or two further remarks which I want to add.

One is that, in stressing the nature of the empirical propositions of which

[26] [In the original 1937 version, this line read ". . . such claims have usually been rejected by sociologists, . . ."—Ed.]

we must make use if the formal apparatus of equilibrium analysis is to serve for an explanation of the real world, and in emphasizing that the propositions about how people will learn, which are relevant in this connection, are of a fundamentally different nature from those of formal analysis, I do not mean to suggest that there opens here and now a wide field for empirical research. I very much doubt whether such investigation would teach us anything new. The important point is rather that we should become aware of what the questions of fact are on which the applicability of our argument to the real world depends, or, to put the same thing in other words, at what point our argument, when it is applied to phenomena of the real world, becomes subject to verification.

The second point is that I do of course not want to suggest that the sorts of problems I have been discussing were foreign to the arguments of the economists of the older generations. The only objection that can be made against them is that they have so mixed up the two sorts of propositions, the *a priori* and the empirical, of which every realistic economist makes constant use, that it is frequently quite impossible to see what sort of validity they claimed for a particular statement. More recent work has been free from this fault—but only at the price of leaving more and more obscure what sort of relevance their arguments had to the phenomena of the real world. All I have tried to do has been to find the way back to the common-sense meaning of our analysis, of which, I am afraid, we are likely to lose sight as our analysis becomes more elaborate. You may even feel that most of what I have said has been commonplace. But from time to time it is probably necessary to detach oneself from the technicalities of the argument and to ask quite naïvely what it is all about. If I have only shown not only that in some respects the answer to this question is not obvious but that occasionally we even do not quite know what it is, I have succeeded in my purpose.

TWO

THE FACTS OF THE SOCIAL SCIENCES[1]

I

There exists today no commonly accepted term to describe the group of disciplines with which we shall be concerned in this paper. The term 'moral sciences', in the sense in which John Stuart Mill used it, did approximately cover the field, but it has long been out of fashion and would now carry inappropriate connotations to most readers. While it is for that reason necessary to use the familiar 'social sciences' in the title, I must begin by emphasizing that by no means all the disciplines concerned with the phenomena of social life present the particular problems we shall discuss. Vital statistics, for example, or the study of the spreading of contagious diseases, undoubtedly deal with social phenomena but raise none of the specific questions to be considered here. They are, if I may call them so, true natural sciences of society and differ in no important respect from the other natural sciences. But it is different with the study of language or the market, of law and most other human institutions. It is this group of disciplines which alone I propose to consider and for which I am compelled to use the somewhat misleading term 'social sciences.'

Since I shall contend that the rôle of experience in these fields of knowledge is fundamentally different from that which it plays in the natural sciences, I had, perhaps, better explain that I myself originally approached my subject, economics, thoroughly imbued with a belief in the universal validity of the methods of the natural sciences. Not only was my first technical training largely scientific in the narrow sense of the word but also what little training I had in philosophy or scientific method was entirely in the school of Ernst

[1] Read before the Cambridge University Moral Science Club, November 19, 1942. Reprinted from *Ethics*, vol. 54, October, 1943, 1–13. [This essay was reprinted in F. A. Hayek, *Individualism and Economic Order* (Chicago: University of Chicago Press, 1948), pp. 57–76.—Ed.] Some of the issues raised in this essay are discussed at greater length in the author's article on "Scientism and the Study of Society", which appeared in three instalments in *Economica*, 1942–1944. [The "Scientism" essay now appears in F. A. Hayek, *Studies on the Abuse and Decline of Reason: Texts and Documents*, ed. Bruce Caldwell, volume 13 (2010) of *The Collected Works of F. A. Hayek* (Chicago: University of Chicago Press; London: Routledge), pp. 75–166.—Ed.]

Mach and later of the logical positivists.[2] Yet all this had the effect only of creating an awareness, which became more and more definite as time went on, that, certainly in economics, all the people who are universally regarded as talking sense are constantly infringing the accepted canons of scientific method evolved from the practice of the natural sciences; that even the natural scientists, when they begin to discuss social phenomena, as a rule—at least in so far as they preserve any common-sense—do the same; but that, in the not infrequent instances when a natural scientist seriously tries to apply his professional habits of thought to social problems, the result has almost invariably been disastrous—that is, of a sort which to all professional students of these fields seems utter nonsense. But, while it is easy to show the absurdity of most concrete attempts to make the social sciences 'scientific', it is much less easy to put up a convincing defence of our own methods, which, though satisfying to most people in particular applications, are, if looked at with a critical eye, suspiciously similar to what is popularly known as 'medieval scholasticism.'

II

But enough of introduction. Let me plunge directly to the middle of my subject and ask with what kind of facts we have to deal in the social sciences. This question immediately raises another which is in many ways crucial for my problem: What do we mean when we speak of 'a certain *kind* of facts'? Are they given to us as facts of a certain kind, or do we make them such by looking at them in a certain way? Of course all our knowledge of the external world is in a way derived from sense perception and therefore from our knowledge of physical facts. But does this mean that all our knowledge is of physical facts only? This depends on what we mean by 'a kind of facts.'

An analogy from the physical sciences will make the position clear. All levers or pendulums which we can conceive have chemical and optical properties. But, when we talk about levers or pendulums, we do not talk about chemical or optical facts. What makes a number of individual things facts of a kind are the attributes which we select in order to treat them as members of a class. This is, of course, commonplace. But it means that, though all the social phenomena with which we can possibly deal may have physical attributes, they need not be physical facts for our purpose. That depends on how we shall find it convenient to classify them for the discussion of our problems. Are the

[2] [For more the Austrian physicist, psychologist, and philosopher of science Ernst Mach's influence, see Hayek's essay, "Ernst Mach (1838–1916) and the Social Sciences in Vienna", chapter 7 of *The Fortunes of Liberalism*, ed. Peter Klein, vol. 4 (1992) of *The Collected Works of F. A. Hayek*. —Ed.]

human actions which we observe, and the objects of these actions, things of the same or a different kind because they appear as physically the same or different to us, the observers—or for some other reason?

Now the social sciences are without exception concerned with the way in which men behave towards their environment —other men or things—or I should say rather that these are the elements from which the social sciences build patterns of relationships between many men. How must we define or classify the objects of their activity if we want to explain or understand their actions? Is it the physical attributes of the objects—what *we* can find out about these objects by studying them—or is it by something else that we must classify the objects when we attempt to explain what men do about them? Let me first consider a few examples.

Take such things as tools, food, medicine, weapons, words, sentences, communications, and acts of production—or any one particular instance of any of these. I believe these to be fair samples of the kind of objects of human activity which constantly occur in the social sciences. It is easily seen that all these concepts (and the same is true of more concrete instances) refer not to some objective properties possessed by the things, or which the observer can find out about them, but to views which some other person holds about the things. These objects cannot even be defined in physical terms, because there is no single physical property which any one member of a class must possess. These concepts are also not merely abstractions of the kind we use in all physical sciences; they abstract from *all* the physical properties of the things themselves. They are all instances of what are sometimes called 'teleological concepts', that is, they can be defined only by indicating relations between three terms: a purpose, somebody who holds that purpose, and an object which that person thinks to be a suitable means for that purpose. If we wish, we could say that all these objects are defined not in terms of their 'real' properties but in terms of opinions people hold about them. In short, in the social sciences the things are what people think they are. Money is money, a word is a word, a cosmetic is a cosmetic, if and because somebody thinks they are.

That this is not more obvious is due to the historical accident that in the world in which we live the knowledge of most people is approximately similar to our own. It stands out much more strongly when we think of men with a knowledge different from our own, for example, people who believe in magic. That a charm believed to protect the wearer's life, or a ritual intended to secure good harvests, can be defined only in terms of people's beliefs about them is obvious. But the logical character of the concepts we have to use in attempts to interpret people's actions is the same whether our beliefs coincide with theirs or not. Whether a medicine is a medicine, for the purpose of understanding a person's actions, depends solely on whether that person believes it to be one, irrespective of whether we, the observers, agree or not. Sometimes

80

it is somewhat difficult to keep this distinction clearly in mind. We are likely, for example, to think of the relationship between parent and child as an 'objective' fact. But, when we use this concept in studying family life, what is relevant is not that x is the natural offspring of y but that either or both believe this to be the case. The relevant character is not different from the case where x and y believe some spiritual tie to exist between them in the existence of which we do not believe. Perhaps the relevant distinction comes out most clearly in the general and obvious statement that no superior knowledge the observer may possess about the object, but which is not possessed by the acting person, can help us in understanding the motives of their actions.

The objects of human activity, then, for the purposes of the social sciences are of the same or of a different kind, or belong to the same or different classes, not according to what we, the observers, know about the objects, but according to what we think the observed person knows about it. We somehow, and for reasons which I shall presently consider, impute knowledge to the observed person. Before I go on to ask on what grounds such an imputation to the acting person of knowledge about the object is based, what this means, and what follows from the fact that we define the objects of human action in such a way, I must turn for a moment to consider the second kind of elements with which we have to deal in the social sciences: not the environment towards which the human beings behave but human action itself. When we examine the classification of different kinds of actions which we must use when we discuss intelligible human behaviour, we meet precisely the same situation as we did in analysing the classification of objects of human actions. Of the examples I have given before, the last four fall into this category: words, sentences, communications, and acts of production are instances of human actions of this kind. Now, what makes two instances of the same word or the same act of production actions of the same kind, in the sense that is relevant when we discuss intelligible behaviour? Surely not any physical properties they have in common. It is not because I know explicitly what physical properties the sound of the word 'sycamore' pronounced at different times by different people has in common but because I know that x or y intend all these different sounds or signs to mean the same word, or that they understand them all as the same word, that I treat them as instances of the same class. It is not because of any objective or physical similarity but because of the (imputed) intention of the acting person that I regard the various ways in which in different circumstances he may make, say, a spindle, as instances of the same act of production.

Please note that neither with respect to the objects of human activity nor with respect to the different kinds of human activity themselves do I argue that their physical properties do not come into the process of classification. What I am arguing is that no physical properties can enter into the explicit definition of any of these classes, because the elements of these classes need not possess common physical attributes, and we do not even consciously or explicitly know which are the various physical properties of which an object would have to possess at least one to be a member of a class. The situation may be described schematically by saying that we know that the objects $a, b, c, \ldots$, which may be physically completely dissimilar and which we can never exhaustively enumerate, are objects of the same kind because the attitude of X towards them all is similar. But the fact that X's attitude towards them is similar can again be defined only by saying that he will react towards them by any one of the actions $\alpha, \beta, \gamma, \ldots$, which again may be physically dissimilar and which we will not be able to enumerate exhaustively, but which we just know to 'mean' the same thing.

This result of reflecting about what we are actually doing is no doubt a little disturbing. Yet there seems to me no possible doubt that this not only is precisely what we are doing, in ordinary life as well as in the social sciences, when we talk about other people's intelligible action, but that it is the *only* way in which we can ever 'understand' what other people do; and that, therefore, we *must* rely on this sort of reasoning whenever we discuss what we all know as specifically human or intelligible activities. We all know what we mean when we say that we see a person 'playing' or 'working', a man doing this or that 'deliberately', or when we say that a face looks 'friendly' or a man 'frightened.' But, though we might be able to explain how we recognize any one of these things in a particular case, I am certain none of us can enumerate, and no science can—at least as yet—tell us all the different physical symptoms by which we recognize the presence of these things. The common attributes which the elements of any of these classes possess are not physical attributes but must be something else.

From the fact that whenever we interpret human action as in any sense purposive or meaningful, whether we do so in ordinary life or for the purposes of the social sciences, we have to define both the objects of human activity and the different kinds of actions themselves, not in physical terms but in terms of the opinions or intentions of the acting persons, there follow some very important consequences; namely, nothing less than that we can, from the concepts of the objects, analytically conclude something about what the actions will be. If we define an object in terms of a person's attitude towards it, it follows, of course, that the definition of the object implies a statement about the attitude of the person towards the thing. When we say that a person possesses food or money, or that he utters a word, we imply that he knows that the first can be eaten, that the second can be used to buy something with, and that the third can be understood—and perhaps many other things. Whether this implication is in any way significant, that is, whether to make it explicit adds in any way to our knowledge, depends on whether, when we say to a person that this or that thing is food or money, we state thereby merely the observed facts from which we derive this knowledge or whether we imply more than that.

How can we ever know that a person holds certain beliefs about his environment? What do we mean when we say that we know he holds certain beliefs—when we say that we know that he uses this thing as a tool or that gesture or sound as a means of communication? Do we mean merely what we actually observe in the particular case, for example, that we see him chewing and swallowing his food, swinging a hammer, or making noises? Or do we not always when we say we 'understand' a person's action, when we talk about 'why' he is doing this or that, impute to him something beyond what we can observe—at least beyond what we can observe in the particular case?

If we consider for a moment the simplest kinds of actions where this problem arises, it becomes, of course, rapidly obvious that, in discussing what we regard as other people's conscious actions, we invariably interpret their action on the analogy of our own mind: that is, that we group their actions, and the objects of their actions, into classes or categories which we know solely from the knowledge of our own mind. We assume that the idea of a purpose or a tool, a weapon or food, is common to them with us, just as we assume that they can see the difference between different colors or shapes as well as we. We thus always supplement what we actually see of another person's action by projecting into that person a system of classification of objects which we know, not from observing other people, but because it is in terms of these classes that we think ourselves. If, for example, we watch a person cross a square full of traffic, dodging some cars and pausing to let others pass, we know (or we believe we know) much more than we actually perceive with our eyes. This would be equally true if we saw a man behave in a physical environment quite unlike anything we have ever seen before. If I see for the first time a big boulder or an avalanche coming down the side of a mountain towards a man and see him run for his life, I know the meaning of this action because I know what I would or might have done in similar circumstances.

There can be no doubt that we all constantly act on the assumption that we can in this way interpret other people's actions on the analogy of our own mind and that in the great majority of instances this procedure *works*. The trouble is that we can never be sure. On watching a few movements or hearing a few words of a man, we decide that he is sane and not a lunatic and thereby exclude the possibility of his behaving in an infinite number of 'odd' ways which none of us could ever enumerate and which just do not fit into what we know to be reasonable behaviour—which means nothing else than that those actions cannot be interpreted by analogy of our own mind. We can neither explain precisely how, for practical purposes, we know that a man is sane and not a lunatic, nor can we exclude the possibility that in one case in a thousand we may be wrong. Similarly, I shall, from a few observations, be able rapidly to conclude that a man is signalling or hunting, making love to or punishing another person, though I may never have seen these things done in this particular way; and yet my conclusion will be sufficiently certain for all practical purposes.

The important question which arises is whether it is legitimate to employ in scientific analysis such concepts as these, which refer to a state of affairs which we all recognize 'intuitively' and which we not only unhesitatingly use in daily life but on which all social intercourse, all communication between men, is based; or whether we should be precluded from doing so because we cannot state any physical conditions from which we can derive with certainty that the postulated conditions are really present in any particular case, and because for this reason we can never be certain whether any particular instance is really a member of the class about which we talk—although we all agree that in the great majority of cases our diagnosis will be correct. The hesitation which we at first feel about this is probably due to the fact that the retention of such a procedure in the social sciences seems to be in conflict with the most marked tendency of the development of scientific thought in modern times. But is there really such a conflict? The tendency to which I refer has been correctly described as one towards the progressive elimination of all 'anthropomorphic' explanations from the physical sciences. Does this really mean that we must refrain from treating man 'anthropomorphically'—or is it not rather obvious, as soon as we put it in this way, that such an extrapolation of past tendencies is absurd?

I do not wish, of course, in this connection to raise all the problems connected with the behaviourist program, though a more systematic survey of my subject could hardly avoid doing so. Indeed, the question with which we are here concerned is nothing else than whether the social sciences could possibly discuss the kind of problems with which they are concerned in purely behaviouristic terms—or even whether consistent behaviourism is possible.

Perhaps the relation between the strictly empirical factor and the part which we add from the knowledge of our own mind in interpreting another person's action can be stated with the help of a (somewhat questionable) use of the distinction between the denotation and the connotation of a concept. What I shall in particular circumstances recognize as a 'friendly face', the denotation of the concept, is largely a matter of experience. But what I mean when I say that this is a 'friendly face', no experience in the ordinary sense of the term can tell me. What I mean by a 'friendly face' does not depend on the physical properties of different concrete instances, which may conceivably have nothing in common. Yet I learn to recognize them as members of the same class—and what makes them members of the same class is not any of their physical properties but an imputed meaning.

The importance of this distinction grows as we move outside the familiar surroundings. As long as I move among my own kind of people, it is probably the physical properties of a bank note or a revolver from which I conclude that they are money or a weapon to the person holding them. When I see a savage holding cowrie shells or a long, thin tube, the physical properties of the thing will probably tell me nothing. But the observations which suggest to me that the cowrie shells are money to him and the blowpipe a weapon will throw much light on the object—much more light than these same observations could possibly give if I were not familiar with the conception of money or a weapon. In recognizing the things as such, I begin to understand the people's behaviour. I am able to fit into a scheme of actions which 'make sense' just because I have come to regard it not as a thing with certain physical properties but as the kind of thing which fits into the pattern of my own purposive action.

If what we do when we speak about understanding a person's action is to fit what we actually observe into patterns we find ready in our own mind, it follows, of course, that we can understand less and less as we turn to beings more and more different from ourselves. But it also follows that it is not only impossible to recognize, but meaningless to speak of, a mind different from our own. What we mean when we speak of another mind is that we can connect what we observe because the things we observe fit into the way of our own thinking. But where this possibility of interpreting in terms of analogies from our own mind ceases, where we can no longer 'understand'—there is no sense in speaking of mind at all; there are then only physical facts which we can group and classify solely according to the physical properties which we observe.

An interesting point in this connection is that, as we go from interpreting the actions of men very much like ourselves to men who live in a very different environment, it is the most concrete concepts which first lose their usefulness for interpreting the people's actions and the most general or abstract which remain helpful longest. My knowledge of the everyday things around me, of the particular ways in which we express ideas or emotions, will be of little use in interpreting the behaviour of the inhabitants of Tierra del Fuego. But my understanding of what I mean by a means to an end, by food or a weapon, a word or a sign, and probably even an exchange or a gift, will still be useful and even essential in my attempt to understand what they do.

III

So far the discussion has been limited to the question of how we classify individual actions and their objects in the discussion of social phenomena. I must now turn to the question of the purpose for which we use this classification. Even though concern with classifications takes up a great deal of our energies in the social sciences—so much, indeed, in economics, for example, that one of the best-known modern critics of the discipline has described it as a purely 'taxonomic' science—this is not our ultimate purpose.[3] Like all classifications, it is merely a convenient way of arranging our facts for whatever we want to explain. But before I can turn to this, I must, first, clear a common misunderstanding from our way and, second, explain a claim frequently made on behalf of this process of classification—a claim which to anyone brought up in the natural sciences sounds highly suspicious but which nevertheless follows merely from the nature of our object.

The misunderstanding is that the social sciences aim at *explaining* individual behaviour and particularly that the elaborate process of classification which we use either is, or serves, such an explanation. The social sciences do in fact nothing of the sort. If conscious action can be 'explained', this is a task for psychology but not for economics or linguistics, jurisprudence or any other social science. What we do is merely to classify types of individual behaviour which we can understand, to develop their classification—in short, to provide an orderly arrangement of the material which we have to use in our further task. Economists, and the same is probably also true in the other social sciences, are usually a little ashamed to admit that this part of their task is 'only' a kind of logic. I think that they would be wise frankly to recognize and to face this fact.

The claim to which I have referred follows directly from this character of the first part of our task as a branch of applied logic. But it sounds startling enough at first. It is that we can derive from the knowledge of our own mind in an '*a priori*' or 'deductive' or 'analytic' fashion, an (at least in principle) *exhaustive* classification of all the possible forms of intelligible behaviour. It is against this claim, rarely openly made, but always implied, that all the taunts against the economists are directed, when we are accused of spinning knowledge out of our inner consciousness and what other similar abusive epithets there are. Yet when we reflect that, whenever we discuss intelligible behaviour, we discuss actions which we can interpret in terms of our own mind, the claim loses its startling character and in fact becomes no more than a truism. If we can understand only what is similar to our own mind, it necessarily follows that we must be able to find all that we can understand in our own mind. Of course, when I say that we can *in principle* achieve an exhaustive classification of all possible forms of intelligible behaviour, this does not mean that we may not discover that, in interpreting human actions, we do use processes of thought which we have not yet analysed or made explicit. We constantly do. What I meant is that when we discuss any particular class of intelligible action which

---

[3] [Hayek refers here to the American institutionalist economist Thorstein Veblen (1857–1929), who made the claim in "The Preconceptions of Economic Science", *Quarterly Journal of Economics*, vol. 14, February 1900, p. 255.—Ed.]

we have defined as actions of one kind, in the sense in which I have used that term, then we can, within that field, provide a completely exhaustive classification of the forms of action which fall within it. If, for example, we define as economic actions all acts of choice which are made necessary by the scarcity of means available for our ends, we can, step by step, proceed to subdivide the possible situations into alternatives so that at each step there is no third possibility: a given means may be useful only for one or for many ends, a given end can be achieved by one or by several different means, different means may be wanted for a given end either alternatively or cumulatively, etc.

But I must leave what I have called the first part of my task and turn to the question of the use we make of these elaborate classifications in the social sciences. The answer is, briefly, that we use the different kinds of individual behaviour thus classified as elements from which we construct hypothetical models in an attempt to reproduce the patterns of social relationships which we know in the world around us. But this still leaves us with the question whether this is the right way to study social phenomena. Have we not in these social structures at last definite tangible social facts which we ought to observe and measure, as we observe and measure physical facts? Should we not here at least derive all our knowledge by observing and experiencing, instead of by 'constructing models' from the elements found in our own thought?

The belief that, when we turn from the action of the individual to the observation of social collectivities, we move from the realm of vague and subjective speculation to the realm of objective fact is very widespread. It is the belief held by all who think that they may make the social sciences more 'scientific' by imitating the model of the natural sciences. Its intellectual basis has been most clearly expressed by the founder of 'sociology', Auguste Comte, when in a famous statement he asserted that in the field of social phenomena, as in biology, "the whole of the object is certainly much better known and more immediately accessible" than the constituent parts.[4] Most of the science he attempted to create is still based on this or similar beliefs.

I believe that this view which regards social collectivities such as 'society' or the 'state', or any particular social institution or phenomenon, as in any sense more objective than the intelligible actions of the individuals is sheer illusion. I shall argue that what we call 'social facts' are no more facts in the specific sense in which this term is used in the physical sciences than are individual actions or their objects; that these so-called 'facts' are rather precisely the same kind of mental models constructed by us from elements which we find in our

---

[4] Auguste Comte, *Cours de philosophie positive*, ed. Émile Littré, 2nd ed. (Paris: J. B. Baillière et fils, 1864), vol. 4, p. 286. [The ideas of the French polymath philosopher and sociologist Auguste Comte (1798–1857) are explicated and criticized by Hayek in his essay "The Counter-Revolution of Science", now reprinted in Hayek, *Studies on the Abuse and Decline of Reason*. See especially chapters 13, 16, and 17.—Ed.]

own minds as those which we construct in the theoretical social sciences; so that what we do in those sciences is in a logical sense exactly the same thing as what we always do when we talk about a state or a community, a language or a market, only that we make explicit what in everyday speech is concealed and vague.

I cannot attempt here to explain this in connection with any one of the theoretical social disciplines—or, rather, in connection with the only one among them where I should be competent to do this, economics. To do so, I should have to spend far more time than I have on technicalities. But it will perhaps be even more helpful if I attempt to do so with respect to the pre-eminently descriptive and, in a sense, pre-eminently empirical discipline in the social field, namely, history. To consider the nature of 'historical facts' will be particularly appropriate, since the social scientists are constantly advised, by those who want to make the social sciences more 'scientific', to turn to history for their facts and to use the 'historical method' as a substitute for the experimental. Indeed, outside the social sciences themselves (and, it seems, particularly among logicians)[5] it appears to have become almost accepted doctrine that the historical method is the legitimate path towards generalizations about social phenomena.[6]

What do we mean by a 'fact' of history? Are the facts with which human history is concerned significant to us as physical facts or in some other sense? What sort of things are the Battle of Waterloo, the French government under Louis XIV, or the feudal system? Perhaps we shall get further if, instead of tackling this question directly, we ask how we decide whether any particular bit of information we have constitutes part of the 'fact' 'Battle of Waterloo.' Was the man plowing his field just beyond the extreme wing of Napoleon's guards part of the Battle of Waterloo? Or the chevalier who dropped his snuff-box on hearing the news of the storming of the Bastille part of the French Revolution? To follow up this kind of question will show at least one thing: that we cannot define a historical fact in terms of spatio-temporal co-ordinates. Neither is everything which takes place at one time and in one place part of the same historical fact, nor must all parts of the same historical fact belong to the same time and place. The classical Greek language or the organization

---

[5]Cf., e.g., L. S. Stebbing, *A Modern Introduction to Logic*, 2nd ed. (London: Methuen, 1933), p. 383.

[6]I am sure that I need not here especially guard myself against the misunderstanding that what I shall have to say about the relation between history and theory is meant in any sense to diminish the importance of history. I should like even to emphasize that the whole purpose of theory is to help our understanding of historical phenomena and that the most perfect knowledge of theory will be of very little use indeed without a most extensive knowledge of a historical character. But this has really nothing to do with my present subject, which is the nature of 'historical facts' and the respective rôles which history and theory play in their discussion.

of the Roman legions, the Baltic trade of the eighteenth century or the evolution of common law, or any move of any army—these are all historical facts where no physical criterion can tell us what are the parts of the fact and how they hang together. Any attempt to define them must take the form of a mental reconstruction, of a model, in which intelligible individual attitudes form the elements. In most instances, no doubt, the model will be so simple that the interconnection of its parts are readily visible; and there will consequently be little justification for dignifying the model with the name of a 'theory.' But, if our historical fact is such a complex as a language or a market, a social system or a method of land cultivation, what we call a fact is either a recurrent process or a complex pattern of persistent relationships which is not 'given' to our observation but which we can only laboriously reconstruct—and which we can reconstruct only because the parts (the relations from which we build up the structure) are familiar and intelligible to us. To put it paradoxically: what we call historical facts are really theories which, in a methodological sense, are of precisely the same character as the more abstract or general models which the theoretical sciences of society construct. The situation is not that we first study the 'given' historical facts and then perhaps can generalize about them. We rather use a theory when we select from the knowledge we have about a period certain parts as intelligibly connected and forming part of the same historical fact. We never observe states or governments, battles or commercial activities, or a people as a whole. When we use any of these terms, we always refer to a scheme which connects individual activities by intelligible relations; that is, we use a theory which tells us what is and what is not part of our subject. It does not alter the position that the theorizing is usually done for us by our informant or source who, in reporting the fact, will use terms like 'state' or 'town' which cannot be defined in physical terms but which refer to a complex of relationships which, made explicit, constitute a 'theory' of the subject.

Social theory, in the sense in which I use the term, is, then, logically prior to history. It explains the terms which history must use. This is, of course, not inconsistent with the fact that historical study frequently forces the theorist to revise the constructions or to provide new ones in terms of which he can arrange the information which he finds. But in so far as the historian talks, not merely about the individual actions of particular people but about what, in some sense, we can call social phenomena, his facts can be explained as facts of a certain kind only in terms of a theory about how its elements hang together. The social complexes, the social wholes which the historian discusses, are never found ready given as are the persistent structures in the organic (animal or vegetable) world. They are created by him by a work of construction or interpretation—a construction which for most purposes is done spontaneously and without any elaborate apparatus. But in some connections where, for example, we deal with such things as languages, economic systems, or bodies of law, these structures are so complicated that, without the help of an elaborate technique, they can no longer be reconstructed without the danger of going wrong and being led into contradictions.

This is all the theories of the social sciences aim to do. They are not *about* the social wholes as wholes; they do not pretend to discover by empirical observation laws of behaviour or change of these wholes. Their task is rather, if I may so call it, to *constitute* these wholes, to provide schemes of structural relationships which the historian can use when he has to attempt to fit together into a meaningful whole the elements which he actually finds. The historian cannot avoid constantly using social theories in this sense. He may do so unconsciously, and in fields in which the relationships are not too complex his instinct may guide him aright. When he turns to more complex phenomena such as those of language, law, or economics, and still disdains to make use of the models worked out for him by the theorists, he is almost certain to come to grief. And this 'coming to grief' will significantly show itself by the theoretician either demonstrating to him that he has involved himself in contradictions or showing him that in his explanations he has asserted a sequence of 'causation' which, as soon as his assumptions are made explicit, he will have to admit does not follow from his assumptions.

There are two important consequences which follow from this and which can here be only briefly stated. The first is that the theories of the social sciences do not consist of 'laws' in the sense of empirical rules about the behaviour of objects definable in physical terms. All that the theory of the social sciences attempts is to provide a technique of reasoning which assists us in connecting individual facts, but which, like logic or mathematics, is not about the facts. It can, therefore, and this is the second point, never be verified or falsified by reference to facts. All that we can and must verify is the presence of our assumptions in the particular case. We have already referred to the special problems and difficulties which this raises. In this connection a genuine 'question of fact' arises—though one it will often not be possible to answer with the same certainty as is the case in the natural sciences. But the theory itself, the mental scheme for the interpretation, can never be 'verified' but only tested for its consistency. It may be irrelevant because the conditions to which it refers never occur; or it may prove inadequate because it does not take account of a sufficient number of conditions. But it can no more be disproved by facts than can logic or mathematics.

There still remains, however, the question whether this kind of 'compositive' theory, as I like to call it, which 'constitutes' the social 'wholes' by constructing models from intelligible elements, is the *only* kind of social theory, or whether we might not also aim at empirical generalizations about the behaviour of these wholes as wholes, at laws of the changes of languages or institutions—the kind of laws which are the aim of 'historical method.'

I shall not enlarge here on the curious contradiction into which the defendants of this method usually involve themselves when they first emphasize that all historical phenomena are unique or singular and then proceed to claim that their study can arrive at generalizations. The point I wish to make is rather that if, of the infinite variety of phenomena which we can find in any concrete situation, only those can be regarded as part of one object which we can connect by means of our mental models, the object can possess no attributes beyond those which can be derived from our model. Of course, we can go on constructing models which fit concrete situations more and more closely—concepts of states or languages which possess an ever richer connotation. But as members of a class, as similar units about which we can make generalizations, these models can never possess any properties which we have not given to them or which do not derive deductively from the assumptions on which we have built them. Experience can never teach us that any particular kind of structure has properties which do not follow from the definition (or the way we construct it). The reason for this is simply that these wholes or social structures are never given to us as natural units, are not definite objects given to observation, that we never deal with the whole of reality but always only with a selection made with the help of our models.[7]

I have not space to discuss more fully the nature of 'historical facts' or the objects of history, but I should like briefly to refer to one question which, though not strictly germane to my subject, is yet not quite irrelevant. It is the very fashionable doctrine of 'historical relativism', the belief that different generations or ages must of necessity hold different views about the same historical facts. It seems to me that this doctrine is the result of the same illusion that historical facts are definitely given to us and not the result of a deliberate selection of what we regard as a connected set of events relevant to the answer of a particular question—an illusion which seems to me to be due to the belief that we can define a historical fact in physical terms by its spatio-temporal co-ordinates. But a thing so defined, say, 'Germany between 1618 and 1648', just is not *one* historical object. Within the space-time continuum thus defined we can find any number of interesting social phenomena which to the historian are altogether different objects: the history of Family X, the development of printing, the change of legal institutions, etc., which may or may not be connected but which are no more part of one social fact than any

---

[7] Incidentally, I am not convinced that this last point really constitutes a difference between the social and the natural sciences. But, if it does not, I think that it is the natural scientists who are mistaken in believing that they ever deal with the *whole* of reality and not merely with selected 'aspects' of it. But this whole problem whether we can ever talk about, or perceive, an object which is indicated to us in a purely demonstrative manner, and which in this sense is an individual as distinguished from a 'unit class' (which is really concrete and not an abstraction), would lead too far beyond my present subject.

other two events in human history. This particular period, or any other period, is, as such, no definite 'historical fact', no single historical object. According to our interests we can ask any number of different questions referring to this period and accordingly shall have to give different answers and shall have to construct different models of connected events. And this is what historians *do* at different times because they are interested in different questions. But as it is only the question that we ask which singles out, from the infinite variety of social events which we can find at any given time and place, a definite set of connected events which can be termed one historical fact, the experience that people give different answers to different questions does, of course, not prove that they hold different views about the same historical fact. There is no reason whatever, on the other hand, why historians at different times, but possessing the same information, should answer the same question differently. This alone, however, would justify the thesis about an inevitable relativity of historical knowledge.

I mention this because this historical relativism is a typical product of that so-called 'historicism' which is, in fact, a product of the misapplication of the scientistic prejudice to historical phenomena—of the belief that social phenomena are ever given to us as the facts of nature are given to us. They are accessible to us only because we can understand what other people tell us and can be understood only by interpreting other people's intentions and plans. They are not physical facts, but the elements from which we reproduce them are always familiar categories of our own mind. Where we could no longer interpret what we know about other people by the analogy of our own mind, history would cease to be human history; it would then, indeed, have to run in purely behaviouristic terms such as the history we might write of an ant heap or the history an observer from Mars might write of the human race.

If this account of what the social sciences are actually doing appears to you as a description of a topsy-turvy world in which everything is in the wrong place, I beg you to remember that these disciplines deal with a world at which from our position we necessarily look in a different manner from that in which we look at the world of nature. To employ a useful metaphor: while at the world of nature we look from the outside, we look at the world of society from the inside; while, as far as nature is concerned, our concepts are about the facts and have to be adapted to the facts, in the world of society at least some of the most familiar concepts are the stuff from which that world is made. Just as the existence of a common structure of thought is the condition of the possibility of our communicating with one another, of your understanding what I say, so it is also the basis on which we all interpret such complicated social structures as those which we find in economic life or law, in language, and in customs.

THREE

THE USE OF KNOWLEDGE IN SOCIETY[1]

I

What is the problem we wish to solve when we try to construct a rational economic order? On certain familiar assumptions the answer is simple enough. *If* we possess all the relevant information, *if* we can start out from a given system of preferences, and *if* we command complete knowledge of available means, the problem which remains is purely one of logic. That is, the answer to the question of what is the best use of the available means is implicit in our assumptions. The conditions which the solution of this optimum problem must satisfy have been fully worked out and can be stated best in mathematical form: put at their briefest, they are that the marginal rates of substitution between any two commodities or factors must be the same in all their different uses.

This, however, is emphatically *not* the economic problem which society faces. And the economic calculus which we have developed to solve this logical problem, though an important step towards the solution of the economic problem of society, does not yet provide an answer to it. The reason for this is that the 'data' from which the economic calculus starts are never for the whole society 'given' to a single mind which could work out the implications, and can never be so given.

The peculiar character of the problem of a rational economic order is determined precisely by the fact that the knowledge of the circumstances of which we must make use never exists in concentrated or integrated form but solely as the dispersed bits of incomplete and frequently contradictory knowledge which all the separate individuals possess. The economic problem of society is thus not merely a problem of how to allocate 'given' resources—if 'given' is taken to mean given to a single mind which deliberately solves the problem set by these 'data.' It is rather a problem of how to secure the best use of resources known to any of the members of society, for ends whose relative

[1]Reprinted from the *American Economic Review*, vol. 35, September 1945, pp. 519–30. [This essay was reprinted in F. A. Hayek, *Individualism and Economic Order* (Chicago: University of Chicago Press, 1948), pp. 77–91.—Ed.]

importance only these individuals know. Or, to put it briefly, it is a problem of the utilization of knowledge which is not given to anyone in its totality.

This character of the fundamental problem has, I am afraid, been obscured rather than illuminated by many of the recent refinements of economic theory, particularly by many of the uses made of mathematics. Though the problem with which I want primarily to deal in this paper is the problem of a rational economic organization, I shall in its course be led again and again to point to its close connections with certain methodological questions. Many of the points I wish to make are indeed conclusions towards which diverse paths of reasoning have unexpectedly converged. But, as I now see these problems, this is no accident. It seems to me that many of the current disputes with regard to both economic theory and economic policy have their common origin in a misconception about the nature of the economic problem of society. This misconception in turn is due to an erroneous transfer to social phenomena of the habits of thought we have developed in dealing with the phenomena of nature.

II

In ordinary language we describe by the word 'planning' the complex of inter-related decisions about the allocation of our available resources. All economic activity is in this sense planning; and in any society in which many people collaborate, this planning, whoever does it, will in some measure have to be based on knowledge which, in the first instance, is not given to the planner but to somebody else, which somehow will have to be conveyed to the planner. The various ways in which the knowledge on which people base their plans is communicated to them is the crucial problem for any theory explaining the economic process, and the problem of what is the best way of utilizing knowledge initially dispersed among all the people is at least one of the main problems of economic policy—or of designing an efficient economic system.

The answer to this question is closely connected with that other question which arises here, that of *who* is to do the planning. It is about this question that all the dispute about 'economic planning' centers. This is not a dispute about whether planning is to be done or not. It is a dispute as to whether planning is to be done centrally, by one authority for the whole economic system, or is to be divided among many individuals. Planning in the specific sense in which the term is used in contemporary controversy necessarily means central planning—direction of the whole economic system according to one unified plan. Competition, on the other hand, means decentralized planning by many separate persons. The half-way house between the two, about which many people talk but which few like when they see it, is the delegation of planning to organized industries, or, in other words, monopolies.

Which of these systems is likely to be more efficient depends mainly on the question under which of them we can expect that fuller use will be made of the existing knowledge. This, in turn, depends on whether we are more likely to succeed in putting at the disposal of a single central authority all the knowledge which ought to be used but which is initially dispersed among many different individuals, or in conveying to the individuals such additional knowledge as they need in order to enable them to dovetail their plans with those of others.

III

It will at once be evident that on this point the position will be different with respect to different kinds of knowledge. The answer to our question will therefore largely turn on the relative importance of the different kinds of knowledge; those more likely to be at the disposal of particular individuals and those which we should with greater confidence expect to find in the possession of an authority made up of suitably chosen experts. If it is today so widely assumed that the latter will be in a better position, this is because one kind of knowledge, namely, scientific knowledge, occupies now so prominent a place in public imagination that we tend to forget that it is not the only kind that is relevant. It may be admitted that, as far as scientific knowledge is concerned, a body of suitably chosen experts may be in the best position to command all the best knowledge available—though this is of course merely shifting the difficulty to the problem of selecting the experts. What I wish to point out is that, even assuming that this problem can be readily solved, it is only a small part of the wider problem.

Today it is almost heresy to suggest that scientific knowledge is not the sum of all knowledge. But a little reflection will show that there is beyond question a body of very important but unorganized knowledge which cannot possibly be called scientific in the sense of knowledge of general rules: the knowledge of the particular circumstances of time and place. It is with respect to this that practically every individual has some advantage over all others because he possesses unique information of which beneficial use might be made, but of which use can be made only if the decisions depending on it are left to him or are made with his active co-operation. We need to remember only how much we have to learn in any occupation after we have completed our theoretical training, how big a part of our working life we spend learning particular jobs, and how valuable an asset in all walks of life is knowledge of people, of local conditions, and of special circumstances. To know of and put to use a machine not fully employed, or somebody's skill which could be better utilized, or to be aware of a surplus stock which can be drawn upon during an interruption of supplies, is socially quite as useful as the knowledge of better alternative techniques. The shipper who earns his living from using otherwise empty or half-filled journeys of tramp-steamers, or the estate agent whose whole knowledge is almost exclusively one of temporary opportunities, or the *arbitrageur* who gains from local differences of commodity prices—are all performing eminently useful functions based on special knowledge of circumstances of the fleeting moment not known to others.

It is a curious fact that this sort of knowledge should today be generally regarded with a kind of contempt and that anyone who by such knowledge gains an advantage over somebody better equipped with theoretical or technical knowledge is thought to have acted almost disreputably. To gain an advantage from better knowledge of facilities of communication or transport is sometimes regarded as almost dishonest, although it is quite as important that society make use of the best opportunities in this respect as in using the latest scientific discoveries. This prejudice has in a considerable measure affected the attitude towards commerce in general compared with that towards production. Even economists who regard themselves as definitely immune to the crude materialist fallacies of the past constantly commit the same mistake where activities directed towards the acquisition of such practical knowledge are concerned—apparently because in their scheme of things all such knowledge is supposed to be 'given.' The common idea now seems to be that all such knowledge should as a matter of course be readily at the command of everybody, and the reproach of irrationality levelled against the existing economic order is frequently based on the fact that it is not so available. This view disregards the fact that the method by which such knowledge can be made as widely available as possible is precisely the problem to which we have to find an answer.

IV

If it is fashionable today to minimize the importance of the knowledge of the particular circumstances of time and place, this is closely connected with the smaller importance which is now attached to change as such. Indeed, there are few points on which the assumptions made (usually only implicitly) by the 'planners' differ from those of their opponents as much as with regard to the significance and frequency of changes which will make substantial alterations of production plans necessary. Of course, if detailed economic plans could be laid down for fairly long periods in advance and then closely adhered to, so that no further economic decisions of importance would be required, the task of drawing up a comprehensive plan governing all economic activity would be much less formidable.

It is, perhaps, worth stressing that economic problems arise always and only in consequence of change. As long as things continue as before, or at least as they were expected to, there arise no new problems requiring a decision, no need to form a new plan. The belief that changes, or at least day-to-day adjustments, have become less important in modern times implies the contention that economic problems also have become less important. This belief in the decreasing importance of change is, for that reason, usually held by the same people who argue that the importance of economic considerations has been driven into the background by the growing importance of technological knowledge.

Is it true that, with the elaborate apparatus of modern production, economic decisions are required only at long intervals, as when a new factory is to be erected or a new process to be introduced? Is it true that, once a plant has been built, the rest is all more or less mechanical, determined by the character of the plant, and leaving little to be changed in adapting to the ever changing circumstances of the moment?

The fairly widespread belief in the affirmative is not, as far as I can ascertain, borne out by the practical experience of the business man. In a competitive industry at any rate—and such an industry alone can serve as a test—the task of keeping cost from rising requires constant struggle, absorbing a great part of the energy of the manager. How easy it is for an inefficient manager to dissipate the differentials on which profitability rests and that it is possible, with the same technical facilities, to produce with a great variety of costs are among the commonplaces of business experience which do not seem to be equally familiar in the study of the economist. The very strength of the desire, constantly voiced by producers and engineers, to be allowed to proceed untrammeled by considerations of money costs, is eloquent testimony to the extent to which these factors enter into their daily work.

One reason why economists are increasingly apt to forget about the constant small changes which make up the whole economic picture is probably their growing preoccupation with statistical aggregates, which show a very much greater stability than the movements of the detail. The comparative stability of the aggregates cannot, however, be accounted for—as the statisticians occasionally seem to be inclined to do—by the 'law of large numbers' or the mutual compensation of random changes. The number of elements with which we have to deal is not large enough for such accidental forces to produce stability. The continuous flow of goods and services is maintained by constant deliberate adjustments, by new dispositions made every day in the light of circumstances not known the day before, by B stepping in at once when A fails to deliver. Even the large and highly mechanized plant keeps going largely because of an environment upon which it can draw for all sorts of unexpected needs: tiles for its roof, stationery for its forms, and all the thousand and one kinds of equipment in which it cannot be self-contained and which the plans for the operation of the plant require to be readily available in the market.

This is, perhaps, also the point where I should briefly mention the fact that the sort of knowledge with which I have been concerned is knowledge of the kind which by its nature cannot enter into statistics and therefore cannot be conveyed to any central authority in statistical form. The statistics which such a central authority would have to use would have to be arrived at precisely by abstracting from minor differences between the things, by lumping together, as resources of one kind, items which differ as regards location, quality, and other particulars, in a way which may be very significant for the specific decision. It follows from this that central planning based on statistical information by its nature cannot take direct account of these circumstances of time and place and that the central planner will have to find some way or other in which the decisions depending on them can be left to the 'man on the spot.'

V

If we can agree that the economic problem of society is mainly one of rapid adaptation to changes in the particular circumstances of time and place, it would seem to follow that the ultimate decisions must be left to the people who are familiar with these circumstances, who know directly of the relevant changes and of the resources immediately available to meet them. We cannot expect that this problem will be solved by first communicating all this knowledge to a central board which, after integrating all knowledge, issues its orders. We must solve it by some form of decentralization. But this answers only part of our problem. We need decentralization because only thus can we ensure that the knowledge of the particular circumstances of time and place will be promptly used. But the 'man on the spot' cannot decide solely on the basis of his limited but intimate knowledge of the facts of his immediate surroundings. There still remains the problem of communicating to him such further information as he needs to fit his decisions into the whole pattern of changes of the larger economic system.

How much knowledge does he need to do so successfully? Which of the events which happen beyond the horizon of his immediate knowledge are of relevance to his immediate decision, and how much of them need he know?

There is hardly anything that happens anywhere in the world that *might* not have an effect on the decision he ought to make. But he need not know of these events as such, nor of *all* their effects. It does not matter for him *why* at the particular moment more screws of one size than of another are wanted, *why* paper bags are more readily available than canvas bags, or *why* skilled labour, or particular machine tools, have for the moment become more difficult to obtain. All that is significant for him is *how much more or less* difficult to procure they have become compared with other things with which he is also concerned, or how much more or less urgently wanted are the alternative things he produces or uses. It is always a question of the relative importance of the particular things with which he is concerned, and the causes which alter their relative importance are of no interest to him beyond the effect on those concrete things of his own environment.

It is in this connection that what I have called the 'economic calculus' (or the Pure Logic of Choice) helps us, at least by analogy, to see how this problem can be solved, and in fact is being solved, by the price system. Even the single controlling mind, in possession of all the data for some small, self-contained economic system, would not—every time some small adjustment in the allocation of resources had to be made—go explicitly through all the relations between ends and means which might possibly be affected. It is indeed the great contribution of the Pure Logic of Choice that it has demonstrated conclusively that even such a single mind could solve this kind of problem only by constructing and constantly using rates of equivalence (or 'values', or 'marginal rates of substitution'), that is, by attaching to each kind of scarce resource a numerical index which cannot be derived from any property possessed by that particular thing, but which reflects, or in which is condensed, its significance in view of the whole means-end structure. In any small change he will have to consider only these quantitative indices (or 'values') in which all the relevant information is concentrated; and, by adjusting the quantities one by one, he can appropriately rearrange his dispositions without having to solve the whole puzzle *ab initio* or without needing at any stage to survey it at once in all its ramifications.

Fundamentally, in a system in which the knowledge of the relevant facts is dispersed among many people, prices can act to co-ordinate the separate actions of different people in the same way as subjective values help the individual to co-ordinate the parts of his plan. It is worth contemplating for a moment a very simple and commonplace instance of the action of the price system to see what precisely it accomplishes. Assume that somewhere in the world a new opportunity for the use of some raw material, say, tin, has arisen, or that one of the sources of supply of tin has been eliminated. It does not matter for our purpose—and it is significant that it does not matter—which of these two causes has made tin more scarce. All that the users of tin need to know is that some of the tin they used to consume is now more profitably employed elsewhere, and that, in consequence, they must economize tin. There is no need for the great majority of them even to know where the more urgent need has arisen, or in favour of what other needs they ought to husband the supply. If only some of them know directly of the new demand, and switch resources over to it, and if the people who are aware of the new gap thus created in turn fill it from still other sources, the effect will rapidly spread throughout the whole economic system and influence not only all the uses of tin but also those of its substitutes and the substitutes of these substitutes, the supply of all the things made of tin, and their substitutes, and so on; and all this without the great majority of those instrumental in bringing about these substitutions knowing anything at all about the original cause of these changes. The whole acts as one market, not because any of its members survey the whole field, but because their limited individual fields of vision sufficiently overlap so that through many intermediaries the relevant information is communicated to all. The mere fact that there is one price for any commodity—or rather that local prices are connected in a manner determined by the cost of transport, etc.—brings about the solution which (it is just conceptually possible) might have been arrived at by one single mind possessing all the information which is in fact dispersed among all the people involved in the process.

VI

We must look at the price system as such a mechanism for communicating information if we want to understand its real function—a function which, of course, it fulfills less perfectly as prices grow more rigid. (Even when quoted prices have become quite rigid, however, the forces which would operate through changes in price still operate to a considerable extent through changes in the other terms of the contract.) The most significant fact about this system is the economy of knowledge with which it operates, or how little the individual participants need to know in order to be able to take the right action. In abbreviated form, by a kind of symbol, only the most essential information is passed on and passed on only to those concerned. It is more than a metaphor to describe the price system as a kind of machinery for registering change, or a system of telecommunications which enables individual producers to watch merely the movement of a few pointers, as an engineer might watch the hands of a few dials, in order to adjust their activities to changes of which they may never know more than is reflected in the price movement.

Of course, these adjustments are probably never 'perfect' in the sense in which the economist conceives of them in his equilibrium analysis. But I fear that our theoretical habits of approaching the problem with the assumption of more or less perfect knowledge on the part of almost everyone has made us somewhat blind to the true function of the price mechanism and led us to apply rather misleading standards in judging its efficiency. The marvel is that in a case like that of a scarcity of one raw material, without an order being issued, without more than perhaps a handful of people knowing the cause, tens of thousands of people whose identity could not be ascertained by months of investigation, are made to use the material or its products more sparingly; that is, they move in the right direction. This is enough of a marvel even if, in a constantly changing world, not all will hit it off so perfectly that their profit rates will always be maintained at the same even or 'normal' level.

I have deliberately used the word 'marvel' to shock the reader out of the complacency with which we often take the working of this mechanism for granted. I am convinced that if it were the result of deliberate human design, and if the people guided by the price changes understood that their decisions have significance far beyond their immediate aim, this mechanism would have been acclaimed as one of the greatest triumphs of the human mind. Its misfortune is the double one that it is not the product of human design and that the people guided by it usually do not know why they are made to do what they do. But those who clamor for 'conscious direction'—and who cannot believe that anything which has evolved without design (and even without our understanding it) should solve problems which we should not be able to solve consciously—should remember this: The problem is precisely how to extend the span of our utilization of resources beyond the span of the control of any one mind; and, therefore, how to dispense with the need of conscious control and how to provide inducements which will make the individuals do the desirable things without anyone having to tell them what to do.

The problem which we meet here is by no means peculiar to economics but arises in connection with nearly all truly social phenomena, with language and with most of our cultural inheritance, and constitutes really the central theoretical problem of all social science. As Alfred Whitehead has said in another connection, "It is a profoundly erroneous truism, repeated by all copy-books and by eminent people when they are making speeches, that we should cultivate the habit of thinking of what we are doing. The precise opposite is the case. Civilization advances by extending the number of important operations which we can perform without thinking about them."[2] This is of profound significance in the social field. We make constant use of formulas, symbols, and rules whose meaning we do not understand and through the use of which we avail ourselves of the assistance of knowledge which individually we do not possess. We have developed these practices and institutions by building upon habits and institutions which have proved successful in their own sphere and which have in turn become the foundation of the civilization we have built up.

The price system is just one of those formations which man has learned to use (though he is still very far from having learned to make the best use of it) after he had stumbled upon it without understanding it. Through it not only a division of labour but also a co-ordinated utilization of resources based on an

---

[2] [Alfred North Whitehead (1861–1947) was a British philosopher, logician, and mathematician whose writings ranged from the monumental *Principia Mathematica* (1910–1913) with Bertrand Russell, to the popular *Science and the Modern World* (1925). The quote is from his *Introduction to Mathematics* (London: Williams and Norgate, 1911), p. 61. Hayek used part of the quote again at the head of chapter 2 of *The Constitution of Liberty.*—Ed.]

THE MARKET AND OTHER ORDERS

equally divided knowledge has become possible. The people who like to deride any suggestion that this may be so usually distort the argument by insinuating that it asserts that by some miracle just that sort of system has spontaneously grown up which is best suited to modern civilization. It is the other way round: man has been able to develop that division of labour on which our civilization is based because he happened to stumble upon a method which made it possible. Had he not done so, he might still have developed some other, altogether different, type of civilization, something like the 'state' of the termite ants, or some other altogether unimaginable type. All that we can say is that nobody has yet succeeded in designing an alternative system in which certain features of the existing one can be preserved which are dear even to those who most violently assail it—such as particularly the extent to which the individual can choose his pursuits and consequently freely use his own knowledge and skill.

VII

It is in many ways fortunate that the dispute about the indispensability of the price system for any rational calculation in a complex society is now no longer conducted entirely between camps holding different political views. The thesis that without the price system we could not preserve a society based on such extensive division of labour as ours was greeted with a howl of derision when it was first advanced by von Mises twenty-five years ago.[3] Today the difficulties which some still find in accepting it are no longer mainly political, and this makes for an atmosphere much more conducive to reasonable discussion. When we find Leon Trotsky arguing that "economic accounting is unthinkable without market relations"; when Professor Oskar Lange promises Professor von Mises a statue in the marble halls of the future Central Planning Board; and when Professor Abba P. Lerner rediscovers Adam Smith and emphasizes that the essential utility of the price system consists in inducing the individual, while seeking his own interest, to do what is in the general interest, the differences can indeed no longer be ascribed to political prejudice.[4] The remaining

[3] [Hayek refers to Ludwig von Mises's classic article, "Die Wirtschaftsrechnung im sozialistischen Gemeinwessen", *Archiv für Sozialwissenschaft*, vol. 47, 1920, pp. 86–121, translated by S. Adler as "Economic Calculation in the Socialist Commonwealth", in *Collectivist Economic Planning: Critical Studies on the Possibilities of Socialism*, ed. F. A. Hayek (London: Routledge and Sons, 1935; reprinted, Clifton: NJ: Kelley, 1975), pp. 87–130.—Ed.]

[4] [Russian revolutionary leader and Marxist theorist Leon Trotsky (1879–1940) penned these words for an article published in 1932 in *The Militant* titled "The Soviet Economy in Danger", now reprinted in *Writings of Leon Trotsky—1932* (New York: Pathfinder Press, 1973), p. 276. Polish economist Oskar Lange (1904–1965) was a leading proponent of market socialism, a doctrine which purported to combine the efficiency characteristics of a competitive market regime with the redistributive aims of socialism. Acknowledging Mises's insight about the importance of

dissent seems clearly to be due to purely intellectual, and more particularly methodological, differences.

A recent statement by Joseph Schumpeter in his *Capitalism, Socialism and Democracy* provides a clear illustration of one of the methodological differences which I have in mind. Its author is pre-eminent among those economists who approach economic phenomena in the light of a certain branch of positivism. To him these phenomena accordingly appear as objectively given quantities of commodities impinging directly upon each other, almost, it would seem, without any intervention of human minds. Only against this background can I account for the following (to me startling) pronouncement. Professor Schumpeter argues that the possibility of a rational calculation in the absence of markets for the factors of production follows for the theorist "from the elementary proposition that consumers in evaluating ('demanding') consumers' goods *ipso facto* also evaluate the means of production which enter into the production of those goods."[5]

Taken literally, this statement is simply untrue. The consumers do nothing of the kind. What Professor Schumpeter's "*ipso facto*" presumably means is that the valuation of the factors of production is implied in, or follows necessarily from, the valuation of consumers' goods. But this, too, is not correct. Implication is a logical relationship which can be meaningfully asserted only

---

prices as a tool for the rational allocation of resources, Lange proposed the erection of a statue in "On the Economic Theory of Socialism", in *On the Economic Theory of Socialism*, ed. Benjamin E. Lippincott (Minneapolis: University of Minnesota Press; reprinted, New York: McGraw Hill, 1956), pp. 57–58. In *The Economics of Control* (New York: Macmillan, 1944; reprinted, New York: Kelley, 1970), p. 67, the market socialist Abba Lerner (1905–1982) said about the price mechanism, "If it is appropriately used it induces each member of society, while seeking his own benefit, to do that which is in the general social interest. Fundamentally this is the great discovery of Adam Smith and the Physiocrats."—Ed.]

[5]Joseph Schumpeter, *Capitalism, Socialism and Democracy* (New York: Harper, 1942), p. 175. Professor Schumpeter is, I believe, also the original author of the myth that Pareto and Barone have 'solved' the problem of socialist calculation. What they, and many others, did was merely to state the conditions which a rational allocation of resources would have to satisfy and to point out that these were essentially the same as the conditions of equilibrium of a competitive market. This is something altogether different from showing how the allocation of resources satisfying these conditions can be found in practice. Pareto himself (from whom Barone has taken practically everything he has to say), far from claiming to have solved the practical problem, in fact explicitly denies that it can be solved without the help of the market. See his *Manuel d'économie politique*, translated by Alfred Bonnet, 2nd ed. (Paris: Marcel Giard, 1927), pp. 233–34. The relevant passage is quoted in an English translation at the beginning of my article on "Socialist Calculation: The Competitive 'Solution'", in *Economica*, n.s., vol. 8, May 1940, p. 125. [Cf. Hayek, "Socialist Calculation: The Competitive 'Solution'", in *Socialism and War*, ed. Bruce Caldwell, vol. 10 (1997) of *The Collected Works of F. A. Hayek* (Chicago: University of Chicago Press; London: Routledge), chapter 3, pp. 117–18. See also Vilfredo Pareto, *Manual of Political Economy*, ed. Ann S. Schwier and Alfred N. Page, translated by Ann S. Schwier (New York: Kelley, 1971). The passage Hayek refers to appears on p. 171.—Ed.]

of propositions simultaneously present to one and the same mind. It is evident, however, that the values of the factors of production do not depend solely on the valuation of the consumers' goods but also on the conditions of supply of the various factors of production. Only to a mind to which all these facts were simultaneously known would the answer necessarily follow from the facts given to it. The practical problem, however, arises precisely because these facts are never so given to a single mind, and because, in consequence, it is necessary that in the solution of the problem knowledge should be used that is dispersed among many people.

The problem is thus in no way solved if we can show that all the facts, if they were known to a single mind (as we hypothetically assume them to be given to the observing economist), would uniquely determine the solution; instead we must show how a solution is produced by the interactions of people each of whom possesses only partial knowledge. To assume all the knowledge to be given to a single mind in the same manner in which we assume it to be given to us as the explaining economists is to assume the problem away and to disregard everything that is important and significant in the real world.

That an economist of Professor Schumpeter's standing should thus have fallen into a trap which the ambiguity of the term 'datum' sets to the unwary can hardly be explained as a simple error. It suggests rather that there is something fundamentally wrong with an approach which habitually disregards an essential part of the phenomena with which we have to deal: the unavoidable imperfection of man's knowledge and the consequent need for a process by which knowledge is constantly communicated and acquired. Any approach, such as that of much of mathematical economics with its simultaneous equations, which in effect starts from the assumption that people's *knowledge* corresponds with the objective *facts* of the situation, systematically leaves out what is our main task to explain. I am far from denying that in our system equilibrium analysis has a useful function to perform. But when it comes to the point where it misleads some of our leading thinkers into believing that the situation which it describes has direct relevance to the solution of practical problems, it is high time that we remember that it does not deal with the social process at all and that it is no more than a useful preliminary to the study of the main problem.

FOUR

THE MEANING OF COMPETITION[1]

I

There are signs of increasing awareness among economists that what they have been discussing in recent years under the name of 'competition' is not the same thing as what is thus called in ordinary language. But, although there have been some valiant attempts to bring discussion back to earth and to direct attention to the problems of real life, notably by J. M. Clark and Fritz Machlup,[2] the general view seems still to regard the conception of competition currently employed by economists as the significant one and to treat that of the businessman as an abuse. It appears to be generally held that the so-called theory of 'perfect competition' provides the appropriate model for judging the effectiveness of competition in real life and that, to the extent that real competition differs from that model, it is undesirable and even harmful.

For this attitude there seems to me to exist very little justification. I shall attempt to show that what the theory of perfect competition discusses has little claim to be called 'competition' at all and that its conclusions are of little use as guides to policy. The reason for this seems to me to be that this theory throughout assumes that state of affairs already to exist which, according to the truer view of the older theory, the process of competition tends to bring about (or to approximate) and that, if the state of affairs assumed by the theory of perfect competition ever existed, it would not only deprive of their scope all the activities which the verb 'to compete' describes but would make them virtually impossible.

If all this affected only the use of the word 'competition', it would not matter a great deal. But it seems almost as if economists by this peculiar use of

---

[1] This essay reproduces the substance of the Stafford Little Lecture delivered at Princeton University on May 20, 1946. [This essay was reprinted in F. A. Hayek, *Individualism and Economic Order* (Chicago: University of Chicago Press, 1948), pp. 92–106.—Ed.]

[2] J. M. Clark, "Toward a Concept of Workable Competition", *American Economic Review*, vol. 30, June 1940, pp. 241–56; Fritz Machlup, "Competition, Pliopoly, and Profit", *Economica*, n.s., vol. 9, February and May, 1942, pp. 1–23, 153–73.

language were deceiving themselves into the belief that, in discussing 'competition', they are saying something about the nature and significance of the process by which the state of affairs is brought about which they merely assume to exist. In fact, this moving force of economic life is left almost altogether undiscussed.

I do not wish to discuss here at any length the reasons which have led the theory of competition into this curious state. As I have suggested elsewhere in this volume,[3] the tautological method which is appropriate and indispensable for the analysis of individual action seems in this instance to have been illegitimately extended to problems in which we have to deal with a social process in which the decisions of many individuals influence one another and necessarily succeed one another in time. The economic calculus (or the Pure Logic of Choice) which deals with the first kind of problem consists of an apparatus of classification of possible human attitudes and provides us with a technique for describing the interrelations of the different parts of a single plan. Its conclusions are implicit in its assumptions: the desires and the knowledge of the facts, which are assumed to be simultaneously present to a single mind, determine a unique solution. The relations discussed in this type of analysis are logical relations, concerned solely with the conclusions which follow for the mind of the planning individual from the given premises.

When we deal, however, with a situation in which a number of persons are attempting to work out their separate plans, we can no longer assume that the data are the same for all the planning minds. The problem becomes one of how the 'data' of the different individuals on which they base their plans are adjusted to the objective facts of their environment (which includes the actions of the other people). Although in the solution of this type of problem we still must make use of our technique for rapidly working out the implications of a given set of data, we have now to deal not only with several separate sets of data of the different persons but also—and this is even more important—with a process which necessarily involves continuous changes in the data for the different individuals. As I have suggested before, the causal factor enters here in the form of the acquisition of new knowledge by the different individuals or of changes in their data brought about by the contacts between them.

The relevance of this for my present problem will appear when it is recalled that the modern theory of competition deals almost exclusively with a state of what is called 'competitive equilibrium' in which it is assumed that the data for the different individuals are fully adjusted to each other, while the problem which requires explanation is the nature of the process by which the data are thus adjusted. In other words, the description of competitive equilibrium

---

[3] See the essays "Economics and Knowledge" and "The Use of Knowledge in Society." [See this volume, chapters 1 and 3, respectively.—Ed.]

does not even attempt to say that, if we find such and such conditions, such and such consequences will follow, but confines itself to defining conditions in which its conclusions are already implicitly contained and which may conceivably exist but of which it does not tell us how they can ever be brought about. Or, to anticipate our main conclusion in a brief statement, competition is by its nature a dynamic process whose essential characteristics are assumed away by the assumptions underlying static analysis.

II

That the modern theory of competitive equilibrium *assumes* the situation to exist which a true explanation ought to account for as the effect of the competitive process is best shown by examining the familiar list of conditions found in any modern textbook. Most of these conditions, incidentally, not only underlie the analysis of 'perfect' competition but are equally assumed in the discussion of the various 'imperfect' or 'monopolistic' markets, which throughout assume certain unrealistic 'perfections.'[4] For our immediate purpose, however, the theory of perfect competition will be the most instructive case to examine.

While different authors may state the list of essential conditions of perfect competition differently, the following is probably more than sufficiently comprehensive for our purpose, because, as we shall see, those conditions are not really independent of each other. According to the generally accepted view, perfect competition presupposes:

1. A homogeneous commodity offered and demanded by a large number of relatively small sellers or buyers, none of whom expects to exercise by his action a perceptible influence on price.
2. Free entry into the market and absence of other restraints on the movement of prices and resources.
3. Complete knowledge of the relevant factors on the part of all participants in the market.

We shall not ask at this stage precisely for what these conditions are required or what is implied if they are assumed to be given. But we must inquire a little further about their meaning, and in this respect it is the third condition which is the critical and obscure one. The standard can evidently not be perfect knowledge of everything affecting the market on the part of every person taking part in it. I shall here not go into the familiar paradox of the paralysing

---

[4] Particularly the assumptions that *at all times* a uniform price must rule for a given commodity throughout the market and that sellers know the shape of the demand curve.

effect really perfect knowledge and foresight would have on all action.[5] It will be obvious also that nothing is solved when we assume everybody to know everything and that the real problem is rather how it can be brought about that as much of the available knowledge as possible is used. This raises for a competitive society the question, not how we can 'find' the people who know best, but rather what institutional arrangements are necessary in order that the unknown persons who have knowledge specially suited to a particular task are most likely to be attracted to that task. But we must inquire a little further what sort of knowledge it is that is supposed to be in possession of the parties of the market.

If we consider the market for some kind of finished consumption goods and start with the position of its producers or sellers, we shall find, first, that they are assumed to know the lowest cost at which the commodity can be produced. Yet this knowledge which is assumed to be given to begin with is one of the main points where it is only through the process of competition that the facts will be discovered. This appears to me one of the most important of the points where the starting point of the theory of competitive equilibrium assumes away the main task which only the process of competition can solve. The position is somewhat similar with respect to the second point on which the producers are assumed to be fully informed: the wishes and desires of the consumers, including the kinds of goods and services which they demand and the prices they are willing to pay. These cannot properly be regarded as given facts but ought rather to be regarded as problems to be solved by the process of competition.

The same situation exists on the side of the consumers or buyers. Again the knowledge they are supposed to possess in a state of competitive equilibrium cannot be legitimately assumed to be at their command before the process of competition starts. Their knowledge of the alternatives before them is the result of what happens on the market, of such activities as advertising, etc.; and the whole organization of the market serves mainly the need of spreading the information on which the buyer is to act.

The peculiar nature of the assumptions from which the theory of competitive equilibrium starts stands out very clearly if we ask which of the activities that are commonly designated by the verb 'to compete' would still be possible if those conditions were all satisfied. Perhaps it is worth recalling that, according to Dr. Johnson, competition is "the act of endeavouring to gain what another endeavours to gain at the same time."[6] Now, how many of the devices

[5] See Oskar Morgenstern, "Vollkommene Voraussicht und wirtschaftliches Gleichgewicht", *Zeitschrift für Nationalökonomie*, vol. 6, August 1935, pp. 337–57.

[6] [This is the first definition offered of the term 'competition' in *Chambers's Encyclopedia: A Dictionary of Universal Knowledge for the People*, rev. ed. (London: W. & R. Chambers, 1886), vol. 3, p. 163, where it is attributed to Dr. Johnson.—Ed.]

adopted in ordinary life to that end would still be open to a seller in a market in which so-called 'perfect competition' prevails? I believe that the answer is exactly none. Advertising, undercutting, and improving ('differentiating') the goods or services produced are all excluded by definition—'perfect' competition means indeed the absence of all competitive activities.

Especially remarkable in this connection is the explicit and complete exclusion from the theory of perfect competition of all personal relationships existing between the parties.[7] In actual life the fact that our inadequate knowledge of the available commodities or services is made up for by our experience with the persons or firms supplying them—that competition is in a large measure competition for reputation or good will—is one of the most important facts which enables us to solve our daily problems. The function of competition is here precisely to teach us *who* will serve us well: which grocer or travel agency, which department store or hotel, which doctor or solicitor, we can expect to provide the most satisfactory solution for whatever particular personal problem we may have to face. Evidently in all these fields competition may be very intense, just because the services of the different persons or firms will never be exactly alike, and it will be owing to this competition that we are in a position to be served as well as we are. The reasons competition in this field is described as imperfect have indeed nothing to do with the competitive character of the activities of these people; it lies in the nature of the commodities or services themselves. If no two doctors are perfectly alike, this does not mean that the competition between them is less intense but merely that any degree of competition between them will not produce exactly those results which it would if their services were exactly alike. This is not a purely verbal point. The talk about the defects of competition when we are in fact talking about the necessary difference between commodities and services conceals a very real confusion and leads on occasion to absurd conclusions.

While on a first glance the assumption concerning the perfect knowledge possessed by the parties may seem the most startling and artificial of all those on which the theory of perfect competition is based, it may in fact be no more than a consequence of, and in part even justified by, another of the presuppositions on which it is founded. If, indeed, we start by assuming that a large number of people are producing the same commodity and command the same objective facilities and opportunities for doing so, then indeed it might be made plausible (although this has, to my knowledge, never been attempted) that they will in time all be led to know most of the facts relevant for judging the market of that commodity. Not only will each producer by his experience

---

[7] Cf. G. J. Stigler, *The Theory of Price* (New York: Macmillan, 1946), p. 24: "Economic relationships are never perfectly competitive if they involve any personal relationships between economic units" (see also ibid., p. 226).

learn the same facts as every other but also he will thus come to know what his fellows know and in consequence the elasticity of the demand for his own product. The condition where different manufacturers produce the identical product under identical conditions is in fact the most favourable for producing that state of knowledge among them which perfect competition requires. Perhaps this means no more than that the commodities can be identical in the sense in which it is alone relevant for our understanding human action only if people hold the same views about them, although it should also be possible to state a set of physical conditions which is favourable to all those who are concerned with a set of closely interrelated activities learning the facts relevant for their decisions.

However that be, it will be clear that the facts will not always be as favourable to this result as they are when many people are at least in a position to produce the same article. The conception of the economic system as divisible into distinct markets for separate commodities is after all very largely the product of the imagination of the economist and certainly is not the rule in the field of manufacture and of personal services, to which the discussion about competition so largely refers. In fact, it need hardly be said, no products of two producers are ever exactly alike, even if it were only because, as they leave his plant, they must be at different places. These differences are part of the facts which create our economic problem, and it is little help to answer it on the assumption that they are absent.

The belief in the advantages of perfect competition frequently leads enthusiasts even to argue that a more advantageous use of resources would be achieved if the existing variety of products were reduced by *compulsory* standardization. Now, there is undoubtedly much to be said in many fields for assisting standardization by agreed recommendations or standards which are to apply unless different requirements are explicitly stipulated in contracts. But this is something very different from the demands of those who believe that the variety of people's tastes should be disregarded and the constant experimentation with improvements should be suppressed in order to obtain the advantages of perfect competition. It would clearly not be an improvement to build all houses exactly alike in order to create a perfect market for houses, and the same is true of most other fields where differences between the individual products prevent competition from ever being perfect.

III

We shall probably learn more about the nature and significance of the competitive process if for a while we forget about the artificial assumptions underlying the theory of perfect competition and ask whether competition would be any less important if, for example, no two commodities were ever exactly alike. If it were not for the difficulty of the analysis of such a situation, it would be well worthwhile to consider in some detail the case where the different commodities could not be readily classed into distinct groups, but where we had to deal with a continuous range of close substitutes, every unit somewhat different from the other but without any marked break in the continuous range. The result of the analysis of competition in such a situation might in many respects be more relevant to the conditions of real life than those of the analysis of competition in a single industry producing a homogeneous commodity sharply differentiated from all others. Or, if the case where no two commodities are exactly alike be thought to be too extreme, we might at least turn to the case where no two producers produce exactly the same commodity, as is the rule not only with all personal services but also in the markets of many manufactured commodities, such as the markets for books or musical instruments.

For our present purpose I need not attempt anything like a complete analysis of such kinds of markets but shall merely ask what would be the rôle of competition in them. Although the result would, of course, within fairly wide margins be indeterminate, the market would still bring about a set of prices at which each commodity sold just cheap enough to outbid its potential close substitutes—and this in itself is no small thing when we consider the insurmountable difficulties of discovering even such a system of prices by any other method except that of trial and error in the market, with the individual participants gradually learning the relevant circumstances. It is true, of course, that in such a market correspondence between prices and marginal costs is to be expected only to the degree that elasticities of demand for the individual commodities approach the conditions assumed by the theory of perfect competition or that elasticities of substitution between the different commodities approach infinity. But the point is that in this case this standard of perfection as something desirable or to be aimed at is wholly irrelevant. The basis of comparison, on the grounds of which the achievement of competition ought to be judged, cannot be a situation which is different from the objective facts and which cannot be brought about by any known means. It ought to be the situation as it would exist if competition were prevented from operating. Not the approach to an unachievable and meaningless ideal but the improvement upon the conditions that would exist without competition should be the test.

In such a situation how would conditions differ, if competition were 'free' in the traditional sense, from those which would exist if, for example, only people licensed by authority were allowed to produce particular things, or prices were fixed by authority, or both? Clearly there would be not only no likelihood that the different things would be produced by those who knew best how to do it and therefore could do it at lowest cost but also no likelihood that all those things would be produced at all which, if the consumers had the choice, they would like best. There would be little relationship between actual prices and the lowest cost at which somebody would be able to produce these commodities; indeed, the alternatives between which both producers and consumers would be in a position to choose, their data, would be altogether different from what they would be under competition.

The real problem in all this is not whether we will get *given* commodities or services at *given* marginal costs but mainly by what commodities and services the needs of the people can be most cheaply satisfied. The solution of the economic problem of society is in this respect always a voyage of exploration into the unknown, an attempt to discover new ways of doing things better than they have been done before. This must always remain so as long as there are any economic problems to be solved at all, because all economic problems are created by unforeseen changes which require adaptation. Only what we have not foreseen and provided for requires new decisions. If no such adaptations were required, if at any moment we knew that all change had stopped and things would forever go on exactly as they are now, there would be no more questions of the use of resources to be solved.

A person who possesses the exclusive knowledge or skill which enables him to reduce the cost of production of a commodity by 50 per cent still renders an enormous service to society if he enters its production and reduces its price by only 25 per cent—not only through that price reduction but also through his additional saving of cost. But it is only through competition that we can assume that these possible savings of cost will be achieved. Even if in each instance prices were only just low enough to keep out producers which do not enjoy these or other equivalent advantages, so that each commodity were produced as cheaply as possible, though many may be sold at prices considerably above costs, this would probably be a result which could not be achieved by any other method than that of letting competition operate.

IV

That in conditions of real life the position even of any two producers is hardly ever the same is due to facts which the theory of perfect competition eliminates by its concentration on a long-term equilibrium which in an ever changing world can never be reached. At any given moment the equipment of a particular firm is always largely determined by historical accident, and the problem is that it should make the best use of the given equipment (including the acquired capacities of the members of its staff) and not what it should do if it were given unlimited time to adjust itself to constant conditions. For the problem of the best use of the given durable but exhaustible resources the long-term equilibrium price with which a theory discussing 'perfect' competition must be concerned is not only not relevant; the conclusions concerning policy to which preoccupation with this model leads are highly misleading and even dangerous. The idea that under 'perfect' competition prices should be equal to long-run costs often leads to the approval of such anti-social practices as the demand for an 'orderly competition' which will secure a fair return on capital and for the destruction of excess capacity. Enthusiasm for perfect competition in theory and the support of monopoly in practice are indeed surprisingly often found to live together.

This is, however, only one of the many points on which the neglect of the time element makes the theoretical picture of perfect competition so entirely remote from all that is relevant to an understanding of the process of competition. If we think of it, as we ought to, as a succession of events, it becomes even more obvious that in real life there will at any moment be as a rule only one producer who can manufacture a given article at the lowest cost and who may in fact sell below the cost of his next successful competitor, but who, while still trying to extend his market, will often be overtaken by somebody else, who in turn will be prevented from capturing the whole market by yet another, and so on. Such a market would clearly never be in a state of perfect competition, yet competition in it might not only be as intense as possible but would also be the essential factor in bringing about the fact that the article in question is supplied at any moment to the consumer as cheaply as this can be done by any known method.

When we compare an 'imperfect' market like this with a relatively 'perfect' market as that of, say, grain, we shall now be in a better position to bring out the distinction which has been underlying this whole discussion—the distinction between the underlying objective facts of a situation which cannot be altered by human activity and the nature of the competitive activities by which men adjust themselves to the situation. Where, as in the latter case, we have a highly organized market of a fully standardized commodity produced by many producers, there is little need or scope for competitive activities because the situation is such that the conditions which these activities might bring about are already satisfied to begin with. The best ways of producing the commodity, its character and uses, are most of the time known to nearly the same degree to all members of the market. The knowledge of any important change spreads so rapidly and the adaptation to it is so soon effected that we usually simply disregard what happens during these short transition periods and confine ourselves to comparing the two states of near-equilibrium which exist before and after them. But it is during this short and neglected interval that the forces of competition operate and become visible, and it is the events during this interval which we must study if we are to 'explain' the equilibrium which follows it.

It is only in a market where adaptation is slow compared with the rate of change that the process of competition is in continuous operation. And though the reason why adaptation is slow *may* be that competition is weak, e.g., because there are special obstacles to entry into the trade, or because of some other factors of the character of natural monopolies, slow adaptation does by no means necessarily mean weak competition. When the variety of near-substitutes is great and rapidly changing, where it takes a long time to find out about the relative merits of the available alternatives, or where the need for a whole class of goods or services occurs only discontinuously at irregular intervals, the adjustment must be slow even if competition is strong and active.

The confusion between the objective facts of the situation and the character of the human responses to it tends to conceal from us the important fact that competition is the more important the more complex or 'imperfect' are the objective conditions in which it has to operate. Indeed, far from competition being beneficial only when it is 'perfect', I am inclined to argue that the need for competition is nowhere greater than in fields in which the nature of the commodities or services makes it impossible that it ever should create a perfect market in the theoretical sense. The inevitable actual imperfections of competition are as little an argument against competition as the difficulties of achieving a perfect solution of any other task are an argument against attempting to solve it at all, or as little as imperfect health is an argument against health.

In conditions where we can never have many people offering the same homogeneous product or service, because of the ever changing character of our needs and our knowledge, or of the infinite variety of human skills and capacities, the ideal state cannot be one requiring an identical character of large numbers of such products and services. The economic problem is a problem of making the best use of what resources we have, and not one of what we should do if the situation were different from what it actually is. There is no sense in talking of a use of resources 'as if' a perfect market existed, if this means that the resources would have to be different from what they are, or in discussing what somebody with perfect knowledge would do if our task must be to make the best use of the knowledge the existing people have.

V

The argument in favour of competition does not rest on the conditions that would exist if it were perfect. Although, where the objective facts would make it possible for competition to approach perfection, this would also secure the most effective use of resources, and, although there is therefore every case for removing human obstacles to competition, this does not mean that competition does not also bring about as effective a use of resources as can be brought about by any known means where in the nature of the case it must be imperfect. Even where free entry will secure no more than that at any one moment all the goods and services for which there would be an effective demand if they were available are in fact produced at the least current[8] expenditure of resources at which, in the given historical situation, they can be produced, even though the price the consumer is made to pay for them is considerably higher and only just below the cost of the next best way in which his need could be satisfied, this, I submit, is more than we can expect from any other known system. The decisive point is still the elementary one that it is most unlikely that, without artificial obstacles which government activity either creates or can remove, any commodity or service will for any length of time be available only at a price at which outsiders could expect a more than normal profit if they entered the field.

The practical lesson of all this, I think, is that we should worry much less about whether competition in a given case is perfect and worry much more whether there is competition at all. What our theoretical models of separate industries conceal is that in practice a much bigger gulf divides competition from no competition than perfect from imperfect competition. Yet the current tendency in discussion is to be intolerant about the imperfections and to be silent about the prevention of competition. We can probably still learn more about the real significance of competition by studying the results which regularly occur where competition is deliberately suppressed than by concentrating on the shortcomings of actual competition compared with an ideal which is irrelevant for the given facts. I say advisedly "where competition is deliberately suppressed" and not merely "where it is absent", because its main effects are usually operating, even if more slowly, so long as it is not outright suppressed with the assistance or the tolerance of the state. The evils which experience has shown to be the regular consequence of a suppression of competition are on a different plane from those which the imperfections of competition may cause. Much more serious than the fact that prices may not correspond to marginal cost is the fact that, with an entrenched monopoly, costs are likely to be much higher than is necessary. A monopoly based on superior efficiency, on the other hand, does comparatively little harm so long as it is assured that it will disappear as soon as anyone else becomes more efficient in providing satisfaction to the consumers.

In conclusion I want for a moment to go back to the point from which I started and restate the most important conclusion in a more general form. Competition is essentially a process of the formation of opinion: by spreading information, it creates that unity and coherence of the economic system which we presuppose when we think of it as one market. It creates the views

---

[8] 'Current' cost in this connection excludes all true bygones but includes, of course, 'user cost.'

people have about what is best and cheapest, and it is because of it that people know at least as much about possibilities and opportunities as they in fact do. It is thus a process which involves a continuous change in the data and whose significance must therefore be completely missed by any theory which treats these data as constant.

PART II

FROM CHICAGO TO FREIBURG
Further Development

FIVE

THE POLITICAL IDEAL OF
THE RULE OF LAW

NATIONAL BANK OF EGYPT

Fiftieth Anniversary Commemoration Lectures

The Political Ideal of the Rule of Law

by

F. A. HAYEK, F. B. A.

Dr. jur. et Dr. rer. pol. (Vienna)

Dr. Sc. (Econ.) (London)

Professor of Social and Moral Science

in the

University of Chicago

(Committee on Social Thought)

CAIRO, 1955

CONTENTS

Preface

When I was honoured with the invitation to deliver the Commemoration Lectures of the National Bank of Egypt the best I had to offer were the tentative results of a study on which I had been engaged for some time but which is not yet concluded. I have availed myself of the opportunity to give an outline of the conclusions at which I have arrived though they may still require modification in some respect. The following lectures should therefore be regarded as an advance sketch of an argument which needs to be developed on a larger canvass. I have nevertheless acceded with pleasure to the suggestion of the National Bank of Egypt to print the lectures as delivered because I hope to profit for a later and more detailed treatment from the criticisms and comments of those who read them. In view of the sketchy character of the text I have thought it appropriate to give in the notes rather fuller references than is perhaps usual in a set of lectures, in order that those who are not content with the bare bones of the argument should be able to pursue further some of the questions raised. Some of the references I owe to the kindness of Dr. Shirley Letwin, Irene Shils, and Dr. Gerald Stourzh, whose friendly interest in my efforts I gratefully acknowledge.

F. A. HAYEK
February 1955

Lecture I
Freedom and the Rule of Law
A Historical Survey

> The power which is at the root of all liberty to dispose and economise, in the land which God has given them, as masters of family in their own inheritance. —John Milton[1]

1. Principles and Drift in the Democratic Process

If in these lectures I hold up an ideal which for the world was once embodied in the example of Britain, I shall ask you to remember, as I have to add with regret, that I shall be speaking mainly about the past of that great country. I shall be speaking about an ideal which at one time she taught the world and the pursuit of which made her great, though it may now sometimes seem as if she had turned her back upon it. Yet I do not think that for that reason it is necessarily an antiquated ideal which could not still be of immense value to the world. And whatever may be true of countries which by following a policy of individual liberty have become great centers of a creative civilization— and I do not know of an instance in the human history where a country has achieved this by another path—whether such a country can then afford the luxury of replacing the old ideal by some new conception of justice, I do not doubt that the path to greatness is still the same hard and perhaps harsh one: that for countries who are striving to rise, or to recover the wealth they have lost, the stimulus to all individual energies that the reign of freedom brings alone will lead to the goal.

Though I shall begin with certain developments which in modern times commenced in Britain, it will be with a universal and not with a national problem with which I shall be concerned. Sixty or eighty years ago the ideal about which I shall speak had fully conquered the minds if not the practice of all the Western nations and few doubted that it was destined soon to rule the world. The material civilization which surrounds us and which at least the ruling classes of all the peoples of the world have adopted, is still the product of the dominance of that ideal; and since we still describe our political ideals with the same terms which our grandfathers used, few people are aware how

---

[1]John Milton, *The Tenure of Kings and Magistrates*, in *The Prose Works of John Milton*, with an Introductory Review by Robert Fletcher (London: Westley and Davis, 1835), p. 241. [This is the correct citation. In the Cairo lectures, Hayek managed to get the date of publication, Fletcher's first name, and the page wrong. In addition, the passage from Milton in fact reads, "That power, which is the root and source of all liberty, to dispose and economise in the land which God hath given them, as masters of family in their own house and free inheritance."—Ed.]

much their meaning has changed and how far we have moved away from the ideals for which they once stood.

Indeed the main reason why I have decided to approach my subject historically is to make you aware how greatly the whole framework of governmental power already has changed, how little the legal position even in the freest countries still corresponds to the ideals and concepts to which we still pay lip-service. I want to draw your attention to a silent revolution, which during the past two or three generations, has proceeded in the sanctuaries of the law largely unobserved by the general public. This revolution has gradually whittled away most of the guarantees of individual liberty for which at one time those people had been willing to fight. It is a peculiar kind of revolution in which what is often regarded as the most conservative of professions, in working out the implications of the popular will, have more completely changed the legal framework of governmental power than either the sovereign people or its representatives ever comprehended. The crucial steps were changes in the juridical attitude on issues which to the laymen must have appeared nice legal points which only the lawyer could understand or care for, but on which in fact the foundations of their liberty depended.

So little aware of this, indeed, are often the very same people who have been most active in bringing about the change that, though they will never tire of telling you that you 'cannot turn the clock back', they will at the same time indignantly deny that anything essential has been lost or that any of the important achievements of the liberal era have been sacrificed. And this transformation of the whole conception of law and of the powers of the state, has of course even more escaped the attention of the ordinary man in the street. Indeed, who cares for what happens in the dull sphere of administrative law the very name of which to most people spells annoyance and boredom. Yet it is in the technical discussion of this sphere that the fate of our liberty is being decided and to which we must attend if we want to know how to preserve it.

The mechanism by which the interaction of democratic decisions and their implementation by the experts often produces results which nobody has desired is a subject which would deserve much more careful attention than it usually receives. Once administration becomes a specialty, and it is left to the expert to draw the conclusions from what another group of men has laid down as policy, this division of labour is almost bound to bring about undesigned consequences. The lawyer who regards himself merely as the executive of the popular will frequently will have to work out consequences of a democratic decision which, though unquestionably implied by it, were very far from being present to the minds of those who made it. Yet the fact that certain consequences follow from a decision is often taken as evidence that these consequences were wanted. The lawyer who is nothing but a lawyer cannot but draw those conclusions. Perhaps it is right that the lawyer, as the servant

126

of the democratic will, should concern himself exclusively with what in fact is the law. But then, with all due respect, it must be said that the law which guards our liberty is too important a matter to be left entirely in the hands of the lawyers.[2] It is perhaps easy to explain why today the discussion of the law is almost entirely conducted among the people whose professional concern is what the law *is* rather than what it ought to be, but it is certainly unfortunate. Such a situation becomes decidedly dangerous when it is combined with a tendency, so often found among contemporary legal theorists, to treat the fact that a law has been passed as proof that it was necessary—because, as we are often told, chaos would otherwise have arisen—and to treat the actual development as evidence that it was inevitable or desirable. Though their professional concerns may explain this attitude of many lawyers, they are certainly speaking beyond their book in thus defending the development of which they were the instrument. A democracy, if it is to achieve its aspirations, probably needs, even more urgently than any other kind of political order, systematic criticism of the total result which its separate acts jointly produce.

I shall in my last lecture discuss the process by which the traditional safeguards of freedom have in fact gradually been eroded and show how more recently they have even become the object of systematic attack by a whole school of socialist jurists, especially in England. But before I turn to an examination of the contemporary conflict, between an old ideal and modern tendencies, I must try to make it quite clear what that ideal has been, both in its origins and when it was the central aim of the great liberal movement of the nineteenth century.

2. *The State of Liberty*

A historical approach to our problem is also very helpful for a different reason. Abstract discussions of the meaning of liberty have rarely been very fruitful. They usually arise among people who have so long enjoyed the essentials of freedom that they take them for granted and are hardly any longer aware what they are. Because men will always be mainly concerned to surmount the remaining obstacles to the fulfillment of their wishes, new aims always come into the centre of their vision as soon as the older barriers have been overcome. A people who for generations has been in the secure possession of freedom will thus often be more interested in 'new freedoms' than in the liberty he pos-

---

[2]This is not meant as an apology for intruding into the field of law since, as I ought perhaps to mention here, I am by original training myself a lawyer. It is rather intended to stress that we still need, besides the study of the positive law, a critical science of legislation, which requires at least as much knowledge of economics as of law.

sesses, and he may even be seduced by the promise of such new freedoms to sacrifice some of his old liberty.

But if long enjoyment of liberty sometimes blunts a people's sense for its nature and value, we can generally trust those who have been deprived of liberty to recognize it when they see it. If we want to understand what are the essentials of the individual liberty which not so long ago seemed the foundation of Western civilization, we shall do well to glance back at the time when this liberty was still a new thing, a value to be fought and striven for.

In the modern world, general human liberty, as distinguished from the liberties that are the privileges of the few, hardly existed before the England of the seventeenth century.[3] There can be no doubt that it was the development in that country which during the following century became the admired model for the rest of Europe and which provided the foundations for further developments in the New World. Today it is difficult to realize how great then the difference in personal liberty in England and in the rest of Europe has been and how acutely this difference was felt on both sides.[4] If we are no longer so much aware of it, this is probably not so much due to the fact that for a short period before the first Great War the situation in many European countries had come fairly close to English conditions, as to the fact that so much of the characteristic features of freedom in Britain have since disappeared: indeed much of what a generation ago British or American observers regarded as the irksome or intolerable restrictions on freedom existing in the Continental countries have since become so familiar in Britain that many of the younger generation hardly know any longer in what the vaunted British freedom consisted—or indeed are likely to notice any important differences in this respect when they cross the Channel.

It is possible of course to trace the beginnings of English liberty further back than the seventeenth century. For our purposes, however, there would be little justification for such antiquarian inquiries. Although at the beginning of that century, when the English set out on their struggle for liberty, they were able to draw for support on some celebrated documents from their early history, it was in effect a new development which then commenced. It is true that

---

[3] A fuller account of this development ought to give more attention to sixteenth- and seventeenth-century developments in Holland of which too little is known outside that country and of which I am largely ignorant. But I suspect that they had more direct influence on English thought than is commonly realized.

[4] Cf. Charles de Secondat, Baron de Montesquieu, *De l'esprit des lois*, in *Œuvres complètes*, ed. André Masson (Paris: Éditions Nagel, 1950), vol. 1, Book XI, chapter 5: "Il y a aussi une nation dans le monde qui a pour objet direct de sa constitution la liberté politique. Nous allons examiner les principes sur lesquels elle la fonde." This precedes the famous account of the English constitution in the following chapter. [See Montesquieu, *The Spirit of Laws*, translated by Thomas Nugent (London: G. Bell and Sons, 1914), vol. 1, p. 162: "One nation there is also in the world that has for the direct end of its constitution political liberty. We shall presently examine the principles on which this liberty is founded."—Ed.]

the Middle Ages had all over Europe known more about guarantees of personal liberty, both in theory and in practice, than is now commonly believed.[5] But these largely disappeared with the rise of absolute monarchy and they were in Tudor England nearly as much in danger of being swamped by the organized power of the new national state as in other parts of Europe. The conception of limited government, which arose from the English struggle of the seventeenth century, was thus truly a new departure. If the English documents, from Magna Carta, the great "Constitutio Libertatis",[6] downwards, are significant for the development of the modern liberty of the individual, it is because they served as effective weapons in that struggle. They had probably never become entirely forgotten or ineffective;[7] but there can be little doubt that it was only through their use in the disputes of the seventeenth century that their terms received their modern meaning and significance.

But if for our purposes we need not trace the modern history of liberty further back, I must not pass over entirely another source of the conceptions with which we shall be mainly concerned. Even if Thomas Hobbes had not told us of the rebellious spirit of his period that "one of the most frequent causes of it is the reading of the books of policy and histories of the ancient Greeks and Romans" and that for this reason "there was never anything so dearly bought, as these Western parts have bought the learning of the Greek and Latin tongues",[8] there could be no doubt that the inspiration of the new movements derived largely from the study of the classics.

[5] Cf. Robert von Keller, *Freiheitsgarantien für Person und Eigentum im Mittelalter: Eine Studie zur Vorgeschichte moderner Verfassungsgrundrechte* (Heidelberg: C. Winter, 1933), esp. pp. 187–215; Hans Planitz, "Zur Ideengeschichte der Grundrechte", in *Die Grundrechte und Grundpflichten der Reichsverfassung: Kommentar zum zweiten Teil der Reichsverfassung,* ed. Hans Carl Nipperdey (Berlin: Verlag Reimar Hobbing, 1929–1930), vol. 3, p. 597 *et. seq.*; Otto Friedrich von Gierke, *Johannes Althusius und die Entwicklung der naturrechtlichen Staatstheorien: Zugleich ein Beitrag zur Geschichte der Rechtssystematik,* 2nd ed. (Breslau: Verlag Marcus, 1902); Eugen Rosenstock-Huessy, *The Driving Power of Western Civilization: The Christian Revolution of the Middle Ages* (Boston: Beacon Press, 1950); and on the earlier English development especially Charles Howard McIlwain, *The High Court of Parliament and Its Supremacy: An Historical Essay on the Boundaries Between Legislation and Adjudication in England* (New Haven: Yale University Press, 1910), and John Neville Figgis, *The Divine Rights of Kings,* 2nd ed. (Cambridge: Cambridge University Press, 1914).

[6] Magna Carta was so described by Henry de Bracton, *De legibus et consuetudinibus Angliæ,* fol. 168b. [Now see Henry Bracton, *De legibus et consuetudinibus Angliæ,* ed. George Edward Woodbine (New Haven: Yale University Press, 1940), vol. 3, p. 35.—Ed.] Today, when the term 'constitution' is generally taken in its specific meaning of the legal foundations of political organization, the sense in which it was used then, about the same in which we still speak about the constitution of a man, is probably better rendered by 'condition' or perhaps by 'state.'

[7] Cf. Max Radin, "The Myth of Magna Carta", *Harvard Law Review,* vol. 60, 1947, pp. 1060–91.

[8] Thomas Hobbes, *Leviathan,* Part 2, chapters 29 and 21. [See, e.g., Thomas Hobbes, *Leviathan,* ed. Edwin Curley (Indianapolis, IN: Hackett, 1994), chapter 29, sec. 14, p. 214, and chapter 21, sec. 9, p. 141.—Ed.]

3. Isonomy

Yet though the fact of the great influence of the classical tradition of the modern ideal of liberty is indisputable, the nature of this influence is not always understood. It has been obscured by a tendency to deny that the ancients knew individual liberty in the modern sense.[9] But though this may be true of some places and periods, it is certainly not true of Athens at the time of its greatness. Though the degenerate democracy against which Plato reacted may justify some of the doubts, there is surely no place for such doubts in respect to those Athenians who at the moment of supreme danger during the Sicilian expedition, were reminded by their general that they were fighting for a country in which they had "unfettered discretion allowed in it to all to live as they pleased."[10]

But in what did this freedom of the "freest of free countries", as Nikias called Athens on the same occasion, appear to consist both to the Greeks themselves and later to the Elizabethans whose imagination it fired?

The answer seems to be provided at least in part by a Greek word which the Elizabethans borrowed from the Greeks but which has since gone into disuse. Its history, both in ancient Greece and later, is instructive. *Isonomia* appears in England at the end of the sixteenth century in a dictionary as an Italian word meaning "equalitie of lawes to all manner of persons"[11] and shortly afterwards, in 1600, it is already freely used in its English form "isonomy" in a translation of Livy[12] to render his description of a state of equal laws for all and of responsibility of the magistrates. It continued to be used frequently

---

[9]This traces back to the still often quoted essay by Benjamin Constant, "De la liberté des anciens comparée à celle des Modernes" (1819), reprinted in *Cours de politique constitutionnelle; ou Collection des ouvrages publiés sur le gouvernement représentatif* (Paris: Guillaumin et cie, 1861), vol. 2, pp. 539–60, and Numa Denis Fustel de Coulanges, *La cité antique* (Paris: Durand, 1864). On the whole matter see Georg Jellinek, *Das Recht des modernen Staates*, vol. 1 of *Allgemeine Staatslehre*, 2nd ed. (Berlin: O. Haring, 1905), pp. 285–305.

[10]Thucydides, vii, 69. [See Thucydides, *History of the Peloponnesian War*, translated by Charles Forster Smith (Cambridge: Harvard, Loeb Classical Library, 1923), vol. 4, book 7, sec. 69, p. 137.—Ed.] Very instructive for our understanding of the classical Greek conception of liberty is a recent study by Professor W. L. Westerman, based on the numerous decrees for the freeing of slaves found in Delphi: "Between Slavery and Freedom", *American Historical Review*, vol. 50, 1945, pp. 213–27. The definition of freedom which emerges resembles surprisingly and does not compare unfavourably with the conception of English eighteenth-century lawyers. The four essential elements of freedom which always occur in these manumission decrees are (1) the legal status as a protected member of the community, (2) immunity from arbitrary seizure and arrest, (3) the right to work at whatever a man desires to do, and (4) the right to movement according to his own choice.

[11]In the Italian dictionary by John Florio, *World of Wordes, or Most Copious and Exact Dictionarie in Italian and English* (London: Printed by Arnold Hatfield for Edw. Blount, 1598), p. 195.

[12]Titius Livius, *Roman Historie*, translated by Philemon Holland (London: Printed by Adam Islip, 1600).

throughout the seventeenth century. 'Equality before the Law', 'Government of Law' and 'Rule of Law' seem all to be later renderings of the concept then described by that Greek term.

The history of the term in ancient Greece already provides a curious lesson. It is perhaps the first instance of a cycle which civilizations appear to repeat.[13] Originally it described the conditions which Solon had established in Athens when he "gave the people not so much control of public policy, as the certainty of being governed legally in accordance with known rules."[14] As such it was contrasted with the arbitrary government of tyrants[15] and it was isonomy which the Athenians praised in a popular drinking song celebrating the assassination of one of their tyrants.[16] The concept was both older and more general than that of *demokratia*; and the demand for equal participation of all citizens in the government was apparently one of the consequences in turn drawn from it. It is isonomy rather than democracy which to Herodotus appears as "the most beautiful of all names of a political order."[17] And even after democracy had been achieved the term continued to be used for some time as a justification of democracy—and later, as has been justly said,[18] increasingly as a disguise of the true character democracy assumed: because democratic government soon proceeded to destroy that very equality before the law from which it derived its justification. The Greeks were fully aware that the two ideals, though related, were not the same. Thucydides, for instance, speaks without hesitation of an "isonomic oligarchy"[19] and later we find *iso-*

---

[13]Cf. Roscoe Pound, *The Spirit of the Common Law* (Boston: Marshall Jones, 1921), p. 72 *et. seq.*

[14]Sir Ernest Barker, *Greek Political Theory: Plato and His Predecessors*, 2nd ed. (London: Methuen, 1925), p. 44.

[15]Cf. Georg Busolt, *Griechische Staatskunde*, Part 1 of *Allegemeine Darstellung des griechischen Staates*, 3rd rev. ed. (Munich: Beck, 1920), pp. 417–18; Rudolph Hirzl, *Themis, Dike und Verwandtes: Ein Beitrag Geschichte der Rechtsidee bei den Griechen* (Leipzig: S. Hirzel, 1907), p. 240 *et seq.*; *Pauly's Real-Encyclopädie der classischen Altertumswissenschaft*, ed. August Friedrich Pauly, Supplement 7, ed. Georg Wissowa (Stuttgart: J. B. Metzler, 1940), s.v. "Isonomia", by Victor Ehrenberg (pp. 293–301); Jakob Aall Ottesen Larsen, "Cleisthenes and the Development of the Theory of Democracy in Athens", *Essays in Political Theory Presented to George H. Savine*, ed. Milton Ridvas Konvitz and Arthur Edward Murphy (Ithaca, NY: Cornell University Press, 1948), pp. 1–16; and Erik Wolf, *Griechisches Rechtsdenken* (Frankfurt am Main: Vittorio Klostermann, 1952), vol. 2, p. 367.

[16]See Ernst Diehl, *Anthologia Lyrica Graeca* (Leipzig: Teubner, 1925), vol. 2, scolia 10 (9), pp. 184–85, and 13 (12), p. 185.

[17]Herodotus, *Histories*, iii. 80 [See Herodotus, *Histories*, translated by A. D. Godley (1921; rev. ed., Cambridge: Harvard, Loeb Classical Library, 1938), vol. 2, p. 107.—Ed.]; compare also iii. 142 and v. 37. [See ibid., vol. 2, p. 177, and vol. 3 (1922), p. 41.—Ed.]

[18]See Busolt, *Allgemeine Darstellung des griechischen Staates*, p. 417, and Ehrenberg, in *Pauly*, Sup., s.v. "Isonomia", p. 299; see also the important article by Victor Ehrenberg, "Origins of Democracy", *Historia: Zeitschrift für Alte Geschichte*, vol. 1, 1950, pp. 515–48, esp. 535, which has come to my knowledge only after these lectures were completed.

[19]Thucydides, *Peloponnesian War*, iii. 62. 3–4; cf. also iii. 82. 8; and Isokrates, *Areopagiticus*, vii. 20 and *Panathenaicus*, xii. 178. [See *History of the Peloponnesian War*, vol. 2 (1930), pp. 110, 112; 147, 149; Isocrates, *Areopagiticus*, ed. George Norlin (Cambridge: Harvard, Loeb Classical Library,

nomia used by Plato in quite deliberate contrast to democracy rather than in vindication of it.[20]

In the light of this development the famous passages in Aristotle's *Politics* in which he discusses the different kinds of democracy appear in effect as a defense of the ideal of *isonomia*. It is well known how he stresses there that "it is more proper that the law should govern than any of the citizens", that the persons holding supreme power "should be appointed to be only guardians and the servants of the law",[21] and particularly how he condemns the kind of government under which "the people govern and not the law" and where "everything is determined by a majority vote and not by a law." Such a government, according to him, cannot be regarded as that of a free state: "for, when the government is not in the laws, then there is no free state, for the law ought to be supreme over all things." He even contended that any such establishment which centered all power in the votes of the people could not, "properly speaking, be a democracy: for their decrees cannot be general in their extent."[22] Together with the equally famous passage in his *Rhetoric* in which he argues that "it is of great moment that well drawn laws should themselves define all the points they possibly can, and leave as few as possible to the decision of the judges",[23] this provides a fairly complete doctrine of government by law.

How fundamental this conception remained for the Athenians is shown by a law which Demosthenes quotes in one of his orations[24] as a law "as good as ever law was." The Athenian who introduced it was of the opinion that, as every citizen had an equal share in civil rights, so everybody should have an equal share in the laws; and he proposed, therefore, "that it should not be lawful to propose a law affecting any individual, unless the same applied to all Athenians." This became the law of Athens. We do not know when this happened—Demosthenes referred to it in 352 B.C. But it is interesting to see how by that time democracy had already become the primary concept from which the older one of equality before the law was now derived. Although Demos-

---

1929), 115, 117; *Panathenaicus*, ed. George Norlin (Cambridge: Harvard, Loeb Classical Library, 1929), pp. 483, 485.—Ed.]

[20] Plato, *Republic*, viii. 557bc, 559d, 561e. [See Plato, *The Republic*, ed. Paul Shorey (Cambridge: Harvard, Loeb Classical Library, 1935), pp. 285, 287; 295, 303.—Ed.]

[21] Aristotle, *Politics*, 1287a. [See Aristotle, *Politics*, translated by H. Rackham (Cambridge: Harvard, Loeb Classical Library, 1944), book 3, chapter 11, sec. 3, pp. 264–65.—Ed.]

[22] *Ibid.* 1292a. [Ibid., book 4, chapter 4, pp. 303–4.—Ed.]

[23] Aristotle, *Rhetoric*, 1354ab. [See Aristotle, *The "Art" of Rhetoric*, translated by John Henry Freese (Cambridge: Harvard, Loeb Classical Library, 1926), book 1, chapter 1, p. 5.—Ed.]

[24] Demosthenes, *Orations 21–26: Against Meidias. Against Androtion. Against Aristocrates. Against Timocrates. Against Aristogeiton 1 and 2*, translated by J. H. Vince (Cambridge: Harvard, Loeb Classical Library, 1935), vol. 3, pp. 275, 411. [The Loeb translation renders the law thus: "And it shall not be lawful to propose a statute directed against an individual, unless the same apply to all Athenians."—Ed.]

thenes, as is true of Aristotle, no longer uses the term *isonomia*, his account of this incident is little more than a paraphrase of that old concept.

The direct influence which these Greek conceptions exercised in the seventeenth century on English thought appears clearly from an exchange between Thomas Hobbes and James Harrington from which the modern use of the phrase "government of laws and not of men" seems to derive. Hobbes had described it as "another error of Aristotle's politics, that in a well-ordered commonwealth, not men should govern, but the laws."[25] Harrington replied that the "art whereby a civil society of men is instituted and preserved upon the foundation of common right or interest . . . [is], to follow Aristotle and Livy, . . . the empire of laws, and not of men."[26]

In the course of the seventeenth century the influence of the Greek thinkers on English political thought was increasingly superseded by that of the Romans. Livy, whose translation popularized in England the term *isonomia*, and to whom we have just seen Harrington refer, Tacitus, and above all Cicero became the main sources from which the same tradition was received. To Cicero we owe many of the formulations of the ideals of freedom under the law which in the mouths of the English protagonists of political freedom and later in the writing of Montesquieu were to prove most effective. The conception that we obey the law in order that we may be free,[27] and that the judge ought to be merely the mouth through whom the law speaks[28] are his. During this classical period of Roman law it was once more understood that there was no conflict between freedom and law, and that it depended on certain general characteristics of the law, its generality and certainty, and the restrictions which it places on the discretion of authority, whether it would give us freedom.

But once again that freedom which equality before the laws creates was destroyed to meet new popular demands for another kind of equality: during the later Empire the strict law was progressively abandoned, as in the interest of a new social policy the state aimed at an increasing control of economic life,[29]

<hr/>

[25] Thomas Hobbes, *Leviathan*, chapter 46. [See, e.g., *Leviathan*, ed. Edwin Curley, chapter 46, sec. 36, p. 465.—Ed.]

[26] James Harrington, *The Common-wealth of Oceana* (London: Printed by J. Streater for Livewell Chapman, 1656), p. 2. [The brackets are Hayek's.—Ed.]

[27] Marcus Tullius Cicero, *Pro Cluentio*, 53. 146: "Omnes legum servi sumus ut liberi esse possimus." [The passage from Cicero reads, "Legum ministri magistratus, legum interpretes iudices, legum denique idcirco omnes servi sumus, ut liberi esse possimus." ("The magistrates who administer the law, the jurors who interpret it—all of us, in short—obey the law to the end that we may be free.")—Ed.]

[28] Marcus Tullius Cicero, *De legibus*, iii. 122: "magistratum legem esse loquentem." ["The magistrate is the law speaking."—Ed.]

[29] Cf. Friedrich Oertel, "The Economic Life of the Empire", in *Cambridge Ancient History* (Cambridge: Cambridge University Press, 1939), vol. 12, pp. 270 *et. seq.*

and in the end, as a distinguished student of Roman law has described the process which started under the Emperor Constantine, "the absolute empire proclaimed together with the principle of equity the authority of the imperial will unfettered by the barrier of law. Justinian with his learned professors brought this process to its conclusion."[30]

4. The Fight against Privilege

Today it is not always realized that the great struggle between King and Parliament in England, in which these old principles were once again victorious, was fought mainly over problems of economic policy similar to those which today are again in the forefront of political discussion. To the nineteenth-century historians, the measures of James I and Charles I which provoked the conflict, may well have seemed antiquated abuses without topical interest. To us, some of the disputes produced by the recurrent attempts of the Kings to set up industrial monopolies have a very familiar ring: Charles I even intended to nationalize the whole coal industry and was dissuaded from it only when he was told that this would probably provoke a rebellion.[31]

Ever since in the famous Case of Monopolies[32] a court had decided that the grant of the exclusive rights to produce an article was "against the common law and the liberty of the subject", it remained the demand for equal laws for all citizens by which Parliament opposed the King's efforts. Englishmen then seem to have understood better than we do today that the control of production always means the creation of privilege, to give permission to Peter to do what Paul is not allowed to do. The first great statement of the ideal of the Rule of Law was, however, induced by another kind of economic measure: the Petition of Grievances of 1610 was caused by new regulations passed by the King for building in London and for prohibiting the making of starch from wheat. I must quote this celebrated plea of the House of Commons at some length, emphasizing the passages which state the central doctrine:

[30] Fritz Pringsheim, "Jus aequum und jus strictum", *Zeitschrift der Savigny-Stiftung für Rechtsgeschichte, Romanistische Abteilung*, vol. 42, 1921, p. 668.

[31] Cf. John U. Nef, *Industry and Government in France and England: 1540–1640* (Philadelphia: American Philosophical Society, 1940), p. 114.

[32] *Darcy v. Allen* [also spelled "Allin" or "Allein"—Ed.] ("The Case of Monopolies") 74 Eng. Rep. 1131 (K.B. 1602). Cf. William Lewis Letwin, "The English Common Law Concerning Monopolies", *University of Chicago Law Review*, vol. 21, 1953–54, pp. 355–85, and the two articles by Donald Owen Wagner, "Coke and the Rise of Economic Liberalism", *Economic History Review*, vol. 6, 1935–36, pp. 30–44, and "The Common Law and Free Enterprise: An Early Case of Monopoly", *Economic History Review*, vol. 7, 1936–37, pp. 217–20.

Amongst many other points of happiness and freedom which Your Majesty's subjects of this kingdom have enjoyed under your royal progenitors, kings and queens of this realm, there is none which they have accounted more dear and precious than this, *to be guided and governed by the certain rule of law*, which giveth to the head and the members that which of right belongeth to them *and not by any uncertain or arbitrary form of government*. Which, as it hath proceeded from the original good constitution and temperature of this estate, so hath it been the principal means of upholding the same in such sort, as that their kings have been just, beloved, happy and glorious, and the kingdom itself peaceable, flourishing and durable so many ages. . . . *Out of this root hath grown that indubitable right of the people of this kingdom not to be made subject to any punishments that shall extend to their lives, lands, bodies or goods, other than such as are ordained by the common laws of this land, or the statutes made by their common consent in parliament.*[33]

The further development of this Whig doctrine of the Rule of Law, as socialist lawyers have contemptuously dubbed it, was closely connected with the continued fight against government-conferred monopoly and particularly with the discussion around the Statute of Monopolies of 1624. It was mainly in this connection that the great source of Whig principles, Sir Edward Coke, developed his interpretation of Magna Carta which led him to state (with reference to the Case of Monopolies) that: "if a grant be made to any man to have the sole making of cards, or the sole dealing with any other trade, that grant is against the liberty and freedom of the subject . . . and consequently against this Great Charter."[34]

I must not attempt to trace the further development of these ideas throughout the intellectual and political struggle of the century and I will even refer only briefly to the classical exposition of them by John Locke in his *Second Treatise of Civil Government*. I will merely remind you of what is probably the most important passage in which, in conscious contrast to those who interpret freedom as the absence of all legal ties, he defines it as follows: "Freedom of men under government, is, to have a standing rule to live by, common to every one of that society, and made by the legislative power erected in it . . .

[33] Great Britain, Public Record Office, *Calendar of State Papers, Domestic Series, of the Reign of James I*, ed. Mary Anne Everett Green (London: Longman, Brown, Green, Longmans, and Roberts, 1857–72), vol. 5, July 7, 1610. Italics by the author. [The *Calendar of State Papers* generally does not include the full text of documents; for the passage quoted, see *House of Commons*, vol. 2 of *Proceedings in Parliament, 1610*, ed. Elizabeth Read Foster (New Haven, CT: Yale University Press, 1966), pp. 258–59.—Ed.]
[34] Sir Edward Coke, *The Second Part of the Institutes of the Laws of England. Containing the Exposition of Many Ancient and Modern Statutes* (London: Printed for E. and R. Brooke, 1797), p. 47.

and not to be subject to the inconstant, uncertain, unknown, arbitrary will of another man."[35]

The rest of Locke's central doctrine I will quote in the summary by a great American legal scholar: "Law must be general; it must afford equal protection for all; it may not validly operate retroactively; it must be enforced through courts—legislative power does not include judicial power."[36] In addition I will merely point out that for Locke this restriction of the arbitrary will of all authority, including the legislature, presupposes a protected sphere of the individuals, their "lives, liberties and estates, which" he says, "I call by the general name, property";[37] and draw your attention to the rarely noticed modern justification which he gives his whole program: what we now call the "taming of power." In Locke's words: "The end why [men] choose and authorize a legislative, is, that there may be laws made, and rules set as guards and fences to the properties of all the members of the society, to limit the power, and moderate the dominion of every part and member of society."[38]

5. The Eighteenth-Century Tradition

If the struggles of the seventeenth century have successfully vindicated the basic principle, the full establishment of the Rule of Law in England was essentially the work of the eighteenth.[39] What the achievement of the revolution came to mean in the course of time is perhaps most clearly seen in the work of the historians who interpreted it to their contemporaries. It has been said with much justice that to David Hume the real meaning of the history of England was the evolution from a "government of will to a government of laws."[40] There is particularly one passage, referring to the abolition of the Star

[35] John Locke, *An Essay concerning the true original Extent and End of Civil Government* (1690), section 22. [This is Locke's second of his *Two Treatises of Government*. See, e.g., John Locke, *Two Treatises of Government*, ed. Peter Laslett, student edition (Cambridge: Cambridge University Press, 1988). —Ed.]

[36] Edward Samuel Corwin, *The "Higher" Law Background of American Constitutional Law* (Ithaca, NY: Cornell University Press), p. 68.

[37] John Locke, *An Essay concerning the true original Extent and End of Civil Government*, section 123.

[38] Ibid., section 222. [In the Cairo lectures, Hayek's endnotes got out of order: notes 37 and 38 were both marked "Ibid." and so appeared to refer to Corwin rather than Locke. The brackets are Hayek's.—Ed.]

[39] Cf. George Macaulay Trevelyan, *English Social History: A Survey of Six Centuries, Chaucer to Queen Victoria* (London: Longmans, Green, 1942), pp. 245 and 350 *et seq.*, esp. p. 351: "The specific work of the earlier Hannoverian epoch was the establishment of the rule of law; and that law, with all its grave faults, was at least a law of freedom. On that solid foundation all our subsequent reforms were built."

[40] Friedrich Meinecke, *Die Entstehung des Historismus* (Munich and Berlin: R. Oldenbourg, 1936), vol. 1, p. 234.

Chamber in 1641,[41] in which he shows clearly what he regarded as the most significant feature of the constitutional development of the preceding century:

> No Government, at that time, appeared in the world, nor is perhaps to be found in the records of any history, which subsisted without the mixture of some arbitrary authority, committed to some magistrate; and it might reasonably, beforehand, appear doubtful, whether human society could ever arrive at that state of perfection, as to support itself with no other control, than the general and rigid maxims of law and equity. But the Parliament justly thought, that the King was too eminent a magistrate to be trusted with discretionary power, which he might so easily turn to the destruction of liberty. And in the event it has been found, that, though some inconveniencies arise from the maxim of adhering strictly to law, yet the advantages so much overbalance them, as should render the English forever grateful to the memory of their ancestors, who, after repeated contests, at last established that noble principle.[42]

During the second half of the century we find the principle constantly appealed to as the undoubted foundation of English liberty both in political controversy and in the more systematic statements of the political philosophers. It has found classic expression in many familiar passages of Edmund Burke. For more detailed statements we must, however, turn to some of his lesser contemporaries.[43] I must confine myself here to a few especially significant passages.

---

[41] The best short description of the Star Chamber is probably that in Frederic William Maitland's *The Constitutional History of England: A Course of Lectures* (Cambridge: Cambridge University Press, 1909), p. 263, "a court of politicians enforcing a policy, not a court of judges administering the law."

[42] David Hume, *History of England from the Invasion of Julius Caesar to the Revolution of 1688*, new ed., corrected (London: Printed for A. Miller, 1762), vol. 5, p. 280. Cf. David Hume, *Essays: Moral, Political and Literary*, ed. Thomas Hill Green and Thomas Hodge Grose (London: Longmans, Green, 1875), "Of the Origin of Government", vol. 1, p. 117; "Of Civil Liberty", vol. 1, p. 161; and particularly the following passage in "Of the Rise and Progress of the Arts and Sciences", vol. 1, p. 178: "All general laws are attended with inconveniencies, when applied to particular cases; and it requires great penetration and experience, both to perceive that these inconveniencies are fewer than what results from full discretionary powers in every magistrate; and also to discern what general laws are, upon the whole, attended with fewest inconveniencies. This is a matter of so great difficulty, that men have made some advance, even in the sublime arts of poetry and eloquence, where a rapidity of genius and imagination assist their progress, before they arrived at any great refinement in their municipal laws, where frequent trial and diligent observation can alone direct their improvements." See also Hume's *Enquiry Concerning the Principles of Morals*, Essay II, section 2, "Of Justice", and appendix 3, "Some farther Considerations with regard to Justice", vol. 2, pp. 179–96 and 272–78.

[43] A characteristic statement which I find attributed to Sir Philip Francis and which probably occurs somewhere in the *Letters of Junius* runs: "The government of England is a government of

The occasion for one of them was given by an incidental reference to the principle in Adam Smith's *Wealth of Nations* which also shows how much of a matter of course the tradition had by his time become in England. He briefly explains that in England "the public safety does not require that the sovereign be trusted with any discretionary power", even for suppressing "the rudest, the most groundless, and most licentious remonstrances", because he "is secured by a well regulated standing army."[44]

The remarkable assumption which underlies this, that in "a steady and thoroughly legal government" the sovereign at the head of an army will "wait to set himself into motion, till he has received leave for that purpose, that is, till he has been trusted with a power for so doing", has led one of the acutest foreign students of the British constitution to an important discussion of the unique position then achieved in Britain. De Lolme's description of "the most characteristic circumstance in the English Government, and the most pointed proof that can be given of the true freedom which is the consequence of its frame" is essentially that in England "all the individual's actions are supposed to be lawful, till the law is pointed out which makes them otherwise. . . . The foundation of that law principle, or doctrine, which confines the exertion of the power of the government to such cases only as are expressed by a law in being", though tracing back to Magna Carta, was only put into actual force by the abolition of the Star Chamber: "it has appeared by the event, that the very extraordinary restriction upon governing authority we are alluding to, and its execution, are no more than what the intrinsic situation of things, and the strength of the constitution, can bear."[45]

The fullest account of the rationale of the whole doctrine which I know,

---

law. We betray ourselves, we contradict the spirit of our laws, and we shake the whole system of English jurisprudence, whenever we entrust a discretionary power over the life, liberty, or fortune of the subject, to any man or set of men whatsoever upon a presumption that it will not be abused." [See Junius (William Petty-Fitzmaurice, Earl of Shelburne), *Letters of Junius*, ed. Charles Warren Everett (London: Faber and Gwyer, 1927), letter 47, dated May 25, 1771, p. 208.—Ed.] Cf. also Adam Ferguson, *An Essay on the History of Civil Society*, 5th ed. (Edinburgh: Printed for A. Millar and T. Caddel, London, and A. Kincaid and J. Bell, Edinburgh, 1782), p. 205.

[44] Adam Smith, *An Inquiry into the Nature and Causes of the Wealth of Nations*, ed. Edwin Cannan (London: Methuen, 1904), vol. 2, p. 201. [Now see Adam Smith, *An Inquiry into the Nature and Causes of the Wealth of Nations*, ed. W. B. Todd, vol. 2 of *The Glasgow Edition of the Works and Correspondence of Adam Smith* (Glasgow: University of Glasgow, 1976; reprinted, Indianapolis, IN: Liberty Fund, 1981), book 5, chapter 1, part 1, p. 707. In the quotation in the Cairo lecture, Hayek left out the word 'standing', a rather significant omission.—Ed.]

[45] Jean Louis de Lolme, *Constitution of England; or, An Account of the English Government: In Which it is Compared Both with the Republican Form of Government, and the Other Monarchies in Europe* [1784], new ed., corrected (London: G. G. and J. Robinson, 1800), p. 441.

occurs in the chapter "Of the Administration of Justice" of Archdeacon Paley's *Principles of Moral and Political Philosophy*:

> The first maxim of a free state is, that the laws be made by one set of men, and administered by another; in other words, that the legislative and the judicial characters be kept separate. When these offices are united in the same person or assembly, particular laws are made for particular cases, springing oftentimes from partial motives, and directed to private ends: whilst they are kept separate, general laws are made by one body of men, without foreseeing whom they may affect; and, when made, must be applied by the other, let them affect whom they will. . . . When the parties and the interests to be affected by the laws were known, the inclinations of the law makers would inevitably attach to one side or the other; and where there were neither any fixed rules to regulate their determinations, nor any superior power to control their proceedings, these inclinations would interfere with the integrity of public justice. The consequence of which must be, that the subjects of such a constitution would live either without any constant laws, that is, without any known pre-established rules of adjudication whatever: or under laws made for particular cases and particular persons, and partaking of the contradictions and iniquity of the motives to which they owed their origin.
>
> Which dangers, by the division of the legislative and judicial functions, are in this country effectually provided against. Parliament knows not the individuals upon whom its acts will operate; it has no cases or parties before it; no private designs to serve: consequently, its resolutions will be suggested by the considerations of universal effects and tendencies, which always produce impartial, and commonly advantageous regulations.[46]

Even though the last part of Paley's exposition may breathe a complacent optimism which we find difficult to share, the passage seems to me of great importance because it brings together, so far as I know, for the first time, all the elements which the nineteenth century came to take for granted under the name of the Rule of Law. Indeed, it does more: in stating the criterion of the unforeseeability of the incidence of the effects of a law on particular people, it provides the clearest statement of its rationale I have found anywhere. I shall have to come back to this point in my systematic discussion of the whole complex of principles which secure a reign of law. But before I can do this I must conclude this sketch of its evolution.

So far as England is concerned, this development is in the main complete

---

[46]William Paley, *The Principles of Moral and Political Philosophy* [1785] (London: Printed for T. Tegg, 1824), p. 308 *et seq.*

with the end of the eighteenth century. There are a few further contributions of importance, such as John Austin's efforts to provide a sharp distinction between genuine laws, which are general, and commands or orders which are occasional or particular.[47] But on the whole the Rule of Law is no longer problematical in the England of the nineteenth century; it was scarcely again discussed until towards its close. Although, in some respects the results of this evolution were left curiously incomplete, what was achieved became a firmly accepted political tradition which was not again seriously challenged until our own time.

6. The Foundation of Liberty in America

The task of systematizing and completing this development was performed mainly by Continental, and in the first instance, French writers who endeavoured to interpret to the world what England had achieved. But although the work of some of them, especially that of Montesquieu, had in turn considerable influence on the evolution in England and particularly in the United States (the passage by Paley which I quoted clearly shows his influence) before considering in my next lecture that distinct Continental development, I shall, at least briefly indicate how profoundly the English tradition on these matters has affected the American conception of freedom. There are particularly three points which are here of significance: firstly, the great rôle which the formula of the "government of laws and not of men" played in the American tradition. It appears in the Constitution of Massachusetts of 1780,[48] in the decisions of Chief Justice Marshall,[49] and in many other decisions down to recent times. Secondly, the efforts made in many of the constitutions of the states of the Union to draw a sharp line between true laws and specific commands[50]—and of course also their frequent explicit prohibition of retroactive laws. Thirdly, the interesting appearance, again in a decision of Chief Justice Marshall, of the emphasis on the characteristic unpredictability of the incidence of impartial laws.[51] It is true that the famous phrase about the "general laws, formed upon deliberation, under the influence of no resentment, and

[47] John Austin, *Lectures on Jurisprudence; or, The Philosophy of Positive Law*, ed. Robert Campbell, 5th rev. ed. (London: J. Murray, 1885), vol. 1, p. 92.

[48] Constitution of Massachusetts (March 2, 1780), part 1, "Declaration of Rights", art. 30: "To the end it may be a government of laws, and not of men."

[49] *Marbury v. Madison*, 5 U.S. (1 Cranch) 137 (1803).

[50] See the Constitutions of Arkansas (1874), art. 5, sec. 25; Georgia (1877), art. 1, sec. 4, par. 1; Kansas (July, 1859), art. 2, sec. 17; Michigan (1863), art. 4, sec. 29; and Ohio (1851), sec. 2, art. 26.

[51] *Ex Parte Bollman*, 8 U.S. (4 Cranch) 75 (1807).

without knowing upon whom they will operate", refers in the first instance only to penal law. But its significance is much wider.

There is, however, also a great original American contribution to the whole tradition which I must here mention and which was later taken over by the French and from them was taken into most of the constitutions of the countries of Continental Europe: it is the attempt explicitly to delimit the free sphere of the individual by a Bill of Rights incorporated in a written Constitution. We shall later see how important this is if the protection of the individual against arbitrary coercion is to be given definite meaning. For the present I will content myself to illustrate the significance of these Bills of Rights by a quotation from a recent judicial decision: "The very purpose of a Bill of Rights", wrote the late Justice Jackson, "was to withdraw certain subjects from the vicissitudes of political controversy, to place them beyond the reach of majorities and officials, and to establish them as legal principles to be applied by the courts. One's right to life, liberty, and property, to free speech, a free press, freedom of worship and assembly, and other fundamental rights may not be submitted to the vote; they depend on the outcome of no elections."[52]

I will not enter here into any discussion of the particular procedural safeguards which, as a result of the 'due process' clause in the Bill of Rights in the early amendments to the Federal Constitution, the American judicature has built up. I will only say that it seems to me that, because of the accidental wording of this clause, American discussion during the last hundred years, even more so than is true of the English tradition, has turned more upon procedural safeguards than upon what there was to be safeguarded—though perhaps the former is all that can be effectively provided by the law. My concern throughout will be not with the particular legal norms of any one country, but with those features to which during the nineteenth century American judges used to refer as "the essential features of all free governments" and which a great English lawyer at the end of the century could describe as "the normal and necessary marks, in a civilized commonwealth, of justice administered according to the law."[53]

Let me conclude this all-too-brief discussion of the American tradition by a quotation from one of the great founders of the American Republic who more clearly than anyone else, has expressed the ultimate considerations from which all I have said follows. It was Thomas Jefferson, now curiously enough often represented as an advocate of unlimited powers of a democratic government, who wrote: "Free government is founded in jealousy, not in confidence; it is jealousy and not confidence which prescribes limited constitutions, to bind

[52] *West Virginia State Board of Education v. Barnette*, 319 U.S. 624 (1943).

[53] Sir Frederick Pollock, *A First Book of Jurisprudence for Students of the Common Law*, 3rd ed. (London: Macmillan, 1911), p. 37.

those we are obliged to trust with power; . . . our Constitution has accordingly fixed the limits to which, and no further, our confidence may go. . . . In questions of power, then, let no more be heard of confidence in man, but bind him down from mischief by the chains of the Constitution."[54]

---

[54] Thomas Jefferson, "Draft of Kentucky Resolution of 1798", in Ethelbert Dudley Warfield, *The Kentucky Resolutions of 1798*, 2nd ed. (New York: Putman, 1894), pp. 157–58. Characteristic for Jefferson's attitude to these problems is also his letter to Madison of December 20, 1787, in which he writes: "The instability of our laws is really a very serious inconvenience. I think we ought to have obviated it by deciding that a whole year should always be allowed to elapse between the bringing in of a bill and the final passing of it. It should afterwards be discussed and put to the vote without the possibility of making any alterations in it; and if the circumstances of the case required a more speedy decision, the question should not be decided by a simple majority, but by a majority of at least two-thirds of each house." [Jefferson's words actually are as follows: "The instability of our laws is really an immense evil. I think it would be well to provide in our constitutions that there shall always be a twelve-month between the ingrossing a bill & passing it: that it should then be offered to it's [*sic*] passage without changing a word: and that if circumstances should be thought to require a speedier passage, it should take two thirds of both houses instead of a bare majority." See Thomas Jefferson, *Writings* (New York: Library of America, Viking Press, 1984), p. 918. It is understandable that Hayek might change the wording of the first part of Jefferson's second sentence to make its meaning more clear. It is unfortunate that he would not indicate that he was doing so, and doubly so that he would change Jefferson's "immense evil" to "very serious inconvenience." To say the least, this undermines his complaint in Lecture IV, p. 189, note 52.—Ed.]

Lecture II
Liberalism and Administration
The Rechtsstaat

> Nothing is more fertile in prodigies than the art of being free; but there is
> nothing more arduous than the apprenticeship of liberty. . . . Liberty . . . is
> generally established with difficulty in the midst of storms; it is perfected by
> civil discord; and its benefits cannot be appreciated until it is already old.
>
> —A. De Tocqueville[1]

7. Montesquieu, Rousseau, and the French Revolution

Long before the development in the countries of the common law had reached
the point at which I left it in my last lecture, Continental, and particularly
French, writers had commenced to interpret it to their compatriots. Indeed,
on its political side, the 'Enlightment', from Voltaire downwards, was little
else than a spreading of the ideal of freedom as its leaders saw it realized in
England. The interpretation of a bundle of traditions which had grown up
there through generations of political struggle inevitably involved some artificial schematization and idealization. However well the set of institutions
which had grown up in England had worked in the environment of traditions
and beliefs to which it belonged, its evolution had left some strange gaps. Any
attempt at a 'rational reconstruction' of how it worked and what it achieved
required that principles be made explicit which had never been stated, and
that gaps be filled which would at once have made themselves felt if the institutions had been simply transplanted into a different atmosphere. Not only
had the English tradition never explicitly drawn such obvious conclusions from
its basic ideals as the formal recognition of the principle *nulla poena sine lege*;
it had also failed, until quite recently to give the citizen an effective remedy
against wrongs done to him by the State (as distinguished from its individual
agents), and it lacked almost any built-in safeguards against the infringement
of the Rule of Law by routine legislation. These anomalies could not escape
the Continental students who by deliberate legislation hoped to equal and improve upon what Britain had achieved by slow growth.

   The work of the greatest of these political theorists, Montesquieu, I have
already mentioned because of the strong influence it exercised even in England and America. It is now frequently alleged that the most famous of his
doctrines, that of the separation of powers, misrepresented the English con-

---

[1] Alexis de Tocqueville, *Democracy in America*, translated by Henry Reeve, translation edited by
Phillips Bradley (New York: Alfred A. Knopf, 1945), vol. 1, chap. 14, pp. 246–47.

stitution; and so far as the actual position in England is concerned there is some truth in this. But there can be no question that in expounding it he merely stated an ideal which he had found in the English political literature and which, if not as a recognized constitutional principle yet as one of the guiding political ideals behind it, had had great influence on the English evolution.[2] I shall have to show in my next lecture to what extent and in which sense this great principle is an essential element of the Rule of Law.

Hardly less important in the evolution of our ideal was the second of the great political thinkers of the French pre-revolutionary period, Jean Jacques Rousseau. However many tendencies leading in quite the opposite direction may have sprung from his work, his ambivalent concept of the 'general will' led to important elaborations of one of our basic concepts. This 'general will', which was to be the foundation of law, was to be general in two quite different respects: in order to be law it was to be general not only in the sense of being the will of all or at least the will of the majority, but also in intent. As Rousseau has explained it in a classical passage of his *Contrat Social*:

> When I say that the object of laws is always general, I mean that the law always considers the subject in the round and actions in the abstract and never any individual man or one particular action. For instance, a law may provide that there shall be privileges, but it must not name the persons who are to enjoy them; the law may create several classes of citizens and even designate the qualifications which will give entry into each class, but it must not nominate for admission such and such persons; it may establish a royal government with a hereditary succession, but it must not select the king or nominate a royal family; in a word, anything that relates to a named individual is outside the scope of legislative authority.[3]

It was of course during the French Revolution that all these ideas suddenly became live forces. There is a great deal of truth in it, at least in so far as the beginning of the Revolution and the aims of the more moderate groups are concerned, when the historian Michelet describes it in a memorable phrase as *l'avènement de la loi*.[4] Much of its work was guided by the ideal of a govern-

---

[2] Cf. Joseph Dedieu, *Montesquieu et la tradition politique anglaise en France: Les sources anglaises de "L'Esprit des lois"* (Paris: J. Gabalda, 1909); Ernst Klimowsky, *Die englische Gewaltenteilungslehre bis zu Montesquieu* (Berlin-Grunewald: Rothschild, 1927); and for the United States Benjamin F. Wright, Jr., "The Origins of the Separation of Powers in America", *Economica*, no. 40, May, 1933, pp. 169–85.

[3] Jean Jacques Rousseau, *Du contrat social*, book 2, chapter 6, in *Œuvres complètes de J. J. Rousseau: Avec des éclaircissements et des notes historiques*, 2nd ed. (Paris: Baudouin frères, 1826), vol. 6, p. 72.

[4] Jules Michelet, *Histoire de la révolution française* (Paris: Chamerot, 1847–50), vol. 1, p. xxiii. [The phrase might be translated, 'the advent of the law.'—Ed.]

ment of law[5] and a great part of the writings of its chief theoretician, Condorcet, and of the various constitution-making bodies were concerned with questions which lie right at the heart of the matter, such as the distinction between true laws in the sense of general rules and mere orders. Some of the constitutional drafts attempted to embody definitions of law in this sense into their framework,[6] and the whole conception underlying them is perhaps best expressed in a passage of Condorcet: "L'exécutif a pour 'fonction de faire un syllogisme dont la loi est la majeure; un fait plus ou moins général, la mineure; et la conclusion, l'application de la loi. Par exemple, chaque citoyen sera tenu de contribuer à la dépense nécessaire pour les besoins publics, proportionnellement au produit net de sa terre; voilà une loi. Telle dépense doit faire partie des besoins publics; voilà un fait. Donc, chaque citoyen doit contribuer à cette dépense, voilà l'application de la loi.'"[7]

This conception of the law and of the separation of powers, together with the guarantees of the Rights of Men, which the *Déclaration des droits de l'homme et du citoyen* had both declared to be essential parts of any constitution,[8] were aimed entirely at the establishment of a strict reign of law.

Yet, though the French Revolution was so largely inspired by the ideal of the Rule of Law, it is questionable whether it really helped the advance towards that ideal. In its course too many different aspirations gained influence which it was difficult to reconcile with that ideal.[9] Perhaps no revolution, even if its aim is to make the law sovereign, is likely to increase the respect for the law.

---

[5]Cf. Jean Ray, "La révolution française et la pensée juridique: L'idée du règne de la loi", *Revue philosophique*, vol. 218, 1939, pp. 364–425; and Jean Belin, *La logique d'une idée-force: L'idée d'utilité sociale et la révolution française, (1789–1792)* (Paris: Hermann and Cie, 1939).

[6]See especially the "Projet Girondin" in *Archives parlementaires de 1787 à 1860: Recueil complet des débats législatifs et politiques des chambres françaises*, ed. Jérome Mavidal and Émile Laurent (Paris: Imprimé par ordre du Corps législatif, 1900), series 1 (1787–99), vol. 58, title 7, sec. 2, arts. 1–7, pp. 617–18. [In the Cairo lectures, notes 6 and 7 were switched.—Ed.]

[7]Quoted from Condorcet without reference by Joseph Barthélemy, *Le rôle du pouvoir exécutif dans les républiques modernes* (Paris: Giard et Brière, 1906), p. 489, note 3; but compare the similar passages in *Œuvres de Condorcet*, ed. Arthur Condorcet O'Connor and François Arago (Paris: Didot frères, 1847–49), vol. 12, pp. 356–58 and 367. ["The executive's 'function is to construct a syllogism in which the law is the major premise; a fact, which can be more or less general, the minor premise; and the conclusion, the application of the law. For example, each citizen will be required to contribute to the expenditures that are necessary for public needs, proportionally to the net product of his land; here is a law. Each such contribution will be used to fund public needs; here is a fact. That every citizen will contribute to these funds, therefore, is the application of the law.'"—Ed.]

[8]*Declaration des droits de l'homme et du citoyen* (August 26, 1789): "16. Toute société dans laquelle la garantie des droits n'est assurée, ni la séparation des pouvoirs déterminée, n'a point de Constitution." ["16. A society in which the observance of the law is not assured, nor the separation of powers defined, has no constitution whatsoever."—Ed.]

[9]Cf. Jean Ray, "La révolution française", p. 372.

And if the government is to be tied strictly by the law, this certainly makes it more difficult to achieve quick results. In fact, the desire to make equity supersede the harsh rule of the strict law soon again opened the doors for that arbitrary will against which the Revolution had originally been directed. Perhaps the most important factor, however, which weakened the striving for the Rule of Law, was the feeling that, since at last the control of all power had been placed in the hands of the people, all safeguards against any abuse of that power had become unnecessary. The jealousy of the elected representatives of the people of their exclusive rights also made them much more anxious to assure that the executive organs should in all respects carry out their will than that the individual should be protected against the power of the executive. In the later stages of the Revolution, moreover, the precursors of modern socialism already began to raise their voices against the whole principle of merely formal equality before the law and demanded *égalité de fait* instead of mere *égalité de droit*.

8. I. Kant and the German Rechtsstaat

Contrary to widespread beliefs, eighteenth-century Prussia provided a rather favourable climate for the acceptance of the principle of the Rule of Law. It was only later, during the reaction of the second quarter of the nineteenth century, that that country came to be regarded as the archetype of the police state against which all the guns of the liberal movement were directed. Under the enlightened despotism of the eighteenth century its government was in some respects indeed remarkably liberal and in no field more so than in that of law. Significant in this respect is the wide currency of the legend of the miller of Sans-Souci. As every German child knows, Frederick II is supposed to have been annoyed by an old wind-mill close to his palace of Sans-Souci which impaired its appearance, and finally to have personally threatened the miller with eviction. The miller is said to have replied, "We still have courts of justice in Prussia."[10] This suggests a limit to kingly power of which I am not sure whether it applies today to heads of democratic states: a hint to their town planners would quickly lead to the forcible removal of such an eye-sore— though of course purely in the public interest and not to please anybody's whim!

No less important than this political background was the philosophical atmosphere in which the German liberal movement grew up. German writers indeed are accustomed to place the theories of Immanuel Kant at the beginning of their account of the movement for the *Rechtsstaat*. But though

[10] "Es gibt noch ein Kammergericht in Berlin!" is the phrase usually quoted.

this seems to me to overestimate the originality and influence of his legal philosophy,[11] there can be little doubt that his more general conceptions were profoundly important for that evolution. His celebrated "categorical imperative" is indeed little more than an extension to the field of morals of the basic idea underlying the Rule of Law. The principle that you should always "act only on that maxim whereby thou canst at the same time will that it should become a universal law"[12] is exactly that. Like the Rule of Law, it provides of course only one criterion to which good maxims must conform, and it is not sufficient to enable us to derive from it what these rules ought to be. Kant's ideas in the field of law were further developed and widely spread by his successor as the leading philosopher of Germany, J. G. Fichte, who in his early liberal period was particularly concerned with these problems.[13]

Significant is also the fact that Frederick II with his civil code of 1751 initiated in effect[14] that movement for the codification of all laws which soon spread and achieved its best known result in the Napoleonic codes (1800–1810). This whole movement is one of the most important parts of the Continental endeavour to establish the Rule of Law and it determined both its peculiar character and whatever advances it achieved, at least in theory, over the prototype in the countries of the common law. Of course, the possession even of the most perfectly drawn up legal codes can be no adequate substitute for a deeply rooted tradition, and the advantages which the former may give may not outweigh those of the latter. But this should not blind us to the fact that there is some inherent conflict between a system of case law and the ideal of the Rule of Law. Since under case law the judge constantly creates law, the principle that he merely applies pre-existing rules can under that system be approached even less perfectly than where the law is codified. And though the much lauded flexibility of the common law may have been favourable to the rise of the Rule of Law so long as general opinion tended in that direction, the common law also shows, I am afraid, less resistance to its decay once that vigilance is relaxed which alone can keep liberty alive.

[11] See particularly Immanuel Kant, *Die Metaphysik der Sitten* (1785), vol. 1, *Anfangsgründe der Rechtslehre*, part 2: "Das Staatsrecht", secs. 45–49. [For a translation, see Immanuel Kant, *Practical Philosophy*, translated and edited by Mary J. Gregory (Cambridge: Cambridge University Press, 1999), which contains Kant's *Groundwork of the Metaphysics of Morals* (*Grundlegung zur Metaphysik der Sitten*).—Ed.]

[12] Immanuel Kant, *Fundamental Principles of Morals*, translated by A. D. Lindsay, p. 421. [As Ronald Hamowy notes, the "Exhaustive Bibliography of English Translations of Kant" lists no translation by Lindsay of the *Grundlegung zur Metaphysik der Sitten*. See F. A. Hayek, *The Constitution of Liberty*, ed. Ronald Hamowy, vol. 15 (2011) of *The Collected Works of F. A. Hayek* (Chicago: University of Chicago Press; London: Routledge), p. 296, note 18.—Ed.]

[13] See especially Johann Gottlieb Fichte, *Grundlage des Naturrechts nach Principien der Wissenschaftslehre*, vol. 3 (1796) of *Sämmtliche Werke*, ed. Immanuel Hermann Fichte (Berlin: Veit, 1845), p. 105.

[14] It had been preceded by a Swedish code in 1734 and an even earlier Danish code.

The main force which led to codification on the Continent was the demand for greater certainty of the law and the desire for its revision in the direction of more perfect generality and equality. One of the first fruits of this was significantly the explicit recognition of the principle that no act must be treated as a crime or be punished which was not declared as such by a pre-existing law. This principle was first formally recognized by the Austrian penal code of 1787[15] and then found its way into the Declaration of the Rights of Man of 1789.[16] The famous Latin tag *nulluns crimen, nulla poena sine lege* is due to the German lawyer Anselm Feuerbach who, not much later, expounded the principle in an influential treatise of penal law.[17]

Yet the most important contribution which eighteenth-century Prussia made to the development of the Rule of Law was in the crucial field of the control of administration.[18] Here the task which the Continental countries faced was very different from that which the English had met in the preceding century; and the solutions attempted on the Continent are for this reason in some respects of greater significance for the problems of today than the English institutions. While in England the Rule of Law had been achieved before the elaborate administrative machinery of the modern state had grown up, and later had in the same measure prevented or delayed its growth, the Continental countries had to attempt to establish a government of law when a highly developed administrative apparatus was already in existence. Since they did not want to dispense with the advantages which they derived from this machinery which the absolute monarchs had built up, their problem was to bring an operating bureaucracy with a great variety of firmly established functions under the control of the law. In France, after the Revolution, an over-rigid interpretation of the principle of the separation of powers in effect

[15] This code sets out in paragraph 1: "Only such illegal acts are to be considered and treated as crimes which have been enumerated in the present law." [For an English translation of the Austrian Criminal Code of 1787, see *The Emperor's New Code of Criminal Laws, Published at Vienna, the 15th of January 1787*, translated from the German by an officer (Dublin: Printed by John Rea for Messrs. Moncrieffe, White, Byrne, and Moore, 1787).—Ed.]

[16] "8. La Loi ne doit établir que des peines strictement et évidemment nécessaires, et nul ne peut être puni qu'en vertu d'une loi établie et promulguée antérieurement au délit, et légalement appliquée." ["8. The law shall provide for such punishments only as are strictly and obviously necessary, and no one shall suffer punishment except it be legally inflicted in virtue of a law passed and promulgated before the commission of the offense."—Ed.]

[17] Paul Johann Anslem Feuerbach, *Lehrbuch des gemeinen in Deutschland gültigen peinlichen Rechts* (Giessen: G. H. Heyer, 1801), p. 20. Cf. on all this Heinrich Balthassar Gerland, "Nulla poena sine lege", in *Die Grundrechte und Grundpflichten der Reichsverfassung: Kommentar zum zweiten Teil der Reichsverfassung*, ed. Hans Carl Nipperdey (Berlin: Reimar Hobbing, 1929), vol. 1, pp. 368–86.

[18] Cf. Edgar Loening, *Gerichte und Verwaltungsbehörden in Brandenburg-Preussen: Ein Beitrag zur preussischen Rechts- und Verfassungsgeschichte* (Halle: Waisenhaus, 1914), and the important review article on this work by Otto Hintze, "Preussens Entwicklung zum *Rechtsstaat*", reprinted in the author's *Geist und Epochen der preussischen Geschichte* (Leipzig: Koehler and Amelang, 1943), chapter 4, pp. 105–71.

led to the administration being largely freed from such control and to the perpetuation of that independence of the administration from judicial review which had existed before the Revolution. But Prussia attacked the problem already in the eighteenth century with great thoroughness and thereby contributed much to shape the ideals which guided the liberal movement of the nineteenth. In fact, in its most far-reaching experiment in this field, a law of 1797, which applied only to her new provinces in the East, Prussia went so far as to subject all disputes between administrative authorities and private citizens to the jurisdiction of the ordinary courts; she thereby created one of the prototypes around which the nineteenth-century discussion of the *Rechtsstaat* was to center. These beginnings disappeared again, however, and during the height of the liberal agitation for the *Rechtsstaat* from about 1830 to 1860 Prussia was in this respect indeed very far from being a model which could be held up for imitation.

Up to the end of this period, the German contribution to the ideal of the Rule of Law was indeed largely a theoretical one, and in some measure this remained so since it was never given to the Germans fully to realize the ideal which they had elaborated. But we must not underrate the value of their theoretical contribution. The gradual development of the concept of the *Rechtsstaat*, largely the work of German scholars, had a profound influence on the whole Continental tradition and the mere fact that this concept, as the *état du droit* or *stato di diritto*, has entered French and Italian legal terminology, shows the extent of this influence. The German term seems to appear first, still with a rather vague connotation, in a German treatise of 1813[19] and to have been given definite meaning and wider currency by Robert Mohl, who in 1824, in a noteworthy study of the constitution of the United States,[20] held up their example as that of a highly developed *Rechtsstaat* and who then for the next thirty years untiringly elaborated and expounded its principles.[21]

9. The Continental Liberal Movement

The great period in the growth of Continental Liberalism, the fourth and fifth decade of the nineteenth century, is also the period in which it became most closely allied with the movement for the *Rechtsstaat*; indeed it may be said

[19] Karl Teodor Welcker, *Die letzten Gründe von Recht, Staat und Strafe: Philosophisch und nach den Gesetzen der merkwürdigsten Völker rechtshistorisch entwickelt* (Giessen: Heyer, 1813), which distinguishes three types of state: despotism, theocracy, and *Rechtsstaat*.

[20] Robert von Mohl, *Das Bundes-Staatsrecht der Vereinigten Staaten von Nord-Amerika* (Stuttgart: J. G. Cotta, 1824).

[21] Robert Mohl, *Staatsrecht des Königreiches Württemberg* (Tübingen: H. Laupp, 1829–1831); *Die Polizei-Wissenschaft nach den Grundsätzen des Rechtsstaates* (Tübingen: Laupp, 1832–34); *Die Geschichte und Literatur der Staatswissenschaften* (Erlangen: Ferdinand Enke, 1855–58).

that the latter became its main aim. In France this is roughly the period of the July monarchy and for a time it seemed that under its 'bourgeois king' she would go far to realize the ideal. Benjamin Constant, Guizot and the group of the so-called 'doctrinaires' had developed a doctrine of *garantism*, a system of checks designed to protect the rights of the individual against the encroachment of the state, which in a fuller account of the history of the ideal of the Rule of Law would have to occupy a good deal of space.[22] King Louis Philippe himself, at the beginning of his reign, seemed to proclaim the establishment of the Rule of Law as his guiding ideal. As he stated it in a public speech: "La liberté ne consiste que dans le règne des lois. Que chacun ne puisse pas être tenu de faire autre chose que ce que la loi exige de lui, et qu'il puisse faire tout ce que la loi n'interdit pas, telle est la liberté: C'est vouloir la détruire que de vouloir autre chose."[23]

But in fact little use was made of that opportunity to adapt French institutions to the ideal. The pre-revolutionary institutions in the field of administration proved too strong for the ideological movement to make much impression, and in the end the disappearance of the July monarchy with the revolution of 1848 prematurely also discredited its ideals. Neither the reign of Napoleon III nor the Third Republic provided a very favourable climate for their further growth. Not that there were not some developments in this direction which deserve to be better understood.[24] But I have no time to discuss here developments both in France and in Germany, and since for a number of reasons developments in Germany seem to me to be both less known and more significant, I shall, for the rest of this lecture have to concentrate on them.

[22] Cf. Guido de Ruggiero, *The History of European Liberalism*, translated by R. G. Collingwood (Oxford: Oxford University Press, 1927); and Luis Diez del Corral, *El Liberalismo Doctrinario* (Madrid: Instituto de estudios políticos, 1945).

[23] Speech to the National Guard reported in an essay by H. F. R. de Lamennais in *L'Avenir* of May 23, 1831, and reprinted in *Troisièmes mélanges* (Paris: P. Daubrée et Cailleux, 1835), p. 266. ["Liberty consists solely in the rule of law. That no one may be held to do other than what the law demands of him and that he may act in any manner not prohibited by the law, therein lies one's liberty. To desire other than this is tantamount to destroying it."—Ed.]

[24] There are now available in English two excellent accounts of the growth and significance of the French system of administrative jurisdiction: Marguerite A. Sieghart, *Government by Decree* (London: Stevens, 1950), and Bernard Schwartz, *French Administrative Law and the Common-Law World* (New York: New York University Press, 1954). This is part of the reason for the comparative neglect of the French development in what follows. But I also believe that the Germans have made more important contributions to the subject and that though this is less understood, the German development has in fact exercised considerable indirect influence on development elsewhere, including especially the United States. On the importance of the German theoretical development compare Paul Alexéef, "L'État—le droit—et le pouvoir discrétionnaire des autorités publiques", *Revue internationale de la théorie du droit*, vol. 3, 1928–29, p. 216; and Charles Howard McIlwain, *Constitutionalism and the Changing World: Collected Papers* (Cambridge: Cambridge University Press, 1939), p. 270.

In Southern Germany[25] the character of the movement was largely determined by the fact that the intellectual leaders of the whole liberal agitation of
the time were two constitutional lawyers, Carl von Rotteck and K. T. Welcker
(the man who seems to have coined the word *Rechtsstaat*) and who combined
Mohl's *Rechtsstaat* ideal with conceptions drawn from B. Constant and Guizot.
A kind of political encyclopedia which they issued and in which those ideals
were expanded became a sort of handbook for the whole liberal movement.[26]
Gradually the *Rechtsstaat* conception advanced against the original opposition
of the conservatives and made considerable headway even in official quarters.
We soon find, for instance, the president of the highest court of one of the
South German states arguing that wherever a question arises whether any
private rights are well founded or have been violated by official action the matter must be decided by the ordinary courts.[27] The success of the doctrine can
be best gauged by the fact that it entered even the treatise on the philosophy
of law of the man who was to become the leader of the arch-conservatives
in Prussia. G. F. Stahl's definition of the *Rechtsstaat* is in fact probably more
frequently quoted than any other, and as it will provide me with an opportunity to correct a common mistake I shall quote it once more. "The State", he
wrote in 1837,

> should be a state of law (*Rechtsstaat*), this is the watchword and, in truth, also
> the tendency of recent times. It should exactly and irrevocably determine
> and secure the *directions* and the *limits* of its activity and the free sphere of the
> citizen, and not enforce on its own behalf or directly any moral ideas beyond
> the sphere of law. This is the conception of the '*Rechtsstaat*' and not that the
> state should confine itself to administering the law and pursue no adminis-
> trative purpose or *only* protect the rights of the individual. It says nothing
> about the *content* or *aim* of the state but defines only the manner and method
> of achieving them.[28]

[25] The best account of the rôle of the *Rechtsstaat* ideal in the German liberal movement will be
found in Franz Schnabel, *Monarchie und Volksouveränität*, vol. 2 of *Deutsche Geschichte im Neunzehnten
Jahrhundert* (Freiburg im Breisgau: Herder, 1933), pp. 90–214, especially pp. 99–109.

[26] *Staats-Lexikon oder Enzyklopaedie der Staatswissenschaften*, ed. Karl von Rotteck and Karl T.
Welcker (Altona: Hammerich, 1834–1848). Among the collaborators especially important in
this connection, is K. R. Mittermaier (cf. his "Beiträge zu den Gegenständen des bürgerlichen
Prozesses", *Archiv für die zivilistische Praxis*, 1820).

[27] Ludwig Minnigerode, *Beitrag zur Beanwortung der Frage: Was ist Justiz- und was ist Administrativ-
Sache?* (Darmstadt: Meyer, 1835).

[28] Friedrich Julius Stahl, *Rechts-und Staatslehre*, vol. 2 of *Die Philosophie des Rechts*, 5th ed. (Tübingen and Leipzig: J. C. B. Mohr, 1878), part 2 [1837], p. 137. Significant for the general rejection
of the *Rechtsstaat* ideal by the conservatives is the draft of a novel by the Swiss poet Jeremias Gotthelf which was to be called *Joggli, der Schuldenbauer oder der Rechtsstaat*. Cf. Franz Oswald, "Jeremias
Gotthelf über Staat, Recht und Gesellschaft", *Deutsche Juristen-Zeitung*, 1934, esp. p. 1263.

The restrictions added to this definition were well justified by the confusion between the argument that in exercising coercion the state should be strictly bound by law and the contention (represented by W. von Humboldt's essay on the *Sphere and Duties of Government* and many other followers of Kant) that the enforcement of the law should be its *only* activity. The *Rechtsstaat* principle has reference only to the coercive activities of the state and has nothing to say about any other governmental activities which do not involve coercion. This correct view, however must of course not be taken to mean, as it was later taken, that all that was required was mere legality of all government action.

How generally the ideal had become accepted by the middle of the century is shown by the draft constitution for Germany accepted by the Frankfurt parliament in 1848. This provided that all administrative jurisdiction (in the sense in which the term was then understood) was to cease and all violations of private rights were to be adjudicated by courts of justice.[29] This constitution never became law and the struggle for a satisfactory regulation of these problems continued. It was directed very largely against the state of affairs which had developed in Prussia which during the period of reaction had grown into the most notorious instance of a police state with which the ideal of the *Rechtsstaat* was constantly contrasted. The leader in this North German fight for the *Rechtsstaat*, which drew more on the English model and on older German traditions than on the French example, was the Prussian parliamentarian Eduard Lasker, the "idealist of the *Rechtsstaat*" as he has been called, and one of Bismarck's most hated enemies. His writings on the subject are important because of the vivid picture they give of the extent to which unchecked and arbitrary administrative control had returned in the Prussia of the 1860's.[30]

On the theoretical side this phase of the development found its conclusion with the works of the famous legal historian Otto von Giercke[31] and the special study devoted to the *Rechstsstaat* by O. Bähr.[32] It was characteristic of this phase that it aimed, somewhat on the English model, at entrusting the whole control of the lawfulness of the acts of administration to the ordinary courts. This view of the *Rechtsstaat*, which was later usually referred to as 'judicialism',[33] was however soon to be superseded by different conceptions.

---

[29]Cf. Ernst Forsthoff, *Allgemeiner Teil*, vol. 1 of *Lehrbuch des Verwaltungsrechts* (Munich: C. H. Beck, 1950), p. 394.

[30]Eduard Lasker, "Polizeigewalt und Rechtsschutz in Preussen", *Deutsche Jahrbücher für Politik und Literatur*, vol. 1, October 1861, pp. 27–48, reprinted in *Zur Verfassungsgeschichte Preussens* (Leipzig: F. A. Brockhaus, 1874), pp. 179–212.

[31]Otto Friedrich von Gierke, *Das deutsche Genossenschaftsrecht* (Berlin: Weidmann, 1868).

[32]Otto Bähr, *Der Rechtsstaat: Eine Publicistische Skizze* (Cassel: Wigand, 1864).

[33]The German phrase was *Justizstaat*. Cf. Gerhard Anschütz, "Verwaltungsrecht", in *Systematische Rechtswissenschaft*, ed. Rudolf Stammler, *Kultur der Gegenwart*, vol. 2, no. 7 (Leipzig and Berlin: Taeubner, 1906), p. 352. It is certainly not correct with regard to this earlier phase of the German development when Franz Leopold Neumann, "The Concept of Political Freedom", *Co-*

10. Theory and Practice in Continental Administration

There are two distinct reasons why it may be argued that ordinary jurisdiction and the judicial control of administrative action should be kept apart; though they both contributed to the ultimate establishment of a separate system of administrative courts in Germany (and probably also to the preservation of the French system of *droit administratif*), and though they have frequently been confused, they ought to be kept clearly distinct since they aim at quite different and even incompatible ends.

One argument is that the kind of problem which is raised by disputes over administrative actions requires knowledge both of law and of fact which the ordinary judge, trained mainly in the civil or common law, cannot be expected to possess. It is a very strong and probably conclusive argument, but it leads to no greater separation of administrative from ordinary courts than is the case with separate criminal or commercial courts (or with the Admiralty and Divorce Division of the High Court in London). Such separate administrative courts could still be as independent of the government as the civil courts and be concerned solely with the administration of the law, i.e., with the application of a body of pre-existing rules.

Separate administrative courts may on the other hand be thought necessary because it is believed that differences about the legitimacy or administrative actions cannot be decided simply as a matter of law but will always involve questions of administrative policy or expediency. Such courts will be concerned with the aims of the government of the moment and cannot be fully independent, but must form part of the administrative machinery, subject to directions at least by its executive head. They are intended not so much to protect the individual against encroachments by the government on his private sphere than to assure that this is not being done against the intentions and instructions of the government. They are thus more a device to ensure that the subordinate agencies carry out the will of the government (including that of the legislature where it goes beyond laying down of general rules) than a means of protection for the individual.

This distinction would have been clear enough at a time when there existed a body of detailed legal rules for guiding and limiting the actions of the ad-

---

lumbia Law Review, vol. 53, 1953, p. 910, contends that "The English rule of law and the German *Rechtsstaat* doctrines have really nothing in common." This is true enough of the emasculated concept of the *Rechtsstaat* of the end of the century which we shall have to discuss below but neither of the conceptions which inspired the liberal movement of the first half of the century nor of the ideas which led to the reforms of administrative jurisdiction in Prussia. Both the earlier theorists and R. Gneist quite deliberately made the English position their model and aimed at the establishment of the rule of law in the strict original English meaning of the term. Its German equivalent, *Herrschaft des Gesetzes*, was in fact frequently used as a synonym for *Rechtsstaat*.

ministration; but it becomes inevitably blurred when administrative courts are created at a time when the formulation of such rules is a task yet to be achieved by future legislation and jurisdiction. In this case it becomes necessarily one of the tasks of the courts to formulate as legal norms what so far has been merely internal rules of the administration; and it will in such a situation be exceedingly difficult to distinguish between what in fact has the character of such general rules and what were merely the particular aims of policy.

This, however, was essentially the position in Germany when in the 1860's and 1870's a series of attempts was made to translate the long cherished ideal of the *Rechtsstaat* into practice. The argument which carried the day and which finally defeated the long maintained arguments of 'justicialism' was the argument that it was impracticable to leave to ordinary judges, mainly concerned with civil matters, the highly technical issues which would arise in disputes over administrative actions. The new administrative courts which were then created were however meant to be independent courts, concerned with questions of law, and it was hoped that in the course of time they would achieve complete legal control of administrative action. In this sense the creation of a separate administrative jurisdiction appeared both to its main theoretical advocate of the time, Rudolf Gneist,[34] and to most later German theorists of administrative law,[35] as the capping stone of the edifice of the *Rechtsstaat*, as the final realization of the Rule of Law. It seemed merely a minor and temporary defect, and it was unavoidable that for the time being a large number of loopholes were left open for what in effect was still arbitrary action because, if the administrative apparatus was to continue to function, it had to be given wide discretion until the body of rules guiding this action was gradually being evolved. It is significant however, that at least in Prussia, where the English and native German traditions were stronger, judicial review was at least in principle extended to questions which were within the discretionary powers of the administrative authorities, while in Southern Germany, where the French influence was predominant, these were explicitly excluded from judicial review from the outset.[36]

But while the creation of the system of administrative courts was justly regarded by the contemporaries as the decisive step in the achievement of the government of law, the most important task still lay in the future if it was to become a reality. The superimposition of a machinery of judicial control over an old established bureaucratic apparatus could become effective only if the task of rule-making continued in the spirit in which that machinery was conceived. It so happened, however, that the creation of the long wished

[34] Rudolph von Gneist, *Der Rechtsstaat* (Berlin: Julius Springer, 1872).

[35] See for instance Gustav Radbruch, *Einführung in die Rechtswissenschaft*, 2nd ed. (Leipzig: Quelle und Meyer, 1913), p. 108, and Fritz Fleiner, *Institutionen des deutschen Verwaltungsrechts*, 8th ed. (Tübingen: Mohr, 1928), p. 39.

[36] See Ernst Forsthoff, *Allgemeiner Teil*, p. 396.

for edifice of the *Rechtsstaat* coincided in time with the abandonment of the ideas which had given rise to that ideal; there occurred, in fact, at the same time a major reversal of intellectual trends which can only be described as the abandonment of that liberalism for which the *Rechtsstaat* had been the main goal. The 1870's and 1880's during which in the German States (and also in France) the system of administrative courts received its final form, were also the time during which, in these countries, the new movement towards state socialism and the welfare state was getting under way. There was, thereafter, little willingness to implement the conception of limited government which the administrative courts had been designed to serve by legislation progressively narrowing those discretionary powers of the administrative authorities which the reform had had to leave in existence. There was, on the contrary, a strong temptation to widen the loopholes progressively by explicitly exempting administrative decisions from judicial review.

11. The Historicist and Positivist Reaction

In so far as this retreat from the *Rechtsstaat* ideal was the result of new conceptions of economic and social policy it will be the main topic of my last lecture. Today I must briefly consider another influence which became operative at about the same time and which, though connected with those other new tendencies I shall not have time to examine. I am referring to the allied movements of historicism and legal positivism which contributed much to weaken the ideal of the Rule of Law and to empty the concept of its significance.

I have so far deliberately not mentioned the close historical connection which existed between the ideal of the *Rechtsstaat* and that of the law of nature or *Naturrecht*. I have avoided it because this connection, though historically very important, somewhat confuses the main issues. The Rule of Law, as a limitation on the power of all government, is, of course, also a rule, but, as we shall see, an extra-legal rule which cannot itself be a law but can only exist as the governing opinion about the attributes good laws should possess. It is too easy a solution to ascribe to that principle existence elsewhere than in the conviction of men, to impute to it objective validity apart from human will. It may have permanent validity in the sense that any man who shares certain fundamental values and possesses the understanding of human affairs which the experience of generations has accumulated, will recognize it as desirable. But this does not alter the fact that its comprehension requires an ever renewed act of the understanding and of the will and that to preserve it demands constant self-discipline. The traditional treatment of the Rule of Law, however, often represented it as a form of Higher Law that had its foundation elsewhere than in the will of man. This connection was greatly strengthened by the fact that modern Continental theory on the subject (and in part also English views) trace back to the teaching of the founder of the modern theory of the law of nature, Hugo Grotius.[37]

It was against this apparent foundation of the principle of the Rule of Law that the criticism of the historical school and of the positivists was directed. They refused to recognize—rightly enough so far as the word 'law' in the strict sense was concerned—the existence of any permanent or immutable laws which could not be altered by the legislative authority. Both, in their ways, were schools of pure lawyers, interested only in what the law in fact was at a particular time, and who did not regard it as their concern to inquire what the law ought to be. In consequence, they did not possess any standards by which to judge any particular rule except the principle of legality or constitutionality. The whole idea of the Rule of Law or of the *Rechtsstaat*, however, implied an ideal standard by which the actual legal position was judged; it was an ideal in the name of which modern liberty had been achieved and which had been closely approached because it had governed and guided the minds of men. Like most of the governing ideas of any age, it was held not because its *rationale* was fully understood, but rather because the success of the groups and civilizations who had held it had brought it to dominance. It had become part of that sense of justice which a process of natural selection among societies produces by making those flourish which have evolved beliefs most conducive to the best use of the capacities of their members.

The historical approach which attempted to explain the development of law by the needs and aims of each time tended to destroy the belief in such principles to which all laws should conform. With its stress on the changeability of the law it encouraged the belief that there was nothing which should not be tried if it seemed the most efficient means for a particular purpose, no rule which the legislator should not be free to alter if it seemed expedient to him. It created a moral and legal relativism which, somewhat contrary to the attitude which a real understanding of the non-rational forces in history should produce, implied a denial of the value of any experience that is embodied in traditions and institutions.[38]

Legal positivism is a logical consequence of these beliefs.[39] As it knows no

---

[37] Hugo Grotius, *De jure belli ac pacis* (1625); see especially the significant discussion of the generality of laws, L.I, chapter 3, sec. 6. It was probably in an attempt to provide a theoretical foundation for the rule of law so largely achieved in Holland at an early date that Grotius developed his theory of natural law, but these connections of the whole tradition with the developments in Holland still need investigation. [See Hugo Grotius, *The Rights of War and Peace*, ed. Richard Tuck (Indianapolis, IN: Liberty Fund, 2005), book 1, chapter 3, section 6, titled "In what Things the Civil Power consists", pp. 257–59.—Ed.]

[38] Cf. Emil Brunner, *Justice and Social Order* (New York: Harper, 1945), pp. 6–7.

[39] Cf. Hermann Heller, "Bemerkungen zur staats- und rechtstheoretischen Problematik der Gegenwart", *Archiv für öffentliches Recht*, vol. 16, 1929, p. 336.

principles beyond the positive laws, it has no criteria to judge whether a law is good or bad. It is solely concerned with what the law is and whether according to it a particular action is legal or not. A law which gives the executive unlimited authority to do whatever pleases him is from this point of view just as good as any other. Since the Rule of Law as a limitation upon legislation is a sort of meta-legal principle which cannot be a part of a positive law but to which the positive law may or may not conform, it could have no meaning within the compass of positive jurisprudence. Consequently, the principle of the *Rechtsstaat* or of the Rule of Law came to mean to the representatives of these schools merely the demand for legality, the requirement of a legal foundation for any act of the state.[40] As such it ceased to have any significance as a guarantee of individual freedom, since any oppression, however arbitrary or discriminatory, could be legalized by a law authorizing an authority to act in such a manner.

This view which deprived the concept of the *Rechtsstaat* of all distinctive meaning became widely accepted at the end of the last century but reached its fullest development only in the present one. How in its extremest form, as the "pure theory of law", it has indeed removed all theoretical objections to calling even the most tyrannical rule a *Rechtsstaat*—a possibility of which the totalitarian regimes have made ample use—is clearly shown by a statement of its best known representative, Professor Hans Kelsen. "Entirely meaningless", he argued in his chief treatise of 1925,

> is the assertion that under despotism there exists no order of law (*Rechtsordnung*) [but] that there the arbitrary will of the despot reigns. . . . The despotically governed state also represents some order of human behaviour. This order is the order of law. To deny to it the name of an order of law is nothing but naïveté and presumption deriving from natural-law thinking. . . . What is interpreted as arbitrary will is merely the legal possibility of the autocrat's taking on himself every decision, determining unconditionally the activities of subordinate organs and rescinding or altering at any time norms once announced, either generally or for a particular case. Such a condition is a condition of law even when it is felt to be disadvantageous. It has also its good aspects. The demand for dictatorship not uncommon in the modern *Rechtsstaat* shows this very clearly.[41]

---

[40] Cf. John Hamilton Hallowell, *The Decline of Liberalism as an Ideology, with Particular Reference to German Politico-Legal Thought* (Berkeley: University of California Press, 1943); Gustav Radbruch, *Rechtsphilosophie*, 4th ed. (Stuttgart: K. F. Koehler, 1950); and Friedrich Darmstädter, *Die Grenzen der Wirksamkeit des Rechtsstaates: Eine Untersuchung zur gegenwärtigen Krise des liberalen Staatsgedankens* (Heidelberg: C. Winter, 1930), and *Rechtsstaat oder Machtstaat?* (Berlin: Rothschild, 1932).

[41] Hans Kelsen, *Allgemeine Staatslehre* (Berlin: Julius Springer, 1925), p. 335–36. [The brackets are Hayek's.—Ed.]

12. Dicey's Misunderstanding of the Continental Tradition

The conditions which towards the end of last century generally existed on the Continent thus showed a curious contrast between theory and practice. This contrast partly accounts for a fateful misunderstanding by Anglo-Saxon observers of the institutions which had grown up there, a misunderstanding which had grave consequences for the development in England and the United States. In principle, the ideal of the Rule of Law had not only been long recognized on the Continent, but important institutional advances had been made which were intended to adapt the ideal to the conditions of a modern state with its extensive and multiform administrative activities. Though the success of the administrative courts was somewhat restricted, they still constituted the only original attempt to place this kind of administrative activity under the control of definite rules. The system had indeed never had a chance fully to show its possibilities; not only did certain features of the pre-*Rechtsstaat* days never fully disappear, but the advance towards the welfare state, so much ahead of developments in England or the United States, soon added new ones. The result was that any Englishman or American who observed the daily practice in France or Germany would feel that the situation was still very far from what according to his way of thought was required by the Rule of Law. The difference between the powers and behaviour of a policeman in London and one in Berlin—to mention an often quoted example—seemed as great as ever. Or, as a typical discussion of the contrast in a once widely read American text described it: "In some cases, it is true, [even in England] an officer of the local board is given by statute power to make regulations. The Local Government Board (in Great Britain) and our boards of health furnish examples of this; but such cases are exceptional, and most Anglo-Saxons feel that this power is in its nature arbitrary, and ought not to be extended any further than is absolutely necessary."[42]

It was in this situation that A. V. Dicey,[43] in a work that was to become a classic and after giving a brilliant though somewhat one-sided exposition of the principle of the Rule of Law as it prevailed in England, proceeded to contrast it with the position on the Continent and gave an altogether misleading picture. Starting from the accepted and undeniable assumption that the Rule of Law did only very imperfectly prevail on the Continent, and seeing that this was somehow connected with the fact that administrative coercion was largely exempt from judicial review, he made, somewhat on the lines of the earlier

[42] Abbott Lawrence Lowell, *Governments and Parties in Continental Europe* (New York: Houghton, Mifflin, 1896), vol. 1, p. 44. [Hayek added the bracketed material.—Ed.]

[43] Albert Venn Dicey, *Introduction to the Study of the Law of the Constitution*, 9th ed., introduction and appendix by E. C. S. Wade (London: Macmillan, 1939). Originally delivered as lectures in 1884.

German 'justicialists', the possibility of a review of administrative action by the *ordinary* courts the kingpin of his argument. He appears to have known only the French system of administrative jurisdiction and to have known that rather imperfectly, and to have been practically ignorant of the German developments. With regard to the French system, his severe strictures may in fact have been somewhat more justified, though even there the *Conseil d'État* had already initiated a development which, as a modern observer remarks, "might in time succeed in bringing all discretionary powers of the administration . . . within the range of judicial control."[44] But they were even more inapplicable to the *principle* of the German administrative courts which from the beginning had been constituted as independent judicial bodies with the very purpose of securing that Rule of Law which Dicey was so anxious to preserve. It should of course be remembered that in 1885, when Dicey published his famous *Lectures*, the German administrative courts were only just taking shape and even the French system had only recently received its definite form. Nevertheless, the "fundamental mistake" of Dicey, as it has been called by one of his learned admirers, "so fundamental that it is difficult to understand or excuse in a writer of his eminence",[45] had the most unfortunate consequences. The very idea of separate administrative courts—and by a naïve confusion even the term 'administrative law'—came to be regarded in England as the denial of the Rule of Law. Thus, by his attempt to vindicate the Rule of Law as he saw it, Dicey in effect blocked the development which perhaps offered the best chance of preserving it. He could not prevent the growth of an administrative apparatus similar to that which the Continental countries already possessed. But he did contribute much to prevent or delay the growth of institutions suitable to subjecting that new bureaucratic machinery to effective control by independent courts.

[44] M. A. Sieghart, *Government by Decree* (London: Stevens, 1950), p. 221.

[45] Sir Carlton Kemp Allen, *Law and Orders: An Inquiry into the Nature and Scope of Delegated Legislation and Executive Powers in England* (London: Stevens, 1945), p. 28.

Lecture III
The Safeguards of Individual Liberty

> Order is not a pressure imposed upon society from without, but an equilib-
> rium which is set up from within. —J. Ortega Y. Gasset[1]

13. Law and Order

The main purpose of this lecture will be to examine the connection between
the various principles which together constitute the Rule of Law. But before I
turn to this I want briefly to draw your attention to a more general aspect of
the relation between law and order.

It is a deeply ingrained tendency of the human mind that whenever it discovers an orderly pattern, it believes that this must have been designed by a
mind like itself and assumes that there can be no order without such conscious
design. But if a multitude of individual elements obey certain general laws,
this may of course produce a definite order of the whole mass without the interference of an outside force. This applies to the laws obeyed by men no less
than to the laws of nature; and however much the two meanings of the term
law may have moved apart, if we look for a moment at the most general aspects of that relationship, the general nature of our problem would be placed
in a clearer light.

There are of course innumerable instances in nature where the regularities
in the behaviour of many independent parts or elements result in the formation of distinct order of any complex they will form; and more than this: we
very often employ our knowledge of such laws to bring about an organization
of matter which we could not possibly produce by individually placing each
particle just where we want it. Think of the manner in which we produce a
complex chemical compound or in which the most elaborate and beautiful
structure of snow crystals is formed. They are the result of the behaviour of
the individual molecules, each of which will respond only to the actions upon
it of its immediate environment. Yet this mutual adjustment of the elements
to their immediate neighbors creates an equilibrium of the whole, an order in
which every element takes its appropriate part. We meet here what Michael
Polanyi has described as the spontaneous formation of a polycentric order;[2]
an order which is not the result of all the factors being taken into account by

---

[1] José Ortega y Gasset, *Mirabeau o El Político* (1927), vol. 3 of *Obras Completas* (Madrid: Revista de Occidente, 1947), p. 603.

[2] Michael Polanyi, *The Logic of Liberty: Reflections and Rejoinders* (London: Routledge and Kegan Paul, 1951), especially pp. 114 *et seq.* and 154 *et seq.* [Hayek refers to the section titled "Spontane-ous Order Compared with Corporate Order" in chapter 8, and to chapter 10, "Manageability of Social Tasks", which begins with a discussion of "Two Kinds of Order."—Ed.]

a single centre, but which is produced by the responses of the individual elements to their respective surroundings.

The use of such properties of the individual elements enables us to arrange them in an order which we might never be able to achieve by placing them individually at the appropriate point. We could never produce a complex organic compound if this depended on our putting each molecule of the different elements individually in the appropriate relation to other individual molecules of the same or different elements so as to produce the complex structure of the compound. We must rely on the fact that whenever certain conditions are satisfied, the molecules will themselves enter into relations with others which will show certain characteristics. But this reliance on the spontaneous forces, which is our *only* means to achieve this result, also means that we cannot control certain aspects of the process. We could, e.g., not at the same time rely on those forces and make sure that particular individual molecules will occupy particular places in the resulting structure. We might, for instance, for some reason dislike the idea that on successive occasions on which we produce the compound from a given material, the identical molecules should always occupy the topmost position in the resulting solid. But though this would be unlikely to happen, we should have no way of preventing it with certainty. We shall have no choice but either to leave to chance the particular places which the individual molecules will occupy or not to produce the compound at all.

There is a further point about the manner in which such spontaneous orders are formed in nature which deserves attention. The behaviour of the elements need not be determined in all respects but must conform merely to some abstract conditions in order that a structure with definite characteristics should be formed. All that is necessary is that whenever some selected features of the environment are given, the behaviour of the elements will also show some general characteristics. In other words, it is not necessary for the formation of a spontaneous order that the behaviour of the elements is predictable in every respect: even a very partial regularity of their action may be sufficient to produce a definite order of the whole.

All this is of course of the greatest importance for our efforts to produce an order in complex phenomena wherever we do not know all the details. And this is precisely the problem in creating an order in society. The most important fact which we have here to face is the necessary and irremediable ignorance, of any one person or group of persons, of most of the circumstances which at any moment determine the needs and opportunities of all the different individuals.[3] This is evidently knowledge which can exist only

---

[3] For a fuller account of these considerations see F. A. Hayek, *Individualism and Economic Order* (Chicago: University of Chicago Press, 1948). [Hayek is referring here to two articles from that volume, both of which are reprinted in the present volume: namely, "Economics and Knowledge" and "The Use of Knowledge in Society."—Ed.]

dispersed among all the different members of society and can never be concentrated in a single head, or be deliberately manipulated by any man or any group of men. Yet we desire that as much of this knowledge as possible should be utilized in directing an orderly process, that the individual activities should be integrated into a whole in which each individual profits from the co-ordination of the activities of all which is thus brought about.

Where intelligent human beings form the elements of such an order, men whom we wish to use their individual knowledge as successfully as possible in the pursuit of their individual ends, we must desire to bring about a mutual adjustment of the individual plans and actions by each adapting himself to those circumstances which he can himself observe. The two devices for this purpose on which man has stumbled and on which our civilization has been built are that every man has a known sphere of things which we can control and which we call his property, and that these things can be transferred from the sphere of one to that of another only by mutual consent. These two general principles are of course capable of a great deal of variety in detail—indeed the different systems of private law are little more than variations on this theme.

Very general as these two principles may seem, they yet suffice, as is shown by the analysis of economic theory, to secure an arrangement of human actions which satisfies certain conditions of rational co-ordination—an arrangement which may not be all we might wish but which we can achieve only by leaving the individuals free and by enabling them to act with the maximum degree of certainty according to their individual plans. One of the main aims of the rules which are to achieve this must therefore be to eliminate for the individual as much avoidable uncertainty as possible. This means that he must be able to ascertain from the circumstances which he can know what he is free to do, and under what circumstances and in what manner other human forces will constrain him. If he is to use his knowledge to the best advantage for achieving his aims, the world around him must be, as far as possible, given to him. Of course, in a changing world much of his task and his merit will be to foresee changes correctly, to adapt himself successfully to ever changing conditions. But if the resulting order is to be the effect of the polycentric adjustment of many equilibria, his decision must not be overridden by any interference with that freedom on the ground of circumstances which are beyond the sphere of his observation.

It has taken man a very long time to discover this possibility of creating order by maintaining general laws—or perhaps I should say to learn to use it without really understanding it; because this method of producing order was certainly not 'invented' but its advantages were rather recognized after it had grown up. And until the present day, man has scarcely yet quite understood how he can indirectly make those spontaneous forces work more beneficially by improving the rules according to which the individual acts. Indeed, whenever man is faced with new problems, his first reaction is still to bring about the required adjustment by the crude method of force rather than by operating through the spontaneous interplay of the individuals.

14. A Meta-legal Principle

It is this reliance on the action of abstract rules governing the relations between individuals which is the essential basis of the Rule of Law. Since this Rule of Law means that the government must never coerce an individual except in enforcement of a rule which has been announced beforehand and from which the particular act of coercion necessarily follows, it is of course a limitation upon the powers of all government and especially a limitation upon legislation. It is therefore a doctrine *about* what the law ought to be, or about certain general attributes which the laws must possess in order to conform to it. This is important because the Rule of Law is sometimes confounded with the demand for mere legality of all government action. But although the Rule of Law of course presupposes complete legality in this sense, this is not enough: if a constitutional law gave the government unlimited power to act according to its desire, it would certainly no longer operate under the Rule of Law, although all its acts would be legal. The Rule of Law is, therefore, also more than mere Constitutionalism: it implies certain requirements concerning the contents of the Constitution.

From the fact that the Rule of Law is a limitation upon all legislation it follows that it cannot itself be a law in the same sense as the laws passed by the legislator. Constitutional provisions may make infringements of the Rule of Law more difficult, or delay the process. But the ultimate legislator can never by law limit his own powers, because he can also abrogate any law he has made. The Rule of Law is, therefore, not a rule of the law but a rule about the law, a meta-legal doctrine, or a political ideal. It will be effective only in so far as the legislator feels himself bound to abide by it. In a democracy this means in effect that whether the Rule of Law will be obeyed or not will depend on whether it is accepted by public opinion, that is, in effect, on whether it is part of the sense of justice prevailing in the community.

This dependence on the ideals governing public opinion makes the persistent attacks on the principle, of which I shall have to speak in my next lecture, so very ominous. As we shall presently see that, many of the applications of the Rule of Law are ideals also in the sense that we can hope only to approach them more and more closely, but can probably never fully realize them. But how far they will be realized will depend on the state of public opinion. If belief in the Rule of Law is part of the underlying convictions, both legislation and jurisdiction will tend to approach it more and more. If, on the other hand, its principles are represented as impracticable or perhaps even as undesirable, and people cease to strive for their realization, they will rapidly disappear; a society where this happens will quickly move backwards towards that state of arbitrary tyranny against which the movement for the Rule of Law was directed. This, as we shall see, is exactly what has been happening all over the world during the last two or three generations.

15. Generality, Equality, and Certainty of the Law

I have already suggested more than once that the Rule of Law is really a complex of doctrines which have been formulated at different times and which are connected only by serving the same end.[4] This end is to limit coercion by the power of the state to instances where it is explicitly required by general abstract rules which have been announced beforehand and which applied equally to all people, and refer to circumstances known to them. Since the means of coercion of the individual by the state is punishment, the most important application of the principle is the rule *nullum crimen, nulla poena sine lege*, that is, the rule that nothing must be treated as a crime and punished without a previously existing law providing for it. Yet, clear and definite as this rule may appear at first, we at once encounter all the problems raised by the Rule

---

[4]The literature on the meaning of the Rule of Law is of course enormous and I can list here only a few of the more important publications to which I have not had occasion to refer elsewhere; Sir Ernest Barker, "The Rule of Law", *Political Quarterly*, vol. 1, 1914, pp. 117–40; Felice Battaglia, "Stato etico e Stato di diritto", *Revista internazionale di filosofia di diritto*, vol. 17, 1937, pp. 237–87; Franz Böhm, "Freiheitsordnung und soziale Frage", in *Grundsatzfragen der Wirtschaftsordnung, Wirtschaftswissenschaftliche Abhandlungen*, vol. 2 (Berlin: Duncker and Humblot, 1954); Carl Joachim Friedrich, *Constitutional Government and Democracy: Theory and Practice in Europe and America* (Boston: Little, Brown, 1941); Fernando Garzoni, *Die Rechtsstaatsidee im schweizerischen Staatsdenken des 19. Jahrhunderts* (Zürich: Polygraphischer Verlag, 1952); Werner Kägi, *Die Verfassung als rechtliche Grundordnung des Staates: Untersuchungen über die Entwicklungstendenzen im modernen Verfassungsrecht* (Zürich: Polygraphischer Verlag, 1945), and "Rechtsstaat—Sozialstaat—sozialer Rechtsstaat", in *Die Schweiz, Ein nationales Jahrbuch* (Bern: Jahrbuch Verlag, 1945); Robert Morrison MacIver, *The Modern State* (Oxford: The Clarendon Press, 1928), chapter 8, sec. 3; Charles Howard McIlwain, "Government by Law", *Foreign Affairs: An American Quarterly Review*, vol. 14, 1935–36, pp. 185–98; Maxime Leroy, *La loi: Essai sur la théorie de l'autorité dans la démocratie* (Paris: V. Giard and E. Brière, 1908), chapter 10; Herman von Mangoldt, *Rechtsstaatsgedanke und Regierungsformen in den Vereinigten Staaten von Amerika: Die geistigen Grundlagen des amerikanischen Verfassungsrechts* (Essen: Essener Verlagsanstalt, 1938), and *Geschriebene Verfassung und Rechtssicherheit in den Vereinigten Staaten von Amerika*, (Breslau-Neukirch: A. Kurtze, 1934); James Roland Pennock, *Administration and the Rule of Law* (New York: Farrer and Rinehart, 1941); Albert Picot, "L'État fondé sur le droit et le droit penal", in *Actes de la Société Suisse des Juristes* (Basel: Helbling and Lichtenhahn, 1944), pp. 201a–8a; Roscoe Pound, "Rule of Law", *Encyclopedia of the Social Sciences*, vol. 13, 1934, pp. 463–66; Marcel Waline, *L'Individualisme et le droit*, 2nd ed. (Paris: Éditions Domat Montchrestien, 1949).

of Law if we ask what precisely in this formula is meant by 'law.' Would the rule be satisfied if the law merely said that whoever disobeys the orders of some official, say of a policeman, will be punished in such and such a manner? Clearly, not. Yet even in the freest of countries the law does in fact always provide for something which at a first glance seems very similar to that. There is probably no country on earth where you may not in certain circumstances, if you disobey a policeman, become liable to be punished for an 'act done to the public mischief', for 'disturbing the public order', for 'obstructing the police', or whatever else the local law may call your act. We cannot understand this part of the doctrine without examining at the same time most of the others.

It will be useful to begin by considering the three classical requirements which any legal system must fulfill above all others in order that it may have any claim to be considered as constituting the Rule of Law. They are that the laws must be general, equal, and certain.

The requirement that the law which binds the ordinary citizen must be *general* at once reminds us that we use today the term 'law' in two different and largely independent senses.[5] We call a law every act of the legislative authority; but only some, today probably a small minority of them, are general rules applying to private persons. The state has its own means which it has to use for common ends, and its own servants to administer these means. It is today everywhere the task of the same legislatures to direct the use of these means, and to lay down general rules which the private citizen must observe. But while the government must administer the means put at its disposal, including the services of all those it has hired to carry out its instructions, this does not mean that it should or may in the same manner 'administer' the efforts of the private citizen. It is perhaps the main difference between a free and a socialist or totalitarian society that in the former there is a private sphere, clearly different from the public, and that the private citizen cannot be ordered about but can only be held to obey the general rules applicable to all. This distinction, very definite in the past, is becoming increasingly blurred. It used to be the pride of free men that so long as they obeyed the known laws, no authority and no official could give them an order, and that they did not have to ask anybody's permission in their daily pursuits. I rather doubt whether there is still anybody in the world who can boast that this applies to him.

Of the two kinds of legislative acts which I have mentioned, those which decide about the use of the means which are put at the state's disposal are in effect orders to its servants. All these rules which determine the organization of the apparatus of the state, which regulate the expenditure of its means, the direction of its efforts, and its actions towards other states, are also called laws,

---

[5] See Albert Haenel, *Die organisatorische Entwicklung der deutschen Reichsverfassung: Gesetz im formellen und materiellen Sinne*, vol. 2 of *Studien zum deutschen Staatsrechte* (Leipzig: Verlag H. Haessel, 1888).

though they have not the form of general rules but refer to specific circumstances of time and place. They govern the internal working of the machinery of the state, and bind all those who are part of this machinery: but unless the citizen has voluntarily—or temporarily in obedience to general rules, such as military conscription—become part of this machinery, he is supposed to be outside it. The machinery is supposed to serve him, and it can be used to coerce him only in order to enforce the general rules which apply alike to the relations between citizens and to those between them and the state.

These latter kinds of rules alone are true laws in the specific sense in which we distinguish laws from orders: they are general not only in the sense of applying equally to all people, but also in the sense that they do not refer to particulars but apply whenever certain abstractly defined conditions are satisfied. We have seen in our more general considerations what this means: that only certain selected aspects of the complex situations of real life are singled out as relevant for the application of the rule. I will now merely remind you, that if the rule is to govern behaviour by being known to the people to whom it applies, it must refer only to circumstances which can be presumed to be known to these people and to no other circumstances.

At this point the requirement of generality touches most closely on the second, most difficult and perhaps most important requirement, that of *equality* before the law. There is an enormous and in part very profound literature on this subject[6] and in the little time I can devote to it I can hardly hope to add anything new although I must admit that in spite of all the efforts devoted to it the concept is still far from clear. It seems to be one of those ideals which indicate a direction without clearly defining the goal. Nevertheless, though the ideal may forever remain beyond our complete grasp, it is no less essential that we always strive towards it. Though complete equality before the law, in the sense that no attribute belonging to some individuals but not to others should alter their position under the law, is probably both unattainable and undesirable, there clearly is a meaning in the demand that the laws must be the same for all. Nor can we be satisfied with the easy evasion of saying that the law must not make any irrelevant distinctions, that it must not discriminate between persons for reasons which have no connection with the purpose of the law. These frequently used phrases either evade the issue or admit in effect

---

[6] See Gerhard Leibholz, *Die Gleichheit vor dem Gesetz: Eine Studie auf rechtsvergleichender und rechstphilosophischer Grundlage* (Berlin: O. Liebmann, 1925); Max Friedrich Rümelin, *Die Gleichheit vor dem Gesetz: Rede gehalten bei der akademischen Preisverteilung am 6 November 1928* (Tübingen: Mohr, 1928); Carl Schmitt, *Unabhängigkeit der Richter, Gleichheit vor dem Gesetz und Gewährleistung des Privateigentums nach der Weimarer Verfassung: Ein Rechtsgutachten zu den Gesetzentwürfen über die Vermögensauseinandersetzung mit den frührer regierenden Fürstenhäusern* (Berlin: Walter de Gruyter, 1926); Eduardo Luis Llorens, *La Igualdad ante la Ley* (Murcia: Instituto de estudios políticos de la Universidad de Murcia, 1934); Hans Nef, *Gleichheit und Gerechtigkeit* (Zürich: Polygraphischer Verlag, 1941).

all discriminations the lawyers may wish to make. The real point probably is that, although the law must recognize certain generic differences between human beings, such as the difference between men and women, the differentiation which it makes must not be aimed at benefitting particular people.

Finally we have the requirement which for the functioning of the economic activities of society is probably the most important, that of the *certainty* of the law.[7] I doubt whether the significance which the certainty of the law has for the smooth and efficient working of economic life can be exaggerated, and there is probably no single factor which has contributed more to the greater prosperity of the Western world compared with the Orient than the relative certainty of the law which in the West had early been achieved. Of course it also is an ideal which can be only approached but never fully realized. Yet the extent to which the law is inevitably uncertain can easily be exaggerated and there are reasons why lawyers are especially prone to do so. They are concerned mostly with cases which may lead to litigation because the issue is uncertain. But the degree of certainty of the law which has been achieved in any country must of course be measured by the disputes which do *not* lead to litigation, because as soon as the legal position is examined the outcome is practically certain. It is the cases which never come before the courts, not those which do, which are the measure of the certainty of the law. If there will always remain an irreducible minimum of uncertainty this is the result of the imperfection of all human institutions. The modern tendency to exaggerate the magnitude of this uncertainty appears to be part of that campaign against the ideal of the Rule of Law which will occupy me later. It is curious, however, that this agitation should so frequently come from the same authors who regard the prediction of judicial decisions as the sole purpose of legal science. If the law were as uncertain as these men assert, there could, on their own showing, exist no science of jurisprudence whatsoever.

16. The Separation of Powers

In one sense the principle of the separation of powers is an important part of the doctrine of the Rule of Law;[8] but it is liable to so many misunderstandings and confusions that it has to be handled with special care. It can even be

---

[7]See Sir Henry William Wade, "The Concept of Legal Certainty: A Preliminary Skirmish", *Modern Law Review*, vol. 4, 1941, pp. 183–99; Carl August Emge, *Sicherheit und Gerechtigkeit: Ihre gemeinsame meta-juristische Wurzel* (Berlin: Akademie der Wissenschaften in Kommission bei W. de Gruyter, 1940); and Paul Roubier, *Théorie générale du droit: Histoire des doctrines juridiques et philosophie des valuers sociales* (Paris: Recueil Sirey, 1946), esp. pp. 269 *et seq.*

[8]In connection with the following see particularly the important Review by William Searle Holdsworth of the 9th edition of A. V. Dicey's *Introduction to the Study of the Law of the Constitution*

interpreted in such a manner—as has to some extent happened in France—
that its effects are contrary to the ideal of the Rule of Law which it is intended
to uphold. Like the prohibition of any delegation of legislation which is really
a part of the principle of the separation of powers, the latter is one of those
procedural rules which are beneficial in so far as they serve and safeguard the
Rule of Law, but which should always be viewed under that aspect and not be
treated as if they had independent validity.

The significance of the demand for the separation of powers is fairly clear
in so far as the relation between legislature and judicature is concerned. The
principle that the general rules should be laid down apart from their application to particular instances almost requires that these distinct functions should
also be performed by distinct groups of people. This is perhaps not the only
conceivable but almost certainly the only practicable safeguard that the rules
are not made to fit particular instances but because of their general significance. Other precautions which might be suggested for the same purpose, as,

---

in *The Law Quarterly Review*, vol. 55, 1939, pp. 587–88, from which I would like to quote here at
least the most important passage:

> It is a corollary from this conception of the rule of law that the judicial power of the
> State is, to a large extent, separate from the executive and the Legislature. This corol-
> lary, which had been implicit in the conception of the rule of law from the beginning,
> was emphasized, and rightly emphasized, by Montesquieu and Blackstone. The con-
> cept of the rule of law, therefore, is one of those survivals of medieval law, adapted
> to the needs of a modern State, which helped Parliament to limit the power of the
> Crown and establish constitutional government. Now if this be the true meaning of
> the concept of the rule of law it is clearly not true to say that judges who are allowed,
> for reasons of State, to impose sentences not prescribed by the law are acting in ac-
> cordance with the rule of law. In such a case they are acting not as judges but as agents
> of the executive. If it be said that they are acting in accordance with the rule of law
> because the law allows them so to act, the answer is that if the laws permits such a
> course of action, the rule of law has in effect been abrogated by the Legislature; for in
> such a case the separation between the judicial power and the executive, which is an
> essential feature of the rule of law, has been eliminated. Similarly, if the Stuart Kings
> had defeated the Parliament, and if they had got power to legislate and tax and to
> dictate to the Courts what their judgments should be, the rule of law, in the sense in
> which that concept has been understood by Coke and Blackstone and later lawyers,
> would have been abrogated. In fact the concept of the rule of law is a true juridical
> concept: it is no mere 'principle of political action.' Dr. Jennings's statement to the
> contrary is the exact opposite of the truth.
>
> The rule of law is as valuable a principle today as it has ever been. For it means
> that the Courts can see to it that the powers of officials, and official bodies of persons
> entrusted with government, are not exceeded and are not abused, and that the rights
> of citizens are determined in accordance with the law enacted and unenacted. In so
> far as the jurisdiction of the Courts is ousted, and officials or official bodies of persons
> are given a purely administrative discretion, the rule of law is abrogated. It is not abro-
> gated if these officials or official bodies are given a judicial or quasi-judicial discretion,
> although the machinery through which the rule is applied is not that of the Courts.

for instance, that no rule should be applied sooner than after some considerable interval of time, such as one year, after it has been promulgated, would
hardly seem effective. It would always be difficult to get any body to bind itself
strictly by the words of a rule it has itself formulated. Since what should count
ought not to be the hidden intentions of the maker of the rules but what the
rules as they have been promulgated must mean to an impartial observer, it
would seem necessary that their applications should be left to an independent
authority. I need not enter here into any detailed discussion of why this demands an independent position of the judges, bound by nothing but the law
and secured against all pressure by irremovability and similar safeguards—
and I will also pass over such other corollaries of the principle as the explicit
prohibition of retroactive laws or bills of attainder. I will only add that if this
ideal could ever be fully achieved the judge could hardly be regarded as a
separate power but would rather become a kind of machine applying the law:
Cicero's and Montesquieu's famous "mouth which pronounces the law." But
since it is probably inevitable that certain general conceptions enter into the
interpretation of the law which are not explicitly stated in the law, and since in
the actual struggle of forces the persons who have to apply the law are among
the most important, there is at least some good justification for describing
them as a distinct 'power.'

It is much more doubtful whether, under a strict application of the Rule of
Law, it would not be misleading to describe the executive or the administration
as a distinct and separate power, co-ordinated on equal terms with the other
two. It would certainly not be compatible with the Rule of Law if this was
interpreted to mean that in its dealings with the private citizen the administration is not always subject to the law laid down by the legislature and applied
by independent courts. The assertion of such a power of the administrative
authorities is in fact the very antithesis of the Rule of Law. There are undoubtedly many powers which the administrative authorities will possess and which,
under almost any conceivable system, will not be subject to the control by
independent courts, but under the Rule of Law "Administrative Powers over
Persons and Property" (to quote the title of an influential work)[9] cannot be
among them. Under the Rule of Law the executive must in its coercive action
be bound by rules which not only prescribe where it may act, but also how it
has to act. And the only way to ensure that the administrative authorities will
be so bound is to make the substance of their actions of this sort subject to
judicial review.

It is to a much greater extent a matter of expediency rather than of principle whether these rules need be laid down by the legislature or may be dele-

[9]Ernest Freund, *Administrative Powers Over Persons and Property: A Comparative Study* (Chicago:
University of Chicago Press, 1928).

gated by it to some other body; or perhaps I should say that this question does not so much bear on the principle of the Rule of Law as on the quite distinct principle of the democratic control of Government. So far as the principle of the Rule of Law is concerned, there is no objection against delegation as such, though the actual reasons which today so frequently lead to delegation give much ground for concern. Clearly, the delegation of rule-making to local legislative bodies, such as provincial legislatures or town councils, is from both points of view not objectionable. Even the delegation of rule-making to some kind of non-elective authority need not be contrary to the Rule of Law so long as this authority is bound to state and publish the rules in advance of their application, and so long as it can effectively be made to adhere to them. The trouble with the widespread modern use of delegation is that not the power of making general rules is delegated, but that authorities are in effect given power to wield coercion without rule, because no general rule can be formulated for the exercise of the powers in question. This has really little to do with the delegation of the power of making laws in the substantive sense of the word 'law': it merely means that the decision on the particular issues by some authorities is given the formal validity of a law, that is, that it has to be accepted by the courts as legal. I have already referred to this ambiguity of the term law which here again clouds the issue. What is often called the delegation of law-making power is not the delegation of the power to make rules—which might be politically unwise but not necessarily dangerous to individual liberty—but the delegation of the privilege that whatever the authority decides, within the sphere in which it is given such power, shall have the force of law and must, like an act of the legislature, be unquestioningly accepted by the courts.

17. The Limits of Administrative Discretion

This brings me to the crucial and in the last resort decisive problem of the limits of administrative discretion. The discussion of this problem has been obscured by a confusion between several meanings of the term 'discretion.' One of these meanings is closely connected with the unavoidable degree of uncertainty of the law which I have already discussed. This uncertainty makes it necessary that anybody who has to apply the law, whether as a judge or as an administrative officer, must be given a certain discretion in interpreting it. But authority to interpret a rule is not really discretion in the relevant sense:[10]

---

[10] See particularly Ernst Forsthoff, *Allgemeiner Teil*; also Paul Alexéef, "L'État—le droit—et le pouvoir discrétionnaire des autorités publiques", *Revue internationale de la théorie du droit*, vol. 3, 1928–29, pp. 195–219; and G. E. Treves, "Administrative Discretion and Judicial Control", *Modern Law Review*, vol. 10, 1947, pp. 276–91.

it is the task of discovering what is in the spirit of the whole system of valid rules of law, a task of finding what the imperfect wording or foresight of the legislator has not explicitly expressed but which should and could be expressed as a general rule. That the task of interpretation of the law is not really one of discretion in the strict sense is evident from the fact that it can and usually is made subject to review by another authority, a court or a higher court. Indeed, that the substance of the decision can be made subject to review by such an independent body which needs to know only the existing rules and the facts which can be supposed to have been known to the parties involved is probably the best criterion whether a decision is bound by rule and not left to the discretion of the authority. It is a question on which it is possible to argue whether a particular interpretation of the law is correct or incorrect; and though it may seem sometimes be impossible to arrive at an absolutely convincing conclusion, it is still a question which must be decided by an appeal to the rules and not by a simple act of the will.

An entirely different, and again for our purposes irrelevant meaning of discretion arises in the relation between principal and agent as it appears throughout the whole hierarchy of government, from the sovereign legislature through the heads of the administrative departments down to the lowest government official. Here the question is really what part of the authority of the government as a whole is delegated to a particular office or official. As this assignment of tasks is also to a large extent regulated by law, the question what a particular agency is entitled to do, i.e., what part of the powers of government it is allowed to exercise, is also often referred to as discretion. It is clear that not all the acts of government can be bound by fixed rules and that at every stage of the hierarchy considerable discretion must be granted. And so far as the government administers its own resources for the ends for which it has been given them, there are of course strong arguments in favor of giving it as much discretion as any business management would have had in similar circumstances. As A. V. Dicey once wrote, "in the management of its own business, properly so called, the government will be found to need that freedom of action, necessarily possessed by every private person in the management of his own personal concerns."[11] It may well be true that the jealousy of legislative bodies often hampers in these matters the discretion of the administrative agencies more than is good for the efficient performance of their tasks. If this may be unavoidable to some extent, and bureaucratic organizations may always have to be bound by rules to a much greater extent than business concerns, this also is due to reasons which have little to do with our problem: it is to be ascribed to the impossibility of devising automatic tests

[11] Albert Venn Dicey, "The Development of Administrative Law in England", *Law Quarterly Review*, vol. 31, 1915, p. 150.

of efficiency, such as money profits provide in commercial affairs.[12] There are indeed quite a number of reasons why in a large organization the action of individuals must to some extent be bound by rules and where in consequence the problem of discretion arises—in a form, however, which has no connection with our problem and should not be confused with it.

The problem of discretionary powers which is relevant in connection with the Rule of Law is not a problem of the limitations of the powers of particular agents of government but of the powers of government as a whole; or perhaps I should say it is a problem of the scope of administration in general. That the government must be able, for the efficient use of the means put at its disposal, to exercise a great deal of discretion is not to be disputed. But the important point is that the private citizen and his property are in this sense not an object of administration by the government, not a means to be used by it for its purposes in the way its agents think most expedient; that the way to induce the private citizen to use his resources for the common good is not to direct him but to make him obey general rules. It is only in so far as administration involves interference with this private sphere of the citizen that the question of discretion is relevant in this connection, and that the principle of the Rule of Law requires in effect that the administrative authorities should have no discretionary powers in this sense.

As I have mentioned before, it is only in its acts of coercion towards the private citizen that the powers of the executive must be strictly limited by law and that discretion must be precluded. In acting according to the rules of law, the administrative agencies will still often have to exercise discretion, in the same sense in which the judge exercises discretion in interpreting the rules of law. But this will be a discretion which can and must be controlled by the possibility of a review of the substance of the administrative decision by an independent court. This means that the decision must be deducible from the rules of law and from those circumstances to which the law refers and which can be known to private parties affected. What must *not* enter into the decision are the momentary ends of government, the particular values which it attaches to different concrete purposes, or its preferences between the effects of its actions on different people. We come here to the important distinction between law and policy and what I am arguing about is essentially the old but somewhat forgotten principle that coercion is admissible under the Rule of Law only in execution of a general rule but not in the service of a particular aim of policy. It is this distinction which in the last resort makes the difference between arbitrary government and the Rule of Law.

Although I have repeatedly spoken of the requirement that the substance of administrative decisions should be subject to review by independent courts,

---

[12] Cf. Ludwig von Mises, *Bureaucracy* (New Haven: Yale University Press, 1944).

I have perhaps not yet sufficiently brought out the distinction to which I refer here by the word 'substance.' Yet it is here where, as I have mentioned in my first lecture, our liberty depends on what at first may appear to the layman as a minor technicality, a fine legal point, in which he is not interested and which he rarely understands. But unless public opinion fully awakens to the importance of this point, and it becomes the recognized central issue in the struggle for the limitation of the powers of government, we shall not succeed in putting an effective curb on arbitrary power.

While in all countries which make any pretence to legality of their administration some kinds of tribunals are given power to pass on the legality of the actions of the administrative authorities, this power refers often and with increasing frequency merely to the question whether the agency in question had power to act on the issue in question and not to the question whether the particular decision which it made was required by the law. Or, to use the established legal terms, the powers of the reviewing court frequently extend only to the question whether the administrative was *intra vires* or *ultra vires* of the authority concerned, but not to the question whether the decision within these limits was such as follows from a pre-existing law.[13] We have seen how this distinction became necessary when administrative courts were first set up in the Continental countries in order to place some limits on the established functions of a highly developed bureaucracy, but no detailed rules had yet been formulated to guide its actions. In recent times, however, and in the countries of the common law even more than in those of codified law, it has become increasingly the rule that legislation explicitly limits judicial review to the question of whether an act was *ultra vires*, or not, and that it gives the administrative authorities full powers to act within these limits with complete freedom. It is here where administrative despotism begins.

Once more I must emphasize that this raises serious issues only in so far as the administrative acts involve coercion of private citizens, i.e., in so far as they interfere with their protected private sphere. But it makes no essential difference of course, whether this coercion takes the form of an individual being constrained by a specific order to perform or to omit a particular act, or whether a general law imposes such duties on all citizens, and administrative authority is given powers to allow exceptions. The two methods differ merely in form and the result is exactly the same. The decisive point is that in either case the same rules do not apply to all, that one person is permitted or forced to do things which another is not allowed or compelled to do, that an administrative authority has power to discriminate between people, not in accordance

---

[13] [*Intra vires* means 'within the powers'; *ultra vires* means 'beyond the powers.' Thus if an administrative action was judged to be legally authorized, it would be deemed *intra vires*; if it went beyond that authorization, it would be *ultra vires.*—Ed.]

with an objective rule but as it deems expedient in view of the results it wants to achieve.

18. Legislation and Policy

I must here say a few more words about the important distinction between legislation and policy, though this subject is so big that I can give it here no more than a passing glance. In current usage the distinction is often obscured, but there is good sense in it where the two concepts are deliberately contrasted. Of course, in a certain sense legislation always involves policy, namely long-run policy. Yet there is clearly a difference between laying down rules which in the whole are likely, in circumstances which cannot be foreseen, to benefit all affected, and the direction of activities to specific, concrete ends. What might be the most efficient action for the government to achieve a particular result at a particular moment, and what is the most beneficial rule to apply to such situations if people are to follow the same rule in all situations of the kind, are clearly different and often conflicting considerations. If the government is to be bound in its actions by formal rules so that what it will be required to do depends on the situations which the citizens create, it would be impossible for the government to determine the effects its actions would have on particular people. If, on the other hand, the government wants to achieve particular effects for particular people, it must not be bound by formal rules and cannot allow the people to make what use they can of such rules.

Policy, in the narrow sense in which it is contrasted with legislation, is the task of adjusting the means at the government's disposal to the ever changing needs of the day—but only those means which have been placed at its disposal, which in a free society do not normally include the private citizen and his property. Administration in the technical meaning of the word is the execution of policy in this sense: the decision of what is the most important and urgent task at the moment. All the services which the government offers to the citizen, from defense to road-building and sanitary policy, involve such day-to-day decisions of policy. But whether and how any individual citizen may be coerced is, under the Rule of Law, not a matter of policy in this sense but a matter of rule which must be decided by an authority which knows nothing about the momentary aims of government but which recognizes only the rules of the law.

The matter is further obscured by the fact that the word 'policy' is often used in connection with principles which the courts have to apply. If it is said that 'it is public policy' not to enforce contracts for immoral purposes or in restraint of trade, this does not refer to 'policy' in the specific sense in which it is different from legislation, but on the contrary to a principle which is recognized as a rule of the law.[14]

19. Fundamental Rights and the Protected Private Sphere

I come now to the last main element of the doctrine of the Rule of Law. I have already had to mention on several occasions that if the concept of coercion is to have a definite meaning, it is necessary that a definite sphere be circumscribed within which the individual can follow his own plans. He must know that so long as he keeps within the rules defining that sphere, nobody can prevent him from doing what he wants, and that he needs no permission from any authority for doing what anybody else is allowed to do under the same circumstances. It is in order to designate this free sphere of the individual that a list of fundamental individual rights is often specifically enumerated in Constitutions. Its most important elements are still indicated by classic formula of 'Life, Liberty, and Property', though of course liberty of speech, of religion, of the press and of assembly are also essential. I need here consider specifically only that one among these fundamental rights which in modern times has been so often questioned, especially by so-called progressives, and which yet, next to freedom from bodily constraint, is the most crucial: the right to private property. There can be no free sphere for the individual unless he knows which things in the material world he can control and how he can control them, unless he knows at any moment what means he can use for the ends which he pursues. Indeed, it is very doubtful whether there could be anything like what we call law at all without the institution of private property. If the law is to provide rules determining the relations between the individual private spheres, these rules must above all determine the boundaries of these spheres in the material world and say how these boundaries can be changed by the voluntary action of the individuals.

There is a great variety possible in the particular content of these rules and the classical formulae about the 'private property' and the 'freedom of contract' do not tell us much about what the content of these rules ought to be. The important point, however, is merely that they should be stated in terms of general rules, that the sphere in which the individual can follow his own will and the conditions and the manner in which he can be coerced shall be clearly known.

[14]All the instances which William A. Robson, *Justice and Administrative Law*, 3rd ed. (London: Stevens, 1951), pp. 410–11, quotes as illustrations of how "policy" enters "every department of English law" are significantly all instances of general rules and not of policy in the specific sense in which it is commonly said that administration is guided by policy.

The recognition of such a private sphere can, of course, not mean that it must be sacrosanct under all circumstances, and the precise character of the rules which determine when it can be infringed are perhaps as important as its delimitation. We have seen that under the Rule of Law, in order that the individual should be able to plan his own affairs successfully, he should be in a position to predict from the circumstance which he can be presumed to know or foresee what we will be allowed to do and what not. This means that as a general rule circumstances which are beyond his field of vision must not be made a ground for his coercion. We must recognize, however, that there will occur exceptional circumstances in which it would be in the highest interest of the Community that particular individuals should be made to do things as a result of events which they do not know and in a manner for which no rule provides. Natural catastrophes, war or other sudden dangers which require concerted action directed by those who know the facts, do occur and have to be met. If in ordinary circumstances the individual probably contributes most to the common welfare if he attends to his own affairs, we cannot *always* leave it to him to decide whether some common purpose is not more important than his particular concern. There are various considerations which for one reason or another may not be reflected in the price relations which normally help the individual to adjust his actions to events of which he may know nothing. And the speed of action required may on occasions demand that even the private citizen must place himself under the command of authority.

If, however, for everyday purposes, we are to rely on the free decisions of the individuals, it is important that such interferences with their private sphere should be exceptional and that those who have to submit to them are not made to suffer for the disappointment of their legitimate expectations. While there must be guardians of the common interest who can exercise emergency powers, it is essential that these powers be kept in check by an independent authority. The devices which have been developed for this purpose and which are closely connected are the limitations of such powers to specific purposes (such as the law of eminent domain) and particular conditions (such as the American rule of 'clear and present danger'), and the provision that the full costs to the individual of such interference are borne by the community, or, in other words, that full compensation for every infringement of the rights of private property or other legally acquired rights is given. There is in such instances no justification for demanding a sacrifice from the particular individual, and indeed every case for limiting such interference to instances where the social gain is so large as to leave an ample margin for generous compensation. It is evidently desirable that in all such instances an independent tribunal should have to decide on general abstract principles not only about the legitimacy of the interference but also about the appropriate compensation—not only in order to protect the freedom of the individual but hardly less in order to force the administrative agency to count all the costs, since it is an inherent tendency of all expert administration to overestimate the importance of its immediate objectives and to pay inadequate attention to the more indirect damages it causes.

What all this amounts to, then, is that the Rule of Law requires that administrative discretion in coercive action (i.e., in interfering with the person and property of the private citizen) must always be subject to review by an independent court which is not an instrument of, or even privy to, the aims of current governmental policy; that its review must in all such instances extend to the substance of the administrative act and not merely to the question whether it was *infra* or *ultra vires*; and that, if such a court finds that the rights of private citizens have been infringed, it will assess damages just as if the right of this person had been violated by another private citizen. This, in addition to the familiar requirements of generality, equality, and certainty of the law is really the crux of the matter, the decisive point on which it depends whether the Rule of Law prevails or not.

Lecture IV
The Decline of the Rule of Law

> Necessity is the plea for every infringement of human freedom. It is the argument of tyrants; it is the creed of slaves. —William Pitt[1]

20. A Minimum Program for Liberty

The most obvious objection against the rôle as the chief safeguard of individual freedom which I have assigned to the Rule of Law is that it is insufficient to achieve that purpose. There is some justification for this. The Rule of Law gives us only a necessary and not a sufficient condition of individual freedom: within the scope that it leaves for legislation and administration these might still become very irksome and harmful. But it still seems to me not only an essential minimum condition of freedom but in practice also to secure what is most important. In consequence, all laws and institutions which offend against the ideal of the Rule of Law are objectionable in principle, while any law which conforms to it will have to be judged on its individual merits. Such a law may still be stupid or harmful, but the grounds on which it can be opposed must be its specific effects, not that it infringes some general principle, such as non-intervention, laissez-faire, or the like. Indeed the concept of the Rule of Law seems to me to provide the only sensible meaning of the concept of 'intervention' for which the demand for non-intervention is justified. None of those who opposed state intervention of course meant to argue that the state should do nothing at all: but whenever the state acts it 'interferes' with something. What the principle of non-interference really means is that the state should not intrude into a private sphere of the citizen which is clearly defined by general rules.[2] I believe this is also what the more serious defenders of *'laissez-faire'* meant by that phrase.

The field which our principle still leaves open for possible state action is enormous. Anything which can be achieved by laying down and enforcing general rules, equally applicable to all people, is in principle admissible under it. This includes in particular all the regulations of production setting up requirements concerning safety, health, or the quality of the product. It provides no ground for objecting against the state engaging in production and commerce so long as the state does not prevent private people from also doing what it does. And the principle even allows general prohibitions of the pro-

---

[1] William Pitt in the House of Commons, 18 November 1783.

[2] Cf. Ludwig von Mises, *Kritik des Interventionismus: Untersuchungen zur Wirtschaftspolitik und Wirtschaftsideologie der Gegenwart* (Jena: G. Fischer, 1929), pp. 5 *et seq.* [See now Ludwig von Mises, *A Critique of Interventionism*, translated by Hans Sennholz (New Rochelle, NY: Arlington House, 1977), pp. 19 *et. seq.*—Ed.]

duction or use of certain articles including such absurd regulations as luxury laws, and it might be used to enforce a high degree of uniformity in manners and behaviour so long as these rules were really general and nobody had powers to grant exceptions. It would thus in principle even be possible, while strictly conforming to the requirements of the Rule of Law, to enforce something like religious conformity—certainly one of the most objectionable forms of oppression to any freedom-loving person.

Yet while a great deal of silly and harmful legislation would still be possible under the Rule of Law, it is at least not *likely* that oppressive legislation would be passed under it. The requirement that the laws must be equally applicable to all, that nobody must have the power of dispensing from them, makes this highly improbable. I will admit that some religious fanatics might wish to enforce general rules which others would feel as very severe restrictions of their liberty. But there are at least few rational grounds on which men could wish to impose upon all such restrictions—and where it might be attempted, as in the case of the prohibition of alcoholic drinks and the like, such restrictions are not likely to remain long effective if a substantial number of people regard them as oppressive.

21. What Can Not Be Done Under the Rule of Law

Why should then a principle which leaves such a wide field open to the activities of the state, and under which there seems to be scope for an almost infinite variety of experimentation and improvement, have come under the most persistent attack and in consequence have been gradually abandoned? The answer is, that it does prevent certain kinds of state activity and in particular the very kind which under the influence of socialistic doctrines has become most popular during the last hundred years. The principle of the Rule of Law is most intimately connected with the recognition of private property, especially private property in the means of production, which socialism denies; and it is incompatible with that central direction of economic activity, today known as 'economic planning', which socialism wants to substitute for the system of private property and the market.

The incompatibility of the two conceptions of the order of society is really so obvious that the founders of socialism had little doubt about it, though their present followers like to deny it. With individuals who are by nature very different in their individual capacities, inclinations and temperament, the application of equal rules must have very unequal effects on their position. If you want to make people equal who in many respects are very unequal you must treat them differently. If you wish to see people rewarded not according to the value which their product has to society, but according to their subjective merit, you must give somebody power to determine that merit and to assign a reward accordingly. If you wish the action of the state on the individuals to produce specific results for that and other particular individuals, you cannot let the action of the state be uniquely determined by abstract rules but must allow it to adjust its action to the particular circumstances of time and place, to be guided by what to the acting authority appears expedient in the light of its knowledge and of the particular aims it pursues at the moment.

It is impossible to decide what and how much is to be produced without at the same time deciding how the different productive forces are to be used, which means, above all, without deciding who is to do what. This shows itself at once when the government undertakes to control quantities or prices of commodities. In order to maintain a price different from the market price it is necessary to decide who is to be allowed to buy or to sell at the price so fixed. It is equally impossible to make sure that a certain quantity of a commodity is produced without deciding who is to produce it and who not. This appears already in the simplest instances where licensing is used to adjust supplies to 'local needs' or to some similar consideration. The 'needs' might, perhaps, be determined according to some objective criterion, though even this is doubtful in most cases. But *who* is to supply these needs can be decided only by arbitrary discrimination.

The direction of economic activity thus necessarily involves discrimination between persons, the creation of monopoly and privilege, while the aim of the Rule of Law is the abolition of all privilege, be it in favor of the strong or of the weak. And it is no less fatal to freedom if exemption from general legal rules is granted to the weak than when it is granted to the strong. Once the door is opened to differentiation on the ground of deserts or needs, it will be arbitrary will instead of objective rule which will govern men.

Apart from the instances where outright direction of economic activity is attempted, administrative expediency is often made the excuse for conferring exclusive and discretionary powers on governmental agencies where the nature of the activities would not require it. This applies particularly to such fields as education and the various social services where there is probably much to be said for the state helping in the organization and finance of such services, but where the dangers arise from the tendency of most states to assume exclusive powers and to make the participation in its organizations compulsory. It is of course not to be denied that this frequently offers administrative advantages and that it is also often the quickest and in this sense most effective way of achieving the immediately perceived goal. It should be remembered, however, that in thus excluding a whole field from the scope of spontaneous growth, the immediate advantage may in the long run be bought at a very high price: it may be true that, e.g., by instituting a single, unified and compulsory system of health insurance we shall probably achieve our present goals more quickly than by any other means; but we also prevent the gradual development of new types of solutions for the problem which, as the American example shows, competitive experimentation is likely sooner or later to produce.

I must touch here briefly upon another point which I have no time to de-velop at any length: it might be said, in apparent objection to the distinction I have drawn, that *all* state activity involves coercion, if in no other form at least through the method of financing it. And as I have admitted that in much of its activities the administration cannot effectively be bound by rules, it would seem that coercion must inevitably be used in connection with discretionary powers. This is in a way true enough, yet not in a sense which conflicts with the general principle. If we agree to contribute to a common pool according to a uniform rule and then instruct an agent to spend the money as he thinks expedient for a specified purpose, this does not restrict our freedom. There are in fact few fields where administrative coercion can be so strictly bound by legal rules as is true of taxation. Whether the actual principles of taxation now widely accepted conform to the principle of equality before the law is a different question. Per-sonally I have grave doubts whether the principle of progressive or graduated income taxation in particular, which always involves that people will receive unequal pay for equal work, can be reconciled with the ideal of equality before the law. But this is another matter into which I must not enter here.

22. The Socialist Revolt against the Rule of Law

I have already referred to the fact that socialists early recognized that to treat un-equal people equally must result in inequality, and that at least since the French Revolution they have persistently opposed the demand for material equality to the ideal of purely 'formal' equality before the law. It became in the course of the nineteenth century one of the standard objections to the capitalist system and was given its classical expression in the famous gibe of Anatole France about "la majestueuse égalité des lois, qui interdit au riche comme au pauvre de coucher sous les ponts, de mendier dans les rues et de voler du pain."[3]

There are few phrases which have been so often unthinkingly repeated by well-meaning people without realizing that they were deriding the foundations of all impersonal justice.

These ideas were systematically developed by the legal theorists of socialism. One of the clearest statements is to be found in the writings of the Austrian lawyer Anton Menger (the brother of the famous economist Carl Menger):

> By treating in a perfectly equal manner all citizens regardless of their per-sonal qualities and economic position, and by allowing unlimited competi-

---

[3]Anatole France, *Le Lys rouge* (Paris: Calmann-Lévy, 1894), pp. 117–18. A. France was of course a close friend and associate of the leading French socialists of his time such as Guesde, Laurès and Leon Blum. ["The majestic equality of the law that forbids the rich as well as the poor to sleep under bridges, to beg in the streets, and to steal bread."—Ed.]

tion between them, it came about that the production of goods was increased without limit; but the poor and weak had only a small share in that output. The new economic and social legislation therefore attempts to protect the weak against the strong and to secure for them a moderate share in the good things of life. This is because today *it is understood that there is no greater injustice than to treat as equal what in fact is unequal!*[4]

The culmination of this development came with the rise of a school of Marxist lawyers in communist Russia who clearly recognized what Jeremy Bentham had already known, that "property and law are born and must die together",[5] and who drew the consistent conclusion that with the disappearance of private property, law and justice as we know them must also disappear. Pashukanis, at one time the leader of this school, disposed of the ideal of the Rule of Law as a mere mirage very convenient for the bourgeois.[6] According to him the very ideal of justice as we know it, is derived from the exchange relations and apart from them has no meaning:[7] "To the administrative technical direction by subordination to a general economic plan corresponds the method of direct, technologically determined direction in the shape of programs for production and distribution. The gradual victory of this tendency means the gradual extinction of law as such."[8] In short, ". . . as, in a socialist community, there was no scope for autonomous private legal relations, but only for regulation in the interest of the community, all law was converted into administration; all fixed rules into discretion and utility."[9]

Though Pashukanis later become a victim of one of the periodic changes in official doctrines,[10] he was by no means alone in this view but merely the most outspoken representative of a school which consistently drew the conclu-

[4] Anton Menger, *Das bürgerliche Recht und die besitzlosen Volksklassen* [1890], 3rd ed. (Tübingen: H. Laupp, 1904), p. 30. Italics not in the original.

[5] Jeremy Bentham, "Principles of the Civil Code", in *The Works of Jeremy Bentham, Vol. 1, Part 2,* ed. John Bowring (Edinburgh: William Tait, 1838) p. 309. [In the Cairo lectures, this note and note 6 were switched.—Ed.]

[6] Evgenii Bronislavovich Pashukanis, *Allgemeine Rechtslehre und Marxismus: Versuch einer Kritik der juristischen Grundbegriffe*, translated from the second Russian edition by Edith Hajós (Vienna: Verlag für Literatur und Politik, 1929), p. 127. An English translation of this and of a later work by Pashukanis has been published in *Soviet Legal Philosophy*, translated by Hugh Webster Badd, introduction by John Newbold Hazard (Cambridge, MA: Harvard University Press, 1951).

[7] Pashukanis, *Allgemeine Rechtslehre und Marxismus*, p. 143.

[8] Ibid., p. 117.

[9] This summary of Pashukanis's argument is taken from Wolfgang Gaston Friedmann, *Law and Social Change in Contemporary Britain* (London: Stevens and Sons, 1951), p. 154.

[10] On Pashukanis's fate, Roscoe Pound, *Administrative Law: Its Growth, Procedure, and Significance* (Pittsburgh: University of Pittsburg Press, 1942), p. 127 observes: "The professor is not with us now. With the setting up of a plan by the present government in Russia, a change of doctrine was called for and he did not move fast enough in his teaching to conform to the doctrinal exigencies

sions inherent in socialism. P. J. Stuchka, the President of the Soviet Supreme Court, similarly explained in 1927 in an official handbook of civil law that: "Communism means not the victory of socialist law, but the victory of socialism over any law, since with the abolition of classes with antagonistic interests, law will disappear altogether."[11]

Elsewhere things moved of course less fast, but the tendencies inherent in socialism made themselves no less clearly felt. There are many reasons why the instance of Germany, where the reversal of the trend commenced and was carried furthest till the Russians took over, is the most interesting. It would deserve much closer attention than I can give it here or than it usually receives in foreign countries. We have seen how the completion of the machinery of the *Rechtsstaat* coincided with a general change of opinion in the direction of state socialism. It began to affect the law early and in many directions. As early as 1893 a famous criminologist noted that "the rising socialist generation, which emphasizes the common interests more than their predecessors and for whose ears the word 'freedom' has an archaic sound, is shaking the foundations."[12]

By the turn of the century it had become accepted doctrine that the individualist *Rechtsstaat* was a thing of the past, "vanquished by the creative powers of national and social ideas",[13] or, as another student of administrative law described the process in retrospect:

> We have returned to the principles of the police state to such an extent that we again recognize the idea of a *Kulturstaat*. The only difference is in the means. On the basis of laws the modern state permits itself everything, much more than the police state did. Thus, in the course of the nineteenth century, the term *Rechtsstaat* was given a new meaning. We understand by it a state whose whole activity takes place on the basis of laws and in legal form. On the purpose of the state and the limits of its competence the term *Rechtsstaat* in its present-day meaning says nothing.[14]

---

of the new order. If there had been law instead of only administrative orders it might have been possible for him to lose his job without losing his life."

[11] Quoted by Vladmir Gsovski, *Soviet Civil Law: Private Rights and Their Background Under the Soviet Regime; Comparative Survey and Translation of the Civil Code, Code of Domestic Relations, Judiciary Act, Code of Civil Procedures, Laws on Nationality, Corporations, Patents, Copyright, Collective Farms, Labor, and Related Laws* (Ann Arbor: University of Michigan Law School, 1948–49), vol. 1, p. 170, from Peter Ivanovitch Stuchka, *Encyclopedia of State and Law [Entsiklopediia gosudarstva I prava—Ed.]* (Moscow: Izd-vo Kommunisticheskoi Akademii, 1925–1927), p. 1593.

[12] Franz von Liszt, *1892 bis 1904*, vol. 2 of *Strafrechtliche Aufsätze und Vorträge* (Berlin: J. Guttentag, 1905), p. 60.

[13] Richard Thoma, "Rechtsstaatsidee und Verwaltungstrechtswissenschaft", *Jahrbuch des offentlichen Rechts der Gegenwart*, vol. 4, 1910, p. 199.

[14] Edmund Bernatzik, *Die Ausgestaltung des Nationalgefühls im 19. Jahrhundert. Rechtsstaat und Kulturstaat: Zwei Vorträge gehalten in der Vereinigung für staatswissenschaftliche Fortbildung in Coln im April 1912*

He emphasizes that this is a result of the great movement which in the 1870's rose against Liberalism.[15]

This process which had gone very far even under the empire was greatly accelerated under the Weimar Republic. Its character and its causes were then already clearly recognized by some observers. In a detailed study of the effects of the efforts "to realize the socialist state, the opposite of the *Rechtsstaat*",[16] a German lawyer in 1930 pointed out that the doctrinal developments had already removed all obstacles to the final disappearance of the *Rechtsstaat* ideal and opened the doors to the victory and sole dominance of the fascist and bolshevist will of the state.[17] This is of course exactly what happened in Germany three years later. But it must be added that not only the Germans in general but also the German socialists have in some measure learned the dreadful lesson of twenty-two years of arbitrary totalitarian power. It is very significant that the revered dean of socialist philosophers of law, the late Gustav Radbruch, in one of his last publications wrote that: "though democracy is certainly a praiseworthy value, the *Rechtsstaat* is like the daily bread, like the water we drink and the air we breathe; and the greatest merit of democracy is that it alone is adapted to preserve the *Rechtsstaat*."[18]

That in fact democracy does not necessarily or invariably do so is only too clear from Radbruch's own exposition of the evolution in Germany. It would probably be truer to put it the other way round and to say that democracy will not exist long unless it preserves the Rule of Law.[19]

I can only refer in passing to the very similar developments which have taken place in France. I wish I had time at least briefly to summarize the alarming description which Professor George Ripert has given, in a book under that title, of the *Déclin de droit*[20] in that country or of the similar account which we find in Professor Paul Roubier's *Theorie générale du droit*.[21] I must confine myself to quoting some of Professor Ripert's conclusions. He finds that,

---

(Hannover: Helwing, 1912), p. 56. Compare also the same author's "Polizei und Kulturpflege", in *Systematische Rechtswissenschaft*, part 2, sec. 8 of *Die Kultur der Gegenwart*, edited by Paul Hinneberg (Berlin: Teubner, 1906), pp. 387–426.

[15] Bernatzik, *Die Ausgestaltung des Nationalgefühls im 19. Jahrhundert* , p. 57.

[16] Friedrich Darmstaedter, *Die Grenzen der Wirksamkeit des Rechtsstaates: Eine Untersuchung zur gegenwärtigen Krise des liberalen Staatsgedankens* (Heidelberg: Carl Winter, 1930), p. 268.

[17] Ibid., p. 84.

[18] Gustav Radbruch, *Rechtsphilosophie*, 4th ed. (Stuttgart: K. F. Koehler, 1950), p. 357.

[19] See Carel Henrik Frederik Polak, *Ordening en Rechtsstaat* (Zwolle: W. E. J. Tjeenk Willenk, 1951); and the essays by Werner Kägi and Hans Huber in *Demokratie und Rechtsstaat: Festgabe zum 60. Geburtstag von Zaccaria Giacometti* (Zürich: Polygraphischer Verlag, 1953).

[20] Georges Ripert, *Le Déclin du droit* (Paris: Pichon and Durand-Auzias, 1949). ['The Decline of the Law.' Hayek used the phrase as the title of chapter 16 of *The Constitution of Liberty*.—Ed.]

[21] Paul Roubier, *Théorie générale du droit: Histoire des doctrines juridiques et philosophie des valeurs sociales* (Paris: Recueil Sirey, 1946).

"Le jour où l'État entreprit de diriger l'économie, la servitude devint autrement étroite."[22] The reason is that, "Si la loi se borne à poser un principe en laissant à un règlement administratif le soin de donner les règles d'application, elle consacre une véritable abdication de pouvoir et le législateur livre les sujets de droit aux décisions de l'Administration. Une telle politique est devenue de pratique habituelle dans la direction de l'économie."[23] And he finds that, as is true with other countries, the responsibility for this development rests largely with the jurists:

> Il nous faut tout d'abord faire le procès des juristes. Ce sont eux qui depuis un demi-siècle ont affaibli la notion de droit individuel sans avoir conscience qu'ils livraient ainsi ces droits à la toute puissance de l'État politique. Les uns étaient désireux de se classer parmi les hommes de progrès. Les autres croyaient retrouver une doctrine traditionnelle étouffée par l'individualisme libéral du XIX siècle. Les hommes de science ont souvent une certaine candeur qui ne leur permet pas d'apercevoir les conséquences pratiques que d'autres tireront de leurs doctrines désintéressées.[24]

23. English Socialist Jurisprudence

While however, in spite of all this, the magic of the never fully achieved *Rechtsstaat* ideal was such in most Continental countries that even when it was most completely perverted under the totalitarian rules, the name was still sometimes used as a means of disguising the reality, the country where the Rule of Law has come under the most direct attack has been the country of its origin. For a long time it had, in Great Britain, been a process of gradual undermining of the traditional ideal of which few people were aware. As late

[22] Ripert, *Le Déclin du droit*, p. 84. ["The day that the State decided to manage the economy, servitude became much more widespread."—Ed.]

[23] Ibid., p. 158. ["If the law limits itself to the statement of principles, and the rules or decisions regarding its application are left to the administration, it effectively sanctions the abdication of power and legislators turn the subjects over to the decisions of the administration. Such a political setup became commonplace in the management of the economy."—Ed.]

[24] Ibid., p. 192. ["Above all, we must put the blame on the jurists. It was they who for half a century undermined the conception of individual rights without being aware that they thereby delivered these rights to the omnipotence of the political state. Some of them wished to prove themselves progressive, while others believed that they were rediscovering traditional doctrine which the liberal individualism of the nineteenth century had obliterated. Scholars often show a certain single-mindedness which prevents them from seeing the practical conclusions which others will draw from their disinterested doctrines." This is Hayek's own translation of the passage; see F. A. Hayek, *The Constitution of Liberty*, ed. Ronald Hamowy, vol. 17 (2011) of *The Collected Works of F. A. Hayek* (Chicago: University of Chicago Press; London: Routledge), pp. 363–64.—Ed.]

as 1929 the Rule of Law could still be described as "perhaps the political principle nearest the heart of England."[25] But as early as 1915 A. V. Dicey observed, in a new Introduction to the last edition of his book on the *Law of the Constitution* which he himself edited, that "the ancient veneration for the rule of law has in England suffered during the last thirty years a marked decline."[26] During the next twenty-five years this process continued at an accelerating rate, yet still largely in a haphazard way and unobserved by the general public until at last no less a person than the then Lord Chief Justice of England uttered a strong protest. Lord Hewart's book *The New Despotism* in 1929 at last forced the issue into the open.[27] It caused immense indignation among the so-called progressives and was thoroughly abused as a reactionary pamphlet.[28] But it led to the appointment by the Lord Chancellor of a "Committee on Ministers' Powers", whose Report,[29] however, while mildly reasserting A. V. Dicey's doctrines, tended on the whole to minimize the dangers. The inquiry turned largely on the question of delegation which, as we have seen, is only indirectly connected with the main problem, in so far as it is not the rule-making power which is delegated but as the reason for delegation is that in fact no general rules are or can be laid down to bind the executive agencies and it is intended to give them power to act in each particular case as expediency indicates. This comes out only occasionally in the Report itself as when it gives

[25] Alfred Cobban, *Edmund Burke and the Revolt against the Eighteenth Century* (London: G. Allen and Unwin, 1929), p. 41.

[26] A. V. Dicey, *Introduction to the Study of the Law of the Constitution*, 8th ed. (London: Macmillan, 1915), p. xxxviii.

[27] Gordon Hewart, Baron Hewart, *The New Despotism* (London: Ernest Benn Ltd., 1929).

[28] Characteristic for the treatment which this serious warning received even in the United States are the following sentences Professor Felix Frankfurter (now a Judge at the U.S. Supreme Court) published in 1938: "As late as 1929 Lord Hewart attempted to give fresh life to the moribund unrealities of Dicey by garnishing them with alarm. Unfortunately, the eloquent journalism of this book carried the imprimatur of the Lord Chief Justice. His extravagant charges demanded authoritative disposition and they received it" (Foreword to "Current Developments in Administrative Law", *Yale Law Journal*, vol. 47, 1938, p. 517). Few people who have watched the further development in England will now doubt the justice of Lord Hewart's apprehensions. Recently *The Economist* ("What Is the Public Interest?", June 19, 1954, p. 952) wrote: "The 'new despotism', in short, is not an exaggeration, it is a reality. It is a despotism that is practised by the most conscientious, incorruptible and industrious tyrants that the world has ever seen." [In his book *The New Despotism*, Lord Chief Justice Hewart warned about the dangers of the delegation of powers by Parliament to administrative tribunals that then would act independently of Parliament's authority.—Ed.]

[29] Committee on Ministers' Powers, *Report Presented by the Lord High Chancellor to Parliament by Command of His Majesty, April 1932*, chaired from 30 October 1929 to 2 May 1931 by the Rt. Hon. The Earl of Donoughmore. Cmd. 4060 (London: His Majesty's Stationary Office, 1932); see also Committee on Ministers' Powers, *Memoranda Submitted by Government Departments in Reply to Questionnaire of November 1929 and Minutes of Evidence* (London: His Majesty's Stationary Office, 1932).

it as one of the reasons for delegation that "many of the laws affect people's lives so closely that elasticity is essential."[30]

It was however in the attacks on this Report that a whole school of socialist lawyers emerged, almost all colleagues or pupils of the late Professor Harold Laski (who himself had been a member of the Committee). The efforts of this school, which has gained influence far beyond England and beyond professed socialists, and whose views are now often represented as the modern view of the Anglo-Saxon world on these matters, deserve close attention. The attack was opened by two review articles on the Report and the documents on which it was based by Mr. (now Sir Ivor) Jennings.[31] In these he argued that the doctrine of the Rule of Law in the sense in which it was used in the Report, that is, meaning "equality before the law, the ordinary law of the land, administered by the ordinary courts . . . taken literally . . . is just nonsense."[32] In his view, this rule of law "is either common to all nations or does not exist."[33] While he admits that "the fixity and certainty of the law have been part of the English tradition for centuries" he evidently was impatient that this tradition was "but reluctantly breaking down."[34] And all his irony was directed against the belief shared "by most of the members of the Committee, and most of the witnesses . . . that there was a clear distinction between the functions of a judge and the functions of an administrator."[35]

In only slightly modified form these views then entered into a widely used textbook by the same author.[36] Here it is denied that "the rule of law and

---

[30]Committee on Ministers' Powers, *Report*, p. 23.

[31]Sir William Ivor Jennings, "The Report on Ministers' Powers", *Public Administration* (London), vol. 10, 1932, pp. 333–51, and his book review, "Official Ministers' Powers", vol. 11, 1933, pp. 109–14.

[32]Ibid., vol. 10, p. 342.

[33]Ibid., p. 343.

[34]Ibid., p. 345.

[35]Ibid., p. 345. [This quotation actually appears in Jennings's review "Official Ministers' Powers", p. 111.—Ed.]

[36]Sir William Ivor Jennings, *The Law and the Constitution*, 4th ed. (London: University of London Press, 1952). The book is dedicated to Harold Laski. After these lectures were written I have seen with great pleasure a new book by Sir Ivor Jennings, *The Queen's Government* (London: Penguin Books, 1954), which begins and ends with sections in praise of the Rule of Law and even gives a somewhat idealized picture of the extent to which it actually prevails in England at the present day. The statement (p. 152) that "there is nowhere in the law a general power of *règlementation*—a word for the making of general rules in execution of the laws which has to be put into French because the idea itself does not exist in Britain" would probably have been more appropriate in the nineteenth century than it is today. [In the original Cairo lectures, the quotation from Jennings was rendered, "There is now here in the law a general power of *règlementation* . . ." The change from "nowhere" to "now here" was a mistake that reversed the meaning of Jennings's sentence.—Ed.]

discretionary powers are contradictory",[37] or that there is any opposition "between 'regular law' and 'administrative powers.'"[38] In the sense in which Dicey had interpreted the principle to mean that public authorities ought not to have wide discretionary powers, the Rule of Law is said to be "a rule of action for Whigs and may be ignored by others."[39] But at least Mr. Jennings then recognizes that "to a constitutional lawyer of 1870, or even 1880, it might have seemed that the British Constitution was essentially based on the individualist rule of law, and that the British State was the *Rechtsstaat* of individualist political and legal theory."[40] "The Constitution frowned on 'discretionary' powers, unless they were exercised by judges. When Dicey said that 'Englishmen are ruled by the law and the law alone' he meant that Englishmen 'are ruled by judges, and by judges alone.' That would have been an exaggeration, but it was good individualism."[41]

In some ways even more alarming because of the apparent moderation of the argument which nevertheless in effect advocates the complete abandonment of the basic principles of the Rule of Law is the widely used treatise of Professor W. A. Robson.[42] He combines a commendable zeal for regularizing the chaotic state of the control over administrative action with a view about the tasks of administrative tribunals which would make them completely ineffective as protectors of individual liberty. The work indeed aims mainly at describing and accelerating that "break-away from that Rule of Law which the late Professor A. V. Dicey regarded as an essential feature of the English Constitutional System."[43] It commences with a systematic attack on what the author calls "the legendary separation of powers", "that antique and rickety chariot."[44] To Professor Robson the whole distinction between law and policy is "utterly false"[45] and the traditional conception that the judge is not concerned with governmental ends but with the administration of justice, a matter for ridicule.[46] In fact he regards it as one of the main advantages of separate administrative tribunals that such a tribunal "can enforce a policy unhampered by rules of law and judicial precedents. . . . Of all the characteristics of administrative law, none is more advantageous, when rightly used for the public good, than the power of the tribunal to decide the cases coming

---

[37] Jennings, *Law and the Constitution*, p. 54.

[38] Ibid,. p. 291.

[39] Ibid., p. 292.

[40] Ibid., p. 294.

[41] Ibid., p. 294.

[42] William A. Robson, *Justice and Administrative Law*, 3rd ed. (London: Stevens, 1951).

[43] Ibid., p. xi.

[44] Ibid., p. 16.

[45] Ibid., p. 433

[46] Ibid., p. 506. [No such distinction is made on p. 506. Hayek may have had in mind the discussion in the section titled "Popular Notions of the Judicial Process" that begins on p. 40.—Ed.]

before it with the avowed object of furthering a policy of social improvement in some particular field; and of adapting their attitude towards the controversy so as to fit the needs of that policy."[47]

Minor lights of the same group have carried these views even further. In an essay on "The Planned State and the Rule of Law" Professor W. Friedmann[48] first undertakes, in the approved fashion of all who are out to destroy traditional liberties, to "redefine" the Rule of Law.[49] It emerges from that mauling at "whatever parliament as the supreme lawgiver makes it."[50] This, of course, enables Professor Friedmann to "assert with confidence that the incompatibility of planning with the rule of law is a myth sustainable only by prejudice or ignorance."[51] The views of this author are now also spread in a widely used textbook in which the views which he opposes are by misquotation distorted beyond recognition.[52] Can one be surprised that yet another member of this group[53] has seriously replied to the rhetorical question I had asked in *The Road to Serfdom*, whether, assuming that Hitler had obtained his unlimited powers in a constitutional manner, the Rule of Law would still have prevailed in Nazi Germany: "The answer is Yes; the majority would be right: the Rule of Law would be in operation, *if* the majority *voted* him into power. The majority might be unwise, and it might be wicked, but the Rule of Law would prevail. For in a democracy right is what the majority makes it to be."[54]

---

[47] Ibid., pp. 572–73.

[48] Wolfgang Gaston Friedmann, *The Planned State and the Rule of Law* (Melbourne: Melbourne University Press, 1948), reprinted in *Law and Social Change in Contemporary Britain* (London: Stevens and Sons, 1951), pp. 277–310. References will be to that reprint.

[49] Ibid., p. 281: "Living as we do in a planned society, we have to accept it for purposes of legal analysis, and in particular, for the redefinition of the rule of law."

[50] Ibid., p. 284.

[51] Ibid., p. 310.

[52] Wolfgang Gaston Friedmann, *Legal Theory*, 2nd ed. (London: Stevens, 1949). Quoting on p. 458 the definition of the rule of law from my *Road to Serfdom*, this lawyer, whom one must presume to be capable of exact quotation, completely alters five out of forty-six words with a corresponding alteration in the punctuation. [Friedmann: "Government in all its actions is bound by rules fixed and announced beforehand—rules which make it possible to foresee with fair certainty which authority will use its concise powers in giving considerations and to plan one's individual affairs on the basis of this knowledge." Hayek: "Government in all its actions is bound by rules fixed and announced beforehand—rules which make it possible to foresee with fair certainty how the authority will use its coercive powers in given circumstances and to plan one's individual affairs on the basis of this knowledge." See Hayek, *The Road to Serfdom: Texts and Documents*, ed. Bruce Caldwell, vol. 2 (2007) of *The Collected Works of F. A. Hayek*, p. 112. Though five words were altered, there does not seem to be any change in punctuation.—Ed.]

[53] For the characterization of Harold Laski, Ivor Jennings, William A. Robson and Herman Finer as members of the same group see William Ivor Jennings, "Administrative Law and Administrative Jurisdiction", *Journal of Comparative Legislation and International Law*, 3rd series, vol. 20, 1938, p. 103.

[54] Herman Finer, *The Road to Reaction* (Boston: Little, Brown, 1945), p. 60.

Here of course we have the fatal confusion of our time expressed in the most flagrant form.

24. The Decline of the Rule of Law in America

It might be expected that in the United States, where the movement towards socialism has in practice made so much less progress, the tendencies I have been describing should also be less advanced. This, however, is not the case. Contrary to what one would expect, it is here where in the field of administration the theoreticians of law have exercised the greatest influence and where, little noticed by public or legislatures, they have built up a conception of administrative law which has already led very far away from the ideal of the Rule of Law. This has happened in a comparatively short time and has meant a change of extraordinary magnitude, since in nineteenth-century America at least some of the checks upon administrative discretion had been more stringent and effective than in perhaps any other country. The developments which have led away from this position are part of the same intellectual movement which prepared the New Deal, and probably nowhere else has, in the ideological field, the conflict between the true liberals and those socialists who in the United States call themselves liberals, been so clearly on the issues which concern us here as in that country.

The peculiar character of the American discussion was determined by the far-reaching powers which, under the Federal Constitution and most of the state constitutions, the courts had acquired over administrative and even legislative action. The reaction against this commenced even before the first World War and as an issue of practical politics reached its first high point with Senator La Follette's campaign for the Presidency which made the curbing of the authority of the courts one of the chief issues of the campaign. Ever since it has been the so-called progressives or radicals who in the United States have become the advocates of wide administrative discretion and the enemies of a strict limitation of government by law.

As early as 1921 one of the most eminent American students of law, Dean Roscoe Pound of Harvard University, could speak of "a tendency away from courts and law and a reversion to justice without law in the form of revival of executive and even of legislative justice and reliance upon arbitrary governmental power",[55] a tendency which he justly compared with English developments in the sixteenth century. This movement received strong support from a whole school of legal theorists. The late 1920's and the early 1930's saw a flood of publications of this kind which has exercised a profound influence on legislative and judicial developments. I can here mention only one or two of

---

[55] Roscoe Pound, *The Spirit of the Common Law* (Boston: Marshall Jones, 1921), p. 72.

the most characteristic and influential works of that literature. Among those who led the frontal attack on the American tradition of a *Government of Law and Not of Men* the most prolific writer was Professor Charles G. Haines who, in an essay under that title not only treated the whole ideal as an "illusion"[56] but seriously pleaded that the American people, in direct conflict to the ideal of the makers of the Constitution, should "establish governments on a theory of trust in men in public affairs."[57]

Perhaps the most characteristic and symptomatic work of this kind, significant also for the success which it enjoyed and which to the reader of today is difficult to understand, is a book published in 1930 by the present U.S. Justice Jerome Frank entitled *Law and the Modern Mind*. This work is a violent attack on the ideal of certainty of the law in which the author attempts, with the help of psychoanalysis, to ridicule as the result of a "childish need for an authoritative father."[58] This attack on the endeavor to achieve certainty by laying down general rules developed into a general attack on the principle of impersonal justice and a plea for wide judicial discretion.

I have no space here to show in detail how even by the late 1920's it had, as a result of this development, become accepted doctrine that

> every public officer has, marked out for him by law, a certain area of 'juris-
> diction.' Within the boundaries of that area he can act freely according to his
> own discretion, and the courts will respect his action as final and not inquire
> into its rightfulness. But if he oversteps those bounds, then the court will
> intervene. In this form, the law of court review of the acts of public officers
> becomes simply a branch of the law of *ultra vires*. The only question before
> the courts is one of jurisdiction, and the court has no control of the officer's
> exercise of discretion within that jurisdiction.[59]

Just before the entry of the United States into the second World War the apprehension which these developments had caused in some circles led, as had happened in England ten years earlier, to the appointment of an official committee of inquiry, the U.S. Attorney General's Committee on Administrative Procedure, whose majority tended in its Report on the whole to represent what was happening as both inevitable and innocuous. The character of this report is probably best described by the concluding passages of an article which Dean Roscoe Pound devoted to its review:

[56] Charles Grove Haines, *A Government of Laws or a Government of Men: Judicial or Legislative Supremacy* (Berkeley: University of California Press, 1929), p. 37.

[57] Ibid., p. 18.

[58] Jerome Frank, *Law and the Modern Mind* (New York: Brentano's, 1930), p. 21; see also p. 118.

[59] John Dickinson, *Administrative Justice and the Supremacy of Law in the United States* (Cambridge: Harvard University Press, 1927), p. 41.

Even if quite unintended, the majority [of the Committee] are moving in the line of administrative absolutism which is a phase of the rising absolutism throughout the world. Ideas of the disappearance of law, of a society in which there will be no law, or only one law, namely that there are no laws but only administrative orders; doctrines that there are no such things as rights and that laws are only threats of exercise of state force, rules and principles being nothing but superstition and pious wish; a teaching that separation of powers is an outmoded eighteenth-century fashion of thought, that the common law doctrine of the supremacy of law has been outgrown, and expounding of a public law which is to be a 'subordinating law', subordinating the interests of the individual to those of the public official and allowing the latter to identify one side of a controversy with the public interest and so give it a greater value and ignore the other; and finally a theory that law is whatever is done officially and so whatever is done officially is law and beyond criticism by lawyers—such is the setting in which the proposals of the majority must be seen.[60]

25. The Task for Liberty-Loving Statesmen

But I must cease speaking about the past. I hope that what I have said has made clear to you the dangers created by tendencies which have now been operating for a long time all over the world. I must use what little time I have left to return to the issue on which I have touched at the beginning of this lecture and ask what we can still do if we wish to stem this development and keep future evolution within the limits which make the survival of freedom and of the Rule of Law possible.

If our aim is to assist the formation of a spontaneous order and to restrict the use of coercion as much as possible, our main task must be to adjust our rules so as to make the spontaneous forces of society work as beneficially as possible. The first need in order that we should be able to do so is that we learn to understand the working of those forces. The most important among the forces on which we must rely in an advanced society are those of the market which will function in a desirable manner only if as much competition prevails or is at least possible as the nature of the various fields allow. The first task then must be to create an appropriate legal framework for the effective working of competition. This is a task which has never been systematically taken in hand and where a great deal still remains to be done. We have still gradually to learn to shape our rules so as to minimize the chances of deliberate inhibi-

---

[60]Roscoe Pound, "Administrative Procedure Legislation for the 'Minority Report'", *American Bar Association Journal*, vol. 27, 1941, p. 678. [The brackets are Hayek's.—Ed.]

tion of competition and of the creation of contrived scarcities. We may indeed never succeed in entirely eliminating such harmful efforts. But though I am very skeptical of the supposed advantages of monopoly which some authorities are able to discover, I am also not convinced that those temporary monopolies based on superior efficiency or even exceptionally large size of some single firms are as harmful as is often suggested. I am on the whole inclined to believe that if we intelligently adjusted the relevant rules of law, especially the law of corporations and the law of industrial patents, and if, what is still more important, governments refrained from deliberately fostering monopoly by protection and similar measures, we could reduce its extent to a point where it would cease to be a serious problem. The apparent failure of past efforts in this direction is partly due to our use as a standard of some unrealistic ideal of 'perfect' competition which in many fields probably could not possibly exist, but even more so to our own unwillingness to accept competition as a general rule and systematically to outlaw all attempts at 'restraint of trade.' There has always been and still is in this field a tendency prevalent which is not only bound to lead to failure but which is fraught with serious dangers: the tendency to allow competition only where we like its immediate effects and to prevent its suppression only where it is visibly harmful. This is not only impracticable but makes it almost inevitable that we equip the authorities charged with such a supervision of the markets with discretionary and arbitrary powers and thus re-introduce the very element which a system based on the spontaneous forces of the market should enable us to eliminate. I am in this respect not at all happy about the modern tendencies in the anti-cartel and anti-trust policies of the major industrial countries. Indeed, if it were really an alternative of either equipping authorities with such discretionary powers of interfering with what the general rules of the law permit, and putting up with some degree of monopoly, I should decidedly prefer the latter. But I do not think that this is the practical issue because, as I have already suggested, we probably could, if we seriously wanted, restrict the dangers of monopoly to insignificant proportions if we were only willing to create conditions which favor competition whenever it is possible.

In order to be able to discuss these matters in any detail I should have to stand at the beginning rather than at the end of such a course of lectures as this. What I have said with regard to a particularly important field of economic legislation could of course be no more than an illustration of the implementation of the general principle to which these lectures were devoted. A serious discussion would have to range over the whole field of modern economic and social policy and have to attempt to show what form our efforts would have to take if they were to conform to this general principle. This, I cannot now attempt and I must hope that the illustration I have given will be sufficient to indicate the general character which such a discussion would have to assume.

To those who have been brought up in the beliefs which were current during the last half century the limits I am inclined to place on what the state can beneficially and successfully undertake, though not as narrow as they may at first appear, may still seem disappointing and disillusioning. But I have become profoundly convinced that most of the evils we have been experiencing during that period were largely due to the fact that we have been expecting the state to do wonders, and that if we want to preserve the essential creative forces of a free civilization the first need is that we reduce our aspirations in this field to sensible proportions. We shall never create Utopia by state action. After all it is still as true as ever

> How small of all that human hearts endure
> That part which kings or states can cure.[61]

What we have learnt since these lines were written in the eighteenth century is probably that the evils which the state can cause are even greater than anyone then imagined. I believe that the main lesson which our generation has learnt is that we must find a new limit for the activities of government, a limit which leaves ample scope for sensible experimentation but which secures the freedom of the individual as the mainspring of all social and political activity. The whole purpose of these lectures has been to suggest that we can find such a limit if we are willing to revive and develop the ancient ideal of the Rule of Law.

---

[61] [Hayek misquotes a passage from Oliver Goldsmith's poem *The Traveller*, a passage that had been supplied by Samuel Johnson. See Oliver Goldsmith, *The Traveller*, 4th ed. (London: J. Newbery, 1765), p. 22: "How small of all that human hearts endure, / That part which laws or kings can cause or cure."—Ed.]

DEGREES OF EXPLANATION[1]

I

The discussion of scientific method has been guided almost entirely by the example of classical physics. The reason for this is mainly that certain features of scientific method can be most easily illustrated by instances from this field, and partly a belief that, because physics is the most highly developed of all the empirical sciences, it ought to be held up to all the others for imitation. Whatever truth there may be in this second consideration ought not, however, to make us overlook the possibility that some of the characteristic procedures of physics may not be of universal applicability, and that the procedure of some of the other sciences, 'natural' or 'social', may differ from that of physics, not because the former are less advanced, but because the situation in their fields differs in significant respects from that of physics. More particularly, what we regard as the field of physics may well be the totality of phenomena where the number of significantly connected variables of different kinds[2] is sufficiently

---

[1] Reprinted from the *British Journal for the Philosophy of Science*, vol. 6, November 1955, pp. 209–25, with the last four paragraphs of the original manuscript restored which had been omitted on the occasion of the first publication for reasons of space.

The subject of this and chapter 2, "The Theory of Complex Phenomena", are closely connected, so closely indeed that they might be regarded as treatments of the same subject at an interval of about eight years. I have nevertheless decided not only to reprint them both but even to give the earlier one first place, because they approach the subject from somewhat different angles and cover different aspects of the problem. ["Degrees of Explanation" and "The Theory of Complex Phenomena" appeared as the first two chapters of F. A. Hayek, *Studies in Philosophy, Politics and Economics* (Chicago: University of Chicago Press, 1967), pp. 3–21 and 22–42, respectively. For "The Theory of Complex Phenomena", see this volume, chapter 9.—Ed.]

[2] Modern physics has of course resorted to statistics to deal with systems of very large numbers of variables, but this does not appear to me to be in conflict with the observation in the text. The statistical technique is in effect a manner of reducing the number of separate entities, connected by laws which have to be stated, to comparatively few (namely the statistical collectives) and not a technique for dealing with the interplay of a large number of such significantly independent variables as the individuals in a social order. The problems of complexity to which the further discussion refers are of the kind which Warren Weaver has described as "problems of organized complexity" as distinguished from those "problems of disorganized complexity" with which we

small to enable us to study them as if they formed a closed system for which we can observe and control all the determining factors; and we may have been led to treat certain phenomena as lying outside physics precisely because this is not the case. If this were true it would certainly be paradoxical to try to force methods made possible by these special conditions on disciplines regarded as distinct because in their field these conditions do not prevail.

For our attempt to bring out certain aspects of scientific method that are not generally appreciated we will start from the now widely accepted interpretation of theoretical science as a 'hypothetico-deductive' system. One may accept most of the basic ideas underlying this approach and yet feel that it can be interpreted in a manner which makes it inappropriate to some subjects. Its basic conception lends itself to a somewhat narrow interpretation according to which the essence of *all* scientific procedure consists in the discovery of *new* statements ('natural laws' or 'hypotheses') from which testable predictions can be derived. This interpretation may become a serious bar to the penetration of our understanding into fields where certainly at present, and perhaps forever, a different procedure may be our only effective means of obtaining guidance in the complex world in which we live.

The conception of science as a hypothetico-deductive system has been expounded by Karl Popper in a manner which brings out clearly some very important points.[3] He has made it clear that the theoretical sciences are all essentially deductive, that there can be no such logical procedure as 'induction' which leads with necessity from the observation of facts to the formulation of general rules, and that the latter are products of creative acts of the mind which cannot be formalized. He has also emphasized the important point that the conclusions to which theories lead are essentially of the nature of prohibitions: they 'forbid' the occurrence of certain kinds of events and can never be

---

can deal by statistical techniques. Cf. Warren Weaver, "Science and Complexity", *American Scientist*, vol. 36, October 1948, pp. 536–44, and now the fuller version of his views in "A Quarter Century in the Natural Sciences", *The Rockefeller Foundation Annual Report, 1958* (New York: Rockefeller Foundation, 1958), pp. 7–16. [Chapter 1 of Weaver's lengthy "A Quarter Century in the Natural Sciences" is titled "Science and Complexity" and, aside from a few marginal changes, reproduces about half of his original 1948 article. Hayek's characterization of the 1958 piece as a "fuller version" is therefore inaccurate.—Ed.]

[3] Although on some particular points Professor Popper has in recent publications, such as *The Poverty of Historicism* (London: Routledge and Kegan Paul, 1957), especially sections 11 and 12, and *The Open Society and Its Enemies*, rev. ed. (Princeton: Princeton University Press, 1950) improved on his formulations, it is still necessary to go for a full account to his *The Logic of Scientific Discovery* (London: Hutchinson, 1959), which was translated from the German version, *Logik der Forschung* (Vienna: J. Springer, 1935). In many respects what follows is little more than an elaboration of some of Popper's ideas, particularly of his conception of degrees of testability and of his 'relativization' of his falsifiability criterion. My critical observations are therefore directed solely against certain positivist and operationalist interpretations of the 'hypothetico-deductive' thesis but not against Popper's or similar variants.

definitely 'verified' but only increasingly confirmed by persistently unsuccessful attempts to prove them false. For what follows, this part of the argument will be accepted.

There is, however, a further and no less illuminating idea contained in this approach which, if accepted too literally, is apt to become misleading. It is what Popper has occasionally expressed in conversation[4] by saying that science does not explain the unknown by the known, as is commonly believed, but, on the contrary, the known by the unknown. What is meant by this apparent paradox is that the advance of knowledge consists in the formulation of new statements which often refer to events which cannot be directly observed and from which, in combination with other statements about particulars, we can derive statements capable of disproof by observation. I do not doubt that it is important to emphasize that additions to knowledge in such instances will be contained in new statements (hypotheses or natural laws) which form part of the basis of our deductive argument; but this seems to me to represent not a general characteristic of all scientific procedure, but one which may be the rule in physics and occasionally also be successful in the biological sciences, but which presupposes conditions which are not present in many other fields.

II

Even in so far as the physical sciences are concerned, the emphasis on the procedure from the hypothesis to be tested to the conclusions which can be proved false may go too far. A large part of the value of these disciplines un-doubtedly derives from the fact that once their hypotheses are well accredited we can confidently derive from them conclusions applicable to new circum-stances and treat these as true without testing them. The work of the theorist is not concluded when his hypotheses seem sufficiently confirmed. The activ-ity of thinking through all their implications is evidently an activity important and valuable in its own right; and it may sometimes be an activity of great complexity and difficulty, requiring the highest forms of intelligence. Nobody will deny that constant efforts in this direction are part of the regular task of science; in fact, whole theoretical disciplines are concerned almost exclusively with this kind of activity. The question of what is the range of application or the capacity of a theory, whether it can or cannot account for a certain group of observed phenomena, or whether the observed events are within the range of what might have been predicted from it if all the relevant factual data had

[4] See now, however, Sir Karl Popper's *Conjectures and Refutations* (London: Routledge and Kegan Paul, 1963), especially p. 63: "scientific explanation is . . . the reduction of the known to the un-known", as well as ibid., pp. 102 and 174.

been known and if we were capable of manipulating them adequately, is often as interesting a problem as that whether the particular conclusion derived from the theory can be confirmed; and it is clearly independent of that question.

These aspects of the work of the theorist become increasingly prominent as we turn from the 'pure' theory of physics to disciplines like astrophysics or the various branches of geophysics (seismology, meteorology, geology, ocean-ography, etc.) which are sometimes described as 'applied' sciences. This name hardly describes the distinct kind of effort which those disciplines involve. It is used in this context neither to express that, like technology, they serve particular human needs, nor in order to indicate that their applicability is confined to particular regions of time and space. They all aim at developing generic explanations which, at least in principle, are significant apart from the particular events for which they have been worked out: much of the theory of tides as developed in terrestrial oceanography would be applicable to oceans on Mars, etc. What is characteristic of these theories is that they are, in a sense, derivative: they consist of deductions derived from combinations of known laws of physics, and do not, strictly speaking, state distinct laws of their own but elaborate the laws of physics into explanatory patterns appropriate to the peculiar kind of phenomena to which they refer. It is, of course, conceivable that the study of the tides might lead to the discovery of a new natural law; but if it did it would presumably be a new law of physics and not one of oceanography. Yet oceanography will still contain general statements which are not just plain physics but which have been elaborated from the laws of physics in order to account for the joint effects of certain typical constellations of physical events—specific patterns of argument developed to deal with recurring types of situations.

It is, no doubt, desirable that in working out such deductive systems the conclusions should be tested against the facts at every step. We can never exclude the possibility that even the best accredited law may cease to hold under conditions for which it has not yet been tested. But while this possibility always exists, its likelihood in the case of a well-confirmed hypothesis is so small that we often disregard it in practice. The conclusions which we can draw from a combination of well-established hypotheses will therefore be valuable though we may not be in a position to test them.

In a certain sense such a deductive argument, developed to account for an observed phenomenon, does not contain *new* knowledge. To those who are not regularly concerned with the elaboration of such patterns of explanation for typical complex situations the tasks of merely deducing the combined effects of known laws may seem trivial. But this is true only in the sense in which it is also true of mathematics. That certain conclusions are implied by what we know already does not necessarily mean that we are aware of these conclusions, or are able to apply them whenever they would help us to explain what we observe. Nobody could, in fact, work out all the consequences implied by our existing knowledge, or even those of some of the most trivial and undoubted propositions which we employ in daily life; it will often be an exceedingly difficult task to decide how much of what we observe can be explained by laws already known, or could be so explained if we possessed all the relevant data. To squeeze out of what we already know as many significant conclusions as possible is, of course, not a purely deductive task: it must be guided by observation in its choice of problems. But, though observation will raise the problems, the answer will rest on deduction alone.

In the disciplines mentioned, thus, the important question usually is not whether the hypotheses or laws used for the explanation of the phenomena are true, but whether we have selected the appropriate hypotheses from our store of accepted statements and have combined them in the right manner. What will be new about such a 'new' explanation of some phenomena will be the particular combination of theoretical statements with statements about facts regarded as significant for the particular situation (the 'initial' and 'marginal conditions'), not any one of the theoretical statements from which it starts. And the problem will not be whether the model as such is true, but whether it is applicable to (or true *of*) the phenomena it is meant to explain.

We have up to this point spoken mainly of what are called applied branches of physics in order to show that even there much of the undoubtedly theoretical work does not aim at the discovery of new laws and at their confirmation, but at the elaboration from accepted premises of deductive patterns of argument which will account for complex observed facts. If in these instances we can speak of hypotheses which require to be tested, they must be sought in the assertion that this or that pattern fits an observable situation, and not in the conditional statements of which the explanatory pattern itself consists and which is assumed to be true. We shall later discuss the peculiarities of this procedure more fully. At present our aim was merely to stress how comparatively rare an event in the progress even of the physical sciences the discovery of a true new law of nature is, and to suggest how special may be the conditions under which we can hope to discover such new laws of nature.

III

By a scientific prediction we mean the use of a rule or law in order to derive from certain statements about existing conditions statements about what will happen (including statements about what we will find if we search at a particular point). Its simplest form is that of a conditional or 'if then' statement combined with the assertion that the conditions stated in the antecedent are satisfied at a particular time and place. What in this connection is usually not explicitly considered is how specific need be the description of the events mentioned in the law, in the statement of the initial and marginal conditions, and in the prognosis, in order to merit the name of prediction. From the simple examples commonly adduced from physics it is readily concluded that it will generally be possible to specify all those aspects of the phenomenon in which we are interested with any degree of precision which we may need for our purposes. If we represent this form of statement by 'if u and v and w then z', it is often tacitly assumed that at least the description of z will contain all the characteristics of z which are deemed significant for the problem in hand. Where the relations we are studying are between a comparatively small number of measurements, this appears to present no serious difficulties.

The situation is different, however, where the number of significantly interdependent variables is very large and only some of them can in practice be individually observed. The position will here frequently be that if *we already knew* the relevant laws, we could predict that if several hundred specified factors had the values $x_1, x_2, x_3, \ldots x_n$, then there would always occur $y_1, y_2, y_3, \ldots y_n$. But in fact all that our observation suggests may be that if x_1, x_2, x_3, and x_4, then there will occur either (y_1 and y_2) or (y_1 and y_3) or (y_2 and y_3), or some similar situation—perhaps that if x_1, x_2, x_3, and x_4, then there will occur some y_1 and y_2 between which either the relation P or the relation Q will exist. There may be no possibility of getting beyond this by means of observation, because it may in practice be impossible to test all the possible combinations of the factors $x_1, x_2, x_3, x_4, \ldots x_n$. If in the face of the variety and complexity of such a situation our imagination cannot suggest more precise rules than those indicated, no systematic testing will help us over the difficulty.

In situations like these the observation of the complex facts will therefore not enable us to invent new hypotheses from which we can deduce predictions for situations we have not yet observed. We shall not be in a position to discover new natural laws for the kind of complex in question which would enable us to arrive at new predictions. The current view often seems to regard such a situation as beyond the limits of the application of scientific method (at least for the existing state of observational technique) and to accept that for the time being science must stop there. If this were correct, it would be very serious. There is no guarantee that we shall ever be able, physically or conceptually, to handle phenomena of any degree of complexity, nor that phenomena of a degree of complexity exceeding this limit may not be very important.

But if there is no reason to assume that the conditions presupposed by the standard method of physics will be satisfied by all events in which we are interested, there is still no need to despair about our prospects of learning at least something of importance about phenomena where they are not satisfied. But this will require a kind of reversal of what has been described as the standard procedure of physics; we shall here have to proceed in our deductions, not from the hypothetical or unknown to the known and observable, but—as used to be thought to be the normal procedure—from the familiar to the unknown. This is not an entirely satisfactory description of the procedure we shall now have to examine; but it is still true that the older conception of explaining the new by the familiar fits this procedure better than the conception that we proceed from the unknown to the known.

IV

'Explanation'[5] and 'prediction' of course do not refer to an individual event but always to phenomena of a certain kind or class; they will always state only some and never all the properties of any particular phenomenon to which they refer. In addition, each property stated will be expressed not as a unique value or magnitude but as a range, however narrow, within which the property will fall. Because of the limitations of the possible precision of measurement this is true even of the most exact predictions of physics which, strictly speaking, never say more than that the magnitude in question will fall within a certain interval; and it is still more obviously the case where the prediction is not quantitative.

In ordinary usage we are inclined to admit as predictions only statements which narrow down the admitted phenomena fairly closely, and to draw a distinction between 'positive' predictions such as "the moon will be full at 5h 22′ 16″ tomorrow", and merely negative predictions such as "the moon will not be full tomorrow." But this is no more than a distinction of degree. Any statement about what we will find or not find within a stated temporal and spatial interval is a prediction and may be exceedingly useful: the information that I will find no water on a certain journey may indeed be more important than most positive statements about what I will find. Even statements which specify no single specific property of what we will find but which merely tell us disjunctively that we will find either x or y or z must be admitted as predictions, and may be important predictions. A statement which excludes only one of all conceivable events from the range of those which may occur is no less a prediction and as such may prove to be false.

---

[5] I assume that the prejudice of certain earlier positivists against the word 'explanation' is now a thing of the past and that it may be taken for granted that prediction and explanation are merely two aspects of the same process where, in the first instance, known rules are used to derive from the known facts what will follow upon them, while in the second instance these rules are used to derive from the known facts what preceded them. For the purposes of this article it would indeed make no important difference if instead of 'degrees of explanation' we spoke throughout of 'degrees of prediction.' Cf. Popper, *The Open Society*, p. 446.

V

Where we have to deal with a complex situation in which observation discloses only very limited regularities, be it in the 'applied' branches of physics or in biology or in the social sciences, we usually ask to what extent our existing knowledge of the forces at work, or of the properties of some of the elements of the complex, may account for what we observe. We endeavour to find out whether this may be derived by deduction from what we know about the behaviour under simpler conditions of some of the factors involved. Of course we can never be certain that what we know about the action of those forces under simpler conditions will apply to more complex situations, and we will have no direct way of testing this assumption, since our difficulty is precisely that we are unable to ascertain by observation the presence and specific arrangement of the multiplicity of factors which form the starting point of our deductive reasoning. Neither the assumption that factors of the kind assumed are present, nor of course the validity of the deductive reasoning, need, therefore, be regarded as disproved if the conclusions at which we arrived are not borne out by observation. But though observation of such complex situations cannot decide whether our conditional ('if then') statement is true, it will help us to decide whether to accept it as an explanation of the facts which we observe.

It will be of interest, of course, if we succeed in deducing from our premises precisely those partial regularities of the complex from which we started. But this, though it may give us satisfaction, does not add to our knowledge. Yet the assertion that what we observe is due to a certain constellation of familiar factors, though we may not be able to test it directly, will usually imply consequences which we can test. The mechanism which we believe to have produced the observed phenomena will be capable of producing some further results but not others. This means that if what we have observed of a given complex of events is due to the assumed mechanism, that complex will also possess certain other characteristics and not be capable of definite other kinds of behaviour. Our tentative explanation will thus tell us what *kinds* of events to expect and which not, and it can be proved false if the phenomena observed show characteristics which the postulated mechanism could not produce. It will thus give us new information by indicating the *range* of phenomena to expect. By providing a schema or framework for the possible results, it not only helps us to order the observational knowledge which we already possess, but it will also provide *niches* for new observations likely to occur, and indicate the directions in which we must expect the phenomena to vary. Not only will the observed facts thus come to 'make sense' and to 'fall into their places', but we shall be able to make predictions about the combinations of events which will not occur if our explanation is correct.

This procedure differs from the supposedly normal procedure of physics in that we do here not *invent* new hypotheses or constructs but merely *select* them from what we know already about some of the elements of the phenomena; in consequence we do not ask whether the hypotheses we used are true or whether the constructs are appropriate, but whether the factors we have singled out are in fact present in the particular phenomena we want to explain, and whether they are relevant and sufficient to explain what we observe. The answer will depend on whether what we observe is of the kind which according to our deductions would occur *if* the postulated factors were present.

VI

The most familiar instance in the natural sciences of this sort of mere 'explanation of the principle'[6] is probably provided by the theory of evolution by natural selection of the different organisms. It is a theory which neither aims at specific predictions of particular events, nor is based on hypotheses in the sense that the several statements from which it starts are expected to be confirmed or refuted by observation. Although, as is true of any scientific theory, it does delimit a range of facts which are permitted by it against others which it 'forbids', our purpose in examining the facts is not to ascertain whether the different individual premises from which the theory starts are true, but to test whether the particular combination of undoubted premises is adequate to arrange the known facts in a meaningful order, and (what in a sense is the same thing) to show why only certain kinds of events are to be expected while others are precluded.

However we prefer to phrase the individual premises from which we deduce the theory of evolution, they will all be of such a kind that we do not doubt their truth and should not regard them as refuted if the conclusions drawn from them jointly should be contradicted by observation. We can get a considerable distance by starting from the following three assumptions: (i) Organisms which survive to the reproductive stage produce on the average a number of offspring much greater than their own; (ii) While organisms of any one kind produce as a rule only similar organisms, the new individuals are not all completely similar to their parents, and any new properties will in turn be inherited by their offspring; and (iii) Some of these mutations will alter the probability that the individuals affected will in turn produce offspring.[7]

[6] Though this term is rarely defined, theoretical discussion in biology abounds with statements qualified by the addition of 'in principle', such as 'is in principle specifiable', 'can in principle be ascertained', 'such a reduction is in principle possible', etc. Cf. A. S. Sommerhoff, *Analytical Biology* (London: Geoffrey Cumberlege, 1950), pp. iv, v, 27, 30, 198.

[7] For a similar listing of these basic assumptions see Julian S. Huxley, *Evolution: The Modern Synthesis* (London: Harper, 1942), p. 14.

Few people will doubt that these statements are true, or believe that the problem of the theory of evolution is whether they are true or not. The problem is rather whether they are adequate and sufficient to account for the phenomena which we do observe and for the absence of others which do not occur. We want to know what this mechanism of reduplication with transmittable variations and competitive selection can achieve, and this question we can answer only by deductively working out all the implications of these assumptions. We shall accept the conclusions drawn from the premises and regard them as a satisfactory explanation if they not only allow us to derive from them a process by which the observed phenomena might have been brought about, but if the explanation also points to new (not yet observed) distinctions between what is and what is not possible which are later confirmed by observation.[8]

In some instances such a theory may in fact produce practically no new conclusions but will merely provide a rational foundation for the biologist's knowledge that 'nature does not work that way.' It has even been suggested of the theory of evolution by natural selection that the main objection to it is that it cannot be disproved because "it appears impossible to indicate any biological phenomenon that would plainly disprove it."[9] This is true only in a limited sense. The individual statements from which it is derived are indeed unlikely to be disproved. But the assertion that the observed differentiation of species is always due to the operation of these factors could be refuted, e.g., if it were observed that after a sudden change in the environment the individuals then living would at once begin to produce offspring possessing a new adaptation to the changed environment. And, in the form in which the premises have been stated before, their adequacy as an explanation has in fact been shown insufficient by the inheritance of specific attributes of the non-sexual members of certain types of social insects. To account for these, the premises have to be enlarged to include situations wherein not only the properties of the individual but also properties of other members of the group will affect the chances of successful procreation.

It is worthwhile to pursue a little further the question how much the theory of evolution explains or predicts, and what the causes are of the limitations

---

[8] A very neat statement of the relation between theory and observation in this field, which is of wider application, occurs in G. S. Carter, *Animal Evolution* (London: Sidgwick and Jackson, 1951), p. 9: "The palaeontologist may be able to exclude some theories of evolution on the ground that they demand change not in accord with his facts; he claimed to be able to do so for Mendelian theories in their earliest forms at the start of this century. . . . The part of palaeontology in the study of evolutionary theory resembles that of natural selection in the process of evolution; it serves to remove the inefficient but cannot itself initiate." See also Popper, *The Poverty of Historicism*, as cited.

[9] Ludwig von Bertalanffy, *Problems of Life* (New York: Wiley, 1952), p. 89.

to what it can do. It can explain or predict only *kinds* of phenomena, defined by very general characteristics: the occurrence, not at a narrowly defined time and place but within a wide range, of changes of certain *types*; or rather the absence of other types of changes in the structure of the succeeding organisms. Disputes which have arisen in the course of the growth of the theory of evolution have thus significantly turned not so much on facts but on such questions as whether the postulated mechanism can account for the evolution having taken place in the time which has been available. And the answer has frequently come, not from the discovery of new facts, but from purely deductive arguments such as the mathematical theory of genetics, while "experiment and observation did not quite keep pace with the mathematical theory of selection."[10] If we can test the deductions by observation, so much the better: if we conclude, e.g., that mice of a colour little different from that of the ground are less likely to be caught by owls and will therefore multiply more rapidly than those with a contrasting colour and ultimately dominate the species, it is no doubt desirable that we should be able to confirm this by experiment (as has been done); because it is at least conceivable that such a tendency may be counteracted by another, e.g., by the frequent losses to owls stimulating the fecundity of the species affected (as the proportion of male births among humans was once believed to increase in wartime). But even if such direct confirmation by experiment is not possible, it will be reasonable to accept the deductive conclusions until they are disproved.

VII

The kind of explanation with which we are concerned is in current discussion often referred to as 'model-building.' This expression does not emphasize quite the distinction with which we are concerned since even the most precise predictions of physics are based on the use of 'models' of a formal or material kind.[11] But if the term model is meant to stress that a model always represents only some but not all the features of the original (so that an exact replica of a

---

[10] Ibid., p. 83.

[11] See Arturo Rosenblueth and Norbert Weiner, "The Role of Models in Science", *Philosophy of Science*, vol. 12, October 1945, p. 317: "A material model is the representation of a complex system by a system which is assumed simpler and which is also assumed to have some properties similar to those selected for study in the original complex system. A formal model is a symbolic assertion in logical terms of an idealized relatively simple situation sharing the structural properties of the original factual system." In connection with what follows see also Karl W. Deutsch, "Mechanism, Organism, and Society: Some Models in Natural and Social Science", *Philosophy of Science*, vol. 18, July 1951, pp. 230–52; "Mechanism, Teleology, and Mind", *Philosophy and Phenomenological Research*, vol. 12, December 1951, p. 185.

machine could not appropriately be called a model), it indeed brings out an important feature which all explanations possess but to very different degrees.

This difference of degree is well illustrated by the suspicion with which the physicist frequently regards the formal models employed in the biological and social sciences. To the physicist the value of a model (especially of a mathematical model represented by a set of equations) normally consists in the fact that he can ascertain and insert the relevant variables and thus derive the quantitative values of the events to be predicted or explained. Yet in the disciplines mentioned above similar models are regularly used although the values of the variables cannot in fact be ascertained, and often though there is no prospect of ever ascertaining them. Yet explanatory value is claimed for these models irrespective of this possibility, i.e., although they do not enable us to predict that such and such a specific event will occur at a particular time and place. Wherein does their explanatory value, then, consist?

The answer should now be obvious. Any model defines a certain range of phenomena which can be produced by the type of situation which it represents. We may not be able directly to confirm that the causal mechanism determining the phenomenon in question is the same as that of the model. But we know that, *if* the mechanism is the same, the observed structures must be capable of showing some kinds of action and unable to show others; and if, and so long as, the observed phenomena keep within the range of possibilities indicated as possible, that is so long as our expectations derived from the model are not contradicted, there is good reason to regard the model as exhibiting the principle at work in the more complex phenomenon.

The peculiar thing about these kinds of models is that, because we have to draw deductions from what we know about some factors contributing to the phenomenon and know nothing about others, our conclusions and predictions will also refer only to some properties of the resulting phenomenon, in other words, to a *kind* of phenomenon rather than to a particular event. Strictly speaking, as we have seen, this is true of all explanations, predictions, or models. Yet there is of course a great difference between the prediction that upon turning a switch the pointer of a measuring instrument will be at a particular figure and the prediction that horses will not give birth to hippogriffs or that, if all commodity prices are fixed by law and demand afterwards increases, people will not be able to buy as much of every commodity as they would wish to buy at these prices.

If we consider a formal model consisting of a system of algebraic equations or 'propositional equations',[12] it will contain assertions about a structure of relations even if we do not know the value of any of the variables, and even

---

[12] I.e., propositional functions for whose variables we will admit only values which make the propositions true. See Popper, *Logic of Scientific Discovery*, p. 73.

if we have only the most general information about the character of the functions occurring in it: it will still exclude the possibility of the occurrence of certain combinations of values in any phenomenon which the model is asserted
to represent;[13] it will tell us both what combinations of variables can occur at
any time and what range of values the other variables can assume when the
value of one or more of the variables is known. Of course, as we become able
to insert more and more definite values for the variables, this range will be nar-
rowed until we reach the point when the system is completely determined and
only one value of the remaining variable possible.

It is often not recognized that even the most formal system of equations can
thus be used to make predictions and therefore will possess empirical content
(though this content would be small), and that it will thus provide an explanation of the common features of a wide range of phenomena—or an explanation of the principle of this kind of phenomenon. This needs to be stressed
because of the widespread misconception that the value of such models rests
entirely on our ability to specify the values of the variables occurring in them
and that they are useless so long as we cannot do this. This is not so: such
models are valuable on their own, irrespective of their use for determining
particular situations, and even where we know that we shall never have the
information which would make this possible. They still do tell us something
about the facts and allow us to make prognoses.

But is it not still true that our aim everywhere, as has been said of the theoretical description of nature,[14] should be to formulate theories that can be
'falsified' as easily as possible, i.e., which have as great an empirical content
as possible? It is undoubtedly a drawback to have to work with theories which
can be refuted only by statements of a high degree of complexity, because anything below that degree of complexity is on that ground alone permitted by
our theory.[15] Yet it is still possible that in some fields the more generic theories
are the more useful ones and further specification may be of little practical
value. Where only the most general patterns can be observed in a considerable number of instances, the endeavour to become more 'scientific' by further
narrowing down our formulae may well be a waste of effort; to strive for this
in some subjects such as economics has often led to the illegitimate assumption
of constants where in fact we have no right to assume the factors in question
to be constant.

[13] Ibid. "Even if the system of equations does not suffice for a unique solution, it does not
allow every conceivable combination of values to be substituted for the 'unknowns' (variables).
Rather, the system of equations characterizes certain combinations of values or value systems
as admissible."
[14] Ibid., p. 68. [This reference does not seem right. A better reference might be Popper, *Logic of
Scientific Discovery*, chapter 6, section 31, pp. 112–13.—Ed.]
[15] Ibid., p. 127.

VIII

Though our conclusions are most readily seen to apply to those disciplines which, like mathematical biology or mathematical economics, employ formalized symbolic models, they are no less true of those biological and social theories which are expressed in ordinary language. While it would be equally incorrect, however, to say that these theories do not lead to predictions, and while their value does indeed rest on what they predict, it must be recognized that those predictions are so different in character from what is usually understood by this word that not only the physicist but also the ordinary man may well hesitate to accept them as such. They will be mostly negative predictions that such and such things will not occur, and more especially predictions that such and such phenomena will not occur together. These theories equip us with ready-made schemes which tell us that when we observe given patterns of phenomena, certain other patterns are to be expected but not some others. They will show their value through the manner in which the isolated facts which have been known will begin to make sense, will fill the *niches* which the theory provides, and only those. In some respects such theories may seem little more than schemes of classification, yet schemes which provide in advance only for such phenomena or combinations of phenomena as the theories allow to occur. They indicate the range of phenomena to be expected: if the taxonomic scheme of zoology does not provide for winged vertebrates with more than two legs, this is the result of a theory which makes it unlikely that such organisms have arisen. If economics tells us that we cannot at the same time maintain fixed rates of foreign exchange and at will control the internal price level of a country by changing the quantity of money, the character of such a 'prediction' is essentially the same as in the previous case. It is because its predictions possess this character that economics, in particular, appears so often to consist merely of variations upon the theme that 'you cannot have your cake and eat it.' The practical value of such knowledge consists indeed largely in that it protects us from striving for incompatible aims. The situation in the other theoretical sciences of society, such as theoretical anthropology, seems to be very much the same: what they tell us is in effect that certain types of institutions will not be found together, that because such and such institutions presuppose certain attitudes on the part of the people (the presence of which can often not be confirmed satisfactorily), only such and such other institutions will be found among people possessing the former (which can be confirmed or refuted by observation).

The limited character of the predictions which these theories enable us to make should not be confused with the question whether they are more or less uncertain than the theories which lead to more specific predictions. They are more uncertain only in the sense that they *leave* more uncertain because they say less about the phenomena, not in the sense that *what* they say is less certain. In so far as the latter sometimes may also be the case, it will be due to a different factor with which we are not here concerned: where we deal with very complex phenomena the *recognition* of the presence of the conditions to which the theory applies may often require the ready perception of patterns or configurations which will demand a special skill which few acquire. The selection and application of the appropriate theoretical scheme thus becomes something of an art where success or failure cannot be ascertained by any mechanical test.[16] The possession of such a ready-made pattern of significant relationships gives us a sort of sense for the physiognomy of events which will guide us in our observation of the environment. But even this constitutes no more than a distinction of degree from the physical sciences: the reading of many instruments also requires very special skills and there will be no other test for its correctness than that the great majority of properly trained observers agree.

IX

The service of a theory which does not tell us what particular events to expect at a definite moment, but only what kinds of events we are to expect within a certain range, or on complexes of a certain type, would perhaps be better described by the term *orientation* than by speaking of prediction. Although such a theory does not tell us precisely what to expect, it will still make the world around us a more familiar world in which we can move with greater confidence that we shall not be disappointed because we can at least exclude certain eventualities. It makes it a more orderly world in which the events make sense because we can at least say in general terms how they hang together and are able to form a coherent picture of them. Though we are not in a position to specify precisely what to expect, or even to list all the possibilities, each observed pattern has meaning in the sense that it limits the possibilities of what else may occur.

Where our predictions are thus limited to some general and perhaps only negative attributes of what is likely to happen, we evidently also shall have

---

[16]This is perhaps the place to mention that what we are discussing here is of course not the only difference between the physical and the social sciences, but rather a peculiarity which the latter share with those natural sciences which deal with comparatively complex phenomena. Another and perhaps more important peculiarity of the social sciences is due to the fact that here the *recognition* of the different kinds of facts rests largely on a similarity between the observer and the observed persons. On this see now my essay on "Rules, Perception and Intelligibility", reprinted as the third essay in the present volume. [Hayek's essay "Rules, Perception and Intelligibility" is reprinted below as chapter 8.—Ed.]

little power to control developments.[17] Yet the knowledge of what kinds of events are to be expected and what not, will nevertheless help us to make our action more effective. Even if we cannot control the external circumstances at all, we may adapt our actions to them. And sometimes, though we may not be able to bring about the particular results we would like, knowledge of the principle of the thing will enable us to make circumstances more favourable to the kinds of events we desire. Of the different classes of events which are to be expected under various combinations of circumstances which we can bring about, some may with greater probability include desirable results than others. An explanation of the principle will thus often enable us to create such favourable circumstances even if it does not allow us to control the outcome. Such activities in which we are guided by a knowledge merely of the principle of the thing should perhaps better be described by the term *cultivation* than by the familiar term 'control'—cultivation in the sense in which the farmer or gardener cultivates his plants, where he knows and can control only some of the determining circumstances, and in which the wise legislator or statesman will probably attempt to cultivate rather than to control the forces of the social process.[18]

But if it is true that in subjects of great complexity we must rely to a large extent on such mere explanations of the principle, we must not overlook some disadvantages connected with this technique. Because such theories are difficult to disprove, the elimination of inferior rival theories will be a slow affair, bound up closely with the argumentative skill and persuasiveness of those who employ them. There can be no crucial experiments which decide between them. There will be opportunities for grave abuses: possibilities for pretentious, over-elaborate theories which no simple test but only the good sense of those equally competent in the field can refute. There will be no safeguards even against sheer quackery. Constant awareness of these dangers is probably the only effective precaution. But it does not help to hold up against this the example of other sciences where the situation is different. It is not because of a failure to follow better counsel, but because of the refractory nature of certain subjects that these difficulties arise. There is no basis for the contention that they are due to the immaturity of the sciences concerned. It would be a complete misunderstanding of the argument of this essay to think that it deals with a provisional and transitory state of the progress of those sciences which they are bound to overcome sooner or later. This may in some instances be possible—but in some of the fields there is good reason to believe that these

[17] While it is evidently possible to predict precisely without being able to control, we shall clearly not be able to control developments further than we can predict the results of our action. A limitation of prediction thus implies a limitation of control, but not *vice versa*.

[18] The following paragraphs were for reasons of space omitted on the occasion of the first publication of this essay.

limitations will be permanent, that explanations of the principles will remain the best we can achieve in them, and that the nature of the subject puts forever beyond our reach the sort of explanation of detail which would enable us to make specific predictions. It is certainly not helpful to discredit what may be the only sort of knowledge we can achieve in these fields.

It seems indeed not improbable that, as the advance of the sciences penetrates further and further into more complex phenomena, theories which merely provide explanations of the principle, or which merely describe a range of phenomena which certain types of structures are able to produce, may become more the rule than the exception. Certain developments of recent years, such as cybernetics, the theory of automata or machines, general system theory, and perhaps also communication theory, seem to belong to this kind. And the more we move into the realm of the very complex, the more our knowledge is likely to be of the principle only, of the significant outline rather than of the detail. Especially where we have to deal with the extreme complexity of human affairs, the hope of ever achieving specific predictions of particulars seems vain. It would appear to be an evident impossibility for a human brain to specify in detail that "way of acting, feeling, and thinking channelled by a society out of an infinite number and variety of potential ways of thinking", which, in the words of an eminent anthropologist, is the essence of culture.[19]

It cannot be our task here to inquire whether what we have considered with regard to the disciplines which had, from their very beginning, to deal with relatively complex phenomena, may not also become increasingly true of the discipline which was at least able to start with the relatively simple: that is, whether not even physics, as it ceases to treat of a few connected events as if they were closed systems, and at the same time develops in a manner which makes it necessary to define its terms in relation to each other, and in consequence only the theoretical system as a whole but no longer in part can be really falsified,[20] will increasingly have to face the same difficulties with which we are familiar from the biological and social sciences. This would mean that because of the nature of its subject physics comes only at a later stage up against the same sort of obstacles which other disciplines have met earlier, and that the latter, far from being able to learn from physics on this point, indeed had already to grapple for a long time with problems of a kind which physicists meet only at a later stage of the development of their science.

[19] A. L. Kroeber, "Values as a Subject of Natural Science Inquiry", in A. L. Kroeber, *The Nature of Culture* (Chicago: Chicago University Press, 1952), p. 136. [In Kroeber's original statement, the word "habitual" preceded "acting", and the final word was "living" instead of "thinking."—Ed.]

[20] Cf. F. A. Hayek, *The Sensory Order: An Inquiry into the Foundations of Theoretical Psychology* (London: Routledge and Paul, 1952), pp. 170 *et seq.* [A *Collected Works* edition of this volume is anticipated.—Ed.]

In conclusion it should perhaps be stressed that there can never be competition between the two procedures, because what we have called an explanation of the principle will always give us only part of the information which a full explanation would yield where it can be achieved, and because in this sense the former is a less powerful instrument. But it is more powerful in the sense that it can be applied to fields to which the other procedure, for the time being or permanently, cannot be applied at all. Though scientists sometimes talk as if there could be no such fields not accessible to what they regard as the normal scientific method, i.e., fields where we cannot hope to establish by observation the laws of complex phenomena, few would seriously maintain this after reflecting that this belief implies that the human mind must be equipped to deal with the full details of phenomena of any conceivable degree of complexity. This may have some plausibility so long as we think exclusively of the physical world in the narrow sense of the term: it becomes highly doubtful when we think of biological phenomena; and it certainly ceases to be true when we have to deal with some of the activities of man himself. Especially in those fields where the object of our investigation, and our means of investigating and communicating the results, that is our thoughts, our language, and the whole mechanism of communication between men, are partly identical and where in consequence in discussing a system of events we must at the same time move within that system, there are probably definite limits to what we can know. These limits can be ascertained only by studying the *kind* of relations which exist between what can be said within a given system and what can be said about that system. To gain an understanding of such problems it may prove necessary deliberately to cultivate the techniques of explanation of the principle, i.e., the reproduction of a principle on greatly simplified models; and with regard to them the systematic use of this technique may prove the only path to definite knowledge—especially of the limits of what our thought can achieve.

SEVEN

THE ECONOMY, SCIENCE AND POLITICS[1]

I

The assumption of new duties and the entry into a new sphere of activities are for the academic teacher a salutary occasion for giving an account of the aims of his efforts. This is even more true when, after long years of study in various parts of the world which were devoted more to research than to teaching, he speaks for his first time from the place at which he hopes during the remainder of his active life to pass on the fruits of his experience.

I do not know to what good star I owe it that for the third time in the course of one life that faculty has honoured me with the offer of a chair which I would have chosen if an absolutely free choice in such things were possible. Not only is the move to this place in the heart of Europe, exactly half-way between Vienna and London, the two places which have shaped me intellectually, and in addition in *Vorder-Österreich*,[2] after a dozen years in the New World, for me something like coming home—even though my acquaintance with Freiburg counts only in days. I also value particularly the opportunity to teach again in a faculty of law, in the atmosphere to which I owe my own schooling. After one has endeavoured for thirty years to teach economics to students possessing no knowledge of law or the history of legal institutions, one is sometimes tempted to ask whether the separation of legal and economic studies was not perhaps, after all, a mistake. For my own person, although I have retained little knowledge of positive law, I have at any rate always been grateful that when I commenced the study of economics, this was possible only as part of the study of law.

---

[1] Inaugural lecture delivered (in German) at the assumption of the professorship of Political Economy at the University of Freiburg i. B., June 18, 1962, and published under the title, *Wirtschaft, Wissenschaft und Politik* (Freiburg i. B.: Hans Ferdinand Schulz, 1963), pp. 1–24. Footnotes have been added to the translation. [Reprinted in F. A. Hayek, *Studies in Philosophy, Politics and Economics* (Chicago: University of Chicago Press, 1967), pp. 251–69.—Ed.]

[2] Hither-Austria: The Breisgau in which Freiburg is situated and some connected territories used to be called *Vorder-Österreich* during the centuries when they were part of the domain of the Habsburgs.

Special mention is due to the personal contacts with professional colleagues which have for decades provided for me a connection with this university. Unfortunately these ties have been severed by the premature death of those contemporaries to whom community of convictions had drawn me. With Adolf Lampe and with my predecessor in this chair, Alfons Schmitt, whom I unfortunately never met in person, I have long been connected by common interests which occasionally had led to an exchange of views by correspondence.[3] With Leonhard Miksch I shared in addition common efforts for the elaboration of an economic philosophy for a free society.[4] By far the most important for me was, however, the friendship of many years' standing, based on the closest agreement on scientific as well as on political questions, with the unforgettable Walter Eucken.[5] During the last four years of his life this friendship had led to close collaboration; and I would like to use this opportunity to tell you of the extraordinary reputation which Eucken had gained in the world during this period.

More than fifteen years ago—less than two years after the end of the war—I had undertaken to call an international conference of some economists, lawyers and historians of the Western world who were passionately concerned about the preservation of personal freedom. The conference was held in Switzerland and it was at that time not only still incredibly difficult to make it possible for a German to enter Switzerland, but also the problem of a meeting between scholars from what so recently had been enemy camps was at that time, curious as this fortunately sounds fifteen years later, a cause of some apprehension and hesitation. My friends and I had initially hoped to get the his-

[3] [Both Adolf Lampe (1897–1948) and Alfons Schmitt (1903–1960) taught at Freiburg. Lampe together with Eucken were prominent critics of the views expressed by Martin Heidigger in his rectorial address at Freiburg in May 1933, an address about the rôle of the German university ("The Self-Assertion of the German University") that was peppered with Nazi language and allusions. Lampe was arrested by the Gestapo in September 1944 and spent some time in a concentration camp but escaped when Soviet forces neared the camp. Schmitt was the director of an institute for regional policy and logistics (Institut für Regionalpolitik und Verkehrswissenschaft). That post that was passed on to J. Heinz Müller, while his chair for economics (Volkswirtschaftslehre) was taken over by Hayek in 1962.—Ed.]

[4] [Leonhard Miksch (1901–1950) was a professor of economics and finance at the University of Freiburg. Nils Goldschmidt and Arnold Berndt note that he was "a key figure in the evolution of ordo-liberalism to constitutional economics" in their article "Leonhard Miksch (1901–1950): A Forgotten Member of the Freiburg School", *American Journal of Economics and Sociology*, vol. 64, October 2005, p. 974.—Ed.]

[5] [Walter Eucken (1891–1950) was the principal founder of ordo-liberalism, the doctrine that a strong state should set up the legal rules and political order under which a freely competitive market society will best function. He influenced Ludwig Erhard, whose currency reforms and abolition of price controls in 1948 initiated 'the German Miracle', Germany's rapid post-war economic recovery.—Ed.]

torian Franz Schnabel[6] and Walter Eucken to Switzerland, but we succeeded in overcoming all the technical difficulties only with regard to Eucken, who, in consequence, was the only participant from Germany at the conference on Mont Pèlerin. This made it the more significant that he became the great personal success of the conference and that his moral stature made the most profound impression on all participants. He has thereby contributed much to restore in the West the belief in the existence of liberal thinkers in Germany, and he has further strengthened this impression at a further conference of the Mont Pèlerin Society and on a visit to London in 1950 from which he was not to return.[7]

You know better than I what Eucken has achieved in Germany. I need therefore not explain further what it means if I say here today that I shall regard it as one of my chief tasks to resume and continue the tradition which Eucken and his friends have created at Freiburg and in Germany. It is a tradition of the greatest scientific integrity and at the same time of outspoken conviction on the great issues of public life. The extent to which, and the conditions under which, these two aims can be combined in the academic work of an economist will be the main subject of my further observations.

II

In spite of the fact that at least the first half of my career as an economist has been wholly devoted to pure theory, and because I have since devoted much time to subjects entirely outside the field of economics, I do welcome the prospect that my teaching is to concern in future mainly problems of economic policy. I am very anxious, however, to state clearly and publicly, even before I start on my regular courses, what seem to me the aims and the limits of the contributions of science and the tasks of academic instruction in the field of economic policy.

In this I will not dwell longer than necessary on the much discussed problem which arises here in the first instance and which I cannot wholly pass over even though I have nothing new to say about it: the rôle of value judgments in the social sciences in general and in the discussion of questions of economic and

[6][The German historian Franz Schnabel (1887–1966) was the author of the multivolume *Deutsche Geschichte im neunzehnten Jahrhundert* (*History of Germany in the Nineteenth Century*). A Catholic, he was dismissed from the Higher Technical School in Karlsruhe in 1935. After the war he taught at the University of Munich.—Ed.]

[7][In 1950 Eucken went to England to deliver a series of five lectures at the University of London. He had a stroke and died on March 20, 1950; his final lecture was read to the audience by Alan Peacock. Though Hayek had initiated the invitation, he had moved to the United States by this time so was not on hand for the lectures or his friend's death.—Ed.]

social policy in particular. It is now almost fifty years since Max Weber stated the essentials of this issue, and if one now re-reads his careful formulations one finds little that one wishes to add.[8] The effects of his admonitions may perhaps sometimes have gone too far. But we must not be surprised that at a time when economics threatened to degenerate in Germany into a doctrine of social reform, and a school of economics could describe itself as the 'ethical school', he pushed his argument to a point where it could also have been misunderstood.[9] This unfortunately has often produced a fear of expressing any value judgments and even to an avoidance of some of the most important problems which the economist ought frankly to face in his teaching.

The general principles which we ought to follow in this respect are really very simple—however difficult may often be their application in a particular case. It is of course an elementary duty of intellectual honesty to distinguish clearly between connections of cause and effect, on which science is competent to pronounce, and the desirability or undesirability of particular results. Science as such has of course nothing to say on the relative values of ultimate aims. It is equally obvious that the very selection of our problems for scientific examination implies valuations and that therefore the clear separation of scientific knowledge and valuations cannot be achieved by avoiding all valuations, but only by an unmistakable statement of the guiding values. It seems equally incontestable that the academic teacher should not pretend to be neutral or indifferent but should make it easier for his audience to recognize the dependence of his practical conclusions on value judgment by openly stating his personal ideals as such.

It appears to me today as if, at the time when I was a student and for some time thereafter, under the influence of Max Weber's powerful argument, we had been more restrained in this respect than was desirable. When, more than thirty years ago, and somewhat more than a year after I had assumed a professorship at the University of London, I gave my first inaugural lecture and used the opportunity to explain my general economic philosophy,[10] I still felt

[8] [German sociologist and political economist Max Weber (1864–1920) wrote extensively about the necessity of keeping positive analysis and judgments of value separate in science. Hayek hoped to go to Munich to study with Weber after completing his degree in Vienna, but Weber died before he could do so. See F. A. Hayek, *Hayek on Hayek: An Autobiographical Dialogue*, ed. Stephen Kresge and Leif Wenar (Chicago: University of Chicago Press, 1994), p. 64.—Ed.]

[9] [Though he identified himself as a member of the school, Weber's writings on the importance of value neutrality were directed against other members of the younger German historical school. The German historical school was a direct rival to the Austrian school of economics. For more on this, see Bruce Caldwell, *Hayek's Challenge: An Intellectual Biography of F. A. Hayek* (Chicago: University of Chicago Press, 2004), chapters 2–4.—Ed.]

[10] "The Trend of Economic Thinking", *Economica*, n.s., vol. 13, May 1933, pp. 121–37. [See F. A. Hayek, "The Trend of Economic Thinking", in *The Trend of Economic Thinking: Essays on*

gratified when I discovered that the students were surprised and disappointed to find that I did not share their predominantly socialist views. It is true that my lectures until then had been confined to questions of pure theory and that I had had no special occasion to deal explicitly with political questions. Today I ask myself whether, rather than being proud of my impartiality, I ought not to have had a bad conscience when I discovered how successfully I had hidden the presuppositions which had guided me at least in the choice of problems I thought to be important.

It was partly that experience which made me desire that on the present occasion my inaugural lecture should really be my first lecture to you, and made me desire to state in it certain views which will be presupposed in much that I shall have to say in the discussion of particular issues.

Concerning the question of the rôle of value judgments and the appropriateness of taking in academic teaching a position on politically contested issues, I want to add two more observations. The first is that I believe that if Max Weber had lived twenty years longer he would probably have changed his emphasis a little. When in his day he represented intellectual honesty as the only virtue which the academic teacher has to support, it might still have seemed as if this demand had nothing to do with politics. We have since learnt that there exist political systems which make very difficult even such intellectual honesty as is a basic condition for all genuine science. It is certainly possible to preserve intellectual honesty in the most difficult conditions. But we are not all heroes, and if we value science we must also advocate a social order which does not make such intellectual honesty too difficult. There seems to me to exist in this respect a close connection between the ideals of science and the ideals of personal liberty.

The second point is that it seems to me a clear duty of the social scientist to ask certain questions the mere raising of which will seem to imply the taking of a political position. One illustration will suffice to explain what I have in mind. It is probably sufficient to mark a scholar in many circles as an enemy of the working class if he merely asks whether it is true, as is almost universally believed, that the wage policies of the trade unions have resulted in raising the real wages of the workers as a whole to a level higher than it would otherwise be. There exist in fact not only good reasons to doubt this but even a fair

---

Political Economists and Economic History, ed. W. W. Bartley III and Stephen Kresge, vol. 3 (1991) of *The Collected Works of F. A. Hayek* (Chicago: University of Chicago Press; London: Routledge), pp. 17–34. In an interview Hayek recalled, "One of the more intelligent students had the cheek to come to see me for the sole purpose of telling me that, though hitherto admired by the students, I had wholly destroyed my reputation by taking, in this lecture, a clearly anti-socialist position." W. W. Bartley III, "Hayek Biography: 'Inductive Base'", unpublished manuscript, p. 78. —Ed.]

probability that the opposite is true and that as a necessary consequence of the wage policy of the unions the real wages—or at least the real income—of the whole working class is lower than it would have been without it.

The considerations which lead to this apparently paradoxical and certainly not generally understood conclusion are fairly simple and rest on theorems which are scarcely disputed. The power of any particular union to push up the wages of its members, that is, to make them higher than they would be without the activity of the union, rests entirely on its ability to prevent the entry into the trade of workers willing to work for a lower wage. This will have the effect that the latter either must work elsewhere at still lower wages or that they will remain unemployed. It is, of course, in general true that the unions will be strong in prospering and rapidly developing trades and less powerful in stagnating or declining trades. This means that the power of any one union to raise the wages of its members rests on their preventing the movement of workers from points where their marginal productivity is low to points where their marginal productivity is high. This must result in the overall marginal productivity of labour and therefore the level of real wages being kept lower than it would otherwise be.

If we represent this as only a probable and not a certain effect the reason for this is that we cannot exclude the possibility that the gain of that group of workers whose wages are pushed up beyond the level which would establish itself on a free market may be greater than the loss of the group whose wages will be lower than they would be if they had access to the prospering trade. The increased wages of one group will thus certainly be bought at the expense of greater inequality and probably also at the price of a lower real income of the working class as a whole.

I need hardly stress that all these considerations apply only to real wages and not to money wages—and that the fact that the wage policy of the unions may lead to a general rise of money wages, and to inflation, is the reason for the persistence of the illusion that thanks to the unions wages in general are higher than they would otherwise be.

You will observe that the answer to this problem, although likely to arouse intense political passion, depends in no way on value judgments. The answer I have sketched may be true or false—and it is certainly not as simple as such a brief sketch makes it appear—but its truth or falsity depends on the correctness of the theory and perhaps on some particular facts of the concrete situation, but not on our opinion of the desirability or undesirability of the aims we pursue. This is fortunately true of a very great part of the problems of economic policy—I believe of far the greater part. But even where at first there appears to exist unbridgeable contrasts of moral valuations, it usually proves that if the disputing parties can agree on the alternatives between which they have to choose, their differences tend to disappear.

III

Let me show this in somewhat greater detail with respect to the central problem on which socialists and the supporters of a free economy are still in disagreement. I speak of their *still* being in disagreement, because one argument which at one time was seriously advanced in support of socialism has been pretty generally abandoned as a result of the scientific discussion of the problem. This is the contention that a centrally directed economy would be more productive than one guided by the market. I shall later, in another context, return to this question and mention it here only in order to point out that, even if the falsity of this belief were conceded, this does not yet dispose of the argument in support of socialism. Because for most socialists as important as, if not even more important than, the increased general supply of goods is the distribution of those we get. It would be wholly consistent, even though perhaps not very expedient politically, if a socialist guided solely by ethical considerations were to maintain that even a considerable reduction of the aggregate real social income would not be too high a price to pay for achieving a more just distribution of that income.

Even the advocate of a free economy must concede that the conception of justice which inspires socialism can be realized, if at all, only in a centrally directed economy. Yet the question remains whether the socialist would really be prepared to accept *all* the effects which a realization of his ideal of justice would bring about and of which the reduction of material productivity may not be the most important. If that were the case, we could indeed only admit a difference on ultimate values which no rational discussion could remove. This, however, seems to me by no means to be the case, and a somewhat more searching analysis of the different but usually vague conceptions which the disputing parties have of what they call 'social justice' will soon show this. In the terminology current since Aristotle we can express the difference by saying that a free economy can always achieve only commutative justice, while socialism— and in a great measure the popular ideal of social justice—demands distributive justice. Commutative justice means here a reward according to the value which a person's services actually have to those of his fellows to whom he renders them, and which finds expression in the price the latter are willing to pay. This value has, as we must concede, no necessary connection with moral merit. It will be the same, irrespective of whether a given performance was in the case of one man the result of great effort and painful sacrifice while it is rendered by another with playful ease and perhaps even for his own enjoyment, or whether he was able to meet a need at the right moment as a result of prudent foresight or by sheer chance. Commutative justice takes no account of personal or subjective circumstances, of needs or good intentions, but solely of how the results of a man's activities are valued by those who make use of them.

The results of such remuneration according to the value of the product must appear as highly unjust from the point of view of distributive justice. It will rarely correspond to what we regard as the subjective merit of a performance. That the speculator who by chance has guessed correctly may earn a fortune in a few hours while the life-long efforts of an inventor who has been anticipated by another by a few days remains unremunerated, or that the hard work of the peasant who clings to his soil barely brings him enough to keep going, while a man who enjoys writing detective stories thereby earns enough to afford a luxurious life, will appear unjust to most people. I understand the dissatisfaction produced by the daily observation of such cases and honour the feeling which calls for distributive justice. If it were a question whether fate or some omnipotent and omniscient power should reward people according to the principles of commutative or according to those of distributive justice, we would probably all choose the latter.

This, however, is not the position in the existing world. In the first instance, we cannot assume that, if the system of remuneration were altogether different, the individual men would still do what they do now. Indeed we can now leave them to decide for themselves what they want to do because they bear the risk of their choice and because we remunerate them not according to their effort and the honesty of their intentions but solely according to the value of the results of their activity. Free choice of occupation and free decision by each of what he wants to produce or what services he wants to render are irreconcilable with distributive justice. The latter is a justice which remunerates each according as he discharges duties which he owes in the opinions of others. It is the kind of justice which may and perhaps must prevail within a military or bureaucratic organization in which each member is judged according to the measure in which in the opinion of his superiors he discharges tasks set to him; and it can extend no further than the group that acts under one authority for the same purposes. It is the justice of a command-society or command-economy and irreconcilable with the freedom of each to decide what he wants to do.

It is irreconcilable, moreover, not only with freedom of action but also with freedom of opinion—because it requires that all men are made to serve a unitary hierarchy of values. In fact, of course, neither do we agree on what represents greater or lesser merit, nor can we objectively ascertain the facts on which such a judgment is based. The merit of an action is in its nature something subjective and rests in a large measure on circumstances which only the acting person can know and the importance of which different people will assess very differently. Does it constitute greater merit to overcome personal loathing or pain, physical weakness or illness? Does it constitute greater merit to have risked one's life or to have damaged one's reputation? Individually each of us may have very definite answers to such questions, but there is little probability that we shall all agree and evidently no possibility to prove to others that our opinion is right. This means, however, that for an attempt to remunerate men according to their subjective merit it must always be the opinion of a few which must be imposed upon the rest. Distributive justice therefore demands not only personal unfreedom but the enforcement of an indisputable hierarchy of values, in other words, a strictly totalitarian regime.

Whether this conclusion is inevitable is of course, again, a matter which one might discuss at considerable length. But for my present purpose the point is solely that it depends only on scientific analysis and not on any value judgments. Only after we have agreed what would be the consequences of enforcing either kind of justice will the choice between them depend on valuations. Personally it seems to me that scarcely anyone who has understood and admits that distributive justice can be realized generally only in a system of personal unfreedom and personal arbitrariness is likely to decide in favour of distributive justice. There are of course many people to whom my argument does not appear cogent, and with them discussion may be instructive and worthwhile. But if anybody concedes the conclusion and asserts that he still prefers a system which realizes an ideal of distributive justice at the price of personal unfreedom and unlimited authority of a few to a system in which personal freedom is combined with merely commutative justice which to him may appear as supreme injustice, science indeed has nothing further to say.

In many instances, in fact, after we have brought out the consequences of alternative decisions, it will appear not only as very pedantic but almost a mockery to add that it is now left to the listener or reader to choose. Already in the first great theoretical work of our science, Richard Cantillon's *Essai sur la nature du commerce en général*, in which more than two hundred years ago the distinction was clearly drawn, it is sometimes difficult not to feel that the author has no doubt about the answer when, for example, he breaks off his discussion of the population problem with the remark that it cannot be the task of science to decide whether it is better to have a numerous but poor or a small but rich population.[11] But we should probably not be afraid of this sort of pedantry which is often resented as a kind of *reductio ad absurdum* and does not tend to make popular those who employ it.

[11] [The Irish economist Richard Cantillon (c. 1680–1734) lived most of his life in France. His *Essai* was first published in 1755, well after his death (he died in a fire, possibly set by his former cook) in 1734. Though it had some influence in its day, it was not until it was rediscovered by the English economist William Stanley Jevons more than a century later that it became famous: Jevons declared the book "the cradle of political economy." See Richard Cantillon, *Essai sur la nature du commerce en général*, edited with an English translation and other materials by Henry Higgs (London: Royal Economic Society, 1931; reprinted, New York: Kelley, 1964). Hayek wrote an essay on Cantillon that was published in German in 1931. For a translation by Grete Heinz, see F. A. Hayek, "Richard Cantillon (c. 1680–1734)", in *The Trend of Economic Thinking*, chapter 13. —Ed.]

IV

It is necessary now to turn to another limitation of the possibility of a scientific justification of particular political measures which is less familiar but probably more important. This is a consequence of the fundamental difficulty of any complete explanation of highly complex phenomena and not merely of an insufficient development of economic theory. Although there are undoubtedly still many open questions of this theory, it seems to me that it is on the whole in a fairly satisfactory state. My opinion is that the source of our difficulties lies elsewhere than in an insufficiently advanced state of theory which, I sometimes feel, has been refined to a point where in fact we can no longer apply it to the real world.

I take it that I need not defend here the view that only theory can be regarded as science in the strict sense. Knowledge of facts as such is not science and does not help us to control or influence the course of things. But even theoretical insight, even where it enables us to understand in a large measure why things happen as they do, does not always make it possible to predict particular events or to shape things as we desire—if we do not *also* know the particular facts which constitute the data which we must insert into the formulae of our theory. This is where the great obstacle to a full explanation or to effective control of really complex phenomena appears. It seems to me as if in this respect economists often forget the limits of their power and give the unjustified impression that their advanced theoretical insight enables them in concrete instances to predict the particular consequences of given events or measures.

The difficulty I am going to discuss arises not only in economics but in all subjects which deal with processes in highly complex structures. It exists as much in theoretical biology and psychology as in all the social sciences and for this reason deserves somewhat careful consideration, particularly as the example of the physical sciences has often led to a false approach in those fields.

All theory consists in the statement of abstract and schematic orders or patterns. The kinds of order which are characteristic for different groups of phenomena may be relatively simple or relatively complex, by which I mean that the characteristic principle which gives the class of phenomena their distinct character can be exhibited by models which consist of comparatively few elements or only by models which consist of comparatively large numbers of elements. In this sense the phenomena of mechanics are comparatively simple—or, rather, we call mechanical those processes whose principles can be represented by relatively simple models. This does not mean that in particular cases those simple relations cannot be combined into extremely complex structures. But the mere multiplication of the elements does here not produce something new, however difficult may be the application of the simple theory to some of those complex structures.

222

Because in those fields the theoretical formulae (the description of the characteristic kind of order or pattern) are relatively simple, it will as a rule also be possible to insert into them all the concrete data which must be known to make particular events predictable. For the physicist or chemist the theory, the general description of the kind of order, is for this reason generally of interest only to the extent that, by the insertion of concrete data, he can derive from it specific predictions of individual events. And though he has of course also his difficulties in thus applying his theory, he will generally assume that the particular data which he has to insert into his mathematical formulae can be ascertained to any degree of exactness required to make precise predictions. To him it often appears therefore as incomprehensible that the economist should bother to construct theories which look very much like physical theories and may for instance be stated in the form of systems of simultaneous equations, although the latter admits that he can never ascertain all the data which he would have to insert into the equations before he can solve them.

It is, however, by no means evident that the prediction (or the explanation of the appearance) of an abstract order or pattern of a certain kind is useful or interesting only if we can explain also its concrete manifestation. In the case of simple orders the difference between their general character and their particular manifestation is indeed not very significant. But the more complex the order is, and particularly as several ordering principles are superimposed over each other, the more important this distinction becomes. The prediction merely of the fact that we shall find a certain arrangement of elements will often be an interesting, and above all a refutable and therefore empirical prediction, even if we can say little about the particular properties of those elements, their magnitude or distance, etc. Even in the physical sciences there occur many instances in which our knowledge justifies only the prediction of a general arrangement. The mineralogist, for example, who knows that a certain substance will form hexagonal crystals, will often not be in a position to predict what the size of these crystals will be. But what is rather the exception in the physical sciences is the rule in the sciences of the more highly organized structures. We often know enough to determine the general character of the order which we shall find. Our theory may even be adequate to derive from it the particular events which will occur, provided that we assume that the particular circumstances are known. The difficulty is merely that these particular circumstances are so numerous that we can never ascertain them all!

This, I believe, is true of a large part of theoretical biology, especially of the biological theory of evolution, and certainly of the theoretical social sciences. One of the best examples is the systems of equations of the mathematical theory of prices. They show in an impressive and on the whole probably true manner how the whole system of prices of goods and services is determined by the desires, the resources and the knowledge of all the individuals and enterprises. But, as the creators of the theory perfectly understood, the purpose of those equations is *not* to arrive at a numerical determination of those prices, since, as Vilfredo Pareto put it, it would be "absurd" to assume that we could ever ascertain all the particular data.[12] Their purpose is exclusively to describe the general character of the order that will form itself. Since this order implies the existence of certain relations between the elements, and the actual presence or absence of such relations can be ascertained, the prediction of such an order can be shown to be false, and the theory will thus be empirically testable. But we shall always be able to predict only the general character of the order and not its detail. So far as I know, no economist has yet succeeded in using his knowledge of theory to make a fortune by a prediction of future prices. (This applies even to Lord Keynes who is sometimes thought to have done so. But so long as he speculated in the field in which one might have thought that his theoretical knowledge would have helped him, namely in foreign exchange, he lost more than he possessed; and only later, when he turned to speculation in commodities where admittedly his theoretical knowledge was of no use to him, did he succeed in acquiring a substantial fortune.)[13]

That our theory does not enable us to predict particular prices, etc., says nothing against its validity. It means merely that we never know all the particular circumstances on which, according to that theory, the several prices depend. These circumstances are in the first instance the desires and the knowledge of all the persons taking part in the economic process.

That we never can know all that the people know whose actions determine the formation of prices and the methods and direction of production is, of course, of decisive importance not only for theory. It has also the greatest significance for political action. The fact that much more knowledge contributes to form the order of a market economy than can be known to any one mind or used by any one organization is the decisive reason why a market economy is more effective than any other known type of economic order.

Before I take up this subject, however, I want to mention that it seems to me that the whole modern development of what is called macro-economic theory is a result of the erroneous belief that theory will be useful only if it puts us in a position to predict particular events. As it appeared obvious that the data necessary for such a use of macro-economic theory could never be ascertained, it was attempted to overcome this difficulty by so reconstructing theory that the data which had to be inserted into its formulae were no longer information about individuals but statistical magnitudes, sums or averages. Most of these efforts seem to me to be mistaken. The result is merely that we

---

[12] [See Vilfredo Pareto, *Manual of Political Economy*, ed. Ann S. Schwier and Alfred N. Page, translated by Ann S. Schwier (New York: Kelley, 1971), p. 171.—Ed.]

[13] [For more on Keynes's speculative adventures, see D. E. Moggridge, *Maynard Keynes: An Economist's Biography* (London: Routledge, 1992), pp. 348–52.—Ed.]

lose insights we can gain into the structure of the relations between men, and that, as those statistical magnitudes inform us only about the past and provide no justification for the assumption that they will remain constant, we still do not achieve successful prediction of particular events. Apart perhaps from certain problems of the theory of money, those endeavours seem to me to promise little. They certainly offer no escape from the difficulties I have discussed, because the prices and quantities produced of particular commodities are not determined by any averages but by particular circumstances, the knowledge of which is dispersed among hundreds of thousands of men.

V

One of the chief results of the theory of the market economy is thus that in certain conditions, which I cannot further consider here, competition produces an adaptation to countless circumstances which in their totality are not known and cannot be known to any person or authority, and that therefore this adaptation cannot be brought about by a central direction of all economic activity. This means in the first instance that, contrary to a widely held opinion, economic theory has much of importance to say about the effectiveness of different kinds of economic systems, that is, on the very questions of the discussion of which scholars are sometimes afraid because they are so closely connected with opposing political opinions; and that it has comparatively little to say on the concrete effects of particular measures in given circumstances. We know the general character of the self-regulating forces of the economy and the general conditions in which these forces will function or not function, but we do not know all the particular circumstances to which they bring about an adaptation. This is impossible because of the general interdependence of all parts of the economic process, that is because, in order to interfere successfully on any point, we would have to know all the details of the whole economy, not only of our own country but of the whole world.

In so far as we want to avail ourselves of the forces of the market—and there can probably be no doubt that we must do so if we want even approximately to preserve our standard of life—it would seem that a rational economic policy should confine itself to creating the conditions in which the market will function as well as possible, but should not regard it as its task deliberately to influence or guide the individual activities. The chief task of economic policy would thus appear to be the creation of a framework within which the individual not only can freely decide for himself what he wants to do, but in which also this decision based on his particular knowledge will contribute as much as possible to aggregate output. And our evaluation of any particular measure of policy will have to depend not so much on its particular results, all of which in most instances we shall in any case not know, but on its being in conformity with the whole system (what I believe W. Eucken was the first to describe as *systemgerecht*).[14] This also means that we shall often have to act in all cases on assumptions which in fact are true only of most but not of all instances: a good example of this is the fact that all the exceptions from the rule that free international exchange will benefit both partners have been discovered by convinced advocates of free trade, which did not prevent them from continuing to advocate universal free trade, because they also understood that it is hardly ever possible to establish the actual presence of those unusual circumstances which would justify an exception. Perhaps even more instructive is the case of the late Professor A. C. Pigou, the founder of the theory of welfare economics—who at the end of a long life devoted almost entirely to the task of defining the conditions in which government interference might be used to improve upon the results of the market, had to concede that the practical value of these theoretical considerations was somewhat doubtful because we are rarely in a position to ascertain whether the particular circumstances to which the theory refers exist in fact in any given situation.[15] Not because he knows so much, but because he knows how much he would have to know in order to interfere successfully, and because he knows that he will never know all the relevant circumstances, it would seem that the economist should refrain from recommending isolated acts of interference even in conditions in which the theory tells him that they may sometimes be beneficial.

The recognition of this limitation of our knowledge is important if we do not want to become responsible for measures which will do more harm than good. The general conclusion we ought to draw from the insight seems to me

[14] [The term *systemgerecht* may be translated as 'system-compatible.' Eucken used it in his *Grundsätze der Wirtschaftspolitik* (Bern: A. Francke, 1952), or *Principles of Economic Policy*. Eucken used the term to claim, for example, that it would be 'systemgerecht' if local natural monopolies arose as a consequence of cost advantages.—Ed.]

[15] Cf. his article on "Some Aspects of the Welfare State", *Diogenes*, vol. 2, June 1954, p. 6. [Cambridge economics professor A. C. Pigou (1877–1959), author of *The Economics of Welfare* (1920; 4th ed, 1932), was the creator of the British variant of (or 'old') welfare economics, a theory calling for government intervention to improve welfare by maintaining full production, redistributing income, and correcting for various forms of 'market failure.' Hayek perhaps overstates the case about Pigou's recantation, though the British economist does say on p. 6 in reference to externalities, "It must be confessed, however, that we seldom know enough to decide in what fields and to what extent the State, on account of [the gaps between private and social costs] could usefully interfere with individual freedom of choice. Moreover, even though economists were able to provide a perfect blueprint for beneficial State action, politicians are not philosopher kings and a blueprint might quickly yield place on their desks to the propaganda of competing pressure groups." On p. 10, in discussing at what point further income redistribution might lead to a decrease in total production, Pigou acknowledges, "It is beyond our powers to determine where at any given time in any given circumstances, in any given country it [the tipping point] actually is."—Ed.]

to be that in our evaluation of measures of economic policy we should allow ourselves to be guided only by their general character and not by their particular effects on certain persons or groups. That a certain measure assists somebody deserving is by itself no sufficient justification of it if we are not prepared generally to recommend measures of the kind in question.

This attitude is likely to be criticized as a dogmatic adherence to rigid principles. This, however, is a reproach which ought not to deter us but which we should proudly accept, because principles are the most important contributions we can make to questions of policy. It is no accident that in our subject the term 'principles' is so often used in the titles of general treatises. Especially so far as economic policy is concerned, principles are practically all that we have to contribute.

Principles are particularly important, however, when the one political aim which we may take for granted is personal freedom. I have attempted in a recent work to show that the ultimate reason why personal freedom is so important is the unavoidable ignorance of most of the circumstances which determine the conduct of all others from which we nevertheless constantly benefit. And I have already used the last opportunity I had on a visit to Freiburg to explain in a lecture[16] how greatly this freedom must be constantly endangered if in our political decisions we consider exclusively their foreseeable effects, because the immediate effects which indicate a measure will necessarily be predictable, while the developments which have been prevented by the restriction of freedom will in their very nature be unforeseeable. I need not therefore dwell further on this point.

VI

I wish rather to use the remaining minutes to forestall two possible misunderstandings of what I have said so far. The first is that the clear position which I feel it is both appropriate and desirable that an academic teacher should take on certain great principles by no means implies that he should commit himself on particular current issues of politics, and still less that he should tie himself to a political party. The latter seems to me to be most undesirable and hardly compatible with the duties of an academic teacher in the social sciences. I quite understand the urge to take a part in the solution of the pressing problems of the public policy of the day, and if special circumstances had not prevented me from doing so I should probably myself have succumbed to the temptation to devote a great part of my energy to such tasks.

---

[16]F. A. Hayek, "Die Ursachen der ständigen Gefährdung der Freiheit", published in *Ordo*, vol. 12, 1960–61, pp. 103–9.

Already in my young days in Austria, however, we used to joke that we were better theorists than our colleagues in Germany because we had so little influence on practical affairs. I have later observed the same difference between the English and the American economists: at least in the 1930's the English economists were undoubtedly the better theoreticians and at the same time were much less involved in the conduct of current policy. This has somewhat changed since and I am not sure that the effect has been altogether beneficial for the state of scientific economics in England.

If I look back on the last thirty years I become, at any rate, very much aware of how much I owe to the fact that during the greater part of this time I was a foreigner in the countries in which I worked and for this reason felt it inappropriate to pronounce on the political problems of the day. If I have succeeded during this period in building up something like a fairly systematic body of opinion on economic policy this is not least due to the circumstance that all this time I had to be content with the rôle of a spectator and had never to ask what was politically possible or would assist any group with which I was connected. This will not be different in the future.

The second point on which I want to prevent possible misunderstandings is my emphasis on the limitations of our theoretical knowledge. I hope none of you has interpreted this to mean that I feel that because the utility of theory is so restricted we had better concentrate on facts. This was certainly not what I meant to convey.[17] Although it is one of the tasks of an academic teacher to show how to ascertain and interpret facts, knowledge of facts does not make a science, and that knowledge of facts which you will some day need in order to apply your scientific knowledge you will constantly have to learn anew on the job. The chief gain from your study at the university must be an understanding of theory, and it is the only profit which you can gain nowhere else. The knowledge of the particular facts to which you will have to apply your scientific knowledge will come soon enough. I hope it has never too seriously detracted from my effectiveness as a teacher that for the reason already mentioned I generally knew less about the particular conditions of the country in which I taught than my students did, and I hope that you will not be too disappointed when you soon discover that for some time at any rate the same will again be true.

The real conflict which arises today in the study of economics—and I do in this not refer to particular curricula or examination requirements about which I know little, but to the ideal aims of study—does not exist between the knowledge of facts and the understanding of theory. If that were the whole problem I should not hesitate to advise you to devote the precious years of

---

[17] [As Hayek made very clear in section 10 of "Economics and Knowledge", reprinted in this volume as chapter 1.—Ed.]

study to entire concentration on theory and to let the learning of the concrete facts wait until you meet them in your professional work. And, in spite of certain qualifications which I am going to add, this indeed seems to me desirable at least for a part of one's years at the university. Only those who have really mastered one science—and in spite of all the respect I have for history I am inclined to say one theoretical science—know what science is. Such mastery of a theoretical discipline can, however, today be acquired only in the course of a period of narrow specialization on its problems.

The difficulties lie elsewhere. They are a consequence of the fact that in order to arrive at an answer to those questions of principle on which, on the one hand, we have most to say, economic theory is, on the other, a necessary but not a sufficient equipment. I have said on another occasion, and it seems to me important enough to repeat it here, that he who is only an economist cannot be a good economist. Much more than in the natural sciences, it is true in the social sciences that there is hardly a concrete problem which can be adequately answered on the basis of a single special discipline. Not only are political science and jurisprudence, anthropology and psychology, and of course history, subjects of which we all ought to know much more than any man can know. Even more do all our problems touch on questions of philosophy. It is certainly no accident that in the country which has so long been leading in economics, England, almost all the great economists were also philosophers and, at least in the past, all the great philosophers also economists. There are indeed among the economists two conspicuous exceptions: two of the greatest, David Ricardo and Alfred Marshall. But I am not sure that this does not account for certain shortcomings in their work. If we leave them aside, however, and mention only the most important names, John Locke, George Berkeley and David Hume, Adam Smith and Jeremy Bentham, Samuel Bailey, James and John Stuart Mill, William Stanley Jevons, Henry Sidgwick and finally John Neville and John Maynard Keynes, such a list will appear to the philosophers as a list of important philosophers or logicians, and to the economists as a list of leading economists.[18]

Although the instances of such combinations of philosophy and economics which I encountered as a student in German literature[19] might rather have

---

[18] [Cf. Hayek's more extended discussion in his paper "Economists and Philosophers", which may be found in the appendix of the present volume.—Ed.]

[19] Especially such figures as Othmar Spann, F. von Gottl-Ottlilienfeld, R. Stolzmann or Werner Sombart. [Othmar Spann (1878–1950) was one of Hayek's professors at the University of Vienna; for Hayek's disparaging assessment, see *Hayek on Hayek*, p. 54; cf. Caldwell, *Hayek's Challenge*, pp. 138–39. Friedrich von Gottl-Ottlilienfeld (1868–1958) was the author of such books as *Die Grenzen der Geschichte* (1904) (*The Limits of History*) and *Der wirthschaftliche Charakter der technischen Arbeit* (1910) (*The Economic Character of Technical Work*). He was a proponent of *Fordismus* (the mass production philosophy of Henry Ford that was to transform the German economy) in Weimar

been a deterrent, I have come to the conclusion that it can be very fertile—and I do not think this belief is merely a result of the often noticed propensity of the old to turn from their special subject to philosophy. Most of the problems upon which I have touched today raise economic as well as philosophical problems. While it is somewhat doubtful whether such a thing as a single theoretical science of society is possible, all the sciences of society certainly do raise the same philosophical problems—many of them problems which have occupied philosophers for two thousand years before they were considered by more specialized disciplines. The problems of the formation of our civilization and institutions are closely connected with the problems of the development of our mind and its tools. The economist can only gain, for instance, if he occasionally looks into the problem of theoretical linguistics, and the common problems which he then discovers are in the last instance philosophical problems.

I mention this not only in order to justify the occasional excursions into philosophy into which I shall certainly be tempted. I speak of it also because I hope to find again this spirit of general intellectual curiosity and spiritual adventure which I remember from my student days in Vienna and which, if not unknown, is at least much more rare in American universities. However much the mastery of the discipline must be the chief aim of study, in the social sciences technical competence in one subject should not be the only purpose. For those who feel that the problems in our field are really important, the specialized study ought to be the beginning of a struggle for achieving a comprehensive philosophy of society—a struggle which will be fruitful only if one's studies have opened one's eyes not merely for the problems of one's special discipline.

It was my wish to talk on these general questions before I commenced my regular course of lectures. I am very conscious, however, that such a *confessio fidei* publicly made before one has become familiar with the peculiar atmosphere of a place incurs certain risks. It is one of the lessons I have learnt in moving from country to country that the intellectual frontiers on which one has to fight shift in the process. I have noticed this for the first time in what was then my special field, the theory of industrial fluctuations, when I moved to England. In the German discussion I was regarded as a pronounced representative of monetary explanations of the trade cycle, and my efforts had

---

Germany and in later years claimed to have created a new economics comparable to Hitler's new world order. Rudolf Stolzmann (1852–1930) was the author of *Der Zweck der Volkswirtschaft: Die Volkswirtschaft als social-ethisches Zweckgebilde* (1909) (*Purpose in the National Economy: The National Economy as a Social and Ethical Construction*). Werner Sombart (1863–1941) chronicled the history of the development of capitalism. In a chapter titled "The Socialist Roots of Nazi Germany" in *The Road to Serfdom*, Hayek took Sombart's gradual movement from socialism towards fascism as representing a natural tendency. See F. A. Hayek, *The Road to Serfdom: Text and Documents*, ed. Bruce Caldwell, vol. 2 (2007) of *The Collected Works of F. A. Hayek*, pp. 183–84.—Ed.]

indeed been directed to emphasizing the rôle money played in these processes. But in England I encountered a much more extreme form of a purely monetary explanation which regarded the fluctuations of the general price level as the essence of the phenomena. The consequence was that my arguments had soon to be directed against the dominant kind of monetary theory of the trade cycles and to aim at stressing the importance of the real factors, perhaps somewhat to the bewilderment of those who regarded me as a typical representative of monetary explanations.

Something similar happened to me in the philosophical field. At Vienna I had at least been close to the logical positivism of the Vienna circle, even though I could not accept some of the application of their views to the social sciences. In England, and still more later in the U.S., I found it, however, soon necessary to oppose certain more extreme forms of empiricism which I found there to be prevalent.[20] I should not be surprised if longer acquaintance with the present state of thinking in Germany should again seem to make it appear that such a change of front is indicated. It may well be, for instance, that I shall find that such an emphasis on the importance of theory as I felt today to be desirable was not really appropriate. My general impression, however, is that American fashions are spreading so rapidly that what I intended to say is not altogether out of place. But in case my emphasis should have been misplaced, I wanted in conclusion at least to mention the special difficulty which anyone encounters who after a long absence returns to an environment which was at one time familiar to him.

---

[20] [For more on Hayek's experiences in the United States and Britain, see the editor's introduction of F. A. Hayek, *Studies on the Abuse and Decline of Reason*, ed. Bruce Caldwell, vol. 13 (2010) of *The Collected Works of F. A. Hayek*, pp. 18–30.—Ed.]

EIGHT

RULES, PERCEPTION AND INTELLIGIBILITY[1]

1. Rule-guided Action

The most striking instance of the phenomenon from which we shall start is the ability of small children to use language in accordance with the rules of grammar and idiom of which they are wholly unaware. "Perhaps there is", Edward Sapir wrote thirty-five years ago, "a far-reaching moral in the fact that even a child may speak the most difficult language with idiomatic ease but that it takes an unusually analytical type of mind to define the mere elements of that incredibly subtle linguistic mechanism which is but a plaything in the child's unconscious."[2]

---

[1] Reprinted from the *Proceedings of the British Academy*, vol. 48, 1962, pp. 321–44. [Reprinted in F. A. Hayek, *Studies in Philosophy, Politics and Economics* (Chicago: University of Chicago Press, 1967), pp. 43–65. The references were listed as endnotes there but have been changed to footnotes for this edition.—Ed.]

[2] Edward Sapir, "The Unconscious Patterning of Behavior in Society" (1927), in *Selected Writings of Edward Sapir*, ed. D. G. Mandelbaum (Berkeley: University of California Press, 1949), p. 549. Further insight into the nature of grammatical order makes this achievement of children appear even more remarkable, and Robert B. Lees, in "Review of Noam Chomsky's *Syntactic Structures*", *Language*, vol. 33, July–September 1957, p. 408, was recently moved to observe that "in the case of this typically human and culturally universal phenomenon of speech, the simplest model that we can construct to account for it reveals that a grammar is of the same order as a predictive theory. If we are to account adequately for the indubitable fact that a child by the age of five or six has somehow reconstructed for himself the theory of his language, it would seem that our notions of human learning are due for some considerable sophistication."

Compare also on the whole issue Michael Polanyi, *Personal Knowledge, Towards a Post-Critical Philosophy* (London: Routledge and Kegan Paul, 1958), especially the chapters on "Skills" and "Articulation", and the penetrating observations in Adam Ferguson, *An Essay on the History of Civil Society* (Edinburgh: Printed for A. Millar and T. Caddel, London, and A. Kincaid and J. Bell, Edinburgh, 1767), pp. 50–51: "It is fortunate in this, as in other articles to which speculation and theory are applied, that nature proceeds in her course, whilst the curious are busied in the search of her principles. The peasant, or the child, can reason, and judge, and speak his language, with a discernment, a consistency, and a regard to analogy, which perplex the logician, the moralist, and the grammarian, when they would find the principle upon which the proceeding is founded, or when they would bring to general rules, what is so familiar, and so well sustained in particular cases."

The phenomenon is a very comprehensive one and includes all that we call skills. The skill of a craftsman or athlete which in English is described as 'knowledge how' (to carve, to ride a bicycle, to ski, or to tie a knot) belongs to this category. It is characteristic of these skills that we are usually not able to state explicitly (discursively) the manner of acting which is involved. A good example is given in another connection by Milton Friedman and L. J. Savage:

> Consider the problem of predicting, before each shot, the direction of travel of a billiard ball hit by an expert billiard player. It would be possible to construct one or more mathematical formulas that would give the directions of travel that would score points and, among these, would indicate the one (or more) that would leave the balls in the best positions. The formulas might, of course, be extremely complicated, since they would necessarily take account of the location of the balls in relation to one another and to the cushions and of the complicated phenomena introduced by 'english.' Nonetheless, it seems not at all unreasonable that excellent predictions would be yielded by the hypothesis that the billiard player made his shots *as if* he knew the formulas, could estimate accurately by eye the angles, etc., describing the location of the balls, could make lightning calculations from the formulas, and could then make the ball travel in the direction indicated by the formulas.[3]

(A being endowed with intellectual powers of a higher order would probably describe this by saying that the billiards player acted as if he could think.)

So far as we are able to describe the character of such skills we must do so by stating the rules governing the actions of which the actors will usually be unaware. Unfortunately, modern English usage does not permit generally to employ the verb 'can' (in the sense of the German *können*) to describe all those instances in which an individual merely 'knows how' to do a thing. In the instances so far quoted it will probably be readily granted that the 'know how' consists in the capacity to act according to rules which we may be able to discover but which we need not be able to state in order to obey them.[4] The

[3] Milton Friedman and L. J. Savage, "The Utility Analysis of Choice Involving Risk", *Journal of Political Economy*, vol. 56, August 1948, p. 298, reprinted in George J. Stigler and Kenneth E. Boulding, eds., *Readings in Price Theory* (Chicago: University of Chicago Press, 1952), p. 87.

[4] Cf. Gilbert Ryle, "Knowing How and Knowing That", *Proceedings of the Aristotelian Society*, vol. 46, 1945–46, pp. 1–16, and *The Concept of Mind* (London: Hutchinson's University Library, 1949), chapter 2. The almost complete loss of the original connotation of 'can' in English, where it can scarcely any longer be used in the infinitive form, is not only an obstacle to the easy discussion of these problems but also a source of confusion in the international communication of ideas. If a German says 'Ich weiß, wie man Tennis spielt' this does not necessarily imply that he knows how to play tennis, which a German would express by saying 'Ich kann Tennis spielen.' In German the former phrase states the explicit knowledge of the rules of the game and may— if the speaker had made special motion studies—refer to the rules by which the skill of a player

problem is, however, of much wider significance than will perhaps be readily conceded. If what is called the *Sprachgefühl* consists in our capacity to follow yet unformulated rules,[5] there is no reason why, for example, the sense of justice (the *Rechtsgefühl*) should not also consist in such a capacity to follow rules which we do not know in the sense that we can state them.[6]

From these instances where action is guided by rules (movement patterns, ordering principles, etc.) which the acting person need not explicitly know (be able to specify, discursively to describe, or 'verbalize'),[7] and where the nervous system appears to act as what may be called a 'movement pattern effector', we must now turn to the corresponding and no less interesting instances where the organism is able to recognize actions conforming to such rules or patterns without being consciously aware of the elements of these patterns, and therefore must be presumed to possess also a kind of 'movement pattern detector.'

2. Rule-guided Perception

Again the capacity of the child to understand various meanings of sentences expressed by the appropriate grammatical structure provides the most conspicuous example of the capacity of rule-perception. Rules which we cannot state thus do not govern only our actions. They also govern our perceptions, and particularly our perceptions of other people's actions. The child who speaks grammatically without knowing the rules of grammar not only understands all the shades of meaning expressed by others through following the rules of grammar, but may also be able to correct a grammatical mistake in the speech of others.

---

can be described, a skill which the speaker who claims to know these rules need not possess. German, in fact, has three terms for the English 'to know': *wissen*, corresponding to 'know that', *kennen*, corresponding to 'be acquainted with', and *können*, corresponding to 'know how.' See the interesting discussion in Hermann von Helmholtz, *Populäre wissenschaftliche Vorträge* (Braunschweig: Friedrich Vieweg und Sohn, 1871), Book 2, pp. 92 *et seq.* The passage is inevitably rendered only imperfectly in the English translation of this work. [For the translation, see Hermann von Helmholtz, *Popular Lectures on Scientific Subjects*, translated by E. Atkinson (London: Longmans, Green, 1904), pp. 270 *et seq.*—Ed.]

[5] Cf. Friedrich Kainz, *Psychologie der Sprache* (Stuttgart: Ferdinand Enke, 1956), vol. 4, p. 343: "Die Normen, die das Sprachverwenden steuern und kontrollieren, das Richtige vom Falschen sondern, bilden in ihrer Gesamtheit das Sprachgefühl." [The passage might be translated, "The norms that control and check the use of language, separating right usage from wrong, constitute in their entirety the sense for language."—Ed.]

[6] Cf. L. Wittgenstein, *Philosophical Investigations*, translated by G. E. M. Anscombe (Oxford: Basil Blackwell, 1953), p. 185e: " 'Knowing' it only means: being able to describe it."

[7] Since the meaning of many of the terms we shall have to use is somewhat fluid, we shall occasionally resort to the device of cumulating near-synonyms which, although not identical in their meaning, by the range of overlap of meaning define more precisely the sense in which we use these terms.

This capacity of perceiving rules (or regularity, or patterns) in the action of others is a very general and important phenomenon. It is an instance of *Gestalt* perception, but of a perception of configurations of a peculiar kind. While in the more familiar instances we are able to specify (explicitly or discursively to describe, or explicate) the configurations which are recognized as the same, and therefore also are able deliberately to reproduce the stimulus situation which will produce the same perception in different people, all we often know in the instances which belong here and which will be the main subject of this paper is that a particular situation is recognized by different persons as one of a certain kind.

To these classes of structures of events which are "known by none, and understood by all"[8] belong in the first instance gestures and facial expressions. It is significant that the capacity to respond to signs of which we are not conscious decreases as we move from members of our own culture to those of different cultures, but that in some measure it also exists in our mutual relations to (and also between) higher animals.[9] The phenomenon has in recent years received a good deal of attention under the heading of 'physiognomy perception';[10] it seems, however, to be of much wider occurrence than this

---

[8] Sapir, "The Unconscious Patterning", p. 556: "In spite of these difficulties of conscious analysis, we respond to gestures with an extreme alertness and, one might almost say, in accordance with an elaborate and secret code that is written nowhere, known by none, and understood by all." Compare also Goethe's expression "Ein jeder lebt's, nicht vielen ist's bekannt." [The quotation, taken from Goethe's *Faust: Vorspiel auf dem Theater*, line 168, spoken by the jester or comedian and referring to life, might be rendered, "We are all doing it; very few of us understand what we are doing." Indeed, this translation was the one used by Philip Wicksteed when he chose the sentence as the epigraph to the introduction of his *The Common Sense of Political Economy*. See Philip H. Wicksteed, *The Common Sense of Political Economy and Selected Papers and Reviews on Economic Theory*, ed. Lionel Robbins (London: Routledge and Kegan Paul, 1933), vol. 1.—Ed.]

[9] Wolfgang Köhler, *The Mentality of Apes* (New York: Harcourt, 1925), p. 307, reports that the chimpanzee "at once correctly interprets the slightest changes of human expression, whether menacing or friendly"; and H. Hediger, *Skizzen zu einer Tierpsychologie im Zoo und im Zirkus* (Stuttgart: Europa Verlag, 1954), p. 282, writes: "Im Tierreich, namentlich bei Säugetieren, besteht eine weitverbreitete und überraschend hoch entwickelte Fähigkeit, menschliche Ausdruckserscheinungen ganz allgemein aufs feinste zu interpretieren." ["In the animal kingdom, especially among mammals, there is a widespread and surprisingly sophisticated ability to interpret the most subtly general types of human expression."—Ed.] Robert E. Miller, John V. Murphy, and I. Arthur Mirsky, "Non-verbal Communication of Affect", *Journal of Clinical Psychology*, vol. 15, April 1959, p. 158, have shown "that the affect of fear and/or anxiety can be perceived and discriminated by rhesus monkeys in the facial expression and posture of other monkeys." For an illustration of the reverse relation, man recognizing the actions of apes as meaningful, see the description of observations of chimpanzees in the wild in Adriaan Kortlandt, "Chimpanzees in the Wild", *Scientific American*, vol. 206, May 1962, pp. 128–38.

[10] See Heinz Werner, *Comparative Psychology of Mental Development*, rev. ed. (Chicago, Follett, 1948); Heinz Werner et. al., "Studies in Physiognomic Perception", *Journal of Psychology*, volumes 38–46, 1954–58; Fritz Heider, *The Psychology of Interpersonal Relations* (New York: Wiley, 1958); and now Joseph Church, *Language and the Discovery of Reality: A Developmental Psychology of Cognition* (New York: Random House, 1961) where, after completing this paper, I found much support for its argument.

term at first suggests. It guides not only our perception of expression but also our recognition of action as directed or purposive;[11] and it colours also our perception of non-human and inanimate phenomena. It would lead too far to consider here the important contributions made to the knowledge of these phenomena by ethology, particularly by the studies of birds by Oskar Heinroth, Konrad Lorenz, and Niko Tinbergen,[12] though their descriptions of the 'infective' character of certain types of movement and of the 'innate releasing mechanism' as a 'perceptual function' are highly relevant. We shall on the whole have to confine ourselves to the problems in man with an occasional look at other higher animals.

3. Imitation and Identification

The main difficulty which has to be overcome in accounting for these phenomena is most clearly seen in connection with the phenomenon of imitation. The attention paid to this by psychologists has fluctuated greatly and after a period of neglect it seems again to have become respectable.[13] The aspect which concerns us here probably has not again been stated more clearly since it was first pointed out at the end of the eighteenth century by Dugald Stewart.[14] It concerns a difficulty which is commonly overlooked because imitation is most frequently discussed in connection with speech where it is at least plau-

[11] See, particularly, Franz From, "Perception of Human Action", in *Perspectives in Personality Research*, ed. Henry P. David and J. C. Brengelmann (New York: Springer, 1960); Edgar Rubin, "Bemerkungen über unser Wissen von anderen Menschen", in *Experimenta Psychologica*, ed. Edgar Rubin (Copenhagen: Munksgaard, 1949); as well as Gordon W. Allport, *Pattern and Growth in Personality* (New York: Holt, Rinehart, and Winston, 1961), p. 520, who sums up by saying that "the key to person perception lies in our attention to what the other is *trying to do*."

[12] See Oskar Heinroth, "Ueber bestimmte Bewegungsweisen der Wirbeltiere", *Sitzungsberichte der Gesellschaft naturforschender Freunde* (Berlin: n.p., 1930), pp. 333–42; Konrad Lorenz, "The Comparative Method in Studying Innate Behaviour Patterns", in *Physiological Mechanisms in Animal Behaviour: Proceedings of the Fourth Symposium of the Society for Experimental Biology, Cambridge, July 1949* (Cambridge: Cambridge University Press, 1950), pp. 221–68, and "The Role of Gestalt Perception in Animal and Human Behaviour", in *Aspects of Form: A Symposium on Form in Nature and Art*, ed. Lancelot E. White (London: Lund Humphries, 1951), pp. 157–78; and Niko Tinbergen, *The Study of Instinct* (Oxford: Clarendon, 1951), respectively.

[13] For a survey see Neal E. Miller and John Dollard, *Social Learning and Imitation* (New Haven: Yale University Press, 1941), especially appendix 2; cf. also Harry F. Harlow, "Social Behavior in Primates", in *Comparative Psychology*, ed. C. P. Stone (New York: Prentice-Hall, 1951), p. 443; Kurt Koffka, *The Growth of the Mind: An Introduction to Child-Psychology* (New York: Harcourt, Brace, 1925), pp. 307–19; and Gordon Allport, *Pattern and Growth in Personality*, chapter 1. [Allport does not discuss imitation in chapter 1 but does on pp. 103–5 and 533–37 of his book.—Ed.]

[14] Dugald Stewart, *Elements of the Philosophy of the Human Mind*, vol. 4 of *The Collected Works of Dugald Stewart* (Edinburgh: Thomas Constable, 1854), chapter 2 on "Of the Principle or Law of Sympathetic Imitation."

sible to assume that the sounds emitted by an individual are perceived by him as similar to those produced by another.

The position is very different, however, in the case of gestures, postures, gait, and other movements and particularly in that of facial expressions, where the movements of one's own body are perceived in a manner altogether different from that in which the corresponding movements of another person are perceived. Whatever in this respect may be the capacities of the newborn infant,[15] there can be no doubt that not only do human beings soon learn to recognize and to imitate complex movement patterns, but also that the various forms of 'infection' which occur in all forms of group life presuppose some such identification of the observed movements of another with one's own movements.[16] Whether it is the bird which is induced to fly (or preen, scratch, shake itself, etc.) by the sight of other birds doing so, or man induced to yawn or stretch by seeing others doing the same, or the more deliberate imitation practiced in mimicry or learning a skill, what happens in all these instances is that an observed movement is directly translated into the corresponding action, often without the observing and imitating individual being aware of the elements of which the action consists or (in the case of man) being able to state what he observes and does.[17]

[15] For the latest experimental results and the earlier literature on the smiling response of infants, see R. Ahrens, "Beitrag zur Entwicklung des Physiognomie- und Mimikerkennens, Teil I", *Zeitschrift für experimentelle und angewandte Psychologie*, vol. 2, 1954, pp. 412–54; Kurt Goldstein, "The Smiling of the Infant and the Problem of Understanding the 'Other'", *Journal of Psychology*, vol. 44, 1957, pp. 175–91; H. Plessner, "Die Deutung des mimischen Ausdrucks: Ein Beitrag zur Lehre vom Bewusstsein des anderen Ichs" (1925–26), reprinted in Helmuth Plessner, *Zwischen Philosophie und Gesellschaft: Ausgewählte Abhandlungen und Vorträge* (Bern: Francke, 1953), pp. 132–79; and F. J. J. Buytendijk, "Das erste Lächeln des Kindes", *Psyche*, vol. 2, 1948, pp. 57–70.

[16] Cf. Dugald Stewart, *Elements*, p. 139: "To bestow upon [this theory of imitation] even the shadow of plausibility, it must be supposed farther, that the infant has the aid of a mirror, to enable it to know the existence of its own smiles, and what sort of appearance these smiles exhibit to the eye . . . this throws no light whatever on the present difficulty, till it is farther explained by what process the child learns to *identify* what it feels, or is conscious of, in its own countenance, with what it sees on the countenance of another." (Italics added and original italics omitted.) [Hayek added the bracketed material in this quote.—Ed.]

[17] Cf. Paul Schilder, *The Image and Appearance of the Human Body: Studies in the Constructive Energies of the Psyche* (London: Kegan Paul, Trench, Trubner, 1935), p. 244: "real imitation actions . . . are due to the fact that the visual presentation of the movement of another is apt to evoke the representation of a similar movement of one's own body, which, like all motor representation, tends to realize itself immediately in movements. Many of the imitative movements of children are of this class." The extensive experimental work done on this phenomenon in recent times with the help of elaborate apparatus, photography, etc., has not taught us much more than Adam Smith knew when he wrote in *The Theory of Moral Sentiments*, in *Essays* (London: Alex Murray, 1869), p. 10, that "the mob, when they are gazing at a dancer on the slack rope, naturally writhe and twist and balance their own bodies, as they see him do, and as they feel that they themselves must do if in his situation." [Now see Adam Smith, *The Theory of Moral Sentiments*, ed. D. D. Raphael

Our capacity to imitate someone's gait, postures, or grimaces certainly does not depend on our capacity to describe these in words. We are frequently unable to do the latter, not merely because we lack the appropriate words but because we are unaware both of the elements of which these patterns are made up and of the manner in which they are related. We may well have a name for the whole,[18] or sometimes use comparisons with movements of animals ('creeping', 'ferocious') and the like, or describe conduct as expressive of an attribute of character such as 'furtive', 'timid', 'determined', or 'proud.' In one sense we thus know what we observe, but in another sense we do not know what it is that we thus observe.

Imitation is of course only one particularly obvious instance of the many in which we recognize the actions of others as being of a known kind, of a kind, however, which we are able to describe only by stating the 'meaning' which these actions have to us and not by pointing out the elements from which we recognize this meaning. Whenever we conclude that an individual is in a certain mood, or acts deliberately or purposively or effortlessly, seems to expect[19] something or to threaten or comfort another, etc., we generally do not know, and would not be able to explain, how we know this. Yet we generally act successfully on the basis of such 'understanding' of the conduct of others.

All these instances raise a problem of 'identification', not in the special psycho-analytical but in the ordinary sense of the term, the sense in which some movement (or posture, etc.) of our own which is perceived through one sense is recognized as being of the same kind as the movements of other people which we perceive through another sense. Before imitation is possible, identification must be achieved, i.e., the correspondence established between movement patterns which are perceived through different sense modalities.

4. The Transfer of Learnt Rules

The recognition of a correspondence between patterns made up of different sensory elements (whether belonging to the same or to different sense modalities) presupposes a mechanism of sensory pattern transfer, that is, a mechanism for the transfer of the capacity to discern an abstract order or arrangement

---

and A. L. Macfie, vol. 1 (1976) of *The Works and Correspondence of Adam Smith* (Oxford: Oxford University Press; reprinted, Indianapolis, IN: Liberty Fund, 1982), p. 10.—Ed.]

[18] Getrude Kietz, *Der Ausdrucksgehalt des menschlichen Ganges* (Beiheft 93 to *Zeitschrift für angewandte Psychologie und Charakterkunde*, Leipzig 1948), lists 59 verbs and 67 adjectives which are used in the region of Leipzig to describe distinguishable kinds of gait.

[19] Even William S. Verplanck, the author of *A Glossary of Some Terms Used in the Objective Science of Behavior*, supplement to *Psychological Review*, vol. 64, November 1957, p. 14, (s.v. 'expect') finds himself forced to say that "If one does not 'intuitively know' what *expect* means, one is lost."

from one field to another. That such a capacity should exist seems not implausible as a similar transfer of learning in the motor sphere is a well-established fact: skills learnt with one hand are readily transferred to the other, etc.[20] It has recently also been demonstrated that, for example, monkeys trained to respond to differences in simple rhythms of light signals (opening a door on two signals of equal duration and not opening it on two signals of unequal duration) at once transferred this response to the corresponding rhythms of sound signals.[21] In the field of perception many of the *Gestalt* phenomena, such as the transposition of a melody, also imply the operation of the same principle. The prevalent views on the nature of perception, however, do not supply us with an adequate account of how such a transfer is brought about.[22]

Such a mechanism is not difficult to conceive. The main point to keep in mind is that in order that any two different sensory elements ('elementary sense qualities' or more complex percepts) should be capable of taking the same place in a pattern of a certain kind, they must have certain attributes in common. Unless both can vary along some such scale as large : small, strong : weak, of long duration : of short duration, etc., they cannot serve in the same place as constituents of similar patterns. The most important of these common properties of different kinds of sensations which enables them to take the same place in a pattern of a certain kind is their common space-time framework: while visual, tactile, kinesthetic, and auditory sensations may have the same rhythm, and the first three of them also form the same spatial patterns, this is not possible for sensations of smell and taste.[23]

[20] A convenient survey of the facts is given by Robert S. Woodworth and Harold Schlosberg, *Experimental Psychology*, rev. ed. (New York: Holt, 1954), chapter 24, where also instances of the transfer of 'perceptual skills' are given. See also K. S. Lashley, "The Problem of Serial Order in Behavior", in *Cerebral Mechanisms in Behavior: The Hixon Symposium*, ed. Lloyd Jeffress (New York: Wiley, 1951), pp. 112–36, a paper full of significant suggestions on our problem.

[21] Lucjan C. Stepien, J. Pierre Cordeau, and Theodore Rasmussen, "The Effect of Temporal Lobe and Hippocampal Lesions on Auditory and Visual Recent Memory in Monkeys", *Brain*, vol. 83, September 1960, pp. 472–73.

[22] In modern discussions of these problems resort is generally had to the somewhat vague conception of the 'schema.' For recent discussions of this, see R. C. Oldfield and O. L. Zangwill, "Head's Concept of the Schema and Its Application in Contemporary British Psychology, I–IV", *British Journal of Psychology* (General Section), vol. 32, April 1942, pp. 267–86; vol. 33, July 1942, pp. 58–64; October 1942, pp. 113–29; January 1943, pp. 143–49; R. C. Oldfield, "Memory Mechanisms and the Theory of Schemata", *British Journal of Psychology* (General Section), vol. 45, February 1954, pp. 14–23; and M. D. Vernon, "The Function of Schemata in Perceiving", *Psychological Review*, vol. 62, May 1955, pp. 180–92. We shall not use it here as a technical term because by its various uses it has acquired a penumbra of undesirable connotations.

[23] It is becoming increasingly clear that even the perception of spatial patterns, which we are inclined to ascribe to the simultaneous occurrence of the sensory elements from which the patterns are made up, rests largely on a process of visual or tactual scanning and on the perception of 'gradients', i.e., on the particular sequence of stimuli being recognized as following a

These common attributes that the separate sensations must possess in order to be capable of forming the same abstract patterns must evidently have some distinct neural correlates (impulses in particular groups of neurons which represent them), because only thus can they in some respect have the same effect on our mental processes and actions: if different sensations lead us to describe them as 'large' or 'intense' or 'long', the impulses corresponding to them must at some stage of the hierarchical order of evaluation (classification)[24] reach the same pathways. Once, however, we recognize that in order to possess similar attributes the sensations caused by different nerve impulses must have some identical elements among the 'following'[25] which determines their quality, the problem of the transfer of a pattern that has been learnt in one sensory field to another presents no serious difficulty.

If a certain order or sequence of sensory elements possessing given attributes has acquired a distinctive significance, this significance will be determined by the classification as equivalent of the neural events standing for those attributes and it will thus automatically apply to them also when they are evoked by other sensations than those in connection with which the pattern has been learnt in the first instance. Or, to put this differently, sensations which have common attributes will be capable of forming elements of the same pattern and this pattern will be recognized as one of the same kind even if it has never been experienced before in connection with the particular elements, because the otherwise qualitatively different sensations will have among the impulses determining their quality some which uniquely determine the abstract attribute in question; and whenever the capacity of recognizing an abstract rule which the arrangement of these attributes follows has been acquired in one field, the same master mould will apply when the signs for those abstract attributes are evoked by altogether different elements. It is the classification of

---

rule. Hence, as K. S. Lashley, "The Problem of Serial Order", p. 128, has pointed out, "spatial and temporal order thus appear to be almost completely interchangeable in cerebral action." It would seem as if the task of the theory of perception were increasingly becoming the discovery of the rules according to which various constellations of physical data are translated into perceptual categories so that a great variety of sets of physical facts are interpreted as the same phenomenal situation. This development traces back to Hermann von Helmholtz's conception of the "unconscious inference", in Helmholtz, *Populäre wissenschaftliche Vorträge*, p. 92. [In the English translation, see p. 269, where Helmholtz's "unbewusste Schlüsse" is rendered "unconscious judgment."—Ed.] This has been developed particularly by James J. Gibson, *The Perception of the Visual World* (Boston: Houghton Mifflin, 1950), and has recently produced the most remarkable results in Ivo Kohler's demonstration, in Ivo Kohler, "Experiments with Goggles", *Scientific American*, vol. 206, May 1962, pp. 62–72, of the 'general rules' by which the visual system learns to correct exceedingly complex and variable distortions produced by prismatic spectacles when the eye or the head moves.

[24] For a systematic exposition of the theory underlying this statement see F. A. Hayek, *The Sensory Order* (Chicago: University of Chicago Press, 1952). [A *Collected Works* edition of this work is anticipated.—Ed.]

[25] See Hayek, *Sensory Order*, para. 3.34.

the structure of relationships between these abstract attributes which constitutes the recognition of the patterns as the same or different.

5. Behaviour Patterns and Perception Patterns

In the course of its development[26] any organism will acquire a large repertoire of such perceptual patterns to which it can specifically respond, and among this repertoire of patterns some of the earliest and most firmly embedded will be those due to the proprioceptive (kinesthetic) recording of movement patterns of its own body, movement patterns which in many instances will be guided by innate organization and probably be directed sub-cortically, yet reported to and recorded at higher levels. The term 'movement pattern' in this connection hardly suggests the complexity or variety of the attributes of the movements involved. Not only does it include relative movements of rigid bodies and various bending or elastic movements of flexible bodies, but also continuous and discontinuous, rhythmic and a-rhythmic changes of speed, etc. The opening and closing of jaws or beaks or the characteristic movements of limbs are relatively simple instances of such patterns. They can generally be analysed into several separate movements which together produce the pattern in question.

The young animal for which every day begins with the sight of his elders and siblings yawning and stretching, grooming and defecating, scanning the environment, and so on, and who soon learns to recognize these basic schemata as the same as its own innate movement patterns connected with certain moods (or dispositions, or sets), will tend to place into these perceptual categories everything which approximately fits them. These patterns will provide the master moulds (templates, schemata, or *Schablonen*) in terms of which will be perceived many other complex phenomena in addition to those from which the patterns are derived. What at first may have originated with an innate and fairly specific movement pattern may thus become a learnt and abstract mould for classifying perceived events. ('Classifying' stands here, of course, for a process of channelling, or switching, or 'gating', of the nervous impulses so as to produce a particular disposition or set.)[27] The effect of perceiving that events occur according to a rule will thus be that another rule is imposed upon the further course of the processes in the nervous system.

[26] The expression 'development' is used to include not only ontogenetic but also phylogenetic processes.

[27] See F. A. Hayek, "Scientism and the Study of Society", *Economica*, n.s., vol. 9, August 1942, pp. 276–84, reprinted in *The Counter-Revolution of Science* (Glencoe, IL: The Free Press, 1952), chapter 3. [Now see F. A. Hayek, "Scientism and the Study of Society", in *Studies on the Abuse and Decline of Reason*, ed. Bruce Caldwell, vol. 13 (2010) of *The Collected Works of F. A. Hayek* (Chicago: University of Chicago Press; London: Routledge), pp. 88–98.—Ed.]

The phenomenal (sensory, subjective, or behavioural)[28] world in which such an organism lives will therefore be built up largely of movement patterns characteristic of its own kind (species or wider group). These will be among the most important categories in terms of which it perceives the world and particularly most forms of life. Our tendency to personify (to interpret in anthropomorphic or animistic terms) the events we observe is probably the result of such an application of schemata which our own bodily movements provide. It is they which make, though not yet intelligible, at least perceivable (comprehensible or meaningful) complexes of events which without such perceptual schemata would have no coherence or character as wholes.

It is not surprising that the explicit evoking of these anthropomorphic interpretations should have become one of the main tools of artistic expression by which the poet or painter can conjure up the character of our experiences in an especially vivid manner. Expressions such as that a thundercloud leans threateningly over us, or that a landscape is peaceful or smiling or sombre or wild, are more than merely metaphors. They describe true attributes of our experiences in the terms in which they occur. This does not mean that these attributes belong to the objective events in any other sense than that we intuitively ascribe them to those events. But they are nevertheless part of the environment as we know it and as it determines our conduct. And, as we shall see, if our perceptions in those instances do not in fact help us to understand nature, the fact that sometimes those patterns we read (or project) into nature are all that we know and all that determines our action makes it an essential datum in our efforts to explain the results of human interaction.

The conception that we often perceive patterns without being aware of (or even without perceiving at all) the elements of which they are made up conflicts with the deeply ingrained belief that all recognition of 'abstract' forms is 'derived' from our prior perception of the 'concrete': the assumption that we must first perceive particulars in all their richness and detail before we learn to abstract from them those features which they have in common with other experiences. But, although there exists some clinical evidence that the abstract is often dependent on the functioning of higher nervous centres and that the capacity to form abstract conceptions may be lost while more concrete images are still retained, this is clearly not always so.[29] Nor would it prove that the concrete is chronologically prior. It is at least highly probable that we often perceive only highly abstract features, that is, an order of stimuli which individually are not perceived at all or at least are not identified.[30]

[28] In contrast to objective, physical, scientific, etc. See Hayek, *Sensory Order*, paragraph 1.10.

[29] Cf. Roger W. Brown, *Words and Things* (Glencoe, IL: The Free Press, 1958), pp. 264–98, and Hayek, *Sensory Order*, paras. 6.33–6.43.

[30] Cf. Church, *Language and the Discovery of Reality*, p. 111: "It is perfectly possible to see something well enough to sense that it is something dangerous or something attractive but not well enough to know what it is."

6. Specifiable and Non-specifiable Patterns

The fact that we sometimes perceive patterns which we are unable to specify has often been noticed, but it has scarcely yet been given its proper place in our general conception of our relations to the outside world. It will therefore be useful to contrast it explicitly with the two more familiar ways in which patterns play a rôle in the interpretation of our surroundings. The instance which is familiar to everybody is that of the sensory perception of patterns, such as geometrical figures, which we can also explicitly describe. That the ability intuitively to perceive and the ability discursively to describe a pattern are not the same thing, however, has become evident in the course of the advance of science, which has increasingly led to the interpretation of nature in terms of patterns which can be constructed by our intellect but not intuitively pictured (such as patterns in multidimensional space). Mathematics and logic are largely occupied with the making of new patterns which our perception does not show us but which later may or may not be found to describe relations between observable elements.[31]

In the third case, the one which interests us here, the relation is the reverse: our senses recognize (or better: 'project', or 'read into' the world) patterns which we are in fact not able discursively to describe[32] and perhaps may never be able to specify. That there exist instances where we do recognize such patterns intuitively long before we can describe them the instance of language alone sufficiently demonstrates. But once the existence of some such cases is demonstrated, we must be prepared to discover that they are more numerous and significant than we are immediately aware of. Whether in all such instances we shall, even in principle, be able explicitly to describe the structures which our senses spontaneously treat as instances of the same pattern we shall have to consider at the end of this paper.

The fact that we recognize patterns which we cannot specify does not, of course, mean that such perceptions can legitimately serve as elements of scientific explanation (though they may provide the 'intuitions' which usually pre-

[31] Cf. F. A. Hayek, "The Theory of Complex Phenomena", now reprinted as the second essay in the present volume. [In this note, Hayek is referring to *Studies in Philosophy, Politics and Economics* when he says "second essay in the present volume." "The Theory of Complex Phenomena" appears as chapter 9 of the present volume.—Ed.]

[32] Compare Goethe's remark that "Das Wort bemüht sich nur umsonst, Gestalten schöpferisch aufzubauen." [The passage is from Goethe's *Faust: Eine Tragödie Zweiter Teil*, lines 8691–92. In *Faust: Part Two*, translated by David Luke (Oxford: Oxford University Press, 1994), p. 129, the passage is rendered, "For ever vainly words attempt to recreate and recompose the forms we see."—Ed.] See also E. H. Gombrich, *Art and Illusion: A Study in the Psychology of Pictorial Representation* (New York: Pantheon, 1960), pp. 103–5 and 307–13, and particularly his observation on p. 307 that "it almost looks as if the eye knew of meanings of which the mind knows nothing."

cede the conceptual formulation).[33] But, though such perceptions do not provide a scientific explanation, they not only raise a problem for explanation; we must also take into account in explaining the effects of men's actions that they are guided by such perceptions. We shall have to return to this problem later. At this stage it should merely be pointed out that it is entirely consistent, on the one hand, to deny that 'wholes' which are intuitively perceived by the scientist may legitimately figure in his explanations and, on the other, to insist that the perception of such wholes by the persons whose interactions are the object of investigation must form a datum for scientific analysis. We shall find that perceptions of this sort, which the radical behaviourists wish to disregard because the corresponding stimuli cannot be defined in 'physical terms', are among the chief data on which our explanations of the relations between men must be built.[34]

In a certain sense it is generally true that the requirement that the terms in which an explanation runs must be fully specifiable applies only to the theory (the general formula or the abstract pattern) and not to the particular data which must be inserted in place of the blanks to make it applicable to particular instances. So far as the recognition of the particular conditions is concerned to which a theoretical statement is applicable, we always have to rely on interpersonal agreement, whether the conditions are defined in terms of sensory qualities such as 'green' or 'bitter', or in terms of point coincidences, as is the case where we measure. In these familiar instances this raises in general no difficulty, not only because agreement between different observers is very high, but also because we know how to create the conditions in which different persons will experience the same perceptions. The physical circumstances which produce these sensations can be deliberately manipulated and generally as-

[33] It is a different matter that in medical and other diagnoses 'physiognomy perception' plays a very important rôle as a guide to practice. Even here, however, it cannot directly enter theory. On its rôle cf. Michael Polanyi, "Knowing and Being", *Mind*, vol. 70, October 1961, pp. 458–70. See on these problems also Heinrich Klüver, *Behavior Mechanisms in Monkeys* (Chicago: University of Chicago Press, 1933) pp. 7–9, and Lorenz, "The Role of Gestalt Perception", p. 176, who suggests that "no important scientific fact has ever been 'proved' that had not previously been simply and immediately seen by intuitive *Gestalt* perception."

[34] It is difficult to say how far such perceptions of non-specifiable patterns fit the usual conception of 'sense data', 'data of observation', 'perceptual data', 'empirical ultimates', or 'objective facts', and perhaps even whether we can still speak of perception by the senses or should rather speak of perception by the mind. It would seem as if the whole phenomenon we are considering could not be fitted into the sensualist philosophy from which those conceptions derive. It is clearly not true, as is implied in those terms, that all we experience we must also be in a position to describe. Though we may have a name for such unspecifiable perceptions which our fellows understand, we should have no way of explaining what they are to a person who does not already in some sense perceive the same complexes of events of which we cannot further explain what they have in common.

signed to defined space-time regions which are for the observer 'filled' with the sensory quality in question. We will also find in general that what appears as alike to different people will also have the same effects on other objects; and we regard it as a rather surprising exception if what appears as alike to us acts differently on other objects, or if what appears different to us acts alike on other objects.[35] Yet we can experiment with the stimuli to which such perceptions are due, and though in the last resort the applicability of our theoretical model also rests on agreement on sense perceptions, we can push these, as it were, as far back as we wish.

The situation is different where we cannot specify the structures of elements which people in fact treat as the same pattern and call by the same name. Though in one sense people know in those instances what they perceive, in another they do not know what it is that they thus perceive. While all observers may in fact agree that a person is happy, or acts deliberately or clumsily, or expects something, etc., they cannot for persons who do not know what these terms mean provide what is sometimes misleadingly called an 'ostensive' definition because they cannot point to those parts of the observed environment from which they recognize those attributes.

The intelligibility of communications intended to be understood (or the comprehension of their meaning) on the basis of the perception of the rules which they follow is merely the most conspicuous instance of a phenomenon of much wider occurrence. What we perceive in watching other people (and in some measure also in watching other living things)[36] is not so much particular movements but a purpose or mood or attitude (disposition or set) which we recognize from we do not know what. It is from such perceptions that we derive most of the information which makes the conduct of others intelligible to us. What we recognize as purposive conduct is conduct following a rule with which we are acquainted but which we need not explicitly know. Similarly, that an approach of another person is friendly or hostile, that he is playing a game or willing to sell us some commodity or intends to make love, we recognize without knowing what we recognize it from. In general, we do not know in those instances what psychologists call the 'clues' (or 'cues') from which men recognize what to them is the significant aspect of the situation; and in most instances there will in fact be no specific clues in the sense of single events but merely a pattern of a certain kind which has a meaning to them.

[35] See Hayek, *The Sensory Order*, paras. 1.6–1.21, and "Scientism and the Study of Society", chapter 1.

[36] If the vitalists find causal explanations of the phenomena of life so unsatisfactory, it is probably because such explanations do not fully account for those features by which we intuitively recognize something as living.

7. The Multiple Chain of Rules

We have called the phenomena we are discussing 'rule perception' (though 'regularity perception' would perhaps be more appropriate).[37] That expression has the advantage over such terms as 'pattern perception' and the like in that it more strongly suggests that such perceptions may be of any degree of generality or abstractness, that it clearly includes temporal as well as spatial orders, and that it is compatible with the fact that the rules to which it refers interact in a complex structure. It is also helpful in bringing out the connection between the rules governing perception and the rules governing action.[38]

No attempt will be made here to define 'rule.' It should be noted, however, that in describing the rules on which a system acts, at least some of these rules will have to be given the form of imperatives or norms, i.e., the form 'if A, then do B', though once a framework of such imperatives has been established, within it indicative rules such as 'if A, then B' may be used to determine the premises of the imperative rules. But while all the indicative rules could be restated as imperative rules (namely in the form 'if A, then do as if B'), the reverse is not true.

The unconscious rules which govern our action are often represented as 'customs' or 'habits.' These terms are somewhat misleading, however, because they are usually understood to refer to very specific or particular actions. But the rules of which we are speaking generally control or circumscribe only certain aspects of concrete actions by providing a general schema which is then adapted to the particular circumstances. They will often merely determine or limit the range of possibilities within which the choice is made consciously.[39] By eliminating certain kinds of action altogether and providing certain routine ways of achieving the object, they merely restrict the alternatives on which a conscious choice is required. The moral rules, for example, which have become part of a man's nature will mean that certain conceivable choices will not appear at all among the possibilities between which he chooses. Thus even

[37] Cf. Oliver G. Selfridge, "Pattern Recognition and Learning", in *Information Theory: Papers Read at a Symposium on "Information Theory" Held at the Royal Institution, London, September 12th to 16th, 1955*, ed. Colin Cherry (London: Butterworths Scientific Publications, 1956), p. 345: "A pattern is equivalent to a set of rules for recognizing it", and p. 346: "By 'pattern recognition' is meant classifying a set of data into the learnt categories."

[38] The crucial significance of the concept of rule in this connection was brought home to me by reading Thomas S. Szasz, *The Myth of Mental Illness: Foundations of a Theory of Personal Conduct* (New York: Hoeber-Harper, 1961), and R. S. Peters, *The Concept of Motivation* (London: Routledge and Kegan Paul, 1958), which helped me to bring together various strands of thought starting from different origins.

[39] Cf. G. Humphrey, *The Nature of Learning in its Relation to the Living System* (London: Kegan Paul, Trench, Trubner, 1933), especially p. 255, who distinguishes with respect to habits between the fixed strategy and the variable tactics.

decisions which have been carefully considered will in part be determined by rules of which the acting person is not aware. Like scientific laws,[40] the rules which guide an individual's action are better seen as determining what he will not do rather than what he will do.

The relations between rules of perception and rules of action are complex. So far as the perception of actions of other individuals is concerned, we have seen that in the first instance the perceiving individual's own action patterns provide the master moulds by which the action patterns of other individuals are recognized. But recognizing an action pattern as one of a class determines merely that it has the same meaning as others of the same class, but not yet what that meaning is. The latter rests on the further pattern of action, or set of rules, which in response to the recognition of a pattern as one of a certain kind the organism imposes upon its own further activities.[41] Every perception of a rule in the external events as well as every single perceived event, or any need arising out of the internal processes of the organism, thus adds to or modifies the set of rules governing the further responses to new stimuli. It is the total of such activated rules (or conditions imposed upon further action) which constitutes what is called the 'set' (disposition) of the organism at any particular moment, and the significance of newly received signals consists in the manner in which they modify this complex of rules.[42]

The complexity of the arrangement in which these rules may be superimposed and interrelated is difficult briefly to indicate. We must assume that there exists not only on the perceptual side a hierarchy of superimposed classes of classes, etc., but that similarly also on the motor side not merely dispositions to act according to a rule but dispositions to change dispositions and so on will

---

[40]Cf. Karl R. Popper, *The Logic of Scientific Discovery* (London: Hutchinson, 1959). [Hayek doubtless had in mind Popper's statement on p. 41 of *Logic*: "Not for nothing do we call the laws of nature 'laws': the more they prohibit the more they say."—Ed.]

[41]I presume that it is this circular connection between action patterns and perception patterns which Viktor von Weizsäcker, *Der Gestaltkreis: Theorie der Einheit von Wahrnehmen und Bewegen*, 3rd ed. (Stuttgart: Thieme, 1947), had in mind in speaking of the *Gestaltkreis*. In this connection it should be mentioned that, apart from the *Gestalt* theorists, those who have given most attention to the phenomena discussed here were mainly students influenced by phenomenologist or existentialist conceptions, though I find myself unable to accept their philosophical interpretations. See particularly F. J. J. Buytendijk, *Allgemeine Theorie der menschlichen Haltung und Bewegung als Verbindung und Gegenüberstellung von physiologischer und psychologischer Betrachtungsweise* (Berlin-Heidelberg: Springer, 1956); Maurice Merleau-Ponty, *La structure du comportement* (Paris: Presses universitaires de France, 1942); and Plessner, "Die Deutung des mimischen Ausdrucks." Cf. also Hayek, *Sensory Order*, paras. 4.45–4.63 and 5.63–5.75.

[42]That the arrival of additional modifiers of an action that may already be sufficiently determined by other circumstances does not lead to over-determination presupposes an organization more complex than that represented, for example, by a system of simultaneous equations, something in which a 'normal' (general purpose or routine) instruction can be superseded by another containing more specific information.

operate chains which may be of considerable length. Indeed, in view of the inter-connections between the sensory and the motor elements on all levels, it becomes impossible clearly to distinguish between an ascending (sensory) and descending (motor) branch of the process; we should conceive of the whole rather as one continuous stream in which the connection between any group of stimuli and any group of responses is effected by many arcs of different length, with the longer ones not only controlling the results of the shorter ones but in turn being controlled by the ongoing processes in the higher centres through which they pass. The first step in the successive classification of the stimuli must thus be seen as at the same time the first step in a successive imposition of rules on action, and the final specification of a particular action as the last step of many chains of successive classifications of stimuli according to the rules to which their arrangement corresponds.[43]

It would seem to follow from this that the meaning (connotation, intension) of a symbol or concept will normally be a rule imposed on further mental processes which itself need not be conscious or specifiable. This would imply that such a concept need not be accompanied by an image or have an external 'referent': it merely puts into operation a rule which the organism possesses. This rule imposed upon the further processes should, of course, not be confused with the rule by which the symbol or action having the meaning is recognized. Nor must we expect to find any simple correspondence between the structure of any system of symbols and the structure of meaning: what we have to deal with is a set of relations between two systems of rules. A great part of the current philosophies of 'symbolism' seem in this respect to be barking up the wrong tree—not to speak of the paradox of a 'theory of communication' which believes that it can account for communication while disregarding meaning or the process of understanding.

8. Γνῶσις τοῦ ὁμοίου τῷ ὁμοίῳ[44]

We have yet to consider more closely the rôle which the perception of the meaning of other people's action must play in the scientific explanation of the interaction of men. The problem which arises here is known in the discussion of the methodology of the social sciences as that of *Verstehen* (understanding). We have seen that this understanding of the meaning of actions is of the same kind as the understanding of communications (i.e., of action intended to be understood). It includes what the eighteenth-century authors described

---

[43]Cf. Hayek, *Sensory Order*, paras. 4.45–4.63 and 5.63–5.75.

[44][Aristotle's summary of Empedocles's doctrine of perception might be translated as "knowledge of like is by means of like"—that is, the senses are similar to what they sense.—Ed.]

as sympathy and what has more recently been discussed under the heading of 'empathy' (*Einfühlung*). Since we shall be concerned chiefly with the use of these perceptions as data for the theoretical social sciences, we shall concentrate on what is sometimes called rational understanding (or rational reconstruction), that is, on the instances where we recognize that the persons in whose actions we are interested base their decisions on the meaning of what they perceive. The theoretical social sciences do not treat all of a person's actions as an unspecifiable and unexplainable whole but, in their efforts to account for the unintended consequences of individual actions, endeavour to reconstruct the individual's reasoning from the data which to him are provided by the recognition of the actions of others as meaningful wholes. We shall indicate this limitation by speaking of *intelligibility* and of *comprehending the meaning* of human action rather than of understanding.[45]

The chief question we shall have to consider is that of what, and how much, we must have in common with other people in order to find their actions intelligible or meaningful. We have seen that our capacity to recognize action as following rules and having meaning rests on ourselves already being equipped with these rules. This 'knowledge by acquaintance' presupposes therefore that some of the rules in terms of which we perceive and act are the same as those by which the conduct of those whose actions we interpret is guided.

The contention that intelligibility of human action presupposes a certain likeness between actor and the interpreter of his actions has led to the misunderstanding that this means that, for example, "only a war-like historian can tackle a Genghis Khan or a Hitler."[46] This, of course, is not implied in the contention. We need not be wholly alike or even have a similar character with those whose communications or other actions we find intelligible, but we must be made up of the same ingredients, however different the mixture may be in the particular instances. The requirement of likeness is of the same kind as in the case of understanding language, although in the latter case the specificity of languages to particular cultures adds an extra requirement which is not needed for the interpretation of the meaning of many other actions. One need

[45]See Ludwig von Mises, "Begreifen und Verstehen" (1930), translated by George Reisman as "Conception and Understanding", in Ludwig von Mises, *Epistemological Problems of Economics* (Princeton, NJ: D. Van Nostrand, 1960), pp. 130–45, and Ludwig von Mises, *Human Action: A Treatise on Economics*, 3rd ed. (Chicago: Henry Regnery, 1966), where he distinguishes between *Begreifen* and *Verstehen*, though I prefer to render his *Begreifen* by 'comprehension' rather than by his own English term 'conception.' To the first of his works cited I owe also the quotation from Empedocles used as the heading of this section, which is derived from Aristotle, *Metaphysics* B, 1000b5. A careful analysis of the whole problem of *Verstehen* which deserves to be better known will be found in Heinrich Gomperz, *Über Sinn und Sinngebilde, Verstehen und Erklären* (Tübingen: Mohr, 1929).

[46]J. W. N. Watkins, "Ideal Types and Historical Explanation", in *Readings in the Philosophy of Science*, ed. Herbert Feigl and May Brodbeck (New York: Appleton-Century-Crofts, 1953), p. 740.

clearly not be frequently or even ever violently angry to be familiar with the rage pattern or to recognize and interpret a choleric temper.[47] Nor need one be at all like Hitler to understand his reasoning in a way one cannot understand the mental processes of an imbecile. Nor does one have to like the same things as another to know what 'liking' means.[48] Intelligibility is certainly a matter of degree and it is a commonplace that people who are more alike also understand each other better. Yet this does not alter the fact that even in the limiting case of the restricted understanding which occurs between men and higher animals, and still more in the understanding between men of different cultural backgrounds or character, intelligibility of communications and other acts rests on a partial similarity of mental structure.

It is true that there is no systematic procedure by which we are able to decide in a particular instance whether our comprehension of the meaning of the action of others is correct, and also that for this reason we can never be certain of this sort of fact. But of this those who guide their action by physiognomic perceptions are generally also aware, and the degree of confidence they attach to their knowledge of the meaning of another man's action is as much a datum by which they orient themselves as the meaning itself, and must therefore in the same manner enter our scientific account of the effects of the interactions of many men.

9. Supra-conscious Rules and the Explanation of Mind

So far our argument has rested solely on the uncontestable assumption that we are not in fact able to specify all the rules which govern our perceptions and actions. We still have to consider the question whether it is conceivable that we should ever be in a position discursively to describe all (or at least any one we like) of these rules, or whether mental activity must always be guided by some rules which we are in principle not able to specify.

If it should turn out that it is basically impossible to state or communicate

---

[47]Cf. Robert Redfield, "Social Science among the Humanities", *Measure: A Critical Journal*, vol. 1, Winter 1950, p. 71: "The anthropologist demonstrates the existence of human nature whenever he finds out what an exotic people are thinking and feeling. He can do this only by supposing that they have in common with him certain acquired propensities of attitude; these are human nature. To be able to find out what it is that a Zuni Indian is ashamed of, one must first know what it is to be ashamed."

[48]Cf. Heinrich Klüver, "Functional Significance of the Geniculo-Striate System", in *Visual Mechanisms*, ed. Heinrich Klüver, vol. 7 of *Biological Symposia*, ed. Jaques Cattell (Lancaster, PA: Jaques Cattell Press, 1942), p. 286: "It should be realized that 'emotional' or 'affective' qualities may become visible as 'physiognomic' properties of objects without emotional states or events occurring in the observer or the observed object. We may see, for instance, 'sadness' or 'aggressiveness' in a face without being emotionally affected."

all the rules which govern our actions, including our communications and explicit statements, this would imply an inherent limitation of our possible explicit knowledge and, in particular, the impossibility of ever fully explaining a mind of the complexity of our own. Yet, though I am not able to supply a strict proof, this seems to me indeed to follow from the preceding considerations.

If everything we can express (state, communicate) is intelligible to others only because their mental structure is governed by the same rules as ours, it would seem that these rules themselves can never be communicated. This seems to imply that in one sense we always know not only more than we can deliberately state but also more than we can be aware of or deliberately test; and that much that we successfully do depends on presuppositions which are outside the range of what we can either state or reflect upon. This application to all conscious thought of what seems obviously true of verbal statements seems to follow from the fact that such thought must, if we are not to be led into an infinite regress, be assumed to be directed by rules which in turn cannot be conscious—by a supra-conscious[49] mechanism which operates upon the contents of consciousness but which cannot itself be conscious.[50]

The main difficulty of admitting the existence of such supra-conscious processes is probably our habit of regarding conscious thought and explicit statements as in some sense the highest level of mental functions. While we are clearly often not aware of mental processes because they have not yet risen to the level of consciousness but proceed on what are (both physiologically and psychologically) lower levels, there is no reason why the conscious level should be the highest level, and there are many grounds which make it probable that, in order to be conscious, processes must be guided by a supra-conscious order which cannot be the object of its own representations. Mental events may thus be unconscious and incommunicable because they proceed on too high a level as well as because they proceed on too low a level.

To put this differently: if 'to have meaning' is to have a place in an order

[49] Or better, perhaps, 'meta-conscious', since the problem is essentially the same as those which have given rise to meta-mathematics, meta-languages, and meta-legal rules.
[50] Twenty years ago I suggested in "Scientism and the Study of Society", p. 86 [*Studies on the Abuse and Decline of Reason*, pp. 112–13.—Ed.], that it would seem that any mechanism of classification would always have to possess a degree of complexity greater than any one of the different objects it classifies, and if this is correct it would follow that it is impossible that our brain should ever be able to produce a complete explanation of the particular ways in which it classifies stimuli (as distinguished from a mere explanation of the principle); and ten years later I attempted to state the argument more fully in *The Sensory Order*, paras. 8.66–8.86. It now seems to me as if this would follow from what I understand to be Georg Cantor's theorem in the theory of sets according to which in any system of classification there are always more classes than things to be classified, which presumably implies that no system of classes can contain itself. But I do not feel competent to attempt such a proof.

which we share with other people, this order itself cannot have meaning because it cannot have a place in itself. A point may have a distinct place in a network of lines which differentiates it from all other points in that network; and, similarly, a complex structure of relationships may be distinguished from all other similar structures by a place in a more comprehensive structure which gives each element of the first structure and its relations a distinct 'place.' But the distinguishing character of such an order could never be defined by its place in itself, and a mechanism possessing such an order, though it may be able to indicate meaning by reference to such a place, can never by its action so reproduce the set of relations which defines this place as to distinguish it from another such set of relations.

It is important not to confuse the contention that any such system must always act on some rules which it cannot communicate with the contention that there are particular rules which no such system could ever state. All the former contention means is that there will always be some rules governing a mind which that mind in its then prevailing state cannot communicate, and that, if it ever were to acquire the capacity of communicating these rules, this would presuppose that it had acquired further higher rules which make the communication of the former possible but which themselves will still be incommunicable.

To those familiar with the celebrated theorem due to Kurt Gödel it will probably be obvious that these conclusions are closely related to those Gödel has shown to prevail in formalized arithmetical systems.[51] It would thus appear that Gödel's theorem is but a special case of a more general principle applying to all conscious and particularly all rational processes, namely the principle that among their determinants there must always be some rules which cannot be stated or even be conscious. At least all we can talk about and probably all we can consciously think about presupposes the existence of a framework which determines its meaning, i.e., a system of rules which operate us but which we can neither state nor form an image of and which we can merely evoke in others in so far as they already possess them.

It would lead too far if we were here to attempt an examination of the processes by which the manipulation of rules of which we are conscious may lead to the building up of further meta-conscious rules, in terms of which we may then be able explicitly to formulate rules of which we were formerly unconscious. It seems probable that much of the mysterious powers of scientific creativity are due to processes of this sort which involve a restructuring of the supra-conscious matrix in which our conscious thought moves.

We must be content here with providing a framework within which the

---

[51] See Ernest Nagel and James R. Newman, *Gödel's Proof* (New York: New York University Press, 1958) for a semi-popular exposition.

problem of meaning (intelligibility, significance, understanding) can be meaningfully discussed. To pursue it further would demand the construction of a formal model of a causal system capable not only of recognizing rules in the observed events and responding to them according to another set of rules, different from, yet related to the former, but also able to communicate its perceptions and actions to another system of the same sort, and the demonstration that two such communicating systems must be governed by a common set of rules which cannot be communicated between them. This, however, is a task which would exceed not only the scope of this paper but also the powers of its author.

PART III

A GENERAL THEORY OF ORDERS, WITH APPLICATIONS

NINE

THE THEORY OF COMPLEX PHENOMENA[1]

1. Pattern Recognition and Pattern Prediction

Man has been impelled to scientific inquiry by wonder and by need. Of these wonder has been incomparably more fertile. There are good reasons for this. Where we wonder we have already a question to ask. But however urgently we may want to find our way in what appears just chaotic, so long as we do not know what to look for, even the most attentive and persistent observation of the bare facts is not likely to make them more intelligible. Intimate acquaintance with the facts is certainly important; but systematic observation can start only after problems have arisen. Until we have definite questions to ask we cannot employ our intellect; and questions presuppose that we have formed some provisional hypothesis or theory about the events.[2]

---

[1] Reprinted from *The Critical Approach to Science and Philosophy: In Honor of Karl R. Popper*, ed. Mario Bunge (New York: The Free Press, 1964), pp. 332–49. The article was there printed (apart from a few stylistic emendations by the editor) in the form in which I had completed the manuscript in December 1961 and without my ever having seen proofs. I have now availed myself of this opportunity to insert some references I had intended to add in the proofs. [Reprinted in F. A. Hayek, *Studies in Philosophy, Politics and Economics* (Chicago: University of Chicago Press, 1967), pp. 22–42.—Ed.]

[2] See already Aristotle, *The Metaphysics*, translated by Hugh Tredennick (London: William Heinemann, Loeb Classical Library, 1933), Book I, part 2, section 9982b, (Loeb. ed., p. 13): "It is through wonder that men now begin and originally began to philosophize . . . it is obvious that they pursued science for the sake of knowledge, and not for any practical utility"; also Adam Smith, "The Principles which Lead and Direct Philosophical Enquiries, Illustrated by the History of Astronomy", in *Essays* (London: Alexander Murray, 1869), p. 340: "Wonder, therefore, and not any expectation of advantage from its discoveries, is the first principle which prompts mankind to the study of Philosophy, of that science which pretends to lay open the concealed connections that unite the various appearances of nature; and they pursue this study for its own sake, as an original pleasure or good in itself, without regarding its tendency to procure them the means of many other pleasures." [See now Adam Smith, "The Principles which Lead and Direct Philosophical Enquiries, Illustrated by the History of Astronomy", in *Essays on Philosophical Subjects*, ed. W. P. D. Wightman and J. C. Bryce, vol. 3 of *The Glasgow Edition of the Works and Correspondence of Adam Smith* (Glasgow: University of Glasgow, 1976; reprinted, Indianapolis, IN: Liberty Fund, 1981), p. 51.—Ed.] Is there really any evidence for the now popular contrary view that, e.g., "hunger in the Nile Valley led to the development of geometry" (as Gardner Murphy, in

257

Questions will arise at first only after our senses have discerned some recurring pattern or order in the events. It is a re-cognition of some regularity (or recurring pattern, or order), of some similar feature in otherwise different circumstances, which makes us wonder and ask "why?"[3] Our minds are so made that when we notice such regularity in diversity we suspect the presence of the same agent and become curious to detect it. It is to this trait of our minds that we owe whatever understanding and mastery of our environment we have achieved.

Many such regularities of nature are recognized 'intuitively' by our senses. We see and hear patterns as much as individual events without having to resort to intellectual operations. In many instances these patterns are of course so much part of the environment which we take for granted that they do not cause questions. But where our senses show us new patterns, this causes surprise and questioning. To such curiosity we owe the beginning of science.

Marvellous, however, as the intuitive capacity of our senses for pattern recognition is, it is still limited.[4] Only certain kinds of regular arrangements (not

"Social Motivation", in the *Handbook of Social Psychology*, ed. Gardner Lindzey (Cambridge, MA: Addison-Wesley, 1954), vol. 2, p. 616, tells us)? Surely the fact that the discovery of geometry turned out to be useful does not prove that it was discovered because of its usefulness. On the fact that economics has in some degree been an exception to the general rule and has suffered by being guided more by need than by detached curiosity, see my lecture on "The Trend of Economic Thinking" in *Economica*, vol. 13, May 1933, pp. 121–37. [Now see F. A. Hayek, "The Trend of Economic Thinking", in *The Trend of Economic Thinking*, ed. W. W. Bartley and Stephen Kresge, vol. 3 (1991) of *The Collected Works of F. A. Hayek* (Chicago: University of Chicago Press; London: Routledge), pp. 17–34.—Ed.]

[3]See Karl Popper, *The Poverty of Historicism* (London: Routledge and Kegan Paul, 1957), p. 121: "Science . . . cannot start with observations, or with the 'collection of data', as some students of method believe. Before we can collect data, our interest in *data of a certain kind* must be aroused: the *problem* always comes first." Also in his *The Logic of Scientific Discovery* (London: Hutchinson, 1959), p. 59: "observation is always *observation in the light of theories.*"

[4]Although in some respects the capacity of our senses for pattern recognition clearly also exceeds the capacity of our mind for specifying these patterns. The question of the extent to which this capacity of our senses is the result of another kind of (pre-sensory) experience is another matter. See, on this and on the general point that all perception involves a theory or hypothesis, my book *The Sensory Order* (Chicago: University of Chicago Press, 1952), esp. paragraph 7.37 [A *Collected Works* edition of this volume is anticipated.—Ed.]; also the remarkable thought expressed by Adam Ferguson (and probably derived from George Berkeley) in *An Essay on the History of Civil Society* (Edinburgh: Printed for A. Millar and T. Caddel, London, and A. Kincaid and J. Bell, Edinburgh, 1767), p. 39, that "the inferences of thought are sometimes not to be distinguished from the perceptions of sense"; as well as Hermann von Helmholtz's theory of the "unconscious inferences" involved in most perceptions. [See Hermann von Helmholtz, *Popular Lectures on Scientific Subjects*, translated by E. Atkinson (London: Longmans, Green, 1904), pp. 269 *et seq.*—Ed.] For a recent revival of these ideas see Norwood R. Hanson, *Patterns of Discovery: An Inquiry into the Conceptual Foundations of Science* (Cambridge: Cambridge University Press, 1958), esp. p. 19, and the views on the rôle of 'hypotheses' in perception as developed in recent 'cognition theory' by Jerome S. Bruner, Leo Postman and others. [The interested reader might consult

necessarily the simplest) obtrude themselves on our senses. Many of the patterns of nature we can discover only *after* they have been constructed by our mind. The systematic construction of such new patterns is the business of mathematics.[5] The rôle which geometry plays in this respect with regard to some visual patterns is merely the most familiar instance of this. The great strength of mathematics is that it enables us to describe abstract patterns which cannot be perceived by our senses, and to state the common properties of hierarchies or classes of patterns of a highly abstract character. Every algebraic equation or set of such equations defines in this sense a class of patterns, with the individual manifestation of this kind of pattern being particularized as we substitute definite values for the variables.

It is probably the capacity of our senses spontaneously to recognize certain kinds of patterns that has led to the erroneous belief that if we look only long enough, or at a sufficient number of instances of natural events, a pattern will always reveal itself. That this often is so means merely that in those cases the theorizing has been done already by our senses. Where, however, we have to deal with patterns for the development of which there has been no biological reason, we shall first have to invent the pattern before we can discover its presence in the phenomena—or before we shall be able to test its applicability to what we observe. A theory will always define only a kind (or class) of patterns, and the particular manifestation of the pattern to be expected will depend on the particular circumstances (the 'initial and marginal conditions' to which, for the purposes of this article, we shall refer as 'data'). How much in fact we shall be able to predict will depend on how many of those data we can ascertain.

The description of the pattern which the theory provides is commonly regarded merely as a tool which will enable us to predict the particular manifestations of the pattern that will appear in specific circumstances. But the prediction that in certain general conditions a pattern of a certain kind will appear is also a significant (and falsifiable) prediction. If I tell somebody that if he goes to my study he will find there a rug with a pattern made up of diamonds and meanders, he will have no difficulty in deciding "whether that prediction was verified or falsified by the result",[6] even though I have said nothing about the arrangement, size, colour, etc., of the elements from which the pattern of the rug is formed.

The distinction between a prediction of the appearance of a pattern of a

---

Jerome S. Bruner et al., *Contemporary Approaches to Cognition: A Symposium Held at the University of Colorado* (Cambridge, MA: Harvard University Press, 1957), or Leo Postman, *Learned Principles of Organization in Memory* (Washington, DC: American Psychological Association, 1954).—Ed.]

[5]Cf. G. H. Hardy, *A Mathematician's Apology* (Cambridge: Cambridge University Press, 1941), p. 24: "A mathematician, like a painter or a poet, is a maker of patterns."

[6]Charles Dickens, *The Personal History of David Copperfield* (London: Bradbury and Evans, 1850), p. 1.

certain class and a prediction of the appearance of a particular instance of this class is sometimes important even in the physical sciences. The mineralogist who states that the crystals of a certain mineral are hexagonal, or the astronomer who assumes that the course of a celestial body in the field of gravity of another will correspond to one of the conic sections, make significant predictions which can be refuted. But in general the physical sciences tend to assume that it will in principle always be possible to specify their predictions to any degree desired.[7] The distinction assumes, however, much greater importance when we turn from the relatively simple phenomena with which the natural sciences deal, to the more complex phenomena of life, of mind, and of society, where such specifications may not always be possible.[8]

2. Degrees of Complexity

The distinction between simplicity and complexity raises considerable philosophical difficulties when applied to statements. But there seems to exist a fairly easy and adequate way to measure the degree of complexity of different kinds of abstract patterns. The minimum number of elements of which an instance of the pattern must consist in order to exhibit all the characteristic attributes of the class of patterns in question appears to provide an unambiguous criterion.

It has occasionally been questioned whether the phenomena of life, of mind, and of society are really more complex than those of the physical world.[9] This

---

[7] Though it may be permissible to doubt whether it is in fact possible to predict, e.g., the precise pattern which the vibrations of an airplane will at a particular moment produce in the standing wave on the surface of the coffee in my cup.

[8] Cf. Michael Scriven, "A Possible Distinction between Traditional Scientific Disciplines and the Study of Human Behavior", in *The Foundations of Science and the Concepts of Psychology and Psychoanalysis*, ed. Herbert Feigl and Michael Scriven, vol. 1 (1956) of *Minnesota Studies in the Philosophy of Science* (Minnesota: University of Minnesota Press), p. 332: "The difference between the scientific study of behavior and that of physical phenomena is thus partly due to the relatively greater complexity of the simplest phenomena we are concerned to account for in a behavioral theory."

[9] Ernest Nagel, "Explanation and Understanding in the Social Sciences", in *The Structure of Science: Problems in the Logic of Scientific Explanation* (New York: Harcourt, Brace and World: 1961), p. 505: "though social phenomena may indeed be complex, it is by no means certain that they are in general more complex than physical and biological phenomena." See, however, John von Neumann, "The General and Logical Theory of Automata", in *Cerebral Mechanisms in Behavior: The Hixon Symposium*, ed. Lloyd A. Jeffress (New York: John Wiley and Sons, 1951), p. 24: "we are dealing here with parts of logics with which we have practically no past experience. The order of complexity is out of all proportion to anything we have ever known." It may be useful to give here a few illustrations of the orders of magnitude with which biology and neurology have to deal. While the total number of electrons in the Universe has been estimated at 10^{79} and the number of electrons and protons at 10^{100}, there are in chromosomes with 1,000 locations [genes]

seems to be largely due to a confusion between the degree of complexity characteristic of a peculiar *kind* of phenomenon and the degree of complexity to
which, by a combination of elements, any kind of phenomenon can be built
up. Of course, in this manner physical phenomena may achieve any degree of
complexity. Yet when we consider the question from the angle of the minimum
number of distinct variables a formula or model must possess in order to reproduce the characteristic patterns of structures of different fields (or to exhibit
the general laws which these structures obey), the increasing complexity as we
proceed from the inanimate to the ('more highly organized') animate and social
phenomena becomes fairly obvious.

It is, indeed, surprising how simple in these terms, i.e., in terms of the number of distinct variables, appear all the laws of physics, and particularly of
mechanics, when we look through a collection of formulae expressing them.[10]
On the other hand, even such relatively simple constituents of biological phenomena as feedback (or cybernetic) systems, in which a certain combination of
physical structures produces an overall structure possessing distinct characteristic properties, require for their description something much more elaborate
than anything describing the general laws of mechanics. In fact, when we ask
ourselves by what criteria we single out certain phenomena as 'mechanical'
or 'physical', we shall probably find that these laws are simple in the sense defined. Non-physical phenomena are more complex because we call physical
what can be described by relatively simple formulae.

The 'emergence' of 'new' patterns as a result of the increase in the number

---

with 10 allelomorphs 10^{1000} possible combinations; and the number of possible proteins is estimated at 10^{2700} (Ludwig von Bertalanffy, *Problems of Life* [New York: John Wiley and Sons, 1952],
p. 103). [The brackets around 'genes' are Hayek's.—Ed.] C. Judson Herrick, in *Brains of Rats
and Men: A Survey of the Origin and Biological Significance of the Cerebral Cortex* (Chicago: University of
Chicago Press, 1926), p. 9, suggests that "during a few minutes of intense cortical activity the
number of interneuronic connections actually made (counting also those that are activated more
than once in different associational patterns) may well be as great as the total number of atoms
in the solar system" (i.e., 10^{56}); and Ralph W. Gerard, in "What Is Memory?", *Scientific American*,
vol. 189, September 1953, p. 118, has estimated that in the course of seventy years a man may
accumulate 15 x 10^{12} units of information ('bits'), which is more than 1,000 times larger than
the number of nerve cells. The further complications which social relations superimpose upon
this are, of course, relatively insignificant. But the point is that if we wanted to 'reduce' social
phenomena to physical events, they would constitute an additional complication, superimposed
upon that of the physiological processes determining mental events.

[10]Cf. Warren Weaver, "A Quarter Century in the Natural Sciences", *The Rockefeller Foundation
Annual Report* (New York: Rockefeller Foundation, 1958), chapter 1, "Science and Complexity",
which, when writing this, I knew only in the abbreviated version which appeared in the *American
Scientist*, vol. 36, October 1948, pp. 536–44. [As noted in "Degrees of Explanation", p. 196,
note 2, this volume, the first chapter of "A Quarter Century in the Natural Sciences" is actually
only about half the length of Weaver's original "Science and Complexity" essay in the *American
Scientist*. Hayek therefore was wrong to refer to the 1948 version as "abbreviated."—Ed.]

of elements between which simple relations exist, means that this larger structure as a whole will possess certain general or abstract features which will recur independently of the particular values of the individual data, so long as the general structure (as described, e.g., by an algebraic equation) is preserved.[11] Such 'wholes', defined in terms of certain general properties of their structure, will constitute distinctive objects of explanation for a theory, even though such a theory may be merely a particular way of fitting together statements about the relations between the individual elements.

It is somewhat misleading to approach this task mainly from the angle of whether such structures are 'open' or 'closed' systems. There are, strictly speaking, no closed systems within the universe. All we can ask is whether in the particular instance the points of contact through which the rest of the universe acts upon the system we try to single out (and which for the theory become the data) are few or many. These data, or variables, which determine the particular form which the pattern described by the theory will assume in the given circumstances, will be more numerous in the case of complex wholes and much more difficult to ascertain and control than in the case of simple phenomena.

What we single out as wholes, or where we draw the 'partition boundary',[12] will be determined by the consideration whether we can thus isolate recurrent patterns of coherent structures of a distinct kind which we do in fact encounter in the world in which we live. Many complex patterns which are conceivable and might recur we shall not find it worthwhile to construct. Whether it will be useful to elaborate and study a pattern of a particular kind will depend on whether the structure it describes is persistent or merely accidental. The coherent structures in which we are mainly interested are those in which a complex pattern has produced properties which make self-maintaining the structure showing it.

---

[11] Lloyd Morgan's conception of 'emergence' derives, *via* George Henry Lewes (*Problems of Life and Mind, First Series: The Foundations of a Creed* [Boston: Osgood, 1875]), vol. 2, Problem V, chapter 3, section headed "Resultants and Emergents", p. 368), from John Stuart Mill's distinction of the 'heteropathic' laws of chemistry and other complex phenomena from the ordinary 'composition of causes' in mechanics, etc. See his *A System of Logic, Ratiocinative and Inductive, Being a Connected View of the Principles of Evidence, and the Methods of Scientific Investigation* (London: John W. Parker, West Strand, 1843), vol. 1, book III, chapter 6, p. 431 [Now see John Stuart Mill, *A System of Logic Ratiocinative and Inductive: Being a Connected View of the Principles of Evidence and the Methods of Scientific Investigation*, ed. John Robson, vol. 7 (1973) of *Collected Works of John Stuart Mill* (Toronto: University of Toronto Press, 1963–1991; reprinted, Indianapolis, IN: Liberty Fund, 2006), p. 374.—Ed.], and C. Lloyd Morgan, *The Emergence of Novelty* (London: Williams and Norgate, 1933), p. 12.

[12] Lewis White Beck, "The 'Natural Science Ideal' in the Social Sciences", *The Scientific Monthly*, vol. 68, June 1949, p. 388.

3. Pattern Prediction with Incomplete Data

The multiplicity of even the minimum of distinct elements required to produce (and therefore also of the minimum number of data required to explain) a complex phenomenon of a certain kind creates problems which dominate the disciplines concerned with such phenomena and gives them an appearance very different from that of those concerned with simpler phenomena. The chief difficulty in the former becomes one of in fact ascertaining all the data determining a particular manifestation of the phenomenon in question, a difficulty which is often insurmountable in practice and sometimes even an absolute one.[13] Those mainly concerned with simple phenomena are often inclined to think that where this is the case a theory is useless and that scientific procedure demands that we should find a theory of sufficient simplicity to enable us to derive from it predictions of particular events. To them the theory, the knowledge of the pattern, is merely a tool whose usefulness depends entirely on our capacity to translate it into a representation of the circumstances producing a particular event. Of the theories of simple phenomena this is largely true.[14]

There is, however, no justification for the belief that it must always be possible to discover such simple regularities and that physics is more advanced because it has succeeded in doing this while other sciences have not yet done so. It is rather the other way round: physics has succeeded because it deals with phenomena which, in our sense, are simple. But a simple theory of phenomena which are in their nature complex (or one which, if that expression be preferred, has to deal with more highly organized phenomena) is probably merely of necessity false—at least without a specified *ceteris paribus* assumption, after the full statement of which the theory would no longer be simple.

We are, however, interested not only in individual events, and it is also not only predictions of individual events which can be empirically tested. We are equally interested in the recurrence of abstract patterns as such; and the prediction that a pattern of a certain kind will appear in defined circumstances is a falsifiable (and therefore empirical) statement. Knowledge of the conditions in which a pattern of a certain kind will appear, and of what depends on its preservation, may be of great practical importance. The circumstances or conditions in which the pattern described by the theory will appear are defined

---

[13] Cf. Hayek, *The Sensory Order*, paras. 8.66–8.86.

[14] Cf. Ernest Nagel, "Problems of Concept and Theory Formation in the Social Sciences", in *Science, Language and Human Rights*, American Philosophical Association, Eastern Division (Philadelphia: University of Pennsylvania Press, 1952), p. 62: "In many cases we are ignorant of the appropriate initial and boundary conditions, and cannot make precise forecasts even though available theory is adequate for that purpose."

by the range of values which may be inserted for the variables of the formula. All we need to know in order to make such a theory applicable to a situation is, therefore, that the data possess certain general properties (or belong to the class defined by the scope of the variables). Beyond this we need to know nothing about their individual attributes so long as we are content to derive merely the sort of pattern that will appear and not its particular manifestation.

Such a theory destined to remain 'algebraic',[15] because we are in fact unable to substitute particular values for the variables, ceases then to be a mere tool and becomes the final result of our theoretical efforts. Such a theory will, of course, in Popper's terms,[16] be one of small empirical content, because it enables us to predict or explain only certain general features of a situation which may be compatible with a great many particular circumstances. It will perhaps enable us to make only what Michael Scriven has called 'hypothetical predictions',[17] i.e., predictions dependent on yet unknown future events; in any case the range of phenomena compatible with it will be wide and the possibility of falsifying it correspondingly small. But as in many fields this will be for the present, or perhaps forever, all the theoretical knowledge we can achieve, it will nevertheless extend the range of the possible advance of scientific knowledge.

The advance of science will thus have to proceed in two different directions: while it is certainly desirable to make our theories as falsifiable as possible, we must also push forward into fields where, as we advance, the degree of falsifiability necessarily decreases. This is the price we have to pay for an advance into the field of complex phenomena.

4. Statistics Impotent to Deal with Pattern Complexity

Before we further illustrate the use of those mere 'explanations of the principle'[18] provided by 'algebraic' theories which describe only the general character of higher-level generalities, and before we consider the important conclusions which follow from the insight into the boundaries of possible knowledge

[15]The useful term 'algebraic theories' was suggested to me by J. W. N. Watkins.
[16]Popper, *Logic of Scientific Discovery*, p. 113.
[17]M. Scriven, "Explanation and Prediction in Evolutionary Theory", *Science*, vol. 130, August 28, 1959, p. 478; and cf. Karl R. Popper, "Prediction and Prophecy in the Social Sciences" (1949), reprinted in his *Conjectures and Refutations* (London: Routledge and Kegan Paul, 1963), especially pp. 339 *et seq.*
[18]Cf. F. A. Hayek, "Degrees of Explanation", *The British Journal for the Philosophy of Science*, vol. 6, November 1955, pp. 209–25, now reprinted as the first essay of the present collection. [In this note, Hayek is referring to where the essay may be found in *Studies in Philosophy, Politics and Economics*. "Degrees of Explanation" appears in the current volume as chapter 6.—Ed.]

which our distinction provides, it is necessary to turn aside and consider the method which is often, but erroneously, believed to give us access to the understanding of complex phenomena: statistics. Because statistics is designed to deal with large numbers it is often thought that the difficulty arising from the large number of elements of which complex structures consist can be overcome by recourse to statistical techniques.

Statistics, however, deals with the problem of large numbers essentially by eliminating complexity and deliberately treating the individual elements which it counts as if they were not systematically connected. It avoids the problem of complexity by substituting for the information on the individual elements information on the frequency with which their different properties occur in classes of such elements, and it deliberately disregards the fact that the relative position of the different elements in a structure may matter. In other words, it proceeds on the assumption that information on the numerical frequencies of the different elements of a collective is enough to explain the phenomena and that no information is required on the manner in which the elements are related. The statistical method is therefore of use only where we either deliberately ignore, or are ignorant of, the relations between the individual elements with different attributes, i.e., where we ignore or are ignorant of any structure into which they are organized. Statistics in such situations enables us to regain simplicity and to make the task manageable by substituting a single attribute for the unascertainable individual attributes in the collective. It is, however, for this reason irrelevant to the solution of problems in which it is the relations between individual elements with different attributes which matters.

Statistics might assist us where we had information about many complex structures of the same kind, that is, where the complex phenomena and not the elements of which they consist could be made the elements of the statistical collective. It may provide us, e.g., with information on the relative frequency with which particular properties of the complex structures, say of the members of a species of organisms, occur together; but it presupposes that we have an independent criterion for identifying structures of the kind in question. Where we have such statistics about the properties of many individuals belonging to a class of animals, or languages, or economic systems, this may indeed be scientifically significant information.[19]

How little statistics can contribute, however, even in such cases, to the explanation of complex phenomena is clearly seen if we imagine that computers were natural objects which we found in sufficiently large numbers and whose

---

[19]See F. A. Hayek, *The Counter-Revolution of Science* (Glencoe, Ill.: The Free Press, 1952), pp. 60–63 [pp. 107–10—Ed.]. [Now see F. A. Hayek, "Scientism and the Study of Society", in *Studies on the Abuse and Decline of Reason*, ed. Bruce Caldwell, vol. 13 (2010) of *The Collected Works of F. A. Hayek*, pp. 124–25.—Ed.]

behaviour we wanted to predict. It is clear that we should never succeed in this unless we possessed the mathematical knowledge built into the computers, that is, unless we knew the theory determining their structure. No amount of statistical information on the correlation between input and output would get us any nearer our aim. Yet the efforts which are currently made on a large scale with regard to the much more complex structures which we call organisms are of the same kind. The belief that it must be possible in this manner to discover by observation regularities in the relations between input and output without the possession of an appropriate theory in this case appears even more futile and naïve than it would be in the case of the computers.[20]

While statistics can successfully deal with complex phenomena where these are the elements of the population on which we have information, it can tell us nothing about the structure of these elements. It treats them, in the fashionable phrase, as 'black boxes' which are presumed to be of the same kind but about whose identifying characteristics it has nothing to say. Nobody would probably seriously contend that statistics can elucidate even the comparatively not very complex structures of organic molecules, and few would argue that it can help us to explain the functioning of organisms. Yet when it comes to accounting for the functioning of social structures, that belief is widely held. It is here of course largely the product of a misconception about what the aim of a theory of social phenomena is, which is another story.

5. The Theory of Evolution as an Instance of Pattern Prediction

Probably the best illustration of a theory of complex phenomena which is of great value, although it describes merely a general pattern whose detail we can never fill in, is the Darwinian theory of evolution by natural selection. It is significant that this theory has always been something of a stumbling block for the dominant conception of scientific method. It certainly does not fit the orthodox criteria of 'prediction and control' as the hallmarks of scientific method.[21] Yet it cannot be denied that it has become the successful foundation of a great part of modern biology.

Before we examine its character we must clear out of the way a widely held misconception as to its content. It is often represented as if it consisted of an assertion about the succession of particular species of organisms which gradually changed into each other. This, however, is not the theory of evolution but

[20] Cf. J. G. Taylor, "Experimental Design: A Cloak for Intellectual Sterility", *The British Journal of Psychology*, vol. 49, May 1958, esp. pp. 107–8.

[21] Cf., e.g., Stephen Toulmin, *Foresight and Understanding: An Enquiry into the Aims of Science* (London: Hutchinson, 1961), p. 24: "No scientist has ever used this theory to foretell the coming-into-existence of creatures of a novel species, still less verified his forecast."

an application of the theory to the particular events which took place on Earth during the last two billion years or so.[22] Most of the misapplications of evolutionary theory (particularly in anthropology and the other social sciences) and its various abuses (e.g., in ethics) are due to this erroneous interpretation of its content.

The theory of evolution by natural selection describes a kind of process (or mechanism) which is independent of the particular circumstances in which it has taken place on Earth, which is equally applicable to a course of events in very different circumstances, and which might result in the production of an entirely different set of organisms. The basic conception of the theory is exceedingly simple and it is only in its application to the concrete circumstances that its extraordinary fertility and the range of phenomena for which it can account manifests itself.[23] The basic proposition which has this far-reaching implication is that a mechanism of reduplication with transmittable variations and competitive selection of those which prove to have a better chance of survival will in the course of time produce a great variety of structures adapted to continuous adjustment to the environment and to each other. The validity of this general proposition is not dependent on the truth of the particular applications which were first made of it: if, for example, it should have turned out that, in spite of their structural similarity, man and ape were not joint descendants from a comparatively near common ancestor but were the product of two convergent strands starting from ancestors which differed much more from each other (such as is true of the externally very similar types of marsupial and placental carnivores), this would not have refuted Darwin's general theory of evolution but only the manner of its application to the particular case.

The theory as such, as is true of all theories, describes merely a range of possibilities. In doing this it excludes other conceivable courses of events and thus can be falsified. Its empirical content consists in what it forbids.[24] If a sequence of events should be observed which cannot be fitted into its pattern,

---

[22] Even Professor Popper seems to imply this interpretation when he writes in *Poverty of Historicism*, p. 107, that "the evolutionary hypothesis is not a universal law of nature but a particular (or, more precisely, singular) historical statement about the ancestry of a number of terrestrial plants and animals." If this means that the essence of the theory of evolution is the assertion that particular species had common ancestors, or that the similarity of structure always means a common ancestry (which was the hypothesis from which the theory of evolution was derived), this is emphatically not the main content of the present theory of evolution. There is, incidentally, some contradiction between Popper's treatment of the concept of 'mammals' as a universal in *Logic*, p. 65, and the denial that the evolutionary hypothesis describes a universal law of nature. The same process might have produced mammals on other planets.

[23] Charles Darwin himself well knew, as he once wrote to Lyell, that "all the labour consists in the application of the theory", as quoted by C. C. Gillispie, *The Edge of Objectivity: An Essay in the History of Scientific Ideas* (Princeton: Princeton University Press, 1960), p. 314.

[24] Popper, *Logic of Scientific Discovery*, p. 41.

such as, e.g., that horses suddenly should begin to give birth to young with wings, or that the cutting off of a hind-paw in successive generations of dogs should result in dogs being born without that hind-paw, we should regard the theory as refuted.[25]

The range of what is permitted by the theory is undeniably wide. Yet one could also argue that it is only the limitation of our imagination which prevents us from being more aware of how much greater is the range of the prohibited—how infinite is the variety of conceivable forms of organisms which, thanks to the theory of evolution, we know will not in the foreseeable future appear on Earth. Common-sense may have told us before not to expect anything widely different from what we already knew. But exactly what kinds of variations are within the range of possibility and what kinds are not, only the theory of evolution can tell us. Though we may not be able to write down an exhaustive list of the possibilities, any specific question we shall, in principle, be able to answer.

For our present purposes we may disregard the fact that in one respect the theory of evolution is still incomplete because we still know only little about the mechanism of mutation. But let us assume that we knew precisely the circumstances in which (or at least the probability that in given conditions) a particular mutation will appear, and that we similarly knew also the precise advantages which any such mutation would in any particular kind of environment confer upon an individual of a specific constitution. This would not enable us to explain why the existing species or organisms have the particular structures which they possess, nor to predict what new forms will spring from them.

The reason for this is the actual impossibility of ascertaining the particular circumstances which, in the course of two billion years, have decided the emergence of the existing forms, or even those which, during the next few hundred years, will determine the selection of the types which will survive. Even if we tried to apply our explanatory scheme to a single species consisting of a known number of individuals each of which we were able to observe, and assuming that we were able to ascertain and record every single relevant fact, their sheer number would be such that we should never be able to manipulate them, i.e., to insert these data into the appropriate blanks of our theoretical formula and then to solve the 'statement equations' thus determined.[26]

---

[25] Cf. Morton Beckner, *The Biological Way of Thought* (New York: Columbia University Press, 1954), p. 241. [Beckner's book has only two hundred pages and was published in 1959, so this citation is wrong in detail. There is a chapter on "Selection Theory" in which Beckner defends evolutionary theory against assertions that it is not a theory or that it is "so elastic that it can be accommodated to any empirical facts" (p. 163), and in which Hayek's friend Ludwig von Bertalanffy is prominently mentioned, but there is no reference to winged horses or legless dogs.—Ed.]

[26] Popper, *Logic of Scientific Discovery*, p. 73.

What we have said about the theory of evolution applies to most of the rest of biology. The theoretical understanding of the growth and functioning of organisms can only in the rarest of instances be turned into specific predictions of what will happen in a particular case, because we can hardly ever ascertain all the facts which will contribute to determine the outcome. Hence, "prediction and control, usually regarded as essential criteria of science, are less reliable [in biology]."[27] It deals with pattern-building forces, the knowledge of which is useful for creating conditions favourable to the production of certain kinds of results, while it will only in comparatively few cases be possible to control all the relevant circumstances.

6. Theories of Social Structures

It should not be difficult now to recognize the similar limitations applying to theoretical explanations of the phenomena of mind and society. One of the chief results so far achieved by theoretical work in these fields seems to me to be the demonstration that here individual events regularly depend on so many concrete circumstances that we shall never in fact be in a position to ascertain them all; and that in consequence not only the ideal of prediction and control must largely remain beyond our reach, but also the hope remain illusory that we can discover by observation regular connections between the individual events. The very insight which theory provides, for example, that almost any event in the course of a man's life may have some effect on almost any of his future actions, makes it impossible that we translate our theoretical knowledge into predictions of specific events. There is no justification for the dogmatic belief that such translation must be possible if a science of these subjects is to be achieved, and that workers in these sciences have merely not yet succeeded in what physics has done, namely to discover simple relations between a few observables. If the theories which we have yet achieved tell us anything, it is that no such simple regularities are to be expected.

I will not consider here the fact that in the case of mind attempting to explain the detail of the working of another mind of the same order of complexity, there seems to exist, in addition to the merely 'practical' yet nevertheless insurmountable obstacles, also an absolute impossibility: because the conception of a mind fully explaining itself involves a logical contradiction. This I have discussed elsewhere.[28] It is not relevant here because the practical limits deter-

[27] Ralph S. Lillie, "Some Aspects of Theoretical Biology", *Philosophy of Science*, vol. 15, April 1948, p. 119. [The editor added the brackets because the phrase "in biology" did not appear in the original article by Lillie.—Ed.]
[28] See *The Sensory Order*, 8.66–8.86, also *The Counter-Revolution of Science*, p. 48 [pp. 85–86—Ed.], [Now see "Scientism and the Study of Society", in *Studies on the Abuse and Decline of Reason*, vol. 13

mined by the impossibility of ascertaining all the relevant data lie so far inside the logical limits that the latter have little relevance to what in fact we can do.

In the field of social phenomena only economics and linguistics[29] seem to have succeeded in building up a coherent body of theory. I shall confine myself here to illustrating the general thesis with reference to economic theory, though most of what I have to say would appear to apply equally to linguistic theory.

Schumpeter well described the task of economic theory when he wrote that "the economic life of a non-socialist society consists of millions of relations or flows between individual firms and households. We can establish certain theorems about them, but we can never observe all of them."[30] To this must be added that most of the phenomena in which we are interested, such as competition, could not occur at all unless the number of distinct elements involved were fairly large, and that the overall pattern that will form itself is determined by the significantly different behaviour of the different individuals so that the obstacle of obtaining the relevant data cannot be overcome by treating them as members of a statistical collective.

For this reason economic theory is confined to describing kinds of patterns which will appear if certain general conditions are satisfied, but can rarely if ever derive from this knowledge any predictions of specific phenomena. This is seen most clearly if we consider those systems of simultaneous equations which since Léon Walras have been widely used to represent the general relations between the prices and the quantities of all commodities bought and sold.[31] They are so framed that *if* we were able to fill in all the blanks, i.e., *if* we knew all the parameters of these equations, we could calculate the prices and quantities of all the commodities. But, as at least the founders of this theory clearly understood, its purpose is not "to arrive at a numerical calculation

---

(2010) of *The Collected Works of F. A. Hayek*, pp. 112–13.—Ed.], and the following essay in the present volume. [Hayek refers here to the position of "Rules, Perception and Intelligibility" in his 1967 collection *Studies in Philosophy, Politics and Economics*. "Rules, Perception and Intelligibity" appears as chapter 8 of the present volume.—Ed.]

[29]See particularly Noam Chomsky, *Syntactic Structures* ('s-Gravenhage: Mouton, 1957), who characteristically seems to succeed in building up such a theory after frankly abandoning the striving after an inductivist 'discovery procedure' and substituting for it the search after an 'evaluation procedure' which enables him to eliminate false theories of grammars and where these grammars may be arrived at "by intuition, guess-work, all sorts of partial methodological hints, reliance on past experience, etc." (p. 56).

[30]Joseph A. Schumpeter, *History of Economic Analysis* (Oxford: Oxford University Press, 1954), p. 241.

[31][The French economist Léon Walras (1834–1910), a co-founder (with William Stanley Jevons and Carl Menger) of the 'Marginal Revolution', introduced the general equilibrium approach in his book *Eléments d'économie politique pure, ou, Théorie de la richesse sociale* (1874–1877), translated by William Jaffé as *Elements of Pure Economics, or, the Theory of Social Wealth* (London: Allen and Unwin, 1954; reprinted, New York: A. M. Kelley, 1969).—Ed.]

of prices", because it would be "absurd" to assume that we can ascertain all the data.[32]

The prediction of the formation of this general kind of pattern rests on certain very general factual assumptions (such as that most people engage in trade in order to earn an income, that they prefer a larger income to a smaller one, that they are not prevented from entering whatever trade they wish, etc.—assumptions which determine the scope of the variables but not their particular values); it is, however, not dependent on the knowledge of the more particular circumstances which we would have to know in order to be able to predict prices or quantities of particular commodities. No economist has yet succeeded in making a fortune by buying or selling commodities on the basis of his scientific prediction of future prices (even though some may have done so by selling such predictions).

To the physicist it often seems puzzling why the economist should bother to formulate those equations although admittedly he sees no chance of determining the numerical values of the parameters which would enable him to derive from them the values of the individual magnitudes. Even many economists seem loath to admit that those systems of equations are not a step towards specific predictions of individual events but the final results of their theoretical efforts, a description merely of the general character of the order we shall find under specifiable conditions which, however, can never be translated into a prediction of its particular manifestations.

Predictions of a pattern are nevertheless both testable and valuable. Since the theory tells us under which general conditions a pattern of this sort will form itself, it will enable us to create such conditions and to observe whether a pattern of the kind predicted will appear. And since the theory tells us that this pattern assures a maximization of output in a certain sense, it also enables us to create the general conditions which will assure such a maximization, though we are ignorant of many of the particular circumstances which will determine the pattern that will appear.

It is not really surprising that the explanation of merely a sort of pattern may be highly significant in the field of complex phenomena but of little interest in the field of simple phenomena, such as those of mechanics. The fact is that in studies of complex phenomena the general patterns are all that is characteristic of those persistent wholes which are the main object of our interest, because a number of enduring structures have this general pattern in common and nothing else.[33]

---

[32] Vilfredo Pareto, *Manuel d'économie politique*, translated by Alfred Bonnet, 2nd ed. (Paris: Marcel Giard, 1927), pp. 233–34. [Cf. Vilfredo Pareto, *Manual of Political Economy*, ed. Ann S. Schwier and Alfred N. Page, translated by Ann S. Schwier (New York: Kelley, 1971), p. 171.—Ed.]

[33] A characteristic instance of the misunderstanding of this point (quoted by E. Nagel, *Structure of Science*, p. 61) occurs in Charles A. Beard, *The Nature of the Social Sciences in Relation to Objectives of*

7. The Ambiguity of the Claims of Determinism

The insight that we will sometimes be able to say that data of a certain class (or of certain classes) will bring about a pattern of a certain kind, but will not be able to ascertain the attributes of the individual elements which decide which particular form the pattern will assume, has consequences of considerable importance. It means, in the first instance, that when we assert that we know how something is determined, this statement is ambiguous. It may mean that we merely know what class of circumstances determines a certain kind of phenomena, without being able to specify the particular circumstances which decide which member of the predicted class of patterns will appear; or it may mean that we can also explain the latter. Thus we can reasonably claim that a certain phenomenon is determined by known natural forces and at the same time admit that we do not know precisely how it has been produced. Nor is the claim invalidated that we can explain the principle on which a certain mechanism operates if it is pointed out that we cannot say precisely what it will do at a particular place and time. From the fact that we do know that a phenomenon is determined by certain kinds of circumstances it does not follow that we must be able to know even in one particular instance all the circumstances which have determined all its attributes.

There may well be valid and more grave philosophical objections to the claim that science can demonstrate a universal determinism; but for all practical purposes the limits created by the impossibility of ascertaining all the particular data required to derive detailed conclusions from our theories are probably much narrower. Even if the assertion of a universal determinism were meaningful, scarcely any of the conclusions usually derived from it would therefore follow. In the first of the two senses we have distinguished we may, for instance, well be able to establish that every single action of a human being is the necessary result of the inherited structure of his body (particularly of its nervous system) and of all the external influences which have acted upon it since birth. We might even be able to go further and assert that if the most important of these factors were in a particular case very much the same as with most other individuals, a particular class of influences will have a certain kind of effect. But this would be an empirical generalization based on a *ceteris paribus* assumption which we could not verify in the particular instance. The chief fact would continue to be, in spite of our knowledge of the principle on which the human mind works, that we should not be able to state the full set

---

Instruction (New York: Scribner's, 1934), p. 29, where it is contended that if a science of society "were a true science, like that of astronomy, it would enable us to predict the essential movements of human affairs for the immediate and the indefinite future, to give pictures of society in the year 2000 or the year 2500 just as astronomers can map the appearances of the heavens at fixed points of time in the future."

of particular facts which brought it about that the individual did a particular thing at a particular time. The individual personality would remain for us as much a unique and unaccountable phenomenon which we might hope to influence in a desirable direction by such empirically developed practices as praise and blame, but whose specific actions we could generally not predict or control, because we could not obtain the information on all the particular facts which determined it.

8. The Ambiguity of Relativism

The same sort of misconception underlies the conclusions derived from the various kinds of 'relativism.' In most instances these relativistic positions on questions of history, culture, or ethics are derived from the erroneous interpretations of the theory of evolution which we have already considered. But the basic conclusion that the whole of our civilization and all human values are the result of a long process of evolution in the course of which values, as the aims of human activity appeared, continue to change, seems inescapable in the light of our present knowledge. We are probably also entitled to conclude that our present values exist only as the elements of a particular cultural tradition and are significant only for some more or less long phase of evolution— whether this phase includes some of our pre-human ancestors or is confined to certain periods of human civilization. We have no more ground to ascribe to them eternal existence than to the human race itself. There is thus one possible sense in which we may legitimately regard human values as relative and speak of the probability of their further evolution.

But it is a far cry from this general insight to the claims of the ethical, cultural, or historical relativists or of evolutionary ethics. To put it crudely: while we know that all those values are relative to something, we do not know to what they are relative. We may be able to indicate the general class of circumstances which have made them what they are, but we do not know the particular conditions to which the values we hold are due, or what our values would be if those circumstances had been different. Most of the illegitimate conclusions are the result of the erroneous interpretation of the theory of evolution as the empirical establishment of a trend. Once we recognize that it gives us no more than a scheme of explanation which might be sufficient to explain particular phenomena *if* we knew all the facts which have operated in the course of history, it becomes evident that the claims of the various kinds of relativism (and of evolutionary ethics) are unfounded. Though we may meaningfully say that our values are determined by a class of circumstances definable in general terms, so long as we cannot state which particular circumstances have produced the existing values, or what our values would be under

273

any specific set of other circumstances, no significant conclusions follow from the assertion.

It deserves brief notice in passing how radically opposed are the practical conclusions which are derived from the same evolutionary approach according as it is assumed that we can or cannot in fact know enough about the circumstances to derive specific conclusions from our theory. While the assumption of a sufficient knowledge of the concrete facts generally produces a sort of intellectual hubris which deludes itself that reason can judge all values, the insight into the impossibility of such full knowledge induces an attitude of humility and reverence towards that experience of mankind as a whole that has been precipitated in the values and institutions of existing society.

A few observations ought to be added here about the obvious significance of our conclusions for assessing the various kinds of 'reductionism.' In the sense of the first of the distinctions which we have repeatedly made—in the sense of general description—the assertion that biological or mental phenomena are 'nothing but' certain complexes of physical events, or that they are certain classes of structures of such events, these claims are probably defensible. But in the second sense—specific prediction—which alone would justify the more ambitious claims made for reductionism, they are completely unjustified. A full reduction would be achieved only if we were able to substitute for a description of events in biological or mental terms a description in physical terms which included an exhaustive enumeration of all the physical circumstances which constitute a necessary and sufficient condition of the biological or mental phenomena in question. In fact such attempts always consist—and can consist only—in the illustrative enumeration of classes of events, usually with an added 'etc.', which might produce the phenomenon in question. Such 'etc.-reductions' are not reductions which enable us to dispense with the biological or mental entities, or to substitute for them a statement of physical events, but are mere explanations of the general character of the kind of order or pattern whose specific manifestations we know only through our concrete experience of them.[34]

9. The Importance of Our Ignorance

Perhaps it is only natural that in the exuberance generated by the successful advances of science the circumstances which limit our factual knowledge,

[34] Cf. my *Counter-Revolution of Science*, pp. 48 [p. 85—Ed.] *et seq.* [Now see "Scientism and the Study of Society", in *Studies on the Abuse and Decline of Reason*, vol. 13 (2010) of *The Collected Works of F. A. Hayek*, pp. 112 *et. seq.*—Ed.], and William Craig, "Replacement of Auxiliary Expressions", *The Philosophical Review*, vol. 65, January 1956, pp. 38–55.

and the consequent boundaries imposed upon the applicability of theoretical knowledge, have been rather disregarded. It is high time, however, that we take our ignorance more seriously. As Popper and others have pointed out, "the more we learn about the world, and the deeper our learning, the more conscious, specific, and articulate will be our knowledge of what we do not know, our knowledge of our ignorance."[35] We have indeed in many fields learnt enough to know that we cannot know all that we would have to know for a full explanation of the phenomena.

These boundaries may not be absolute. Though we may never know as much about certain complex phenomena as we can know about simple phenomena, we may partly pierce the boundary by deliberately cultivating a technique which aims at more limited objectives—the explanation not of individual events but merely of the appearance of certain patterns or orders. Whether we call these mere explanations of the principle or mere pattern predictions or higher-level theories does not matter. Once we explicitly recognize that the understanding of the general mechanism which produces patterns of a certain kind is not merely a tool for specific predictions but important in its own right, and that it may provide important guides to action (or sometimes indications of the desirability of no action), we may indeed find that this limited knowledge is most valuable.

What we must get rid of is the naïve superstition that the world must be so organized that it is possible by direct observation to discover simple regularities between all phenomena and that this is a necessary presupposition for the application of the scientific method. What we have by now discovered about the organization of many complex structures should be sufficient to teach us that there is no reason to expect this, and that if we want to get ahead in these fields our aims will have to be somewhat different from what they are in the fields of simple phenomena.

---

[35] Karl R. Popper, "On the Sources of Knowledge and of Ignorance", *Proceedings of the British Academy*, vol. 46, 1960, p. 69. See also Warren Weaver, "A Scientist Ponders Faith", *Saturday Review*, vol. 42, January 3, 1959: "Is science really gaining in its assault on the totality of the unsolved? As science learns one answer, it is characteristically true that it also learns several new questions. It is as though science were working in a great forest of ignorance, making an ever larger circular clearing within which, not to insist on the pun, things are clear. . . . But as that circle becomes larger and larger, the circumference of contact with ignorance also gets longer and longer. Science learns more and more. But there is an ultimate sense in which it does not gain; for the volume of the appreciated but not understood keeps getting larger. We keep, in science, getting a more and more sophisticated view of our ignorance." [Weaver's article was comparing faith and science, and the sentence that Hayek quotes actually begins, "First, then, which—science or religion—is really gaining in its assault . . .—Ed.]

10. A Postscript on the Rôle of 'Laws' in the Theory of Complex Phenomena[36]

Perhaps it deserves to be added that the preceding considerations throw some doubt on the widely held view that the aim of theoretical science is to establish 'laws'—at least if the word 'law' is used as commonly understood. Most people would probably accept some such definition of 'law' as that 'a scientific law is the rule by which two phenomena are connected with each other according to the principle of causality, that is to say, as cause and effect.'[37] And no less an authority than Max Planck is reported to have insisted that a true scientific law must be expressible in a single equation.[38]

Now the statement that a certain structure can assume only one of the (still infinite) number of states defined by a system of many simultaneous equations is still a perfectly good scientific (theoretical and falsifiable) statement.[39] We might still call, of course, such a statement a 'law', if we so wish (though some people might rightly feel that this would do violence to language); but the adoption of such a terminology would be likely to make us neglectful of an important distinction: for to say that such a statement describes, like an ordinary law, a relation between cause and effect would be highly misleading. It would seem, therefore, that the conception of law in the usual sense has little application to the theory of complex phenomena, and that therefore also the description of scientific theories as 'nomologic' or 'nomothetic' (or by the German term *Gesetzeswissenschaften*) is appropriate only to those two-variable or perhaps three-variable problems to which the theory of simple phenomena can be reduced, but not to the theory of phenomena which appear only above a certain level of complexity. If we assume that all the other parameters of

---

[36] This last section of this essay was not contained in the version originally published and has been added to this reprint.

[37] The particular wording which I happened to come across while drafting this is taken from Hans Kelsen, "The Natural-Law Doctrine Before the Tribunal of Science" [1949], reprinted in *What is Justice? Justice, Law, and Politics in the Mirror of Science: Collected Essays* (Berkeley, CA: University of California Press, 1960), p. 139. It seems to express well a widely held view. [Kelsen's statement actually reads, "A scientific law of nature is the rule by which . . .—Ed.]

[38] Sir Karl Popper comments on this that it seems extremely doubtful whether any *single* one of Maxwell's equations could be said to express anything of real significance if we knew none of the others; in fact, it seems that the repeated occurrence of the symbols in the various equations is needed to secure that these symbols have the intended meanings. [I was unable to find any written source by Popper for this statement. We may want to take Hayek's use of the word 'comments' literally and assume that this was something that Popper said to Hayek in a conversation.—Ed.]

[39] Cf. Popper, *Logic of Scientific Discovery*, p. 73: "Even if the system of equations does not suffice for a unique solution, it does not allow every conceivable combination of values to be substituted for the 'unknowns' (variables). Rather, the system of equations characterizes certain combinations of values or value systems as admissible, and others as inadmissible; it distinguishes the class of admissible value systems from the class of inadmissible value systems." Note also the application of this in the following passages to 'statement equations.'

such a system of equations describing a complex structure are constant, we can of course still call the dependence of one of the latter on the other a 'law' and describe a change in the one as 'the cause' and the change in the other as 'the effect.' But such a 'law' would be valid only for one particular set of values of all the other parameters and would change with every change in any one of them. This would evidently not be a very useful conception of a 'law', and the only generally valid statement about the regularities of the structure in question is the whole set of simultaneous equations from which, if the values of the parameters are continuously variable, an infinite number of particular laws, showing the dependence of one variable upon another, could be derived.

In this sense we may well have achieved a very elaborate and quite useful theory about some kind of complex phenomenon and yet have to admit that we do not know of a single law, in the ordinary sense of the word, which this kind of phenomenon obeys. I believe this to be in a great measure true of social phenomena: though we possess theories of social structures, I rather doubt whether we know of any 'laws' which social phenomena obey. It would then appear that the search for the discovery of laws is not an appropriate hallmark of scientific procedure but merely a characteristic of the theories of simple phenomena as we have defined these earlier; and that in the field of complex phenomena the term 'law' as well as the concepts of cause and effect are not applicable without such modification as to deprive them of their ordinary meaning.

In some respect the prevalent stress on 'laws', i.e., on the discovery of regularities in two-variable relations, is probably a result of inductivism, because only such simple co-variation of two magnitudes is likely to strike the senses before an explicit theory or hypothesis has been formed. In the case of more complex phenomena it is more obvious that we must have our theory first before we can ascertain whether the things do in fact behave according to this theory. It would probably have saved much confusion if theoretical science had not in this manner come to be identified with the search for laws in the sense of a simple dependence of one magnitude upon another. It would have prevented such misconception as that, e.g., the biological theory of evolution proposed some definite 'law of evolution' such as a law of the necessary sequence of certain stages or forms. It has of course done nothing of the kind and all attempts to do this rest on a misunderstanding of Darwin's great achievement. And the prejudice that in order to be scientific one must produce laws may yet prove to be one of the most harmful of methodological conceptions. It may have been useful to some extent for the reason given by Popper, that 'simple statements . . . are to be prized more highly'[40] in all fields where simple statements are significant. But it seems to me that there will always be fields where it can be shown that all such simple statements must be false and where in consequence also the prejudice in favour of 'laws' must be harmful.

[40] Ibid., p. 142.

TEN

NOTES ON THE EVOLUTION OF SYSTEMS OF RULES OF CONDUCT

The Interplay between Rules of Individual Conduct and the Social Order of Actions[1]

I

The purpose of these notes is to clarify the conceptual tools with which we describe facts, not to present new facts. More particularly, their aim is to make clear the important distinction between the systems of rules of conduct which govern the behaviour of the individual members of a group (or of the elements of any order) on the one hand and, on the other hand, the order or pattern of actions which results from this for the group as a whole.[2] It does not matter for this purpose whether the individual members which make up the group are animals or men,[3] nor whether the rules of conduct are innate (transmitted genetically) or learnt (transmitted culturally). We know that cultural transmission by learning occurs at least among some of the higher animals, and there can be no doubt that men also obey some rules of conduct which are innate. The two sorts of rules will therefore often interact. Throughout it should be clearly understood that the term 'rule' is used for a statement by which a regularity of the conduct of individuals can be described, irrespective of whether such a rule is 'known' to the individuals in any other sense than that they normally act in accordance with it. We shall not consider here the interesting question of how such rules can be transmitted culturally long before the individuals are capable of stating them in words and therefore of explicitly teaching them, or how they learn abstract rules 'by analogy' from concrete instances.

That the systems of rules of individual conduct and the order of actions

---

[1] [F. A. Hayek, *Studies in Philosophy, Politics and Economics* (Chicago: University of Chicago Press, 1967), pp. 66–81.—Ed.]

[2] We shall use '(social) order' and '(social) pattern' interchangeably to describe the structure of the actions of all the members of a group, but shall avoid the more common term 'social organization', because 'organization' has an intentionalist (anthropomorphic) connotation and is therefore better reserved for orders which are the product of design. Similarly we shall occasionally use the pairs of concepts 'order and its elements' and 'groups and individuals' interchangeably, although the former is of course the more general term of which the relation between group and individual is a particular instance.

[3] Or even whether they are living organisms or perhaps some sort of reduplicating mechanical structures. Cf. L. S. Penrose, "Self-Reproducing Machines", *Scientific American*, vol. 200, June 1959, pp. 105–14.

which results from the individuals acting in accordance with them are not the same thing should be obvious as soon as it is stated, although the two are in fact frequently confused. (Lawyers are particularly prone to do so by using the term 'order of law' for both.) Not every system of rules of individual conduct will produce an overall order of the actions of a group of individuals; and whether a given system of rules of individual conduct will produce an order of actions, and what kind of order, will depend on the circumstances in which the individuals act. The classical instance in which the very regularity of the behaviour of the elements produces 'perfect disorder' is the second law of thermodynamics, the entropy principle. It is evident that in a group of living beings many possible rules of individual conduct would also produce only disorder or make the existence of the group as such impossible. A society of animals or men is always a number of individuals observing such common rules of conduct as, in the circumstances in which they live, will produce an order of actions.

For the understanding of animal and human societies the distinction is particularly important because the genetic (and in a great measure also the cultural) *transmission* of rules of conduct takes place *from individual to individual*, while what may be called the natural *selection* of rules will operate on the basis of the greater or lesser efficiency of the resulting *order of the group*.[4] For the purposes of this discussion we shall define the different kinds of elements of which groups consist by the rules of conduct which they obey, and regard the appearance of a transmittable 'mutation' of these rules of individual conduct as the equivalent of the appearance of new elements, or as a progressive change in the character of all the elements of the group.

II

The necessity of distinguishing between the order of actions of the group and the rules of conduct of the individuals may be further supported by the following considerations:

1. A particular order of actions can be observed and described without knowledge of the rules of conduct of the individuals which bring it about: and it is at least conceivable that the same overall order of actions may be produced by different sets of rules of individual conduct.

[4]Cf. Alexander Carr-Saunders, *The Population Problem: A Study in Human Evolution* (Oxford: Clarendon Press, 1922), p. 223: "Those groups practising the most advantageous customs will have an advantage in the constant struggle with adjacent groups." [Hayek uses this quotation again in later works, so perhaps it is best to give the full quotation as it actually reads: "Those groups practising the most advantageous customs will have an advantage in the constant struggle between adjacent groups over those that practise less advantageous customs."—Ed.]

2. The same set of rules of individual conduct may in some circumstances bring about a certain order of actions, but not do so in different external circumstances.

3. It is the resulting overall order of actions but not the regularity of the actions of the separate individuals as such which is important for the preservation of the group; and a certain kind of overall order may in the same manner contribute to the survival of the members of the group whatever the particular rules of individual conduct which bring it about.

4. The evolutionary selection of different rules of individual conduct operates through the viability of the order it will produce, and any given rules of individual conduct may prove beneficial as part of one set of such rules, or in one set of external circumstances, and harmful as part of another set of rules or in another set of external circumstances.

5. Although the overall order of actions arises in appropriate circumstances as the joint product of the actions of many individuals who are governed by certain rules, the production of the overall order is of course not the conscious aim of individual action since the individual will not have any knowledge of the overall order, so that it will not be an awareness of what is needed to preserve or restore the overall order at a particular moment but an abstract rule which will guide the actions of the individual.

6. The concrete individual action will always be the joint effect of internal impulses, such as hunger, the particular external events acting upon the individual (including the actions of other members of the group), and the rules applicable to the situation thus determined. The rules upon which different individual members of a group will at any moment act may therefore be different either because the drives or external circumstances acting upon them make different rules applicable, or because different rules apply to different individuals according to age, sex, status, or some particular state in which each individual finds itself at the moment.

7. It is important always to remember that a rule of conduct will never by itself be a sufficient cause of action but that the impulse for actions of a certain kind will always come either from a particular external stimulus or from an internal drive (and usually from a combination of both), and that the rules of conduct will always act only as a restraint on actions induced by other causes.

8. The orderliness of the system of actions will in general show itself in the fact that actions of the different individuals will be so co-ordinated, or mutually adjusted to each other, that the result of their actions will remove the initial stimulus or make inoperative the drive which has been the cause of activity.

9. The difference between the orderliness of the whole and the regularity of the actions of any of its individual parts is also shown by the fact that a whole may be orderly without the action of any particular individual element showing any regularity. This might be the case, for instance, if the order of the whole were brought about by an authority commanding all particular actions and choosing the individuals who have to perform any one action at a given moment at random,

say by drawing lots. There might in such a group well exist a recognizable order in the sense that certain rôles were always filled by somebody; but no rules guiding the actions of any one individual (other than perhaps the commanding authority) could be formulated. The actions taken there by any one individual would not be derived by means of a rule from any of its properties or any of the circumstances acting on it (other than the commands of the organizer).

III

The most easily observed instances in which the rules of individual conduct produce an overall order are those where this order consists in a spatial pattern such as will occur in the marching, defence, or hunting of a group of animals or men. The arrow formation of migrating wild geese, the defensive ring of the buffaloes, or the manner in which lionesses drive the prey towards the male for the kill, are simple instances in which presumably it is not an awareness of the overall pattern by the individual but some rules of how to respond to the immediate environment which co-ordinate the actions of the several individuals.

More instructive are the abstract and more complex orders based on a division of labour which we find in such insect societies as those of bees, ants, and termites. There is perhaps less temptation in these instances to ascribe the changes in the activities of the individual either to a central command or to an 'insight' on the part of the individual into what at the particular moment is needed by the whole. There can be little doubt that the successive activities which a worker bee performs at the different stages of its career, at intervals varying in length according to the requirements of the situation[5] (and apparently even reverting to stages already passed when the 'needs' of the hive require it), could be explained by comparatively simple rules of individual conduct, if we only knew them. Similarly the elaborate structures which termites build, the genetics of which A. E. Emerson has so revealingly described,[6] must ultimately be accounted for by innate rules of conduct of the individuals of which we are largely ignorant.

When we are concerned with primitive human societies, on the other hand, it is often easier to ascertain the rules of individual conduct than to trace from them the resulting overall and often highly abstract order. The individuals will often themselves be able to tell us what they regard as appropriate action in

[5] See K. von Frisch, *The Dancing Bees: An Account of the Life and Senses of the Honey Bee* (New York: Harcourt, Brace, 1955).

[6] Alfred E. Emerson, "Termite Nests—A Study of Phylogeny of Behavior", *Ecological Monographs*, vol. 8, April 1938, pp. 247–84.

different circumstances, though they may be able to do this only for particular instances but not to articulate the rules in accordance with which they act;[7] but the 'functions' which these rules serve we shall be able to discover only after we have reconstructed the overall order which is produced by actions in accordance with them. The individual may have no idea what this overall order is that results from his observing such rules as those concerning kinship and intermarriage, or the succession to property, or which function this overall order serves. Yet all the individuals of the species which exist will behave in that manner because groups of individuals which have thus behaved have displaced those which did not do so.[8]

IV

The overall order of actions in a group is in two respects more than the totality of regularities observable in the actions of the individuals and cannot be wholly reduced to them. It is so not only in the trivial sense in which a whole is more than the mere *sum* of its parts but presupposes also that these elements are related to each other in a particular manner.[9] It is more also because the existence of those relations which are essential for the existence of the whole cannot be accounted for wholly by the interaction of the parts but only by their interaction with an outside world both of the individual parts and the whole. If there exist recurrent and persistent structures of a certain type (i.e., showing a certain order), this is due to the elements responding to external influences which they are likely to encounter in a manner which brings about the preservation or restoration of this order; and on this, in turn, may be dependent the chances of the individuals to preserve themselves.

From any given set of rules of conduct of the elements will arise a steady structure (showing 'homeostatic' control) only in an environment in which there prevails a certain probability of encountering the sort of circumstances to which the rules of conduct are adapted. A change of environment may require, if the whole is to persist, a change in the order of the group and

---

[7] Cf. Edward Sapir, *Selected Writings of Edward Sapir*, ed. David G. Mandelbaum (Berkeley: University of California Press, 1949), p. 548 *et seq.*

[8] Ample further illustrations of the kind of orders briefly sketched in this section will be found in V. C. Wynne-Edwards, *Animal Dispersion in Relation to Social Behaviour* (Edinburgh: Oliver and Boyd, 1962); Anne Roe and George Gaylord Simpson, eds., *Behavior and Evolution* (New Haven: Yale University Press, 1958); and Robert Ardrey, *The Territorial Imperative: A Personal Inquiry into the Animal Origins of Property and Nations* (New York: Atheneum, 1966).

[9] Cf. Karl R. Popper, *The Poverty of Historicism* (London: Routledge and Kegan Paul, 1957), section 7, and Ernest Nagel, *The Structure of Science* (New York: Harcourt, Brace and World, 1961), pp. 380–97.

therefore in the rules of conduct of the individuals; and a spontaneous change of the rules of individual conduct and of the resulting order may enable the group to persist in circumstances which, without such change, would have led to its destruction.

These considerations are mainly intended to bring out that systems of rules of conduct will develop as wholes, or that the selection process of evolution will operate on the order as a whole; and that, whether a new rule will, in combination with all the other rules of the group, and in the particular environment in which it exists, increase or decrease the efficiency of the group as a whole, will depend on the order to which such individual conduct leads. One consequence of this is that a new rule of individual conduct which in one position may prove detrimental, may in another prove to be beneficial. Another is that changes in one rule may make beneficial other changes, both of a behavioural or somatic character, which before were harmful. It is thus likely that even culturally transmitted patterns of individual behaviour (or the resulting patterns of action of the group) may contribute to determine the selection among genetic changes of a behavioural or somatic kind.[10]

It is evident that this interplay of the rules of conduct of the individuals with the actions of other individuals and the external circumstances in producing an overall order may be a highly complex affair. The whole task of social theory consists in little else but an effort to reconstruct the overall orders which are thus formed, and the reason why that special apparatus of conceptual construction is needed which social theory represents is the complexity of this task. It will also be clear that such a distinct theory of social structures can provide only an explanation of certain general and highly abstract features of the different types of structures (or only of the 'qualitative aspects'), because these abstract features will be all that all the structures of a certain type will have in common, and therefore all that will be predictable or provide useful guidance for action.

Of theories of this type economic theory, the theory of the market order of free human societies, is so far the only one which has been systematically developed over a long period and, together with linguistics, perhaps one of a very few which, because of the peculiar complexity of their subject, require such elaboration. Yet, though the whole of economic theory (and, I believe, of linguistic theory) may be interpreted as nothing else but an endeavour to reconstruct from regularities of the individual actions the character of the resulting order, it can hardly be said that economists are fully aware that this is what they are doing. The nature of the different kinds of rules of individual conduct (some voluntarily and even unconsciously observed and some enforced), which

---

[10]Cf. Sir Alister Hardy, *The Living Stream: A Restatement of Evolution Theory and Its Relation to the Spirit of Man* (London: Collins, 1965), especially Lecture II.

the formation of the overall order presupposes, is frequently left obscure.[11] The important question of which of these rules of individual action can be deliberately and profitably altered, and which are likely to evolve gradually with or without such deliberate collective decisions as legislation involves, is rarely systematically considered.

V

Although the existence and preservation of the order of actions of a group can be accounted for only from the rules of conduct which the individuals obey, these rules of individual conduct have developed because the individuals have been living in groups whose structures have gradually changed. In other words, the properties of the individuals which are significant for the existence and preservation of the group, and through this also for the existence and preservation of the individuals themselves, have been shaped by the selection of those from the individuals living in groups which at each stage of the evolution of the group tended to act according to such rules as made the group more efficient.

Thus for the explanation of the functioning of the social order at any one time the rules of individual conduct must be assumed to be given. Yet these rules have been selected and formed by the effects they have on the social order; and in so far as psychology does not wish to content itself with describing the rules which individuals actually obey, but undertakes to explain why they observe these rules, at least a great part of it will have to become evolutionary social psychology. Or, to put this differently, though social theory constructs social orders from the rules of conduct assumed to be given at any one time, these rules of conduct have themselves developed as part of a larger whole, and at each stage of this development the then prevailing overall order determined what effect any one change in the rules of individual conduct had.

Though we cannot here further pursue the question of the relation of psychology to social theory, it will contribute to the main purpose of these notes if we add a few remarks on the difference between an order which is brought about by the direction of a central organ such as the brain, and the formation of an order determined by the regularity of the actions towards each other of the elements of a structure. Michael Polanyi has usefully described this distinction as that between a monocentric and a polycentric order.[12] The first

---

[11] As is shown by the unprofitable discussions about the degree of 'rationality' which economic theory is alleged to assume. What is said above, incidentally, also implies that social theory is, strictly speaking, not a science of behaviour and that to regard it as part of 'behavioural science' is at least misleading.

[12] Michael Polanyi, *The Logic of Liberty* (London: Routledge and Kegan Paul, 1951 [reprinted, Indianapolis: Liberty Fund, 1998—Ed.]), especially chapters 8 and 9. [Hungarian-born chemist

NOTES ON THE EVOLUTION OF SYSTEMS OF RULES OF CONDUCT

point which it is in this connection important to note is that the brain of an organism which acts as the directing centre for that organism is itself in turn a polycentric order, that is, that its actions are determined by the relation and mutual adjustment to each other of the elements of which it consists.

As we are all tempted to assume that wherever we find an order it must be directed by a central organ, which, if we applied this to the brain, evidently would lead to an infinite regress, it will be useful briefly to consider the advantage derived from the fact that one such polycentric order is set aside in a part of the whole and governs the action of the rest. This advantage consists in the possibility of trying out beforehand on a model the various alternative complexes of actions and selecting from them the most promising before action is taken by the whole organism. There is no reason why any one of these complex patterns of actions should not be determined by the direct interaction of the parts without this pattern being first formed in another centre, and then directed by it. The unique attribute of the brain is that it can produce a representative model on which the alternative actions and their consequences can be tried out beforehand. The structure which the brain directs may have a repertoire of possible patterns of actions quite as big as the one the brain can preform; but if it actually had to take that action before it was tried out on a model, it might discover its harmful effects only when it was too late and it might be destroyed as a result. If, on the other hand, such action is first tried out on a model in a separate part of the whole set aside for the purpose, not the actual effect but a representation of the effect to be expected will act as a signal that the particular action is not to be taken.

There is, therefore, no reason why a polycentric order in which each element is guided only by rules and receives no orders from a centre should not be capable of bringing about as complex and apparently as 'purposive' an adaptation to circumstances as could be produced in a system where a part is set aside to preform such an order on an analogue or model before it is put into execution by the larger structure. In so far as the self-organizing forces of a structure as a whole lead at once to the right kind of action (or to tentative actions which can be retraced before too much harm is done), such a single-stage order need not be inferior to a hierarchic one in which the whole merely carries out what has first been tried out in a part. Such a non-hierarchic order dispenses with the necessity of first communicating all the information on which its several elements act to a common centre and conceivably may make the use of more information possible than could be transmitted to, and digested by, a centre.

---

and philosopher Michael Polanyi (1891–1976) had known and corresponded with Hayek since the 1930's. Polanyi used the idea of polycentric orders in his critique of attempts to plan science, a critique that Hayek endorsed. Polanyi also originated the notion of tacit knowledge, one that fit nicely with Hayek's own writings about localized, dispersed knowledge.—Ed.]

Such spontaneous orders as those of societies, although they will often produce results similar to those which could be produced by a brain, are thus organized on principles different from those which govern the relations between a brain and the organism which it directs. Although the brain may be organized on principles similar to those on which a society is organized, society is not a brain and must not be represented as a sort of super-brain, because in it the acting parts and those between which the relations determining the structure are established are the same, and the ordering task is not deputized to any part in which a model is preformed.

VI

The existence of such ordered structures as galaxies, solar systems, organisms, and social orders in a multiplicity of instances showing certain common features and observing as wholes regularities which cannot be wholly reduced to the regularities of the parts, because they also depend on the interaction of the whole with the environment which placed and keeps the part in the order necessary for the specific behaviour of the whole, creates certain difficulties for a theory of scientific method which regards as its aim the discovery of 'universal laws of nature.' Though it is reasonable to believe that structures of the kind will in a definable environment always behave as they do, the existence of such structures may in fact depend not only on that environment, but also on the existence in the past of many other environments, indeed on a definite sequence of such environments which have succeeded in that order only once in the history of the universe. The theoretical disciplines which are concerned with the structures of such complexes have thus an object the very existence of which is due to circumstances (and a process of evolution determined by them) which, though in principle repeatable, may in fact have been unique and never occur again. In consequence, the laws which govern the behaviour of these complexes, though 'in principle universally valid' (whatever that means), apply in fact only to structures to be found in a particular space-time sector of that universe.

Just as apparently the existence of life on earth is due to events which could have happened only in the peculiar conditions prevailing during an early phase of its history, so the existence of our kind of society, and even of human beings thinking as we do, may be due to phases in the evolution of our species without which neither the present order nor the existing kinds of individual minds could have arisen, and from the legacy of which we can never wholly free ourselves. We can judge and modify all our views and beliefs only within a framework of opinions and values which, though they will gradually change, are for us a given result of that evolution.

Yet the problem of the formation of such structures is still a theoretical and not a historical problem, because it is concerned with those factors in a sequence of events which are in principle repeatable, though in fact they may have occurred only once. We may call the answer 'conjectural history' (and much of modern social theory derives indeed from what the eighteenth-century thinkers called conjectural history), if we remain aware that the aim of such 'conjectural history' is not to account for all particular attributes which a unique event possesses, but only for those which under conditions which may be repeated can be produced again in the same combination. Conjectural history in this sense is the reconstruction of a hypothetical kind of process which may never have been observed but which, if it had taken place, would have produced phenomena of the kind we observe. The assumption that such a process has taken place may be tested by seeking for yet unobserved consequences which follow from it, and by asking whether all regular structures of the kind in question which we find can be accounted for by that assumption.

As was clearly recognized by Carl Menger, in the sphere of complex phenomena *"this genetic element is inseparable from the idea of theoretical sciences."*[13] Or, to put it differently, the existence of the structures with which the theory of complex phenomena is concerned can be made intelligible only by what the physicists would call a cosmology, that is, a theory of their evolution.[14] The problem of how galaxies or solar systems are formed and what is their resulting structure is much more like the problems which the social sciences have to face than the problems of mechanics; and for the understanding of the methodological problems of the social sciences a study of the procedures of geology or biology is therefore much more instructive than that of physics. In all these fields the structures or steady states which they study, the kind of objects with which they are concerned, though they may within a particular space-time region occur in millions or billions of instances, can be fully accounted for only by considering also circumstances which are not properties of the structures themselves but particular facts of the environment in which they have developed and exist.

---

[13] Carl Menger, *Untersuchungen über die Methode der Socialwissenschaften und der Politischen Oekonomie insbesondere* (Leipzig: Duncker & Humblot, 1883), p. 88, English translation by Francis J. Nock, edited by Louis Schneider under the title *Problems of Economics and Sociology* (Urbana, IL: University of Illinois Press, 1963), p. 94. Italics in the original. [The Schneider edition of Menger's book was subsequently reissued as *Investigations into the Method of the Social Sciences with Special Reference to Economics* (New York and London: New York University Press, 1985).—Ed.]

[14] I assume it need not be stressed here that a theory of evolution does not imply 'laws of evolution' in the sense of necessary sequences of particular forms or stages, a mistake often made by the same people who interpret the genetical as a historical problem. A theory of genetics describes a mechanism capable of producing an infinite variety of particular results.

VII

Societies differ from simpler complex structures by the fact that their elements are themselves complex structures whose chance to persist depends on (or at least is improved by) their being part of the more comprehensive structure. We have to deal here with integration on at least two different levels,[15] with, on the one hand, the more comprehensive order assisting the preservation of ordered structures on the lower level, and, on the other, the kind of order which on the lower level determines the regularities of individual conduct assisting the prospect of the survival of the individual only through its effect on the overall order of the society. This means that the individual with a particular structure and behaviour owes its existence in this form to a society of a particular structure, because only within such a society has it been advantageous to develop some of its peculiar characteristics, while the order of society in turn is a result of these regularities of conduct which the individuals have developed in society.

This implies a sort of inversion of the relation between cause and effect in the sense that the structures possessing a kind of order will exist because the elements do what is necessary to secure the persistence of that order. The 'final cause' or 'purpose', i.e., the adaptation of the parts to the requirements of the whole, becomes a necessary part of the explanation of why structures of the kind exist: we are bound to explain the fact that the elements behave in a certain way by the circumstance that this sort of conduct is most likely to preserve the whole—on the preservation of which depends the preservation of the individuals, which would therefore not exist if they did not behave in this manner. A 'teleological' explanation is thus entirely in order so long as it does not imply design by a maker but merely the recognition that the kind of structure would not have perpetuated itself if it did not act in a manner likely to produce certain effects,[16] and that it has evolved through those prevailing at each stage who did.

The reason why we are reluctant to describe such actions as purposive is that the order which will form as the result of these actions is of course in no

[15] Cf. Robert Redfield, ed., *Levels of Integration in Biological and Social Systems*, in Jacques Cattell, ed., vol. 8 (1941) of *Biological Symposia* (Lancaster, Penn.: Jacques Cattell, 1940–47). 'Integration', in this context, means of course simply the formation of an order or the incorporation in an already existing order.

[16] Cf. David Hume, *Dialogues Concerning Natural Religion*, in *The Philosophical Works*, ed. Thomas Hill Green and Thomas Hodge Grose, new rev. ed. (London: Longmans, Green, 1890), vol. 2, pp. 428–29: "I would fain know how an animal could subsist, unless its parts were so adjusted? . . . No form . . . can subsist, unless it possess those powers and organs, requisite for its subsistence: some new order or oeconomy must be tried, and so on, without intermission, till at last some order, which can support and maintain itself, is fallen upon."

sense 'part of the purpose' or of the motive of the acting individuals. The immediate cause, the impulse which drives them to act, will be something affecting them only; and it is merely because in doing so they are restrained by rules that an overall order results, while this consequence of observing these rules is wholly beyond their knowledge or intentions. In Adam Smith's classical phrase, man "is led to promote an end which was no part of his intention",[17] just as the animal defending its territory has no idea that it thereby contributes to regulate the numbers of its species.[18] It was indeed what I have elsewhere called the twin ideas of evolution and spontaneous order,[19] the great contributions of Bernard Mandeville and David Hume, of Adam Ferguson and Adam Smith, which have opened the way for an understanding, both in biological and social theory, of that interaction between the regularity of the conduct of the elements and the regularity of the resulting structure. What they did not make clear, and what even in the subsequent development of social theory has not been brought out with sufficient clarity, is that it is always some regularity in the behaviour of the elements which produces, in interaction with the environment, what may be a wholly different regularity of the actions of the whole.

Earlier groping efforts towards such an understanding which have left their traces on modern jurisprudence ran in terms of the adequacy of the rules of individual conduct to the *natura rei*, the nature of the thing. By this was meant just that overall order which would be affected by a change in any one of the rules of individual conduct—with the consequence that the effects of such a change in any one rule can be assessed only out of an understanding of all the factors determining the overall order. The true element in this is that the normative rules often serve to adapt an action to an order which exists as a fact. That there always exists such an order beyond the regularities of the actions of any one individual, an order at which the particular rules 'aim' and into which any one new rule has to be fitted, is the insight which only a theory of the formation of that overall order can adequately give.

[17] Adam Smith, *An Inquiry into the Nature and Causes of the Wealth of Nations* [1776], ed. Edwin Cannan (London: Methuen, 1904), vol. 1, p. 421. [See now Adam Smith, *An Inquiry into the Nature and Causes of the Wealth of Nations*, ed. W. B. Todd, vol. 2 of *The Glasgow Edition of the Works and Correspondence of Adam Smith* (Glasgow: University of Glasgow, 1976; reprinted, Indianapolis, IN: Liberty Fund, 1981), book 4, chapter 2, p. 456. Smith's sentence actually reads, "[Man] is led by an invisible hand to promote an end which was no part of his intention." It is rather curious that Hayek should decide to suppress here any reference to the invisible hand.—Ed.]

[18] See V. C. Wynne-Edwards, *Animal Dispersion*.

[19] See my lecture, 'Dr. Bernard Mandeville', *Proceedings of the British Academy* (London: Oxford University Press), vol. 52, 1966, pp. 125–41. [See now F. A. Hayek, "Dr. Bernard Mandeville (1670–1733)", in *The Trend of Economic Thinking*, ed. W. W. Bartley III and Stephen Kresge, vol. 3 (1991) of *The Collected Works of F. A. Hayek* (Chicago: University of Chicago Press; London: Routledge), pp. 79–100.—Ed.]

VIII

A few observations may be added in conclusion on certain peculiarities of social orders which rest on learnt (culturally transmitted) rules in addition to the innate (genetically transmitted) ones. Such rules will presumably be less strictly observed and it will need some continuous outside pressure to secure that individuals will continue to observe them. This will in part be effected if behaviour according to the rules serves as a sort of mark of recognition of membership of the group. If deviant behaviour results in non-acceptance by the other members of the group, and observance of the rules is a condition of successful co-operation with them, an effective pressure for the preservation of an established set of rules will be maintained. Expulsion from the group is probably the earliest and most effective sanction or 'punishment' which secures conformity, first by mere actual elimination from the group of the individuals who do not conform while later, in higher stages of intellectual development, the fear of expulsion may act as a deterrent.

Such systems of learnt rules will probably nevertheless be more flexible than a system of innate rules and a few more remarks on the process by which they may change will be in place. This process will be closely connected with that by which individuals learn by imitation how to observe abstract rules; a process of which we know very little. One factor influencing it will be the order of dominance of the individuals within the group. There will be, on the one end of the scale, a greater margin of tolerance for the young who are still in the process of learning and who are accepted as members of the group, not because they have already learnt all the rules peculiar to the group, but because as natural offspring they are attached to particular adult members of the group. On the other end of the scale there will be dominant old individuals who are firmly set in their ways and not likely to change their habits, but whose position is such that if they do acquire new practices they are more likely to be imitated than to be expelled from the group. The order of rank is thus undoubtedly an important factor in determining what alterations will be tolerated or will spread, though not necessarily in the sense that it will always be the high-ranking who initiate change.[20]

A point which deserves more consideration than it usually receives, however, is that the preference for acting according to established rules, and the fear of the consequences if one deviates from them, is probably much older and more basic than the ascription of these rules to the will of a personal,

---

[20] It would seem, e.g., that among monkeys new food habits are acquired more readily by the young and may then spread to the older members of the group: see the observations by J. Itani reported by Syunzo Kawamura, "The Process of Sub-culture Propagation among Japanese Macaques", in *Primate Social Behavior*, ed. Charles H. Southwick (Princeton, NJ: D. Van Nostrand, 1963), p. 85.

human or super-natural, agent, or to the fear of punishment that may be in-flicted by such an agent. The partial awareness of a regularity of the world, of the difference between a known and predictable and an unknown and unpredictable part of the events in the environment, must create a prefer-ence for the kinds of actions whose consequences are predictable and a fear of the kinds of actions whose consequences are unpredictable. Though in an animistically interpreted world this fear is likely to become a fear of retribu-tion by the agent whose will is disregarded, such a fear of the unknown or unusual action must operate much earlier to keep the individual to the tried ways. The knowledge of some regularities of the environment will create a preference for those kinds of conduct which produce a confident expectation of certain consequences, and an aversion to doing something unfamiliar and fear when it has been done. This establishes a sort of connection between the knowledge that rules exist in the objective world and a disinclination to devi-ate from the rules commonly followed in action, and therefore also between the belief that events follow rules and the feeling that one 'ought' to observe rules in one's conduct.

Our knowledge of fact (and especially of that complex order of society within which we move as much as within the order of nature) tells us mainly what will be the consequences of some of our actions in some circumstances. While this will help us to decide what to do if we want to obtain a particular result, or are driven by a particular impulse, it needs to be supplemented in a largely unknown world by some principle which inhibits actions to which our internal drives might lead us but which are inappropriate to the circum-stances. The rules of fact which one knows can be relied upon only so long as one plays the game oneself according to the rules, i.e., keeps within the kind of actions the consequences of which are tolerably predictable. Norms are thus an adaptation to a factual regularity on which we depend but which we know only partially and on which we can count only if we observe those norms. If I know that if I do not observe the rules of my group, not only will I not be accepted and in consequence not be able to do most of the things I want to do and must do to preserve my life, but also that, if I do not observe these rules, I may release the most terrifying events and enter a world in which I can no longer orient myself, such rules will be as much a necessary guidance to successful action as rules that tell me how the objects in my environment will behave. The factual belief that such and such is the only way in which a certain result can be brought about, and the normative belief that this is the only way in which it ought to be pursued, are thus closely associated. The indi-vidual will feel that it exposes itself to dangers by transgressing the rules even if there is nobody there to punish it, and the fear of this will keep even the animal to the customary way. But once such rules are deliberately taught, and taught in an animistic language, they come almost inevitably to be associated with the will of the teacher or the punishment or the super-natural sanctions threatened by him.

Man does not so much choose between alternative actions according to their known consequences as prefer those the consequences of which are predictable over those the consequences of which are unknown. What he most fears, and what puts him in a state of terror when it has happened, is to lose his bearings and no longer to know what to do. Though we all tend to associate conscience with the fear of blame or punishment by another will, the state of mind which it represents is psychologically little different from the alarm experienced by somebody who, while manipulating a powerful and complicated machinery, has inadvertently pulled the wrong levers and thereby produced wholly unexpected movements. The resulting feeling that something dreadful is going to happen because one has infringed rules of conduct is but one form of the panic produced when one realizes that one has entered an unknown world. A bad conscience is the fear of the dangers to which one has thus exposed oneself by having left the known path and entered such an unknown world. The world is fairly predictable only so long as one adheres to the established procedures, but it becomes frightening when one deviates from them.

In order to live successfully and to achieve one's aims within a world which is only very partially understood, it is therefore quite as important to obey certain inhibiting rules which prevent one from exposing oneself to danger as to understand the rules on which this world operates. Taboos or negative rules acting through the paralysing action of fear will, as a kind of knowledge of what *not* to do, constitute just as significant information about the environment as any positive knowledge of the attributes of the objects of this environment. While the latter enables us to predict the consequences of particular actions, the former just warns us not to take certain kinds of action. At least so long as the normative rules consist of prohibitions, as most of them probably did before they were interpreted as commands of another will, the 'Thou shalt not' kind of rule may after all not be so very different from the rules giving us information about what is.[21]

---

[21] The possibility contemplated here is not that all normative rules can be interpreted as descriptive or explanatory rules, but that the latter may be meaningful only within a framework of a system of normative rules.

ELEVEN

THE RESULTS OF HUMAN ACTION
BUT NOT OF HUMAN DESIGN[1] [2]

The belief in the superiority of deliberate design and planning over the spontaneous forces of society enters European thought explicitly only through the rationalist constructivism of Descartes. But it has its sources in a much older erroneous dichotomy which derives from the ancient Greeks and still forms the greatest obstacle to a proper understanding of the distinct task of both social theory and social policy. This is the misleading division of all phenomena into those which are 'natural' and those which are 'artificial.'[3] Already the sophists of the fifth century B.C. had struggled with the problem and stated it as the false alternative that institutions and practices must be either due to nature (*physei*) or due to convention (*thesei* or *nomō*); and through Aristotle's adoption of this division it has become an integral part of European thought.[4]

---

[1] A French translation of this essay was published in: *Les fondements philosophiques des systèmes économiques: Textes de Jacques Rueff et essais rédigés en son honneur*, ed. Emil Claassen (Paris: Payot, 1967), pp. 98–106. [Reprinted in F. A. Hayek, *Studies in Philosophy, Politics and Economics* (Chicago: University of Chicago Press, 1967), pp. 96–105.—Ed.]

[2] Adam Ferguson, *An Essay on the History of Civil Society* (Edinburgh: Printed for A. Millar and T. Caddel, London, and A. Kincaid and J. Bell, Edinburgh, 1767), p. 187: "Nations stumble upon establishments, which are indeed the result of human action, but not the execution of any human design." Ferguson refers in this connection to the *Mémoires du Cardinal de Retz* (Paris: E. Ledoux, 1820), vol. 2, p. 497, presumably the reference to President de Bellièvre's statement that Cromwell once told him that "on ne montait jamais si haut que quand on ne sait où l'on va." [The next sentence of Ferguson's text reads, "If Cromwell said, that a man never mounts higher, than when he knows not whither he is going; it may with more reason be affirmed of communities, that they admit of the greatest revolutions where no change is intended, and that the most refined politicians do not always know whither they are leading the state by their projects."—Ed.]

[3] Cf. Felix Heinimann, *Nomos und Physis: Herkunft und Bedeutung einer Antithese im griechischen Denken des 5. Jahrhunderts* (Basel: Friedrich Reinhardt, 1945).

[4] [In his paper "Nature, Custom, and Reason as the Explanatory and Practical Principles of Aristotelian Political Science" (*Review of Politics*, vol. 64, Summer 2002, pp. 469–95), James Murphy argues that Aristotle, like Hayek, employed a three part division in explaining social orders, a "nested hierarchy" consisting of nature, habit, and reason, such that "our habits presuppose human nature but cannot be reduced to it, just as our stipulated rational ideals presuppose our habits but cannot be reduced to them" (p. 473). Murphy thus would reject Hayek's lumping Aristotle in with the sophists on this matter.—Ed.]

It is misleading, however, because those terms make it possible to include a large and distinct group of phenomena either under the one or the other of the two terms, according as to which of two possible definitions is adopted that were never clearly distinguished and are to the present day constantly confused. Those terms could be used to describe either the contrast between something which was independent of human action and something which was the result of human action, or to describe the contrast between something which had come about without, and something which had come about as a result of, human design. This double meaning made it possible to represent all those institutions which in the eighteenth century Adam Ferguson at last clearly singled out as due to human action but not to human design either as natural or as conventional according as one or the other of these distinctions was adopted. Most thinkers, however, appear to have been hardly aware that there were two different distinctions possible.

Neither the Greeks of the fifth century B.C. nor their successors for the next two thousand years developed a systematic social theory which explicitly dealt with those unintended consequences of human action or accounted for the manner in which an order or regularity could form itself among those actions which none of the acting persons had intended. It therefore never became clear that what was really required was a three-fold division which inserted between the phenomena which were natural in the sense that they were wholly independent of human action, and those which were artificial or conventional[5] in the sense that they were the product of human design, a distinct middle category comprising all those unintended patterns and regularities which we find to exist in human society and which it is the task of social theory to explain. We still suffer, however, from the lack of a generally accepted term to describe this class of phenomena; and to avoid continuing confusion it seems to be urgently necessary that one should be adopted. Unfortunately the most obvious term which should be available for that purpose, namely 'social', has by a curious development come to mean almost the opposite of what is wanted: as a result of the personification of society, consequent on the very failure to recognize it as a spontaneous order, the word 'social' has come to be generally used to describe the aims of deliberate concerted action. And the new term 'societal' which, conscious of the difficulty, some sociologists have attempted to introduce, appears to have small prospect of establishing itself to fill that urgent need.[6]

[5] The ambiguity of the term 'conventional', which may refer either to explicit agreement or to habitual practices and their results, has further contributed to enhance the confusion.

[6] See F. Stuart Chapin, *Cultural Change* (New York: Century, 1928), and Maurice Mandelbaum, "Societal Facts", in *Theories of History*, ed. Patrick Gardiner (London, Allen and Unwin, 1959), pp. 476–88. The term 'cultural' which social anthropologists have adopted as a technical term to describe these phenomena will hardly do for general usage, since most people would hesitate to include, e.g., cannibalism under 'cultural' institutions.

It is important to remember, however, that up to the appearance of modern social theory in the eighteenth century, the only generally understood term through which it could be expressed that certain observed regularities in human affairs were not the product of design was the term 'natural.' And, indeed, until the rationalist reinterpretation of the law of nature in the seventeenth century, the term 'natural' was used to describe an orderliness or regularity that was not the product of deliberate human will. Together with 'organism' it was one of the two terms generally understood to refer to the spontaneously grown in contrast to the invented or designed. Its use in this sense had been inherited from the stoic philosophy, had been revived in the twelfth century,[7] and it was finally under its flag that the late Spanish Schoolmen developed the foundations of the genesis and functioning of spontaneously formed social institutions.[8]

It was through asking how things would have developed if no deliberate acts of legislation had ever interfered that successively all the problems of social and particularly economic theory emerged. In the seventeenth century, however, this older natural law tradition was submerged by another and very different one, a view which in the spirit of the then rising constructivist rationalism interpreted the 'natural' as the product of designing reason.[9] It was

[7] Cf. particularly the account in Sten Gagnér, *Studien zur Ideengeschichte der Gesetzgebung* (Stockholm: Almquist and Wiksell, 1960), pp. 225–40, of the work of Guillaume des Conches, especially the passage quoted on p. 231: "Et est positiva que est ab hominibus inventa. . . . Naturalis vero que non est homine inventa." ["The positive is that which is contrived by men. . . . The natural is that which is not contrived by men."—Ed.]

[8] See particularly Luis Molina, *De iustitia et iure*, Cologne, 1596–1600, especially Tome II, disputatio 347, no. 3, where he says of natural price that "naturale dicitur, quoniam et ipsis rebus, seclusa quacumque humana lege eo decreto consurgit, dependetur tamen a multis circumstantiis, quibus variatur, atque ab hominum affectu, ac aestimatione, comparatione diversum usum, interdum pro solo hominum beneplacito et arbitrio." ["It is called natural because it derives from the thing itself, exclusive of any human law or decree, but is dependent on the many circumstances which alter it, and on the sentiments and opinions of men in comparing various uses, even sometimes on the pleasures and whims of men."—Ed.] In an interesting but unpublished doctoral thesis of Harvard University (William Seavey Joyce, *The Economics of Louis de Molina: A Study in the Development of Scholastic Economics in the Sixteenth Century*, 1949, pp. 2–3 of the Appendix, "Molina on Natural Law"), the author rightly says that "Molina explains that, unlike positive law, natural law is 'de objecto'—an untranslatable, but very handy scholastic term which means pretty much, 'in the nature of the case'—because from the very nature of the thing (*ex ipsamet natura rei*) it follows that, for the preservation of virtue or the avoiding of vice, that action should be commanded or forbidden, which the (natural) law commands or forbids. . . . 'Hence', Molina continues, 'what is commanded or forbidden results from the nature of the case and not from the arbitrary will (*ex voluntate et libito*) of the legislator.'"

[9] The change in the meaning of the concept of reason which this transition involves is clearly shown by a passage in John Locke's early *Essays on the Law of Nature*, ed. W. von Leyden (Oxford: Clarendon Press, 1954), p. 111, in which he explains that "By reason, however, I do not think is meant here that faculty of the understanding which forms trains of thought and deduces proofs, but certain definite principles of action from which spring all virtues and whatever is necessary

finally in reaction to this Cartesian rationalism that the British moral philosophers of the eighteenth century, starting from the theory of the common law
as much as from that of the law of nature, built up a social theory which made
the undesigned results of individual action its central object, and in particular
provided a comprehensive theory of the spontaneous order of the market.

There can be little question that the author to whom more than to any
other this 'anti-rationalist' reaction is due was Bernard Mandeville.[10] But the
full development comes only with Montesquieu[11] and particularly with David
Hume,[12] Josiah Tucker, Adam Ferguson, and Adam Smith. The uncompre-

---

for the proper moulding of morals." Cf. also ibid., p. 149: "For right reason of this sort is nothing
but the law of nature itself already known."

[10]The basic idea is already contained in many passages of the original poems of 1705, especially

> The worst of all the multitude
> Did something for the common good,

but the fully developed conception occurs only in the second part of the prose commentary
added more than twenty years later to *The Fable of the Bees* (see Bernard Mandeville, *The Fable of
the Bees: Or, Private Vices, Publick Benefits*, ed. F. B. Kaye (Oxford: Clarendon, 1924), vol. 2, especially pp. 142, 287–88, and 349–50, and compare Chiaki Nishiyama, *The Theory of Self-Love. An
Essay on the Methodology of the Social Sciences, and Especially of Economics, with Special Reference to Bernard
Mandeville*, Chicago Ph.D. thesis, June 1960, especially for the relation of Mandeville's theories
to Menger's). [Hayek was Chiaki Nishiyama's dissertation supervisor; the title of the dissertation is evidently patterned on Menger's *Investigations into the Method of the Social Sciences, with Special
Reference to Economics.*—Ed.]

[11]On the influence of Mandeville on Montesquieu see Joseph Dedieu, *Montesquieu et la tradition
politique anglaise en France: Les sources anglaise de "L'Esprit des lois"* (Paris: J. Gabalda, 1909).

[12]David Hume, *The Philosophical Works*, ed. Thomas Hill Green and Thomas Hodge Grose (London: Longmans, Green, 1890), vols. 1 and 2, *A Treatise of Human Nature*, vols. 3 and 4, *Essays, Moral,
Political, and Literary*, esp. vol. 2, p. 296: "advantageous to the public; though it be not intended for
that purpose by the inventors"; also vol. 3, p. 99: "if the particular checks and controls, provided
by the constitution . . . made it not the interest, even of bad men, to act for the public good"; as
well as vol. 2, p. 289: "I learn to do a service to another, without bearing him any real kindness";
and vol. 4, p. 195: "all these institutions arise merely from the necessities of human society." It is
interesting to observe the terminological difficulties into which Hume is led because, as a result
of his opposition to contemporary natural law doctrines, he has chosen to describe as 'artifact',
'artifice', and 'artificial' precisely what the older natural law theorists had described as 'natural',
cf. esp. vol. 2, p. 258: "where an invention is obvious and absolutely necessary, it may as properly
be said to be natural as anything that proceeds immediately from original principles; without the
intervention of thought or reflection. Though the rules of justice be *artificial*, they are not *arbitrary*.
Nor is the expression improper to call them *Laws of Nature*; if by natural we understand what is
common to any species, or even if we confine it to mean what is inseparable from the species."
Cf. my essay on "The Legal and Political Philosophy of David Hume", reprinted in *Studies in
Philosophy, Politics and Economics.* [This essay is now reprinted as chapter 7 of *The Trend of Economic
Thinking*, ed. W. W. Bartley III and Stephen Kresge, vol. 3 (1991) of *The Collected Works of F. A. Hayek*
(Chicago: University of Chicago Press; London: Routledge), pp. 101–18.—Ed.] Professor Bruno
Leoni has drawn my attention to the fact that Hume's use of 'artificial' in this connection derives
probably from Edward Coke's conception of law as 'artificial reason' which is of course closer to
the meaning the later scholastics had given to 'natural' than to the usual meaning of 'artificial.'

hending ridicule later poured on the latter's expression of the 'invisible hand' by which 'man is led to promote an end which was no part of his intention',[13] however, once more submerged this profound insight into the object of all social theory, and it was not until a century later that Carl Menger at last resuscitated it in a form which now, yet another eighty years later, seems to have become widely accepted,[14] at least within the field of social theory proper.

There was perhaps some excuse for the revulsion against Smith's formula

[13] Adam Smith, *An Inquiry into the Nature and Causes of the Wealth of Nations* [1776], ed. Edwin Cannan (London: Methuen, 1904), vol. 1, p. 421. [See now Adam Smith, *An Inquiry into the Nature and Causes of the Wealth of Nations*, ed. W. B. Todd, vol. 2 of *The Glasgow Edition of the Works and Correspondence of Adam Smith* (Glasgow: University of Glasgow, 1976; reprinted, Indianapolis, IN: Liberty Fund, 1981), book 4, chapter 2, p. 456.—Ed.]

[14] Carl Menger, *Untersuchungen über die Methode der Socialwissenschaften und der Politischen Ökonomie insbesondere* (Leipzig: Duncker & Humblot, 1883), p. 182: ". . . die unbeabsichtigte Resultante individueller d. i. individuelle Interessen verfolgender Bestrebungen der Volksglieder . . . die unbeabsichtigte sociale Resultante individuel-teleologischer Faktoren", in the English translation of this work by F. J. Nock, *Problems of Economics and Sociology*, ed. Louis Schneider (Urbana, IL: University of Illinois Press, 1963), p. 158. [See now the retitled edition of Menger's work, *Investigations into the Method of the Social Sciences, with Special Reference to Economics*, ed. Louis Schneider, translated by Francis Nock (New York: New York University Press, 1985), p. 158, where this translation is offered: "the unintended result of individual efforts of members of society, i.e., of efforts in the pursuit of individual interests . . . the unintended social result of individually teleological factors."—Ed.] The more recent revival of this conception seems to date from my own article on "Scientism and the Study of Society", *Economica*, n.s., vol. 9, August 1942, p. 276, or in the reprint in *The Counter-Revolution of Science* (Glencoe, IL: The Free Press, 1952), p. 41, where I argued that the aim of social studies is "to explain the unintended or undesigned results of the actions of many men." [Now see F. A. Hayek, *Studies on the Abuse and Decline of Reason: Texts and Documents*, ed. Bruce Caldwell, vol. 13 (2010) of *The Collected Works of F. A. Hayek*, p. 88.—Ed.] From this it appears to have been adopted by Karl Popper, "The Poverty of Historicism", *Economica*, n.s., vol. 11, August 1944, p. 122, or in the book edition (London: Routledge and Kegan Paul, 1957), p. 65, where he speaks of "the undesigned results of human actions" and adds in a note that "undesigned social institutions may develop as *unintended consequences of rational actions*"; as well as in *The Open Society and Its Enemies*, 4th ed. (Princeton: Princeton University Press, 1963), vol. 2, p. 93, where he speaks of "the indirect, the unintended and often the unwanted by-products of such actions" (i.e., "conscious and intentional human actions"). (I cannot agree, however, with the statement, ibid., p. 323, based on a suggestion of Karl Polanyi, that "it was Marx who first conceived social theory as the study of the *unwanted social repercussions of nearly all our actions*." The idea was clearly expressed by Adam Ferguson and Adam Smith, to mention only the authors to whom Marx was unquestionably indebted.) The conception is also used (though perhaps not adopted) by Ernest Nagel, "Problems of Concept and Theory Formation in the Social Sciences", in *Science, Language and Human Rights*, American Philosophical Association, Eastern Division, (Philadelphia: University of Pennsylvania Press, 1952), p. 54, where he says that "social phenomena are indeed not generally the intended resultants of individual actions; nevertheless the central task of social science is the explanation of phenomena as the unintended outcome of springs of action." Similar though not identical is K. R. Merton's conception of "the unanticipated consequences of purposive social action"; see his article under that title in *American Sociological Review*, vol. 1, December 1936, pp. 894–904, and the further discussion in *Social Theory and Social Structure*, rev. ed. (Glencoe, IL: Free Press, 1957), pp. 61–62.

because he may have seemed to treat it as too obvious that the order which formed itself spontaneously was also the best order possible. His implied assumption, however, that the extensive division of labour of a complex society from which we all profited could only have been brought about by spontaneous ordering forces and not by design was largely justified. At any rate, neither Smith nor any other reputable author I know has ever maintained that there existed some original harmony of interests irrespective of those grown institutions. What they did maintain, and what one of Smith's contemporaries, indeed, expressed much more clearly than Smith himself ever did, was that institutions had developed by a process of the elimination of the less effective which did bring about a reconciliation of the divergent interests. Josiah Tucker's claim was not that "the universal mover in human nature, self love" always did receive, but that it "may receive such a direction in this case (as in all others) as to promote the public interest by those efforts it shall make towards pursuing its own."[15]

The point in this which was long not fully understood until at last Carl Menger explained it clearly, was that the problem of the origin or formation and that of the manner of functioning of social institutions was essentially the same: the institutions did develop in a particular way because the co-ordination of the actions of the parts which they secured proved more effective than the alternative institutions with which they had competed and which they had displaced. The theory of evolution of traditions and habits which made the formation of spontaneous orders possible stands therefore in a close relation to the theory of evolution of the particular kinds of spontaneous orders which we call organisms, and has in fact provided the essential concepts on which the latter was built.[16]

But if in the theoretical social sciences these insights appear at last to have firmly established themselves, another branch of knowledge of much greater

[15]Josiah Tucker, *The Elements of Commerce and Theory of Taxes* (1755), reprinted in *Josiah Tucker: A Selection from His Economic and Political Writings*, ed. Robert L. Schuyler (New York: Columbia University Press, 1931), p. 92. Cf. also my *Individualism and Economic Order* (Chicago: University of Chicago Press, 1948), p. 7. [Hayek refers to his essay "Individualism: True and False", now reprinted in *Studies on the Abuse and Decline of Reason*, vol. 13 (2010) of *The Collected Works of F. A. Hayek*. Josiah Tucker (1712–1799) was an English rector, pamphleteer, and controversialist who wrote on a wide variety of subjects.—Ed.]

[16]Carl Menger, *Untersuchungen*, p. 88: "Dies genetische Element ist untrennbar von der Idee theoretischer Wissenschaften." [In the English translation, this is rendered, "This genetic element is inseparable from the idea of theoretical sciences."—Ed.]; also Nishiyama, *Theory of Self-Love*. It is interesting to compare this with the insight from the biological field stressed by Ludwig von Bertalanffy, *Problems of Life* (New York: John Wiley and Sons, 1952), p. 134: "What are called structures are slow processes of long duration, functions are quick processes of short duration. If we say that a function such as the contraction of a muscle is performed by a structure, it means that a quick and short process wave is superimposed on a long-lasting and slowly running wave."

practical influence, jurisprudence, is still almost wholly unaffected by it. The philosophy dominant in this field, legal positivism, still clings to the essentially anthropomorphic view which regards all rules of justice as the product of deliberate invention or design, and even prides itself to have at last escaped from all influence of that 'metaphysical' conception of 'natural law' from the pursuit of which, as we have seen, all theoretical understanding of social phenomena springs. This may be accounted for by the fact that the natural law concept against which modern jurisprudence reacted was the perverted rationalist conception which interpreted the law of nature as the deductive constructions of 'natural reason' rather than as the undesigned outcome of a process of growth in which the test of what is justice was not anybody's arbitrary will but compatibility with a whole system of inherited but partly inarticulated rules. Yet the fear of contamination by what was regarded as a metaphysical conception has not only driven legal theory into much more unscientific fictions, but these fictions have in effect deprived law of all that connection with justice which made it an intelligible instrument for the inducement of a spontaneous order.

The whole conception, however, that law is only what a legislator has willed and that the existence of law presupposes a previous articulation of the will of a legislator is both factually false and cannot even be consistently put into practice. Law is not only much older than legislation or even an organized state: the whole authority of the legislator and of the state derives from pre-existing conceptions of justice, and no system of articulated law can be applied except within a framework of generally recognized but often unarticulated rules of justice.[17] There never has been and there never can be a 'gap-less' (*lückenlos*) system of formulated rules. Not only does all made law *aim* at justice and *not create* justice, not only has no made law ever succeeded in replacing all the already recognized rules of justice which it presupposes or even succeeded in dispensing with explicit references to such unarticulated conceptions of justice; but the whole process of development, change and interpretation of law would become wholly unintelligible if we closed our eyes to the existence of a framework of such unarticulated rules from which the articulated law receives its meaning.[18] The whole of this positivist conception of law derives from that

[17]Cf. Paulus (*Dig.* 50, 17, 1) "non ex regula ius sumatur, sed ex iure quod est regula fiat"; and Accursius (*Gloss 9* on *Dig.* I, 1, 1) "Est autem ius a iustitia, sicut a matre sua, ergo prius fuit iustitia quam ius." [The first passage, taken from the *Digest*, a compendium of legal writings by ancient jurists that was completed under the reign of the Roman emperor Justinian, might be rendered, "The law may not be derived from a rule, but a rule must arise from the law as it is." The second, a commentary on the *Digest* by the glossator Accursius, might be rendered, "Therefore law is from justice, as if from its mother, because there was justice before law."—Ed.]

[18]Cf. Hermann Kantorowicz, *The Definition of Law*, ed. A. H. Campbell (London: Cambridge University Press, 1958) p. 35: "The whole history of legal science, particularly the work of the

factually untrue anthropomorphic interpretation of grown institutions as the product of design which we owe to constructivist rationalism.

The most serious effect of the dominance of that view has been that it leads necessarily to the destruction of all belief in a justice which can be found and not merely decreed by the will of a legislator. If law is wholly the product of deliberate design, whatever the designer decrees to be law is just by definition and unjust law becomes a contradiction in terms.[19] The will of the duly authorized legislator is then wholly unfettered and guided solely by his concrete interests. As the most consistent representative of contemporary legal positivism has put it, "From the point of view of rational cognition, there are only interests of human beings and hence conflicts of interests. The solution of these conflicts can be brought about either by satisfying one interest at the expense of the other, or by a compromise between the conflicting interests."[20]

All that is proved by this argument, however, is that the approach of rationalist constructivism cannot arrive at any criterion of justice. If we realize that law is never wholly the product of design but is judged and tested within a framework of rules of justice which nobody has invented and which guided people's thinking and actions even before those rules were ever expressed in words, we obtain, though not a positive, yet still a negative criterion of justice which enables us, by progressively eliminating all rules which are incompatible with the rest of the system,[21] gradually to approach (though perhaps never to reach) absolute justice.[22] This means that those who endeavoured to discover something 'naturally' (i.e., undesignedly) given were nearer the truth and therefore more 'scientific' than those who insisted that all law had been set ('posited') by the deliberate will of men. The task of applying the insight

---

Italian glossators and the German pandectists, would become unintelligible if law were to be considered as a body of commands of the sovereign."

[19] Cf. Thomas Hobbes, *Leviathan*, ed. Michael Oakeshott (Oxford: Blackwell, 1946), chapter 30, p. 227: "no law can be unjust."

[20] Hans Kelsen, *What is Justice? Justice, Law, and Politics in the Mirror of Science: Collected Essays* (Berkeley, Ca.: University of California Press, 1957), pp. 21–22.

[21] On the problem of compatibility of the several rules as test, see now the interesting studies by Jürgen von Kempski, collected in *Recht und Politik: Studien zur Einheit der Sozialwissenschaft* (Stuttgart: W. Kohlhammer, 1965), and his essay "Grundlegung zu einer Strukturtheorie des Rechts", *Abhandlungen der Geistes- und Sozialwissenschaftlichen Klasse* (Mainz: Akademie der Wissenschaften und der Literatur, 1961), no. 2.

[22] The conception of a negative test of the justice of legal rules (essentially of the kind at which the legal philosophy of Immanuel Kant aimed) which would enable us continuously to approach justice by eliminating all inconsistencies or incompatibilities from the whole body of rules of justice, of which at any one time a large part is always the common and undisputed possession of the members of a given civilization, is one of the central points of a book on which I am at present working.

of social theory to the understanding of law has, however, yet to be accomplished, after a century of the dominance of positivism has almost entirely obliterated what had already been accomplished in this direction.

Because there has been a period in which those insights of social theory had begun to affect legal theory; Savigny and his older historical school, largely based on the conception of a grown order elaborated by the Scottish philosophers of the eighteenth century, continued their efforts in what we now call social anthropology and even appear to have been the main channel through which those ideas reached Carl Menger and made the revival of their conceptions possible.[23] That in this respect Savigny continued or resumed the aim of the older natural law theorists has been concealed by his rightly directing his argument against the rationalist natural law theories of the seventeenth and eighteenth centuries. But though he thereby helped to discredit that conception of natural law, his whole concern had been to discover how law had arisen largely without design, and even to demonstrate that it was impossible by design adequately to replace the outcome of such natural growth. The natural

---

[23] For the channels through which the ideas of Burke (and through Burke, those of David Hume) appear to have reached Savigny see Heinrich Ahrens, *Die Rechtsphilosophie, oder das Naturrecht, auf philosophisch-anthropologischer Grundlage*, 4th ed. (Vienna: C. Gerold, 1852), p. 64. This book was probably also one of Carl Menger's first sources of information. On Savigny and his school, cf. also the acute observations of Eugen Ehrlich, *Die juristische Logik* (Tübingen: J. C. B. Mohr, 1918), p. 84: "Burke, Savigny and Puchta . . . verstehen, was immer verkannt wird, unter Volk oder Nation dasselbe, was wir heute als Gesellschaft im Gegensatz zum Staate bezeichnen, allerdings in nationaler Begrenzung" ["It has always been thought, incorrectly, that Burke, Savigny, and Puchta identified the 'people' or 'nation' with the 'state', rather than with 'society'; however, they could only conceive of a 'people' or 'nation'—hence 'society'—as existing within national borders."—Ed.]; and Sir Frederick Pollock, *Oxford Lectures and Other Discourses*, (London: Macmillan, 1890), pp. 41–42: "The doctrine of evolution is nothing else than the historical method applied to the facts of nature; the historical method is nothing else than the doctrine of evolution applied to human societies and institutions. When Charles Darwin created the philosophy of natural history . . . he was working in the same spirit and towards the same ends as the great publicists who, heeding his fields of labour as little as he heeded theirs, had laid in the patient study of historical fact the bases of a solid and rational philosophy of politics and law. Savigny, whom we do not yet know or honour enough, and our own Burke, whom we know and honour, but cannot honour too much, were Darwinians before Darwin. In some measure the same may be said of the great Frenchman Montesquieu, whose unequal but illuminating genius was lost in a generation of formalists." The claim to have been 'Darwinians before Darwin' was, however, first advanced by the theorists of language: see August Schleicher, *Die Darwinsche Theorie und die Sprachwissenrchaft* (Weimar, Böhlau, 1863), and Max Müller, "Lectures on Mr. Darwin's Philosophy of Language", *Fraser's Magazine*, vol. 7, June 1893 [1873—Ed.], p. 662, from whom Pollock seems to have borrowed the phrase. [For a translation of Schleicher's book, see *Darwinism Tested by the Science of Language*, translated by Alex. V. W. Bikkers (London: J. C. Hotten, 1869). The German jurist Friedrich Karl von Savigny (1779–1861) was a founder of the German historical school of law.—Ed.]

law which he opposed was not the natural law to be discovered but the natural law which was deductively derived from natural reason.

But if for the older historical school, though they spurned the word 'natural', law and justice were still given objects to be discovered and explained, the whole idea of law as something objectively given was abandoned by positivism, according to which it was regarded as wholly the product of the deliberate will of the legislator. The positivists no longer understood that something might be objectively given although it was not part of material nature but a result of men's actions; and that law indeed could be an object for a science only in so far as at least part of it was given independently of any particular human will: it led to the paradox of a science which explicitly denied that it had an object.[24] Because, if "there can be no law without a legislative act",[25] there may arise problems for psychology or sociology but not for a science of law.

The attitude found its expression in the slogan which governed the whole positivist period: that 'what man has made he can also alter to suit his desires.' This is, however, a complete *non sequitur* if 'made' is understood to include what has arisen from man's actions without his design. This whole belief, of which legal positivism is but a particular form, is entirely a product of that Cartesian constructivism which must deny that there are rules of justice to be discovered because it has no room for anything which is 'the result of human action but not of human design' and therefore no place for social theory. While on the whole we have now successfully expelled this influence from the theoretical sciences of society—and had to, to make them possible—the conceptions which today guide legal theory and legislation still belong almost wholly to this prescientific approach. And though it was French social scientists who earlier than others had clearly seen that from the famous *Discours de la Méthode* "il était sorti autant de déraison sociale et d'aberrations métaphysiques, d'abstractions et d'utopies que de données positives, que s'il menait à Comte il avait aussi mené à Rousseau",[26] it would seem at least to the outsider that in France, even more than elsewhere, law is still under its influence.

---

[24]Cf. Leonard Nelson, *Die Rechtswissenschaft ohne Recht: Kritische Betrachtungen über die Grundlagen des Staats- und Völkerrechts, insbesondere über die Lehre von der Souveränität* (Leipzig: Viet, 1917).

[25]John Austin, *Lectures on Jurisprudence, or the Philosophy of Positive Law*, 3rd ed. (London: John Murray, 1872 [1869—Ed.]), vol. 2, p. 555.

[26]Albert Sorel, "Comment j'ai lu la 'Réforme Sociale'", *Réforme sociale*, November 1, 1906, p. 614, quoted by Albert Schatz, *L'individualisme économique et sociale* (Paris: A. Colin, 1907), p. 41, which together with Henry Michel, *L'idée de l'état*, 3rd ed. (Paris: Hachette, 1898), is most instructive on this influence of Cartesianism on French social thought. [Sorel's claim was that Descartes's *Discourse on Method* "had given vent as much to social unreasonableness, metaphysical aberration, and abstract utopian speculation as to positive data, and that if it led to Comte it had led to Rousseau as well."—Ed.]

Supplementary Notes

1. Sten Gagnér, *Studien zur Ideengeschichte der Gesetzgebung*, pp. 208 and 242, shows that the terms 'natural law' and 'positive law' derive from the introduction by Gellius in the second century A.D. of the Latin adjectives *naturalis* and *positivus* to render the meaning of the Greek nouns *physis* and *thesis*. This indicates that the whole confusion involved in the dispute between legal positivism and the theories of the law of nature traces back directly to the false dichotomy here discussed, since it should be obvious that systems of legal rules (and therefore also the individual rules which have meaning only as part of such a system) belong to those cultural phenomena which are 'the result of human action but not of human design.' See on this also chapter 4 above. [Hayek refers in this citation to where "Notes on the Evolution of Systems of Rules of Conduct" appears in *Studies in Philosophy, Politics and Economics*. In the present volume, that essay is chapter 10.—Ed.]

2. Herr Christoph Eucken has drawn my attention to the fact that the contrast that is drawn in the opening sentence of Herodotus's *Histories* between what has arisen from [the actions of] men (*ta genomena ex anthrōpōn*) and their great and astounding works (*erga megala kai thōmasta*) suggests that he was more aware of the distinction here made than was true of many of the later ancient Greeks. [Hayek added the material in square brackets.—Ed.]

TWELVE

COMPETITION AS A
DISCOVERY PROCEDURE[1]

I

It is difficult to defend economists against the charge that for some 40 to 50 years they have been discussing competition on assumptions that, *if* they were true of the real world, would make it wholly uninteresting and useless. If anyone really knew all about what economic theory calls the *data*, competition would indeed be a very wasteful method of securing adjustment to these facts. It is thus not surprising that some people have been led to the conclusion that we can either wholly dispense with the market, or that its results should be used only as a first step towards securing an output of goods and services which we can then manipulate, correct, or redistribute in any manner we wish. Others, who seem to derive their conception of competition solely from modern textbooks, have not unnaturally concluded that competition does not exist.

Against this, it is salutary to remember that, *wherever* the use of competition can be rationally justified, it is on the ground that we do *not* know in advance the facts that determine the actions of competitors. In sports or in examinations, no less than in the award of government contracts or of prizes for poetry, it would clearly be pointless to arrange for competition, if we were certain beforehand who would do best. As indicated in the title of this lecture, I propose to consider competition as a procedure for the discovery of such facts as, without resort to it, would not be known to anyone, or at least would not be utilized.[2]

---

[1] This lecture was originally delivered, without the present section 2, to a meeting of the Philadelphia Society at Chicago on 29 March 1968 and later, on 5 July 1968, in German, without the present final section, to the *Institut für Weltwirtschaft* of the University of Kiel. Only the German version has been published before, first in the series of "Kieler Vorträge", N.S. 56, Kiel, 1968, and then reprinted in my collected essays entitled *Freiburger Studien* (Tübingen: Mohr, 1969). [Reprinted in F. A. Hayek, *New Studies in Philosophy, Politics, Economics and the History of Ideas* (Chicago: University of Chicago Press, 1978), pp. 179–90.—Ed.]

[2] Since I wrote this my attention has been drawn to a paper by Leopold von Wiese on "Die Konkurrenz, vorwiegend in soziologisch-systematischer Betrachtung", *Verhandlungen des Sechsten Deutschen Soziologentages* (Tübingen: J. C. B. Mohr—Paul Siebeck, 1929), where, on p. 27, he discusses the 'experimental' nature of competition.

This may at first appear so obvious and incontestable as hardly to deserve attention. Yet, some interesting consequences that are not so obvious immediately follow from the explicit formulation of the above apparent truism. One is that competition is valuable *only* because, and so far as, its results are unpredictable and on the whole different from those which anyone has, or could have, deliberately aimed at. Further, that the generally beneficial effects of competition must include disappointing or defeating some particular expectations or intentions.

Closely connected with this is an interesting methodological consequence. It goes far to account for the discredit into which the micro-economic approach to theory has fallen. Although this theory seems to me to be the only one capable of explaining the rôle of competition, it is no longer understood, even by some professed economists. It is therefore worthwhile to say at the outset a few words about the methodological peculiarity of any theory of competition, because it has made its conclusions suspect to many of those who habitually apply an over-simplified test to decide what they are willing to accept as scientific. The necessary consequence of the reason why we use competition is that, *in those cases in which it is interesting*, the validity of the theory can never be tested empirically. We can test it on conceptual models, and we might conceivably test it in artificially created real situations, where the facts which competition is intended to discover are already known to the observer. But in such cases it is of no practical value, so that to carry out the experiment would hardly be worth the expense. If we do not know the facts we hope to discover by means of competition, we can never ascertain how effective it has been in discovering those facts that might be discovered. All we can hope to find out is that, on the whole, societies which rely for this purpose on competition have achieved their aims more successfully than others. This is a conclusion which the history of civilization seems eminently to have confirmed.

The peculiarity of competition—which it has in common with scientific method—is that its performance cannot be tested in particular instances where it is significant, but is shown only by the fact that the market will prevail in comparison with any alternative arrangements. The advantages of accepted scientific procedures can never be proved scientifically, but only demonstrated by the common experience that, on the whole, they are better adapted to delivering the goods than alternative approaches.[3]

The difference between economic competition and the successful procedures of science consists in the fact that the former is a method of discovering

[3]Cf. the interesting studies of the late Michael Polanyi in *The Logic of Liberty* (London: Routledge and Kegan Paul, 1951 [reprinted, Indianapolis, IN: Liberty Fund, 1998—Ed.]), which show how he has been led from the study of scientific method to the study of competition in economic affairs; and see also Karl R. Popper, *The Logic of Scientific Discovery* (London: Hutchinson, 1959).

particular facts relevant to the achievement of specific, temporary purposes, while science aims at the discovery of what are sometimes called 'general facts', which are regularities of events. Science concerns itself with unique, particular facts only to the extent that they help to confirm or refute theories. Because these refer to general, permanent features of the world, the discoveries of science have ample time to prove their value. In contrast, the benefits of particular facts, whose usefulness competition in the market discovers, are in a great measure transitory. So far as the theory of scientific method is concerned, it would be as easy to discredit it on the ground that it does not lead to testable predictions about what science will discover, as it is to discredit the theory of the market on the ground that it fails to predict particular results the market will achieve. This, in the nature of the case, the theory of competition cannot do in any situation in which it is sensible to employ it. As we shall see, its capacity to predict is necessarily limited to predicting the kind of pattern, or the abstract character of the order that will form itself, but does not extend to the prediction of particular facts.[4]

II

Having relieved myself of this pet concern, I shall return to the central subject of this lecture, by pointing out that economic theory sometimes appears at the outset to bar its way to a true appreciation of the character of the process of competition, because it starts from the assumption of a 'given' supply of scarce goods. But which goods are scarce goods, or which things are goods, and how scarce or valuable they are—these are precisely the things which competition has to discover. Provisional results from the market process at each stage alone tell individuals what to look for. Utilization of knowledge widely dispersed in a society with extensive division of labour cannot rest on individuals knowing all the particular uses to which well-known things in their individual environment might be put. Prices direct their attention to what is worth finding out about market offers for various things and services. This means that the, in some respects always unique, combinations of individual knowledge and skills, which the market enables them to use, will not merely, or even in the first instance, be such knowledge of facts as they could list and communicate if some authority asked them to do so. The knowledge of which I speak consists rather of a capacity to find out particular circumstances, which becomes effective only if

---

[4]On the nature of 'pattern prediction' see my essay on "The Theory of Complex Phenomena" in *Studies in Philosophy, Politics and Economics* (Chicago: University of Chicago Press, 1967), pp. 22–42. [This essay appears as chapter 9 of the present volume.—Ed.]

possessors of this knowledge are informed by the market which kinds of things or services are wanted, and how urgently they are wanted.[5]

This must suffice to indicate what kind of knowledge I am referring to when I call competition a discovery procedure. Much would have to be added to clothe the bare bones of this abstract statement with concrete flesh, so as to show its full practical importance. But I must be content with thus briefly indicating the absurdity of the usual procedure of starting the analysis with a situation in which all the facts are supposed to be known. This is a *state* of affairs which economic theory curiously calls 'perfect competition.' It leaves no room whatever for the *activity* called competition, which is presumed to have already done its task. However, I must hurry on to examine a question, on which there exists even more confusion—namely, the meaning of the contention that the market adjusts activities spontaneously to the facts it discovers— or the question of the purpose for which it uses this information.

The prevailing confusion here is largely due to mistakenly treating the order which the market produces as an 'economy' in the strict sense of the word, and judging results of the market process by criteria which are appropriate only to such a single organized community serving a given hierarchy of ends. But such a hierarchy of ends is not relevant to the complex structure composed of countless individual economic arrangements. The latter, unfortunately, we also describe by the same word 'economy', although it is something fundamentally different, and must be judged by different standards. An economy, in the strict sense of the word, is an organization or arrangement in which someone deliberately allocates resources to a unitary order of ends. Spontaneous order produced by the market is nothing of the kind; and in important respects it does not behave like an economy proper. In particular, such spontaneous order differs because it does *not* ensure that what general opinion regards as more important needs are always satisfied before the less important ones. This is the chief reason why people object to it. Indeed, the whole of socialism is nothing but a demand that the market order (or catallaxy, as I like to call it, to prevent confusion with an economy proper)[6] should be turned into an economy in the strict sense, in which a common scale of importance determines which of the various needs are to be satisfied, and which are not to be satisfied.

The trouble with this socialist aim is a double one. As is true of every deliberate organization, only the knowledge of the organizer can enter into the

---

[5]Cf. Samuel Johnson in *Boswell's Life of Johnson*, L. F. Powell's revision of G. B. Hill's edition (Oxford: Clarendon Press, 1934) vol. 2, p. 365 (18 April 1775): "Knowledge is of two kinds. We know a subject ourselves, or we know where we can find information upon it."

[6]For a fuller discussion see now my *The Mirage of Social Justice*, vol. 2 of *Law, Legislation and Liberty*, (Chicago and London: University of Chicago Press and Routledge, 1976), pp. 107–20. [A *Collected Works* edition of this volume is anticipated.—Ed.]

design of the economy proper, and all the members of such an economy, conceived as a deliberate organization, must be guided in their actions by the unitary hierarchy of ends which it serves. On the other hand, advantages of the spontaneous order of the market, or the catallaxy, are correspondingly two. Knowledge that is used in it is that of all its members. Ends that it serves are the separate ends of those individuals, in all their variety and contrariness.

Out of this fact arise certain intellectual difficulties which worry not only socialists, but all economists who want to assess the accomplishments of the market order; because, if the market order does not serve a definite order of ends, indeed if, like any spontaneously formed order, it cannot legitimately be said to *have* particular ends, it is also not possible to express the value of the results as a sum of its particular individual products. What, then, do we mean when we claim that the market order produces in some sense a maximum or optimum?

The fact is, that, though the existence of a spontaneous order not made for a particular purpose cannot be properly said to have a purpose, it may yet be highly conducive to the achievement of many different individual purposes not known as a whole to any single person, or relatively small group of persons. Indeed, rational action is possible only in a fairly orderly world. Therefore it clearly makes sense to try to produce conditions under which the chances for any individual taken at random to achieve his ends as effectively as possible will be very high—even if it cannot be predicted which particular aims will be favoured, and which not.

As we have seen, the results of a discovery procedure are in their nature unpredictable; and all we can expect from the adoption of an effective discovery procedure is to improve the chances for unknown people. The only common aim which we can pursue by the choice of this technique of ordering social affairs is the general kind of pattern, or the abstract character, of the order that will form itself.

III

Economists usually ascribe the order which competition produces as an equilibrium—a somewhat unfortunate term, because such an equilibrium presupposes that the facts have already all been discovered and competition therefore has ceased. The concept of an 'order' which, at least for the discussion of problems of economic policy, I prefer to that of equilibrium, has the advantage that we can meaningfully speak about an order being approached to various degrees, and that order can be preserved throughout a process of change. While an economic equilibrium never really exists, there is some justification for asserting that the kind of order of which our theory describes an ideal type, is approached in a high degree.

This order manifests itself in the first instance in the circumstance that the expectations of transactions to be effected with other members of society, on which the plans of all the several economic subjects are based, can be mostly realized. This mutual adjustment of individual plans is brought about by what, since the physical sciences have also begun to concern themselves with spontaneous orders, or 'self-organizing systems', we have learnt to call 'negative feedback.' Indeed, as intelligent biologists acknowledge, "long before" Claude Bernard, Clerk Maxwell, Walter B. Cannon, or Norbert Wiener developed cybernetics, "Adam Smith had just as clearly used the idea in his *The Wealth of Nations* (1776). The 'invisible hand' that regulates prices to a nicety is clearly this idea. In a free market, says Smith in effect, prices are regulated by negative feedback."[7]

We shall see that the fact that a high degree of coincidence of expectations is brought about by the systematic disappointment of some kind of expectations is of crucial importance for an understanding of the functioning of the market order. But to bring about a mutual adjustment of individual plans is not all that the market achieves. It also secures that whatever is being produced will be produced by people who can do so more cheaply than (or at least as cheaply as) anybody who does not produce it (and cannot devote his energies to produce something else comparatively even more cheaply), and that each product is sold at a price lower than that at which anybody who in fact does not produce it could supply it. This, of course, does not exclude that some may make considerable profits over their costs if these costs are much lower than those of the next efficient potential producer. But it does mean that of the combination of commodities that is in fact produced, as much will be produced as we know to bring about by any known method. It will of course not be as much as we might produce if all the knowledge anybody possessed or can acquire were commanded by some one agency, and fed into a computer (the cost of finding out would, however, be considerable). Yet we do injustice to the achievement of the market if we judge it, as it were, from above, by comparing it with an ideal standard which we have no known way of achieving. If we judge it, as we ought to, from below, that is, if the comparison in this case is made against what we could achieve by any other method—especially against what would be produced if competition were prevented, so that only

[7] Garrett Hardin, *Nature and Man's Fate* (New York: New American Library, Mentor edition, 1961), p. 54. [In his original essay Hayek's quote started with the words "long before" and ended with "negative feedback", but in Hardin's book the references to Bernard, Maxwell, Cannon, and Weiner as the developers of cybernetics were actually mentioned earlier. The quote above has been corrected to reflect this. Though Hayek's manipulation did not change any of the passage's meaning, it is illustrative of a certain creativity of quotation on his part.—Ed.]

those to whom some authority had conferred the right to produce or sell particular things were allowed to do so. All we need to consider is how difficult it is in a competitive system to discover ways of supplying to consumers better or cheaper goods than they already get. Where such unused opportunities seem to exist we usually find that they remain undeveloped because their use is either prevented by the power of authority (including the enforcement of patent privileges), or by some private misuse of power which the law ought to prohibit.

It must not be forgotten that in this respect the market only brings about an approach towards some point on that n-dimensional surface, by which pure economic theory represents the horizon of all possibilities to which the production of any one proportional combination of commodities and services could conceivably be carried. The market leaves the particular combination of goods, and its distribution among individuals, largely to unforeseeable circumstances—and, in this sense, to accident. It is, as Adam Smith already understood,[8] as if we had agreed to play a game, partly of skill and partly of chance. This competitive game, at the price of leaving the share of each individual in some measure to accident, ensures that the real equivalent of whatever his share turns out to be, is as large as we know how to make it. The game is, to use up-to-date language, not a zero-sum game, but one through which, by playing it according to the rules, the pool to be shared is enlarged, leaving individual shares in the pool in a great measure to chance. A mind knowing all the facts could select any point he liked on the surface and distribute this product in the manner he thought right. But the only point on, or tolerably near, the horizon of possibilities which we know how to reach is the one at which we shall arrive if we leave its determination to the market. The so-called 'maximum' which we thus reach naturally cannot be defined as a sum of particular things, but only in terms of the chances it offers to unknown people to get as large a real equivalent as possible for their relative shares, which will be determined partly by accident. Simply because its results cannot be assessed in terms of a single scale of values, as is the case in an economy proper, it is very misleading to assess the results of a catallaxy as if it were an economy.

---

[8]Adam Smith, *The Theory of Moral Sentiments* (London: A. Millar, 1759), Part VI, section 2, chapter 2, penultimate paragraph, and part VII, section 2, chapter 1. [Now see Adam Smith, *The Theory of Moral Sentiments*, ed. D. D. Raphael and A. L. Macfie, vol. 1 of *The Glasgow Edition of the Works and Correspondence of Adam Smith* (Glasgow: University of Glasgow, 1976; reprinted, Indianapolis, IN: Liberty Fund, 1982), pp. 233–34 and pp. 278–80, respectively. The first citation, where Smith talks of "the man of system" who deludes himself into thinking that "he can arrange the different members of a great society with as much ease as the hand arranges the different pieces upon a chess-board", is certainly apt. The second citation is less so: though Smith speaks of life as a great game, he does so in the context of describing the Stoic system of philosophy.—Ed.]

IV

Misinterpretation of the market order as an economy that can and ought to satisfy different needs in a certain order of priority, shows itself particularly in the efforts of policy to correct prices and incomes in the interest of what is called 'social justice.' Whatever meaning social philosophers have attached to this concept, in the practice of economic policy it has almost always meant one thing, and one thing only: the protection of certain groups against the necessity to descend from the absolute or relative material position which they have for some time enjoyed. Yet this is not a principle on which it is possible to act generally without destroying the foundations of the market order. Not only continuous increase, but in certain circumstances even mere maintenance of the existing level of incomes, depends on adaptation to unforeseen changes. This necessarily involves the relative, and perhaps even the absolute, share of some having to be reduced, although they are in no way responsible for the reduction.

The point to keep constantly in mind is that *all* economic adjustment is made necessary by unforeseen changes; and the whole reason for employing the price mechanism is to tell individuals that what they are doing, or can do, has for some reason for which they are not responsible become less or more demanded. Adaptation of the whole order of activities to changed circumstances rests on the remuneration derived from different activities being changed, without regard to the merits or faults of those affected.

The term 'incentives' is often used in this connection with somewhat misleading connotations, as if the main problem were to induce people to exert themselves sufficiently. However, the chief guidance which prices offer is not so much how to act, but *what to do*. In a continuously changing world even mere maintenance of a given level of wealth requires incessant changes in the direction of the efforts of some, which will be brought about only if the remuneration of some activities is increased and that of others decreased. With these adjustments, which under relatively stable conditions are needed merely to maintain the income stream, no 'surplus' is available which can be used to compensate those against whom prices turn. Only in a rapidly growing system can we hope to avoid absolute declines in the position of some groups.

Modern economists seem in this connection often to overlook that even the relative stability shown by many of those aggregates which macro-economics treats as data, is itself the result of a micro-economic process, of which changes in relative prices are an essential part. It is only thanks to the market mechanism that someone else is induced to step in and fill the gap caused by the failure of anyone to fulfill the expectations of his partners. Indeed, all those aggregate demand and supply curves with which we like to operate are not really objectively given facts, but results of the process of competition going on all the time. Nor can we hope to learn from statistical information what changes in prices or incomes are necessary in order to bring about adjustments to the inevitable changes.

The chief point, however, is that in a democratic society it would be wholly impossible by commands to bring about changes which are not felt to be just, and the necessity of which could never be clearly demonstrated. Deliberate regulation in such a political system must always aim at securing prices which appear to be just. This means in practice preservation of the traditional structure of incomes and prices. An economic system in which each gets what others think he deserves would necessarily be a highly inefficient system—quite apart from its being also an intolerably oppressive system. Every 'incomes policy' is therefore more likely to prevent than to facilitate those changes in the price and income structures that are required to adapt the system to new circumstances.

It is one of the paradoxes of the present world that the communist countries are probably freer from the incubus of 'social justice', and more willing to let those bear the burden against whom developments turn, than are the 'capitalist' countries. For some Western countries at least the position seems hopeless, precisely because the ideology dominating their politics makes changes impossible that are necessary for the position of the working class to rise sufficiently fast to lead to the disappearance of this ideology.

V

If even in highly developed economic systems competition is important as a process of exploration in which prospectors search for unused opportunities that, when discovered, can also be used by others, this is to an even greater extent true of underdeveloped societies. My first attention has been deliberately given to problems of preserving an efficient order for conditions in which most resources and techniques are generally known, and constant adaptations of activities are made necessary only by inevitably minor changes, in order to maintain a given level of incomes. I will not consider here the undoubted rôle competition plays in the advance of technological knowledge. But I do want to point out how much more important it must be in countries where the chief task is to discover yet unknown opportunities of a society in which in the past competition has not been active. It may not be altogether absurd, although largely erroneous, to believe that we can foresee and control the structure of society which further technological advance will produce in already highly developed countries. But it is simply fantastic to believe that we can determine in advance the social structure in a country where the chief problem still is to discover what material and human resources are available, or that for such a country we can predict the particular consequences of any measures we may take.

Apart from the fact that there is in such countries so much more to be discovered, there is still another reason why the greatest freedom of competition seems to be even more important there than in more advanced countries. This is that required changes in habits and customs will be brought about only if the few willing and able to experiment with new methods can make it necessary for the many to follow them, and at the same time to show them the way. The required discovery process will be impeded or prevented, if the many are able to keep the few to the traditional ways. Of course, it is one of the chief reasons for the dislike of competition that it not only shows how things can be done more effectively, but also confronts those who depend for their incomes on the market with the alternative of imitating the more successful or losing some or all of their income. Competition produces in this way a kind of impersonal compulsion which makes it necessary for numerous individuals to adjust their way of life in a manner that no deliberate instructions or commands could bring about. Central direction in the service of so-called 'social justice' may be a luxury rich nations can afford, perhaps for a long time, without too great an impairment of their incomes. But it is certainly not a method by which poor countries can accelerate their adaptation to rapidly changing circumstances, on which their growth depends.

Perhaps it deserves mention in this connection that possibilities of growth are likely to be greater the more extensive are a country's yet unused opportunities. Strange though this may seem at first sight, a high rate of growth is more often than not evidence that opportunities have been neglected in the past. Thus, a high rate of growth can sometimes testify to bad policies of the past rather than good policies of the present. Consequently it is unreasonable to expect in already highly developed countries as high a rate of growth as can for some time be achieved in countries where effective utilization of resources was previously long prevented by legal and institutional obstacles.

From all I have seen of the world the proportion of private persons who are prepared to try new possibilities, if they appear to them to promise better conditions, and if they are not prevented by the pressure of their fellows, is much the same everywhere. The much lamented absence of a spirit of enterprise in many of the new countries is not an unalterable characteristic of the individual inhabitants, but the consequence of restraints which existing customs and institutions place upon them. This is why it would be fatal in such societies for the collective will to be allowed to direct the efforts of individuals, instead of governmental power being confined to protecting individuals against the pressures of society. Such protection for private initiatives and enterprise can only ever be achieved through the institution of private property and the whole aggregate of libertarian institutions of law.

313

THIRTEEN

THE PRIMACY OF THE ABSTRACT[1]

I did not bring a written paper as I preferred to leave it to the course of the discussion to determine in what direction I could best supplement it. Perhaps, however, it was quite as much a tacit hope that the discussion would provide me with an excuse to talk about a problem in which at the moment I am much interested but on which my ideas have not yet reached the clarity required for writing a formal paper. As I was listening I have indeed come to the conclusion that this is the most useful thing I can attempt to do and I am now taking my courage in both hands to present to you, as well as I can from a few notes,[2] some half-baked ideas about what I have called 'The Primacy of the Abstract.'[3]

I

What I shall try to explain under this paradoxical heading seems to me in some ways merely a final step in a long development, which would probably have been explicitly formulated some time ago had it not required the overcoming of a barrier built into the language which we have to employ. This is shown by the necessity in which I found myself of describing my subject by an apparent contradiction in terms. We simply have no other suitable term to describe what we call 'abstract' than this expression which implies that we deal

---

[1] Reprinted from *The Alpbach Symposium 1968: Beyond Reductionism: New Perspectives in the Life Sciences*, ed. Arthur Koestler and J. R. Smythies (London: Hutchinson, 1969), for which I had written up from my notes the essence of a talk I had given at Alpbach on 7 June 1968. [Reprinted in F. A. Hayek, *New Studies in Philosophy, Politics, Economics and the History of Ideas* (Chicago: University of Chicago Press, 1978), pp. 35–49.—Ed.]

[2] The numbered paragraphs in the present written paper correspond to the headings of the notes from which I spoke. Beyond this I have followed only partly the transcript of the tape recording. Not everything as now written was contained or came out clearly in the oral presentation. [Sections, not paragraphs, were numbered in the *New Studies* version, from which this text was taken.—Ed.]

[3] I could, of course, instead have spoken of 'the primacy of the general', but this would not have had the shock effect which is the merit of the phrase chosen.

with something 'abstracted' or derived from some other previously existing mental entity or entities which in some respect are richer or 'more concrete.' The contention which I want to expound and defend here is that, on the contrary, all the conscious experience that we regard as relatively concrete and primary, in particular all sensations, perceptions and images, are the product of a superimposition of many 'classifications'[4] of the events perceived according to their significance in many respects. These classifications are to us difficult or impossible to disentangle because they happen simultaneously, but are nevertheless the constituents of the richer experiences which are built up from these abstract elements.

My main concern in all this will not be to argue the truth of my contention but to ask what is its significance if true. I shall in a moment try to show that the phrase of the title merely brings under one heading several conceptions which have emerged independently in different fields. They will not be quoted as conclusive evidence for the truth of my thesis, but merely as a justification for examining the consequences that would follow if it were true. Without entering into a detailed account of the different theories in question, these references must remain very summary and incomplete. But I want to leave as much time as possible for showing in what way the conception suggested might provide a clue to a number of interesting questions, and have a liberating effect on one's thinking.

II

First I want to explain more fully what I mean by the 'primacy' of the abstract. I do not mean by this primarily a genetic sequence, although an evolutionary movement from the perception of abstract patterns to that of particular objects is also involved. The primacy with which I am mainly concerned is a causal one, that is, it refers to what, in the explanation of mental phenomena, must come first and can be used to explain the other. I do not wish to deny that in our conscious experience, or introspectively, concrete particulars occupy the central place and the abstractions appear to be derived from them. But this subjective experience appears to me to be the source of the error with which I am concerned, the appearance which prevents us from recognizing that these concrete particulars are the product of abstractions which the mind must possess in order that it should be able to experience particular sensations, percep-

---

[4]For a justification of this, and a few related terms I shall occasionally use, see my earlier book *The Sensory Order* (Chicago and London: University of Chicago Press and Routledge, 1952), in which, as it now seems to me, much of what I shall have to say was already implicitly contained. [A *Collected Works* edition of this volume is anticipated.—Ed.]

tions, or images. If, indeed, all we are aware of are concrete particulars, this does not preclude our being aware of them only because the mind is capable of operating in accordance with abstract rules which we can discover in that mind, but which it must have possessed before we were able to perceive the particulars from which we believe the abstractions to be derived. What I contend, in short, is that the mind must be capable of performing abstract operations in order to be able to perceive particulars, and that this capacity appears long before we can speak of a conscious awareness of particulars. Subjectively, we live in a concrete world and may have the greatest difficulty in discovering even a few of the abstract relations which enable us to discriminate between different things and to respond to them differentially. But when we want to explain what makes us tick, we must start with the abstract relations governing the order which, as a whole, gives particulars their distinct place.

So far this may sound pretty obvious, but when we reflect on the implications, they would mean little less than that psychology and the theory of knowledge frequently start at the wrong end. From the assertion that the abstract presupposes the concrete rather than the concrete the abstract (in the sense that in the mind the abstract can exist without the concrete, but not the concrete without the abstract) a wholly erroneous approach results which treats as given what most requires explanation.

III

Let me now remind you briefly of the chief developments in the various disciplines concerned, which seem to me instances of my general proposition. The chief support comes, of course, from ethology, and especially from the dummy experiments with fishes and birds that show that they respond in the same manner to a great variety of shapes which have only some very abstract features in common. It seems to follow that probably most animals recognize, not what we would regard as concrete particulars, or particular individuals, but abstract features long before they can identify particulars. This is indicated most clearly by the theoretical framework developed by ethology, which distinguishes between the 'innate releasing patterns' and the mechanism through which these evoke certain 'action patterns', where both concepts refer not to particular events, but to classes of combinations of stimuli and their effects in inducing a preparedness for one of a class of actions, which are both definable only in abstract terms.[5]

Similar insights have been gained by human sensory psychology in the course of its gradual emancipation from the conception of simple elemen-

[5] Cf., for example, W. H. Thorpe, *Learning and Instinct in Animals*, 2nd ed. (London: Methuen, 1963), p. 130.

tary sensations from which, in a mosaic fashion, the representations of the environment were supposed to be built up.[6] From H. von Helmholtz's still insufficiently appreciated conception of 'unconscious inference' and the similar ideas of C. S. Peirce[7] to F. Bartlett's interpretation of perceptions as 'inferential constructs', of which Koestler has reminded us, and culminating in the Gestalt school, which now proves to have emphasized only one aspect of a much wider phenomenon,[8] they all stress in one way or another that our perception of the external world is made possible by the mind possessing an organizing capacity; and that what used to be called elementary qualities are its product rather than its material.[9]

Another important development in a similar direction is the increasing awareness that all our actions must be conceived of as being guided by rules of which we are not conscious but which in their joint influence enable us to exercise extremely complicated skills without having any idea of the particular sequence of movements involved. (This capacity is often inadequately described as 'intuitive knowledge.') From Gilbert Ryle's now familiar distinction between the 'knowledge how' to do a thing and the 'knowledge that' it is so and so,[10]

[6] See on what immediately follows my *The Sensory Order* quoted before.

[7] C. S. Peirce, *The Collected Papers of Charles Saunders Peirce*, ed. Charles Hartshorne and Paul Weiss (Cambridge: Harvard University Press, 1931), vol. 1, p. 38.

[8] In a paper which I have come to know only since delivering this talk, Maurice Merleau-Ponty discusses under a heading very similar to that of this paper, the 'primacy of perception' over sensation. See his volume, *The Primacy of Perception, and Other Essays on Phenomenological Psychology, the Philosophy of Art, History, and Politics*, ed. James M. Edie (Evanston, IL: Northwestern University Press, 1964), pp. 12 ff.

[9] Cf. further James J. Gibson, *The Perception of the Visual World* (Boston: Houghton Mifflin, 1950), W. H. Thorpe, *Learning and Instinct in Animals*, p. 129, and particularly Ivo Kohler, "Experiments with Goggles", *Scientific American*, vol. 206, May 1962, pp. 62–72, who speaks of the 'general rules' by which the visual system learns to correct exceedingly complex and variable distortions produced by prismatic spectacles. [In his long sentence Hayek refers to the German physiologist, psychologist, and physicist Hermann von Helmholtz (1821–1894), whose theory of unconscious inference Hayek previously made note of in "Rules, Perception and Intelligibility", this volume, chapter 8, p. 240, note 23, and "The Theory of Complex Phenomena", this volume, chapter 9, p. 258, note 4, as well as to the American philosopher, mathematician, and scientist Charles Sanders Peirce (1839–1914). Hayek refers to a section titled "Reasoning From Samples" within Peirce's manuscript of notes titled "Lessons from the History of Science", but he might better have referred to the section titled "Kinds of Reasoning", pp. 28–31, where Peirce discusses retroduction, which involves forming a conjecture based on past observations, and analogical thinking, both of which come closer to what Hayek describes. Hayek also refers to the Cambridge psychologist Frederic C. Bartlett (1887–1969), who discusses perceptions as inferential constructs in his book *Thinking: An Experimental and Social Study* (London: Allen and Unwin, 1958), and to the author and organizer of the symposium, Arthur Koestler (1905–1983), who referred to Bartlett on p. 205 of his own symposium paper, "Beyond Atomism and Holism—The Concept of the Holon."—Ed.]

[10] Gilbert Ryle, "Knowing How and Knowing That", *Proceedings of the Aristotelian Society*, vol. 46, 1945–46, pp. 1–16, and *The Concept of Mind* (London: Hutchinson's University Library, 1949). [Cf. Hayek's earlier reference to Ryle's distinction in "Rules, Perception and Intelligibility", this

through Michael Polanyi's analysis of skills (and the closely connected concept of 'physiognomy perception'),[11] to R. S. Peters's highly important discussion of the significance of non-articulated rules in determining action,[12] there has been an increasing stress on mental factors which govern all our acting and thinking without being known to us, and which can be described only as abstract rules guiding us without our knowledge.

The field, however, in which it has come out most clearly that our mental activities are not guided solely or even chiefly by the particulars at which they are consciously directed, or of which the acting mind is aware, but by abstract rules which it cannot be said to know yet which nevertheless guide it, is modern linguistics. I do not know enough about it to discuss it at any length, but the chief point has indeed been brought out as long as 200 years ago by Adam Ferguson in one of my favourite passages of his great work which I cannot refrain from quoting:[13] "The peasant, or the child, can reason, and judge, and speak his language, with a discernment, a consistency, and a regard to analogy, which perplex the logician, the moralist, and the grammarian, when they would find the principle upon which the proceeding is founded, or when they would bring to general rules, what is so familiar, and so well sustained in particular cases." You all know how far this conception of the elaborate theory of the grammar of his language which the small child can observe without having any conscious idea of its existence has been carried by Noam Chomsky[14] and his school of transformational-generative grammar.

IV

When I now turn to the substance of my thesis it will be expedient to begin by considering, not how we interpret the external world, but how this interpretation governs our actions. It is easier first to show how particular actions are determined by the superimposition of various instructions concerning the several attributes of the action to be taken, and only afterwards to consider in

---

volume, chapter 8, p. 233, note 4. In note 2 of that essay Hayek also refers to the citations noted here by Polanyi and Ferguson.—Ed.]

[11] Michael Polanyi, *Personal Knowledge: Towards a Post-Critical Philosophy* (London: Routledge and Kegan Paul, 1959).

[12] [See R. S. Peters, *The Concept of Motivation* (London: Routledge and Kegan Paul, 1958).—Ed.]

[13] Adam Ferguson, *An Essay on the History of Civil Society* (Edinburgh: Printed for A. Millar and T. Caddel, London, and A. Kincaid and J. Bell, Edinburgh, 1767), p. 50.

[14] Noam Chomsky, *Syntactic Structures* ('s-Gravenhage: Mouton, 1957). I notice in R. H. Robins, *A Short History of Linguistics* (London: Longman, 1967), p. 126, that Louis Hjelmslev in his early *Principes de grammaire générale* (Copenhagen: A. F. Høst, 1928), pp. 15, 268, demanded a universal *état abstrait* comprising the possibilities available to language and differently realized in *états concrets* for each particular one which I quote for the interesting use of 'abstract' and 'concrete' in this connection.

what sense the perception of events can also be regarded as a subsummation of particular stimuli, or groups of stimuli, as elements of an abstract class to which a response possessing certain characteristics is appropriate.

The most convenient starting point is the conception of a disposition (or 'set', or propensity, or state) which makes an organism inclined to respond to stimuli of a certain class, not by a particular response, but by a response of a certain kind. What I mean to show in this connection is that what I have called an abstraction is primarily such a disposition towards certain ranges of actions, that the various 'qualities' which we attribute to our sensations and perceptions are these dispositions which they evoke, and that both the specification of a particular experienced event, and the specification of a particular response to it, are the result of a superimposition of many such dispositions to kinds of actions, which result in the connection of particular stimuli with particular actions.

I need not enter here into the detail of the physiological processes involved through which, by raising the threshold of excitation of a great many other neurons, the stream of impulses issuing from one will put a great many others in a state of preparedness to act. The important point is that only very rarely if ever will a single signal sent out from the highest levels of the nervous system evoke an invariable action pattern, and that normally the particular sequence of movements of particular muscles will be the joint result of many superimposed dispositions. A disposition will thus, strictly speaking, not be directed towards a particular action, but towards an action possessing certain properties, and it will be the concurrent effect of many such dispositions which will determine the various attributes of a particular action. A disposition to act will be directed towards a particular pattern of movements only in the abstract sense of pattern, and the execution of the movement will take one of many different possible concrete forms adjusted to the situation taken into account by the joint effect of many other dispositions existing at the moment. The particular movements of, say, a lion jumping on the neck of his prey, will be one of a range of movements in the determination of which account will be taken not only of direction, distance and speed of movement of the prey, but also of the state of the ground (whether smooth or rough, hard or soft), whether it is covered or open territory, the state of fitness of the lion's various limbs—all being present as dispositions together with its disposition to jump. Every one of these dispositions will refer not to a particular action but to attributes of any action to be taken while the dispositions in question last. It will equally govern the lion's action if it decides to slink away instead of jumping.[15]

[15] [Cf. Hayek's discussion in "*The Sensory Order* after Twenty-Five Years", in *Cognition and the Symbolic Processes*, ed. Walter Weimer and David Palermo (Hillsdale, NJ: Erlbaum, 1982), vol. 2, pp. 289–91, about the central rôle of the concept 'disposition' in his theory of psychology, and his lament that he had not sufficiently developed the idea in *The Sensory Order* itself. Hayek's discussion will appear in the forthcoming *Collected Works* edition of *The Sensory Order*.—Ed.]

The difference between such a determination of an action and the unique response of what we usually call a mechanism when we pull a trigger or press a button, is that each of the various signals ultimately determining the action of the organism at first activates merely a tendency towards one of a range of in some respect equivalent movements; and it will be the overlapping of many generic instructions (corresponding to different 'considerations') which will select a particular movement.

These several dispositions towards *kinds* of movements can be regarded as adaptations to typical features of the environment, and the 'recognition' of such features as the activation of the kind of disposition adapted to them. The perception of something as 'round', for example, would thus consist essentially in the arousal of a disposition towards a class of movements of the limbs or the whole body which have in common only that they consist of a succession of movements of the several muscles which in different scales, dimensions and directions lead to what we call a round movement. It will be these capacities to act in a kind of manner, or of imposing upon the movements certain general characteristics adapted to certain attributes of the environment, which operate as the classifiers identifying certain combinations of stimuli as being of the same kind. The action patterns of a very general character which the organism is capable of imposing upon its movements operate thus as moulds into which the various effects upon it of the external world are fitted.

What this amounts to is that all the 'knowledge' of the external world which such an organism possesses consists in the action patterns which the stimuli tend to evoke, or, with special reference to the human mind, that what we call knowledge is primarily a system of rules of action assisted and modified by rules indicating equivalences or differences or various combinations of stimuli. This, I believe, is the limited truth contained in behaviourism:[16] that in the last resort all sensory experience, perceptions, images, concepts, etc., derive their particular qualitative properties from the rules of action which they put into operation, and that it is meaningless to speak of perceiving or thinking except as a function of an acting organism in which the differentiation of the stimuli manifests itself in the differences of the dispositions to act which they evoke.

The chief points I want to drive home here are that the primary characteristic of an organism is a capacity to govern its actions by rules which determine

---

[16]A truth, however, often much more clearly expressed by authors who were very far from being behaviourists: cf., for example, Ernst Cassirer, *Philosophie der symbolischen Formen*, vol. 2 of *Das mythische Denken* (Berlin: Bruno Cassirer, 1925), p. 193: "Nicht das blosse Betrachten, sondern das Tun bildet vielmehr den Mittelpunkt, von dem für den Menschen die geistige Organisation der Wirklichkeit ihren Ausgang nimmt." [In the English translation by Ralph Manheim, *The Philosophy of Symbolic Forms* (New Haven: Yale University Press, 1955), vol. 2, p. 157, this passage is rendered, "It is not mere meditation but action which constitutes the centre from which man undertakes the spiritual organization of reality."—Ed.]

the properties of its particular movements; that in this sense its actions must be governed by abstract categories long before it experiences conscious mental processes, and that what we call mind is essentially a system of such rules conjointly determining particular actions. In the sphere of action what I have called 'the primacy of the abstract' would then merely mean that the dispositions for a kind of action possessing certain properties comes first and the particular action is determined by the superimposition of many such dispositions.

V

There is still one special point to which I must draw your attention in connection with these action patterns by which the organism responds to—and thereby, as I like to call it, 'classifies'—the various effects on it of events in the external world. This is the limited extent in which it can be said that these action patterns are built up by 'experience.' It seems to me that the organism first develops new potentialities for actions and that only afterwards does experience select and confirm those which are useful as adaptations to typical characteristics of its environment. There will thus be gradually developed by natural selection a repertory of action types adapted to standard features of the environment. Organisms become capable of ever greater varieties of actions, and learn to select among them, as a result of some assisting the preservation of the individual or the species, while other possible actions come to be similarly inhibited or confined to some special constellations of external conditions.

Perhaps I should add, in view of what we have discussed earlier, that nothing in this commits us to a choice between nativism and empiricism, although it makes it seem probable that most of the action patterns by which the organism responds will be innate. The important point is that the action patterns are not built up by the mind, but that it is by a selection among mechanisms producing different action patterns that the system of rules of action is built up on which rests what we regard as an interpretation of the external world by the mind.

You may already have noticed that what I have been arguing is in some way related to certain developments in the modern theory of knowledge, especially Karl Popper's argument against 'inductivism'—i.e., the argument that we cannot logically derive generalizations from particular experiences, but that the capacity to generalize comes first and the hypotheses are then tested and confirmed or refuted according to their effectiveness as guides to actions. As the organism plays with a great many action patterns of which some are confirmed and retained as conducive to the preservation of the species, corresponding structures of the nervous system producing appropriate dispositions will first appear experimentally and then either be retained or abandoned.

I cannot here more than just mention that this approach evidently also sheds important light on the significance of purely playful activities in the development both of animal and of human intelligence.

VI

While my chief contention is the primacy of the rules of action (or dispositions), which are abstract in the sense that they merely impose certain attributes on particular actions (which constitute the 'responses' by which the stimuli or combinations of stimuli are classified), I will now turn to the significance of this for the cognitive processes. I will put my main point first by stating that the formation of abstractions ought to be regarded not as actions of the human mind but rather as something which happens to the mind, or that alters that structure of relationships which we call the mind, and which consists of the system of abstract rules which govern its operation. In other words, we ought to regard what we call mind as a system of abstract rules of action (each 'rule' defining a class of actions) which determines each action by a combination of several such rules; while every appearance of a new rule (or abstraction) constitutes a change in that system, something which its own operations cannot produce but which is brought about by extraneous factors.

This implies that the richness of the sensory world in which we live, and which defies exhaustive analysis by our mind, is not the starting point from which the mind derives abstractions, but the product of a great range of abstractions which the mind must possess in order to be capable of experiencing that richness of the particular. The difference between this approach and the still predominant one is perhaps best illustrated by an oft-quoted phrase of William James which is very characteristic of the idea that the primitive mind of a higher animal or a small child perceives concrete particulars but lacks abstract relations. James speaks of the 'blooming, buzzing confusion' of the baby's sensory experience of his environment.[17] This presumably means that the baby can fully perceive such particulars as coloured spots, particular sounds, etc., but that for him these particulars are unordered. I am inclined to believe that, in the case of the baby as well as in that of higher animals, almost the exact opposite is true, namely that they experience a structured world in which the particulars are very indistinct. The baby and the animal

---

[17] [Hayek refers to the American psychologist and philosopher William James's (1842–1910) observation that "The baby, assailed by eyes, ears, nose, skin, and entrails at once, feels it all as one great blooming, buzzing confusion"; see William James, *The Principles of Psychology* [1890] (Cambridge: Harvard University Press, 1981), vol. 1, p. 462. Hayek referred approvingly to the James-Lange theory of emotions in his 1920 student paper on psychology. A translation of that paper will appear in the *Collected Works* edition of *The Sensory Order.*—Ed.]

certainly do not live in the same sensory world in which we live. But this is so, not because, though their 'sense data' are the same, they have not yet been able to derive from them as many abstractions as we have done, but because of the much thinner net of ordering relations which they possess—because the much smaller number of abstract classes under which they can subsume their impressions makes the qualities which their supposedly elementary sensations possess much less rich. Our experience is so much richer than theirs as a consequence of our mind being equipped, not with relations which are more abstract, but with a greater number of abstract relations not derived from given attributes of the elements. It rather confers these attributes on the elements.

VII

Some people are likely to object to this analysis on the ground that the term 'abstract' is properly attributed only to results of conscious thought. I shall later return to this point and in fact question whether we can ever in the same sense be conscious of an abstraction in which we are conscious of the intuitive perceptions of particular events or of images. But before I turn to this question I want to examine a tacit assumption which seems to be uncritically accepted in most discussions of these problems.

It is generally taken for granted that in some sense conscious experience constitutes the 'highest' level in the hierarchy of mental events, and that what is not conscious has remained 'sub-conscious' because it has not yet risen to that level. There can of course be no doubt that many neural processes through which stimuli evoke actions do not become conscious because they proceed on literally too low a level of the central nervous system. But this is no justification for assuming that all the neural events determining action to which no distinct conscious experience corresponds are in this sense sub-conscious. If my conception is correct that abstract rules of which we are not aware determine the sensory (and other) 'qualities' which we consciously experience, this would mean that of much that happens in our mind we are not aware, not because it proceeds at too low a level but because it proceeds at too high a level. It would seem more appropriate to call such processes not 'sub-conscious' but 'super-conscious', because they govern the conscious processes without appearing in them.[18] This would mean that what we consciously experience is only a part, or the result, of processes of which we cannot be conscious, because it is only the multiple classification by the super-structure

---

[18] I did not mention in my oral exposition, and therefore will not enlarge here on, the obvious relation of all this to Kant's conception of the categories that govern our thinking—which I took rather for granted.

which assigns to a particular event that determined place in a comprehensive order which makes it a conscious event.

This brings me back to the question of whether we can ever be conscious of all the higher abstractions which govern our thinking. It is rather significant in this connection that we seem to be unable to use such abstractions without resort to concrete symbols which appear to have the capacity of evoking the abstract operations that the mind is capable of performing, but of which we cannot form an intuitive 'picture', and of which, in this sense, we are not conscious. It seems to me that if we ask whether we can ever strictly be conscious of an abstraction in the same sense in which we are conscious of something that we perceive with our senses, the answer is at least uncertain. Is what we call an abstraction perhaps something which had better be described as an operation of the mind and which it can be induced to perform by the perception of appropriate symbols, but which can never 'figure' in conscious experience? I would suggest that at least those abstractions of which it can in some sense be said that we are aware of them, and can communicate them, are a secondary phenomenon, late discoveries by our mind reflecting on itself, and to be distinguished from their primary significances as guides to our acting and thinking.

VIII

The point in all this which I find most difficult to bring out clearly is that the formation of a new abstraction seems *never* to be the outcome of a conscious process, not something at which the mind can deliberately aim, but always a discovery of something which *already* guides its operation. This is closely connected with the fact that the capacity for abstraction manifests itself already in the actions of organisms to which we surely have no reason to attribute anything like consciousness, and that our own actions certainly provide ample evidence of being governed by abstract rules of which we are not aware.

I may perhaps mention here my interest in two apparently wholly different problems, namely the problem of what makes the observed action of other persons intelligible to us, and the problem of what we mean by the expression 'sense of justice.'[19] In this connection I was driven to the conclusions that both

---

[19]Cf. chapters 3, 4, and 11 in my *Studies in Philosophy, Politics and Economics* (Chicago: University of Chicago Press, 1967), and section 3 of my pamphlet, *The Confusion of Language in Political Thought*. [Hayek refers to "Rules, Perception and Intelligibility" and "Notes on the Evolution of Systems of Rules of Conduct", reprinted in this volume as chapters 8 and 10, respectively; "The Principles of a Liberal Social Order", in F. A. Hayek, *Studies in Philosophy, Politics and Economics*, pp. 160–77; and to section 3 of his pamphlet, *The Confusion of Language in Political Thought*, reprinted as chapter 6 of Hayek, *New Studies*, pp. 71–97. It is anticipated that the latter two papers will be reproduced in a future *Collected Works* volume.—Ed.]

THE PRIMACY OF THE ABSTRACT

our capacity to recognize other people's actions as meaningful, and the capacity to judge actions of our own or of others as just or unjust, must be based on the possession of highly abstract rules governing our actions, although we are not aware of their existence and even less capable of articulating them in words. Recent developments in the theory of linguistics at last make explicit those rules to which older linguists used to refer as the *Sprachgefühl*[20]—which is clearly a phenomenon of the same sort as the sense of justice (*Rechtsgefühl*). Once more the jurists, as they did in ancient Rome,[21] could probably learn a great deal from the 'grammarians.' The point which the lawyers have yet to learn is that what is 'felt but not reasoned' is not, as the word 'feel' might suggest, a matter of emotion, but is determined by processes which, though not conscious, have much more in common with intellectual than with emotional processes.

There is still another problem of language on which I must briefly touch. It is probably because in the development of language concrete terms seem to precede abstract terms that it is generally believed that the concrete precedes the abstract. I suspect that even the terms 'concrete' and 'abstract' were introduced by some ancient Latin grammarian and then taken over by the logicians and philosophers. But even if the evolution of words should proceed from concrete to abstract terms, this would not disprove that mental development proceeds in the opposite direction. Once we realize that the capacity to act in accordance with very abstract rules is much older than language, and that man developing language was already guided by a great many abstract rules of action, the fact (if it is a fact) that language begins with names for relatively concrete things would mean no more than that in the development of language the sequence characteristic of the development of mind is reversed.

Even that may be true, however, only if we mean by language the words of which it is made up and not also the manner in which we handle the words. We do not know, of course, whether vocal signs for such abstract concepts as 'danger' or 'food' actually appeared earlier than names for particular things. But if they did not, this is probably due to the fact, already mentioned, that of such abstractions no conscious image can be formed but that they are represented directly by dispositions to certain kinds of actions, while words were developed largely to evoke images of absent things. However that may be, it

---

[20] Cf. Friedrich Kainz, *Psychologie der Sprache* (Stuttgart: Ferdinand Enke, 1956), vol. 4, p. 343: "Die Normen, die das Sprachverwenden steuern und kontrollieren, das Richtige vom Falschen sondern, bilden in ihrer Gesamtheit das Sprachgefühl." ['Sprachgefühl' translates as 'sense for language.' The passage from Kainz might be translated, "The norms that control and check the use of language, separating right usage from wrong, constitute in their entirety the sense for language."—Ed.]

[21] Peter Stein, *Regulae Iuris, From Juristic Rules to Legal Maxims* (Edinburgh: Edinburgh University Press, 1966).

does not seem to me to mean that if in language abstract terms appear relatively late, we can draw from this any conclusions concerning the development of the mental faculties which govern all action (including speaking).

To identify and name the regularities which govern our own actions may be a much more difficult task than to identify objects of the external world, even though the existence of the former be the condition which makes the latter possible. If, as I suggested, abstractions are something that the conscious mind cannot make but only discover in itself, or something the existence of which constitutes that mind, to become aware of their existence and to be able to give them names may indeed be possible only at a very late stage of intellectual development.

IX

Before I attempt briefly to sum up I should like at least to mention, although I cannot pursue this point at any length, that only the recognition of the primacy of the abstract in the production of mental phenomena can enable us to integrate our knowledge of mind with our knowledge of the physical world. Science can deal only with the abstract. The processes of classification and specification by superimposition of many classes, which would turn out to be the determinants of what we experience subjectively as events in our consciousness, appear then as processes of the same general kind as those with which we are familiar in the physical sciences. And although, as I have argued at length in other places,[22] a complete reduction of the subjectively experienced mental qualities to exhaustively defined places in a network of physical relations is in principle impossible for us, because, as I would now like to put it, we can never become consciously aware of all the abstract relations which govern our mental processes, we can at least arrive at an understanding of what ranges of events lie within the power of those physical forces to produce—even if we cannot aspire to more than what I like to call a limited 'explanation of the principles' involved.

X

In the course of this sketch I have repeatedly used the phrase 'specification by superimposition', meaning that particular actions are selected from fields of in

---

[22]See *The Sensory Order*, chapter 7, and *Studies in Philosophy, Politics and Economics*, pp. 39 and 60–63. [The last two references are to "The Theory of Complex Phenomena", this volume, chapter 9, p. 274, and "Rules, Perception and Intelligibility", this volume, chapter 8, pp. 250–53.—Ed.]

some respect equivalent action patterns for which the threshold of activation is lowered, by those being reinforced which also belong to families of action patterns which are equivalent in other respects. This phrase 'specification by superimposition' seems to me to be the best description of the mechanism for the operation of which I have claimed the 'primacy of the abstract', because each of the causal determinants decides only one of the attributes of the resulting action.

It is this determination of particular actions by various combinations of abstract propensities which makes it possible for a causally determined structure of actions to produce ever new actions it has never produced before, and therefore to produce altogether new behaviour such as we do not expect from what we usually describe as a mechanism. Even a relatively limited repertory of abstract rules that can thus be combined into particular actions will be capable of 'creating' an almost infinite variety of particular actions.

I do not know how far Koestler would be prepared to accept this as a generalization of his account of creation by 'bisociation.'[23] To me it seems to describe much the same process he had in mind in coining that term, except that under my scheme the new may be the result of combination of any number of separately existing features. However, I am concerned with the appearance of the new in a much wider—and more modest—sense than he was in *The Act of Creation*. I am concerned with the fact that almost every action of a complex organism guided by what we call mind is in some respect something new.

I know that we both have in this connection been vainly endeavouring to find a really appropriate name for that stratification or layering of the structures involved which we are all tempted to describe as 'hierarchies.' I have throughout disregarded the fact that the processes I have been considering occur not just on two but on many superimposed layers, that therefore, for instance, I ought to have talked not only of changes in the dispositions to act, but also of changes in the dispositions to change dispositions, and so on. We need a conception of tiers of networks with the highest tier as complex as the lower ones. What I have called abstraction is after all nothing but such a mechanism which designates a large class of events from which particular events are then selected according as they belong also to various other 'abstract' classes.

---

[23] [In his book *The Act of Creation* (London: Hutchison, 1964), Koestler claimed that all creative acts, from scientific discovery to artistic originality to comic inspiration (represented by the sage, the artist, and the jester), involve "bisociation", which occurs when two or more apparently incompatible ideas are brought together.—Ed.]

Appendix
The Primacy of the Abstract—Discussion[1]

KETY: What Dr. Hayek said makes a very beautiful substrate for the talk on pharmacology, of all things, that I shall be trying to give tomorrow. I would really like to discuss this paper tomorrow, but I cannot resist one comment on the essence of his talk, the primacy of the abstract. He presented the novel idea that the abstract comes first and then raised the question how can the child start with the abstract when he has very little experience to draw on. But we must not forget the child has the experience of the species to draw on, and in a way it makes a very useful kind of concept to think that the child starts up with abstracts and in our later intellectual development what we are doing is adding concrete elaborations on them. Well, one example of an abstract the child starts out with is that things which cause pain are bad and should be avoided. Now this is an abstract of a million years of evolution, and yet the child starts out with that notion and we developed and elaborated upon it in terms of what constitutes pain and how it should be avoided.

HAYEK: It becomes an abstraction by being linked up with families of action patterns which may be innate or acquired by the organism.

BRUNER: I would like to mention one example of a very young baby forming an abstraction. A four-week-old baby in the laboratory was shown his mother's face as a reward for doing some task, such as turning his head to the right. Contrary to the experimenter's expectations, the baby cried when he saw his mother's face, and it was soon evident that he expected to be attended to and picked up when his mother appeared. She wasn't supposed to just *sit* there! Babies start developing anticipations as soon as they are born,

---

[1] [Reprinted by permission of Peters Fraser & Dunlop (www.petersfraserdunlop.com) on behalf of Peters Fraser & Dunlop, Drury House, 34-43 Russell Street, London, WC2B 5HA; tel: 020 7344 1000; fax: 020 7836 9539; www.petersfraserdunlop.com; permissions@pfd.co.uk; The Peters Fraser & Dunlop Group Limited Employment Agents, VAT 503209687, registered in England 218 5448. Reprinted from *The Alpbach Symposium 1968: Beyond Reductionism: New Perspectives in the Life Sciences*, ed. Arthur Koestler and J. R. Smithies (London: Hutchinson, 1969), pp. 324–33. The participants in this discussion were Seymour S. Kety, professor of psychiatry at Harvard; Jerome S. Bruner, director of the Center for Cognitive Studies at Harvard; J. R. Smythies, reader in psychiatry at the University of Edinburgh; writer and symposium organizer Arthur Koestler; Paul Weiss, professor emeritus at Rockefeller University, New York; Bärbel Inhelder, professor of developmental psychology at the University of Geneva; the systems theorist and long-time Hayek acquaintance Ludwig von Bertalanffy, then faculty professor at the State University of New York at Buffalo; C. H. Waddington, professor of genetics at Edinburgh; Viktor Frankl, professor of psychiatry and neurology at the University of Vienna; and W. H. Thorpe, director of the Sub-Department of Animal Behaviour in the Department of Zoology at the University of Cambridge.—Ed.]

and it seems to me that anticipatory schema may be considered a form of abstraction.

HAYEK: This reminds me of another fact of which I have often been told: babies are supposed to recognize only the mother individually while 'daddy' remains for a long time the name for any man and only gradually comes to be confined to the actual father.

SMYTHIES: I would like to take up Professor Hayek's point about the sensory order being governed by abstractions. In an adult, the complex, rich sensory order may be to some extent governed by abstractions. It seems to me more helpful to derive the complexity of sensory order, what we perceive, as a function of ordered and specified mechanisms. Now, would it be in accordance with your ideas to suggest that the element of abstraction may operate in the way that these particular mechanisms are constructed—that is, in the way they operate. Obviously the mechanisms in the brain which are concerned with ordering perception are extremely complex. And these may well work by extremely abstruse mathematical operations. For example, you suggested that the brain mechanisms could take square roots; it may well do things of this complexity and mathematical feats of this order. Is that what you mean by the abstracting processes at work—that this is what is responsible for sensory order? This is one way this could be interpreted.

HAYEK: I think yes, but I would not like to give too definite an answer. What I want to stress is simply that the complex operations of the mind are composite products of rather simple elements which do not enter consciousness as such but do so only in their composite results. Each such process elicits a preparedness for a class of actions and the overlapping of the different classes finally selecting a particular action.

KOESTLER: I agree entirely with the first half of Hayek's paper. It does not even seem to me as heretical as Hayek modestly pretended. What it seems to boil down to, in a different terminology, is rule-governed behaviour, behaviour with fixed rules which are general or abstract. If I may quote a sentence from my paper—it may almost serve as a summary of part of yours—"it seems that life in all its manifestations, from morphogenesis to symbolic thought, is governed by rules of the game which lend it order and stability but leave sufficient latitude for more or less flexible strategies, guided by the particular contingencies in the environment; and that these rules, whether innate or acquired, are represented in coded form on various levels of the hierarchy from the genetic code to the structures in the nervous system responsible for symbolic thought."[2] So here we seem to be in complete agreement. Where you talk about abstractions I talk of rules of the

---

[2] [Koestler, "Beyond Atomism and Holism—The Concept of the Holon", *The Alpbach Symposium*, pp. 198–99.—Ed.]

game or canons, which take various forms at various levels. In embryology you have Waddington's chreods and homeorhesis which rule development.[3] You have rules which govern the sensory order in perception, such as the constancy phenomena, you have rules of instinctive behaviour, rules which govern universes or discourse, and so on. You said these rules are abstractions—

HAYEK: May I interrupt? There may be a misunderstanding here. I would avoid saying rules *are* abstractions, I would merely say that the rules are abstract, by which I mean that they merely limit what is going to happen to a fairly wide range. They narrow the range, and even such a limitation by these rules within a wide range of possibilities suffices to specify a particular outcome.

KOESTLER: I agree. The rules impose constraints on behaviour, but leave room for flexibility. But now comes the rub. You spoke about these abstracts or rules as being located in some sort of super-consciousness. Perhaps you just wanted to avoid the term 'sub-conscious', or you wanted to designate a different locality. Now this is where we seem to disagree because I believe that there is a continuous scale of degrees of awareness, from focally conscious processes through fringe-conscious ones like tying one's shoelaces absent-mindedly, and so on, down to quite unconscious actions and physiological processes. It is a continuum. Now when we learn a new skill like piano-playing or chess, then there is no primacy of the abstract because you have to build up that skill bit by bit from the bottom, you must first learn to hit the right typewriter key and how the knight moves on the chessboard, and then you can gradually build up higher levels of the skill. Now this learning has to be done with great concentration, with focal awareness on those bits, but once you have attained mastery of the skill, then the rules function automatically, unconsciously. No chess player has to think of the rules how to move his knight. So these rules were highly conscious to start with, but now they function unconsciously like the rules of grammar and syntax. The rules occupied first the top floor of my mind and now they have been relegated to the boiler room in the basement, according to the law of parsimony. But before that there was this building-up process and abstractive process, the abstracting of the general rules from particulars. So I think you were a bit hard on empiricism in that limited sense.

HAYEK: I would not deny that there are such *learnt* rules. I do not believe they

3 [Waddington discusses these concepts in his symposium paper, "The Theory of Evolution Today." Homeorhesis refers to a situation in which "what is stabilized is not a constant value but is a particular course of change in time" (p. 366). Waddington claims that such stabilized time trajectories "are the most important features of developing biological systems" (ibid.), and labels them in that domain chreods, which is derived from the Greek words *Chre*, 'it is fated or necessary', and *Hodos*, 'a path.'—Ed.]

could explain the process of learning if there were not others. We could not explain the process of learning if there weren't other rules which had not been learned.

KOESTLER: Agreed.

WEISS: This primacy of abstraction conforms perfectly well both with what I said this morning, that is, the progress from the more general to the more specific or particular and of course with what I called the other day the primacy of order, all the way up through the universe, way beyond your super-conscious.

INHELDER: I am, of course, in full agreement with two of your statements: first, that every process of knowledge is an active abstraction, 'active abstraction' meaning transforming reality and being aware of the outcome of this transformation; and, second, the necessity of going beyond the dichotomy of abstract and concrete. From the developmental point of view we see of course that the small infant has first to act on physical reality before as an adolescent he becomes able to utilize abstract combinatorial operations and hypothetical and deductive strategies. In between these two levels we note the formation of two modes of abstraction and it might perhaps be of value for our discussion to show the distinction between them. On the one hand, we have the logico-mathematical type of abstraction, which plays a part in such activities as classification, seriation, numeration, etc. Here the subject makes the abstraction from his own action; evidently, he acts on objects, but the actual nature of the objects is of no importance since they simply act as a support. On the other hand, we have physical abstraction. Here it is a question of exploring—of determining attributes of objects, such as weight, volume, etc.; here the actual nature of the objects is important. In both cases, there is activity of the subject, but in the first the abstraction bears more directly on the formation of thought structures and in the second it mainly concerns knowledge of the physical world. The development of these two modes of abstraction is not successive but synchronous.

HAYEK: That needs to be thought out, I cannot answer it right away.

BERTALANFFY: Your phrase, the primacy of the abstract, is, you said largely synonymous with 'primacy of the general.' This coincides with what biologists, psychologists and system theorists call progressive differentiation, for which any number of examples could be cited. For instance, von Baer's law in embryology says that the developing organism goes from a more 'general' (or 'abstract') state to an ever more specific one—from blastula to gastrula through a general vertebrate state, to a bird, to a chicken.[4] The particular characteristics of phylum, class, order, family, genus, species arise consecu-

---

[4] [The law is named after Karl Ernst von Baer (1792–1876), a German biologist and founder of embryology, the study of how embryos develop.—Ed.]

tively. Differentiation is also a central principle in the developmental psychology of Piaget or H. Werner.[5] The same applies to language which starts with a 'holophrastic' stage; at first all running things are 'wow-wows', later to become dogs and cats, then dachshunds and poodles. This is a general psychological principle starting with the most fundamental differentiation of 'I' and 'world' from the Piagetian primitive adualism. The same again applies at your 'super-conscious' level; only in my vocabulary, I would prefer to call it 'symbolic.' This symbolic world has its own dynamic, it is self-propelling, if I may use this expression. For this very reason mathematics, to quote a famous dictum, is cleverer than the mathematicians. So I certainly agree that the world becomes richer with progression from the abstract to the concrete, only I would call this progressive differentiation.

WADDINGTON: The first point I wanted to make has been largely covered by Bertalanffy. Of course, in the ordinary processes of development in the biological world we do always go from the general to the specific. At the beginning there is a determination of regions of the egg to become some general part of the organism, such as the foreleg, or the head and so on. This is decided long before it is settled whether this particular portion of the egg will become part of the bones or the muscles in the foreleg, or exactly which part of the brain it will turn into.

The rest of what I wanted to say is concerned with the distinction between the abstract and the concrete. The way I use the term may be rather different from yours, but according to my vocabulary the one thing you certainly cannot entertain in your mind is anything concrete [*laughter*]. Everything you can have in your mind is abstract in some sense or other. From this I want to get on to a point that I think I can best approach by referring to a distinction which Whitehead used to make many years ago—this probably needs a good deal of renovation to bring it in line with modern ideas, but the basic notion he advances seems to me sound. He argued that we perceive things according to two different modes, which he called "causal efficacy" and "presentational immediacy."[6] Causal efficacy is comparable to your abstract logical structures. For instance, if I was a specialized botanist, I would know whether these yellow patches in the field you see out of the window there were buttercups or dandelions, and knowing that, I should really be able to perceive them as that. But I do not know the flora of this

---

[5] [Hayek refers to developmental psychologists Jean Piaget (1896–1980) and Heinz Werner (1890–1964).—Ed.]

[6] [The philosopher, mathematician, and logician Alfred North Whitehead (1861–1947) discussed presentational immediacy and causal efficacy in his book *Symbolism: Its Meaning and Effect* (New York: Macmillan, 1927). For a brief explication of Whitehead's views, see D. L. C. MacLachlan, "Whitehead's Theory of Perception", *Process Studies*, vol. 21, Winter 1992, pp. 227–30. —Ed.]

part of the world and from here I cannot see them as any sort of flower in particular. As for the other mode, the presentational immediacy—well, if I were a trained painter, I could see all sorts of little purple dashes and flecks of other colours in that field, which I do not actually perceive there at the present time.

It seems to me that this distinction between two modes of perception is relevant to the question of how you proceed from the general towards the more particular. I should like to suggest that there are two ways of doing this, that seem to me rather different. In one way you begin with a confused or chaotic mass of details, jumbled together in disorder so that the totality has no particular characteristic, then within this you gradually discern an outline of a pattern around which you gradually learn to group the whole collection of items, so that eventually they make sense as something with a particular character of its own. I think this is the kind of process that Koestler was mentioning when he spoke of building up a competence in chess, first learning to move the parts correctly and then getting a feeling of how the moves fit together. It is also surely how you learn to ride a bicycle—you learn the movements necessary to correct your balance and then suddenly all these detailed movements fit together and you can do it without thinking. This process seems to be related to perceiving by presentational immediacy, in which you first perceive merely a lot of patches of colour and tone and only gradually discover how to interpret these as a particular scene.

In the other way of proceeding from the general to the particular, you start with something which lacks particularity, not because it is chaotic, but because it is extremely orderly but abstract, for instance, a general logical rule, or a scientific hypothesis; and you then find particular exemplifications of this rule. This is the path that people conventionally suppose most human thought to take.

Recently, however, I have been thinking about how it could operate, not in the realm of thought but in the material world we observe. As I mentioned a few minutes ago, in the development of the embryo, something determines that a group of cells will form some part or other of a complex organ, such as a leg, rather than part of an arm, before it is decided whether those cells shall be bone or muscle. Now I think this is a very astonishing performance. What kind of material substance can there possibly be which characterizes the whole leg with all its bones, muscles, nerves, blood vessels and so on, and differentiates it from an arm with its bones, muscles and so on? One highly speculative but amusing possibility I've been thinking about is this: we have recently started to realize that we have to think of most living cells and similar systems as oscillators. The important processes in cells are controlled by negative feedback loops, and systems of that kind have an inherent tendency to oscillate. Now, we have a lot of experience of systems that oscillate, or go up and down in a wave-like manner; for instance, sound is an oscillation of the air. Consider what happens in a piece of music—or at least some kinds of music. There is an early statement of something very general—a melodic theme, or perhaps in some forms of jazz only a sequence of chords. The theme or the chord sequence fixes the general character of the subsequent performance, which consists in working out this generality into detailed particulars. In the performance of music, of course, this development is carried out by the intervention of human mentality, but there seems no particular reason why a computer, or even some simpler mechanical system, should not be able to carry out an analogous development of a stated theme. If it did, we should have an example from the non-mental world of the second type of progress from the general to the particular, that corresponding to perception by causal efficacy. It is, I think, an interesting possibility that something of this kind happens normally during embryonic development. This would, I think, be different from the type of building up from chaotic details towards a particular generalization that Koestler was talking about.

HAYEK: On the first point I really completely agree with you and I readily admit that I have been using the terms loosely. Strictly speaking only the real is concrete—it always possesses more properties than we know, and everything mental is abstract compared with the real. But we have to deal with degrees of abstractness and it is inevitable that we should use the word concrete not in the strict sense, but only in the sense of something less abstract. On the other question of how you actually get from the abstract to the concrete. I suggested a superimposition of abstractions, and when you have used a sufficient number of abstractions, you can finally get a combination which in fact defines one unique individual event or action.

WADDINGTON: I would like to make one further point about this. When you go from the general to the particular, the thing that carries you has got to have the character of an instruction. It is a rule of the game, in fact an algorithm. You have got to have something which gives rise to a process. It is that which generates the complexity.

KOESTLER: Somebody has compared the process of generating a sentence with the development of an embryo, and both with the carving out of a figure from a piece of wood. Although one should not carry analogies too far, there are certain basic things they have in common—thus each is a stepwise process. Spelling out step-wise an implicit idea or code in more and more explicit forms, as in the Chomsky schema, or as in your strategy of the genes.[7] There is again a combination of fixed rules and flexible strategies.

---

[7] ["Chomsky schema" probably refers to the linguist Noam Chomsky's (1928–) ideas of an innate universal grammar in which rules for determining whether a sentence is grammatically

FRANKL: May I quote what Koestler said, that the mind itself can never know what governs mental operation? In other words, I would say, it is trans-conscious and one could also say that the mind eludes full self-awareness, self-consciousness. Now in this context what comes to mind is Max Scheler's emphasis on the fact that the person or the subject cannot be fully objectified, it eludes objectification by itself or by others.[8] This in turn might remind us of the statement in the Vedanta that that which does the knowing cannot be known, that which does the seeing cannot be seen. In other words that which does the seeing is not perceptible to itself. Now what is mirrored here is a general law we meet again and again, for instance, in clinical practice. Often we are confronted with patients who are so to speak over-conscious of what they are doing, and this interferes with performance, be it the performance of the sexual act (sexual neurosis) or the performance of any artistic work (vocational neurosis). I have published a series of case histories which indicate that artistic creation and performance are impaired to the extent to which this phenomenon is present—I have coined a word, *hyper-reflection*, for it. Hyper-reflection needs to be counteracted by a therapeutic technique that I call *de-reflection*, i.e., turning away the patient's attention from himself, from his own activity.

Thus one could say that full self-awareness and/or self-consciousness are self-defeating. But we need not stick to such a negative formulation, we may as well reformulate it in positive terms by saying the essence of existence is not based on or characterized by self-reflection, but rather by self-transcendence. That is to say human reality is profoundly characterized by its intentionality, its directionality. To be human means being directed beyond oneself, being directed at something other than itself. And human existence falters and collapses unless this self-transcendent quality is lived out. Let me repeat: that which does the seeing is invisible to itself, cannot see itself. But we have to add: except for pathological cases. There are pathological cases in which the eye may well see itself, but to the same extent the function of the eye, the seeing capacity is impaired. Remember the trivial example of the *mouche volante*: this is something within the eye which the eye yet is capable of seeing. But precisely to this extent the seeing capacity has been impaired all along. It is the exception that proves the rule.

HAYEK: I entirely agree and I am even convinced that the contention can be strictly proved. Yet the proof is very difficult and I have never succeeded in fully working it out. But I can give an example of the sort of proposition it

---

correct are reviewed in a step-by-step, algorithmic manner. Hayek refers to Chomsky's theories in both "The Theory of Complex Phenomena", this volume, p. 270, note 29, and "The Primacy of the Abstract", this volume, p. 318, note 14.—Ed.]

[8][Frankl refers to the views of the German phenomenologist Max Scheler (1874–1928). —Ed.]

would involve. Though it is a very simple one, I think you will see the analogy with the more general proposition. The example is the thesis that on no adding machine with an upper limit to the sum it can show is it possible to compute the number of different operations this machine can perform (if any combination of different figures to be added is regarded as a different operation). Assume the maximum the machine can show is 999,999. Then there will be 500,000 different additions which give 999,999 as the result, 499,999 different additions which give 999,998 as a result, and so on, and thus clearly a total number much greater than 999,999. It seems to me that this can be extended to show that any apparatus for mechanical classification of objects will be able to sort out such objects only with regard to a number of properties which must be smaller than the relevant properties which it must itself possess; or, expressed differently, that such an apparatus for classifying according to mechanical complexity must always be of greater complexity than the objects it classifies. If, as I believe it to be the case, the mind can be interpreted as a classifying machine, this would imply that the mind can never classify (and therefore never explain) another mind of the same degree of complexity. It seems to me that if one follows up this idea it turns out to be a special case of the famous Goedel theorem about the impossibility of stating, within a formalized mathematical system, all the rules which determine that system.

THORPE: Karl Popper has come to much the same conclusion.[9] I was very interested in some of the things you said about ethology, and the point you made that all of us are capable of a wide variety of actions and then learn to limit ourselves to particular actions. That, of course, is true. It is in fact one of the most interesting things about birds; and the reason in fact why I, as an ethologist, took up the study of birds was that some parts of their behaviour are so precisely programmed and so rigid, and other parts so flexible. Now in those contexts where the actions are flexible, birds are capable of a very high degree of learning. There is one particularly interesting case you might like to hear about. If you hand-rear Bee-eaters (*Merops apiaster*) and feed them on artificial food, you soon see the young birds going through shaking movements of the bill; and although these movements serve no function when the animal is being fed on an artificial diet, they continue unabated. Under natural conditions this action serves to stun the bees, or other sting-bearing Hymenoptera, before they are eaten; and there are many other cases of that kind where actions appropriate to dealing with a par-

---

[9] [Thorpe might have had in mind Karl Popper's paper "Indeterminism in Quantum Physics and Classical Physics, Part II", *British Journal for the Philosophy of Science*, vol. 1, November 1950, pp. 179–88, where Popper discusses "Goedelian sentences." I thank Jeremy Shearmur for this suggestion.—Ed.]

ticular special diet to which the species is adapted, so to speak, force themselves out, whether appropriate or not, under artificial conditions of rearing. At one time, I and some of my pupils became interested in the question whether the choice of food was very highly programmed in different Finch species, each of which has differently shaped bills. So, Miss Janet Kear, a pupil of mine took four species of finches, Chaffinch (*Fringilla coelebs*), Bullfinch (*Pyrrhula pyrrhula*), Greenfinch (*Carduelis chloris*) and Hawfinch (*Coccothraustes coccothraustes*): with different sized and shaped bills, with the idea of finding out whether these birds when they meet different kinds of seeds in nature have their feeding methods all innately programmed; whether in fact the bird was programmed with the correct pattern, with the appropriate behavioural apparatus, to cope with a certain kind of seed most efficiently. What she found was that this certainly was not innately programmed. What the young bird does is to sample all the different kinds of seeds offered, and then concentrate on those seeds which could be most easily exploited by the bill of particular size and shape which the species possessed. And so this behavioural adjustment was learned quite quickly by the bird experimenting on various different kinds and sizes of seed. The bird as a result of this experience then confines itself to one or a few particular kinds of seeds which can be exploited most efficiently. To put it picturesquely, one might almost say the bird is carrying out a time and motion study!

This contribution concerning the choice of food by birds is, perhaps, a very minor one but I was very stimulated by your approach, and the phrase 'the primacy of the abstract' will certainly stick with me.

FOURTEEN

THE ERRORS OF CONSTRUCTIVISM[1]

I

It seemed to me necessary to introduce the term 'constructivism'[2] as a specific name for a manner of thinking that in the past has often, but misleadingly, been described as 'rationalism.'[3] The basic conception of this constructivism can perhaps be expressed in the simplest manner by the innocent sounding formula that, since man has himself created the institutions of society and civilization, he must also be able to alter them at will so as to satisfy his desires or wishes. It is almost 50 years since I first heard and was greatly impressed by this formula.[4]

---

[1] An inaugural lecture delivered on 27 January 1970 on the assumption of a visiting professorship at the Paris-Lodron University of Salzburg and originally published as *Die Irrtümer des Konstruktivismus und die Grundlagen legitimer Kritik gesellschaftlicher Gebilde* (Munich: Wilhelm Fink, 1970; reprinted, Tübingen: J. C. B. Mohr, 1975). The first two paragraphs referring solely to local circumstances have been omitted from this translation. [Reprinted in F. A. Hayek, *New Studies in Philosophy, Politics, Economics and the History of Ideas* (Chicago: University of Chicago Press, 1978), pp. 3–22.—Ed.]

[2] See my Tokyo lecture of 1964, "Kinds of Rationalism." [See this volume, prologue.—Ed.]

[3] I have come across occasional references to the fact that the adjective 'constructivist' was a favourite term of W. E. Gladstone, but I have not succeeded in finding it in his published works. [As noted in "Kinds of Rationalism", this volume, p. 42, note 8, Hayek might have come across this idea in Gladstone's letter of February 11, 1885, to Lord Acton, where Gladstone says of the liberalism of his day, "Its pet idea is what they call construction, that is to say, taking into the hands of the State the business of the individual man." See *Selections from the Correspondence of the First Lord Acton*, ed. John Neville Figgis and Reginald Vere Laurence (London: Longmans, Green, 1917), vol. 1, p. 239.—Ed.] More recently it has also been used to describe a movement in art where its meaning is not unrelated to the concept here discussed. See Stephen Bann, ed. *The Tradition of Constructivism* (London: Thames and Hudson, 1974). Perhaps, to show that we use the term in a critical sense, 'constructivistic' is better than 'constructivist.'

[4] In a lecture by W. C. Mitchell at Columbia University in New York during the year 1923. If I had even then some reservations about this statement it was mainly due to the discussion of the effects of 'non-reflected action' in Carl Menger, *Untersuchungen über die Methoden der Socialwissenschaften und der politischen Oekonomie insbesondere* (Leipzig: Duncker & Humblot, 1883). [Cf. Carl Menger, *Investigations into the Method of the Social Sciences with Special Reference to Economics*, ed. Louis

At first the current phrase that man 'created' his civilization and its institutions may appear rather harmless and commonplace. But as soon as it is extended, as is frequently done, to mean that man was able to do this because he was endowed with reason, the implications become questionable. Man did not possess reason before civilization. The two evolved together. We need merely to consider language, which today nobody still believes to have been 'invented' by a rational being, in order to see that reason and civilization develop in constant mutual interaction. But what we now no longer question with regard to language (though even that is comparatively recent) is by no means generally accepted with regard to morals, law, the skills of handicrafts, or social institutions. We are still too easily led to assume that these phenomena, which are clearly the results of human action, must also have been consciously designed by a human mind, in circumstances created for the purposes which they serve—that is, that they are what Max Weber called *wert-rationale* products.[5] In short, we are misled into thinking that morals, law, skills and social institutions can only be justified in so far as they correspond to some preconceived design.

It is significant that this is a mistake we usually commit only with regard to the phenomena of our own civilization. If the ethnologist or social anthropologist attempts to understand other cultures, he has no doubt that their members frequently have no idea as to the reason for observing particular rules, or what depends on it. Yet most modern social theorists are rarely willing to admit that the same thing applies also to our own civilization. We too frequently do not know what benefits we derive from the usages of our society; and such social theorists regard this merely as a regrettable deficiency which ought to be removed as soon as possible.

Schneider, translated by Francis J. Nock (New York: New York University Press, 1985). Lectures notes from Mitchell's 1934–1935 class were stenographically recorded by a student: see Wesley Clair Mitchell, *Lecture Notes on Types of Economic Theory*, 2 vols. (New York: Augustus M. Kelley, 1949); for a fuller collection of his notes, see Wesley Clair Mitchell, *Types of Economic Theory: From Mercantilism to Institutionalism*, ed. Joseph Dorfman, 2 vols. (New York: Kelley, 1967–1969). For a conjecture about the effects of Mitchell's lectures on Hayek, see the editor's introduction to F. A. Hayek, *Studies on the Abuse and Decline of Reason*, ed. Bruce Caldwell, vol. 13 (2010) of *The Collected Works of F. A. Hayek* (Chicago: University of Chicago Press; London: Routledge), pp. 18–24. —Ed.]

[5] See Max Weber, *Wirtschaft und Gesellschaft* (Tübingen: Mohr, 1921), chapter 1, section 2, pp. 12–13, where we get little help, however, since the 'values' to which the discussion refers are soon in effect reduced to consciously pursued particular aims. [See Max Weber, *Economy and Society: An Outline of Interpretive Sociology*, ed. Guenther Roth and Claus Wittich (New York: Bedminster Press, 1968), chapter 1, section 2, pp. 24–26, for Weber's discussion of the types of social action.—Ed.]

II

In a short lecture it is not possible to trace the history of the discussion of these problems to which I have given some attention in recent years.[6] I will merely mention that they were already familiar to the ancient Greeks. The very dichotomy between 'natural' and 'artificial' formations which the ancient Greeks introduced has dominated the discussion for 2,000 years. Unfortunately, the Greeks' distinction between natural and artificial has become the greatest obstacle to further advance; because, interpreted as an exclusive alternative, this distinction is not only ambiguous but definitely false. As was at last clearly seen by the Scottish social philosophers of the eighteenth century (but the late Schoolmen had already partly seen it), a large part of social formations, although the result of human action, is not of human design. The consequence of this is that such formations, according to the interpretation of the traditional terms, could be described either as 'natural', or as 'artificial.'

The beginning of a true appreciation of these circumstances in the sixteenth century was extinguished, however, in the seventeenth century by the rise of a powerful new philosophy—the rationalism of René Descartes and his followers, from whom all modern forms of constructivism derive. From Descartes it was taken over by that unreasonable 'Age of Reason', which was entirely dominated by the Cartesian spirit. Voltaire, the greatest representative of the so-called 'Age of Reason', expressed the Cartesian spirit in his famous statement: "if you want good laws, burn those you have and make yourselves new ones."[7] Against this, the great critic of rationalism, David Hume, could only slowly elaborate the foundations of a true theory of the growth of social formations, which was further developed by his fellow Scotsmen, Adam Smith and Adam Ferguson, into a theory of phenomena that are 'the result of human action but not of human design.'

Descartes had taught that we should only believe what we can prove. Applied to the field of morals and values generally, his doctrine meant that we should only accept as binding what we could recognize as a rational design for a recognizable purpose. I will leave undecided how far he himself evaded difficulties by representing the unfathomable will of God as the creator of all

---

[6]See particularly my essays "The Results of Human Action but Not of Human Design", and "The Legal Philosophy and Political Philosophy of David Hume (1711–1776)" in *Studies in Philosophy, Politics and Economics* (Chicago: University of Chicago Press, 1967), and my lecture on "Dr. Bernard Mandeville" published in this book. [The first essay appears in this volume as the prologue. The latter two now appear in Hayek, *The Trend of Economic Thinking*, ed. W. W. Bartley III and Stephen Kresge, vol. 3 (1991) of *The Collected Works of F. A. Hayek*, as chapters 6 and 7.—Ed.]

[7]Voltaire, *Dictionnaire philosophique*, s.v. 'Lois', reprinted in *Œuvres complètes de Voltaire*, new edition (Paris: Garnier frères, 1879), vol. 19, p. 614. ["Voulez-vous avoir de bonnes lois, brûlez les vôtres, et faites-en de nouvelles."—Ed.]

purposive phenomena.[8] For his successors it certainly became a human will, which they regarded as the source of all social formations whose intention must provide the justification. Society appeared to them as a deliberate construction of men for an intended purpose—shown most clearly in the writing of Descartes's faithful pupil, J.-J. Rousseau.[9] The belief in the unlimited power of a supreme authority as necessary, especially for a representative assembly, and therefore the belief that democracy necessarily means the unlimited power of the majority, are ominous consequences of this constructivism.

III

You will probably most clearly see what I mean by 'constructivism' if I quote a characteristic statement of a well-known Swedish sociologist, which I recently encountered in the pages of a German popular science journal. "The most important goal that sociology has set itself", he wrote, "is to predict the future development and to shape (*gestalten*) the future, or, if one prefers to express it in that manner, to create the future of mankind."[10] If a science makes such

---

[8]Descartes was somewhat reticent about his views on political and moral problems and only rarely explicitly stated the consequence of his philosophical principles for these questions. But compare the famous passage at the beginning of the second part of *Discours de la méthode* where he writes: "je crois que, si Sparte a été autrefois très florissante, ce n'a pas été à cause de la bonté de chacune de ses loin en particulier, vu que plusieurs étaient fort étrange et même contraire aux bonnes mœurs; mais à cause que n'ayant été inventée que par un seul, elles tendaient toutes à même fin." The consequences of the Cartesian philosophy for morals are well shown in Alfred Espinas, *Descartes et la morale* (Paris: Editions Bossard, 1925). [In René Descartes, *A Discourse on Method: Meditations and Principles* (London: Dent, Everyman's Library, 1912), p. 11, the passage that Hayek cites is translated, "I believe that the past pre-eminence of Sparta was due not to the goodness of each of its laws in particular, for many of these were very strange, and even opposed to good morals, but to the circumstance that, originated by a single individual, they all tended to a single end."—Ed.]

[9]Cf. Robert Derathé, *Le Rationalisme de J. J. Rousseau* (Paris: Presses universitaires de France, 1948).

[10]Torgny T. Segerstedt, "Wandel der Gesellschaft", *Bild der Wissenschaft*, vol. 6, May 1969, p. 441. See also the same author's *Gesellschaftliche Herrschaft als soziologiches Konzept* (Neuwied and Berlin: Luchterhand, 1967). Earlier examples of the constantly recurring idea of mankind or reason determining itself, particularly by L. T. Hobhouse and Karl Mannheim, I have given on an earlier occasion in *The Counter-Revolution of Science* (Chicago: University of Chicago Press, 1952), pp. 155–56 [Now see Hayek, "Scientism and the Study of Society", in *Studies on the Abuse and Decline of Reason*, vol. 13 (2010) of *The Collected Works of F. A. Hayek*, pp. 150–51.—Ed.], but I had not expected to find the explicit assertion by a representative of this view such as the psychologist B. F. Skinner, in "Freedom and the Control of Men", *The American Scholar*, vol. 26, 1955–56, p. 49, that "Man is able, and now as never before, to lift himself up by his own bootstraps." The reader will find that the same idea appears also in a statement of the psychiatrist G. B. Chisholm, to be quoted later.

341

claims, this evidently implies the assertion that the whole of human civilization, and all we have so far achieved, could only have been built as a purposive rational construction.

It must suffice for the moment to show that this constructivistic interpretation of social formations is by no means merely harmless philosophical speculation, but an assertion of fact from which conclusions are derived concerning both the explanation of social processes and the opportunities for political action. The factually erroneous assertion, from which the constructivists derive such far-reaching consequences and demands, appears to me to be that the complex order of our modern society is exclusively due to the circumstance that men have been guided in their actions by foresight—an insight into the connections between cause and effect—or at least that it could have arisen through design. What I want to show is that men are in their conduct *never* guided *exclusively* by their understanding of the causal connections between particular known means and certain desired ends, but always also by rules of conduct of which they are rarely aware, which they certainly have not consciously invented, and that to discern the function and significance of this is a difficult and only partially achieved task of scientific effort. Expressing this differently—it means that the success of rational striving (Max Weber's *zweck-rationales Handeln*) is largely due to the observance of values, whose rôle in our society ought to be carefully distinguished from that of deliberately pursued goals.

I can only briefly mention the further fact, that success of the individual in the achievement of his immediate aims depends, not only on his conscious insight into causal connections, but also in a high degree on his ability to act according to rules, which he may be unable to express in words, but which we can only describe by formulating rules. All our skills, from the command of language to the mastery of handicrafts or games—actions which we 'know how' to perform without being able to state how we do it—are instances of this.[11] I mention them here only because action according to rules—which we do not explicitly know and which have not been designed by reason, but prevail because the manner of acting of those who are successful is imitated—is perhaps easier to recognise in these instances than in the field directly relevant to my present concerns.

The rules we are discussing are those that are not so much useful to the individuals who observe them, as those that (if they are *generally* observed) make all the members of the group more effective, because they give them opportunities to act within a social *order*. These rules are also mostly not the result of a deliberate choice of means for specific purposes, but of a process of selection,

[11] See my essay on "Rules, Perception and Intelligibility" in *Studies in Philosophy, Politics and Economics*. [This essay now appears in this volume as chapter 8.—Ed.]

in the course of which groups that achieved a more efficient order displaced (or were imitated by) others, often without knowing to what their superiority was due. This social group of rules includes the rules of law, of morals, of custom and so on—in fact, all the values which govern a society. The term 'value', which I shall for lack of a better one have to continue to use in this context, is in fact a little misleading, because we tend to interpret it as referring to particular aims of individual action, while in the fields to which I am referring they consist mostly of rules which do not tell us positively what to do, but in most instances merely what we ought not to do.

Those taboos of society which are not founded on any rational justification have been the favourite subject of derision by the constructivists, who wish to see them banned from any rationally designed order of society. Among the taboos they have largely succeeded in destroying are respect for private property and for the keeping of private contracts, with the result that some people doubt if respect for them can ever again be restored.[12]

For all organisms, however, it is often more important to know what they must not do, if they are to avoid danger, than to know what they must do in order to achieve particular ends. The former kind of knowledge is usually not a knowledge of the consequences which the prohibited kind of conduct would produce, but a knowledge that in certain conditions certain types of conduct are to be avoided. Our positive knowledge of cause and effect assists us only in those fields where our acquaintance with the particular circumstances is sufficient; and it is important that we do not move beyond the region where this knowledge will guide us reliably. This is achieved by rules that, without regard to the consequences in the particular instance, generally prohibit actions of a certain kind.[13]

That in this sense man is not only a purpose-seeking but also a rule-following animal has been repeatedly stressed in the recent literature.[14] In order to understand what is meant by this, we must be quite clear about the meaning attached in this connection to the word 'rule.' This is necessary because those chiefly negative (or prohibitory) rules of conduct which make possible the formation of social order are of three different kinds, which I now

[12] Cf., for example, Gunnar Myrdal, *Beyond the Welfare State: Economic Planning in the Welfare States and Its International Implications* (London: Gerald Duckworth, 1960), p. 17: "The important property and contract taboos, so basic for a stable liberal society, were forcibly weakened when big alterations were allowed to occur in the real value of currencies"; and ibid., p. 19: "Social taboos can never be established by decisions founded upon reflection and discussion."

[13] I have treated these problems more extensively in my lecture on "Rechtsordnung and Handelnsordnung" in *Zur Einheit der Rechts- und Staatswissenschaften*, ed. Erich Streissler (Karlsruhe: C. F. Müller, 1967), reprinted in my *Freiburger Studien* (Tübingen: J. C. B. Mohr, 1969), as well as in *Rules and Order*, vol. 1 of my *Law, Legislation and Liberty* (London and Chicago: Routledge and the University of Chicago Press, 1973).

[14] R. S. Peters, *The Concept of Motivation* (London: Routledge and Kegan Paul, 1958), p. 5.

spell out. These kinds of rules are: (1) rules that are merely observed in fact but have never been stated in words; if we speak of the 'sense of justice' or 'the feeling for language' we refer to such rules which we are able to apply, but do not know explicitly; (2) rules that, though they have been stated in words, still merely express approximately what has long before been generally observed in action; and (3) rules that have been deliberately introduced and therefore necessarily exist as words set out in sentences.

Constructivists would like to reject the first and second groups of rules, and to accept as valid only the third group I have mentioned.

IV

What then is the origin of those rules that most people follow but few if any-one can state in words? Long before Charles Darwin the theorists of society, and particularly those of language, had given the answer that in the process of cultural transmission, in which modes of conduct are passed on from genera-tion to generation, a process of selection takes place, in which those modes of conduct prevail which lead to the formation of a more efficient order for the whole group, because such groups will prevail over others.[15]

A point needing special emphasis, because it is so frequently misunderstood, is that by no means every regularity of conduct among individuals produces an order for the whole of society. Therefore regular individual conduct does not necessarily mean order, but only certain kinds of regularity of the conduct of individuals lead to an order for the whole. The order of society is therefore a factual state of affairs which must be distinguished from the regularity of the conduct of individuals. It must be defined as a condition in which individu-als are able, on the basis of their own respective peculiar knowledge, to form expectations concerning the conduct of others, which are proved correct by making possible a successful mutual adjustment of the actions of these individ-uals. If every person perceiving another were either to try to kill him or to run away, this would certainly also constitute a regularity of individual conduct, but not one that led to the formation of ordered groups. Quite clearly, certain combinations of such rules of individual conduct may produce a superior kind of order, which will enable some groups to expand at the expense of others.

This effect does not presuppose that the members of the group know to which rules of conduct the group owes its superiority, but merely that it will accept only those individuals as members who observe the rules traditionally

---

[15] See on these 'Darwinians before Darwin' in the social sciences my essays "The Results of Human Action but Not of Human Design" and "The Legal and Political Philosophy of David Hume."

accepted by it. There will always be an amount of experience of individuals precipitated in such rules, which its living members do not know, but which nevertheless help them more effectively to pursue their ends.

This sort of 'knowledge of the world' that is passed on from generation to generation will thus consist in a great measure not of knowledge of cause and effect, but of rules of conduct adapted to the environment and acting like information about the environment although they do not say anything about it. Like scientific theories, they are preserved by proving themselves useful, but, in contrast to scientific theories, by a proof which no one needs to know, because the proof manifests itself in the resilience and progressive expansion of the order of society which it makes possible. This is the true content of the much derided idea of the 'wisdom of our ancestors' embodied in inherited institutions, which plays such an important rôle in conservative thought, but appears to the constructivist to be an empty phrase signifying nothing.

V

Time allows me to consider further only one of the many interesting interrelations of this kind, which at the same time also explains why an economist is particularly inclined to concern himself with these problems: the connection between rules of law and the spontaneously formed order of the market.[16] This order is, of course, not the result of a miracle or some natural harmony of interests. It forms itself, because in the course of millennia men develop rules of conduct which lead to the formation of such an order out of the separate spontaneous activities of individuals. The interesting point about this is that men developed these rules without really understanding their functions. Philosophers of law have in general even ceased to ask what is the 'purpose' of law, thinking the question is unanswerable because they interpret 'purpose' to mean particular foreseeable results, to achieve which the rules were designed. In fact, this 'purpose' is to bring about an abstract order—a system of abstract relations—concrete manifestations of which will depend on a great variety of particular circumstances which no one can know in their entirety. Those rules of just conduct have therefore a 'meaning' or 'function' which no one has given them, and which social theory must try to discover.

It was the great achievement of economic theory that, 200 years before cybernetics, it recognized the nature of such self-regulating systems in which certain regularities (or, perhaps better, 'restraints') of conduct of the elements led to constant adaptation of the comprehensive order to particular facts, affecting in the first instance only the separate elements. Such an order, leading

---

[16] Cf. my lecture "Rechtsordnung and Handelnsordnung", cited above in note 13.

to the utilization of much more information than anyone possesses, could not have been 'invented.' This follows from the fact that the result could not have been foreseen. None of our ancestors could have known that the protection of property and contracts would lead to an extensive division of labour, specialization and the establishment of markets, or that the extension to outsiders of rules initially applicable only to members of the same tribe would tend towards the formation of a world economy.

All that man could do was to try to improve bit by bit on a process of mutually adjusting individual activities, by reducing conflicts through modifications to some of the inherited rules. All that he could deliberately design, he could and did create only within a system of rules, which he had not invented, and with the aim of improving an existing order.[17] Always merely adjusting the rules, he tried to improve the combined effect of all other rules accepted in his community. In his efforts to improve the existing order, he was therefore never free arbitrarily to lay down any new rule he liked, but had always a definite problem to solve, raised by an imperfection of the existing order, but of an order he would have been quite incapable of constructing as a whole. What man found were conflicts between accepted values, the significance of which he only partly understood, but on the character of which the results of many of his efforts depended, and which he could only strive better to adapt to each other, but which he could never create anew.

VI

The most surprising aspect of recent developments is that our undeniably increased understanding of these circumstances has led to new errors. We believe, I think rightly, that we have learnt to understand the general principles which govern the formation of such complex orders as those of organisms, human society, or perhaps even the human mind. Experience in those fields in which modern science has achieved its greatest triumphs leads us to expect that such insights will rapidly also give us mastery over the phenomena, and enable us deliberately to determine the results. But in the sphere of the com-

[17]Cf. in this connection Karl R. Popper, *The Open Society and Its Enemies*, 4th ed. (Princeton: Princeton University Press, 1963), vol. 1, p. 64: "Nearly all misunderstandings [of the statement that norms are man-made] can be traced back to one fundamental misapprehension, namely, to the belief that 'convention' implies 'arbitrariness'"; also David Hume, *A Treatise of Human Nature*, in *The Philosophical Works*, ed. T. H. Green and T. H. Grose, new rev. ed. (London: Longmans, Green, 1890), vol. 2, p. 258: "Tho' the rules of justice be *artificial*, they are not *arbitrary*. Nor is the expression improper to call them *Laws of Nature*; if by natural we understand what is common to any species, or even if we confine it to mean what is inseparable from the species." [Hayek added the bracketed material.—Ed.]

plex phenomena of life, of the mind, and of the society, we encounter a new difficulty.[18] However greatly our theories and techniques of investigation assist us to interpret the observed facts, they give little help in ascertaining all those particulars which enter into the determination of the complex patterns, and which we would have to know to achieve complete explanations, or precise predictions.

If we knew all the particular circumstances which prevailed in the course of the history of the earth (and if it were not for the phenomenon of genetic drift) we should be able with the help of modern genetics to explain why different species of organisms have assumed the specific structures which they possess. But it would be absurd to assume that we could ever ascertain all these particular facts. It may even be true that if at a given moment someone could know the sum total of all the particular facts which are dispersed among the millions or billions of people living at the time, he ought to be in a position to bring about a more efficient order of human productive efforts than that achieved by the market. Science can help us to a better theoretical understanding of the interconnections. But science cannot significantly help us to ascertain all the widely dispersed and rapidly fluctuating particular circumstances of time and place which determine the order of a great complex society.

The delusion that advancing theoretical knowledge places us everywhere increasingly in a position to reduce complex inter-connections to ascertainable particular facts often leads to new scientific errors. Especially it leads to those errors of science which we must now consider, because they lead to the destruction of irreplaceable values, to which we owe our social order and our civilization. Such errors are largely due to an arrogation of pretended knowledge, which in fact no one possesses and which even the advance of science is not likely to give us.

Concerning our modern economic system, understanding of the principles by which its order forms itself shows us that it rests on the use of knowledge (and of skills in obtaining relevant information) which no one possesses in its entirety, and that it is brought about because individuals are in their actions guided by certain general rules. Certainly, we ought not to succumb to the false belief; or delusion, that we can replace it with a different kind of order, which presupposes that all this knowledge can be concentrated in a central brain, or group of brains of any practicable size.

The fact, however, that in spite of all the advance of our knowledge, the results of our endeavours remain dependent on circumstances about which we know little or nothing, and on ordering forces we cannot control, is precisely what so many people regard as intolerable. Constructivists ascribe this interde-

---

[18]Cf. my essay on "The Theory of Complex Phenomena" in *Studies in Philosophy, Politics and Economics*. [Now see this volume, chapter 9.—Ed.]

pendence to still allowing ourselves to be guided by values which are not rationally demonstrated or given positive proof as justification for them. They assert that we no longer need to entrust our fate to a system, the results of which we do not determine beforehand, although it opens up vast new opportunities for the efforts of individuals, but at the same time resembles a game of chance in some respects, since no single person bears responsibility for the ultimate outcome. The anthropomorphic hypostatization of a personified mankind, who pursue aims they have consciously chosen, thus leads to the demand that all those grown values not visibly serving approved ends, but which are conditions for the formation of an abstract order, should be discarded to offer individuals improved prospects of achieving their different and often conflicting goals. Scientific error of this kind tends to discredit values, on the observance of which the survival of our civilization may depend.

VII

This process of scientific error destroying indispensable values commenced to play an important rôle during the last century. It is specially associated with various philosophical views, which their authors like to describe as 'positivist', because they wish to recognize as useful knowledge only insights into the connection between cause and effect. The very name—*positus* meaning 'set down'—expresses the preference for the deliberately created over all that has not been rationally designed. The founder of the positivist movement, Auguste Comte, clearly expressed this basic idea when he asserted the unquestionable superiority of demonstrated over revealed morals.[19] The phrase shows that the only choice he recognized was that between deliberate creation by a human mind and creation by a superhuman intelligence, and that he did not even consider the possibility of any origins from a process of selective evolution. The most important later manifestation of this constructivism in the course of the nineteenth century was utilitarianism, the treatment of all norms in epistemological positivism in general, and legal positivism in particular; and finally, I believe, the whole of socialism.

In the case of utilitarianism, this character is clearly shown in its original, particularistic form, now generally distinguished as 'act utilitarianism' from 'rule utilitarianism.' This alone is faithful to the original idea that every single decision must be based on the perceived social utility of its particular effects;

---

[19] Auguste Comte, *Système de politique positive* (Paris: L. Mathias, 1854), vol. 1, p. 356: "La supériorité de la morale démontrée sur la morale révélée!" [For more of Hayek's views on Comte, see his *Studies on the Abuse and Decline of Reason*, vol. 13 (2010) of *The Collected Works of F. A. Hayek*, especially chapters 13, 16, and 17. Comte's phrase may be translated, "The necessary superiority of demonstrated over revealed moral standards."—Ed.]

while a generic or rule utilitarianism, as has often been shown, cannot be consistently carried through.[20] Side by side with these attempts at constructivistic explanation we find in philosophical positivism, however, also a tendency to dispose of all values as things which do not refer to facts (and, therefore, are 'metaphysical') or a tendency to treat them as pure matters of emotion and therefore rationally not justifiable, or meaningless. The most naïve version of this is probably the 'emotivism' that has been popular in the course of the last 30 years. The expounders of 'emotivism'[21] believed that, with the statement that moral or immoral, or just and unjust, action evokes certain moral feelings, they had explained something—as if the question, why a certain group of actions causes one kind of emotion, and another group of actions another kind of emotion, did not raise an important problem of the significance this has for the ordering of life in society.

The constructivist approach is most clearly to be seen in the original form of legal positivism, as expounded by Thomas Hobbes and John Austin, to whom every rule of law must be derivable from a conscious act of legislation. This, as every historian of law knows, is factually false. But even in its most modern form, which I will briefly consider later, this false assumption is avoided only by limiting the conscious act of creating law to the conferring of validity on rules, about the origin of the content of which it has nothing to say. This turns the whole theory into an uninteresting tautology, which tells us nothing about how the rules can be found which the judicial authorities must apply.

The roots of socialism in constructivistic thought are obvious not only in its original form—in which it intended through socialization of the means of production, distribution and exchange to make possible a planned economy to replace the spontaneous order of the market by an organization directed to particular ends.[22] But the modern form of socialism that tries to use the mar-

---

[20] Concerning the results of the more recent discussion of utilitarianism see David Lyons, *Forms and Limits of Utilitarianism* (Oxford: Clarendon Press, 1965); David H. Hodgson, *Consequences of Utilitarianism: A Study in Normative Ethics and Legal Theory* (Oxford: Clarendon Press, 1967); and the convenient collection of essays in *Contemporary Utilitarianism*, ed. Michael D. Bayles (Garden City, New York: Anchor Books, 1968).

[21] See the writings of Rudolf Carnap, and particularly A. J. Ayer, *Language, Truth and Logic* (London: V. Gollanz, 1936).

[22] The recognition of the defects of these plans is now generally and justly ascribed to the great discussion which was started in the 1920's by the writings of Ludwig von Mises. But we should not overlook how many of the important points had been clearly seen earlier by some economists. As one forgotten instance a statement by Erwin Nasse in an article "Ueber die Verhütung der Produktionskrisen durch staatliche Fürsorge", *Jahrbuch für Gesetzgebung, Verwaltung und Volkswirtschaft im Deutschen Reich*, n.s., 1879, p. 164, may be quoted: "Eine planmässige Leitung der Produktion *ohne* Freiheit der Bedarfs- and Berufswahl würde nicht gerade undenkbar, aber mit einer Zerstörung der Cultur und alles dessen, was das Leben lebenswerth macht, verbunden sein. Eine planmässige Leitung der gesammten wirthschaftlichen Tätigkeit *mit* Freiheit der Bedarfs- and Berufswahl zu vereinigen, ist ein Problem, das nur mit der Quadratur des Kreises verglichen

ket in the service of what is called 'social justice', and for this purpose wants to guide the action of men, not by rules of just conduct for the individual, but by the recognized importance of results brought about by the decisions of authority, is no less based upon it.

VIII

In our century constructivism has in particular exercised great influence on ethical views through its effects on psychiatry and psychology. Within the time at my disposal I can give only two of many examples of that destruction of values by scientific error, which is at work in these fields. With regard to the first example, which I take from a psychiatrist, I must first say a few words about the author I shall quote, lest it be suspected that in order to exaggerate I have chosen some unrepresentative figure. The international reputation of the Canadian scientist, the late Brock Chisholm, is illustrated by the fact that he had been entrusted with building up the World Health Organization, acted for five years as its first Secretary-General and was finally elected President of the World Federation of Mental Health.

Just before Brock Chisholm embarked on this international career he wrote:[23]

---

werden kann. Denn, so wie man Jedem gestattet, die Richtung und Art seiner wirtschaftlichen Tätigkeit und Konsumtion frei zu bestimmen, verliert man die Leitung der Gesammtwirtschaft aus der Hand." ["Direction of production according to a plan *without* freedom of choice with regard to wants and occupation would not be absolutely unthinkable, yet would involve the destruction of culture and of all that makes life worth living. To make the direction of economic activity as a whole according to a plan compatible *with* freedom of choice with regard to wants and occupation is a problem only comparable to squaring the circle. For to the extent that everyone is permitted freely to choose the path and kind of economic activity and of consumption, control over the direction of the economy as a whole will be lost."—Ed.]

[23] George Brock Chisholm, "The Re-establishment of Peacetime Society", The William Alanson White Memorial Lectures, 2nd series, *Psychiatry*, vol. 9, no. 3, February 1946 (with a laudatory introduction by Abe Fortas), pp. 9–11. Cf. also two books by Chisholm, *Prescription for Survival* (New York: Columbia University Press, 1957), and *Can People Learn to Learn? How to Know Each Other* (New York: Harper, 1958), as well as his essay "The Issues Concerning Man's Biological Future" in *The Great Issues of Conscience in Modern Medicine* (Hanover, NH: Dartmouth Medical School, 1960), pp. 15–16, where he argues (p. 16): "We haven't even got a government department in any country that I know of that is set up to concern itself with the 'survival of the human race.' And if there is any question about which we have no government department, it obviously is not very important!"

It would be possible to quote here any number of similar utterances of the last 150 years. The Russian revolutionary Alexander Herzen was able to write: "You want a book of rules, while I think that when one reaches a certain age one ought to be ashamed of having to use one", and "the truly free man creates his own morality", in Alexander Herzen, *From the Other Shore*, translated by Moura Baberg, in *From the Other Shore and The Russian People and Socialism: An Open Letter*

The re-interpretation and eventual eradication of the concept of right and wrong which has been the basis of child training, the substitution of intelligent and rational thinking for faith in the certainties of the old people, these are the belated objectives of practically all effective psychotherapy. . . . The suggestion that we should stop teaching children moralities and right and wrong and instead protect their original intellectual integrity has of course to be met by an outcry of heretic or iconoclast, such as was raised against Galileo for finding another planet, and against the truth of evolution, and against Christ's interpretation of the Hebrew Gods, and against any attempt to change the mistaken old ways and ideas. The pretence is made, as it has been made in relation to the finding of any extension of truth, that to do away with right and wrong would produce uncivilized people, immorality, lawlessness and social chaos. The fact is that most psychiatrists and psychologists and many other respectable people have escaped from these moral chains and are able to observe and think freely. . . . If the race is to be freed from its crippling burden of good and evil it must be psychiatrists who take the original responsibility. This is a challenge which must be met. . . . With the other human sciences, psychiatry must now decide what is to be the immediate future of the human race. No one else can. And this is the prime responsibility of psychiatry.

It never seemed to occur to Chisholm that moral rules do not directly serve the satisfaction of individual desires, but are required to assist the functioning of an order; and even to tame some instincts, which man has inherited from his life in small groups where he passed most of his evolution. It may well be that the incorrigible barbarian in our midst resents these restraints. But are psychiatrists really the competent authorities to give us new morals?

Chisholm finally expresses the hope that two or three million trained psychiatrists, with the assistance of appropriate salesmanship, will soon succeed in freeing men from the 'perverse' concept of right and wrong. It sometimes seems as if they have already had too much success in this direction.

---

to Jules Michelet (London: Weidenfeld and Nicolson, 1956), pp. 28 and 141; this is little different from the views of a contemporary logical positivist such as Hans Reichenbach who argues in *The Rise of Scientific Philosophy* (Berkeley: University of California Press, 1951), p. 141 that "the power of reason must be sought not in rules that reason dictates to our imagination, but in the ability to free ourselves from any kind of rules to which we have been conditioned through experience and tradition." The statement by J. M. Keynes, *Two Memoirs: Dr. Melchior: A Defeated Enemy, and My Early Beliefs*, Introduction by D. Garnett (London: Rupert Hart-Davis, 1949), p. 97, which on earlier occasions I have quoted in this connection [Cf. this volume, prologue, p. 48, note 15.—Ed.], appears to me to have largely lost its significance in this context since Michael Holroyd, in *Lytton Strachey, a Critical Biography* (London: Heinemann, 1967–68), has shown that the majority of the members of the group about which Keynes spoke, including himself, were homosexual, which is probably a sufficient explanation of their revolt against ruling morals.

My second contemporary example of the destruction of values by scientific error is taken from jurisprudence. There is no need in this instance to identify the author of the statement I shall quote as belonging to the same category. It comes from no less a figure than my former teacher at the University of Vienna, Hans Kelsen. He assures us that "justice is an irrational idea", and continues:[24] "from the point of view of rational cognition, there are only interests of human beings and hence conflicts of interests. The solution of these conflicts can be brought about either by satisfying one interest at the expense of the other, or by a compromise between the conflicting interests. It is not possible to prove that only the one or the other solution is just."

Law is thus for Kelsen a deliberate construction, serving known particular interests. This might indeed be necessarily so, if we had ever to create anew the whole body of rules of just conduct. I will even concede to Kelsen that we can never positively prove what is just. But this does not preclude our ability to say when a rule is unjust, or that by the persistent application of such a negative test of injustice we may not be able progressively to approach justice.

It is true that this applies only to the rules of just conduct for individuals, and not to what Kelsen, like all socialists, had primarily in mind—namely, those aims of the deliberate measures employed by authority to achieve what is called 'social justice.' Yet neither positive nor negative criteria of an objective kind exist, from which to define or test so-called 'social justice', which is one of the emptiest of all phrases.

The nineteenth-century ideal of liberty was based on the conviction that there were such objective general rules of just conduct; and the false assertion

[24]Hans Kelsen, *What is Justice? Justice, Law, and Politics in the Mirror of Science: Collected Essays* (Berkeley, Ca.: University of California Press, 1957), pp. 21–22; almost literally the same statement occurs in *General Theory of Law and State* (Cambridge: Harvard University Press, 1945), p. 13. [Cf. "The Results of Human Action but Not of Human Design", this volume, p. 300, note 20.—Ed.] The elimination from the law of the concept of justice was of course not a discovery of Kelsen but is common to the whole of legal positivism and is particularly characteristic of the German theorists of law around the turn of the century of whom Alfred von Martin, *Mensch und Gesellschaft Heute* (Frankfurt a. M.: Knecht, 1965), p. 261, rightly says: "In wilhelminischer Zeit machten schliesslich, wie Graf Harry Kessler in seinen Erinnerungen berichtet, berühmteste deutsche Rechtslehrer etwas wie einen Sport daraus, bei jeder Gelegenheit zu betonen, dass Recht natürlich nicht das geringste mit Gerechtigkeit zu tun habe. Die Frucht war die Lehre von der entscheidenden rechtlichen Potenz 'der Entscheidung' als solcher, der Dezisionismus Carl Schmitts, des Kronjuristen der braunen Diktatur." ["In the times of Emperor Wilhelm II, as Count Harry Kessler reports in his recollections, the most famous German law scholars made something of a sport out of emphasizing, on every occasion, that of course law has not the least to do with justice. The fruit was the doctrine of the crucial legal validity of 'the decision' in itself, the decisionism of Carl Schmitt, the crown jurist of the brown dictatorship."—Ed.]

A good account of the dissolution of German liberalism by legal positivism will be found in John H. Hallowell, *The Decline of Liberalism as an Ideology, with Particular Reference to German Politico-Legal Thought* (Berkeley: University of California Press, 1943).

that justice is always merely a matter of particular interests has contributed a great deal to creating the belief that we have no choice but to assign to each individual what is regarded as right by those who for the time being hold the power.

IX

Let me clearly state the consequences that seem to follow from what I have said about the principles for legitimate criticism of social formations. After laying the previous foundations, this can be done in comparatively few words. I must at once warn you, however, that the conservatives among you, who up to this point may be rejoicing, will now probably be disappointed. The proper conclusion from the considerations I have advanced is by no means that we may confidently accept all the old and traditional values. Nor even that there are *any* values or moral principles, which science may not occasionally question. The social scientist who endeavours to understand how society functions, and to discover where it can be improved, must claim the right critically to examine, and even to judge, every *single* value of our society. The consequence of what I have said is merely that we can never at one and the same time question *all* its values. Such absolute doubt could lead only to the destruction of our civilization and—in view of the numbers to which economic progress has allowed the human race to grow—to extreme misery and starvation. Complete abandonment of all traditional values is, of course, impossible; it would make man incapable of acting. If traditional and taught values formed by man in the course of the evolution of civilization were renounced, this could only mean falling back on those instinctive values, which man developed in hundreds of thousands of years of tribal life, and which are now probably in a measure innate. These instinctive values are often irreconcilable with the basic principles of an open society—namely, the application of the same rules of just conduct to our relations with all other men—which our young revolutionaries also profess. The possibility of such a great society certainly does not rest on instincts, but on the governance of acquired rules. This is the discipline of reason.[25] It curbs instinctive impulses, and relies on rules of conduct which have originated in an interpersonal mental process. As the result of this process, in the course of time all the separate individual sets of values become slowly adapted to each other.

[25] The term 'reason' is here used in the sense explained by John Locke, *Essays on the Law of Nature*, ed. W. von Leyden (Oxford: Clarendon Press, 1954), p. 111: "By reason, however, I do not think is meant here that faculty of the understanding which forms trains of thought and deduces proofs, but certain definite principles of action from which spring all virtues and whatever is necessary for the proper moulding of morals."

The process of the evolution of a system of values passed on by cultural transmission must implicitly rest on criticism of individual values in the light of their consistency, or compatibility, with all other values of society, which for this purpose must be taken as given and undoubted. The only standard by which we can judge particular values of our society is the entire body of other values of that same society. More precisely, the factually existing, but always imperfect, order of actions produced by obedience to these values provides the touchstone for evaluation. Because prevailing systems of morals or values do not always give unambiguous answers to the questions which arise, but often prove to be internally contradictory, we are forced to develop and refine such moral systems continuously. We shall sometimes be constrained to sacrifice some moral value, but always only to other moral values which we regard as superior. We cannot escape this choice, because it is part of an indispensable process. In the course of it we are certain to make many mistakes. Sometimes whole groups, and perhaps entire nations, will decline, because they chose the wrong values. Reason has to prove itself in this mutual adjustment of given values, and must perform its most important but very unpopular task—namely, to point out the inner contradictions of our thinking and feeling.

The picture of man as a being who, thanks to his reason, can rise above the values of his civilization, in order to judge it from the outside, or from a higher point of view, is an illusion. It simply must be understood that reason itself is part of civilization. All we can ever do is to confront one part with the other parts. Even this process leads to incessant movement, which may in the very long course of time change the whole. But sudden complete reconstruction of the whole is not possible at any stage of the process, because we must always use the material that is available, and which itself is the integrated product of a process of evolution.

I hope it has become sufficiently clear that it is not, as may sometimes appear, the progress of science which threatens our civilization, but scientific error, based usually on the presumption of knowledge which in fact we do not possess. This lays upon science the responsibility to make good the harm its representatives have done. Growth of knowledge produces the insight that we can now aim at the goals which the present state of science has brought within our reach thanks only to the governance of values, which we have not made, and the significance of which we still only very imperfectly understand. So long as we cannot yet agree on crucial questions, such as whether a competitive market order is possible without the recognition of private several property in the instruments of production, it is clear that we still understand only very imperfectly the fundamental principles on which the existing order is based.

If scientists are so little aware of the responsibility they have incurred by failing to comprehend the rôle of values for the preservation of the social order, this is largely due to the notion that science as such has nothing to say about the validity of values. The *true* statement that, from our understanding of causal connections between facts alone, we can derive no conclusions about the validity of values, has been extended into the false belief that science has nothing to do with values.

This attitude should change immediately: scientific analysis shows that the existing factual order of society exists only because people accept certain values. With regard to such a social system, we cannot even make statements about the effects of particular events without assuming that certain norms are being generally obeyed.[26] From such premises containing values it is perfectly possible to derive conclusions about the compatibility, or incompatibility, of the various values presupposed in an argument. It is therefore incorrect if, from the postulate that science ought to be free of values, the conclusion is drawn that within a given system problems of value cannot be rationally decided. When we have to deal with an ongoing process for the ordering of society, in which most of the governing values are unquestioned, there will often be only one certain answer to particular questions that is compatible with the rest of the system.[27]

We have the curious spectacle that frequently the very same scientists, who particularly emphasize the *wertfrei* (value free) character of science, use that science to discredit prevailing values as the expression of irrational emotions or particular material interests. Such scientists often give the impression that

[26]Cf. in this connection the argument in H. L. A. Hart, *The Concept of Law* (Oxford: Clarendon Press, 1961), p. 188: "Our concern is with social arrangements for continued existence, not with those of a suicide club. We wish to know whether, among these social arrangements, there are some which may illuminatingly be ranked as natural laws discoverable by reason, and what their relation is to human law and morality. To raise this or any other question concerning *how* men should live together, we must assume that their aim, generally speaking, is to live. From this point the argument is a simple one. Reflection on some very obvious generalizations—indeed truisms—concerning human nature and the world in which men live, show that as long as these hold good, there are certain rules of conduct which any social organization must contain if it is to be viable." Similar considerations of an anthropologist are to be found in S. F. Nadel, *Anthropology and Modern Life: An Inaugural Lecture, Friday, 10 July, 1953* (Canberra: Australian National University, 1953), pp. 16–22.

[27]My position in this respect has become very much like that which Luigi Einaudi has well described in his introduction to a book by Costantino Bresciani-Turroni which I know only in its German translation, *Einführung in die Wirtschaftspolitik* (Bern: A. Francke, 1948), p. 13. He relates there how he used to believe that the economist had silently to accept the goals pursued by the legislator but had become increasingly doubtful about this, and might some day arrive at the conclusion that the economist ought to combine his task of a critic of the means with a similar critique of the ends, and that this may prove as much a part of science as the investigation of the means to which science at present confines itself. He adds that the study of the correspondence of means and ends and of the logical consistency of the posited ends may be much more difficult than, and certainly of equal moral value to, all considerations of the acceptability and evaluation of the separate ends.

the only value judgment that is scientifically respectable is the view that our values have no value. This attitude is therefore the result of a defective understanding of the connection between accepted values and the prevailing factual order.[28] All that we can do—and must do—is to test each and every value about which doubts are raised by the standard of other values, which we can assume that our listeners or readers share with us. At present the postulate that we should avoid all value judgments seems to me often to have become a mere excuse of the timid, who do not wish to offend anyone and thus conceal their preferences. Even more frequently, it is an attempt to conceal from themselves rational comprehension of the choices we have to make between possibilities open to us, which force us to sacrifice some aims we wish also to realize.

One of the noblest tasks of social science, it seems to me, is to show up clearly these conflicts of values.

Thus it is possible to demonstrate that what depends on the acceptance of values, which do not appear as consciously pursued aims of individuals or groups, are the very foundations of the factual order, whose existence we presuppose in all our individual endeavours.

[28] A good illustration of what is said in the text is apparently offered by the lectures of Gunnar Myrdal on *Objectivity in Social Research* from which *The Times Literary Supplement* of 19 February 1970 quotes a definition of 'scientific objectivity' as the freeing of the student from "(1) the powerful heritage of earlier writings in his field of inquiry, ordinarily containing normative and teleological notions inherited from past generations and founded upon the metaphysical moral philosophies of natural law and utilitarianism from which all our social and economic theories have branched off; (2) the influences of the entire cultural, social, economic, and political milieu of the society where he lives, works and earns his living and his status; and (3) the influence stemming from his own personality, as moulded not only by traditions and environment but also by his individual history, constitution and inclinations." [Peter Willmott's brief review of Myrdal's lecture *Objectivity in Social Research* (New York: Pantheon, 1969) actually appears in the July 9, 1970, issue of the *Times Literary Supplement*, and does not contain the passage Hayek cites. The passage may be found on pp. 3–4 of Myrdal's book.—Ed.]

FIFTEEN

NATURE VS. NURTURE ONCE AGAIN[1]

After his authoritative *Genetics and Man* (1964) Dr. C. D. Darlington has now given us a magnificent account of *The Evolution of Man and Society*.[2] This monumental work is bound to have great influence on many who will never trouble to study the former. What is here brought together on the origin of cultivation of plants and animals, the effects of disease, the significance of blood groups, and the recurrent destruction by man of the environment from which he draws his sustenance is a veritable treasure house of fascinating information. If Professor Max Beloff had not already given here (*Encounter*, October) a full account of the scope of the work, I should not wish to turn to criticism before dwelling at length on the merits of this contribution of a biologist to the understanding of history.[3] But it seems to me necessary more explicitly to examine a crucial issue on which the book is likely to give a misleading impression and with which Professor Beloff deals only by implication.

The point I want to consider here is whether in looking at history from the special point of view of the geneticist, Dr. Darlington has not much exaggerated the importance of the factor in which he is chiefly interested. All history is to him grist to his genetic mill which in all instances except those of one-egged twins turns out individuals born with distinct innate capacities which decisively determine their actions.

As a reaction against the behaviourist views expounded 40 years ago, e.g., in the *Encyclopaedia of the Social Sciences*, according to which "at birth human infants, regardless of their heredity, are as equal as Fords", this is most refreshing.[4] But true appreciation of the genetic factor is hardly assisted by ascribing

---

[1] A comment on C. D. Darlington, *The Evolution of Man and Society* (London: Allen and Unwin, 1969), reprinted from *Encounter*, vol. 36, February 1971, pp. 81–83. [Reprinted in F. A. Hayek, *New Studies in Philosophy, Politics, Economics and the History of Ideas* (Chicago: University of Chicago Press, 1978), pp. 290–94.—Ed.]

[2] [Hayek refers to C. D. Darlington, *Genetics and Man* (London: Allen and Unwin, 1964).—Ed.]

[3] [Max Beloff, "The Genetic Approach to World History", *Encounter*, vol. 35, October 1970, pp. 85–88.—Ed.]

[4] [Horace M. Kallen, "Behaviorism", *Encyclopaedia of the Social Sciences* (New York: Macmillan, 1930), vol. 2, p. 498.—Ed.]

to it more than it is really capable of explaining adequately. Dr. Darlington greatly extends what he feels must be ascribed to genetic transmission by the simple device that all actions that are not guided by conscious reason must be genetically determined. He operates with the simple dichotomy between, on the one hand, the genetically determined, innate, instinctive, or unconscious capacities (terms which are treated as equivalent), and, on the other hand, rational or learned activities.

I take it that by 'rational' Dr. Darlington means purposive action based on conscious insight into the relations between cause and effect, or what Professor Gilbert Ryle called 'knowledge that.'[5] If so, there is certainly no justification for assuming that what is not rational must be innate and genetically determined. There is no ground for supposing that those attributes which are normally transmitted only from parents are all transmitted genetically. 'Breeding' in the sense of upbringing includes much more than begetting. As Dr. Darlington duly stresses, man's most distinguishing characteristic is his prolonged infancy, which presumably includes a correspondingly increased capacity for learning by imitation. Most of an individual's aptitudes, propensities, and skills are probably acquired in early infancy, and firmly entrenched by the time he becomes capable of rational thought. These learned action patterns are not tools which he consciously selects, but rather properties in accordance with which he will be selected by a process which nobody controls.

* * *

We still know very little about the process of learning by perceiving and imitating, especially by the small child. I know of no systematic study of the extent to which children resemble foster parents in their conscious behaviour patterns. But the importance of this sort of pre-rational learning can hardly be doubted. While apparently the higher apes 'ape' very little, man must have early developed a great capacity for imitating, that is, of translating perceived into performed movements. This may indeed have been one of the most important steps in the development of his brain. I should not be surprised if we were to discover that something analogous to 'imprinting' played a great rôle in this connection. Once such an innate capacity for learning by imitation is acquired, the transmission of abilities takes a new form—vastly superior to genetic transmission precisely because it includes the transmission of acquired characters which genetic transmission does not.

* * *

Man is clearly genetically adapted to this learning process which he must undergo before he is capable of maintaining himself. But we must not confuse

---

[5] [Gilbert Ryle, "Knowing How and Knowing That", *Proceedings of the Aristotelian Society*, vol. 46, 1945–1946, pp. 1–16.—Ed.]

the inherited capacity to learn a great variety of modes of conduct with a heredity of particular modes of conduct. Nor must we confine 'learning' to what the child is explicitly taught. Much that is learned certainly is not rational or conscious, but, in the loose and incorrect use of these terms, 'intuitive' or even 'instinctive.' Neither the individual who provides the example nor the imitator will be able to state what is merely 'knowledge how', or know what depends on his acting in this particular manner. Much of what we can do rests on skills or aptitudes or propensities acquired by following examples, and selected because they proved successful, but not deliberately chosen for a purpose.

This process of cultural evolution follows in many respects the same pattern as biological evolution. As the late Sir Alexander Carr-Saunders explained nearly 50 years ago: "Men and groups of men are naturally selected on account of the customs they practise just as they are selected on account of their mental and physical characteristics."[6] And, as Sir Alister Hardy has shown recently, culturally transmitted patterns may in turn contribute to determine the selection of genetic properties.[7] The processes of cultural and of genetic evolution will thus constantly interact, and their respective influence will be very difficult to distinguish.

Cultural evolution, because it also rests on a sort of natural selection, looks very much like biological evolution. Both are likely to produce the results which Dr. Darlington stresses, or to operate by 'hybridization', 'recombination', 'assortative mating', or 'stratification.' The 'breeding systems' whose significance Dr. Darlington emphasizes exclusively with reference to the genetic effects are equally important for both forms of evolution. For instance, inbreeding among a group living for generations in the same environment will be apt to lead to the loss of previously possessed skills if failure to transmit them has no deleterious effects on those who have to do without them; but it will disable them from coping with a changed environment, irrespective of whether the transmission of these skills is effected genetically or culturally.

Cultural transmission has however one great advantage over the genetic: it includes the transmission of acquired characters. The child will acquire unconsciously from the example of the parent skills which the latter may have learnt through a long process of trial and error, but which with the child become the starting point from which he can proceed to greater perfection.

It is curious that Dr. Darlington, in his endeavour to play up the genetic aspect, should do less than justice to the comprehensive character of the general principle of evolution, and overlook that it extends far beyond biology—and, incidentally, was used in the theories of language and law long before

[6] [Alexander Carr-Saunders, *The Population Problem: A Study in Human Evolution* (Oxford: Clarendon Press, 1922), p. 223. Hayek changed Carr-Saunders's "characters" to "characteristics", which indeed reads somewhat better.—Ed.]

[7] [See Alister Hardy, *The Living Stream: Evolution and Man* (New York: Harper and Row, 1965), especially chapter 6, "Behavior as a Selective Force."—Ed.]

it was applied to biology. He does not explicitly discuss the distinction which his fellow-biologists, Sir Julian Huxley and Dr. Theodosius Dobzhansky, have made between the biological and the 'psycho-social' or 'super-organic' modes of evolution; perhaps these were not very fortunate terms.[8] And I am not surprised if he should not trust the sociologists properly to develop the theory of cultural evolution since some of them have indeed talked much nonsense about it. But to exclude the *cultural* aspect of evolution and claim almost everything for *genetic* transmission surely is doing violence to the subject. Dr. Darlington has certainly not proved the "universal dependence of the exchange and transmission of ideas and aptitudes on the exchange and transmission of genes."[9]

One might have hoped from a work like this that it would provide us with a criterion or test by which we can recognize what is genetically determined or which of the features on which our culture depends are conditioned by innate properties of the individuals. But on this question the author lets us down. So far as I can see he does not demonstrate at any point that the operative sort of inheritance shows any of the specific characteristics of genetic inheritance, such as the exclusion of acquired characters or Mendelian distributions, though he sometimes writes as if he had done so. It may well be that, e.g., the "gift for narrative" of the Irish requires a special genetic factor; but the suggestion that the resemblance of the Etruscan Lion at Vulci to some Hittite work almost 1,000 years older shows that "the genetic continuity overrides the cultural discontinuity" is to me not very convincing.[10] It would be very helpful if we had a test to decide such questions, but I fear that in the present state of knowledge we can hardly hope for one. If we had, it would probably show how precarious the stability of our present civilization is, precisely because it rests largely on cultural traditions which can be more rapidly destroyed than the genetic endowment of populations.

* * *

All these are comparatively minor points which little affect the merits or even the chief conclusions of the book. If the amendments which seem to me necessary were made, these conclusions would not become much more palatable to some of our professional egalitarians, such as the reviewer in the *New Statesman*, to whom Dr. Darlington's work appeared as a "profoundly reactionary book."[11] The conclusions may seem only just a little less dismal to them if it

---

[8] [See, e.g., Julian Huxley, *Evolution in Action* (New York: Harper and Brothers, 1953), pp. 153ff.; and Theodosius Dobzhansky, *Mankind Evolving: The Evolution of the Human Species* (New Haven: Yale University Press, 1962), pp. 18ff.—Ed.]

[9] [Darlington, *Evolution of Man and Society*, p. 84.—Ed.]

[10] [Darlington discusses these examples on pp. 429 and 238, respectively.—Ed.]

[11] [See Robert Young's review of Darlington's book, "Understanding It All", *The New Statesman*, vol. 78, September 26, 1969, pp. 417–18. Young begins his review with these words: "This book is a snare for the unwary."—Ed.]

is admitted that acquired cultural achievements are passed on by processes which are not genetic, and that growing up within a particular family rather than physical descent may be the more important factor. But what Dr. Darlington says about such phenomena as stratification, or the secondary importance of that part of the environment which we can manipulate, would still remain true.

On the whole we must probably conclude, as does Sir Gavin de Beer in a book on a similar theme (*Streams of Culture*, 1969) which appeared about the same time as Dr. Darlington's, that the old controversy between 'Nature' and 'Nurture' ought to be allowed to die because "it is necessary to regard both nature and nurture as cooperating, without our being able to say in any one case exactly how much has been contributed by either. . . ."[12]

[12] [Sir Gavin de Beer, "The Role of Genetics in the Evolution of Man", in *Streams of Culture* (New York: J. B. Lippincott, 1969), p. 152.—Ed.]

SIXTEEN

THE PRETENCE OF KNOWLEDGE[1]

The particular occasion of this lecture, combined with the chief practical problem which economists have to face today, have made the choice of its topic almost inevitable. On the one hand the still recent establishment of the Nobel Memorial Prize in Economic Science marks a significant step in the process by which, in the opinion of the general public, economics has been conceded some of the dignity and prestige of the physical sciences. On the other hand, the economists are at this moment called upon to say how to extricate the free world from the serious threat of accelerating inflation which, it must be admitted, has been brought about by policies which the majority of economists recommended and even urged governments to pursue. We have indeed at the moment little cause for pride: as a profession we have made a mess of things.

It seems to me that this failure of the economists to guide policy more successfully is closely connected with their propensity to imitate as closely as possible the procedures of the brilliantly successful physical sciences—an attempt which in our field may lead to outright error. It is an approach which has come to be described as the 'scientistic' attitude—an attitude which, as I defined it some thirty years ago, "is decidedly unscientific in the true sense of the word, since it involves a mechanical and uncritical application of habits of thought to fields different from those in which they have been formed."[2] I want today to begin by explaining how some of the gravest errors of recent economic policy are a direct consequence of this scientistic error.

The theory which has been guiding monetary and financial policy during

---

[1] Nobel Memorial Lecture, delivered at Stockholm, 11 December 1974, and reprinted from *Les Prix Nobel en 1974* (Stockholm: Nobel Foundation, 1975), pp. 247–58. [Reprinted in F. A. Hayek, *New Studies in Philosophy, Politics, Economics and the History of Ideas* (Chicago: University of Chicago Press, 1978), pp. 23–34.—Ed.]

[2] "Scientism and the Study of Society", *Economica*, n.s., vol. 9, August 1942, p. 269, reprinted in *The Counter-Revolution of Science* (Chicago: University of Chicago Press, 1952), p. 24. [See now "Scientism and the Study of Society", in *Studies on the Abuse and Decline of Reason*, ed. Bruce Caldwell, vol. 13 (2010) of *The Collected Works of F. A. Hayek* (Chicago: University of Chicago Press; London: Routledge), p. 80.—Ed.]

the last thirty years, and which I contend is largely the product of such a mistaken conception of the proper scientific procedure, consists in the assertion that there exists a simple positive correlation between total employment and the size of the aggregate demand for goods and services; it leads to the belief that we can permanently assure full employment by maintaining total money expenditure at an appropriate level. Among the various theories advanced to account for extensive unemployment, this is probably the only one in support of which strong quantitative evidence can be adduced. I nevertheless regard it as fundamentally false, and to act upon it, as we now experience, as very harmful.

This brings me to the crucial issue. Unlike the position that exists in the physical sciences, in economics and other disciplines that deal with essentially complex phenomena, the aspects of the events to be accounted for about which we can get quantitative data are necessarily limited and may not include the important ones. While in the physical sciences it is generally assumed, probably with good reason, that any important factor which determines the observed events will itself be directly observable and measurable, in the study of such complex phenomena as the market, which depend on the actions of many individuals, all the circumstances which will determine the outcome of a process, for reasons which I shall explain later, will hardly ever be fully known or measurable. And while in the physical sciences the investigator will be able to measure what, on the basis of a *prima facie* theory, he thinks important, in the social sciences often that is treated as important which happens to be accessible to measurement. This is sometimes carried to the point where it is demanded that our theories must be formulated in such terms that they refer only to measurable magnitudes.

It can hardly be denied that such a demand quite arbitrarily limits the facts which are to be admitted as possible causes of the events which occur in the real world. This view, which is often quite naïvely accepted as required by scientific procedure, has some rather paradoxical consequences. We know, of course, with regard to the market and similar social structures, a great many facts which we cannot measure and on which indeed we have only some very imprecise and general information. And because the effects of these facts in any particular instance cannot be confirmed by quantitative evidence, they are simply disregarded by those sworn to admit only what they regard as scientific evidence: they thereupon happily proceed on the fiction that the factors which they can measure are the only ones that are relevant.

The correlation between aggregate demand and total employment, for instance, may only be approximate, but as it is the *only* one on which we have quantitative data, it is accepted as the only causal connection that counts. On this standard there may thus well exist better 'scientific' evidence for a false theory, which will be accepted because it is more 'scientific', than for a valid explanation, which is rejected because there is no sufficient quantitative evidence for it.

Let me illustrate this by a brief sketch of what I regard as the chief actual cause of extensive unemployment—an account which will also explain why such unemployment cannot be lastingly cured by the inflationary policies recommended by the now fashionable theory. This correct explanation appears to me to be the existence of discrepancies between the distribution of demand among the different goods and services and the allocation of labour and other resources among the production of those outputs. We possess a fairly good 'qualitative' knowledge of the forces by which a correspondence between demand and supply in the different sectors of the economic system is brought about, of the conditions under which it will be achieved, and of the factors likely to prevent such an adjustment. The separate steps in the account of this process rely on facts of everyday experience, and few who take the trouble to follow the argument will question the validity of the factual assumptions, or the logical correctness of the conclusions drawn from them. We have indeed good reason to believe that unemployment indicates that the structure of relative prices and wages has been distorted (usually by monopolistic or governmental price fixing), and that in order to restore equality between the demand and the supply of labour in all sectors changes of relative prices and some transfers of labour will be necessary.

But when we are asked for quantitative evidence for the particular structure of prices and wages that would be required in order to assure a smooth continuous sale of the products and services offered, we must admit that we have no such information. We know, in other words, the general conditions in which what we call, somewhat misleadingly, an equilibrium will establish itself: but we never know what the particular prices or wages are which would exist if the market were to bring about such an equilibrium. We can merely say what the conditions are in which we can expect the market to establish prices and wages at which demand will equal supply. But we can never produce statistical information which would show how much the prevailing prices and wages *deviate* from those which would secure a continuous sale of the current supply of labour. Though this account of the causes of unemployment is an empirical theory, in the sense that it might be proved false, for example if, with a constant money supply, a general increase of wages did not lead to unemployment, it is certainly not the kind of theory which we could use to obtain specific numerical predictions concerning the rates of wages, or the distribution of labour, to be expected.

Why should we, however, in economics, have to plead ignorance of the sort of facts on which, in the case of a physical theory, a scientist would certainly be expected to give precise information? It is probably not surprising that those impressed by the example of the physical sciences should find this position very unsatisfactory and should insist on the standards of proof which they find there. The reason for this state of affairs is the fact, to which I have already briefly referred, that the social sciences, like much of biology but unlike most fields of the physical sciences, have to deal with structures of *essential* complexity, i.e., with structures whose characteristic properties can be exhibited only by models made up of relatively large numbers of variables. Competition, for instance, is a process which will produce certain results only if it proceeds among a fairly large number of acting persons.

In some fields, particularly where problems of a similar kind arise in the physical sciences, the difficulties can be overcome by using, instead of specific information about the individual elements, data about the relative frequency, or the probability, of the occurrence of the various distinctive properties of the elements. But this is true only where we have to deal with what has been called by Dr. Warren Weaver (formerly of the Rockefeller Foundation), with a distinction which ought to be much more widely understood, "phenomena of unorganized complexity", in contrast to those "phenomena of organized complexity" with which we have to deal in the social sciences.[3] Organized complexity here means that the character of the structures showing it depends not only on the properties of the individual elements of which they are composed, and the relative frequency with which they occur, but also on the manner in which the individual elements are connected with each other. In the explanation of the working of such structures we can for this reason not replace the information about the individual elements by statistical information, but require full information about each element if from our theory we are to derive specific predictions about individual events. Without such specific information about the individual elements we shall be confined to what on another occasion I have called mere pattern predictions—predictions of some of the general attributes of the structures that will form themselves, but not containing specific statements about the individual elements of which the structures will be made up.[4]

This is particularly true of our theories accounting for the determination of the systems of relative prices and wages that will form themselves on a well-functioning market. Into the determination of these prices and wages there will enter the effects of particular information possessed by every one of the participants in the market process—a sum of facts which in their totality can-

[3] Warren Weaver, "A Quarter Century in the Natural Sciences", *The Rockefeller Foundation Annual Report* (New York: Rockefeller Foundation, 1958), chapter 1, "Science and Complexity."

[4] See my essay "The Theory of Complex Phenomena" in *The Critical Approach to Science and Philosophy: In Honor of Karl R. Popper*, ed. Mario Bunge (New York: The Free Press, 1964), pp. 332–49, and reprinted (with additions) in my *Studies in Philosophy, Politics and Economics* (London and Chicago: Routledge and the University of Chicago Press, 1967), pp. 22–42. [See this volume, chapter 9.—Ed.]

not be known to the scientific observer, or to any other single brain. It is indeed the source of the superiority of the market order, and the reason why, when it is not suppressed by the powers of government, it regularly displaces other types of order, that in the resulting allocation of resources more of the knowledge of particular facts will be utilized which exists only dispersed among uncounted persons, than any one person can possess. But because we, the observing scientists, can thus never know all the determinants of such an order, and in consequence also cannot know at which particular structure of prices and wages demand would everywhere equal supply, we also cannot measure the deviations from that order; nor can we statistically test our theory that it is the deviations from that 'equilibrium' system of prices and wages which make it impossible to sell some of the products and services at the prices at which they are offered.

Before I continue with my immediate concern, the effects of all this on the employment policies currently pursued, allow me to define more specifically the inherent limitations of our numerical knowledge which are so often overlooked. I want to do this to avoid giving the impression that I generally reject the mathematical method in economics. I regard it in fact as the great advantage of the mathematical technique that it allows us to describe, by means of algebraic equations, the general character of a pattern even where we are ignorant of the numerical values which will determine its particular manifestation. We could scarcely have achieved that comprehensive picture of the mutual interdependencies of the different events in a market without this algebraic technique. It has led to the illusion, however, that we can use this technique for the determination and prediction of the numerical values of those magnitudes; and this has led to a vain search for quantitative or numerical constants. This happened in spite of the fact that the modern founders of mathematical economics had no such illusions. It is true that their systems of equations describing the pattern of a market equilibrium are so framed that *if* we were able to fill in all the blanks of the abstract formulae, i.e., *if* we knew all the parameters of these equations, we could calculate the prices and quantities of all commodities and services sold. But, as Vilfredo Pareto, one of the founders of this theory, clearly stated, its purpose cannot be "to arrive at a numerical calculation of prices", because, as he said, it would be "absurd" to assume that we could ascertain all the data.[5] Indeed, the chief point was already seen by those remarkable anticipators of modern economics, the Spanish Schoolmen of the sixteenth century, who emphasized that what they called *pretium mathematicum*, the mathematical price, depended on so many par-

---

[5] Vilfredo Pareto, *Manuel d'économie politique*, translated by Alfred Bonnet, 2nd ed. (Paris: Marcel Giard, 1927), pp. 233–34. [Cf. Vilfredo Pareto, *Manual of Political Economy*, ed. nn S. Schwier and Alfred N. Page, translated by Ann S. Schwier (New York: Kelley, 1971), p. 171.—Ed.]

ticular circumstances that it could never be known to man but was known only to God.[6] I sometimes wish that our mathematical economists would take this to heart. I must confess that I still doubt whether their search for measurable magnitudes has made significant contributions to our *theoretical* understanding of economic phenomena—as distinct from their value as a description of particular situations. Nor am I prepared to accept the excuse that this branch of research is still very young: Sir William Petty, the founder of econometrics, was after all a somewhat senior colleague of Sir Isaac Newton in the Royal Society!

There may be few instances in which the superstition that only measurable magnitudes can be important has done positive harm in the economic field: but the present inflation and employment problems are a very serious one. Its effect has been that what is probably the true cause of extensive unemployment has been disregarded by the scientistically minded majority of economists, because its operation could not be confirmed by directly observable relations between measurable magnitudes, and that an almost exclusive concentration on quantitatively measurable surface phenomena has produced a policy which has made matters worse.

It has, of course, to be readily admitted that the kind of theory which I regard as the true explanation of unemployment is a theory of somewhat limited content because it allows us to make only very general predictions of the *kind* of events which we must expect in a given situation. But the effects on policy of the more ambitious constructions have not been very fortunate and I confess that I prefer true but imperfect knowledge, even if it leaves much indetermined and unpredictable, to a pretence of exact knowledge that is likely to be false. The credit which the apparent conformity with recognized scientific standards can gain for seemingly simple but false theories may, as the present instance shows, have grave consequences.

In fact, in the case discussed, the very measures which the dominant 'macroeconomic' theory has recommended as a remedy for unemployment, namely the increase of aggregate demand, have become a cause of a very extensive misallocation of resources which is likely to make later large-scale unemployment inevitable. The continuous injection of additional amounts of money at points of the economic system where it creates a temporary demand which must cease when the increase of the quantity of money stops or slows down, together with the expectation of a continuing rise of prices, draws labour and other resources into employments which can last only so long as the increase of the quantity of money continues at the same rate—or perhaps even only so long as it continues to accelerate at a given rate. What this policy has produced

[6]See, for example, Luis Molina, *De iustitia et iure*, Cologne, 1596–1600, Tome II, disputatio 347, no. 3, and particularly Johannes de Lugo, *Disputationum de iustitia et iure tomus secundus*, Lyon, 1642, disputatio 26, sect. 4, no. 40.

is not so much a level of employment that could not have been brought about in other ways, as a distribution of employment which cannot be indefinitely maintained and which after some time can be maintained only by a rate of inflation which would rapidly lead to a disorganization of all economic activity. The fact is that by a mistaken theoretical view we have been led into a precarious position in which we cannot prevent substantial unemployment from reappearing; not because, as this view is sometimes misrepresented, this unemployment is deliberately brought about as a means to combat inflation, but because it is now bound to occur as a deeply regrettable but inescapable consequence of the mistaken policies of the past as soon as inflation ceases to accelerate.

I must, however, now leave these problems of immediate practical importance which I have introduced chiefly as an illustration of the momentous consequences that may follow from errors concerning abstract problems of the philosophy of science. There is as much reason to be apprehensive about the long-run dangers created in a much wider field by the uncritical acceptance of assertions which have the *appearance* of being scientific as there is with regard to the problems I have just discussed. What I mainly wanted to bring out by the topical illustration is that certainly in my field, but I believe also generally in the sciences of man, what looks superficially like the most scientific procedure is often the most unscientific, and, beyond this, that in these fields there are definite limits to what we can expect science to achieve. This means that to entrust to science—or to deliberate control according to scientific principles—more than scientific methods can achieve may have deplorable effects. The progress of the natural sciences in modern times has of course so much exceeded all expectations that any suggestion that there may be some limits to it is bound to arouse suspicion. Especially all those will resist such an insight who have hoped that our increasing power of prediction and control, generally regarded as the characteristic result of scientific advance, applied to the processes of society, would soon enable us to mould society entirely to our liking. It is indeed true that, in contrast to the exhilaration which the discoveries of the physical sciences tend to produce, the insights which we gain from the study of society more often have a dampening effect on our aspirations; and it is perhaps not surprising that the more impetuous younger members of our profession are not always prepared to accept this. Yet the confidence in the unlimited power of science is only too often based on a false belief that the scientific method consists in the application of a ready-made technique, or in imitating the form rather than the substance of scientific procedure, as if one needed only to follow some cooking recipes to solve all social problems. It sometimes almost seems as if the technique of science were more easily learnt than the thinking that shows us what the problems are and how to approach them.

The conflict between what in its present mood the public expects science to achieve in satisfaction of popular hopes and what is really in its power is a serious matter because, even if the true scientists should all recognize the limitations of what they can do in the field of human affairs, so long as the public expects more there will always be some who will pretend, and perhaps honestly believe, that they can do more to meet popular demands than is really in their power. It is often difficult enough for the expert, and certainly in many instances impossible for the layman, to distinguish between legitimate and illegitimate claims advanced in the name of science. The enormous publicity recently given by the media to a report pronouncing in the name of science on *The Limits to Growth*, and the silence of the same media about the devastating criticism this report has received from the competent experts,[7] must make one feel somewhat apprehensive about the use to which the prestige of science can be put. But it is by no means only in the field of economics that far-reaching claims are made on behalf of a more scientific direction of all human activities and the desirability of replacing spontaneous processes by 'conscious human control.' If I am not mistaken, psychology, psychiatry, and some branches of sociology, not to speak about the so-called philosophy of history, are even more affected by what I have called the scientistic prejudice, and by specious claims of what science can achieve.[8]

If we are to safeguard the reputation of science, and to prevent the arrogation of knowledge based on a superficial similarity of procedure with that of the physical sciences, much effort will have to be directed towards debunking such arrogations, some of which have by now become the vested interests of established university departments. We cannot be grateful enough to such modern philosophers of science as Sir Karl Popper for giving us a test by which we can distinguish between what we may accept as scientific and what not—a test which I am sure some doctrines now widely accepted as scientific would not pass. There are some special problems, however, in connection with those essentially complex phenomena of which social structures are so important an instance, which make me wish to restate in conclusion in more general terms the reasons why in these fields not only are there absolute obstacles to

---

[7] See Donella H. Meadows et. al., *The Limits to Growth: A Report for the Club of Rome's Project on the Predicament of Mankind* (New York: Universe Books, 1972); for a systematic examination of this by a competent economist, cf. Wilfred Beckerman, *In Defence of Economic Growth* (London: Jonathan Cape, 1974), and, for a list of earlier criticisms by experts, Gottfried Haberler, *Economic Growth and Stability: An Analysis of Economic Change and Policies* (Los Angeles: Nash, 1974), who rightly calls their effect "devastating."

[8] I have given some illustrations of these tendencies in other fields in my inaugural lecture as Visiting Professor at the University of Salzburg, *Die Irrtümer des Konstruktivismus und die Grundlagen legitimer Kritik gesellschaftlicher Gebilde* (Munich: Wilhelm Fink, 1970), now reissued for the Walter Eucken Institute, at Freiburg i. B., by J. C. B. Mohr, Tübingen, 1975. [See "The Errors of Constructivism", this volume, chapter 14.—Ed.]

the prediction of specific events, but why to act as if we possessed scientific knowledge enabling us to transcend them may itself become a serious obstacle to the advance of the human intellect.[9]

The chief point we must remember is that the great and rapid advance of the physical sciences took place in fields where it proved that explanation and prediction could be based on laws which accounted for the observed phenomena as functions of comparatively few variables—either particular facts or relative frequencies of events. This may even be the ultimate reason why we single out these realms as 'physical' in contrast to those more highly organized structures which I have here called essentially complex phenomena. There is no reason why the position must be the same in the latter as in the former fields. The difficulties which we encounter in the latter are not, as one might at first suspect, difficulties about formulating theories for the explanation of the observed events—although they cause also special difficulties about testing proposed explanations and therefore about eliminating bad theories. They are due to the chief problem which arises when we apply our theories to any particular situation in the real world. A theory of essentially complex phenomena must refer to a large number of particular facts; and to derive a prediction from it, or to test it, we have to ascertain all these particular facts. Once we succeeded in this there should be no particular difficulty about deriving testable predictions—with the help of modern computers it should be easy enough to insert these data into the appropriate blanks of the theoretical formulae and to derive a prediction. The real difficulty, to the solution of which science has little to contribute, and which is sometimes indeed insoluble, consists in the ascertainment of the particular facts.

A simple example will show the nature of this difficulty. Consider some ball game played by a few people of approximately equal skill. If we knew a few particular facts in addition to our general knowledge of the ability of the individual players, such as their state of attention, their perceptions and the state of their hearts, lungs, muscles, etc., at each moment of the game, we could probably predict the outcome. Indeed, if we were familiar both with the game and the teams we should probably have a fairly shrewd idea on what the outcome will depend. But we shall of course not be able to ascertain those facts and in consequence the result of the game will be outside the range of the scientifically predictable, however well we may know what effects particular events would have on the result of the game. This does not mean that we can make no predictions at all about the course of such a game. If we know the rules of the different games we shall, in watching one, very soon know which game is being played and what kinds of actions we can expect and what kind

---

[9] [Cf. Hayek's discussion of the limits of prediction in such fields in "The Theory of Complex Phenomena", this volume, chapter 9.—Ed.]

not. But our capacity to predict will be confined to such general characteristics of the events to be expected and not include the capacity of predicting particular individual events.

This corresponds to what I have called earlier the mere pattern predictions to which we are increasingly confined as we penetrate from the realm in which relatively simple laws prevail into the range of phenomena where organized complexity rules. As we advance we find more and more frequently that we can in fact ascertain only some but not all the particular circumstances which determine the outcome of a given process; and in consequence we are able to predict only some but not all the properties of the result we have to expect. Often all that we shall be able to predict will be some abstract characteristic of the pattern that will appear—relations between kinds of elements about which individually we know very little. Yet, as I am anxious to repeat, we will still achieve predictions which can be falsified and which therefore are of empirical significance.

Of course, compared with the precise predictions we have learnt to expect in the physical sciences, this sort of mere pattern predictions is a second best with which one does not like to have to be content. Yet the danger of which I want to warn is precisely the belief that in order to have a claim to be accepted as scientific it is necessary to achieve more. This way lies charlatanism and worse. To act on the belief that we possess the knowledge and the power which enable us to shape the processes of society entirely to our liking, knowledge which in fact we do *not* possess, is likely to make us do much harm. In the physical sciences there may be little objection to trying to do the impossible; one might even feel that one ought not to discourage the over-confident because their experiments may after all produce some new insights. But in the social field the erroneous belief that the exercise of some power would have beneficial consequences is likely to lead to a new power to coerce other men being conferred on some authority. Even if such power is not in itself bad, its exercise is likely to impede the functioning of those spontaneous ordering forces by which, without understanding them, man is in fact so largely assisted in the pursuit of his aims. We are only beginning to understand on how subtle a communication system the functioning of an advanced industrial society is based—a communications system which we call the market and which turns out to be a more efficient mechanism for digesting dispersed information than any that man has deliberately designed.

If man is not to do more harm than good in his efforts to improve the social order, he will have to learn that in this, as in all other fields where essential complexity of an organized kind prevails, he cannot acquire the full knowledge which would make mastery of the events possible. He will therefore have to use what knowledge he can achieve, not to shape the results as the craftsman shapes his handiwork, but rather to cultivate a growth by providing the appropriate environment, in the manner in which the gardener does this for his plants. There is danger in the exuberant feeling of ever growing power which the advance of the physical sciences has engendered and which tempts man to try, 'dizzy with success', to use a characteristic phrase of early communism, to subject not only our natural but also our human environment to the control of a human will. The recognition of the insuperable limits to his knowledge ought indeed to teach the student of society a lesson in humility which should guard him against becoming an accomplice in men's fatal striving to control society—a striving which makes him not only a tyrant over his fellows, but which may well make him the destroyer of a civilization which no brain has designed but which has grown from the free efforts of millions of individuals.

APPENDIX A
A New Look at Economic Theory

Lecture I
The Object of Economic Theory[1]

1. Introduction

In this series of lectures I propose to take a new look at what until about twenty-five years ago was regarded as the central core of economic theory. During that interval of time there has occurred a change not so much in the answers which economists give to particular questions as in the questions which they mainly ask. What used to be the central problems have been relegated to a secondary position and as 'micro-analysis' had to give pride of place to something called 'macro-analysis' because it deals chiefly with such aggregates as income and employment. It is my belief that this shift has gone much too far and that an inadequate understanding of what had been the central problems is now impeding even the advance in the new direction—especially because it prevents an adequate comprehension of the factors governing the volume of investment.

It seems to me that this shift of emphasis was not due entirely to the greater urgency which the problems of fluctuations of income and employment assumed at the time. At least as important was probably the fact that the new macro-analysis both seemed to conform better to the predominant conception of the character of scientific procedure and to make more direct contributions to the problems of day-to-day economic policy, while the exact scientific character of the older micro-analysis was always a little obscure, and its results significant mainly for the choice between alternative economic systems rather than problems of current policy and for this reason often suspect as apologetics for the free enterprise system.

Misconceptions about the character and aim of traditional theoretical analysis—both by its defenders and its critics—have indeed contributed so much to alter our attitude to problems of economic policy that a reconsideration of those theoretical issues seems of considerable practical importance. I believe also that what has gradually become clear about the method of economic theory is significant far beyond our field, and that certain aspects of the tech-

[1] [In spring 1961 the Thomas Jefferson Center for Studies in Political Economy at the University of Virginia sponsored a public lecture series featuring Friedrich Hayek. According to the program, the series of four lectures were held at 8:00 p.m. in the South Meeting Room of Newcomb Hall on February 20, March 16, April 6, and April 27, respectively. The lectures were never published, and some of them contain additions and deletions in Hayek's hand. When legible the changes that Hayek made were incorporated into the present text. Obvious typos were silently corrected, but the text remains much as it is in the original version. The originals may be found in the Hayek Collection, box 138, folders 16–19, Hoover Institution Archives, Stanford University, Calif.—Ed.]

nique of analysis of micro-economic theory should apply also in other fields which deal with phenomena of comparable complexity and therefore meet the same difficulty in applying the more familiar procedures of inquiry. There seems to me to be still much truth in the view that as we move from the comparatively simple phenomena of inanimate nature to the increasingly complex ones of life and society, we may have to become more modest in our aims and be content with results which are much more limited in their predictive content than is the case in the physical sciences.

2. Boundaries of Knowledge

The suggestion that there may be limits to what science can achieve is generally not well received today. It is not only regarded as the expression of a defeatism unwarranted in view of the incredible conquests which science is making every day, and as a prediction of a kind which has been disproved in the past in so many instances as to have lost its plausibility. It is even considered as outright unscientific, because only experience can show what science can and what it cannot do.

I happen to think that so far as the human mind is the object of scientific study, there are indeed demonstrable limits to what explanation can achieve— demonstrable because they are a logical consequence of what we mean by explanation.[2] For my present purposes, however, I do not need such a strong assertion and shall take for my starting point merely the common-sense position that human society presents certain phenomena of such complexity that at least for a considerable time we shall not be able to achieve a complete explanation of them. The question I want to consider is whether there is a procedure which enables us to penetrate the boundary where our knowledge ceases to be adequate for a full explanation leading to prediction and control of particular events, and to obtain at least some knowledge about phenomena outside that range which is both useful as a guide to action and testable.

By a full explanation I mean here a statement which enables us to derive from ascertainable facts a precise prediction of particular events. Such prediction will be possible if we can ascertain (and preferably also control) all the circumstances which influence those events. We need for this both a theory which tells us on what circumstances the events in question will depend, and information on the particular circumstances which may influence the event in

---

[2] Cf. my study *The Sensory Order* (Chicago: University of Chicago Press, and London: Routledge, 1952), chapter. [Hayek does not include a chapter in the typescript, but the discussion of the limits of explanation comes in chapter 8, section 6 of his book. A *Collected Works* edition of this volume is anticipated.—Ed.]

which we are interested. Even a true theory will not enable us to make predictions of specific events unless we are able to ascertain all those relevant facts ('the initial and marginal conditions' as the philosophers of science call them) which govern the particular position. These facts may be few or many and the practical difficulty of applying our theoretical knowledge will evidently increase with the number of such facts which have to be taken into account.

The rapid progress of the physical sciences is in no small degree due to the fact that the laws which govern the phenomena in their field are generally of such character that they can be exhibited on models consisting of comparatively few elements. They refer to closed systems and to the direct relations between the comparatively few elements of which these closed systems must consist and the properties of which are known or easily ascertainable. Though they can be applied to situations involving much larger numbers of elements, their character can be exhibited on models comprising only a very few such elements whose relevant properties can be readily ascertained.

The same can hardly ever be true of the results of the interplay of the independent action of many men. What these men will do depends on the facts which they know and on how they interpret them. Even if we assume that in principle everybody's action is determined by the combined effect of his inherited constitution, all his past experience, and his knowledge of his environment at the moment when he acts, we clearly can never know all these facts for all the men who form part of any particular social structure. Their individual action must therefore remain largely unpredictable.[3] If we were in the same position with regard to the relatively simple systems with which, e.g., mechanics is concerned, because any one of the elements of such a system might at any time act in an unpredictable manner, that would be the end of the matter: no prediction of the events in the system would be possible. It has often been contended that the unpredictability of individual conduct must similarly make all significant theoretical knowledge of society impossible. I shall presently turn to the task of showing how in the case of the relatively complex structures of society it is still possible to arrive at some useful, though limited, theoretical generalizations. Before I attempt this I will however consider why we can in general in the social sciences not resort for this purpose to those techniques which the physical sciences employ in those instances where they cannot obtain sufficient information about the individual elements of a system: namely to rely instead on information about the probability or frequency with which particular attributes occur among a class of events.[4]

I do not intend to deny that there may be some problems of economic

---

[3] [Hayek used 'impredictable' for 'unpredictable' in the original manuscript.—Ed.]

[4] [In the margin Hayek wrote, probably to be inserted here, "That most of what we call relations are not statistical in this sense."—Ed.]

theory, most likely in the field of the theory of money, where such truly statistical information is helpful or perhaps indispensable. Such statistical information can, however, clearly not get us out of the difficulties which we meet in our attempts to explain the allocation of resources, the relations between the prices of commodities, or the distribution of income. While on the one hand the number of individual elements which enter into the determination of these magnitudes is clearly much too large to make it possible for us to know them all individually, they are on the other hand not numerous enough to make it possible to substitute for the information on the individual elements information about classes of such elements (statistical collectives). Prices and quantities of any particular good may be altered by the actions of a few and often even a single individual; moreover, the observable actions of individuals on which we might conceivably get statistical information is not independent of the prices which we want to explain but in fact determined by these prices. The task of the explanation of the structures which are the typical objects of social theory lies here in a range of complexity which is intermediate between the relatively simple structures with few variables with which the physical sciences largely deal, and the phenomena with which we can cope by relying on information on the frequency with which certain properties occur among large numbers of elements. In the convenient terms suggested by Warren Weaver, they are neither "problems of simplicity" nor "problems of disorganized complexity" but "problems of organized complexity."[5]

It is one of the purposes of these lectures to describe the character of the theories which we can form about phenomena where our knowledge of the elements is limited in the manner characteristic of the problems of organized complexity. Though my immediate interest is solely the problems of this sort as they arise in the field of economic theory, I hope it will appear that at least some of the considerations which apply here are equally relevant not only to the other theoretical sciences of society but also to certain problems of biology and psychology.

I will now turn to another aspect of the differences between the position in the physical and in the social sciences which, however, will soon lead me back to the same problems.

3. Intuitive and Abstract Orders

The two chief sources of scientific endeavor have been wonder and need. Of these wonder has been much the more fertile—certainly in the early stages of the growth of science. It was where man began to wonder and not where his

---

[5] Warren Weaver, "Science and Complexity", *American Scientist*, vol. 36, October 1948, pp. 536–44.

need for knowledge was greatest that science began. Astronomy and not mechanics, the phenomena of matter rather than those of life were the first fields where scientific effort succeeded, though the practical need for knowledge was probably much greater elsewhere. The reason for this is that where we wonder we already have a definite question to ask; while, however urgently we may wish to find our way in an environment which seems entirely chaotic, if we do not know what to look for, even the most attentive and persistent examination of the bare facts will not make them more intelligible. Until we have specific questions to ask, we cannot really employ our intellect.

Such questions will arise only after we have discerned some recurring pattern or order in the events. It is only the re-cognition of some such recurring pattern or order, the re-appearance of certain common features in different circumstances, which makes us wonder and ask "why?" Our minds are so made that when we notice such similarities in diversity we suspect the presence of some common agent in different situations and seek to detect it. It is to this trait of our minds that we owe most of the understanding and mastery of our environment that we have achieved.

In the world of nature, unlike the more complex phenomena of society, many such regularities are readily recognized by our senses (or 'intuitively', as the philosophers call it). We see and hear patterns as much as individual events without need for assistance from our intellect. Many of these patterns and regularities we take of course so much for granted that they do not lead to questions. But where our senses discover repeatedly the same new pattern, this causes surprise and questioning. To such curiosity we owe probably the beginning of all systematic knowledge of nature.

Our unaided senses, however, do not enable us to discover such order or patterns everywhere. Marvellous as in this respect their intuitive capacity is, it is still limited. Only relatively simple orders will spontaneously obtrude themselves on our sense perception. While our eyes and ears generally discern shapes and rhythms and similar simple patterns, they will not spontaneously discover orders of a more complex character. In such instances the conceptual capacities of our minds must assist the perceptual capacities of our senses. (This is what we mean when we describe such an order as abstract rather than concrete: it cannot be seen, heard, or touched but only traced by our intellect.) In order to discover such an order we must already possess a conception of the principle of arrangement of the elements, explicitly know of a rule by which they are related. The discipline which normally provides the abstract schemata of possible orders, which the physical sciences then often discover in the events of the world, is mathematics. Man would probably never have discovered regularities in the movements of planets if he had not already been familiar with the abstract concepts of the circle and the ellipse, he would probably never have discovered the laws of gravity if he had not already been familiar with the concept of acceleration, and he would never have formed modern field concepts if the conception of functions of several variables had not already been elaborated by mathematics.

4. Theoretical Problems Raised by Undesigned Orders Only[6]

But while in the case of natural phenomena the need for such abstract schemata of order arises only at a comparatively late stage and the unaided eye will discover all sort of patterns and order,[7] no such order will reveal itself to the observer of society—or at least no order calling for a theoretical explanation. When we look at the life of men in society, our senses discern no such order or regularity as the movement of the stars or the waves, the shapes of the different animals or plants, or even that the mountains and clouds present to us. To the naïve observer the phenomena of society appear entirely disorderly or chaotic. There is no occasion for wonder, no reason to ask "why", because our senses discern no pattern or order in the movements of men—or at least no pattern which surprises us because we do not have a ready explanation. Of course there are such regular movements as that of a body of soldiers on the parade ground, or of a corps de ballet, or of the traffic on the roads, but in these instances we know why they move as they do: they move according to a human design, obeying the instructions of some men, or (as in the case of the spatial and temporal patterns of traffic) in adaptations to circumstances of time and place. Why somebody wants such an organized body of men to move in such a manner and why they obey his wish, or why the traffic moves as it does, may also raise important and interesting questions, but they are questions of a different kind from those which, e.g., the regularities of the market raise.

It is perhaps natural that men were long inclined to ascribe all order they could discern in social phenomena to a designing mind. They tried to do so

---

[6] [This heading was added in longhand by Hayek.—Ed.]

[7] It is probably because of these instances where patterns obtrude themselves on sense observation that the inductivist illusion continues that there is a direct way from observation to theory, or that, if we only look long enough at the phenomena, we shall discover an order in them. Actually the instances in which our senses interpret the events in terms of a pattern involve a process similar to that where the mind forms a hypothesis which then has to be tested, and it has been well said that "there is a sense, then, in which seeing is a 'theory-laden' undertaking." See Norwood R. Hanson, *Patterns of Discovery: An Inquiry into the Conceptual Foundations of Science* (Cambridge: Cambridge University Press, 1958), p. 19. In a way this was understood already by Adam Ferguson, who in a remarkable passage in his *An Essay on the History of Civil Society* (Edinburgh: Printed for A. Millar and T. Caddel, London, and A. Kincaid and J. Bell, Edinburgh, 1767), p. 39, said that "the inferences of thought are sometimes not to be distinguished from the perceptions of sense."

long enough even with regard to the phenomena of nature and it was only much later that it was recognized that in the relations between men there existed also recurring patterns which were not the result of human design and that these regularities—and only these regularities—provided an object for theoretical sciences of social phenomena.

5. Higher Level Regularities

Yet these patterns were not only not intuitively perceptible but possessed an abstract character so that they could be traced only after the theoretical scheme was known; there was also the further difficulty that in any particular instances the number of factors determining the concrete manifestation of the pattern is too large to make their individual ascertainment possible or to derive from them the specific relations between any particular parts. In fact, without the knowledge of all the individual facts determining the pattern that will form itself at a particular place and time, all we are able to do is to speak about the kind of pattern that will form itself, about a pattern that is defined by certain characteristics or attributes, without being able to specify the detail. I shall say that all we know in such instances are certain 'higher level regularities' but not the detail—a distinction which needs careful explanation if it is not to mislead.

A restriction to statements about such 'higher level regularities' is not unknown in the natural sciences. Crystallography, e.g., until about fifty years ago, was almost entirely confined to the description of classes of crystals, such as tetragonal, hexagonal, etc., to which all the different crystals of a particular mineral would belong. Within each class of this kind there would be a number of different crystal shapes which were similar to each other in such respects as the numbers of planes of symmetry and the like. It would thus be possible to state that any crystal of a certain mineral would show certain relations between its parts, but not which of the various crystals satisfying these relations would occur in a particular instance.

The term 'higher level regularities'[8] which I have used to describe the content of such statements about the general character of an order is meant to indicate that it does not refer to relations between particular elements of such an order, but only to relations between relations, or even relations between relations between relations between the elements. It refers to the fact that the pattern that will form itself will possess certain characteristics or satisfy certain conditions, although we may not be in a position to say what the relative position of the elements will be at any particular place.

There is perhaps no better illustration of what I mean by higher level regu-

---

[8] [Hayek indicated a footnote to be inserted here, but none is found on the manuscript.—Ed.]

larities than is provided by those systems of equations in which mathematical economists describe the conditions of market equilibrium. In the general form in which they are stated by the theorist, they contain necessarily a number of 'constants' or 'parameters' for which numerical values would have to be inserted if we were to determine the individual prices and quantities. They are sometimes presented as if such a determination of the particular prices were their main purpose, and I have seen physical scientists sorely puzzled why we should ever bother to state these equations if admittedly we were not in a position to ascertain the constants which would have to be inserted to determine the values of the unknowns in the equation. Even many economists seem to be loath to admit that these systems of equations are not a step towards specific prediction of individual events, but the final results of our efforts in this field, the description of the kind of order or of the higher level regularities which we can expect to find, but which we shall never be able to translate into particular predictions of particular prices or quantities. The description of the pattern or order, which in the natural sciences generally is a tool which enables us to derive from the observable part of such an order the unobserved parts and thus to arrive at a prediction of specific events, is with us the results itself.

This does not mean, of course, that the assertions contained in those systems of equations cannot be tested, at least in principle. Since they do assert that under certain conditions certain relations between the observed magnitudes will prevail, whether they in fact do or do not prevail is an empirical question. The practical difficulty is usually to ascertain whether the conditions under which the statement is asserted to be true are satisfied in any given position rather than whether the asserted relations between the magnitudes do exist.

In an earlier discussion of this kind of problem[9] I have described such explanations as mere "explanations of the principle" as distinguished from explanations of the detail. That expression I had borrowed from the discussions of biology and psychology where we constantly meet statements such as that it is possible "in principle" to explain how this or that phenomenon is produced, though we are not able to give a full explanation of any one particular instance of the phenomenon. Perhaps the expression that in such instances we are able to explain only 'higher level regularities' but not the detail in which they will manifest themselves makes it clearer what is meant.

6. The Rôle of the Economic Calculus

In order to be able to trace in the world of fact an abstract order (or higher level regularities) we must be in possession of a description of such an order:

---

[9]See my article "Degrees of Explanation", *British Journal for the Philosophy of Science*, vol. 6, November 1955, pp. 209–25. [This paper now appears as chapter 6 of the present volume.—Ed.]

we must know the characteristic properties which define it if we are to be able to decide whether any particular arrangements of the elements we find is an instance of such an order. The description of such an order will however itself not be an empirical but a deductive statement: it will consist in the elaboration of the implications of the principles determining the order, and as such a derivation of implications of given assumptions it will, like any statement of mathematics, be valid irrespective of [whether][10] any such order actually exists anywhere in the world.

This does of course not mean that, again as in the case of mathematics, the *occasion* for working out the description of this kind of pattern will not often have been some empirical task. Indeed in the field of these logical foundations of economics, or the 'economic calculus' as I will call them, much of the basic work has been done by men who themselves believed that they were engaged in empirical studies of individual behaviour while what they in fact did was to develop a method for describing or classifying the patterns which are to be found in the world of fact. Much of what we know as the pure theory of utility and of production indeed proves on closer inspection to be no more than such a logical scheme, a description of a significant type of order which, once we know it, we then can indeed discover to exist in the real world. But it tells us nothing about why it exists, what forces bring it about, or what are the conditions for its realization.

In the case of economics the significance of the abstract picture of the order is, however, not merely that it enables us to distinguish orderly arrangements from others—that it describes the peculiar kind of order which is being produced by the forces with which the empirical science of economics deals. It also shows the significance which the constant approach towards such an order has for the achievement of human ends. In fact, once we understand the character of this order, it appears that, though it is not designed by men for this purpose, its constant maintenance is an essential condition for the realization of human ends, and in fact that this order has certain similarities with the arrangements which a directing mind would have to make if he were aiming at the achievement of certain purposes. Like some of the patterns of biological phenomena, those of the market are sometimes best comprehended if we regard them as quasi-teleological, that is, *as if* they were designed for a purpose, although, of course, we know that there is no such directing mind, no 'invisible hand' which directed events to such a purpose. Yet what Adam Smith really meant with his celebrated—and much derided—phrase about the invisible hand was in fact that it was the spontaneous appearance of an order which served human purposes which called for an explanation by a theoretical science.

The elements of the economic calculus, at least up to the point where they become familiar textbook material, will be the object of my next lecture. It

---

[10] [This word was added by the editor to make the sentence make sense.—Ed.]

deals, as must have become clear by now, with the logical connections between the parts of a single plan of action drawn up by an individual mind on the basis of his knowledge of the ends to be served and of the available means. It is in its nature entirely hypothetical and deductive, i.e., of the "if so-and-so, then so-and-so necessarily follows" character. The purpose of elaborating it is to enable us to recognize a certain kind of order when we meet it, by giving us an abstract statement of the conditions which any instance of such an order must satisfy; and also to show what depends for us on the fact that the market tends to bring about at all times at least some approach to such an order.

In some respects the pattern which the economic calculus describes has of course great similarity with the patterns described by those systems of equations to which I referred before and which are intended to describe the conditions of market equilibrium. Compared with the latter the economic calculus has however the advantage, as it seems to me, that it is admittedly no more than an abstract description of a possible kind of pattern and does not involve all those somewhat questionable assumptions which are implied in the assertion of the existence of a market equilibrium. The equilibrium of the market presupposes that both the knowledge and the plans of action of all the individuals participating in it are adjusted to each other in a particular manner, and how this adjustment is being brought about or under what conditions it will be brought about is the main problem which the empirical science of economics has to explain.

7. The Difference from the Empirical Science of Economics

If the economic calculus tells us what to regard as an instance of an order in economic affairs, and what is the significance of this sort of order, it can of course tell us nothing about why or under what conditions such an order will form itself or how closely events in the real world will approach such an order under various conditions. To give such an account of the causal mechanism which produces the order is clearly a task for an empirical science and can never be solved by the deductive methods of pure logic.

It is true that at least one distinguished economist, a scholar whom I greatly admire and to whom I owe much inspiration, insists that the whole theory of human action, including all economic theory, is of such an *a priori* character. But it seems to me that, just as the majority of economists overlook that there is a distinct body of propositions of a purely analytical character which all economists use as tools and which deserves to be separately expounded, so Professor von Mises tends to overlook that this logical groundwork does not yet provide an explanation of how things actually happen but stands to such an explanation of the real events in about the same relation as mathematics stands to physics.

The possession of a description of the significant type of order merely enables us to recognize it when we find it, that is, enables us to distinguish in the world of fact structures which possess certain characteristics from others which do not. But it tells us nothing about the forces which produce this order (or the causal mechanism which brings it about), the conditions under which it will appear, the degree to which this order will in fact be approached and how much any given failure to approximate to this pattern matters for the achievement of human ends. All these are questions where the answers cannot be deduced as logical implications of a given set of premises, but require an account of the modus operandi of a process which brings about a state of affairs corresponding to the pattern described by the economic calculus.

I believe the essence of this causal process which produces the market order is a process of communication of knowledge or information, and that the main function of prices is to serve as means of communicating such knowledge which the different participants in the market must possess in order to fit their action into the overall pattern. I hope in my last lecture in this series to give a brief account of this Communication Function of the market, though I am afraid it will have to be in very general terms. It is an approach which seems to me to be very helpful, but, though I have been interested in it now for many years, I must confess that I have not got much further with it than when I first sketched the conception, and I shall consequently have little to say that is new.

Before that last lecture, however, I have inserted one on a topic that at first may seem not too closely connected with my main theme, the relations between economics and technology. But though these have many aspects which are not directly connected with the central topic of these lectures, I have selected the subject because it will give me an opportunity to illustrate further one of the chief points of my argument, the difference between the co-ordination of the action of many men by direction according to a single plan based on concentrated knowledge, and the mutual adjustment of the independent action of many individuals guided by the fragments of knowledge dispersed among them.

8. Limitations of Knowledge and Policy

In conclusion I want briefly to return to some of the considerations from which I started. It was one of my aims to show that, compared with some of the natural sciences, the aim of economic theory must remain a comparatively modest one, not because of any immaturity of our discipline but because of the nature of its object. Since the particular actions of the individuals which make up the economic system are largely unpredictable, we cannot achieve that natural science ideal of the 'prediction and control' of particular events. It seems to me to be of the greatest importance that we fully recognize and come to terms with this limitation of our knowledge, because the pretence to more knowledge than we possess or can obtain has certain dangerous consequences. It creates a great temptation to create conditions under which we would be able to predict specific economic events and to assure that particular things will happen. But this is incompatible with the main benefit we derive from the market system, namely that it makes use of more knowledge of circumstances than any single mind can possess; but so long as it does this it must also necessarily produce results which nobody can predict.

I have suggested on another occasion[11] that in fields like ours it would probably be more appropriate if instead of speaking of prediction and control we described our aim as 'orientation and cultivation.' Though our knowledge is not sufficient to predict or produce specific events, it enables us not only to comprehend the significance of the events we observe but also to create conditions which improve the prospects of a desirable outcome—or which are conducive to the formation and preservation of that orderliness of which success of our individual efforts so largely depends.

The danger of the pretence of the possession of more knowledge than we in fact possess is that this will tempt us into a suppression of those spontaneous ordering forces on which we depend and which we cannot replace by deliberate control so long as we are not able to master all the factual knowledge of all the men who take part in the free process. It is this realization of the permanent limitations of our knowledge which provides the decisive argument against the attempts at conscious control of the whole economic process. Though it is sometimes said that scientific knowledge by itself can never force on us particular views on political issues, here the two are at least closely connected. I have argued elsewhere that the awareness of our irremediable ignorance of most of what is known to somebody is the chief basis of the argument for liberty.[12] This is especially true in the economic field. If it appears that the market mechanism leads to the effective utilization of more knowledge than any directing agency can possess, this is the chief foundation of the case for economic freedom and it is important that economic science to not by false pretences disguise those limitations of knowledge which are of such decisive importance for our choice of a desirable economic order.

---

[11] "Degrees of Explanation", loc. cit. [See this volume, chapter 6, section 9.—Ed.]

[12] [Hayek refers here to his argument in *The Constitution of Liberty* (Chicago: University of Chicago Press, 1960), e.g., chapter 2, section 4, where he states, "The case for individual freedom rests chiefly on the recognition of the inevitable ignorance of all of us concerning a great many of the factors on which the achievement of our ends and welfare depends." The book was published the year before Hayek's Virginia lectures; now see *The Constitution of Liberty*, ed. Ronald Hamowy, vol. 17 (2011) of *The Collected Works of F. A. Hayek* (Chicago: University of Chicago Press; London: Routledge).—Ed.]

Lecture II
The Economic Calculus[1]

The subject of this lecture is one which has interested me for many years, though I still have not got very far with it. Its elementary parts are deceptively simple, so simple indeed that to economists it seemed generally not worthwhile explicitly to state them. Yet any attempt at a rigorous systematic statement of the main body of what I call the economic calculus soon encounters real difficulties through which I have never quite found my way. I can, of course, in this lecture give you no more than the elements of this calculus—or, what amounts to even less, describe its general characteristics instead of stating its main propositions. It still seems to me, however, a task worth undertaking; at any rate, it is an essential step of the argument of this series of lectures.

In my first lecture I described the economic calculus as a technique for describing the patterns (or the regularity or order) which we find in the economic phenomena—similar to the way in which mathematics serves as a technique for describing the patterns we find in the physical world. It enables us to distinguish some arrangements of economic events as instances of a kind of order from other arrangements which are disorderly, and to understand why the tendency of things to arrange themselves in this kind of order is significant for us. It does of course not relieve us of the task of explaining how, or by what mechanism, and under what conditions, this kind of order will be produced. The latter is the task of the empirical science of economics for which the economic calculus is merely a tool. This seems to me now the correct way of defining its character.

But it was not from this methodological angle that I was originally led to think about the economic calculus. It was rather the question of what is the chief lasting benefit we derive from the study of economics—or what those people had in common whom I recognized as good economists, even though their knowledge of concrete facts might be very different, an attribute which on the other hand I often found lacking in many people who knew a great deal about the facts of economic life and even about the theory of the market, and, I am afraid, also in not a few of the highly specialized econometricians of the younger generation. It seemed to me that at least a substantial part of the benefit I had derived from the study of economics, and of what I accepted as the criterion of a good economist in others, was not any knowledge of fact, or

[1] [The hand-drawn diagrams replicate those found in the manuscript in box 138, folder 17, of the Hayek Collection at the Hoover Institution Archives. It looks like they were hastily drawn in. The interested reader may wish to consult the diagrams in Hayek's LSE lecture notes from 1943 to 1944, given when LSE had evacuated to Cambridge, where many of the diagrams are drawn with more care. These may be found in the Hayek Collection, box 138, folder 10, Hoover Institution Archives, Stanford University, Calif.—Ed.]

even of particular laws which economic phenomena obey, but rather a capacity of discovering and refuting certain kinds of fallacies of reasoning. I don't think there can be any doubt that this is one of the most common and not least important tasks of the economist to correct not errors of fact but errors of reasoning.[2]

I came to a similar result when I asked myself what it chiefly was that we should wish other trained minds, such as scientists or engineers, lawyers, generals or clergymen,[3] to know about economics—or what makes communication with them about problems of economic policy often so difficult. It generally does not matter that they are often not familiar with the institutions and the concrete mechanism of the market—and some of them, especially the engineers, often know more about the facts than the theoretical economist. The real obstacles to communication are the fallacies, in the strict sense of the word, which often seem so plausible to the non-economist and make him attack as instances of obvious waste developments which to the economist seem desirable and to conform to the orderly pattern of a well-functioning economy. I am thinking of such instances as the depletion of the stock of some replaceable natural resource which is very generally regarded as clear evidence of harmful waste, although it may be the perfectly sensible and economic thing to do; or the complaint about the waste of expensive machinery standing idle for long periods, although it may have been entirely rationally installed in the expectation that this would be the case; or if it is adduced as clear evidence of the wastefulness of the market, as I have recently seen it argued with respect to some South American country, if all the best wheat land (i.e., nearly all the land capable of producing the highest wheat yield per acre) was in fact used for growing corn (even though some of it was only of second-best quality for growing corn)—of course because the comparative advantage of using that land rather than other land for corn was greater than in the case of wheat—or, as final illustration, the opposite but equally common complaints that either obsolete equipment is scrapped although it could have lasted for many more years, or that it is not replaced by the more modern equipment available, which are both often quoted as clear evidence of waste, although either may in different circumstances be the economically desirable procedure.

The point about these instances is that where the arguments of the laymen go wrong is not on questions of fact or even on questions of theoretical explanation, but on questions of logic; and that the falsity of the popular views can in consequence be demonstrated by working out the implications of the

---

[2] [Cf. Henry Simons's comment "Economics is primarily useful, both to the student and to the political leader, as a prophylactic against popular fallacies." See Henry Calvert Simons, *The Simons' Syllabus*, ed. Gordon Tullock (Fairfax, VA: Center for the Study of Public Choice, George Mason University, 1983), p. 2.—Ed.]

[3] [Hayek wrote in 'ministers' above 'clergymen' but did not cross out 'clergymen.'—Ed.]

assumptions in the same manner in which we demonstrate a mathematical proposition. This led me to ask the question whether the skill in discovering such fallacies or errors of reasoning on economic matters could not be taught systematically. Evidently a technique of reasoning should be capable of being taught separately from any factual knowledge, just as logic or mathematics are being taught. What was this logical groundwork of economics like?

Some attempts of isolating those issues have traditionally of course been made under the realistic disguise of discussing either the situation of a Robinson Crusoe, or, more rarely, that of the dictator of a communist society.[4] Either of these assumptions however tends to bring in irrelevant factual considerations. What we want is a quite general representation of the problems faced by any person who has to allocate scarce means between alternative uses.

This definition of the specifically economic task, which came to be widely accepted just as I started thinking about these problems, directs our attention to the essentials.[5] I had at first thought that what was required was a general 'Logic of Choice.' But I soon became aware that the word 'choice' was ambiguous and that in economics we were concerned with only one particular kind of choice, that made necessary by the scarcity of means. The distinction is of sufficient importance to justify a few words about it.

We speak of choosing both when we would like to have both, A and B, but can have only either, and when we would like to have only A or B but have to make up our mind which we want. Only the first kind of choice raises economic problems while the second may raise technological or aesthetic or perhaps even ethical problems. A woman choosing from her jewelry box what to wear in the evening, a surgeon choosing the most suitable knife for an incision or anybody else choosing from his toolbox what he wants for a particular task are not choosing between things they want at the same time or cumulatively. They want only one of them and are endeavouring to find out which achieves the desired result more effectively. They are trying to discover their own taste, or the technical efficiency of the means, both of which are data for the economic problem proper.

The choice which is involved in economic tasks is of a different kind. It is a choice between aims all of which we should like to achieve but of which, in the existing conditions, we can achieve only some. What makes them, against

---

[4] [For an example of the latter approach, see F. A. Hayek, *The Pure Theory of Capital* [1941], ed. Lawrence H. White, vol. 12 (2007) of *The Collected Works of F. A. Hayek* (Chicago: University of Chicago Press; London: Routledge), Part II.—Ed.]

[5] [The definition was provided by Hayek's friend and LSE colleague Lionel Robbins in *An Essay on the Nature and Significance of Economic Science*, 2nd ed. (London: Macmillan, 1935), p. 16: "Economics is the science which studies human behaviour as a relationship between ends and scarce means which have alternative uses." Hayek first wrote about the "Logic of Choice" in "Economics and Knowledge", reprinted as chapter 1 of the present volume.—Ed.]

our wishes, alternatives, is that some conditions for their achievement, some 'means' as we call them, are sufficient for the realization of only some of them. It is only choice thus made necessary by the scarcity of means which creates an economic problem. The problem is not what we prefer, but what are the alternatives between which we can choose.[6]

The economic calculus is mainly a technique for describing the different structures which the means-ends relations can produce. It makes one assumption which may somewhat limit its usefulness, namely that means and ends are always clearly distinct. Although probably misleading in some respects, this assumption seems indispensable if we are to achieve a tolerably clear scheme. There are various possible dodges by which we could take account of such obvious facts as that, e.g., work may both itself be a pleasure and therefore be an end, and at the same time a means for achieving other ends. But they are not really satisfactory and too complicated to be considered here.

There are one or two other difficulties which a more systematic exposition would have to clear up at the very beginning, chiefly that of the criteria by which we classify means and ends as being of the same or of different kinds. I can here merely briefly say that the most adequate procedure seems to me to be to start by treating all ends as unique individuals, then class as means of the same kind all those which can be used in the same manner and in the same combinations to satisfy the same ends, and finally to treat as similar (but never as quite the same) ends all those which can be achieved by the identical means. To do this properly is one of the more bothersome steps in systematically building up the economic calculus.

There is, however, another and more interesting point I have to bring out before giving you the general scheme of the economic calculus. This is that to begin with we shall have to take into account not only scarce means but all means which are known to be necessary conditions for the achievement of the ends. The reason for this is that if we really start from the beginning (and do not consider an economic system which has been in operation for some time and has developed fairly continuously), we do not know which of the means are scarce until we have completed the task of allocating them among the competing ends. Why this should be so will become clear presently.

And now to the general scheme. I shall graphically represent the position where a quantity of means of the same kind can be used for achieving a variety of ends thus [see fig. A.1].[7] If that exhausted the economic problem, its solution would of course be exceedingly simple. We should just satisfy the

---

[6] [This sentence was handwritten by Hayek.—Ed.]

[7] [Hayek inserted hand-drawn diagrams to accompany the text. This picture and those that follow were produced by tracing over the hand-drawn diagrams, which accounts for their rough, but authentic, appearance. Hayek's drawings were inserted in-line. The editor added the bracketed callouts to indicate the original placement of the figures.—Ed.]

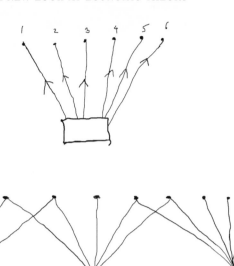

Figure A.1

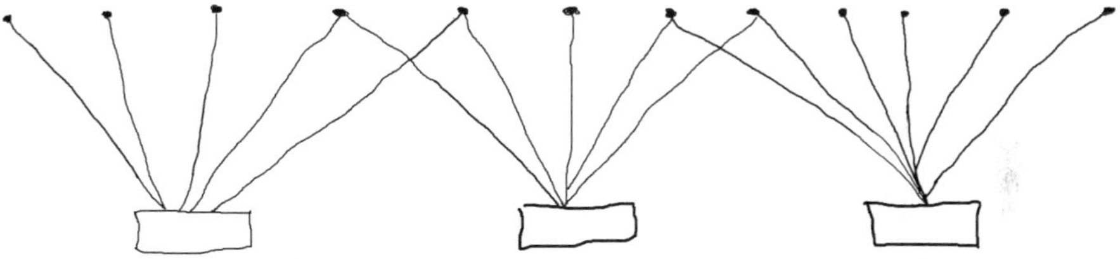

Figure A.2

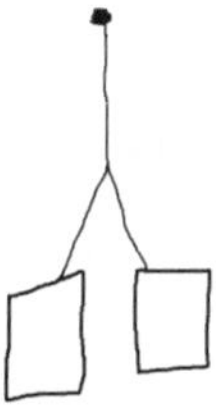

Figure A.3

individual ends in order of their importance and stop when we run out of means. Problems arise only when at least some of the ends either require for their achievement several different means or can be achieved alternatively by different means. This gives us a scheme like this [see fig. A.2]. Strictly speaking I ought here to distinguish between the condition where a given end can be achieved by either the means m or the means n, and the case where m and n are jointly required for that purpose, and perhaps represent the first as I did and the second by[8] [see figure A.3]. Since we shall, however, later see that both the

[8] Similarly there may be instances where a given means can be used not as I have assumed to satisfy the ends A or B but to achieve both ends at the same time, and this may be similarly represented by [figure A.4].

Figure A.4

cumulative and the alternative requirement of different means for the achievement of given ends are merely extreme limiting cases of a continuous range of variation, I shall for the present not further bother about it.

The chief point which my scheme is intended to bring out, however, is the extent of the connectedness between means and ends which is brought about by what I would like to call the 'bi-polarity of the means-ends order', or the fact that the decisions become interdependent both through the commonness of different means for the same ends and the commonness of different ends for the same means. This is in fact the reason why we can speak of one coherent economic system and the task of allocation of resources must be solved for this economic system as a whole. Within such a single economic system we have a general connectedness of all decisions which means that every decision to be appropriate should be part of a single comprehensive plan.

I shall not attempt to show to what complexity the scheme will grow merely as a result of the number of different means and ends which may be part of one and the same economic system. I will specially mention only one kind of elaboration of which it is capable and which is particularly significant, namely that it can be used to show that production is carried on in successive stages and that many kinds of means can be used, not only directly to satisfy final ends, but also (or perhaps only) to produce still other means. We then get some such complication of our scheme as this [see fig. A.5]. Though these elaborate schemes are sometimes quite useful, especially in connection with some problems of capital, the most helpful schemata are generally the simplest. For instance, the characteristic situation which produces rent phenomena can be represented thus [see fig. A.6], where the little circles represent classes of similar ends (or final commodities) and the rectangles, as before, quantities of means or factors of production. The point this diagram is intended to bring out is that if of the two means (or factors of production) m and n one can be used only for the end A (or is highly specific) while the other has a great variety of uses (or is very versatile) a change in the urgency of the end A will clearly have a much stronger effect on the value of m than on that of n, because n has many alternative uses to which or from which it can be shifted whenever it is more or less urgently needed for A.

There are two things which even such a simple illustration shows. The first is that to each type of structure pattern represented by this kind of diagram

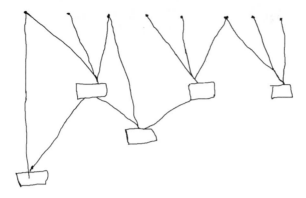

Figure A.5

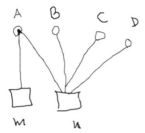

Figure A.6

correspond certain movement patterns—characteristic relations between the changes of values of the different means or ends according to their position in the pattern. The second, which would become more obvious if I had time to modify these schemata a little more, but which probably even so stand out clearly enough, is that these typical schemata can be varied gradually and that in consequence, e.g., such a distinction as that between a 'rent factor' and a 'cost factor' is a matter of degree and not an absolute difference. This is a very important lesson which can hardly be stressed enough. There is an understandable tendency in economic theory to make such distinctions clear by concentrating upon what Ricardo called "strong cases" with the result that frequently the impression is given that we deal with differences in kind rather than differences in degree.[9] This thinking in terms of dichotomies, in either-or terms, is however extremely dangerous in economics. In most of the classifica-

[9]["My object was to elucidate principles, and to do this I imagined strong cases that I might shew the operation of those principles." David Ricardo to Thomas Malthus, May 4, 1820, in David Ricardo, *Letters 1819–June 1821*, vol. 8 (1952) of *The Works and Correspondence of David Ricardo*, ed. Piero Sraffa, with the collaboration of M. H. Dobb (Cambridge: Royal Economic Society), p. 184.—Ed.]

tion of economic objects we have established we actually deal with properties which these objects may possess to different degrees. That applies not only to such distinctions as those between durable and non-durable goods, liquid and non-liquid assets, capital goods and consumers goods, and the like, but even to the distinction between money and goods. I sometimes feel that it would be better if instead of nouns we used adjectives such as capitalish, moneyish, etc., to indicate that objects possessed certain significant attributes to a higher or smaller degree, rather than being compelled to say that they either were capital, or money, or that they were not.

But I have allowed myself to be led away from my main theme and must return to the considerations of the different types of means-ends structures which the economic calculus describes. The overall picture given by the arrow diagram tells us of course only part of the story. It shows what one might call the qualitative aspects of the means-ends structure while to get at the quantitative aspects we have to analyse further the position at the points of inter-communication and the order of rank of the different ends. This is of course essentially what the so-called theory of production and the theory of utility do, and it is useful to think of the former as a technique for describing the variety of positions which can occur at the 'joints' of the arrow diagram.

Of the two aspects of the means-ends structure, the usefulness of any one kind of means for various ends and the achievability of any one end by various different means, I shall explicitly consider only the latter. But most of what I shall have to say can be applied, with appropriate modifications, also to the former. The case of joint products, e.g., raises exactly the same kind of problems as that of the variable or fixed proportions of the factors which I shall consider in a moment.

I have briefly mentioned before that the instances, which I then distinguished, where a given end can be achieved either by one means or by another, and where it could be achieved only by the use of certain combinations of several different means, were in fact merely extreme limiting cases of a continuous range of variations or intermediate positions which it is the object of the theory of production to describe. Since I shall avail myself of the technique it has developed for that purpose I shall also use its terminology and from now onward speak, instead of means and ends, of factors and products. To keep things as simple as possible I shall throughout discuss the problems on the assumption that there are only two different factors and two different products, but the argument can of course be extended to any number of factors or products we like.[10]

---

[10] [In the original typed version, the following sentence appeared as a separate paragraph here, but was scratched out in the revision: "I apologize if I now spend a little time on what to many of you will be familiar textbook matter, but before commenting on the significance of these elements of the theory of production I cannot avoid briefly stating them."—Ed.]

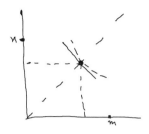

Figure A.7

Figure A.8

The familiar method of representation of the relations between quantities of factors of production and quantities of the product is, of course, to measure the quantities of the factors of production on co-ordinates and then to indicate the different combinations of such factors which will yield a given quantity of the product by equi-product curves of isoquants, which can be conceived as contour lines representing the height of a hill corresponding to the resulting quantity of the product. If we call the two factors required for the product A M and N, then the one extreme case where the quantity a of A can be produced either by m or by n would be indicated by corresponding columns over the points m and n; while the other extreme case would be that in which M and N, to produce A, would have to be used in the fixed proportion $m_1 : n_1$. The intermediate case is of course that in which the given quantity of A can be produced by various combinations of m's and n's, either at a constant marginal rate of substitution or at a variable one. That is, the quantity a of the product could be produced by any combination of m and n represented by the straight line (in the case of constant marginal rates of substitution) or by a curve (in the case of decreasing marginal rates of substitution) [see fig. A.7]. A more familiar way of representing the same situation is this [see fig. A.8].

Historically, the case of fixed proportions of the factors has been regarded as the norm, and I understand that as recently as the beginning of the so-called theory of linear programming this assumption led into serious trouble. The interesting point, which can be demonstrated as a matter of pure logic, that is by means of the economic calculus, is that in order to be scarce (or at least in order to be more than intermittently scarce) the proportion in which a factor

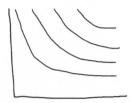

Figure A.9

can be combined with others must be variable at least in some of its uses. If the proportion in which it had to be combined with other factors were fixed in all its uses, it would of course be pure accident if the quantities of the different factors which were available were such that, if used in those fixed proportions, the whole supply of all the factors could be used up; and if by accident this ever should be the case, the slightest change in the relative demand for the different products must bring it about that a surplus of one factor or another would appear, that is, that it would cease to be scarce—not because there was absolutely too much of it, but because some part could not be used for lack of the complementary factor.

That there should be a *logical* necessity that a scarce factor which can be used only in combination with other factors should at least in some of its uses be capable of employment in variable proportions with other factors is one of those conclusions of the economic calculus which at first seem surprising because they look like empirical or testable statements yet are deduced analytically from the definition of scarce factors. The supply of a factor which can be used only in combination with a fixed proportion of other factors can be clearly fully used only if there is enough of that other factor available.

Similarly, it seems that it is a logical necessity that if of two different factors of production which are used in combination both are scarce, changes in their proportion must lead to decreasing returns in terms of the product. In other words, if the quantity of the one factor is kept constant but that of the other increased by constant increments, the resulting increments of the product must be decreasing. If that were not so, the same output could be achieved from the use of a much smaller quantity of the first factor and what we had in excess would be abundant.

This fact of decreasing marginal returns which is a condition that a factor can be scarce must, however, not be confused with the fact of decreasing marginal rates of substitution which we express by drawing the contour lines of our production function as curves rather than as straight lines, i.e., thus [see fig. A.9] rather than thus [see fig. A.10]. That the former is more likely to be true of the majority of cases is an empirical fact and not a necessary conse-

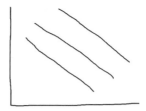

Figure A.10

quence of our assumptions that the factors in question are scarce—although, if the isoquants were in fact all straight lines, this would produce a somewhat peculiar and highly unstable position which I cannot consider here.

The same diagram which I have used to represent the production function can, of course, also be used to represent the relative utility of final products and in that case is called a set of indifference curves because all the points on any such curve represent combinations of the two commodities which are of equal value to the choosing person. Here the situation is slightly different and if the commodities are to be different commodities in the economic sense, the curves must really be curves and not straight lines, because the latter would mean that they are perfect substitutes, which is how commodities of the same kind are defined.

I must now try briefly to show how those parts of the theory of production and utility which state the conditions of optimum use of resources can be fitted into the general scheme of the economic calculus—to which, in my opinion, they really belong. In restating them I shall try to be very brief and thereby probably succeed only in boring those who are familiar with this part of economic theory and be unintelligible to those who are not. Yet it is inevitable that I sketch it at least briefly if I am to show how what I have discussed so far links up with the established parts of economic theory.

On the assumptions I have so far used that there are only two factors m and n and two commodities a and b the question then is reduced to how the available quantities of m and n are to be distributed between the production of a and b. For each of these two commodities we shall have of course different production functions showing the results of using different quantities of m and n [see fig. A.11].

The next step is a device for combining the two production functions so that we can show the result of various distributions of the factors between the two products. The trick by which this is done is of course to turn one of the production functions round by 180° and then so to superimpose it upon the other that we can simultaneously show how much of each of the two factors is used for the production of each of the two commodities. This will be obtained if

Figure A.11

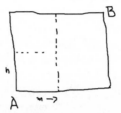

Figure A.12

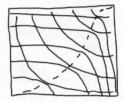

Figure A.13

the sides of the rectangle we have obtained represent the total quantities of the two factors available, so that if we measure the quantity used for the production of one commodity along one co-ordinate, the remaining part represents how much of the factor is left for the production of the other commodity [see fig. A.12]. If we now insert into the diagram the two sets of isoquants it becomes evident at once that only some of the many possible distributions of factors between the production of the two commodities will ever be rational or optimal. If we arbitrarily pick a point representing such a distribution, it will nearly always be possible to increase the output of either or both the commodities by changing the distribution of the factors between the products. We find that only the points at which the isoquants touch and do not intersect are such optimal points and by connecting them we obtain a new curve which represents the locus of all combinations which alone will have to be considered [see fig. A.13].

Except in very special circumstances, which will occur only rarely and accidentally, this new curve will again be a real curve, i.e., not a straight line, and this has a very definite significance. It means that, as we successively transfer factors from the production of A to the production of B, the quantitative proportion in which the two factors are represented in each parcel transferred will constantly change. Evidently it would be a rather unlikely accident if the most efficient distribution of the factors between the two commodities would be such that in the production of each they would be used in the same proportion. In terms of the diagram this would mean that the points of contact between the two curves would lie on a straight line connecting the origins of the two systems of co-ordinates. In that case an expansion of the production of A at the expense of that of B, or vice versa, would mean that factors would be transferred from the one to the other in the same proportion in which they are used in the production of both A and B; and each successive transfer of such constant batches of factors would decrease the output of the one and increase the output of the other by constant amounts, that is, the output of each product could be increased at constant costs in terms of the other.

Usually, however, we shall find that the relative need for the two factors in the two branches of production will be different and that in consequence relatively more of one factor will be used in the production of one commodity and relatively more of the other factor in the production of the second commodity. If that is so, a shift of factors from one to the other will involve the transfer of changing combinations of the two factors. As a result, constant sacrifices of the one product will lead only to decreasing additions to the output of the other, or, what comes to the same thing, constant additions to the output of one product can be obtained only at the cost of increasing reductions of the output of the other.

This situation is most conveniently represented by another diagram, the transformation curve, in which the two co-ordinates measure the quantities of the output of the two commodities A and B which can be produced at the same time from the given supply of factors. If a is the maximum of A which could be produced if no B at all were required and b the corresponding maximum of B, then the case of constant costs (or constant returns) in terms of each other would be represented by a straight line while the case of decreasing returns (or increasing costs) would be represented by a curve [see fig. A.14].

There is a significant difference between the assumptions underlying this diagram and those I have used before. While the production functions represent, as it were, technical data, properties, or capacities which the objects possess as such, the present diagram refers to one particular position determined by the specific quantities of the two factors which are assumed to be available. That I can get so much of B for so much of A is not a general technical fact

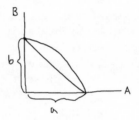

Figure A.14

Figure A.15

but a circumstance determined by the particular quantities of the two factors at my disposal—the result of my solution of the optimum problem by following the path at which the marginal rates of substitution of the two factors are always the same in the production of the two commodities.

I will now rapidly complete the statement of the conditions of optimum use before finally commenting on the significance of it as part of the economic calculus. Since I have already introduced indifference curves as a means of representing the relative importance of the different combinations of the two products, the final step is very simple. All I need to do is to superimpose this diagram expressing preferences and the transformation curve and read off, as it were, the output which gives maximum satisfaction [see fig. A.15].

If you imagine this simple scheme extended to any number of commodities and factors you obtain a general statement of which are usually called the conditions of equilibrium of production and utility. It is, as I mentioned before usually expounded as part of a 'theory' of production and utility as if it explained or described any causal connection. In fact, it does of course no more than make explicit the implications of our assumptions about the relative importance of the various ends and about the different ways in which the means can be used for their satisfaction. It is, as I have said at the beginning of this lecture, a method of describing a kind of pattern which has special significance. But though it makes it intelligible why such patterns will manifest themselves in the plans of persons who have the knowledge and tastes we have assumed, it does of course in no way explain why similar patterns should also appear in the undesigned phenomena of the market. All the economic

400

calculus can do is to enable us to recognize these patterns when they appear and make us see the significance of their existence for the achievement of our ends. But to explain why such patterns form as the result of the separate decisions of many men is a separate task which cannot be solved by pure logic but requires for its solution the causal explanation which only an empirical science can provide.

The main characteristic of this kind of order or pattern is that it is defined in terms, not of properties which the objects possess by themselves, but of properties which they derive from the particular means-ends structure of which at the particular moment they form part. They are rates of equivalence or value relations which serve as the criteria of whether their particular arrangement is an orderly pattern or an instance of the asserted regularity, or whether it is haphazard. There are, of course, various sets of conditions in which this can be expressed: we can do so in terms of equality between marginal rates of substitution, or in terms of equality of the values of the marginal product of any factor in all its different uses, or in terms of equality between marginal costs and the value of the product. But they all come to the same thing. What I am interested in here is however not the technical detail but the general conclusion to which the economic calculus leads, namely that the use and adjustment of such rates of equivalence is a necessary and indispensable tool for the rational solution of the task of allocating scarce resources among competing ends as soon as this means-ends structure becomes at all complex.

If we remember that as recently as thirty years ago it was contended by serious thinkers that the phenomenon of value was peculiar to the capitalist organization of society and that socialist society would be able to dispense with it by relying entirely on what was called calculation 'in natura' or in real terms, it is rather remarkable that this contention can be so clearly disproved by a purely deductive argument.[11] That in this way the economic calculus shows us that economic values are a necessary tool for the rational disposition of the available resources seems to me one of its most valuable services.

I hope that some of the points on which I was today only able to touch I shall have time to elaborate somewhat further in my discussion of the relation between economics and technology in my next lecture. The distinction I shall then attempt to draw between two conceptually different tasks is in a way still part of today's subject. On the relation which the economic calculus has to the explanation of the phenomena of the market I shall be able to comment more systematically only in my last lecture.

[11] [Hayek here refers to the proposals of Otto Neurath (1882–1945), the social science representative of the Vienna Circle of logical positivism. See F. A. Hayek, "The Nature and History of the Problem" [1935], reprinted in *Socialism and War: Essays, Documents, Reviews*, ed. Bruce Caldwell, vol. 10 (1997) of *The Collected Works of F. A. Hayek*, p. 72, and the editor's introduction of that volume, pp. 4–9.—Ed.]

Lecture III
Economics and Technology

I have chosen the relation between economic and technological factors as the subject of the third lecture in this series, partly in order to provide illustrations for the somewhat abstract discussion of my last lecture and partly in order to lead up to the problems with which my next lecture will have to deal. It is one of the benefits we derive from the occupation with the economic calculus that it makes us see the distinct character of economics as distinguished from technological problems.[1] But the relation is also a subject which in its own right deserves attention. Misconceptions about it are not only widespread but have had considerable influence on economic policy and I shall later consider one respect in which at the present time those misconceptions seem to me to be the cause of a serious waste of resources in the 'underdeveloped countries.' But my first task must be to distinguish between the two approaches, to bring out their different significance, and to show how they interact and sometimes conflict.

I am not sure that in ordinary language a sharp distinction is made between what is economic and what is technological. 'Economic' seems frequently to be used to comprise all that determines the productivity of our efforts, including what is more properly called technological. People may be vaguely aware that technology is not all that determines the size of the product and use therefore the term 'economic' to include whatever other factors in addition to the technological may be relevant. It is characteristic, e.g., that we speak of an 'economic interpretation of history' when what is meant is an interpretation of history in terms of technological change, i.e., where the technology is supposed to be the independent variable.[2]

Where, however, the existence of a difference between the two kinds of considerations is recognized, there exists a strong tendency to believe that what is really decisive for the wealth of a nation is the state of its technological knowledge and that compared with this the economic factors are of minor importance. In this country perhaps even more than elsewhere it seems to be generally assumed that the rapid increase of wealth in modern times is entirely and solely due to the growth of technological knowledge. There is of course no question that this growth was a necessary condition and that without the use of modern technology we could not produce anything like as much as we do. This, however, does not mean that the possession (or sufficiently wide dispersion) of this modern technological knowledge is also a sufficient condition for achieving such wealth, as seems to be widely believed. Sir Charles Snow, e.g.,

---

[1] [This sentence was handwritten and it was indicated that it be inserted here.—Ed.]
[2] [The part of this sentence that begins with "where the" was handwritten by Hayek.—Ed.]

402

in his lecture on *The Two Cultures and the Scientific Revolution*, which has attracted much attention, has argued that "for the task of totally industrializing a major country, as in China today, it only takes will to train enough scientists and engineers and technicians."[3] Perhaps I misunderstand what Sir Charles means by "total industrialization of a country"; but if the statement is intended to suggest, as the context makes likely, that this is all that is needed to make a country as rich as the United States or the richer countries of Western Europe, I fear it is just wrong and an error due to not keeping apart the economic and the technological conditions for getting rich. There are certainly countries in Europe where the latest advances in technology are fully known and which are still very much poorer than the U.S. or the other countries which lead in wealth.

That the practical man does not clearly distinguish between the two kinds of problems is not really surprising. In the actual direction of production technological and economic considerations so constantly interact that they are hardly felt to be separate and different. But though they are not always psychologically separable, logically they are distinct and in certain connections it is rather important that we clearly distinguish between them. The danger is probably not that the importance of the technological considerations will ever be overlooked. But there is undoubtedly some danger that the technological considerations may be regarded as alone decisive and that the economic aspects are simply disregarded. Some people at least seem to believe that the organization of production is entirely a matter of technology, and in particular, that technological knowledge alone and unambiguously decides what is the best way of obtaining a given output. It is this error with which I shall be mainly concerned in this lecture.

There are two reasons for the greater importance which is generally attached to technological compared with economic considerations. One is that technological problems have to be solved deliberately by somebody recognizing them as such and consciously seeking for an answer, while the economic problems of society are solved in a large measure by the operation of an impersonal process where nobody needs to be aware of the existence of the problem which is solved by the spontaneous formation of an order. This means that while we must be aware of the significance of the technological problems and know what they are, it is not really necessary that anyone should be aware of the significance of the economic problems in order that they be solved. The second reason for the belief of the uniquely determining character of technological considerations is that in the kind of economic conditions by which the latest development of technology has been guided, the latest and most advanced technological methods will usually also be the most appropri-

---

[3] [C. P. Snow, *The Two Cultures and the Scientific Revolution* (Cambridge: Cambridge University Press, 1960), p. 42.—Ed.]

ate economically—though this does not mean that under different conditions what are at the moment the most advanced methods will also be the best.

I will now try to state the conceptual distinction between the two kinds of considerations rather briefly and shall then endeavor to bring out its significance in connection with more concrete problems.

The basic distinction seems to me that technology informs us of the different ways in which any given result can be produced, while the economic considerations tell us which of these ways to select in view of the other needs which in the particular situation compete for the same means. All technological knowledge is in this sense generic, based on general laws of nature and therefore universally valid—though any one piece of such knowledge may of course often be irrelevant in particular circumstances. Economic considerations on the other hand, always refer to particular circumstances of time and place. It is the latter, however, which determine which of the alternative methods which technology offers to us is appropriate in the particular case.[4]

To put it differently: the various technological possibilities are not necessarily simultaneous possibilities. Which of them can be realized at the same time depends on economic circumstances which are thus chiefly a restraint on what technology pictures as possible. This means that, while technology deals with pleasant facts which give people a thrill, economics deals with unpleasant facts which people would prefer not to be true. Compared with the glamour of technology, economics still is the dismal science which explains why we can't do what we would like to do. In fact, it is still too complimentary to economics to contrast it in this connection to technology, because the two disciplines do not function on the same plane. What I am discussing is really the contrast between technological and economic factors. But while it is the technologist or engineer who contributes the technological knowledge, it is not normally the economist but the businessman and the ordinary consumer who contributes the economic knowledge. The economist is not really needed for the working of the economic process as the technologist is needed: the economist merely looks at the process from the outside and tries to explain how it works, and very frequently has the unpopular task of explaining that the obstacles which stand in the way of realizing all the technological possibilities are not, as might appear, the product of somebody's malice, but the consequences of hard facts.

The difference will come out more clearly if we consider the different meaning in which from the two points of view a particular technique is regarded as

---

[4] [In the typescript two sentences were to be the beginning of the next paragraph, but Hayek crossed them out and instead started the new paragraph that is in the text. The two crossed out sentences read, "The difference will come out most clearly if we consider the different meaning in which from the two points of view a particular technique is regarded as better than another, or as the best. When the technologist speaks of a method being best he usually means that by it a given end is more perfectly achieved with the given means."—Ed.]

better than another, or as the best. When the technologist speaks of a method being best he usually means that by it a given end is more perfectly achieved with the given means than by any others. What he compares are therefore really methods which produce different results, not different ways of producing the same result. If the outlay involved in the two instances is the same, the method which produces the preferable product is of course the better one, whatever economic conditions. Quite a different situation arises, however, when we have to choose between different methods of achieving the same product. There technology really provides no criterion for selecting one of them as better than the others.

The technologist probably will still sometimes regard one solution as more elegant or beautiful than another, but that does not mean that it serves human ends any better. There will also be the simple case where one of the alternative methods requires more of some factors without saving on any others compared with the other methods available, in which case it clearly will be inferior whatever the particular circumstances. But where the technological information is that a given product can be produced either by using so much of x and so much of y, or by producing less of x and more of y, technology has no criterion for deciding which is better. This will be different in different conditions and depend entirely on those particular circumstances of time and place which are taken into account in economic considerations.

If engineers nevertheless often maintain that there are purely technological criteria for selecting a best method of producing a given product, this I believe is due to the fact that they have been so exclusively concerned with one set of economic conditions that they unconsciously assume that they prevail universally. Their concern may have been so exclusively to obtain a maximum utilization of the energy contained in a fuel, or to achieve a maximum economy of labour, that they have come to regard this kind of optimum as an optimum in all circumstances. But though such an optimum may have been the continuous aim of their quest, this does not mean that the technique which extracts the maximum amount of energy from a fuel, or which achieves a given result with a minimum expenditure of labour, is the best or most appropriate in any other sense. There will always be a cost of the extraction of a further amount of energy or of a further saving of labour, and whether it will be worthwhile to incur these costs will depend on whether they are larger or smaller than the value of the amount of energy or labour saved.

It is of course only natural that the engineer in the solution of his tasks will tend to assume that the relations between the values of the different factors will be within the range where they always have been in his experience, or that, because his work has all been done under conditions where labour was becoming increasingly scarce and capital increasingly plentiful, this is a general or necessary state of affairs. I shall presently have to consider the extent to which the development of technological knowledge itself has been guided by particular economic conditions into certain channels and how this raises grave doubts whether the technique which the rich countries of the West have developed is also necessarily the best technology under the very different conditions prevailing in the underdeveloped countries. But before I turn to the consequences which spring from the fact that the appropriateness of different techniques depends on economic conditions, I must yet say something about the different manner in which technological and economic problems are solved—and the different habits of thought which the preoccupation with the one or the other engenders.

It is of course of the essence of a technological task that it not only has a single aim but that all the activities serving that aim are under a single control and guided according to a unitary plan. For this purpose it is necessary that all the facts relevant to the technological choice should be explicitly known to the designer of the plan and therefore that the task should be, as it were, self-contained and of manageable dimensions, i.e., such that it does not exceed the span of capacity of a single mind. Of course in some respects all more complex engineering plans are the product of the collaboration of many minds and are produced by a deliberate or organized division of labour. Yet the separate contributions concern as it were details which have to fit into a predetermined framework, have to satisfy specifications laid down beforehand and can be delegated only because the overall plan into which they have to fit has been decided upon before.

Contrast with this the manner in which the economic problems of society are solved. We can of course speak of problems of society only in a metaphorical sense: society does not know, think, or solve problems. But we have seen how within an economic system all decisions are interdependent and how, if each member is to make the fullest use of his resources for his ends which is possible at least without decreasing the product of others, the resulting arrangement must conform to a certain pattern or order; and, although in a competitive system the use of the resources will not be guided by a single hierarchy of ends but by as many such hierarchies as there are separate individuals or rather families, every one of them is interested in the economical use of all resources since the less is required to supply what others get, the better the chance that more will be left for him. Yet, because of the interdependence of all decisions, nobody knows all the facts which in the last resort determine what the individual decision should be. The economic problem of society is therefore not normally solved deliberately by somebody working out all the implications of the data, because nobody has all the data. It is solved not by somebody beforehand drawing up a comprehensive plan and everybody then acting according to this plan, as a technological problem would be solved, but by the individuals so mutually adjusting their actions that an order is formed.

Each individual will always know only a small fraction of the relevant facts and will usually control not the whole of the actions required to satisfy a given end, but only a part of which he frequently will not even know the ultimate purpose which it serves. The collaboration of the individuals here involves not only a division of labour, as the working according to a single plan usually also would, but also a division of the *knowledge* guiding the action—a division of knowledge which cannot be all conveyed to one designing mind but must be used where it exists, dispersed among many persons who must make their own separate decisions on the basis of the knowledge they individually have.

The manner in which the market conveys to the individuals the information they require in order mutually to adapt their actions to each other will be the subject of my next lecture. All that I need to point out for my present purposes is that it is *because* a modern economy is so *complex* that nobody can know all the facts that it could not effectively be guided by a central plan but must be conducted on the basis of decentralization of decisions. This is worth emphasizing because it is sometimes argued that this very complexity, which in fact prevents effective planning, makes planning necessary.[5]

Before I consider the effect of these views on policy I want at least very briefly to discuss the interplay of the two factors in long-run development. The point with which I am mainly concerned is the extent to which economic considerations will decide not only which of the various known technical processes will be used, but also what technological methods will be known. Of course practical need is not the only factor which decides in which direction technological knowledge will be developed. It is to a large extent a result of the development of the more fundamental research of pure science which presumably follows its own necessities. But the task of technology is essentially to develop the theoretical knowledge of pure science in the directions indicated by practical means. That in some respects the development of technology will be guided by economic conditions is fairly obvious: clearly technological development would have been directed into very different channels if iron had been very scarce but platinum very common, or if oil rather than coal had frequently been found near the surface, or if the relative ease with which any other of the more important materials are obtainable had been very different from what it is.

More important than the relative supplies of particular materials are in this respect the relative quantities available of the three chief classes of factors of production, labour, land, and capital. Clearly the efforts of inventors and designers will be aimed in different directions where labour is scarce and where capital is plentiful from what it would be if the reverse were true. Perhaps it is to be expected that in conditions of rapid advance of technological knowledge

---

[5] [This final sentence was handwritten by Hayek.—Ed.]

the increase of wealth will also lead to a corresponding increase in the supply of capital relatively to labour and that therefore there will be a general tendency towards labour-saving inventions and improvements. But that need by no means generally be the case; it is at least conceivable that technological advance may take place under conditions where population pressure is great and capital very scarce so that inventive effort would be directed mainly towards economizing capital.

So long as a highly developed technology is applied under more or less the kind of economic conditions for which it has been developed, we usually will not be conscious that its appropriateness is confined to these conditions. This is bound, however, to become an important problem once technological knowledge developed in one part of the world is to be applied in other parts where economic conditions are very different. The fact that any technology is 'best' only in the economic conditions for which it has been developed and that the most advanced technology may not be the best under different conditions, is, however, very rarely understood. I shall presently return to this problem, but before I do so must briefly touch on one or two other issues.

At this point I should probably at least mention a problem which many people will expect to hear discussed in a lecture on economics and technology, the problem of technological unemployment. I have nothing new to say on this old issue but since we are again in one of these recurrent phases in which the danger of mass unemployment from imminent technological progress is painted in the darkest colours, I do not want to pass it over altogether. I do not see that the problems which are raised by what is now called automation are really fundamentally different from those discussed under the heading of rationalization thirty or forty years ago, or even those which a hundred years ago were discussed as the effects of the introduction of machinery in general. It is of course still true that the fears caused by the naïve conception that, because we shall soon be able to produce all we consume now with the use of a much smaller labour force, there will be nothing to do for the rest, is just wrong. It is not that in consequence there will be no demand for the labour displaced in their former jobs. But it may well be that the introduction of such labour-saving devices on a very large scale might lead to a fall in the marginal productivity of labour and therefore of the equilibrium wage at which all those seeking work can all be employed. Knut Wicksell's concise statement that "while the capitalist investor is always the friend of labour, the inventor is not infrequently its enemy" is still valid.[6] It may well be that the consequences

---

[6] [See Knut Wicksell, *Lectures on Political Economy*, vol. 1, *General Theory*, translated by E. Classen (London: George Routledge and Sons, 1934; reprinted, Fairfield, NJ: Augustus M. Kelley, 1977), p. 164: "The capitalist saver is thus, fundamentally, the friend of labour, though the technical inventor is not infrequently its enemy."—Ed.]

of the impossibility of lowering any money wages will become an even more serious problem in the years to come, and that the labour unions might be wise if they became aware in time that the pressure for rapidly rising wages may in the future create more harm than it has done in the recent past.

Labour unions have of course long represented it as a beneficial effect of their pressure for higher wages that it often induces the introduction of more modern techniques—and that by adopting more modern techniques the firms can make up for the higher costs of labour. The fact that high labour costs tend to stimulate mechanization is, of course, correct. But though the workers immediately concerned will of course profit by it, it is by no means evident that such a development is beneficial to labour as a whole. So long as the capital available for investment is limited, the result of such mechanization induced by pushing up wages will usually be that fewer workers will be equipped with more capital per head than would otherwise have been the case and nothing[7] will be left to equip the rest; or, to put it differently, that the capital available for investment will be so used as if only that smaller number of workers were available and had to be equipped, while the rest will remain unprovided for and unemployed. Something very similar to this is now, for slightly different reasons, happening on a very large scale in the development of the underdeveloped countries.

I will now turn to the two most important respects in which the greater awareness of the technological as compared with economic conditions has in recent times had a profound effect on public policy. The first is the tendency of the technological approach to predispose those steeped in it in favour of comprehensive planning or central direction of all economic activity. I have discussed this tendency at some length elsewhere and will now consider it only very briefly. I did then describe the attitude guided by the preoccupation with technological tasks as the 'engineering type of approach' largely because its representatives were themselves so fond of speaking of political or social engineering to describe their conception of policy.[8] I have since found that long ago W. E. Gladstone has described exactly this attitude by the term 'constructivism', a much better name, especially as it goes well with the name 'scientism' which I had used for a closely allied attitude.[9] It indeed describes very well a point of view which regards the deliberately constructed as invariably better and superior to any order which forms itself by the mutual adjustment

[7][In the manuscript 'nothing' was crossed out, but the sentence does not make any sense if this is done.—Ed.]

[8][See F. A. Hayek, "Scientism and the Study of Society", especially chapter 10, "Engineers and Planners", in *Studies on the Abuse and Decline of Reason*, ed. Bruce Caldwell, vol. 13 (2011) of *The Collected Works of F. A. Hayek* (Chicago: University of Chicago Press; London: Routledge).—Ed.]

[9][See "The Errors of Constructivism", this volume, p. 338, note 3, and "Kinds of Rationalism", this volume, p. 42, note 8, for more on Gladstone and constructivism.—Ed.]

of independent agents. I do not wish to deny that wherever all the factors that ought to be taken into account are explicitly known to one directing mind, construction is the most satisfactory and appropriate method to arrive at a rational solution of the task. But its limits are exactly where the assumption that all the relevant facts can be known to a single planning agency ceases to be true. Where we want to make use of more knowledge of particular concrete facts than can be concentrated with a single agency, where we want to utilize knowledge widely dispersed among many people, we can do this only by a decentralization of decisions combined with an impersonal mechanism of co-ordination such as the market provides.

All this is of course closely connected with the high esteem which our time attaches to generic or theoretical knowledge and the small esteem or almost contempt it has for knowledge of particular facts, the circumstances of time and place. The term 'knowledge' itself has become largely equivalent with scientific knowledge, i.e., the knowledge of general laws, as if it were the only knowledge the acquisition of which requires special effort, while the possession of information about all the relevant concrete circumstances is taken as a matter of course. There is also a vague yet pervasive feeling that only the permanent facts of science ought to affect our plans, or that they have become so much more important compared with the particular circumstances of any concrete situation that the latter can be increasingly disregarded. There is also an old feeling that, while it is meritorious to succeed by the command of better scientific or technological knowledge, it is somewhat disreputable, if not altogether dishonest, to prevail by the knowledge of any particular fact which others do not know. Somehow it is assumed that this concrete knowledge ought to be readily and without any special effort available to all, and that the economic or commercial activities directed towards the utilization of those local and momentary facts ought to be unnecessary.

In some regards, of course, the very nature of the highly elaborate and durable equipment which modern technology demands also makes impossible that continuous adjustment of the volume and methods of production which was possible when techniques were simpler, and often makes the decision to produce a certain product at a certain rate an all-or-nothing and long-period decision, which is adjusted only to the most general kind of circumstances expected to prevail over long periods and cannot be adapted to any of the particular facts which change from day to day. For these reasons the decision of a firm to erect a plant of a certain type seems to have little in common with the typical economic decisions of the merchant and may appear to be dictated solely by technological considerations. How little true this is appears, or at least ought to appear, only when we ask whether the decision ought to be the same if such fundamental factors as the relative values of capital and labour were very different from what they in fact are today in most of the Western world.

This brings me to the chief instance I want to discuss where the confusion between technological and economic considerations seems to me today to produce particularly harmful consequences. This is the widespread belief that the technological methods used in the economically most advanced countries are also the most effective for poor countries trying to become rich. Here the idea that there is at any one time in every field a technological best way of doing things, namely the way things are done in the technologically most advanced countries, is treated as almost self-evident. Yet in fact it is very far from true and may be very misleading. It is, however, as a result of this misconception that much of the capital that becomes available for new investment in underdeveloped countries contributes much less towards raising living standards than it might.

I have just used the phrase 'technologically most advanced countries', and there is of course a sense in which the richest countries will in general also have carried the development of technology further than others, simply because they can invest more in these efforts. But in another sense the assumption that the technology of the richest countries will be the most advanced rather begs the question: they may be very advanced in one particular direction, e.g., in achieving a very high economy of labour; but that may not be the direction in which under different conditions development may be important or even desirable, when it may be much more urgent to achieve an increase in the productivity of labour with a minimum expenditure of capital. It would perhaps be more correct to say, not that the rich countries have the most advanced technology, but that the technology adapted to the conditions in rich countries is likely to be more highly developed than the technology adapted to poor countries. It is this circumstance which is mainly responsible for the belief that what is the best technology for the rich countries is also the best technology for countries which want to become rich.

The harmful consequence of this is that poor countries will use the limited amounts of capital they have to invest so as to equip a small fraction of their labour force with an amount of capital per head similar to that which prevails in the rich countries instead of spreading it widely. It is of course only in this manner that the highly automatized processes developed in the rich countries can be introduced into poorer countries. But it means that techniques which are adapted to conditions in which labour is very scarce and expensive and capital comparatively plentiful are applied in conditions where there is much cheap labour and capital is very scarce. I have a strong suspicion that in this respect the most modern steel mills of which India boasts have been a very wasteful investment, and I am sure this is true of "the most highly automatized and labour-saving rayon plant in the world" which some years ago I was shown in Spain—a country where labour was certainly more plentiful and capital more scarce than anywhere else in Europe. That in order to obtain the maximum benefit from the limited capital available it should be spread thinly and widely rather than concentrated on a few people seems beyond doubt. But this means that very different techniques from those used in the richer countries might have to be used. Speaking generally, it means that better ploughs and carts and draft animals and farm buildings and not combines or even tractors will probably be what is needed.

There are two chief obstacles to the introduction of the kind of technological methods which would be most effective in raising productivity and incomes in the poorer or underdeveloped countries. The first is that the methods adapted to them have usually never been worked out on the basis of present scientific knowledge and would yet have to be developed. The techniques those countries ought to apply if they are to raise their incomes most rapidly are, of course, not those which the Western countries used at the time when they were still as poor as the underdeveloped countries are now. They should be applications of present scientific knowledge to the practical problems of using most effectively relatively small quantities of capital per head under the conditions prevailing in the underdeveloped countries. The development of such a technology is, however, itself a costly and time-consuming process which would require considerable investment. In some circumstances this fact, that the techniques adapted to the conditions in wealthy countries are readily available while the only techniques adapted to the conditions in poor countries are antiquated and not adapted to present knowledge, may of course bring it about that the former are also economically preferable in the second case. This, however, is probably true only where the differences in average wealth are not too large. Where they are of the magnitude of the differences which exist in this respect between, say, China or India or most parts of Africa on the one side, and the United States on the other, it seems to me that investment in the development of a technology appropriate to the much smaller capital equipment per head may be one of the most urgent and beneficial forms of investment and to encourage it one of the most important but also most difficult tasks of economic policy. I must however confess that I have little idea what to suggest in order to stimulate this sort of development. It would seem to require constant interaction between an economic or commercial and a technological approach, such as might take place in the engineering departments of universities or institutes of technology of the countries concerned. But efforts in this direction are likely to encounter not only the resistance of many of the American- or European-trained engineers who want directly to apply what they have learned and admired during their training, but even more from the government planners in whose hands the direction of investment rests so largely in the underdeveloped countries: because, while a great concentration of the available capital in a few very modern works lends itself to the effective direction by a central planning agency, the use of capital which is thinly spread among many people is practically beyond the control of a central planner.

I am quite aware that, on the other hand the problem of distributing capital widely in small driblets is a very difficult one and that beyond a certain point the costs of spreading it thinly may become prohibitive. Nevertheless it seems to me still probable that the optimum use in countries like India is likely to be nearer to providing the individual peasant with better tools than to creating automatized plants American style.

Attempts to make the leaders of the underdeveloped countries see this generally encounter the difficulty that the imitation of the techniques of the economically most advanced countries has become a matter of national pride, a sort of international status symbol. It is scarcely to be expected that political leaders of such countries should have sufficient insight into what is economically most beneficial so as to be satisfied with what to them is likely to appear as a second best, an inferior sort of technology. The belief that because rich countries employ certain technical methods the best way to become rich is to adopt these methods is bound to persist. This is likely to have rather serious consequences. If the limited amounts of capital which can be made available for these undeveloped countries are used to equip comparatively few workers with relatively much capital per head, instead of spreading this capital among many or most, this will of course raise greatly the productivity and the wages of the few fortunate ones who will work in the new plants; but it will leave the great part of the extreme poverty in those countries untouched. The contrast between it and the improved section will grow and the urgent need to remove the extreme poverty never cease. Indeed if the capital given as economic aid to such countries is used to equip them with the sort of technology the wealthy countries use, the demand for economic aid is likely to become practically permanent, namely to last until the now underdeveloped countries are precisely as rich as the wealthy ones.

That a full use of the possibilities and potentialities of modern knowledge under very different economic conditions cannot be a matter of simple imitation but demands the development of new techniques has of course still further policy implications. I will resist the temptation at this late hour to enlarge on the general relation between economic freedom and the speed of technological development, though this is one of the most fascinating subjects in this field, and one where history provides ample illustration of how it was long less lack of theoretical knowledge than opportunity for practical experimentation which held up the development of technology. It seems to me therefore also fairly certain that the development of technology which the underdeveloped countries need will not occur if the individual producers there are not given the opportunity to experiment with alternative tools and techniques offered to them by competing manufacturers of equipment, and the adaptation to the particular circumstances rather than the conformity to an imported standard is made the chief goal.

I hope you do not feel that I have spent a disproportionately long time on this problem of the technology appropriate in underdeveloped countries. I believe that its practical importance is very great and yet very inadequately realized. But I am of course not concerned with it here for its own sake. I meant it to serve merely as an illustration of how an understanding of the logic of resource allocation is of such great importance for questions of economic policy. It seems to me that this comes out most clearly in examining how economic and technological considerations interact—and that this interaction is today seen nowhere else more clearly than where a technology is applied in conditions different from those in which it has been developed.

The economic calculus which I discussed in my second lecture describes the interrelation of the decisions about resource allocation in conditions where all the relevant facts are known to a single mind. Nothing except what is known to that mind matters, and this knowledge is assumed to be fixed for the purpose of that problem. When we pass from this exercise in logic to an account of the events of the market we pass from the world of thought to the world of action, from a world where nothing counts but what is known to the single planner from the beginning, to a world where not only the different people have different knowledge but where their actions lead constantly to the acquisition of new knowledge. The problem is no longer how somebody would act who knew all the facts, but rather how much the different individuals will know— or learn in the course of their action—and how much they need to know in order mutually to adapt their actions and how much of this needed knowledge is conveyed to them.

It is one of the advantages of the separate treatment of the economic calculus that it makes us aware of the highly unrealistic character of the assumption of perfect knowledge which it is necessary to make for certain purposes for describing a kind of order and its significance, but which would be highly misleading if it were carried into the explanation of what happens in the real world. It is one thing to describe a certain pattern or arrangement as that which would be brought about by a person with perfect knowledge, and quite another to explain the appearance of patterns of this kind by the assumption that people have in fact perfect knowledge. In the task of explaining why events conform to a certain pattern, that is, in the empirical science of economics, the assumption of perfect knowledge ought to have no place. To use it at this stage is to assume away the chief problem: how a pattern of order of the sort can be formed without any one person knowing all the facts to which this pattern is adapted. To start with the assumption of perfect knowledge indeed prevents us from asking all the important questions: how much the different individuals need to know in order that such a pattern be formed, and by what process this knowledge is conveyed to them. The theory of market equilibrium which starts from the assumption of perfect knowledge possessed by the partners in the market largely begs the questions it ought to answer by assuming what need be explained. I believe this assumption would never appear at this stage if its character had been made explicit and its usefulness exhausted in that preliminary logical analysis which I have called the economic calculus. The two fundamental new facts which we have to take into account when we pass from the logical analysis of a single plan of resource allocation to the explanation of the action of many men concern the information both concerning means and concerning ends. In the first instance, the available means are now no longer a single set of data, facts known to one mind, but sets of different facts known to a great many people about the existence and possible uses of different things—knowledge not only dispersed among all these people and of which each individual will possess only a part, but often different opinions which may stand in conflict with each other. Secondly, the aims for which these means are to be used are similarly the separate and distinct aims of many individuals. This means not only that there is nobody to whom all these aims are known but also (which the first of course implies) that these aims do not belong to a single order of rank or importance, but constitute as many unconnected hierarchies of ends as there are individuals. This, as is well known, creates serious difficulties with regard to the meaning of the concept of an optimum allocation which I do not propose to follow up here.

Another useful way of bringing out this point is to examine the concept of the 'data' which we use in theoretical analysis. 'Data' means of course the given fact from which we derive our conclusions about what will happen in the situations thus described. In one respect they play exactly the same rôle which in the natural sciences is played by what the philosophers of science call the initial and marginal conditions which must be known in order that we should be able to use a theory to derive from it predictions of particular events. But there are two important differences: firstly, in economics these data are always only hypothetically but never really all known to the observing scientist. The significance of this I have discussed in my first lecture. Secondly, the facts which we call data, to be effective conditions, must not merely be present but must be known or become known to some of the acting persons. But no one person knows, of course, all the facts, neither the observing or explaining economist nor any one of the participants in the market process. Yet all the data, not only those directly known to any one of the parties in the market but also those of which he does not know, may influence his actions and often must influence his actions if resources are to be used effectively.

A single example will suffice to show you not only what I have in mind but also by what means this adaptation of the individual's action to the facts of which he does not know is brought about.[1] It may clearly happen that an American string manufacturer will be led to substitute sisal for jute, not because there has been any change in the demand for his products or in the production of either sisal or jute, of either of which he might be assumed to be informed, but because, say, a reduction of Indian grain imports had decreased the available shipping space out of India and thus increased shipping costs for jute, while at the same time some other industry had substituted ar-

---

[1] [Cf. Hayek's tin example in "The Use of Knowledge in Society", this volume, chapter 3, pp. 99–100.—Ed.]

tificial fibres for sisal. Of course the effect on the relative supplies of jute and sisal may be due to still more remote causes. Of these originating events our string manufacturer would not be *likely* to be informed. But he also *need* not to be informed of them to make the changes in this disposition made desirable by those events. All he needs to know is that the price of jute has gone up relatively to the price of sisal. This will be the signal to which he responds and which will make him do what is made appropriate by facts of which he has never heard. The effect which is significant for his action may have been transmitted to him, not merely through the changes in the prices of the materials with which he is concerned, but before that through the prices of many other materials or services, which in turn have made other people change their dispositions.

The point of this is of course merely the obvious one that all parties in the market are constantly led to adapt their plans to countless events of which they do not know but whose net effects, so far as they are important for these persons, are reflected in the prices which they learn about and which provide them with the chief information on which they base their decisions. What is thus communicated to them are not all the particular events which are the cause why they should change their dispositions, but only those net resultants of all the events occurring at any one time which they need to know to make the appropriate move. It is this process which in the title of this lecture I have described as the communication function of the market.

The question I want to consider is *how much* the individual producer or dealer need in fact to know in order to be able to fit his decisions into the overall pattern of economic activity. By this I mean that they satisfy two conditions which are closely connected but not quite the same. Fitting into the overall pattern means in the first instance that the plans made by any one individual or firm are so matched with the plans of others that there will be partners for the various sales and purchases for which each plans. But this is not quite enough, or rather it is enough only if we add not only that they will be able to exchange at the prices at which they had planned to do so, but also that these prices are such that they do not afterwards feel they could have done better if they had been better informed. In other words, only if the various familiar conditions of equilibrium are satisfied and prices for any one commodity are uniform or vary only in proportion to costs of transportation and the like, if prices of products exceed costs by a uniform rate of profit, etc., will the individual actions fit into the overall pattern.

My question then is how much need the individual participant in the market know in order that such a state be brought about. In trying to answer this I must, at least at first, avoid the most difficult—and I am afraid most important—aspect of this question, namely the extent to which this involves correct anticipation of future events and particularly of future prices. Though this does not lead us very far I shall have to discuss the question largely as if it were enough that activities adjusted themselves to the facts as they are already known to have occurred, because conditions are sufficiently stable for this to bring about adequate adjustment to facts as they will be. How much then does the individual for this purpose need to know of the facts existing at the moment?

If I consider in this connection almost exclusively his knowledge of prices, I do of course not mean to suggest that he need to know only prices. He clearly must possess not only technological knowledge and knowledge of the general social and legal framework of the society in which he acts, but also a good deal of knowledge of particular circumstances and men in his immediate environment. But I am concerned here mainly with the manner in which the individual adjusts himself to the changing conditions of the whole economic system, and to show how the necessary knowledge of particular circumstances is conveyed to him mainly through the intermediary of prices.[2]

Let me begin by considering the market for any *one* commodity or service. How much need the different individuals or firms know in order that such a market should be effective, i.e., that after any change the fairly rapid establishment of a new uniform price (or of prices differing only by transportation costs and the like) is assured? What the individuals need to know for this purpose is of course not just price figures but particular other individuals or firms willing to buy or sell at particular prices. But how many? Is it necessary that every intending seller, or at least some sellers, should know all the potential buyers, and that every intending buyer, or at least some buyers, should know all potential sellers? It seems to me that this sort of perfect knowledge is clearly not necessary to produce an effective market. All that seems necessary is that there should exist a sufficiently pervasive inter-connection by each seller knowing a number of buyers which are also known to other sellers which in turn know other buyers and so on throughout the whole of the market—which indeed becomes *one* market through this kind of inter-connection. How dense this multiple overlap of the range of knowledge of potential partners by the individual buyers and sellers must be in order to create an effective single market, I find very difficult to define. It appears that it would clearly not be sufficient if each seller knew only two potential buyers, each of which in turn were known to one other seller who in turn knew one more buyer and so on: because in such a situation the chain of inter-communication would be broken as soon as one of the sellers found it profitable to offer all his output to one of the buyers only. He might well sell to him at a higher price than the other

---

[2] [The phrase "of particular circumstances" was written in by Hayek. 'Intermediary' was rendered 'intermediaryship' by Hayek.—Ed.]

buyer of whom he knows has to pay if no further quantities of the commodity can be diverted from the latter to the former.

The effectivity of the market will however very rapidly increase as the number of potential partners which each seller knows increases. This tendency is strengthened by the analogous effect of an extended knowledge of potential sellers by the different buyers. The knowledge of a potential buyer by a seller does of course not necessarily imply that the buyer also knows of the seller or that he does not know of other potential sellers who do not know of him. But such one-sided knowledge of opportunities for transactions will of course lead to the party who has the knowledge making itself known to the other by an offer as soon as this becomes profitable. Such one-sided information is therefore likely to become the cause of some parties being told of opportunities of which they did not know before as soon as a change in conditions makes likely a deal profitable for both parties.

This has already brought me to the transition from the consideration of the information people must have in order that the market should be effective at any one moment, to the examination of the mechanism which will assure that after any change the range of information the different individuals will possess will again in the new circumstances assure an effective market. But before I pursue this second question further, I want to say a few more words on the first, the 'static' aspect of the problem.

Our generation of economists, brought up in the tradition of 'perfect competition' are, it seems to me, much too inclined to assume that each party in a market will, if he does not actually know, at least *try* to know all potential partners. This seems to me not only not necessary to make the market effective, but also not normally to be a rational procedure. Making one's offers known to potential partners is always a costly affair and probably an effort where the costs often rapidly increase as the circle of persons to be reached extends. Whether it is worthwhile to make further efforts in this direction will depend on how much one knows already about potential partners—the likelihood of further efforts being wasted increasing as our information becomes less complete or certain. Geographical and other factors will normally limit the sector of the market which it is normally worthwhile for any one to watch closely. Only when within that range signs appear which suggest that there may have occurred major changes outside the region normally watched will there be an inducement to explore further regions.

It is one of the consequences of economic theory starting from the assumption that people act on the basis of knowledge given to them to begin with, rather than emphasizing the process by which people acquire that knowledge, that it has so little to say about all those activities aiming either at acquiring information or at conveying information to others. But though some of the information used by the parties in the market may, as it were, automatically come to them, much more is no doubt the product of a deliberate search, or of effort to communicate information to others. Not only advertising but all endeavours deliberately to organize markets or exchanges and the like are activities on which economics has singularly little to say and which yet are important factors in bringing about the state which economics claims to explain. Yet they are all activities which would not be necessary if all the parties in the market started out with perfect knowledge; they aim at obtaining the required knowledge.

Here I want however to consider not so much these more elaborate and systematic efforts of making oneself known to other potential partners and finding out about other partners, but the much simpler question *when* buyers or sellers who will normally be content to know some section of the market will be induced to look further afield, and whether this will happen whenever it is necessary to prevent disruption of the market. The overlap which secures this coherence would of course disappear if, e.g., some suppliers which had served several users of a commodity switched all their supplies to one of them. This would destroy some of the connecting links unless those who found that they no longer had any rivals in supplying some users were induced by this to find out what had led those former rivals to turn elsewhere. It will thus be the change in the activities of rivals or partners that will indicate that some new exploration might be profitable and that such new exploration will restore the overlap where it has been disrupted.

. I am not sure how far it is worthwhile to spell out in more detail the account of this process which is probably taken for granted by every economist but never explicitly described. It is sometimes useful, however, to say the obvious, and I hope you will bear with me if in a few sentences I sketch this process more fully. Take the case where the initial change is a sudden substantial increase in somebody's demand for a commodity. The first effect of this will be that those who have been supplying this buyer before will be induced by the possibility of getting higher prices to let him have what they before sold to others. If the switch involves large quantities, it will not only leave gaps in the supply to the other users from which the shift has been made and which will be filled by suppliers which knew of them, but not of the one with whom the change initiated, but their attention will be drawn to the fact that an additional demand has arisen somewhere and induce them to make inquiries. The same will happen at the points from which they have switched their supplies, and thus, as supplies move inwards, as it were, towards the place of the initial additional demand, the signals will spread outward; and this process will continue until the effects have spread not only through the whole market of the commodity concerned but to a greater or lesser extent throughout the whole economic system.

The latter will happen because what I have so far described with reference to the market for any one commodity or service applies equally to the connection between different markets. These connections are effected by the different commodities being either substitutes for each other or complementary to each other and somebody knowing this and acting on this knowledge. But again it is of course not necessary that everybody who is concerned with any commodity should know of all other commodities which might be used in its place or in combination with it, or of their prices.[3] Again it will be sufficient if at all times the inter-communication between the markets for the different commodities is assured by a few people knowing of each of these facts and being ready to respond to changes in the relative prices of these commodities: as before, what is required is a constant multiple overlap of knowledge which is being maintained by any sign of change inducing new inquiries.

Among the particular facts which some individuals but not others will know or rather believe there will of course also be expected future events. So far as they are expectations of real future events—as distinguished from the expectations of future prices to which I will turn in a moment—and expectations which affect present action, their significance is very much the same as that of any knowledge or opinion possessed by an individual. Such anticipations of future facts will contribute to determine present demands and supplies and therefore present prices, and through the latter the actions of people who are not concerned about those future events. There are all kinds of interesting problems in this connection about the manner in which conflicting opinions about the future will offset each other in their effect on prices, and how a wide diversity of opinion may bring it about that prices will reflect a sort of average expectation which in a sense may represent a sort of most probable outcome. Into these questions I cannot enter here.

There are, of course, also a few fields in which there exist markets for future commodities, i.e., markets in which it is possible to contract for the future purchase or sale at predetermined prices. Even where these future contracts do not literally constitute inter-temporal exchanges, because both the delivery of the goods and the payment are contracted for for the future date, they extend (through the possibility of borrowing and lending money) the price system into the dimension of time and serve as guides for the allocation of resources to different points in time in exactly the same manner in which the relative prices of commodities in different places or differing in any other manner act.

Neither the manner in which the expectation of particular future facts enters the formation of present prices nor the existence of dealings in futures raises here any particular difficulties. But there is a related problem which has been the subject of a good deal of speculation by theorists but on which theory

---

[3] [Hayek's written-in changes to this sentence are in part ungrammatical and in part illegible, so the original wording has been retained.—Ed.]

still has little useful to say: that is the basis on which the expectation of future prices is formed. By this I mean here of course solely the expectation of particular and relative prices as they govern the allocation of resources, and not the distinct and quite different problem of the movement of the price level and the connected problems of monetary policy. There can probably be little doubt that the expectations of these particular future prices are formed mainly on the basis of present prices and price movements plus the consideration of such particular facts likely to affect the future situation as are known to the individuals. But in spite of all sorts of ingenious hypotheses which have been suggested and experimented with, we really have very little knowledge of the manner in which any given change of prices will affect price expectations—or even reason to believe that there is a constant relation between the two. The fact that a particular price has risen may lead to the expectation that it will remain at the new figure, or that it will continue to rise, or that it will return to where it was before. There are probably some circumstances in which any one of these three possibilities would seem most likely, but I do not see that we can make any useful general statements about them, beyond, perhaps, that unless they know specific facts justifying different expectations, people are most likely to act on the assumption that future prices are more likely to be near present prices (or near the average prices of the recent past) than very different from them. This, at any rate, seems to me to be the only assumption concerning price expectations which would account for the relative stability of the economic system which we in fact find. But I will confess that when in general I speak with so much confidence of the manner in which prices help to adjust individual action to facts of which these individuals do not know, I do so with considerable uneasiness about how far this is also true of expectation of future prices caused by present price movements. I wish I had something more definite to say on this question, but frankly I just have not.

*　*　*

When I chose these problems as topics for this lecture I had rather hoped that I might be able to present a somewhat more worked-out theory of the communication of knowledge through the market than these rather obvious and common-sense reflections I have been able to present. But I have not only not succeeded in working out such a more precise theory but have also become rather doubtful whether there is much more to be said and whether the taking account of this process of the communication of knowledge does not necessarily mean a sort of retreat from the kind of precision achieved by a theory based on the assumption of given and perfect knowledge to something inevitably more vague and indefinite. This may be very disturbing to some people, but I am not sure whether this retreat from pseudo-precision does not in fact bring a gain in realism and usefulness. Of course on any one problem precise knowledge is better than imprecise knowledge. But this does not mean that the questions to which we can give precise answers are necessarily more important than the questions to which we have only imprecise answers. It may well be that an imprecise answer to an important problem is more valuable than a precise answer to an unimportant question and that we may therefore do more good by pushing forward into fields where we can hope for no more than imprecise answers. The only point I feel unhappy about is that, though even an imprecise answer might be very valuable, the chance of persuading others that so far as it goes it is right, and therefore that it will in fact be used as a guide for political action, is very small. There is no simple test, no specific prediction which can be verified, by which even he who does not fully understand the theory can still see that its results are right. It requires intimate familiarity with the argument to be able to recognize that the patterns we can observe in the real world are of the kind which this theory leads us to expect, and its usefulness lies, as I have stressed in an earlier lecture, not so much in enabling us to foresee the consequence of particular measures as in helping us to assess the advantages of alternative arrangements of our economic affairs. And in this respect the argument I have discussed seems to me to lead to a juster picture.[4]

It seems to me that one of the respects in which the usual approach of current theory has a very misleading effect on the evaluation of different kinds of economic orders is the sort of standard of efficiency which it suggests. Making perfect knowledge of all the relevant facts the starting point of its analysis, it tends also to make its test of the efficiency of an economic system that allocation of resources which would follow from perfect knowledge. Of course when we compare any economic system with one run by men endowed with perfect knowledge, reality must appear shockingly wasteful. But this sort of analysis simply assumes that the main practical problem which we face does not exist. Things look very different if instead we use as a standard of comparison a state of affairs in which each individual has knowledge only of such concrete facts as he will learn about in the course of his ordinary action, could not rely on prices as guides, and either each individual had to make his own decisions based on his limited knowledge, or perhaps one directs the activities of all others on the basis of the information he has which will not be much less limited even in the case of the best informed. That in either case the utilization of the sum of knowledge possessed by all would be very much less than that achieved even in a moderately effective market is evident. Indeed without something like a market any co-ordination of the *separate* decisions would be impossible. The alternative to self-sufficiency of every individual would then indeed be to put the decision of resource allocation into the hands of a single

---

[4] [The last sentence of the paragraph was handwritten by Hayek, and the last two words are not quite legible.—Ed.]

central authority. But while this may seem to provide a solution so long as we just assume that this central authority knows all the relevant facts, what really can be achieved in this manner depends entirely on how much of the relevant information can be put into the possession of the central planner. On this point the theoretical discussions of central planning leave us even more in the dark than the theories of the market. While it at least can be shown that the market has a built-in communication system, nothing corresponding to it is inherent in the idea of central planning. The only indication which we are usually given about how this problem is to be solved are vague references to the availability of modern statistical techniques, but these only show how little the nature of the problem is grasped. Information about aggregates or statistical collectives is of little use for deciding what particular people should do at particular moments which is what they would have to be told by the central authority. The statistician, in order to arrive at his aggregates, must largely abstract from those very details which will decide what particular individuals ought to do.

This comes out most clearly when we reflect that the relative stability of statistical aggregates such as production or sales figures is not a result either of a similar stability of the corresponding figures for individual firms, or of the chance compensation of individual variations under the 'law of large numbers', but is due to the deliberate action of individuals who will fill the gap caused by other producers having temporarily dropped out or other buyers temporarily refraining. Effective central planning would demand that the central planner knows all the details which would influence the independent decision of the individuals. How this knowledge is to be constantly and rapidly conveyed to the central planner, and to be taken account of by him, is the problem to which the advocates of central planning never provide an answer. Where they have tried to put their schemes into practice they have of course soon been forced to resort to some sort of simulated market—one in which prices are not formed by the market but fixed, and periodically revised, by authority. But though this solves part of the problem and makes some devolution of decisions to the managers of the individual enterprises possible—and to this extent involves an abandonment of the ideal of central planning—it does not give the planning authority any of the information it needs either for its price-fixing decisions or for whatever supervisions of the decisions of the individual producers it still wants to exercise.

But to return to the main theme: the second field where I feel that the treatment of the knowledge of the acting persons as a datum has had a particularly harmful effect is the whole modern theory of competition. The concept of perfect competition which provides here the standard is indeed closely connected with the conception of perfect knowledge, and in fact often explicitly presupposes perfect knowledge. Yet, as I have attempted to show at some length on another occasion, this *state* of perfect competition presupposes conditions in which most of the *activities* which in ordinary life are described by the verb 'to compete' are excluded. This process of competition seems to me to be best understood as a constant search for information about opportunities, a process of learning in which new knowledge is acquired all the time—where the effects of changes on demand and prices are studied, and generally the possibilities of action explored. To treat such a process, which essentially aims at finding out what will be successful, as if it proceeded on the basis of initially given and unchanging knowledge, is of course completely to miss the most important feature of it. It is true that such a process in the course of which the data constantly change cannot be neatly pictured by a system of simultaneous equations, and also that what we can say about it will be much less precise and much more general than what can be said about the implications of 'given data.' How people will respond to any new facts about which they learn, what conclusions they will draw from new experiences, must always be to some degree uncertain. But again it may well be true that the somewhat indefinite statements we can make about the general character of this process may be more helpful for our understanding of the real market than the more precise statements which we could make on the basis of unrealistic assumptions.

The main practical significance of what I have said seems to me here again to affect the standards which we apply in judging the appropriateness of the existing institutions. It seems to me that the currently predominant fashion in economic theory leads to far too much concern with whether actual markets conform with the picture of perfect competition, which of course they do very rarely and in most instances could never do, and far too little with those competitive activities which bring about some—even if it be only a remote—approach to the conditions described by the theory of perfect competition. I cannot argue here this contention in detail, but I would like to repeat what I have said on the earlier occasion already referred to, namely that competition in the ordinary sense of a process is probably the more important the more complex or imperfect the objective conditions are under which it operates. Indeed, far from believing that competition is beneficial only where it is perfect, it seems to me that the need for competition is nowhere greater than in those fields where the nature of the commodities or services concerned makes it impossible that it should ever create a perfect market in the theoretical sense.

I must conclude now what I called A New Look at Economic Theory. As I told you at the beginning of these lectures, this was meant to be a reconsideration of that part of economic theory, essentially the theory of value and distribution, which until about the last great war was the central core of the subject. The shift of interest which has since taken place has had the consequence that that part of theory has had little development in recent years. I hope I have made it clear why it still seems to me the most important part of economic theory and also why the manner in which it is usually presented is not altogether satisfactory. When I spoke of a new look *at* that old economic theory I was not thinking of suggesting any major changes in its substance but only a change in the interpretation of what it has done. I have suggested that it has become too ambitious by applying standards of rigorousness, which are appropriate to its logical groundwork, to the empirical science of economics where there are definite limits to what we can positively know; that we shall see more clearly what economics can do if we sharply separate that logical groundwork—the economic calculus as I have called it—from its use in the empirical science of economics; and that, though this science is of great help in the all-important issue of the choice of an economic order and of the general principles of economic policy, its power of specific prediction is inevitably limited—limited by the practical impossibility of ascertaining all the data—those very data whose utilization in the allocation of resources is the great merit of the market system.

APPENDIX B
Economists and Philosophers[1]

Seventy years ago James Bonar published a book entitled *Philosophy and Political Economy* which is closely related to the topic of this lecture.[2] A word may be in place about its distinguished author who as early as 1880 had published a study on Malthus,[3] during the eighties had been one of the first to make the English-speaking world familiar with the ideas of the Austrian economists, and in the nineteen thirties was still about to take the chair at my inaugural lecture at the London School of Economics.[4] Like all his works, *Philosophy and Political Economy* has a charm and polish which belongs to a period when economists were still more gentlemen-scholars than technicians. If it is today not more widely known, this is probably because it tells us little about the technicalities of economic theory and is more concerned with the general intellectual sources which determined the approach of economists, with the relation of the political philosophy current at different times and their economic doctrines. The book therefore deals with many philosophers who had little to say on economics as a science and, being concerned almost exclusively with moral philosophy, scarcely touches on the influence of the philosophies of science on

[1] [This is the second lecture delivered by Hayek at the University of Chicago in October 1963, under the sponsorship of the Charles R. Walgreen Foundation. The first part of the paper extends the brief treatment of economists and philosophers to be found in section 6 of his 1962 Freiburg lecture, reprinted in this volume as chapter 7. He then moves to the problem of complex phenomena in economics, something he would deal with on a more general level in "The Theory of Complex Phenomena", reprinted here as chapter 9.—Ed.]

[2] [James Bonar, *Philosophy and Political Economy in Some of Their Historical Relations* (London: Swan Sonnenschein, 1893). James Bonar (1852–1941) was both a civil servant and a lifelong student of the history of economic thought.—Ed.]

[3] [James Bonar, *Parson Malthus* (Glasgow: J. Maclehose, 1881) is the standard reference, though apparently there was an 1880 edition printed for private circulation in Edinburgh.—Ed.]

[4] [Hayek refers to James Bonar, "Austrian Economists and Their View of Value", *Quarterly Journal of Economics*, vol. 3, October 1888–1889, pp. 1–31. Bonar was in the chair for Hayek's inaugural lecture, "The Trend of Economic Thinking", delivered at the London School of Economics on March 1, 1933. The lecture is reprinted as chapter 1 of *The Trend of Economic Thinking*, ed. W. W. Bartley III and Stephen Kresge, vol. 3 (1991) of *The Collected Works of F. A. Hayek* (Chicago: University of Chicago Press; London: Routledge).—Ed.]

economics and on the noticeable contributions which some economists have made to philosophy.

The task I have set myself for today is somewhat different from Bonar's. My starting point will be the surprising number of instances, at least in Britain and until quite recently, where philosophers were also distinguished economists or economists also philosophers, where by philosopher I mean not merely moral philosopher, which until not long ago would have automatically included economics, but highly competent students of scientific method, or the theory of knowledge, or logic, or whatever you regard as the core of philosophy.

Before I present you the list of British economist-philosophers I will mention that I am not unaware of the fact that probably most contemporary economists are rather proud of the fact that their discipline has at last emancipated itself from the traditional connection with philosophy and feel that only since it has achieved this it has become a true science. The tendency has in this respect been somewhat the same as in the other social sciences and particularly in psychology where it seems that contemporary experimenters are discovering anew what was commonplace to philosophers two hundred years ago. I am at least not convinced that it is a great advance of science when, e.g., modern psychologists document by photographs what Adam Smith had described in his discussion of sympathy, namely that "the mob, when they are gazing at a dancer on the slack rope, naturally writhe and twist and balance their own bodies, as they see him do, and as they feel that they themselves must do if in his situation."[5] I could give other instances where those Scottish philosophers were psychologically considerably more sophisticated than many an experimental psychologist of today.

A certain kinship, incidentally, of the position both in economics and psychology to that in philosophy is indicated by the importance which in all three fields the history of their development has for the understanding of their present state. But again this seems to be a state of affairs of which contemporary economists and psychologists seem to be rather ashamed. Surely, so the argument runs, you can be a good physicist without knowing much about the history of physics, and similarly you ought not need to know anything about the history of economics (or psychology) in order to be a good scientist in your own field. It is thought that it should be possible to transmit the essential results of scientific work without that matrix of philosophical speculation within which they were first developed. I am not sure that even the premise is right, and it seems to me that even the physicists begin to experience an increasing need to understand by what path their science reached its present state. And I am fairly convinced that this is even more true of the theory of those more

---

[5] [Adam Smith, *The Theory of Moral Sentiments* [1759], ed. D. D. Raphael and A. L. Macfie, vol. 1 (1976) of *The Works and Correspondence of Adam Smith* (Oxford: Oxford University Press; reprinted, Indianapolis, IN: Liberty Fund, 1982), p. 10.—Ed.]

complex phenomena like mind and society, and I sometimes feel that the ruthless purging of these disciplines of all philosophical elements has sometimes led to the loss of essential insights without which what remains is not fully intelligible.

But let me now turn to what I meant to be the starting point of my discussion today, the personal union of economists and philosophers in most of the greatest British philosophers and economists. That John Locke and David Hume belong to the founders of economics I need merely mention. It is perhaps not so familiar that the third of the classic British philosophers, Bishop Berkeley, also wrote some acute tracts on economic problems.[6] I need probably also just to remind you that not only Adam Smith but also the other great Scotsmen in the field at that time, from Adam Ferguson to Dugald Stewart, were primarily philosophers, and that in particular Adam Smith in his essay on "The History of Astronomy" has made a significant contribution to the philosophy of science.[7] And still partly in the eighteenth century there is, of course, Jeremy Bentham who ranged over most parts of philosophy and, as we now know, made highly interesting contributions to economic theory.[8]

But if in the eighteenth century the connection might perhaps be explained by the fact that economics had simply not yet become an independent science, it is really in the nineteenth century when the series of British philosopher-economists becomes so remarkable. There are first the two Mills, where the name of the father would be remembered for his *Philosophy of the Human Mind* and the name of the son for his *Logic* if they never had written a line on economics.[9] There was that remarkable man, Samuel Bailey, who rivaled Ben-

---

[6] [Bishop Berkeley's (George Berkeley; 1685–1753) principal contribution to economics was the pamphlet *The Querist* (Dublin: Anonymous, 1735–1737); see *"The Querist* and Other Writings on Economics", ed. T. E. Jessop, in vol. 6 (1953) of *The Works of George Berkeley, Bishop of Cloyne* (London: Thomas Nelson), pp. 87–191.—Ed.]

[7] [Adam Ferguson's (1723–1816) most important work, *An Essay on the History of Civil Society* (1767), is the source for one of Hayek's favourite phrases, institutions that are "the results of human action but not of human design"; see the article by that name, this volume, chapter 11. Dugald Stewart (1753–1828) succeeded Ferguson in the chair of moral philosophy at the University of Edinburgh in 1785. Known by economists principally for his biography of Adam Smith, his philosophical works include *Elements of the Philosophy of the Human Mind* (1792–1816) and *Outlines of Moral Philosophy* (1793), both reprinted in *The Collected Works of Dugald Stewart*, ed. Sir William Hamilton, 10 vols. (Edinburgh: Thomas Constable, 1854–1860). Hayek also refers to Adam Smith's "The History of Astronomy" [1795], reprinted in *Essays on Philosophical Subjects*, ed. W. P. D. Wightman and J. C. Bryce, vol. 3 (1980) of *The Works and Correspondence of Adam Smith*, pp. 33–105.—Ed.]

[8] [The utilitarian philosopher Jeremy Bentham's (1748–1832) most famous economic work is his 1787 tract *Defence of Usury*; for a collection of his writings in economics, see W. Stark, ed., *Jeremy Bentham's Economic Writings*, 3 vols. (London: George Allen and Unwin, 1952–1954).—Ed.]

[9] [Hayek may have confused Dugald Stewart's *Elements of the Philosophy of the Human Mind* with James Mill's (1773–1836) *Analysis of the Phenomena of the Human Mind*, 2 vols. (London: Baldwin and Cradock, 1829); John Stuart Mill, *A System of Logic Ratiocinative and Inductive* [1843], now vols.

tham in the range of his interests (was indeed at the time called the Bentham of [Hallem]shire) and who wrote one of the best philosophical critiques of current value theory in addition to an interesting tract on banking.[10] There was Bishop Whately, known mainly for his book on logic but also the first Drummund Professor of Political Economy at Oxford and the founder of a similar chair at Dublin.[11] And still in the first half of the century we find among the men who were primarily philosophers of science William Whewell also writing on economics and generally mentioned as one of the early mathematical economists.[12]

It is perhaps also significant that the best-known figures of the generation following John Stuart Mill, J. E. Cairnes and Walter Bagehot are today remembered more for their studies on the method of economics than for their positive contributions to the subject.[13] About the same time William Stanley Jevons of course gained a considerable reputation as a philosopher of science by his work in *Pure Logic* and his *Principles of Science*.[14] Then there was Henry

---

7 (1973) and 8 (1974) of *Collected Works of John Stuart Mill*, ed. J. M. Robson, with an introduction by R. F. McRae (Toronto: University of Toronto Press; reprinted, Indianapolis: Liberty Fund, 2006).—Ed.]

[10] [In his manuscript Hayek left a space, never filled in, for 'Hallem.' He refers to Samuel Bailey's (1791–1870) *A Critical Dissertation on the Nature, Measure, and Causes of Value, Chiefly in Reference to the Writings of Mr. David Ricardo and His Followers* (London: R. Hunter, 1825; reprinted, New York: A. M. Kelley, 1967), and *Money and Its Vicissitudes in Value; as They affect National Industry and Pecuniary Contracts; with a Postscript on Joint-Stock Banks* (London: E. Wilson, 1837).—Ed.]

[11] [The Archbishop of Dublin from 1831–1863, Richard Whately (1787–1863) was actually the second Drummond Professor of Political Economy at Oxford, from 1829 to 1831, having succeeded Nassau Senior. Hayek refers to Whately's *Elements of Logic* (London: J. Mawman, 1826; 2nd ed., 1827; reprinted, Delmar, NY: Scholars' Facsimiles and Reprints, 1975). According to Mises, Whately was the first to use the term 'catallactics', this in his *Introductory Lectures on Political Economy* (London: B. Fellowes, 1831), p. 6. See Ludwig von Mises, *Human Action: A Treatise on Economics* (1949), 4th ed. (Irvington-on-Hudson, NY: Foundation for Economic Education, 1996), p. 3.—Ed.]

[12] [Cambridge professor William Whewell's (1799–1866) four papers on mathematical economics, originally presented before the Cambridge Philosophical Society, are now collected in *Mathematical Exposition of Certain Doctrines of Political Economy* (New York: A. M. Kelley, 1971).—Ed.]

[13] [John Elliott Cairnes (1823–1875) held for a time the Whately Professorship in Political Economy at Trinity College, Dublin, and later was professor of political economy at University College, London. His defence of the deductive method in political economy is contained in *The Character and Logical Method of Political Economy*, 2nd ed. (London: Macmillan, 1875). Walter Bagehot (1826–1877), editor of *The Economist* from 1859 to 1877, is probably best known today for *Lombard Street: A Description of the Money Market* (London: H. S. King, 1873; reprinted, Homewood, IL: R. D. Irwin, 1962); Hayek probably had in mind Bagehot's *The Postulates of English Political Economy: Student's Edition*, with a preface by Alfred Marshall (New York and London: G. P. Putnam's Sons, 1885).—Ed.]

[14] [William Stanley Jevons (1835–1882), author of *The Theory of Political Economy* [1871], ed. R. D. Collison Black (Harmondsworth: Pelicans Classics edition, Penguin Books, 1970), one of the founding documents of the 'Marginal Revolution', also wrote *Logic* (London: Macmillan,

Sidgwick, primarily a distinguished philosopher but highly esteemed as an economist.[15] Not much younger was John Neville Keynes, who, though mainly a logician who never seems to have written on substantive economics, in 1891 published his justly famous book on *The Scope and Method of Political Economy*.[16] His more famous son John Maynard Keynes began his scientific work with a study of the theory of probability—even though the final product was published only after he had already made a name for himself as an economist.[17] In Cambridge indeed the association of economics and philosophy survived for some time the establishment of a separate 'economic tripos' distinct from the moral science tripos in which it had been included; and even so pure an economist as A. C. Pigou in 1908, four years before he published *Wealth and Welfare*, but already professor of political economy at Cambridge, published a volume called *The Problem of Theism and other Essays* which begins with an essay on the "General Nature of Reality" in which he grapples with Kant and Lotze, Mill and Sidgwick.[18] And among the Cambridge logicians Johnson and Ramsey contributed difficult but highly important articles on pure theory to the *Economic Journal*.[19] I should probably also mention that within the last few

---

1876) and *The Principles of Science: A Treatise on Logic and Scientific Method*, 2nd ed. (London: Macmillan, 1877; reprinted, New York: Dover, 1958).—Ed.]

[15] [Cambridge philosopher and economist Henry Sidgwick (1838–1900) was the author of both *The Methods of Ethics* (London: Macmillan, 1874; reprinted, Chicago: University of Chicago Press, 1962) and *The Principles of Political Economy*, 2nd ed. (London: Macmillan, 1901; reprinted, Cambridge: Cambridge University Press, 2011).—Ed.]

[16] [John Neville Keynes (1852–1949) was the author of both *Studies and Exercises in Formal Logic* (London: Macmillan, 1884) and *The Scope and Method of Political Economy* (London: Macmillan, 1891, 4th ed., 1917; reprinted, New York: A. M. Kelley, 1963).—Ed.]

[17] [Hayek refers here to Keynes's *A Treatise on Probability* (London: Macmillan, 1921), now reprinted as vol. 8 (1973) of *The Collected Writings of John Maynard Keynes* (London: Macmillan for the Royal Economic Society).—Ed.]

[18] [The creation of a separate economics and political science tripos at Cambridge University in 1903, which allowed students there to specialize in the study of economics, was due to the sustained efforts of Alfred Marshall (1842–1924); the story is recounted in lavish detail in Peter Groenewegen, *A Soaring Eagle: Alfred Marshall, 1842–1924* (Aldershot: Edward Elgar, 1995), chapter 15, "The Creator of a New Tripos", and related appendices. Arthur Cecil Pigou (1877–1959), who acceded to Marshall's chair in political economy at Cambridge in 1908, was the author of both *Wealth and Welfare* (London: Macmillan, 1912) and, as Hayek notes, *The Problem of Theism and Other Essays* (London: Macmillan, 1908). For more on Pigou, see this volume, chapter 7, p. 226, note 15. German philosopher Rudolf Hermann Lotze (1817–1881) wrote books on logic and metaphysics.—Ed.]

[19] [William Ernest Johnson (1858–1931) was the author of "The Pure Theory of Utility Curves", *The Economic Journal*, vol. 23, December 1913, pp. 483–513, and Frank P. Ramsey (1903–1930) the author of "A Contribution to the Theory of Taxation", *The Economic Journal*, vol. 37, March 1927, pp. 47–61, and "A Mathematical Theory of Savings", *The Economic Journal*, vol. 38, December 1928, pp. 543–59. Ramsey is also remembered for his telling critique of John Maynard Keynes's theory of probability.—Ed.]

months the Finnish philosopher Von Wright, who for some years has held the Cambridge chair of philosophy after Ludwig Wittgenstein, has published a small book on the theory of choice which I have not yet had time to study but which may prove very significant for economic theory.[20] In Oxford no less F. Y. Edgeworth had started as a lecturer in logic and quite recently Sir Roy Harrod has surprised us with a highly original treatise on the theory of induction.[21]

What is so particularly intriguing about this list is that it includes so many of the most famous economists but not the names of the two most famous (after Adam Smith), Ricardo and Marshall. I would not attach too much importance to the case of Ricardo (and for similar reasons to that of Cantillon, whom I should perhaps also have mentioned as an exception to the rule). Ricardo was a very busy financier with little formal education and his literary career was after a short ten years ended by his early death at the age of 53. Yet, though it is idle to speculate what he would have done if he had lived longer, I feel he had definitely a philosophical turn of mind. The more remarkable becomes the case of Marshall, and I am inclined to think that it was largely through his great influence that economics became a 'technical' (in the sense of non-philosophical) subject—a positive science, as some will describe it approvingly. Am I wrong when I feel that his efforts were very largely guided by the deliberate aim of getting away from philosophical generalities and aimed at turning economics into a science which could vie with the natural sciences in its capacity of predicting particular events?

If we look for a moment at the development of economics in the other great countries, the situation in England stands out as rather unique. It is true that in eighteenth-century France one of the most original works, Condillac's *Essai sur le commerce et le gouvernement*, came from the pen of an outstanding philosopher and psychologist.[22] And perhaps Turgot, in view of his youthful essays on the philosophy of history might also be put in this class.[23] And in the early

---

[20] [Hayek refers to Georg Henrik von Wright's (1916–2003) *The Logic of Preference, An Essay* (Edinburgh: University of Edinburgh Press, 1963).—Ed.]

[21] [Oxford economist Francis Ysidro Edgeworth (1845–1926), founding editor of *The Economic Journal*, was also the author of *Mathematical Psychics: An Essay on the Application of Mathematics to the Moral Sciences* (London: Kegan Paul, 1881; reprinted, New York: Augustus M. Kelley, 1967). Sir Roy Harrod (1900–1978) was, among other things, Keynes's first biographer, as well as the author of *Foundations of Inductive Logic* (London: Macmillan, 1956).—Ed.]

[22] [Hayek refers to Étienne Bonnot, Abbé de Condillac's (1715–1780) *Essai sur le commerce et le gouvernement* [1776], reprinted as vol. 4 of *Œuvres complètes de Condillac* (Paris: Lecointe et Durey: Tourneux, 1822).—Ed.]

[23] [Anne Robert Jacques Turgot (1727–1781) was comptroller general of finance under Louis XVI from 1774 to 1776. Hayek refers to his "Discours sur l'histoire universelle", in *Œuvres de Turgot*, ed. Eugène Daire (Paris: Guillaumin, 1844), vol. 2, pp. 626–71. For a translation and discussion of the essay, see *Turgot on Progress, Sociology, and Economics*, edited and translated by Ronald Meek (Cambridge: Cambridge University Press, 1973).—Ed.]

nineteenth century there is still one of the greatest philosopher-economists, A. A. Cournot.[24] But this seems to be all. And when we turn to the country which above all others is regarded as the country of philosophers, Germany, there are practically no men of this kind. At least if we confine ourselves to Germany proper and exclude Austria (where in modern times Carl Menger and Ludwig von Mises might have some title to be regarded also as philosophers) we find only one significant instance: Karl Marx. Though Kant was as interested in the principles of politics as David Hume, what he had to say on economics is negligible. Of his three most famous successors, Hegel, Fichte, and Schelling, Fichte indeed did write a book on economic problems, *The Closed Economic State*, which is even mentioned in most books on the history of economics.[25] But it is a sort of socialist utopia which contains precious little economic analysis and even shows little understanding of economic problems. Nor were the German economists of the last century more interested in philosophy. Not that Germany did not produce some first-class economic theorists, at least before the historical school became dominant: von Thünen, Hermann, and Mangoldt can bear comparison with the best of their English contemporaries.[26] But none of them approached their subject in a wider philosophical framework—and in so far as they were professional scholars, the character of the academic specialization did not favour such an approach. Thus Karl Marx remains the only German philosopher-economist, a circumstance which perhaps contributed something to his early success in that country.

I should add that the realization how unphilosophical the German tradition in economics was came to me rather as a surprise, because forty years ago when I was myself a student, philosophical systems of economics were rather a vogue, or perhaps better a plague, in German economics, and I should cer-

[24] [In addition to his *Recherches sur les principes mathématiques de la théorie des richesses* (Paris: L. Hachette, 1838), now available in translation as *Mathematical Principles of the Theory of Wealth*, translated by Nathan T. Bacon (New York: Macmillan, 1927; reprinted, New York: Augustus M. Kelley, 1971), Antoine Augustin Cournot (1801–1877) made contributions to philosophy in such works as his *Essai sur les fondemonts de nos connaissances* (Paris: L. Hachette, 1851), now available as *An Essay on the Foundations of our Knowledge*, translated with an introduction by Merritt H. Moore (New York: Liberal Arts Press, 1956).—Ed.]

[25] [The German philosopher Johann Gottlieb Fichte's (1762–1814) book *Der geschlossen Handelsstaat* (Tübingen: J. G. Cotta, 1800) is now available as *The Closed Commercial State*, translated by Anthony Curtis Adler (Albany: State University of New York Press, 2012).—Ed.]

[26] [Johann Heinrich von Thünen's (1783–1850) masterwork *Der isolierte Staat* was published in parts over a thirty-seven-year period; for a translation see *The Isolated State: An English Edition of "Der isolierte Staat"*, ed. Peter Hall, translated by Carla M. Wartenberg (Oxford: Pergamon Press, 1966). Friedrich B. von Hermann (1795–1868) and Hans Karl Emil von Mangoldt (1824–1868) are both part of what Erich Streissler has called the German "proto-neoclassical tradition"; see Erich Streissler, "The Influence of German Economics on the Work of Menger and Marshall", in *Carl Menger and His Legacy in Economics*, ed. Bruce Caldwell (Durham, NC: Duke University Press, 1990), pp. 31–68.—Ed.]

tainly never have expected that I should ever come to plead for a closer liaison between the two subjects. But I doubt whether the work of Othmar Spann, or Gottl-Ottlilienfeld, or Stolzmann, Sombart, or Liefmann, which were then discussed, will leave any lasting impact either on philosophy or economics, and I can probably pass them over as not very relevant to my subject.[27]

So far as I can see, the situation is rather similar to that in Germany in the other countries which have made significant contributions to economics. Perhaps in Italy Galiani's great work on money might be said to be philosophically inspired (by G. Vico), but I know of no later instances, and neither the United States nor Holland nor the Scandinavian countries seem until modern times to have produced a figure of this kind—though Chicago has been fortunate enough to have for so long the most distinguished living economist-philosopher on its faculty.[28]

The conspicuous difference which exists in this respect between the different countries is probably not a matter of national character but the result of the type of philosophy which has been dominant in Britain. I conclude this from the fact that the adherents of the two philosophical traditions which shared the chief influence in other countries, idealism on the one hand and positivism on the other, seem not even in Britain to have shown an interest in economics. Neither Bradley nor T. H. Green, nor Herbert Spencer or the modern positivists from Bertrand Russell down, any more than the French founder of modern positivism, August Comte, are conspicuous for their interest in or understanding of economic problems.[29]

---

[27] [Some are better remembered than others. Othmar Spann (1878–1950), the prophet of intuitive universalism, was for a time Hayek's teacher at the University of Vienna, but they soon had a falling out: see Bruce Caldwell, *Hayek's Challenge: An Intellectual Biography of F. A. Hayek* (Chicago: University of Chicago Press, 2004), pp. 138–39. Friedrich von Gottl-Ottlilienfeld (1868–1958), who taught at a number of German universities, was Spann's thesis supervisor at Brünn, and was the originator of an approach to economics (dubbed 'Allwirtschaftslehre') that analysed the 'essence' of the economy, then showed the historical evolution of different manifestations of the economy, finally culminating in a description of an intrinsically optimal economy. Rudolf Stolzmann (1852–1930) was an adherent of a socio-legal approach to economics. In this approach, all economic phenomena must be analysed within the context of the social and legal system in which they are embedded, so that universal laws of economics cannot exist. Werner Sombart (1863–1941), perhaps the last of the German historical school economists, was a historian of the development of capitalism. Robert Liefmann (1874–1941) was an economist at the University of Freiburg. Additional information on some of these figures may be found in chapter 7, pp. 229–30, note 19.—Ed.]

[28] [Hayek refers to Ferdinando Galiani's (1728–1787) 1751 work, *Della moneta*; now available as *On Money*, translated by Peter R. Toscano (Ann Arbor: University Microfilms International, 1977), and to the Italian philosopher and historian Giambattista Vico (1668–1744). The "most distinguished living economist-philosopher" is Frank Knight.—Ed.]

[29] [Hayek refers to the Oxford idealist philosophers Francis Herbert Bradley (1846–1924) and Thomas Hill Green (1836–1882). Herbert Spencer (1820–1903) made contributions to philos-

Perhaps the explanation is simply that British philosophy, from Locke to Sidgwick (and most markedly in David Hume), was never primarily interested in an absolute mind or the realm of ideas, or in the physical world, but had always regarded human nature as its central object. Perhaps one might even say that British philosophy just was predominantly social philosophy or even social science and little interested in metaphysics and therefore not tempted to carry irrelevant issues into the discussion of economic problems. At any rate, there seems to me no doubt possible that British economics greatly profited from its association with philosophy. The interesting question is whether the separation, which seems to have been effected by Marshall, is a sign of maturity, simply that final step in the technicalization and professionalization which every science must take to become truly scientific, or whether there are not perhaps reasons why it would be desirable that, not only economics but the social sciences generally, should permanently in some sense remain more philosophical than the physical sciences.

I have not been able in preparing these lectures, as I intend to do before I publish them, to look into the question whether the differences between Marshall and Sidgwick at the time of the establishment of the separate economic tripos at Cambridge, in addition to the moral science tripos within which economics had till then been taught, do not, as I rather suspect, turn on this issue.[30] I should not be surprised if their difference should not prove to be of much wider significance than the local Cambridge problems and if the victory of Marshall proved symptomatic of the change in the character of economics which took place at that time.

It is of course not quite easy to define precisely what is meant by 'philosophical' in contrast to 'scientific.' But for my present purpose I am quite content to accept the definition once proposed by Bertrand Russell when he wrote that science is concerned with what we know and philosophy with what we do not know[31] and to admit unashamedly that on this definition many of the most

ophy, biology, and sociology, and was introduced to the ideas of Auguste Comte (1798–1857), the founder of positivism, by George Henry Lewes and George Eliot, though, like John Stuart Mill, he ultimately found much to criticize in the work of Comte. For more on Hayek's views on Comte and positivism, see F. A. Hayek, "The Counter-Revolution of Science" [1941; 1952], now reprinted in Hayek, *Studies in the Abuse and Decline of Reason*, ed. Bruce Caldwell, vol. 13 (2010) of *The Collected Works of F. A. Hayek*, pp. 201–16, 256–304. Bertrand Russell (1872–1970) was a philosopher, mathematician, and logician whose book with Alfred North Whitehead, *Principia Mathematica*, 2nd ed. (Cambridge: Cambridge University Press, 1925–1927), was taken as a foundational document by the logical positivists.—Ed.]

[30] [It certainly appears to have been one of the differences between Sidgwick and Marshall: see Groenewegen, *A Soaring Eagle*, chapter 15.—Ed.]

[31] [See Bertrand Russell, "The Philosophy of Logical Atomism", *Logic and Knowledge: Essays, 1901–1950* (London: George Allen and Unwin, 1956), p. 281: "Science is what you more or less know and philosophy is what you do not know."—Ed.]

important problems of society not only still belong but always will belong to philosophy. The characteristic problems of the social sciences seem to me to arise out of the fact that neither acting man nor the social scientist can ever know all the facts which determine human action and that the problem of the social sciences is essentially how man copes with this essential ignorance. If this is so, the tendency to concentrate on those issues where we can hope to arrive at concrete testable predictions of particular individual events, that is, where the scientist can ever know all the relevant facts in sufficient detail to arrive at an unambiguous determination of the outcome, would seem to exclude the greater part of what economics and the social sciences generally can achieve, from the range of true sciences. It seems to me that this was essentially the aims of Marshall's realism and his predominant concern with empirical facts, even though, extremely cautious a man that he was, he was very cautious in his claims about what had *yet* been achieved in this direction.

Let me illustrate the view of the more philosophically minded economists of the time by a few passages from Jevons's *Principles of Science*. Jevons was certainly as hardheaded or tough minded a thinker as we could wish. Yet he was extremely critical of the naïve conception that by applying 'the scientific method' to social phenomena we could achieve the same sort of 'prediction and control' in this field as we do in the natural sciences. I particularly like the passage where he writes that "we may congratulate ourselves that we have been endowed with minds which, rightly employed, can form some estimate of their *in*capacity to trace out and account for all that proceeds in the simpler actions of material nature" and then points out that "intellectual phenomena are *yet vastly more extensive.*"[32] In consequence, "the sciences of political economy and morality are comparatively *abstract and general*, treating mankind from simple points of view, and attempting to detect *general* principles of action. They are to social phenomena what the abstract sciences of chemistry, heat, and electricity are to . . . meteorology [a subject of which Jevons had made a special study]. Before we can investigate the actions of any aggregate of men, we must have fairly mastered all the more abstract sciences applying to them. . . ."[33] And with reference to the then-popular attempts to discover laws of historical development he observes: "A science of history in the true sense of the term is an absurd notion. A nation is not a mere sum of individuals whom we can treat by *the method of averages*; it is an organic whole, held together *by ties of infinite complexity*. . . . In human affairs . . . the smallest causes may produce the greatest effects, and the *real* application of *scientific method* is out of the question."[34]

---

[32] Jevons, *Principles of Science*, p. 758. All italics in this and the following two quotations added.
[33] Ibid., p. 760. [Hayek added the bracketed material.—Ed.]
[34] Ibid., p. 761.

This may sound in some respect commonplace and in others even confused. But it does show at least an awareness of the problems peculiar to the social sciences which cannot be solved by any routine application of 'the scientific method', if there is such a thing, but only by an adaptation of our procedure to the peculiar nature of the problems. It shows that he knew that the degree of complexity such phenomena possess preclude the application of what is commonly (though I think mistakenly) called 'the' scientific method and that this difficulty could not be overcome by statistics ('the method of averages'). And it shows particularly a real awareness of the central difficulty which necessarily makes the social sciences philosophical in Bertrand Russell's sense, our ignorance of many of the determining circumstances, and the rôle which abstraction, in a very special sense, plays in helping us partially to overcome this difficulty.

The ignorance with which we have to cope and which we must rather circumvent than overcome is, as I have already suggested, a double one. It is on the one hand, the ignorance of the men whose actions we study, and ignorance which we can assume away only at the peril of making our problems disappear (as has happened to some parts of equilibrium analysis). And, on the other, it is the equally unalterable and fundamental ignorance of many of the particular facts which determine the concrete manifestations of the phenomena by the scientist who studies them and which confines him to what Jevons called the general principles, or, as I would say, the abstract overall pattern of the phenomena, and prevent him from ever similarly explaining the concrete detail.

I do not want to claim that Jevons was better or even as clear on these matters as many others among his fellow philosopher-economists. I have quoted him merely as an example, from an author who has not systematically dealt with the special problems of the method of economics, of the attitude to the problems of which the philosopher-economists were generally aware and which made them less ambitious and more modest in their claims than those who endeavoured to apply a standard recipe called the scientific method to the phenomena of society. It is one of the paradoxes of the situation that this unphilosophical and in the true sense also unscientific procedure has regularly produced grandiose 'philosophies of history', while it requires more than acquaintance with the technique of research to produce useful results in fields which have proved more recalcitrant than those in which science achieved its first triumphs.

I believe we can now explain these peculiarities of the social sciences more clearly than was possible at the time of Jevons and Marshall, and I think I ought to spend some little while on it because it seems to me that it is these methodological peculiarities which largely explain the beneficial rôle which philosophically inclined thinkers have played, and I hope will continue to play, in the history of economics.

I shall start, as I have done in a fuller account which is due to appear shortly,[35] from the concept of complexity. Philosophers regard this as a rather difficult concept, but for our purposes it does seem to me fairly clear and unambiguous. There are *kinds* of phenomena which can adequately be explained in terms of theories or models which deal in terms of the relations between comparatively few, often only two or three, variables. These we usually call physical phenomena. Of course, the circumstances that the theories which are sufficient to explain those phenomena can be adequately stated in terms of very few variables does not mean that the phenomena themselves cannot reach any degree of complexity. The theory of oceanic tides is simple; its application to the tides at a particular place may be of insuperable complexity. But the nature of the phenomena remains the same, whether in the particular instance the distinct factors affecting it are few or many. The multiplicity of determining factors does not produce a new kind of phenomenon, requiring a new theory to explain it. The difficulty is merely one of ascertaining and manipulating an increasingly large number of data according to the same formula.

But there are also kinds of phenomena which can occur only if the number of variables is large, where the phenomenon cannot occur at all unless the number of distinct elements exceeds a certain, often quite considerable, number. I shall call them essentially complex phenomena. It is, of course, a commonplace that as we move from mechanics through the other branches of physics through inorganic and organic chemistry to the 'more highly organized' systems of biology we move in an ascending order of essential complexity. It is perhaps less familiar, but I believe no less true, that the *only* criterion by which we in fact single out some phenomena as belonging to physics is that they are essentially simple, i.e., that their theoretical explanation can be achieved by models requiring only very few parts. This remains even true where this is achieved by substituting for a very large number of individual events an assumption about their probability—this indeed is a device for reducing the number of essential data to a very few. In the field of the more complex phenomena even the simplest model which produces their essential features must consist of many elements whose difference from each other is a of crucial importance and which we can therefore not lump together into a statistical aggregate. For a time, as we move up in the ascending scale of complexity this makes little difference in our procedure except making the task more difficult. Whether our models contain two, three, or four variables, they will generally lead to concrete and testable predictions only if we know the particular values of all the variables, because all the relations characteris-

---

[35] [Hayek refers here to "The Theory of Complex Phenomena", reprinted in this volume as chapter 9, which first appeared in 1964, the year following his Walgreen lectures.—Ed.]

tic of the system are relations between the separate variables. The law which connects the temperature and the pressure of a gas tells us nothing about a concrete instance unless we know the magnitude of the other, and as soon as we know the one we know all that is to be known about the system.

As soon as we have to deal with systems with more than two variables we have, however, no longer the simple alternative that the system is either wholly indetermined or fully determined, but the intermediate possibility that, because some but not all the relevant variables are known, the system is partially determined, i.e., we know, not the precise relations between the individual variables but a certain range within which they must lie. Our partial information will restrict the degrees of freedom which the system still possesses, but every such restriction of its degrees of freedom tells us something useful about the world by telling us what will not be the case—thus producing a prediction which can be falsified and which therefore is empirically testable.

The distinction seems not of great importance so long as the degree of complexity remains moderate so that it can be assumed that if it is desirable it will be possible and practicable to determine all the variables entering the system. In the field in which the physical scientist works, he can usually assume that this is at least in principle possible, although he, too, has in practice frequently to be content with information which allows him to deduce only some general characteristics but not all the details of the result. Even the physiologist, or at least the biological chemist, still largely proceeds as if he had to deal with closed systems all of whose determining elements were in principle determinable so that the ultimate aim is the precise determination of every variable. The biologist proper, however, knows only too well that this is beyond his powers. For him prediction of the general pattern, of certain general relationships whose concrete and particular numerical manifestations depend on circumstances he can never hope to ascertain all, has become the recognized terminus of his efforts.

In fact the instances even in the natural sciences where we have learned to be content with which what I have on earlier occasions called explanations of the principle but which I prefer now to call pattern predictions—the prediction of some but not all the characteristics of a kind of order which will form itself—are exceedingly numerous. The abstract description of these patterns is there fully recognized as valuable in its own right and not, as it is so often misleadingly regarded in the social sciences, treated as a mere tool whose value depends on it being a suitable instrument for determining particular individual events. But the natural sciences have probably nowhere stepped so clearly beyond the range where it is even conceivable that we should ever be able to ascertain (and to manipulate) all the particular circumstances on which any one particular event depends, as we have in the social sciences.

Let me recall what the characteristic problem of the social sciences is. It consists in the explanation of the formation of an order which not only none of the participants intends to produce or needs to know but which also depends on a far larger number of circumstances than is known to any one among them. Nor is the observing scientist in a much better position. If he could not say anything useful before he knew all the concrete facts which determine a particular manifestation of that order, he might as well abdicate. But as, at least in economics, one of the first things his theory tells him is that all parts of an economic system are interdependent, i.e., that any of the data which he can never all know, may affect any of the economic magnitudes in which he is interested, it would seem that he can never with any confidence predict any of the particular magnitudes.

I believe this is in fact so. But what, then, remains for him to do? The situation seems hopeless so long as we assume, but only so long as we assume, that the prediction of particular events is the only justification of scientific effort, and the confirmation of such predictions of individual events the only test of the empirical validity of his theory. But this is not so. It may be, and often is, exceedingly valuable—and an empirically testable statement—if we can predict only the general pattern in which individual events will arrange themselves, perhaps even only a few very general or abstract features which this pattern will possess. I believe it is indeed a general feature of all our theories of essentially complex phenomena that the predictions we can derive from them will not be predictions of individual events, but predictions merely of relations between events, or of relations between relations of events, or even patterns of a still higher degree of abstractness. Which of the infinite number of possible concrete instances of this pattern will in fact occur will always depend also on circumstances which we cannot ascertain. But if certain kinds of patterns are for some reason preferable to others, it may be of the greatest importance to know what the general circumstances must be in order that the one kind of pattern rather than another will form itself.

I cannot here further consider the question in what manner the general character of the pattern that will form itself will depend only on some but not all the data, or, rather, on some but not on all the attributes of the determining circumstances, namely on a limited number of general conditions which we can ascertain rather than on all the particular facts acting on it which we cannot. I rather want to confine myself here to one particular aspect of the problem, namely the relation between what are sometimes described as the 'merely' qualitative and the quantitative aspects of the phenomena in question.

I hope that even the brief outline I have been able to give will be sufficient to show that where we have to deal with essentially complex phenomena we shall often be in a position to make predictions on the most general character of a pattern that will form itself on the basis of very limited and merely generic information about the data; that, as the prediction of the resulting pattern is to become more specific, the information on the data has also to be more full and detailed; and that there may be many degrees in this process of decreasing abstraction which in the end, if we had all the relevant information, might allow us to predict every single element of which the pattern will be formed.

I hope it will also be clear by now that in the case of some very complex phenomena we may in fact be permanently confined to prediction of general patterns and never be able to specify the individual events of which it will be formed. It will probably also be clear that the description of the general abstract pattern will generally be non-quantitative or at least non-numerical and that the particular magnitudes of the individual events making up the pattern will be among the last results to be determined, derivable only when we know all the relevant aspects of the data. Till then the general pattern will be determined by much more general relations between classes of elements, such relations as equality or greater or smaller than, which are not sufficient to determine numerical magnitudes.

In this connection there seems to exist a widespread misconception of the chief value of mathematics for economics. It consists *not* in the fact that it enables us to make economics quantitative, but on the contrary that it enables us to disregard the quantitative aspects and to give precise descriptions of abstract patterns irrespective of the particular magnitudes in which they manifest themselves. This is of course familiar enough in obvious cases. From the numerical illustration to the geometrical diagram to the algebraic function and differential equation is a progress not merely in generality but from a presentation which makes assumptions which in fact we cannot verify and are not part of the general theory to a representation which includes only those data which are significant and which we are able to test. But the same seems to me equally true of the more elaborate constructions of mathematical theory. There is a widespread but in my view wholly mistaken belief that, e.g., the systems of simultaneous equations which describe the interdependence of all prices and quantities are merely a tool which acquires scientific value only as we are able to insert numerical values for its 'constants.' This was not the view of the great thinkers who designed these systems. To them the abstract description of the kind of pattern that would form itself was the final product of theory, a result which possessed empirical significance even if it should be altogether impossible, as, e.g., V. Pareto was convinced that it was impossible, ever to obtain the data necessary to solve these systems of equations.[36] It is for these reasons

---

[36] [Cf. Hayek's "The Theory of Complex Phenomena", pp. 270–71, or "The Pretence of Knowledge", pp. 366–67, both in this volume, for more on Hayek's reading of Vilfredo Pareto's views on this matter.—Ed.]

entirely consistent to be most enthusiastic about the use of advanced mathematics in economics, precisely because it helps us to get away from the quantitative aspects and to provide an adequate description of the general character of the overall patterns, and to be in the highest degree skeptical about the possibility of producing any useful quantitative results.

I need hardly dwell on the significance for policy of the insight that all that science can tell us in this field are certain general characteristics of the order that will form itself in different sets of equally generally defined circumstances, but that the particular manifestations of that order will always remain unpredictable. The whole case in favour of a policy which confines itself to provide a general framework within which the market operates but leaves the continuous formation of an order to the operation of that market rests on this general insight. Once one understands this it also becomes clear why methodological and political differences so frequently go together: those who believe that it is in the power of science to predict particular individual events, or the position of individuals, naturally also want to use that power to produce the particular results they desire.

But I must now briefly consider yet another peculiar feature of the social sciences to which those who want to apply in its fields the standard technique of science, 'the scientific method', are usually blind and where problems arise which belong not to any specialized social science but rather to a general science of man. It concerns the nature of the empirical data with which we have to deal, rather than the character of the theories which we form. The fact is that not only the social structures with which we have to deal, but also the particular data which we have to use in explaining them, are in a peculiar sense complex—complex in a manner which makes it difficult or impossible to define them quite as we define the data which we insert in a physical theory in order to arrive at testable predictions. This issue has of course been discussed for some eighty years, but not in a very satisfactory manner. While the one side claimed that our data were not only based on observation but on the same kind of observation as in physics, observation of events which could be defined in terms of sensory elements, the other side claimed that we had to resort to a special procedure of understanding (*Verstehen*) which was sometimes represented as if it were not observation. Neither of these attitudes seems to me to do justice to what is a real problem. The undeniable fact is that we generally recognize the action of other people as intelligible or having a meaning without being able to state from what particular atomic facts we derive this knowledge. All human intercourse, above all, all communication, but also all recognition of the action of others as being directed to a purpose and therefore forming a significant link in the structure of social relationships, rests on this capacity.

The situation appears to be that our capacity of perception does not really work on the basis that we first perceive atomic sensory elements and from them build up complex pictures, but that our senses do perceive as events of the same kind highly abstract patterns of events, particular patterns of movements of our fellow men, which have nothing in common except that they occupy similar places in our common mental structure and indicate to us that those which we observe pursue certain familiar purposes. The Gestalt school of psychology has seen at least some of the problems which arise here. But it seems to me that the basic issue is one which our ingrained philosophical habits still prevent us largely from seeing—or perhaps I should say, for which the standard practices of science, what is regarded as the scientific method, have no place.

I do not want to lead you further into these issues on the borderline of the social sciences, psychology, and philosophy which to me had always a peculiar fascination. I did not want to say more than was necessary in order to indicate that there are here real issues which are common and peculiar to all social sciences, which the technique of no one social science is competent to answer but about which the techniques of the natural sciences did not have to bother. But we do not think we shall get very far in the social sciences if we neglect them. Perhaps someday we shall get something like a general science of man which will provide us with both the required conceptual framework and the appropriate technique which then we as specialists in economics or any other social science can employ as mechanically and unthinkingly as the natural scientist can follow the scientific method he has been brought up to use. But so far these issues have still remained within the general body of philosophy, and since the issues have not yet been clear and to particular parts which are relevant for our purpose sorted out, I feel that it is still largely true that for much of our task we must try to be, as so many of our great forebears were, not only devotees of a specialized science but also, in some measure at least, philosophers.

NAME INDEX

Acton, Lord, 42n8, 53, 338n3
Amonn, A., 73n21
Aristotle, 52, 132, 133, 219, 293, 293n4
Austin, John, 46, 46n13, 140, 349

Bacon, Francis, 42, 42n7
Bagehot, Walter, 430
Bähr, Otto, 152
Bailey, Samuel, 229, 429
Barone, Enrico, 103n5
Bartlett, Frederic, 317, 317n9
Beccaria, Cesare, 46, 46n13
Beer, Gavin de, 361
Beloff, Max, 357
Bellièvre, President de, 293n2
Benham, Frederic, 63n8
Bentham, Jeremy, 46, 46n13, 52, 229, 429, 429n8, 430
Berkeley, George, 229
Bernard, Claude, 309, 309n7
Bertalanffy, Ludwig, 18, 18n48, 29n90, 268n25, 328n1, 331, 332
Blackstone, William, 168n8
Blum, Leon, 181n3
Bonar, James, 427, 428
Bresciani-Turroni, Costantino, 355n27
Bruner, Jerome S., 328, 328n1
Buchanan, James, 19
Burke, Edmund, 137, 301n23

Cairnes, J. E., 430, 430n13
Cannon, Walter B., 309, 309n7
Cantillon, Richard, 221, 221n11

Cantor, Georg, 251n50
Carr-Saunders, Alexander, 359
Charles I, 134
Chisholm, Brock, 341, 350, 351
Chomsky, Noam, 318, 334n7
Christie, Will, 25n73
Cicero, 52, 133, 169
Clark, J. M., 105
Coke, Edward, 135, 168, 296n12
Comte, Auguste, 87, 87n4, 302n26, 348, 348n19, 434, 434, 435n29
Condorcet, Marquis de, 145
Constant, Benjamin, 150, 151
Cournot, A. A., 433
Cromwell, 293n2

Darlington, C. D., 31, 31n100, 32, 357–59, 360, 361
Darwin, Charles, 267, 267n23, 277, 301n23, 344
Demosthenes, 132
Descartes, René, 26, 41, 41n5, 42, 52, 52n18, 293, 302, 302n26, 340–41, 341n8
Dicey, A. V., 158, 159, 171, 186, 188
Dobzhansky, Theodosius, 360

Edgeworth, Francis Ysidro, 432, 432n21
Einaudi, Luigi, 355n27
Eliot, George, 434–35n29
Emerson, A. E., 281
Erhard, Ludwig, 214n5
Eucken, Walter, 214, 214n3, 214n5, 215, 215n7, 226

445

SUBJECT INDEX

The editor's introduction to this volume provides short descriptions of the main themes treated by Hayek in each of his papers and may be a useful supplement to this index.